THE BARBOUR COLLECTION OF CONNECTICUT TOWN VITAL RECORDS

THE BARBOUR COLLECTION OF CONNECTICUT TOWN VITAL RECORDS

ORANGE 1822–1850

OXFORD 1798–1850

PLAINFIELD 1699–1852

Compiled by
Carole Magnuson

General Editor
Lorraine Cook White

Copyright © 2000
Genealogical Publishing Co., Inc.
Baltimore, Maryland
All Rights Reserved
Library of Congress Catalogue Card Number 94-76197
International Standard Book Number 0-8063-1646-2
Made in the United States of America

INTRODUCTION

As early as 1640 the Connecticut Court of Election ordered all magistrates to keep a record of the marriages they performed. In 1644 the registration of births and marriages became the official responsibility of town clerks and registrars, with deaths added to their duties in 1650. From 1660 until the close of the Revolutionary War these vital records of birth, marriage, and death were generally well kept, but then for a period of about two generations until the mid-nineteenth century, the faithful recording of vital records declined in some towns.

General Lucius Barnes Barbour was the Connecticut Examiner of Public Records from 1911 to 1934 and in that capacity directed a project in which the vital records kept by the towns up to about 1850 were copied and abstracted. Barbour previously had directed the publication of the Bolton and Vernon vital records for the Connecticut Historical Society. For this new project he hired several individuals who were experienced in copying old records and familiar with the old script.

Barbour presented the completed transcriptions of town vital records to the Connecticut State Library where the information was typed onto printed forms. The form sheets were then cut, producing twelve small slips from each sheet. The slips for most towns were then alphabetized and the information was then typed a second time on large sheets of rag paper, which were subsequently bound into separate volumes for each town. The slips for all towns were then interfiled, forming a statewide alphabetized slip index for most surviving town vital records.

The dates of coverage vary from town to town, and of course the records of some towns are more complete than others. There are many cases in which an entry may appear two or three times, apparently because that entry was entered by one or more persons. Altogether the entire Barbour Collection--one of the great genealogical manuscript collections and one of the last to be published--covers 137 towns and comprises 14,333 typed pages.

TABLE OF CONTENTS

ORANGE 1

OXFORD 23

PLAINFIELD 87

ABBREVIATIONS

ae.------------age
b. ------------born, both
bd.-----------buried
bf.------------born of
B.G.---------Burying Ground
d.------------died, day, or daughter
dea.----------deacon
decd.--------deceased
f.-------------father
h.-------------hour or husband
J.P.-----------Justice of Peace
m.------------married, month, or minister
page#+*-----* = 1/2, example: 125* = page 125 1/2
res.-----------resident
s.--------------son
st.------------stillborn
w.------------wife
wid.----------widow
wk.-----------week
y.-------------year

THE BARBOUR COLLECTION
OF CONNECTICUT TOWN
VITAL RECORDS

ORANGE VITAL RECORDS
1822 - 1850

	Page
ADRIANCE, John B., of New York, m. Charlotte E. **HINE**, of Orange, Jan. 15, 1845, by Rev. Cyrus Brewster	17
ALLEN, [see also **ALLING**], Elias, m. Catharine B. **RUSSELL**, b. of Orange, Apr. 30, 1843, by Rev. A. Smyth	15
Hull, of Milford, m. Elizabeth A. **CLARK**, of Orange, Nov. 25, 1847, by Rev. Cyrus Brewster	19
ALLING, [see also **ALLEN**], Albert, m. Mary M. **TREAT**, Nov. 22, 1827, by Stephen W. Stebbins	4
Almira, of Orange, m. E. Y. **SHEPHARD**, of New Haven, Aug. 14, 1833, by Horace Woodruff	8
Amos F., m. Sarah E. **PRUDDON**, b. of Orange, Sept. 2, 1847, by Rev. Geo[rge] P. Pruddon	19
Bela, m. Julia **ROGERS**, Sept. 28, 1826, by Erastus Scranton, V.D.M.	4
Charlotte E., m. Lorenzo **ARMSTRONG**, June 20, 1841, by Stephen W. Stebbins	14
Charlotte E., of Orange, m. Marcus L. **BALDWIN**, of Derby, Nov. 17, 1842, by Rev. Anson Smyth	15
Ebenezer, m. Julia B. **TREAT**, b. of Orange, Nov. 18, 1824, by E. Scranton, V.D.M.	2
Eliza, of Orange, m. Joshua **NEWEL**, of New Haven, Nov. 5, 1848, by E. Wright	20
Elizabeth, m. Lester W. **MABRY**, Jan. 30, 1831, by Horatio A. Parsons	7
Elizabeth, m. Henry S. **DAWSON**, June 5, 1839, by Stephen W. Stebbins	12
Esther, m. William **ANDREW**, b. of Orange, Apr. 15, 1835, by Horace Woodruff	10
Ezra, m. Statira **BALL**, June 3, 1832, by Stephen W. Stebbins	7
Harriet, m. William **TREAT**, [Nov.] 9, [1827], by George Foot, V.D.M., North Milford	4
Laura, m. William **WARNER**, Oct. 29, 1826, by Erastus Scranton, V.D.M.	4
Levi, m. Amy P. **RUSSELL**, b. of Orange, Nov. 29, 1849, by W. W. Belden	22
Mary Newton, of Orange, m. Anson Riley **DAVIS**, of Derby, May 8, 1845, by Rev. W[illia]m Bliss Ashley, of Derby	18
Mary T., m. Alpheas N. **MERWIN**, b. of Orange, Oct. [ ], 1849, by W. W. Belden	21
Patty, m. Charles **PHILLIPS**, Sept. 16, [1822], by Rev. Stephen	

	Page
ALLING, (cont.)	
W. Stebbins, in West Haven	1
Rebecca, m. Miles F. **MERRECK**, b. of Orange, Mar. 5, 1850, by W. W. Belden	22
Susan Rogers, m. Ezekiel Mason **BRADLEY**, June 6, 1844, by Rev. Cyrus Brewster	16
Susannah, m. Jeremiah S. **JOHNSON**, Dec. 29, [1822], by Rev. [ ] Perry	1
Thomas, of New Haven, m. Mrs. Sally **DODD**, of Milford, Oct. 15, 1837, by Asa M. Train	11
Zeri, m. Julia **MUNSON**, b. of Orange, [Sept.] 24, [1843], by Rev. Cyrus Brewster. Int.Pub.	15
ANDREWS, ANDREW, Laura, of Orange, m. William G. **UMBERFIELD**, of Woodbridge, Mar. 31, 1831, by Horatio A. Parsons	6
Mary, of Orange, m. Josiah **ISBEL**, of Milford, Mar. 4, 1835, by Asa M. Train, [of] Milford	9
Norris, of New Haven, m. Julia Ann **LYMAN**, of West Haven, Apr. 6, 1849, by Rev. A. B. Chapin, of West Haven	21
Samuel, of Woodbridge, m. Salina **SMITH**, of Orange, Jan. 1, 1824, by Erastus Scranton, V.D.M.	1
William, m. Esther **ALLING**, b. of Orange, Apr. 15, 1835, by Horace Woodruff	10
ARMSTRONG, Eliza, m. John S. T. **RICHARDS**, b. of West Haven, Sept. 8, 1841, by Rev. A. B. Chapin	21
Lorenzo, m. Charlotte E. **ALLING**, June 20, 1841, by Stephen W. Stebbins	14
Philander, of New Haven, m. Charlotte **MELOY**, of West Haven, Sept. 15, 1850, by A. B. Chapin	22
Sereno, m. Celina **CLARK**, May 27, 1832, by Stephen W. Stebbins	7
William, m. Charlotte **THOMAS**, May 22, 1842, by Stephen W. Stebbins, [of] West Haven	14
[AYERS], [see under **EAYRES**]	
BAKER, Otis T., of New Haven, m. Miriam T. **THOMPSON**, of Orange, Nov. 27, 1845, by E. Wright	18
BALDWIN, Edward, m. Harriet **NETTLETON**, July 1, 1832, by Asa M. Train	7
George H., m. Cynthia M. **JOHNSON**, of Derby, Nov. 16, 1845, by Rev. A. B. Chapin, of West Haven	21
Joel, m. Polly M. **NETTLETON**, Oct. 3, [1822], by Erastus Scranton, V.D.M., in North Milford	1
Marcus L., of Derby, m. Charlotte E. **ALLING**, of Orange, Nov. 17, 1842, by Rev. Anson Smyth	15
Merrett, of New Haven, m. Caroline **BROWN**, of Humphreysville, Apr. 26, 1838, by Stephen W. Stebbins, [of] West Haven	12
Phebe, of Orange, m. Selah **STEEL**, of Berlin, Oct. 5, 1825, by Abijah Cunningham, J.P.	2
Ramond, of Woodbridge, m. Martha **PLATT**, of Orange, Nov. 27,	

ORANGE VITAL RECORDS

Page

BALDWIN, (cont.)
   [1823], by Erastus Scranton, V.D.M.   1
BALL, Levi J., m. wid. Lydia **EAYRES**, Mar. 3, 1829, by Stephen W.
   Stebbins   5
   Statira, m. Ezra **ALLING**, June 3, 1832, by Stephen W.
   Stebbins   7
BARNELL, [see also **BURWELL**], Willis, m. Rosettee **SMITH**, July 7,
   [1822], by Rev. Stephen W. Stebbins, in West Haven
   (Perhaps "**BURWELL**"?)   1
BATES, Maruna, m. Syllys **SMITH**, Oct. 7, 1839, by Stephen W.
   Stebbins   12
BEACH, Calvin, m. Urania **PARDEE**, Nov. 14, 1823, by Erastus
   Scranton, V.D.M.   1
BEARDMAN, Josiah, m. Esther C. **FRIEND**, Sept. 2, 1827, by Rev.
   David Baldwin, in the Episcopal Church, West Haven   3
BELDEN, W[illia]m W., Rev. m. Sarah **TREAT**, b. of Orange, Sept. 2,
   [1849], by Rev. George B. Hubbard   20
BENHAM, Almeda, m. James Lester **KIMBERLY**, b. of Orange, June 4,
   [1852], by E. Wright   23
   Ann C., m. Charles H. **WOOSTER**, b. of New Haven, Sept. 13,
   1846, by Rev. A. B. Chapin, of West Haven   21
   Elijah E., m. Mary E. **HINE**, Apr. 29, 1842, by Rev. A. Smyth   14
   Elisha, m. Abby **KIMBERLEY**, Sept. 5, [1822], by Rev. Stephen
   W. Stebbins, in West Haven   1
   Elivra, of Orange, m. Charles B. **STONE**, of Middlebury, May
   11, 1836, by Stephen W. Stebbins   11
   Maria K., m. Gorham **MUNSON**, b. of Orange, Oct. 23, 1844, by
   Rev. Cyrus Brewster   16
BENJAMIN, Everard, m. Esther **MERWIN**, May 21, 1833, by Horace
   Woodruff   8
BLAKESLEY, Ransom, of Plymouth, m. Elizabeth M. **JUDD**, of Orange,
   Sept. 16, 1835, by Horace Woodruff   10
BOMAN, Leonard, m. Sarah **FITTS**, b. of West Hartford, Aug. 14, 1832,
   by Zepheniah Swift, Derby   7
BOOTH, Eaton, of New Haven, m. Eliza Jane **THOMPSON**, of Orange,
   Mar. 14, 1852, by E. Wright   23
   Parnel, of New Haven, m. Nancy M. **SMITH**, of Orange, May 29,
   1836, by Rev. N. Coe, New Haven   11
BRACKETT, [see also **BROCKETT**], Issabella, m. Willys **PARDEE**, July
   4, 1824, by Stephen W. Stebbins   1
BRADBURY, Reuben, m. Martha **SMITH**, Jan. 1, 1837, by Stephen W.
   Stebbins   11
BRADLEY, Densey, m. Christian **FOWLER**, b. of New Haven, Oct. 13,
   1840, by Nehemiah Kimberley, J.P.   13
   Ezekiel Mason, m. Susan Rogers **ALLING**, June 6, 1844, by Rev.
   Cyrus Brewster   16
   Joel, of East Haven, m. Rena **DAWSON**, of West Haven, Dec. 31,
   1832, by Stephen W. Stebbins   8

	Page
BRADLEY, (cont.)	
Mary H., m. Benjamin F. **SOMERS**, b. of Orange, Nov. 19, 1837, by Asa M. Train	11
Oriel, of Woodbridge, m. Eunice **SPERRY**, of Orange, Oct. 9, [1823], by Erastus Scranton, V.D.M.	1
Sarah, m. David **JOHNSON**, Feb. 17, 1833, by Horace Woodruff	8
BROCKETT, [see also **BRACKETT**], Leonard, m. Martha **HILLS**, b. of West Haven, July 30, 1848, by Rev. A. B. Chapin, of West Haven	21
Lyman, m. Angelina **PARDEE**, Aug. 27, [1822], by Rev. Stephen W. Stebbins, in West Haven	1
Lyman, m. Abigail **HITCHCOCK**, Apr. 2, 1833, by Stephen W. Stebbins	8
BROWN, Caroline, of Humphreysville, m. Merrett **BALDWIN**, of New Haven, Apr. 26, 1838, by Stephen W. Stebbins, West Haven	12
Luman A., of Augusta, N.Y., m. Hannah A. **HINE**, of Orange, Mar. 13, 1836, by Stephen W. Stebbins	10
Roswell J., m. Nancy **THOMAS**, Oct. 9, 1831, by Stephen W. Stebbins	7
Spencer B., m. Abigail **SMITH**, b. of Milford, Oct. 10, 1830, by Horatio A. Parsons	6
BRYAN, Mary S., of Orange, m. Samuel **PECK**, of Fishkill, N. Y., Mar. 17, 1836, by Horace Woodruff	10
William, of Watertown, m. Clarrissa **TREAT**, of Orange, May 6, 1825, by Erastus Scranton, V.D.M.	2
BUCKINGHAM, Daniel, of Milford, m. Lucretia **PRINDLE**, of Orange, Aug. 6, 1849, by Rev. A. B. Chapin, of West Haven	21
BUNNET(?), Reuben, m. Mary **SMITH**, Sept. 19, [1822], by Rev. Stephen W. Stebbins, in West Haven	1
BURNS, William E., m. Martha L. **CLARK**, b. of Orange, May 28, 1842, by Rev. A. Smyth	14
BURRELL, [see also **BURWELL**], Emma, of West Haven, m. Thomas W. **HOTCHKISS**, of New Haven, Nov. 21, 1847, by Rev. A. B. Chapin, of West Haven	21
BURWELL, [see also **BURREL** & **BARNELL**], A. S., m. Susan M. **PECK**, Mar. 2, 1843, by D. B. Coe	15
CADY, Esther C., of Orange, m. James S. **LAWRENCE**, of New Haven, Oct. [ ], 1845, by E. Wright	18
Henry P., m. Perlinah **JOHNSON**, Dec. 28, [1845], by E. Wright, West Haven	18
CAFFREY, John, of Franklin, La., m. Frances Ann **SMITH**, of Orange, Sept. 30, 1835, by Stephen W. Stebbins	9
CAN, Rheuben, of Huntington, m. Rhoda **FREEMAN**, of N[ew] Haven, Oct. 25, 1824, by Benjamin L. Lambert, J.P. (**CARR**?)	2
CANDEE, Adeline, m. Newton **CLARK**, Mar. 30, 1831, by Stephen W. Stebbins	6
Albert, m. Eliza A. **SMITH**, Jan. 15, 1840, by Stephen W. Stebbins, West Haven	13

ORANGE VITAL RECORDS 5

	Page
CANDEE, (cont.)	
Ezra, m. Sarah A. **CLARK**, Apr. 22, 1840, by Asa M. Train	13
Loiza, m. John **FLEMING**, Sept. 30, 1839, by Stephen W. Stebbins	12
Lucy, m. Jesse **HODGE**, Apr. 13, 1835, by Stephen W. Stebbins	9
CARR(?), *Rheuben, of Huntington, m. Rhoda **FREEMAN**, of N[ew] Haven, Oct. 25, 1824, by Benjamin L. Lambert, J.P. *(Written "**CAN**")	2
CLARK, CLERK, Abigail A., of Orange, m. Richard W. **PLATT**, of Milford, Mar. 18, 1841, by Rev. A. Smyth	14
Alvin, m. Henry **PECK**, b. of Orange, Dec. 10, 1829, by Asa M. Train, Milford (Both male names in copy)	5
Asahel, m. Sarah **FOWLER**, Apr. 10, 1827, by Erastus Scranton, V.D.M.	4
Bryan, m. Maria **TREAT**, b. of Orange, Mar. 26, 1834, by Stephen W. Stebbins	9
Celina, m. Sereno **ARMSTRONG**, May 27, 1832, by Stephen W. Stebbins	7
Daniel, of Middletown, m. Sarah L. **PLATT**, of Orange, Oct. 3, 1841, by Rev. E. Colton, of Chester	14
Delia, of Orange, m. Richard M. **HUBBELL**, of Bridgeport, May 7, 1835, by Horace Woodruff	10
Elias T., m. Nancy M. **CLARK**, Apr. 10, 1845, by Asa M. Train	18
Elizabeth A., of Orange, m. Hull **ALLEN**, of Milford, Nov. 25, 1847, by Rev. Cyrus Brewster	19
Elizabeth J., of Orange, m. Charles E. **STUART**, of Sherman, Sept. [ ], 1849, by W. W. Belden	21
Joseph, m. Jane **HINE**, b. of Orange, Oct. 7, 1840, by Asa M. Train	13
Leverett J., m. Lucy **TREAT**, Jan. 7, 1847, by Asa M. Train	19
Leverett J., m. Harriet **HINE**, Oct. 5, 1851, by Rev. William W. Belden	23
Martha L., m. William E. **BURNS**, b. of Orange, May 28, 1842, by Rev. A. Smyth	14
Mehetable, m. Richard E. **SMITH**, Apr. 25, 1844, by Asa M. Train	16
Nancy M., m. Elias T. **CLARK**, Apr. 10, 1845, by Asa M. Train	18
Newton, m. Adeline **CANDEE**, Mar. 30, 1831, by Stephen W. Stebbins	6
Samuel, 3rd, of Milford, m. Mary E. **FOWLER**, of Orange, [June] 11, 1828, by John Clark	5
Sarah, m. Albert F. **MILES**, b. of Orange, Sept. 30, 1830, by Horatio A. Parsons	5
Sarah, m. Jonah **ROGERS**, Apr. 12, 1832, by Horatio A. Parsons	7
Sarah A., m. Ezra **CANDEE**, Apr. 22, 1840, by Asa M. Train	13
Susan, m. Dr. Josiah M. **COLBURN**, b. of Orange, Sept. 18,	

	Page
CLARK, (cont.)	
1825, by Erastus Scranton, V.D.M.	2
CLINTON, Rhoda, Mrs. of Orange, m. Joseph **TUTTLE**, late of Oxford, [Nov.] 16, [1825], by Rev. Eli Dennison	2
Simeon, of Waterbury, m. Nancy **SMITH**, of West Haven, Oct. 3, 1830, by Stephen W. Stebbins	5
COGGESHALL, Mary, m. Wales **SMITH**, May 2, 1830, by Stephen W. Stebbins	5
Mehitable, m. Henry **KIMBERLEY**, Mar. 23, 1834, by Stephen W. Stebbins	9
COLBURN, Josiah M. Dr., m. Susan **CLARK**, b. of Orange, Sept. 18, 1825, by Erastus Scranton, V.D.M.	2
COLTON, Erastus, Rev., of Niles, Mich., m. Jane A. **PRUDDON**, of Orange, Aug. 5, 1850, at her house, by Bishop George P. Pruddon	22
COMSTOCK, W[illia]m, m. Alice **GOODELL**, b. of Westville, July 29, [1845], by E. Wright	18
CRANE, Arpha, of New Haven, m. Dea. Enos **SMITH**, of Orange, Feb. 11, 1827, by Stephen W. Stebbins	3
CRITTENDEN, Harriet, m. Egbert **RIGGS**, Mar. 15, 1829, by Asa M. Train	5
CROFOOT, CROFUT, David R., of Reading, m. Harriet M. **TREAT**, of Orange, Sept. 29, 1841, by Rev. A. Smyth	14
Pollina, m. Garrie **NETTLETON**, Dec. 25, 1850, by Rev. Cha[rle]s Dickinson, of Birmingham	23
CURTISS, Alfred, d. Feb. 17, 1822	23
Hailey, ch. of Levi, d. Aug. 26, 1825	23
Jeremiah, s. Levi, d. Aug. 26, 1825	23
Levi, m. Amarilla **TALMAGE**, May 11, 1811, by [ ]	5
Lucy, w. Levi, d. Dec. 16, 1816	23
Sally, w. Levi, d. Nov. 10, 1810	23
Sally, d. Levi & Amarilla, b. Jan. 17, 1812	23
DAVIS, Anson Riley, of Derby, m. Mary Newton **ALLING**, of Orange, May 8, 1845, by Rev. W[illia]m Bliss Ashley, of Derby	18
Francis B., m. Elizabeth **KIMBERLEY**, May 9, 1825, by Stephen W. Stebbins	2
DAWSON, Henry S., m. Elizabeth **ALLING**, June 5, 1839, by Stephen W. Stebbins	12
Rena, of West Haven, m. Joel **BRADLEY**, of East Haven, Dec. 31, 1832, by Stephen W. Stebbins	8
William H., m. Abigail **WILMOTT**, May 4, 1834, by Stephen W. Stebbins, West Haven	9
DODD, Sally, Mrs. of Milford, m. Thomas **ALLING**, of New Haven, Oct. 15, 1837, by Asa M. Train	11
DOREMUS, Peter C., m. Julia A. **STONE**, May 30, 1838, by B. Y. Messenger	12
DOWNS, Abigail, m. Lyman **PRINDLE**, Mar. 27, 1823, by Rev. Stephen W. Stebbins	1

	Page
DOWNS, (cont.)	
Eliza L, m. Sidney **PARDEE**, May 15, 1833, by Stephen W. Stebbins	8
John W., m. Louisa **SMITH**, b. of West Haven, Dec. 3, 1826, by Stephen W. Stebbins	3
Sarah, m. John **JONES**, Mar. 5, 1839, by Rev. Stephen W. Stebbins, of West Haven	12
Sarah W., m. Enoch **SUMMERS**, Mar. 9, 1826, by Stephen W. Stebbins	3
DURAND, Alva J., m. Sarah Ann **PLATT**, Oct. 6, 1824, by Stephen W. Stebbins	2
Eliza A., of Orange, m. Enoch H. **SOMERS**, of New York, Dec. 2, 1850, by Edward Wright	23
EAYRES, Lydia, wid., m. Levi J. **BALL**, Mar. 3, 1829, by Stephen W. Stebbins	5
EVANS, Eliza A., of West Haven, m. Stanly G. **SMITH**, June 19, 1839, by Stephen W. Stebbins	12
FAIRCHILD, Eleanor, m. Philemon **SMITH**, June 10, 1827, by Stephen W. Stebbins	3
FENN*, Aaron W., m. Dianthy **WOODRUFF**, Dec. 16, 1836, by Asa M. Train (*Perhaps "**TRENN**?")	11
Fowler, of Plymouth, m. Mary E. **ROGERS**, of Orange, Oct. 21, 1833, by Asa M. Train	8
Frances A., m. Noyes A. **TREAT**, b. of Orange, May 4, 1851, by W. W. Belden	23
William A., of McDonough, Ga., m. Jane J. **STONE**, of Orange, May 29, 1839, by Rev. D. G. Tomlinson, of Trumbull	14
FERRIN, John, of East Haven, m. Polly **FRISBEE**, of North Branford, Sept. [ ], 1845, by E. Wright	18
FITTS, Sarah, m. Leonard **BOMAN**, b. of West Hartford, Aug. 14, 1832, by Zepheniah Swift, Derby	7
FLEMING, James, of New York City, m. Sarah A. **MELOY**, of Orange, [June] 6, [1844], by Edward Wright	16
John, m. Loiza **CANDEE**, Sept. 30, 1839, by Stephen W. Stebbins	12
FOOT, Jonathan, Jr., m. Sarah **STEVENS**, Jan. 7, 1841, by Stephen W. Stebbins, West Haven	13
FORD, Harriet, m. George **TOLLES**, b. of West Haven, Feb. 22, 1846, by Rev. A. B. Chapin, of West Haven	21
Harriet A., m. Frederick R. **RICHARDS**, b. of West Haven, Apr. 28, 1850, by Rev. A. B. Chapin, of West Haven	22
Nathaniel, of Hamden, m. Mary Ann **MERWIN**, of Milford, May 4, 1834, by Stephen W. Stebbins	9
FOWLER, Christian, m. Densey **BRADLEY**, b. of New Haven, Oct. 13, 1840, by Nehemiah Kimberley, J.P.	13
Martha, m. Alva **GRAHAM**, July 22, 1833, by Stephen W. Stebbins	8
Mary E., of Orange, m. Samuel **CLARK**, 3rd, of Milford, [June] 11, 1828, by John Clark	5

	Page
FOWLER, (cont.)	
Nathan C., m. Matilda M. **LAMBERT**, b. of Orange, Apr. 10, 1836, by Stephen W. Stebbins, West Haven	10
Sarah, m. Asahel **CLARK**, Apr. 10, 1827, by Erastus Scranton, V.D.M.	4
FREEMAN, Rhoda, of N[ew] Haven, m. Rheuben **CAN**, of Huntington, Oct. 25, 1824, by Benjamin L. Lambert, J.P.	2
FRIEND, Esther C., m. Josiah **BEARDMAN**, Sept. 2, 1827, by Rev. David Baldwin, in the Episcopal Church, West Haven	3
FRISBEE, Polly, of North Branford, m. John **FERRIN**, of East Haven, Sept. [ ], 1845, by E. Wright	18
GALPIN, Sylvester, m. Clarissa **SMITH**, Oct. 9, 1831, by Stephen W. Stebbins	17
GOEHLIN, Otto, m. Cornelia **THOMAS**, Nov. 28, 1850, by Edward Wright	23
GOMAR, Mehetable, m. John S. **WILLIAMS**, July 22, 1839, by Stephen W. Stebbins	12
GOODELL, Alice, m. W[illia]m **COMSTOCK**, b. of Westville, July 29, [1845], by E. Wright	18
GRAHAM, Alva, m. Martha **FOWLER**, July 22, 1833, by Stephen W. Stebbins	8
GRAVES, Richard, of Guilford, m. Esther **HINE**, of Orange, Oct. 10, 1824, by E. Scranton, V.D.M.	2
GRISWOLD, William L., m. Huldah **WARD**, b. of West Haven, Nov. 25, 1849, by Rev. A. B. Chapin, of West Haven	21
GUNN, Stephen, Jr., of Milford, m. Mary O. **MERWIN**, of West Haven, May 28, 1845, by Rev. A. B. Chapin, of West Haven	21
HARRISON, Roxanna, m. Roswell **HOMER**, July 14, [1822], by Erastus Scranton, V.D.M., in North Milford	1
HARTSHORN, Sheldon Smith, of Waterbury, m. Margarett Ann **THOMPSON**, of West Haven, Aug. 25, 1850, by Rev. A. B. Chapin, of West Haven	22
HAWLEY, John, m. Julia Ann **WOODRUFF**, Oct. 5, 1826, by Erastus Scranton V.D.M.	4
HEITMAN, Adrian C., of New Haven, m. Louisa **WARD**, of West Haven, Sept. 29, 1842, by Rev. A. B. Chapin, of West Haven	22
HICOCKS, [see also **HOTCHKISS**], Ann B., m. Edwin **SMITH**, b. of West Haven, May 8, [1845], by Edward Wright	17
HILLS, Martha, m. Leonard **BROCKETT**, b. of West Haven, July 30, 1848, by Rev. A. B. Chapin, of West Haven	21
HINE, [see also **KINE**], Charlotte E., of Orange, m. John B. **ADRIANCE**, of New York, Jan. 15, 1845, by Rev. Cyrus Brewster	17
Esther, of Orange, m. Richard **GRAVES**, of Guilford, Oct. 10, 1824, by E. Scranton, V.D.M.	2
Hannah A., of Orange, m. Luman A. **BROWN**, of Augusta, N. Y., Mar. 13, 1836, by Stephen W. Stebbins	10
Harriet, m. Leverett J. **CLERK**, Oct. 5, 1851, by Rev. William	

	Page
HINE, (cont.)	
Belden	23
Jane, m. Joseph **CLARK**, b. of Orange, Oct. 7, 1840, by Asa M. Train	13
Mary E., m. Elijah E. **BENHAM**, Apr. 29, 1842, by Rev. A. Smyth	14
Thomas D., of New Haven, m. Hellen M. **SMITH**, of Franklin, La., Oct. 6, 1843, by Rev. Edward Wright, West Haven	15
HINMAN, Sarah, m. Willis **SMITH**, Nov. 10, 1842, by Stephen W. Stebbins, West Haven	15
HITCHCOCK, Abigail, m. Lyman **BROCKETT**, Apr. 2, 1833, by Stephen W. Stebbins	8
HOADLEY, Olive C., of South Glastonbury, m. George B. **MALLORY**, of Woodbury, Dec. 1, 1850, by W. W. Belden	23
HODGE, Jesse, m. Lucy **CANDEE**, Apr. 13, 1835, by Stephen W. Stebbins	9
HOLT, Samuel E., of East Haven, m. Eunice **WARD**, of West Haven, Aug. 22, 1844, by Rev. A. B. Chapin, of West Haven	21
HOMER, Roswell, m. Roxanna **HARRISON**, July 14, [1822], by Erastus Scranton, V.D.M., in North Milford	1
HOTCHKISS, HITCHKISS, [see also **HICOCKS**], David, m. Julia **TERRELL**, Sept. 19, 1824, by Stephen W. Stebbins	2
Eliza Ann, m. Jesse Seymour **PARDEE**, Nov. 2, 1826, by Erastus Scranton, V.D.M.	4
Thomas W., of New Haven, m. Emma **BURREL**, of West Haven, Nov. 21, 1847, by Rev. A. B. Chapin, of West Haven	21
HUBBARD, Anna A., m. John W. **MERWIN**, Sept. 30, 1831, by Stephen W. Stebbins	7
HUBBELL, Henry B., of Bridgeport, m. Abby C. **MALLETT**, of Milford, Feb. 1, 1836, by Hiram Woodruff	10
Richard M., of Bridgeport, m. Delia **CLARK**, of Orange, May 7, 1835, by Horace Woodruff	10
HULL, Hannah P., of Orange, m. William S. **SMITH**, of New Haven, May 25, 1831, by Rev. Laban C. Cheney	6
HUNTINGTON, Rebecca Loiza, of Orange, m. John W. **MERWIN**, of Norfolk, VA., Nov. 24, 1840, by Rev. H. G. Ludlow, of New Haven	13
ISBEL, Josiah, of Milford, m. Mary **ANDREW**, of Orange, Mar. 4, 1835, by Asa M. Train, Milford	9
IVES, Eli, of Plymouth, m. Mary **JUDD**, of Orange, May 22, 1834, by H. Woodruff	9
George, of New Haven, m. Lydia **SMITH**, of West Haven, May 25, 1838, by Stephen W. Stebbins	12
Henry, m. Angeline **SMITH**, July 25, 1831, by Stephen W. Stebbins	6
JEWETT, Enoch, Capt., m. Leucretia **NEWHALL**, Oct. 13, [1822], by Rev. Erastus Scranton, in North Milford	1
JOHNSON, Betsey, w. Solomon, d. Jan. 22, 1820	23

	Page
JOHNSON, (cont.)	
Cynthia M., of Derby, m. George H. **BALDWIN**, Nov. 16, 1845, by Rev. A. B. Chapin, of West Haven	21
David, m. Sarah **BRADLEY**, Feb. 17, 1833, by Horace Woodruff	8
David Alling, s. Solomon & Eliza T., b. Feb. 8, 1826	23
Ebenezer, d. Nov. 3, 1818	23
Enos L., m. Mary **PLATT**, Apr. 13, 1836, by Stephen W. Stebbins	3
Esther, wid. Eben[eze]r, d. July 12, 1824	23
Homer, of Orange, m. Lovina **PERKINS**, of Woodbridge, Sept. 6, 1835, by Horace Woodruff	10
Jeremiah S., m. Susannah **ALLING**, Dec. 29, [1822], by Rev. [ ] Perry	1
Perlinah, m. Henry P. **CADY**, Dec. 28, [1845], by E. Wright, West Haven	18
Roswell, m. Sally **SMITH**, Aug. 22, 1824, by Stephen W. Stebbins	1
Solomon Punderson, s. Solomon & Eliza T., b. May 30, 1824	23
W[illia]m, m. Naomi **MERRIMAN** (colored), Aug. 20, 1826, by Rev. W[illia]m S. Potter, of West Haven	4
William Holt, s. Solomon & Eliza T., b. Oct. 19, 1828	23
JONES, John, m. Sarah **DOWNS**, Mar. 5, 1839, by Rev. Stephen W. Stebbins, of West Haven	12
Mary, m. Nathaniel **KIMBERLEY**, b. of West Haven, Oct. 19, 1845, by Rev. A. B. Chapin, of West Haven	21
JUDD, Elizabeth M., of Orange, m. Ransom **BLAKESLEY**, of Plymouth, Sept. 16, 1835, by Horace Woodruff	10
Mary, of Orange, m. Eli **IVES**, of Plymouth, May 22, 1834, by H. Woodruff	9
JUDSON, Mary Abigail, of Orange, m. Andrew **PERRY**, of Huntington, Nov. 4, 1827, by Rev. W[illia]m S. Potter, of West Haven	4
KENNEDY, Nathaniel, m. Mabel **THOMAS**, June 23, 1822, by Rev. Stephen W. Stebbins, in West Haven	1
KIMBERLY,KIMBERLEY, Abby, m. Elisha **BENHAM**, Sept. 5, [1822], by Rev. Stephen W. Stebbins, in West Haven	1
Elizabeth, m. Francis B. **DAVIS**, May 9, 1825, by Stephen W. Stebbins	2
Elizabeth A., m. Lucius **STEVENS**, Oct. 21, 1840, by Stephen W. Stebbins, West Haven	13
Francis, of New York, m. Jane E. **PLATT**, of Orange, Jan. 10, 1849, by E. Wright	20
Henry, m. Mehitable **COGGESHALL**, Mar. 23, 1834, by Stephen W. Stebbins	9
James Lester, m. Almeda **BENHAM**, b. of Orange, June 4, [1852], by E. Wright	23
Mary, m. Asahel **THOMAS**, Apr. 29, 1827, by Stephen W. Stebbins	3
Nathaniel, m. Mary **JONES**, b. of West Haven, Oct. 19, 1845, by Rev. A. B. Chapin, of West Haven	21
Sophia, m. Newton **PLATT**, Apr. 22, 1830, by Stephen W. Stebbins	5

ORANGE VITAL RECORDS 11

Page

KINE*, Susan, of Orange, m. John P. **STRONG**, of Milford, Sept. 9, 1840, by Asa M. Train *(Perhaps "**HINE**") 13
KNEEL, Russell, of Westville, m. Charlotte O. **SPERRY**, d. Kneeland, of Orange, [Feb.] 19, 1840, by John Starkweather 13
LAFORGE, Major G., of New Haven, m. Augusta L. **THOMAS**, of Orange, [Oct.*] 25, [1846], by Edward Wright, West Haven (*Perhaps "Nov.") 19
LAMBERT, Esther M., m. Calvin A. **TREAT**, Mar. 21, 1831, by Horatio A. Parsons 6
Matilda M., m. Nathan C. **FOWLER**, b. of Orange, Apr. 10, 1836, by Stephen W. Stebbins, West Haven 10
Sarah B., of Orange, m. Sherman **PETTIBONE**, of Burlington, May 20, 1835, by Horace Woodruff 10
LAWRENCE, James S., of New Haven, m. Esther C. **CADY**, of Orange, Oct. [ ], 1845, by E. Wright 18
LEE, Geo[rge] A., of Guilford, m. Ann T. **STANNARD**, of Orange, Apr. 9, 1846, by Edward Wright, West Haven 19
LINES, Edwin, m. Frances A. **SMITH**, [Apr.] 5, [1846], by Edward Wright 19
LYMAN, Julia Ann, of West Haven, m. Norris **ANDREWS**, of New Haven, Apr. 6, 1849, by Rev. A. B. Chapin, of West Haven 21
Mary C., of West Haven, m. Lynden **RICHARDSON**, of New Haven, Jan. 26, 1849, by Rev. A. B. Chapin, of West Haven 21
MABRY, Lester W., m. Elizabeth **ALLING**, Jan. 30, 1831, by Horatio A. Parsons 7
MACUMBER, Henry Thomas, m. Charlotte **SMITH**, Nov. 7, 1833, by Stephen W. Stebbins 8
MALLETT, Abby C., of Milford, m. Henry B. **HUBBELL**, of Bridgeport, Feb. 1, 1836, by Hiram Woodruff 10
MALLORY, George B., of Woodbury, m. Olive C. **HOADLEY**, of South Glastonbury, Dec. 1, 1850, by W. W. Belden 23
MANSFIELD, Delia, of North Haven, m. Francis N. **STEVENS**, of Orange, Apr. 25, [1847], by Edward Wright, West Haven 19
Minerva, of Orange, m. Adam **POND**, of Milford, Mar. 11, 1827, by Rev. W[illia]m S. Potter, of West Haven 4
MELOY, Charlotte, of West Haven, m. Philander **ARMSTRONG**, of New Haven, Sept. 15, 1850, by A. B. Chapin 22
MELOY(?), Mary, m. Nathan **PLATT**, Jr., Oct. 12, 1825, by Stephen W. Stebbins 2
Sarah A., of Orange, m. James **FLEMING**, of New York City, [June] 6, [1844], by Edward Wright 16
MERRECK, Miles F., m. Rebecca **ALLING**, b. of Orange, Mar. 5, 1850, by W. W. Belden 22
MERREW, Hannah, of Milford, m. Joseph **MINER**, of Orange, Oct. 23, 1825, by Erastus Scranton, V.D.M. 2
MERRIMAN, Naomi, m. W[illia]m **JOHNSON** (colored), Aug. 20, 1826, by Rev. W[illia]m S. Potter, of West Haven 4
MERWIN, Abram T., m. Virginia **SMITH**, b. of Orange, Oct. 24, 1842,

	Page
MERWIN, (cont.)	
by Asa M. Train	14
Alpheas N., m. Mary T. **ALLING**, b. of Orange, Oct. [ ], 1849, by W. W. Belden	21
Daniel, m. Clarissa **MUNSON**, b. of Orange, Mar. 27, 1836, by Horace Woodruff	10
Esther, m. Everard **BENJAMIN**, May 21, 1833, by Horace Woodruff	8
John W., m. Anna A. **HUBBARD**, Sept. 30, 1831, by Stephen W. Stebbins	7
John W., of Norfolk, Va., m. Rebecca Loiza **HUNTINGTON**, of Orange, Nov. 24, 1840, by Rev. H. G. Ludlow, of New Haven	13
Marcus, of Norfolk, Va., m. Abigail **SMITH**, of Orange, [Feb.] 3, [1845], by Edward Wright	17
Mary Ann, of Milford, m. Nathaniel **FORD**, of Hamden, May 4, 1834, by Stephen W. Stebbins	9
Mary O., of West Haven, m. Stephen **GUNN**, Jr., of Milford, May 28, 1845, by Rev. A. B. Chapin, of West Haven	21
Phebe, m. Capt. James **WARD**, Dec. 5, 1827, by Rev. W[illia]m S. Potter, of West Haven	4
Sarah J., m. J. L. **NORTHRUP**, b. of West Haven, Mar. 29, 1842, by Rev. A. B. Chapin, of West Haven	21
MILES, Albert F., m. Sarah **CLARK**, b. of Orange, Sept. 30, 1830, by Horatio A. Parsons	5
MINOR, MINER, Charles P., of Roxbury, m. Susan **WOODRUFF**, of Orange, [June] 11, [1845], by Rev. Cyrus Brewster	17
Joseph, of Orange, m. Hannah **MERREW**, of Milford, Oct. 23, 1825, by Erastus Scranton, V.D.M.	2
MORGAN, George W., m. Loisa **PLATT**, Oct. 20, 1833, by Stephen W. Stebbins	8
MOULTHROP, Charles Street, s. Daniel, b. Nov. 15, 1824	23
Charles Street, s. Daniel, of West Orange, d. Dec. 13, 1827	23
Delia Ann, m. William **STOWE**, Jr., Apr. 18, 1827, by Stephen W. Stebbins	3
William, s. Daniel, b. Aug. 6, 1826	23
MUNSON, Clarissa, m. Daniel **MERWIN**, b. of Orange, Mar. 27, 1836, by Horace Woodruff	10
Garsham, m. Julia **NETTLETON**, b. of Orange, July 11, 1830, by Horatio A. Parsons	5
Gorham, m. Maria K. **BENHAM**, b. of Orange, Oct. 23, 1844, by Rev. Cyrus Brewster	16
Julia, m. Zeri **ALLING**, b. of Orange, [Sept.] 24, [1843], by Rev. Cyrus Brewster. Int.Pub.	15
NETTLETON, Charlotte Emily, m. Jeremiah **WOODRUFF**, Mar. 29, 1837, by Asa M. Train.	11
Garrie, m. Pollina **CROFUT**, Dec. 25, 1850, by Rev. Cha[rle]s Dickinson, of Birmingham	23
Harriet, m. Edward **BALDWIN**, July 1, 1832, by Asa M. Train	7
Julia, m. Garsham **MUNSON**, b. of Orange, July 11, 1830, by	

ORANGE VITAL RECORDS 13

	Page
NETTLETON, (cont.)	
Horatio A. Parsons	5
Polly M., m. Joel **BALDWIN**, Oct. 3, [1822], by Erastus Scranton, V.D.M., in North Milford	1
Sarah E., of Orange, m. John **RIX**, of Ulster Co., N. Y., Aug. 8, [1844], by Edward Wright, West Haven	16
NEWEL, Joshua, of New Haven, m. Eliza **ALLING**, of Orange, Nov. 5, 1838, by E. Wright	20
NEWHALL, Leucretia, m. Capt. Enoch **JEWETT**, Oct. 13, [1822], by Rev. Erastus Scranton, in North Milford	1
NORTHRUP, J. L., m. Sarah J. **MERWIN**, b. of West Haven, Mar. 29, 1842, by Rev. A. B. Chapin	21
OVIATT, Julia Ann, m. Joseph S. **RIGGS**, b. of Orange, May 23, 1844, by Rev. Cyrus Brewster	16
Sidney F., m. Mary Ann **RIGGS**, Oct. 27, 1844, by Rev. Cyrus Brewster	17
Susan E., m. Benjamin W. **RIGGS**, Mar. 19, 1843, by Rev. Zepheniah Swift, of Derby	15
PARDEE, Angelina, m. Lyman **BROCKETT**, Aug. 27, [1822], by Rev. Stephen W. Stebbins, in West Haven	1
Jesse Seymour, m. Eliza A. **HITCHKISS**, Nov. 2, 1826, by Erastus Scranton, V.D.M.	4
Joseph H., m. Eliza M. **STONE**, b. of Orange, [May] 15, [1848], by Edward Wright	20
Sidney, m. Eliza L. **DOWNS**, May 15, 1833, by Stephen W. Stebbins	8
Urania, m. Calvin **BEACH**, b. of Orange, Nov. 14, 1823, by Erastus Scranton, V.D.M.	1
Willys, m. Issabella **BRACKETT**, July 4, 1824, by Stephen W. Stebbins	1
PARSONS, Susan, m. William E. **RUSSELL**, Sept. 8, 1831, by Horatio A. Parsons	7
PECK, Esther, of Orange, m. Ephraim B. **PITCHER**, of Parma, N. Y., Feb. 1, 1835, by H. Woodruff	9
Henry, m. Alvin **CLARK**, b. of Orange, Dec. 10, 1829, by Asa M. Train, Milford (Both male names in copy)	5
Samuel, of Fishkill, N. Y., m. Mary S. **BRYAN**, of Orange, Mar. 17, 1836, by Horace Woodruff	10
Susan M., m. A. S. **BURWELL**, Mar. 2, 1843, by D. B. Coe	15
PERKINS, Lovina, of Woodbridge, m. Homer **JOHNSON**, of Orange, Sept. 6, 1835, by Horace Woodruff	10
Timothy, m. Charlotte **RUSSELL**, b. of Orange, [Sept.] 28, [1843], by Rev. Cyrus Brewster	15
PERRY, Andrew, of Huntington, m. Mary Abigail **JUDSON**, of Orange, Nov. 4, 1827, by Rev. W[illia]m S. Potter, of West Haven	4
PETTIBONE, Norman, of Burlington, m. Susan **WETMORE**, of Orange, July 17, 1831, by H. A. Parsons	6
Sherman, of Burlington, m. Sarah B. **LAMBERT**, of Orange, May	

	Page
PETTIBONE, (cont.)	
20, 1835, by Horace Woodruff	10
PHELPS, Erastus R., m. Nancy M. **PHELPS**, Dec. 21, 1834, by Stephen W. Stebbins	9
Nancy M., m. Erastus R. **PHELPS**, Dec. 21, 1834, by Stephen W. Stebbins	9
PHILLIPS, Charles, m. Patty **ALLING**, Sept. 16, 1822, by Rev. Stephen W. Stebbins, in West Haven	1
PITCHER, Ephraim B., of Parma, N. Y., m. Esther **PECK**, of Orange, Feb. 1, 1835, by H. Woodruff	9
PLATT, Charles N., m. M. Elizabeth **WOODRUFF**, Sept. 26, 1848, by Rev. W. W. Belden	20
Fanlina, m. Stiles H. **THOMPSON**, Aug. 23, 1829, by Stephen W. Stebbins	5
Jane E., of Orange, m. Francis **KIMBERLEY**, of New York, Jan. 10, 1849, by E. Wright	20
Joseph B., m. Marietta **SMITH**, Sept. 25, 1833, by Stephen W. Stebbins	8
Loisa, m. George W. **MORGAN**, Oct. 20, 1833, by Stephen W. Stebbins	8
Martha, of Orange, m. Ramond **BALDWIN**, of Woodbridge, Nov. 27, [1823], by Erastus Scranton, V.D.M.	1
Mary, m. Enos L. **JOHNSON**, Apr. 13, 1826, by Stephen W. Stebbins	3
Nathan, Jr., Mary **MELOY** (?), Oct. 12, 1825, by Stephen W. Stebbins	2
Newton, m. Sophia **KIMBERLEY**, Apr. 22, 1830, by Stephen W. Stebbins	5
Richard W., of Milford, m. Abigail A. **CLARK**, of Orange, Mar. 18, 1841, by Rev. A. Smyth	14
Sarah Ann, m. Alva J. **DURAND**, Oct. 6, 1824, by Stephen W. Stebbins	2
Sarah L., of Orange, m. Daniel **CLARK**, of Middletown, Oct. 3, 1841, by Rev. E. Colton of Chester	14
POND, Adam, of Milford, m. Minerva **MANSFIELD**, of Orange, Mar. 11, 1827, by Rev. W[illia]m S. Potter, of West Haven	4
POPE, Charles R., m. Mary F. **TREAT**, b. of Orange, May 28, 1844, by Rev. Cyrus Brewster	16
[**PRINDLE**], Horatio Halsey, [s. Lyman & Abigail D.], b. Dec. 25, 1830	23
John H. Hobart, [s. Lyman & Abigail D.], b. Mar. 1, 1827	23
Joseph Stephen, [s. Lyman & Abigail D.]b. Aug. 29, 1825	23
Leitia Eliza, [d. Lyman & Abigail D.], b. Mar. 18, 1829	23
Lucretia, [d. Lyman & Abigail D.], b. Jan. 12, 1824	23
Lucretia, of Orange, m. Daniel **BUCKINGHAM**, of Milford, Aug. 6, 1849, by Rev. A. B. Chapin, of West Haven	21
Lyman, m. Abigail **DOWNS**, Mar. 27, 1823, by Rev. Stephen W. Stebbins	1

ORANGE VITAL RECORDS 15

	Page
PRUDDON, Jane A., of Orange, m. Rev. Erastus **COLTON**, of Niles, Mich., Aug. 5, 1850, at her house, by Bishop George P. Pruddon	22
Sarah E., m. Amos F. **ALLING**, b. of Orange, Sept. 2, 1847, by Rev. Geo[rge] P. Pruddon	19
RAWSON, Elijah, m. Sophia E. **STEBBINS**, Sept. 8, 1841, by Stephen W. Stebbins, West Haven	14
RICHARDS, Frederick R., m. Harriet A. **FORD**, b. of West Haven, Apr. 28, 1850, by Rev. A. B. Chapin, of West Haven	22
John S. T., m. Eliza **ARMSTRONG**, b. of West Haven, Sept. 8, 1841, by Rev. A. B. Chapin	21
RICHARDSON, Lynden, of New Haven, m. Mary C. **LYMAN**, of West Haven, Jan. 26, 1849, by Rev. A. B. Chapin, of West Haven	21
RIGGS, Benjamin W., m. Susan E. **OVIATT**, Mar. 19, 1843, by Rev. Zepheniah Swift, Derby	15
Egbert, m. Harriet **CRITTENDEN**, Mar. 15, 1829, by Asa M. Train	5
Joseph S., m. Julia Ann **OVIATT**, b. of Orange, May 23, 1844, by Rev. Cyrus Brewster	16
Mary Ann, m. Sidney F. **OVIATT**, Oct. 27, 1844, by Rev. Cyrus Brewster	17
RIX, John, of Ulster, Co., N. Y., m. Sarah E. **NETTLETON**, of Orange, Aug. 8, [1844], by Edward Wright, West Haven	16
ROGERS, Jonah, m. Sarah **CLARK**, Apr. 12, 1832, by Horatio A. Parsons	7
Julia, m. Bela **ALLING**, Sept. 28, 1826, by Erastus Scranton, V.D.M.	4
Mary E., of Orange, m. Fowler **FENN**, of Plymouth, Oct. 21, 1833, by Asa M. Train	8
ROSE, Joshua, m. Harriet W. **SMITH**, Feb. 5, 1837, by Stephen W. Stebbins	11
RUSSELL, Amy P., m. Levi **ALLING**, b. of Orange, Nov. 29, 1849, by W. W. Belden	22
Catherine B., m. Elias **ALLEN**, b. of Orange, Apr. 30, 1843, by Rev. A. Smyth	15
Charlotte, m. Timothy **PERKINS**, b. of Orange, [Sept.] 28, [1843], by Rev. Cyrus Brewster	15
William E., m. Susan **PARSONS**, Sept. 8, 1831, by Horatio A. Parsons	7
SAGE, Abula, of Orange, m. Stiles **STEVENS**, of New Haven, Aug. 21, 1825, by Erastus Scranton, V.D.M.	2
SEARS, William L., m. Elizabeth A. **SMITH**, June 8, 1834, by Stephen W. Stebbins, West Haven	9
SEELEY, Catharine, of Fair Haven, m. Albert **THOMAS**, of Orange, Nov. 2, 1845, by E. Wright	18
Harriet M., of Fair Haven, m. Alfred **THOMAS**, of Orange, Mar. 23, 1846, by Edward Wright	18
SEGAR, Sarah, m. Brigham **SMITH**, Apr. 27, [1823], by Rev. Stephen W. Stebbins	1

	Page
SHEPHARD, E. Y.*, of New Haven, m. Almira **ALLING**, of Orange, Aug. 14, 1833, by Horace Woodruff (*correction "Elisha Yale" handwritten above E. Y. in the original manuscript)	8
SMITH, Abigail, m. Spencer B. **BROWN**, b. of Milford, Oct. 10, 1830, by Horatio A. Parsons	6
Abigail, of Orange, m. Marcus **MERWIN**, of Norfolk, Va., [Feb.] 3, [1845], by Edward Wright	17
Amanda R., m. Ephraim B. **WILMOT**, Mar. 3, 1834, by Stephen W. Stebbins	9
Angeline, m. Henry **IVES**, July 25, 1831, by Stephen W. Stebbins	6
Brigham, m. Sarah **SEGAR**, Apr. 27, [1823], by Rev. Stephen W. Stebbins	1
Charlotte, [d. Bradford], b. May 31, 1824	23
Charlotte, m. Henry Thomas **MACUMBER**, Nov. 7, 1833, by Stephen W. Stebbins	8
Clarissa, m. Sylvester **GALPIN**, Oct. 9, 1831, by Stephen W. Stebbins	7
Edwin, m. Ann B. **HICOCKS**, b. of West Haven, May 8, [1845], by Edward Wright	17
Eliza A., m. Albert **CANDEE**, Jan. 15, 1840, by Stephen W. Stebbins, West Haven	13
Eliza Ann, [d. Bradford], b. Oct. 5, 1816	23
Elizabeth A., m. William L. **SEARS**, June 8, 1834, by Stephen W. Stebbins, West Haven	9
Enos, Dea., of Orange, m. Arpha **CRANE**, of New Haven, Feb. 11, 1827, by Stephen W. Stebbins	3
Frances A., m. Edwin **LINES**, [Apr.] 5, [1846], by Edward Wright	19
Frances Ann, of Orange, m. John **CAFFREY**, of Franklin, La., Sept. 30, 1835, by Stephen W. Stebbins	9
Granville, m. Abigail **THOMAS**, b. of Orange, Sept. 23, 1827, by Rev. W[illia]m S. Potter, of West Haven	4
Harriet W., m. Joshua **ROSE**, Feb. 5, 1837, by Stephen W. Stebbins	11
Hellen M., of Franklin, La., m. Thomas D. **HINE**, of New Haven, Oct. 6, 1843, by Rev. Edward Wright, West Haven	15
J. A., m. Louisa **TREAT**, b. of Orange, [May] 14, [1848], by Edward Wright, West Haven	20
Jennett, of Orange, m. Richard **TREAT**, Jr., of Milford, Feb. [ ], 1828, by Rev. Stephen W. Stebbins, of West Haven	4
Lockwood, m. Delia Grace **THOMAS**, June 13, 1838, by Rev. E. E. Griswold	12
Louisa, [d. Bradford], b. Aug. 13, 1804	23
Louisa, m. John W. **DOWNS**, b. of West Haven, Dec. 3, 1826, by Stephen W. Stebbins	3
Lydia, of West Haven, m. George **IVES**, of New Haven, May 25, 1838, by Stephen W. Stebbins	12
Marietta, [d. Bradford], b. May 5, 1811	23
Marietta, m. Joseph B. **PLATT**, Sept. 25, 1833, by Stephen W.	

ORANGE VITAL RECORDS

Page

SMITH, (cont.)
Stebbins — 8
Martha, m. Reuben **BRADBURY**, Jan. 1, 1837, by Stephen W.
 Stebbins — 11
Mary, m. Reuben **BUNNET**, Sept. 19, [1822], by Rev. Stephen W.
 Stebbins, in West Haven — 1
Minerva, m. Silas **THOMPSON**, Jan. 14, 1833, by Stephen W.
 Stebbins — 8
Nancy, [d. Bradford], b. Jan. 19, 1806 — 23
Nancy, of West Haven, m. Simeon **CLINTON**, of Waterbury, Oct.
 3, 1830, by Stephen W. Stebbins — 5
Nancy M., of Orange, m. Parnel **BOOTH**, of New Haven, May 29,
 1836, by Rev. N. Coe., New Haven — 11
Nelson, m. Martha **TOLLS**, Apr. 21, 1831, by Stephen W.
 Stebbins, West Haven — 6
Philemon, m. Eleanor **FAIRCHILD**, June 10, 1827, by Stephen W.
 Stebbins — 3
Richard E., m. Mehetable **CLARK**, Apr. 25, 1844, by Asa M.
 Train — 16
Rosette, m. Willis **BARNELL***, July 7, [1822], by Rev. Stephen
 W. Stebbins, in West Haven (*Perhaps "**BURWELL**"?) — 1
Salina, of Orange, m. Samuel **ANDREW**, of Woodbridge, Jan. 1,
 1824, by Erastus Scranton, V.D.M. — 1
Sally, m. Roswell **JOHNSON**, Aug. 22, 1824, by Stephen W.
 Stebbins — 1
Samuel L., of Milford, m. Harriet **WOODRUFF**, of Orange, July
 20, 1837, by Asa M. Train — 11
Sidney, [s. Bradford], b. Mar. 10, 1808 — 23
Stanl[e]y G., m. Eliza A. **EVANS**, of West Haven, June 19, 1839,
 by Stephen W. Stebbins — 12
Virginia, m. Abram T. **MERWIN**, b. of Orange, Oct. 24, 1842, by
 Asa M. Train — 14
Wales, m. Mary **COGGESHALL**, May 2, 1830, by Stephen W.
 Stebbins — 5
William S., of New Haven, m. Hannah P. **HULL**, of Orange, May
 25, 1831, by Rev. Laban C. Cheney — 6
Wyllys, m. Maruna **BATES**, Oct. 7, 1839, by Stephen W. Stebbins — 12
Willis, m. Sarah **HINMAN**, Nov. 10, 1842, by Stephen W.
 Stebbins, West Haven — 15
SOMERS, Benjamin F., m. Mary H. **BRADLEY**, b. of Orange, Nov. 19,
 1837, by Asa M. Train — 11
Enoch H., of New York, m. Eliza A. **DURAND**, of Orange, Dec. 2,
 1850, by Edward Wright — 23
SPARKS, Edward, m. Phebe Ann **STONE**, b. of West Haven, June 10,
 1849, by Rev. A. B. Chapin, of West Haven — 21
SPERRY, Charlotte O., d. Kneeland, of Orange, m. Russell **KNEEL**, of
 Westville, [Feb.] 19, 1840, by John Starkweather — 13
Eunice, of Orange, m. Oriel **BRADLEY**, of Woodbridge, Oct. 9,

	Page
SPERRY, (cont.)	
[1823], by Erastus Scranton, V.D.M.	1
STANNARD, Ann T., of Orange, m. Geo[rge] A. **LEE**, of Guilford, Apr. 9, 1846, by Edward Wright, West Haven	19
STEBBINS, Ann, of West Haven, m. Rev. Richard S. **STORRS**, of Braintree, Mass., Oct. 18, 1835, by Stephen W. Stebbins	10
Edward Reynolds, s. William, b. Apr. 19, 1824	23
Sophia E., m. Elijah **RAWSON**, Sept. 8, 1841, by Stephen W. Stebbins, West Haven	14
Stephen Alfred, s. William, b. Dec. 13, 1828	23
STEEL, Selah, of Berlin, m. Phebe **BALDWIN**, of Orange, Oct. 5, 1825, by Abijah Cunningham, J.P.	2
STEVENS, Emily, of Orange, m. William H. **TALMAGE**, of New Haven, June 7, 1836, by Stephen W. Stebbins	11
Francis N., of Orange, m. Delia **MANSFIELD**, of North Haven, Apr. 25, [1847], by Edward Wright, West Haven	19
Julia Ann, m. James **TOLLES**, June 21, 1833, by Stephen W. Stebbins	8
Lucius, m. Elizabeth A. **KIMBERLY**, Oct. 21, 1840, by Stephen W. Stebbins, West Haven	13
Mary A., m. Frederick S. **WARD**, b. of Orange, [Dec.] 27, [1847], by Edward Wright, West Haven	20
Sarah, m. Jonathan **FOOT**, Jr., Jan. 7, 1841, by Stephen W. Stebbins, West Haven	13
Stiles, of New Haven, m. Abula **SAGE**, of Orange, Aug. 21, 1825, by Erastus Scranton, V.D.M.	2
STONE, Charles B., of Middlebury, m. Elvira **BENHAM**, of Orange, May 11, 1836, by Stephen W. Stebbins	11
Eliza M., m. Joseph H. **PARDEE**, b. of Orange, [May] 15, [1848], by Edward Wright	20
Jane J., of Orange, m. William A. **FENN**, of McDonough, Ga., May 29, 1839, by Rev. D. G. Tomlinson, of Trumbull	14
Julia A., m. Peter C. **DOREMUS**, May 30, 1838, by B. Y. Messenger	12
Phebe Ann, m. Edward **SPARKS**, b. of West Haven, June 10, 1849, by Rev. A. B. Chapin, of West Haven	21
STORRS, STORR, Richard S., Rev., of Braintree, Mass., m. Ann **STEBBINS**, of West Haven, Oct. 18, 1835, by Stephen W. Stebbins	10
William, m. Mary **STREET**, Dec. 11, [1822], by Rev. Stephen W. Stebbins, in West Haven	1
STOWE, William, Jr., m. Delia Ann **MOULTHROP**, Apr. 18, 1827, by Stephen W. Stebbins	3
STREET, Mary, m. William **STORR**, Dec. 11, [1822], by Rev. Stephen W. Stebbins, in West Haven	1
STRONG, John P., of Milford, m. Susan **KINE***, of Orange, Sept. 9, 1840, by Asa M. Train *(Perhaps "**HINE**")	13
STUART, Charles E., of Sherman, m. Elizabeth J. **CLARK**, of Orange,	

ORANGE VITAL RECORDS

	Page
STUART, (cont.)	
Sept. [ ], 1849, by W. W. Belden	21
SUMMERS, Enoch, m. Sarah W. **DOWNS**, Mar. 9, 1826, by Stephen W. Stebbins	3
TALMAGE, Amarilla, m. Levi **CURTISS**, May 11, 1811, by [ ]	5
William H., of New Haven, m. Emily **STEVENS**, of Orange, June 7, 1836, by Stephen W. Stebbins	11
TERRELL, Julia, m. David **HOTCHKISS**, Sept. 19, 1824, by Stephen W. Stebbins	2
THOMAS, Abigail, m. Granville **SMITH**, b. of Orange, Sept. 23, 1827, by Rev. W[illia]m S. Potter, of West Haven	4
Adela G., m. George **THOMAS**, Jan. 14, 1827, by Stephen W. Stebbins, West Haven	3
Albert, of Orange, m. Catharine **SEELEY**, of Fair Haven, Nov. 2, 1845, by E. Wright	18
Alfred, of Orange, m. Harriet M. **SEELEY**, of Fair Haven, Mar. 23, 1846, by Edward Wright	18
Asahel, m. Mary **KIMBERLEY**, Apr. 29, 1827, by Stephen W. Stebbins	3
Augusta L., of Orange, m. Major G. **LAFORGE**, of New Haven, [Oct.*] 25, [1846], by Edward Wright, West Haven (*Perhaps "Nov.")	19
Charlotte, m. William **ARMSTRONG**, May 22, 1842, by Stephen W. Stebbins, West Haven	14
Cornelia, m. Otto **GOEHLIN**, Nov. 28, 1850, by Edward Wright	23
Delia Grace, m. Lockwood **SMITH**, June 13, 1838, by Rev. E. E. Griswold	12
George, m. Adela G. **THOMAS**, Jan. 14, 1827, by Stephen W. Stebbins, West Haven	3
Harriet L., m. Homer **TUTTLE**, of New Haven, Mar. 16, [1845], by Rev. Cyrus Brewster	17
Mabel, m. Nathaniel **KENNEDY**, June 23, 1822, by Rev. Stephen W. Stebbins, in West Haven	1
Nancy, m. Roswell J. **BROWN**, Oct. 9, 1831, by Stephen W. Stebbins	7
THOMPSON, THOMSON, Eliza Jane, of Orange, m. Eaton **BOOTH**, of New Haven, Mar. 14, 1852, by E. Wright	23
Fanny, m. William **WARD**, Oct. 13, 1822, by Rev. Stephen W. Stebbins	1
Margarett Ann, of West Haven, m. Sheldon Smith **HARTSHORN**, of Waterbury, Aug. 25, 1850, by Rev. A. B. Chapin, of West Haven	22
Miriam T., of Orange, m. Otis T. **BAKER**, of New Haven, Nov. 27, 1845, by E. Wright	18
Silas, m. Minerva **SMITH**, Jan. 14, 1833, by Stephen W. Stebbins	8
Stiles H., m. Fanlina **PLATT**, Aug. 23, 1829, by Stephen W. Stebbins	5

	Page
TOLLES, TOLLS, George, m. Harriet **FORD**, b. of West Haven, Feb. 22, 1846, by Rev. A. B. Chapin, of West Haven	21
James, m. Julia Ann **STEVENS**, June 21, 1833, by Stephen W. Stebbins	8
Martha, m. Nelson **SMITH**, Apr. 21, 1831, by Stephen W. Stebbins, West Haven	6
TREAT, Andrew, m. Marrietta N. **TREAT**, Apr. 25, 1823, by Erastus Scranton, V.D.M.	1
Calvin A., m. Esther M. **LAMBERT**, Mar. 21, 1831, by Horatio A. Parsons	6
Clarrissa, of Orange, m. William **BRYAN**, of Watertown, May 6, 1825, by Erastus Scranton, V.D.M.	2
Harriet M., of Orange, m. David R. **CROFOOT**, of Reading, Sept. 29, 1841, by Rev. A. Smyth	14
Jennett J., of Orange, m. Josiah A. **WEED**, of Danbury, Jan. 16, 1845, by Rev. Cyrus Brewster	17
Julia B., m. Ebenezer **ALLING**, b. of Orange, Nov. 18, 1824, by E. Scranton, V.D.M.	2
Louisa, m. J. A. **SMITH**, b. of Orange, [May] 14, [1848], by Edward Wright, West Haven	20
Louisa J., of Orange, m. John **TROWBRIDGE**, of Roxbury, Dec. 3, 1846, by Asa M. Train	19
Lucy, m. Leverett J. **CLARK**, Jan. 7, 1847, by Asa M. Train	19
Maria, m. Bryan **CLARK**, b. of Orange, Mar. 26, 1834, by Stephen W. Stebbins	9
Marrietta N., m. Andrew **TREAT**, Apr. 25, 1823, by Erastus Scranton, V.D.M.	1
Mary F., m. Charles R. **POPE**, b. of Orange, May 28, 1844, by Rev. Cyrus Brewster	16
Mary M., m. Albert **ALLING**, Nov. 22, 1827, by Stephen W. Stebbins	4
Noyes A., m. Frances A. **FENN**, b. of Orange, May 4, 1851, by W. W. Belden	23
Richard, Jr., of Milford, m. Jennett **SMITH**, of Orange, Feb. [ ], 1828, by Rev. Stephen W. Stebbins, of West Haven	4
Sarah, m. Rev. W[illia]m W. **BELDEN**, of Orange, Sept. 2, [1849], by Rev. George B. Hubbard	20
William, m. Harriet **ALLING**, [Nov.] 9, [1827], by George Foot, V.D.M., North Milford	4
TRENN, [see under **FENN**]	
TROWBRIDGE, John, of Roxbury, m. Louisa J. **TREAT**, of Orange, Dec. 3, 1846, by Asa M. Train	19
TUTTLE, Homer, of New Haven, m. Harriet L. **THOMAS**, Mar. 16, [1845], by Rev. Cyrus Brewster	17
Joseph, late of Oxford, m. Mrs. Rhoda **CLINTON**, of Orange, [Nov.] 16, [1825], by Rev. Eli Dennison	2
UMBERFIELD, William G., of Woodbridge, m. Laura **ANDREW**, of Orange, Mar. 31, 1831, by Horatio A. Parsons	6

	Page
WAKELY, Stiles, m. Julia **WILMOT**, Oct. 17, 1830, by Horatio A. Parsons	6
WARD, Eunice, of West Haven, m. Samuel E. **HOLT**, of East Haven, Aug. 22, 1844, by Rev. A.B. Chapin, of West Haven	21
Frederick S., m. Mary A. **STEVENS**, b. of Orange, [Dec.] 27, [1847], by Edward Wright	20
Huldah, m. William L. **GRISWOLD**, b. of West Haven, Nov. 25, 1849, by Rev. A. B. Chapin, of West Haven	21
James, Capt., m. Phebe **MERWIN**, Dec. 5, 1827, by Rev. W[illia]m S. Potter, of West Haven	4
Louisa, of West Haven, m. Adrian C. **HEITMANN**, of New Haven, Sept. 29, 1842, by Rev. A.B. Chapin, of West Haven	22
William, m. Fanny **THOMSON**, Oct. 13, 1822, by Rev. Stephen W. Stebbins	1
WARNER, William, m. Laura **ALLING**, Oct. 29, 1826, by Erastus Scranton, V.D.M.	4
WEED, Josiah A., of Danbury, m. Jennett J. **TREAT**, of Orange, Jan. 16, 1845, by Rev. Cyrus Brewster	17
WETMORE, Susan, of Orange, m. Norman **PETTIBONE**, of Burlington, July 17, 1831, by H. A. Parsons	6
WILLIAMS, John S., m. Mehetable **GOMAR**, July 22, 1839, by Stephen W. Stebbins	12
WILMOT, WILMOTT, Abigail, m. William H. **DAWSON**, May 4, 1834, by Stephen W. Stebbins, West Haven	9
Ephraim B., m. Amanda R. **SMITH**, Mar. 3, 1834, by Stephen W. Stebbins	9
Julia, m. Stiles **WAKELY**, Oct. 17, 1830, by Horatio A. Parsons	6
WOODRUFF, Dianthy, m. Aaron W. **FENN***, Dec. 16, 1836, by Asa M. Train (*Perhaps "TRENN")	11
Harriet, of Orange, m. Samuel L. **SMITH**, of Milford, July 20, 1837, by Asa M. Train	11
Jeremiah, m. Charlotte Emily **NETTLETON**, Mar. 29, 1837, by Asa M. Train	11
Julia Ann, m. John **HAWLEY**, Oct. 5, 1826, by Erastus Scranton, V.D.M.	4
M. Elizabeth, m. Charles N. **PLATT**, Sept. 26, 1848, by Rev. W. W. Belden	20
Susan, of Orange, m. Charles P. **MINOR**, of Roxbury, [June] 11, [1845], by Rev. Cyrus Brewster	17
WOOSTER, Charles H., m. Ann C. **BENHAM**, b. of New Haven, Sept. 13, 1846, by Rev. A.B. Chapin, of West Haven	21

OXFORD VITAL RECORDS
1798 - 1850

	Vol.	Page
ADAMS, Minerva T., m. Barzillar **STEVENS**, b. of Waterbury, Sept. 13, 1835, by Rev. Abraham Browne	1	58
ALLEN, [see also **ALLING**], Lyman, of Woodbridge, m. Mrs. Ruth Ann **HITCHCOCK**, of Oxford, [Mar.] 19, 1848, by Rev. Stephen Topliff	1	100
ALLING, [see also **ALLEN**], Bennett, m. Clarissa **JOHNSON**, b. of Oxford, [Nov.] 29, [1843], by Rev. Stephen Topliff	1	84
ALLIS, Abel A., m. Elizabeth **DUTTON**, May 3, 1818	2	1
Abel Allen, m. Elizabeth **DUTTON**, d. Hosea & Elizabeth, May 3, 1818	1	1
Agur, of Humphreysville, m. Esther Maria **BUCKINGHAM**, of Oxford, Nov. 2, 1835, by Rev. Abraham Browne	1	59
Caroline Amelia, [d. Abel & Elizabeth], b. Dec. 3, 1823	2	48
Elizabeth D., d. Abel & Elizabeth, b. May 21, 1819	2	48
Philomela, d. [Abel & Elizabeth], b. [ ], 1826	2	48
Sebastian Albert Dutton, s. [Abel & Elizabeth], b. Apr. 25, 1821	2	48
ANDREWS, Betsey, [d. Eph[rai]m & Mary], b. Feb. 19, 1793	2	48
Charlotte Augusta, d. John P. & Eunice, b. June 3, 1818	2	48
Eph[rai]m, [d. 1818], ae. 62	2	110
Ezra, [s. Eph[rai]m & Mary], b. Mar. 11, 1790	2	48
John Pierce, s. Benj[ami]n & Hannah, of New Haven, b. Sept. 7, 1788	2	48
John Pierce, m. Eunice **CANDEE**, d. Justus, Sept. 13, 1814	2	1
Lucy, [d. Eph[rai]m & Mary], b. Oct. 4, 1800	2	48
Lucy, of Oxford, m. Grapter **MANTON**, of Martha's Vineyard, Mass., Feb. 15, 1825, by Abel Wheeler, J.P.	1	20
Lucy Rebecca, d. John Peirce, b. Dec. 16, 1815	2	48
Mary, wid., [d. 1832], ae. 77	2	111
Samuel N., m. Amelia **THOMPSON**, Oct. 26, 1846, by Rev. John D. Smith	1	97
ATWOOD, Charles W[illia]m, s. Henry C. & Jane, b. July 27, 1823	2	48
Henry C., of Woodbury, m. Jane **LAMB**, of Oxford, Oct. 6, 1822, by Ephraim G. Swift	1	8
BAINBRIDGE, Brian G., of Southbury, m. Matilda **GRAHAM**, of Oxford, Feb. 27, 1836, by Rev. Abraham Browne	1	60
BAKER, Polly, w. Martin, d. [1811], ae. 47	2	106

	Vol.	Page
BAKER, (cont.)		
-----, his w. [ ], [1816], ae. 34	2	109
BALDWIN, Caleb, m. Sarah **BEARDSLEY**, Mar. 24, 1824, by Rev. Chauncey Prindle	1	14
Elizabeth Ann, m. Reuben L. **WILLIAMS**, Oct. 18, 1840, by John D. Smith	1	75
James, d. [1813], ae. 50	2	107
Laura, m. Isaac R. **BROOKS**, Sept. 17, 1843, by Rev. John D. Smith, of Humphreyville	1	83
Lavina, d. David, b. Sept. 18, 1815	2	50
Marianna, d. Jesse G. & Lydia R., b. Feb. 18, 1831	2	51
Sarah, m. Whiting **MITCHELL**, b. of Oxford, Nov. 15, 1821, by Rev. Abner Smith, of Derby	1	6
Seymour William, m. Mary Elizabeth **CANDEE**, b. of Oxford, Nov. 15, 1831, by Rev. Ashabel Baldwin	1	39
Temperance, m. Thomas **BUNNEL**, Sept. 4, 1826, by Rev. Chauncey Prindle	1	24
Temperance, m. Irenus **BUNNELL**, Sept. 4, 1826	2	3
BANDS, Benjamin, s. Capt. Sam[ue]l & Mabel, m. Almira Clementina **DUTTON**, d. H[osea] & E[lizabeth], Feb. 21, 1810	1	1
BARNES,-----, wid.d. [1812], ae 79 (pauper)	2	106
BARRETT, Philo, m. Nancy **BRYAN**, b. of Oxford, Nov. 2, 1821, by David Tomlinson, J.P.	1	5
BARTHOLOMEW, Claudius, his w. [ ], [d. 1818] ae. 74	2	110
BASSETT, Abraham, [s. Samuel & Abigail], b. July 4, 1808	2	53
Abr[aha]m, Capt. d. [1805], ae. 80	2	104
Abraham, of New Haven, m. Laura A. **FRENCH**, of Oxford, Mar. 20, 1842, by Rev. T. Sparks, Pleasant Vale	1	77
Althea, of Southbury, m. Glover **LEWIS**, of South East, N.Y., [Feb.] 10, [1828], by Noah Smith	1	29
Andrew, [s. Edw[ard] & Polly], b. Sept. 14, 1791	2	52
Ebenezer, [s. Samuel & Abigail], b. Sept. 15, 1792	2	53
Ebenezer, d. [ ], 1794, ae. 88	2	102
Eneas, [s. Samuel & Abigail], b. Aug. 16, 1794	2	53
Garwood, m. Lucy **BASSETT**, b. of Oxford, Feb. 6, 1830, by Rev. W[illia]m A. Curtiss	1	34
Grace, [d. Samuel & Abigail], b. June 1, 1804	2	53
Hannah, [d Samuel & Abigail], b. Aug. 9, 1790	2	53
Hannah, Mrs. of Oxford, m. Sheldon **HUBBELL**, of Monroe, Dec 19, 1826, by Bennett Lum, J.P., at the house of Edward Basset. Int.Pub.	1	25
Hellen, [d. John R. & Maryan], b. Aug. 17, 1842	2	53
Joel, [s. Edw[ar]d & Polly], b. Sept. 21, 1792	2	52
John, [& w. Kezia] had child, b. Nov. 7, 1799	2	52
John, Lieut., d. [1804], ae. 80	2	104
John, Lieut. his 2nd w. [ ], d. [1804	2	104
John, [d. 1832], ae. 74	2	111

	Vol.	Page
BASSETT, (cont.)		
John R., [s. Samuel & Abigail], b. Apr. 30, 1815	2	53
John T., [s. John R. & Maryan], b. Sept. 30, 1838	2	53
Kezia, [d. Samuel & Abigail], b. August 20, 1785	2	53
Laura, m. William **SMITH**, 3rd, Sept. 27, 1840, by Rev. John D. Smith	1	73
Locrasa A., [d. John R. & Maryan], b. July 15, 1840	2	53
Lucy, m. Garwood **BASSETT**, b. of Oxford, Feb. 6, 1830, by Rev. W[illia]m A. Curtiss	1	34
Marima w. Miles d. [1812], ae. 47	2	106
Mark, [d. 1824], ae. 23	2	111
Markus, [s. Samuel & Abigail], b. May 10, 1802	2	53
Mary Elizabeth, d. Enos & Sabra, b. May 8, 1823	2	50
Mary Gilbert, [d. John R. & Maryan], b. Mar. 10, 1845	2	53
Miles, [d. 1813], ae. 50	2	107
Nathan, [s. John & Kezia], b. Mar. 13, 1794	2	52
Nathan T., m. Sarah **SEELEY**, Nov. 3, 1842, by Rev. Abel Nichols	1	86
Nelson, of Derby, m. Lucy **MANTER**, of Oxford, Jan. 13, 1841, by Elias Scott, J.P.	1	75
Philo, [s. John & Kezia], b. June 25, 1796	2	52
Polly, [d. John & Kezia], b. Sept. 28, 1790	2	52
Polly Minervey, [d. Samuel & Abigail], b. Jan. 5, 1800	2	53
Russel, [s. Samuel & Abigail], b. Jan. 23, 1784	2	53
Sally, m. Bennett **WOOSTER**, b. of Oxford, Mar. 16, 1823, by Beardsley Northrop	1	9
Sam[ue]l, his w., d. [1813], ae. 48	2	107
Samuel Allen, [s. John R. & Maryan], b. Feb. 19, 1848	2	53
Samuel McNeil, [s. Samuel & Abigail], b. Dec. 17, 1796	2	53
Thomas, s. Ezra L., d. Apr. 19, 1831, ae. 2	2	3
Thomas, d. [1831], ae. 2	2	111
Wait, his w. [ ], d. [1813], ae. 27	2	107
William, [s. Samuel & Abigail], b. Jan. 13, 1788	2	53
William, [s. Edw[ar]d & Polly], b. Sept. 18, 1794	2	52
BATEMAN, Amma, his wid., d. [1824], ae. 63	2	111
Selena, m. Diodate **MUN[N]**, Nov. 22, 1807	2	27
BATES, Amos, s. Elihu, m. Lydia **LUM**, d. Jonathan, Jan. 29, 1802	2	3
Amos, his w. d. June [ ], [1825], ae. 42	2	111
Benjamin, his wid. [ ], d. Aug. 15, 1800, ae. 70.	2	102
Charles, [s. Amos & Lydia], b. Mar. 17, 1812	2	51
Elihu, d. Dec. 16, 1836, ae. about 82	2	111
Jennett, m. Luther **BEACH**, b. of Oxford, Nov. 25, 1829, by Rev. Nathan Tuttle	1	33
Julia, d. Andrew & Anna, b. Jan. 22, 1798	2	51
Lucy Maria, [d. Amos & Lydia], b. Jan. 17, 1806	2	51
Lydia, [d. Amos & Lydia, b.], Aug. 28, 1804	2	51
Lydia, m. Shelden **BEEBE**, b. of Oxford, Jan. 6, 1833,		

	Vol.	Page
BATES, (cont.)		
by Samuel Wise, J.P.	1	42
Maria, Mrs., m. Merit **BROWN**, b. of Oxford, Sept. 24, 1828, by Bennett LUM, J.P., at the house of Amos Bates, Int.Pub.	1	30
BEACH, Brothwell, [d. 1832], ae. 37	2	111
David, d. Nov. [,1825], ae. 55	2	111
Luther, m. Jannett **BATES**, b. of Oxford, Nov. 25, 1829, by Rev. Nathan Tuttle	1	33
BEARD, Elam, m. Esther **CABLE**, Feb. 15, 1824, by Rev. John M. Garfield	1	13
BEARDSLEY, BEARDSLEE, Beach, m. Julia Ann **TURNER**, Apr. 12, [1835], by Rev. Matthew Batchelor	1	56
Elam, b. Feb. 13, 1800	2	51
Elam, m. Esther **CANDEE**, Mar. 21, 1826, by Rev. Chauncey Prindle	1	22
Eliakim, d. [ ], 1798, ae. 54	2	103
Eliza, m. David **SCOTT**, b. of Oxford, Jan. 7, 1824, by Abel Wheeler, J.P.	1	12
Esther, [d. 1822], ae. 74	2	111
Laura, b. June 17, 1798	2	51
Lemuel, d. Nov. 23, 1841, ae. 70	2	3
Lemuel, Capt. of 1st Co., in Oxford	2	132
Louisa R., of Oxford, m. Marcus S. **MUNN**, of Southbury, [Oct.] 11, [1846], by Rev. Stephen Topliff	1	96
Louisa Ruth, d. Elam & Esther, b. Aug. 31, 1827	2	51
Marietta C., of Oxford, m. George A. **FLAGG**, of New Haven, Jan. 22, 1835, by Rev. Charles Smith	1	54
Mehitable, of Oxford, m. Lampson **SMITH**, of Kinderhook. N. Y., May 22, 1826, by Eph[rai]m Swift	1	23
Philo, d. [1805], ae. 27	2	104
Polly, d. Jared & Betsey, b. Sept. 19, 1799	2	51
Roswell, d. Eliakim & Esther, b. Feb. 25, 1793	2	51
Ruth, m. Alfred **HARGER**, b. of Oxford, Mar. 13, 1830, by Rev. A. Brown	1	35
Sarah, m. Caleb **BALDWIN**, Mar. 24, 1824, by Rev. Chauncey Prindle	1	14
BEEBE, Eliza, m. Agur **LEWIS**, Nov. 5, 1833, by Samuel Meigs, J.P.	1	95
Joseph, m. Maria **TUCKER**, b. of Oxford [1834(?)], by Rev. Abraham Brown. Recorded Nov. 22, 1834	1	54
Martin, d. Sept. [ ], [1819], ae. 64	2	110
Shelden, m. Lydia **BATES**, b. of Oxford, Jan. 6, 1833, by Samuel Wise, J.P.	1	42
BEECHER, BEACHER, Bennett R., of Waterbury, m. Laura E. **TWITCHELL**, of Oxford, [ ], by Rev. Abraham Brown. Recorded Nov. 22, 1834	1	51
David, m. Elizabeth **HAWKINS**, Mar. 22, 1846, by Samuel		

	Vol.	Page
BEECHER, BEACHER, (cont.)		
Meigs, J.P.	1	96
Est[h]er, m. Calvin **LEAVENWORTH**, Oct. 4, 1840, by John D. Smith	1	74
Harriet, of Oxford, m. Jason **CURTISS**, of Southbury, July 25, 1822, by Ephraim G. Swift	1	7
Isaac, s. David & Polly, b. Nov. 20, 1799	2	51
John, Capt. of 1st Co., in Oxford, 1830	2	132
Mary, m. Abel **FRENCH**, of New Stratford, Apr. 24, 1822, by Ephraim G. Swift	1	7
Philo, Capt., [d. 1815], ae. 42	2	109
Philo, Capt. of 1st Co., in Oxford	2	132
Polly Maria, [d. David & Polly], b. June 28, 1800	2	51
BEERS, Jon[atha]n, d. [1824], ae. about 80	2	111
BELANDEE, Frederic, of Hartford, m. Mary **BUCKINGHAM**, of Oxford, Jan. 6, 1833, by Rev. Abraham Brown	1	49
BENHAM, Eber, of Southbury, m. Olive **ROOT**, of Oxford, Apr. 5, 1827, by Tho[ma]s L. Shipman	1	28
Enos, of Woodbury, m. Betsey Ann **WATTERS**, of Oxford, Jan. 24, 1848, by Rev. David P. Sanford	1	100
Garwood B., m. Nancy S. **CLARK**, Feb. 14, 1831, by Rev. Chauncey Prindle	1	36
BENNETT, Geo[rge], his w. [, d. 1818], ae. 30	2	110
Smith, of Monroe, m. Mary Ann **VOSS**, of Oxford, Jan. 28, 1827, by Rev. David Bennett	1	25
BERT, Ann, m. Sylvester **JONES**, Oct. 12, 1845, by Rev. Geo[rge] L. Fuller	1	91
BETTS, Charles, m. Sarah **SHERMAN**, Nov. 22, 1834, by Matthew Batchelor	1	47
Charlotte, m. Charles **EVERETT**, [Mar.] 24, [1844], by Rev. Stephen Topliff	1	84
BIDWELL, Frederic S., [s. Normand A. & Rebecca], b. July 25, 1829	2	50
Geo[rge] A., [s. Norman A. & Rebecca], b. Nov. 26, 1825	2	50
Ja[me]s S., of Oxford, m. Caroline H. **MASON**, of Lowell, Mass., May 1, 1842, by Rev. Tho[ma]s Sparks	1	78
Mary Jane, [d. Normand A. & Rebecca], b. July 4, 1832	2	50
BLACKMAN, Curtiss, of Huntington, m. Augusta **WATERS**, of Oxford, Jan. 1, 1843, by Rev. Abel Nichols	1	86
Harriet, of Oxford, m. Lucius **POWE**, of Derby, Sept. 16, 1844, by Rev. Abel Nichols	1	87
Julia S., of Oxford, m. William C. **WARRIMER**, of Springfield, Mass., July 24, 1831, by Rev. Charles Thompson, of Humphreyville	1	37
Maria L., of Middlebury, m. Lucian **HOTCHKISS**, Sept. 8,		

	Vol.	Page
BLACKMAN, (cont.)		
1841, by Rev. P.L. Hoyt	1	77
Rhoda, m. Lucius **FULLER**, b. of Oxford, Sept. 28, 1835, by Rev. Abraham Browne	1	59
BOOTH, John C., m. Eunice **TUCKER**, Feb. 19, 1840, by Rev. John E. Bray	1	70
-----, of Newtown, m. Roxana **CANDEE**, of Oxford, May 31, 1826, by Eph[rai]m Swift	1	23
BOTSFORD, Clark, of Derby, m. Betsey M. **HINE**, of Oxford, Aug. 5, 1821, by Beardsley Northrop	1	4
Susan, d. Sam[ue]l & Antha, b. Jan. 27, 1803	2	52
BRADBURY, Mary, of Oxford, m. John M. **HART**, of Boston, Mass., Dec. 25, 1833, by Rev. Abraham Brown	1	51
BRADLEY, Andrew, s. [Benjamin & Eunice], b. May 17, 1786	2	51
Benj[amin], d. [July [29*], 1819], ae. 65 (*correction 29 handwritten in brackets in original manuscript)	2	110
Burr, [s. Treat & Sally], b. Feb. 21, 1831	2	50
Caroline A[u]gusta, of Oxford, m. Victory **LAKE**, of Huntington, Sept. 14, 1823, by Rev. Menzies Raynor, of Huntington	1	12
Charles, s. [Benjamin & Eunice], b. May 15, 1800	2	51
Eunice, d. [Benjamin & Eunice], b. Sept. 13, 1797	2	51
Eunice A., m. James **WARNER**, b. of New Haven, June 4, 1837, by Rev. Abraham Browne	1	66
Frederic A., m. Sarah **WATERS**, b. of Oxford, Apr. 30, 1845, by Rev. A. Nichols	1	90
George, of Bethany, m. Sally E. **JOHNSON**, of Oxford, Aug. 10, 1842, by Rev. Sylvester Smith	1	80
Henry N., [s. Treat & Sally], b. June 18, 1822	2	50
Isa[a]c, [d. 1813], ae. 21	2	107
Jennet F., m. Daniel **GILLETT**, b. of Oxford, Apr. 20, 1836, by Rev. Abraham Browne	1	60
Mary Ann, [d. Treat & Sally], b. Sept. 20, 1819	2	50
Merrett, s. [Benjamin & Eunice], b. Apr. 12, 1790	2	51
Nancy, d. Nov. 9, 1828, ae. 43 y.	2	3
Noyes, s. [Benjamin & Eunice], b. May 17, 1794	2	51
Noyes, m. Mrs. Nancy **RIGGS**, b. of Oxford, Mar. 1, 1827, by Nathaniel G. Huntington	1	26
Rhoda, d. Philo & Rhoda, b. Sept. 13, 1800	2	52
Sally, m. Burritt **SKEELS**, b. of Oxford, May 4, 1828, by Nathan D. Benedict	1	29
Seymour, s. [Benjamin & Eunice], b. July 1, 1788	2	51
Treat, s. [Benjamin & Eunice], b. Mar. 15, 1792	2	51
William W., s. Seymour & Parlos B., b. Nov. 25, 1820	2	50
-----, Capt. d. [1813], ae. 46	2	107
-----, d. [1813], ae. 14	2	107
BRIANT, [see also **BRYAN**], Jane, of Oxford, m. Charles		

OXFORD VITAL RECORDS   29

	Vol.	Page
BRIANT, (cont.)		
WHITFORD, of Amenia, Nov. 21, 1838, by Rev. Daniel Miller	1	65
BRISTOL, Abel, [s. Thomas & Betsey B.], b. Mar. 28, 1808	2	50
Angeline, d. Nov. 14, 1828, ae. 10 y.	2	3
Austin, [d. 1820], ae. 83	2	110
Caroline, of Oxford, m. Spencer **JUDD**, of Waterbury, Nov. 1, 1835, by Rev. Charles Smith	1	57
Cynde, [ch. of Thomas & Betsey B.], b. Sept. 12, 1810	2	50
David, d. Nov. 25, 1828, ae. 7 y.	2	3
Eliphalet, d. [, 1803], ae. 90 or more	2	103
Eunice, [d. Aug. [ ], 1821], ae. 44	2	110
Gad, d. [1807], ae. 68	2	105
Justus, his w. [ ], [d. 1818], ae. 79	2	110
Maria, [d. Thomas & Betsey B.], b. July 18, 1817	2	50
Meny, d. Justus & Sarah, d. Nov. 22, 1798, ae. 18	2	102
Polly, [d. Thomas & Betsey B.,], b. May 17, 1802	2	50
Rache[l], wid., d. [1813], ae. 72	2	107
Simeon L., of Milford, m. Lucy **TUCKER**, of Oxford, Sept. 4, 1845, by Rev. Stephen Topliff	1	90
Sylvania, [d. Thomas & Betsey B.], b. June 24, 1804	2	50
Thompson, s. [Thomas & Betsey B.], b. Oct. 2, 1806	2	50
-----, Mrs. midwife, d. [ ], 1796, ae. 81	2	103
BRONSON, BRUNSON, Abel, Dr., of Middlebury, d. [1805], ae. 60	2	104
David, Rev., M.A., d. [1806], ae. 67	2	104
Harvey, of Southbury, m. Esther **BUCKINGHAM**, of Oxford, Jan. 30, 1823, by Beardsley Northrop	1	9
Samuel, of Southbury, m. Delana **TWITCHELL**, of Oxford, Apr. 11, 1827, by Tho[ma]s L. Shipman	1	28
BROOKS, Isaac R., m. Laura **BALDWIN**, Sept. 17, 1843, by Rev. John D. Smith, of Humphreyville	1	83
John, of Yorkshire, m. Mary **WYETT**, of Birmingham, b. of England, Nov. 6, 1834, by Samuel Wise, J.P.	1	47
BROWN, BROWNE, Charlotte, of Oxford, m. Lewis **FOX**, of Woodbury, Dec. 1, 1849, by Alfred Harger, J.P.	1	111
Jane Harrison, d. Rev. Abr[aha]m & Lucy Maria, b. Dec. 6, 1830	2	53
Manerva, m. Clark **TOMLINSON**, Dec. 28, 1838, by Bennett Lum, J.P.	1	63
Merit, m. Mrs. Maria **BATES**, b. of Oxford, Sept. 24, 1828, by Bennett Lum, J.P., at the house of Amos Bates. Int.Pub.	1	30
Moodey M., m. Ellen Jane **TUCKER**, b. of Oxford, Aug. 10, 1834, by Rev. Abraham Browne	1	53
Moody M., Capt. of 1st Co., in Oxford, 1835	2	132
Thomas W., of New Haven, m. Minerva **BUNNELL**, of		

	Vol.	Page
BROWN, BROWNE, (cont.)		
Oxford, Dec. 25, 1822, by Beardsley Northrop	1	8
-----, Mrs. of Woodbury, d. Mar. 27, 1829, ae. 74 y.	2	3
BRYAN, [see also **BRIANT**], Alanson, [s. Isaac & Anna], b.		
Aug. [ ], 1802	2	51
Anna, w. Jos[eph], d. [1809], ae. 42	2	105
Betsey, [d. Isaac & Anna], b. Jan. 20, 1790	2	51
Harvey, [s. Isaac & Anna], b. June 5, 1798	2	51
Ira, [s. Isaac & Anna], b. June 3, 1794	2	51
Nancy, [d. Isaac & Anna], b. Apr. 8, 1798	2	51
Nancy, m. Philo **BARRETT**, b. of Oxford, Nov. 2, 1821, by David Tomlinson, J.P.	1	5
Sally, [d. Isaac & Anna], b. Aug. 6, 1791	2	51
BUCKINGHAM, Abigail, wid. Dr. Eb[enezer], d. July 20, [1811], ae. 79	2	106
Andrew, [& w. Esther] had child d. Aug. 30, 1801	2	53
Andrew, m. Mary **CAMP**, June 23, 1803	2	3
And[re]w, Capt. his w. [ ], [d. 1815], ae. 42	2	109
Ashel, [s. John & Lucy], b. Mar. 23, 1794	2	53
Aurelius, [d. Andrew & Esther], b. Nov. 30, 1793	2	53
Beulah, d. Nathan J., & Selene, b. Apr. 25, 1799	2	53
Clarissa, [d. Eben[eze]r & Olive], b. Aug. 27, 1794	2	53
Clark, [s. Andrew & Esther], b. Sept. 21, 1798	2	53
Clark, d. June 21, 1840, in his 42nd y.	2	3
Cynthia, [d. Eben[eze]r & Olive], b. Aug. 17, 1804	2	53
Cynthia, m. Jason **MORRIS**, b. of Oxford, Apr. 18, 1838, by Rev. Abraham Browne	1	67
David H., of Oxford, m. Maria **SANFORD**, of Wolcott, Dec. 17, 1828, by Sayrs Gazley, V.D.M.	1	31
David W., [s. Eben & Olive], b. Sept. 25, 1797	2	53
Eben, m. Olive **WOODRUFF**, Oct. 28, 1792	2	3
Eben[eze]r, Capt. of 1st Co., in Oxford, 1775	2	132
Ebenezer, Dr., d. [ ], 1795, ae. 68	2	102
Eben[eze]r, [s. Eben[eze]r & Olive], b. June 18, 1809	2	53
Electa M., m. Cornelius **KEHOE**, Oct. 29, 1831, by Rev. Chaunc[e]y Prindle	1	39
Esther, [d. Andrew & Esther], b. Apr. 14, 1796	2	53
Esther, w. And[rew], d. Mar. 4, 1802, ae. 39	2	103
Esther, of Oxford, m. Harvey **BRUNSON**, of Southbury, Jan. 30, 1823, by Beardsley Northrop	1	9
Esther Maria, of Oxford, m. Agur **ALLIS**, of Humphreysville, Nov. 2, 1835, by Rev. Abraham Browne	1	59
Harriet E., m. Harvey **CHATFIELD**, [Apr.] 9, [1844], by Rev. Stephen Topliff	1	85
Henrietta, [d. Nathan L. & Clarissa], b. Apr. 6, 1826	2	50
Henry, [s. Nathan L. & Clarissa], b. Feb. 29, 1828	2	50
Hezekiah, [s. John & Lucy], b. Nov. 28, 1795	2	53
Horace, of Oxford, m. Fanny **HOTCHKISS**, of Waterbury,		

OXFORD VITAL RECORDS

	Vol.	Page
BUCKINGHAM, (cont.)		
[Dec.] 13, [1840], by Rev. Stephen Topliff	1	74
James A., m. Anna **SMITH**, Jan. 29, 1832, by Rev. A. Browne	1	40
James Andrew, [s. Capt. Andrew & Mary], b. Apr. 20, 1809	2	53
Jared, d. [1814], ae. 81	2	107
Joel, m. Hannah **McEWEN**, b. of Oxford, June 5, 1837, by Rev. Abraham Browne	1	66
Joel, [s. Nathan L. & Clarissa], b. July 17, 1839	2	50
John, [& w. Esther], had ch. b. Sept. 30, 1800	2	53
Laura L., of Oxford, m. Joel F. **WEBSTER**, of Waterbury, Nov. 2, 1835, by Rev. Abraham Browne	1	59
Lewis, [d. 1832], ae. 21	2	111
Lucy, [d. John & Lucy], b. Apr. 28, 1797	2	53
Mark, [s. Nathan L., & Clarissa], b. Apr. 3, 1820	2	50
Martha, [d. Nathan L., & Clarissa], b. Oct. 7, 1823	2	50
Mary, [d. Capt. Andrew & Mary], b. May 11, 1811	2	53
Mary, of Oxford, m. Eli **STRONG**, of Southbury, [1820(?)], by Ephraim G. Swift. Int.Pub.	1	2
Mary, of Oxford, m. Frederick **BELANDEE**, of Hartford, Jan. 6, 1833, by Rev. Abraham Brown	1	49
Nancy, [d. Eben[eze]r & Olive], b. Mar. 26, 1806	2	53
Nathan, Dr., [d. 1815], ae. 80	2	108
Philo B., m. Sally C. **PERKINS**, [Oct.] 12, [1842], by Rev. Stephen Topliff	1	81
Polly, [d. Eben & Olive], b. Feb. 6, 1799	2	53
Rowena, [d. Eben & Olive], b. Dec. 20, 1793	2	53
S. Andrew, Capt. of 1st Co., in Oxford	2	132
Sam[ue]ll, d. [1814], ae. 46	2	108
Samuel Andrew, [s. Capt. Andrew & Mary], b. Dec. 2, 1815	2	53
Sherman, [s. Andrew & Esther], b. Nov. 10, 1791	2	53
Sherman, Capt. of 1st Co., in Oxford, 1826	2	132
Susanna, [d. John & Esther], b. Mar. 13, 1799	2	53
Wales Austin, [twin with W[illia]m Woodruff, s. Eben[eze]r & Olive], b. Oct. 6, 1810	2	53
W[illia]m Woodruff, [twin with Wales Austin, s. Eben[eze]r & Olive], b. Oct. 6, 1810	2	53
-----, w. Dr. [ ], d. [1813], ae. 70	2	107
BUNNELL, BUNNEL, Alma, [d. Luke & Sarah], b. [ ], 1795	2	52
Ann, [d. 1822], ae. 82	2	111
Anna, [d. 1832], ae. 66	2	111
Benj[amin], ae. 24, m. Mary **TWITCHELL**, ae. 27, Nov. 22, 1786	2	3
Benjamin, m. Anna **GUNN**, Oct. 8, 1835, by Rev. Charles Smith	1	56

	Vol.	Page
BUNNELL, BUNNEL, (cont.)		
Benjamin, d. Sept. 20, 1840, ae. 77 y.	2	3
Catharine, d. Thomas & Temperance, b. July 7, 1827	2	52
Charles, d. Mar. [ ], 1838, ae. 80 y.	2	3
Charles Burr, s. Erastus & Charlotte, b. Nov. 8, 1822	2	52
Chester, [s. Benjamin & Mary], b. Apr. 12, 1788	2	52
Clary, m. John L. **FAIRCHILD**, Jan. 26, 1825, by Chauncey Prindle	1	20
David, & w. Polly, had ch., b. May 7, 1797	2	52
David, [& w. Polly], had ch., b. Sept. 2, 1800	2	52
Ellen, [d. 1816], ae. 36	2	109
George, m. Sarah A. **TOMLINSON**, b. of Oxford, Feb. 13, 1848, by Rev. David P. Sanford	1	100
Hannah, wid. Isaac, d. Apr., [1802], ae. 44	2	103
Harvey, [s. Luke & Sarah], b. July 6, 1799	2	52
Irenus, m. Temperence **BALDWIN**, Sept. 4, 1826	2	3
Isaac, d. [1808], ae. 72	2	105
Joel, [s. Luke & Sarah], b. Oct. 14, 1796	2	52
Leverett, [s. Luke & Sarah], b. May 13, 1792	2	52
Lewis, [s. Truman & Anna], b. June 16, 1798	2	52
Lockwood, [s. David & Polly], b. Nov. 25, 1798	2	52
Lydia Maria, m. Milo **EDMUNDS**, b. of Oxford, Nov. 19, 1845, by Rev. G. B. Eastman	1	93
Minerva, of Oxford, m. Thomas W. **BROWN**, of New Haven, Dec. 25, 1822, by Beardsley Northrop	1	8
Polly, [d. Truman & Anna], b. June 28, 1796	2	52
Renas, [ch. of Benjamin & Mary], b. May 14, 1799	2	52
Reuben, [s. Benjamin & Mary], b. Oct. 30, 1795	2	52
Ruth, d. [1809], ae. 72	2	105
Sarah, d. [1810], ae. 82	2	106
Thomas, m. Temperance **BALDWIN**, Sept. 4, 1826, by Rev. Chauncey Prindle	1	24
Truman & w. Anna, had d. [ ], b. Aug. 13, 1800	2	52
BURRELL, David, [d. 1817], ae. 80	2	109
BURRETT, BURRITT, Catharine M., of Bridgeport, m. Willard S. **GUNN**, of Waterbury, Mar. 20, 1844, by Nathan J. Wilcoxson, J.P.	1	84
James [s. Sam[ue]l & Maria], b. Feb. 15, 1811, in Derby	2	50
John, [s. Sam[ue]l & Maria], b. Sept. 12, 1804, in Derby	2	50
Marry Ann, [d. Sam[ue]l & Maria], b. Mar. 7, 1813, in Derby	2	50
Sam[ue]l L., [s. Sam[ue]l & Maria], b. Apr. 13, 1806, in Derby	2	50
William H., [s. Sam[ue]l & Maria], b. Apr. 28, 1808, in Derby	2	50

	Vol.	Page
BUXTON, BUXTEN, Ann, Mrs. of Oxford, m. Henry **LUM**, of Derby, [Nov.] 25, [1843], by Rev. Stephen Topliff	1	83
Henry, of Danbury, m. Lucinda **WOOSTER**, of Oxford, Oct. 31, 1831, by Samuel Wise, J.P.	1	40
Thomas, m. Anna **JOHNSON**, b. of Oxford, Dec. 26, 1838, by Chauncey M. Hatch, J.P.	1	66
Thomas, d. May 1, 1841, ae. 38 y.	2	3
C-----, Elias, [s. Elias & Susan], b. Apr. 6, 1811	2	56
Jonah, [s. Elias & Susan], b. Feb. 11, 1813	2	56
Newton, [s. Elias & Susan], b. Dec. 7, 1806	2	56
Sarah, [twin with Susan, d. Elias & Susan], b. Mar. 11, 1809	2	56
Susan, [twin with Sarah, d. Elias & Susan], b. Mar. 11, 1809	2	56
CABLE, CABLES, Agur Edwin, [s. Roswell & Hannah], b. Feb. 3, 1822	2	55
Betsey Maria, [d. Roswell & Hannah], b. Sept. 28, 1830	2	55
David Sanford, [s. Isaac & Julia], b. Dec. 21, 1807	2	55
Esther, m. Elam **BEARD**, Feb. 15, 1824, by Rev. John M. Garfield	1	13
Frederick Abijah, [s. Roswell & Hannah], b. Aug. 29, 1828	2	55
George, d. Apr. 22, [1802], ae. 50	2	103
Julia Elizabeth, [d. Roswell & Hannah], b. May 18, 1826	2	55
Lavinia Lucy, [d. Roswell & Hannah], b. July 24, 1824	2	55
Lucinda, m. Alonzo **LEEK**, July [ ], 1843, by Rev. Abel Nichols	1	87
Mary Anne, [d. Roswell & Hannah], b. Mar. 8, 1820	2	55
Mary Ann, of Oxford, m. George **SPERRY**, of Bethlem, Nov. 19, 1845, by Rev. G. B. Eastman	1	94
Orlando, m. Betsey **WHEELER**, b. of Oxford, Nov. 9, 1825, by Rev. Menzies Raynor, of Huntington	1	21
Polly Eliza, d. Isaac & Julia, b. Sept. 27, 1801	2	55
CAGER, -----, wid., d. [1823], ae. 74	2	111
CAIN, [see under **O'CAIN**]		
CAMP, Betsey M., of Southbury, m. John F. **COREY***, of Humphreysville, Feb. 24, 1845, by Rev. Stephen Topliff *(Perhaps "Casey")	1	89
Eli B., d. Mar. [ ], 1841	2	7
Mary, m. Andrew **BUCKINGHAM**, June 23, 1803	2	3
Sally, m. Simeon **TOWNER**, b. of Oxford, [, 1834(?)], by Rev. Abraham Browne	1	54
CANDEE, Aaron, s. Dan & Lydia, b. Jan. 25, 1804	2	55
Adeline, [d. Levi & Lucy], b. [ ]	2	56
Agnes, [d. Cyrus & Beulah], b. Feb. 14, 1797	2	55
Ann, [twin with John, s. Levi & Lucy], b. Mar. 15, 1822	2	56
Anna, w. Levi, d. [1807], ae. 33	2	105

	Vol.	Page
CANDEE, (cont.)		
Archibald, s. Caleb, Jr. & Sine, b. Oct. 19, 1804	2	55
Avis, m. Ambrose **OSBORN**, b. of Oxford, Dec. 19, 1832, by Rev. Abraham Brown	1	46
Bazil, s. Capt. S[ ], d. [1823], ae. 25	2	111
Burritt, [s. Justus & Eunice], b. Oct. 28, 1786	2	55
Burrett, s. Justus, d. [1807], ae. 21	2	105
Burritt, [s. Levi & Lucy], b. [ ]	2	56
Burritt Dwight, [s. Timothy & Luana], b. Nov. 8, 1811	2	55
Caleb, his w.[, d. , 1817], ae. 76	2	109
Caleb, d. Dec. 1, 1828, ae. 85 y.	2	6
Caroline, m. Abraham E. **SMITH**, b. of Oxford, Nov. 25, 1833, by Rev. Abraham Brown	1	51
Catharine, [d. Levi & Lucy], b. [ ]	2	56
Charles Addison, [s. David & Hannah], b. June 23, 1823	2	56
Charlotte, d. Enos & Elizabeth, b. Sept. [ ], 1823	2	54
Chittenden, [d. Dec. [ ], 1821], ae. 40	2	110
David Bristol, [s. David & Hannah], b. May 2, 1816	2	56
Eliza[be]th Charlotte, [d. Benj[ami]n & Almira], b. Nov. 4, 1810	2	55
Erastus, [d. 1817], ae. 32	2	109
Esther, d. [1813], ae. 86	2	107
Esther, m. Elam **BEARDSLEE**, Mar. 21, 1826, by Rev. Chauncey Prindle	1	22
Eunice, w. [Justus], b. July 12, 1758	2	55
Eunice, [d. Justus & Eunice], b. Oct. 2, 1795	2	55
Eunice, [d. Timothy & Luana], b. Feb. 8, 1806; d. July 28, 1809	2	55
Eunice, d. Justus, m. John Pierce **ANDREWS**, Sept. 13, 1814	2	1
Eunice, of Oxford, m. John Austin **PECK**, of Southbury, Jan. 1, 1840, by Rev. John D. Smith, at the house of Enos Candee	1	72
Eunice Augusta, d. Isaiah & Melissa, b. July 17, 1810	2	54
Frederick A., m. Louisa A. **HOTCHKISS**, b. of Oxford, Oct. 7, 1845, by Rev. G. B. Eastman	1	93
Frederic Augustus, [s. David & Hannah], b. June 15, 1818	2	56
George N., m. Henrietta **CANDEE**, b. of Oxford, Dec. 30, 1832, by Rev. Abraham Brown	1	46
George Newell, [s. David & Hannah], b. Jan. 5, 1811	2	56
George W., s. David & Hannah, d. May 26, 1800	2	6
George Wiard, [s. David & Hannah], b. Oct. 7, 1809	2	56
Henrietta, m. George N. **CANDEE**, b. of Oxford, Dec. 30, 1832, by Rev. Abraham Brown	1	46
Henrietta, [d. Levi & Lucy], b. [ ]	2	56
Horace, Jr., d. May 10, 1831, ae. 4 m.	2	6

	Vol.	Page
CANDEE, (cont.)		
Horace, 2nd, d. [1831], ae. 4 m.	2	111
Horace, Capt. of 1st Co., in Oxford	2	132
Job, Capt. of 1st. Co., in Oxford	2	132
John, [twin with Ann, s. Levi & Lucy], b. Mar. 15, 1822	2	56
Josiah, [s. Justus & Eunice], b. July 31, 1779	2	55
Juliet, m. Burke **TOMLINSON**, Jan. 4, 1840, by Rev. Daniel Burhans	1	70
Juliet, [d. Levi & Lucy], b. [ ]	2	56
Julius, s. Dan & Lydia, b. Feb. 17, 1800	2	55
Justus, s. Caleb & Lois, b. Feb. 17, 1756	2	55
Justus, m. Eunice **NORTON**, Dec. 21, 1778	2	6
Justus, [s. Timothy & Luana], b. Jan. 15, 1804	2	55
Leverett, s. Job & Sarah, b. June [ ], 1795	2	55
Lewis Burton, of Woodbury, m. Betsey Elizabeth **PANGMAN**, of Oxford, [Mar.] 30, [1835], by Rev. Charles Smith	1	55
Lois, of Oxford, m. Joseph **LOUNSBURY**, of Danbury, Mar. 27, 1827, by Rev. Mark Mead	1	26
Lucina, m. Leman **RIGGS**, b. of Oxford, Mar. 27, 1821, by Ephraim G. Swift	1	4
Lucinda, [d. Timothy & Luana], b. Jan. 28, 1802	2	55
Lucy, [d. Justus & Eunice], b. Sept. 26, 1790	2	55
Lucy Ann, d. Isaiah, of Oxford, m. James **IVES**, of Hamden, Nov. 28, 1838, by Rev. J. Atwater	1	65
Lura A., of Oxford, m. Robert E. **ISBEL**, of Naugatuck, Sept. 13, 1848, by Rev. Stephen Topliff	1	101
Mary A., of Oxford, m. Avery J. **SKILTON** (Dr.), of Troy, N.Y., Mar. 2, 1828, by Rev. Daniel Wooster	1	29
Mary Elizabeth, [d. David & Hannah], b. Aug. 2, 1813	2	56
Mary Elizabeth, m. Seymour William **BALDWIN**, b. of Oxford, Nov. 15, 1831, by Rev. Ashbel Baldwin	1	39
Perloxa, [ch. of Cyrus & Beulah], b. Feb. 10, 1799	2	55
Polly, d. Levi & Anna, b. Mar. 27, 1799	2	55
Roxana, of Oxford, m. [ ] **BOOTH**, of Newtown, May 31, 1826, by Eph[rai]m Swift	1	23
Ruth Ann, of Oxford, m. William **PENDLETON**, of Westville, June 27, 1848, by Rev. David P. Sanford	1	101
Sally, m. Abijah **HYDE**, b. of Oxford, Nov. 2, 1820, by Ephraim G. Swift	1	3
Samuel, Jr., of Southbury, m. Lucy **PERRY**, [, 1834(?)], by Rev. Abraham Brown. Recorded Nov. 22, 1834	1	48
Samuel, Capt. of 1st Co., in Oxford	2	132
Sarah, m. Ebenezer **FAIRCHILD**, b. of Oxford, Oct. 14, 1827, by Sayrs Gazley	1	27
Sarah, w. Job, d. Mar. 20, 1840, ae. 75	2	6

	Vol.	Page
CANDEE, (cont.)		
Sarah, wid. Moses, d. Oct. [ ], 1841, ae. 72	2	6
Sheldon, s. [Justus & Eunice], b. July 15, 1781	2	55
Sina, d. Cyrus & Rebecca, b. June 27, 1801	2	55
Timothy, [s. Justus & Eunice], b. Jan. 18, 1784	2	55
William, [s. Levi & Lucy], b. [ ]	2	56
Woodruff, m. Minerva **RIGGS**, Feb. 13, 1822, by Ephraim G. Swift	1	6
-----, Dr., d. Apr. 19, [1820], ae. 75	2	110
CANFIELD, Pamela, m. Sheldon **DURAND**, b. of Derby, May 20, 1831, by Noah Stone, J.P.	1	37
CARPENTER, Harvey, of Derby, m. Eurania **KINGSLEY**, of Oxford, Dec. 20, 1829, by Rev. W[illia]m A. Curtiss	1	34
CARTIER, James, [d. 1818], ae. 102	2	110
CARY, James, m. Mary Ann **TUCKER**, b. of Oxford, Sept. 30, 1821, by Eph[rai]m G. Swift	1	5
CASTLE, Isaac B., m. Julia **EDWARDS**, b. of Watertown, Aug. 11, 1823, by Chauncey Prindle	1	11
Sally, m. Joseph **CLARK**, b. of Oxford, Oct. 8, 1826, by Adonijah French, J.P.	1	24
CASWELL, Alanson, of Bridgeport, m. Mary P. **JOY**, of Oxford, June 6, 1839, by Rev. Joseph Scott, of Derby	1	68
CATLIN, Hannah, d. Abijah, m. David [ ], s. David, b. of Harwinton, Nov. 14, 1808	2	6
CHAMBERS, George Orlando, s. Francis & Ruth, b. Sept. 15, 1801	2	55
CHAPMAN, Austin, [s. Reuben & Polly], b. Apr. 25, 1806	2	55
Collins, [d. 1831], ae. 74	2	111
Eliza, [d. Reuben & Polly], b. June 17, 1808	2	55
Mary, m. David **CHATFIELD**, b. of Oxford, July 7, 1823, by Rev. Abner Smith, of Derby	1	11
Polly Ann, [d. Reuben & Polly], b. Mar. 10, 1813	2	55
Reuben, his w. [ ], d. [1813], ae. 34	2	107
Sam[ue]l, [d. 1817], ae. 60	2	109
CHATFIELD, Amanda, m. Palaski **CHATFIELD**, June 27, 1825, by John Sherman	1	21
Amanda H., of Oxford, m. Samuel C. **SMITH**, of Derby, Nov. 28, 1838, by Rev. Daniel Miller	1	65
Amanda Henrietta, d. Henry & Amanda, b. Jan. 26, 1822	2	56
Apia, [ch. of Dan & Elizabeth], b. May 20, 1790	2	54
Asahel, [s. Dan & Elizabeth], b. Mar. 10, 1792	2	54
Bennett, m. Ruth A. **TURNER**, b. of Oxford, [Apr.] 27, [1835], by Rev. Matthew Batchelor	1	56
Curtis, [s. Isaac & Sarah], b. Nov. 3, 1782	2	54
Dan, his s. [ ], d. [1809], "drowned"	2	105
David, [s. Chester & Clarissa], b. Apr. 18, 1822	2	56
David, m. Mary **CHAPMAN**, b. of Oxford, July 7, 1823, by		

OXFORD VITAL RECORDS

	Vol.	Page
CHATFIELD, (cont.)		
Rev. Abner Smith, of Derby	1	11
Divine, Capt. of 1st Co., in Oxford	2	132
Elias, [s. Dan & Elizabeth], b. July 11, 1794	2	54
Eliza Ann, [d. Dan & Elizabeth], b. Jan. 12, 1799	2	54
Elizabeth, wid. Gideon, d. Mar. 2, 1827, ae. 64 y.	2	7
Elizabeth S., of Oxford, m. Charles B. **NICHOLS**, of Bridgeport, Apr. 19, 1843, by Rev. Abel Nichols	1	87
Frederic H., m. Priscilla **WILLIAMS**, b. of Oxford, Nov. 29, 1840, by Rev. Sylvester Smith	1	74
George, s. Divine & Mariann, b. Dec. 13, 1810	2	54
Gid[eo]n, [d. 1817], ae. 62	2	109
Hannah, w. Abijah, d. Nov. 28, 1826, ae. 73 y.	2	7
Harvey, [twin with Henry, s. Chester & Clarissa], b. May 14, 1819	2	56
Harvey, m. Harriet E. **BUCKINGHAM**, [Apr.] 9, [1844], by Rev. Stephen Topliff	1	85
Henry, [twin with Harvey, s. Chester & Clarissa], b. May 14, 1819	2	56
Henry, d. Mar. 21, 1822, in North Caroline, ae. 30	2	7
Henry, [d. 1822], ae. 30	2	111
Isaac, [s. Isaac & Sarah], b. Oct. 15, 1786	2	54
Jennette, d. Divine & Mamre, d. Oct. 1, 1831, ae. 11 y.	2	7
Jennette, [d. 1831], ae. 11	2	111
John, [s. Isaac & Sarah], b. May 30, 1793	2	54
John, Lieut. d. [ ], 1793, ae. 97	2	102
John, [d.] June [ ], 1837	2	7
John F., s. John & Molly, d. Aug. 3, 1826	2	7
John Lyman, s. Polaski & Amanda, b. Sept. 13, 1826	2	56
Lewis, m. Thirza **PERRY**, b. of Oxford, Feb. 8, 1823, by Beardsley Northrop	1	9
Lois, [d. Isaac & Sarah], b. Oct. 28, 1790	2	54
Lois, m. James **PERRY**, b. of Oxford, Nov. 1, 1823, by Levi Candee, J.P.	1	12
Lucretia Mary, [d. Chester & Clarissa], b. Feb. 23, 1831	2	56
Martha, [d. Chester & Clarissa], b. May 22, 1824	2	56
Mary, w. John, d. Jan. 21, 1827	2	7
Mary, d. Lewis & Thirza, d. Nov. 4, 1831, ae. 2 y. 9 m.	2	7
Mary, [d. 1831], ae. 3	2	111
Nancy, [d. Dan & Elizabeth], b. Apr. [ ], 1796	2	54
Oliver, [s. Isaac & Sarah], b. July 17, 1788	2	54
Palaski, m. Amanda **CHATFIELD**, June 27, 1825, by John Sherman	1	21
Philo, [s. Chester & Clarissa], b. Sept. 21, 1816	2	56
Rachel, [d. Dan & Elizabeth], b. Jan. 21, 1787	2	54
Sally, [d. Dan & Elizabeth], b. Aug. 28, 1789	2	54

	Vol.	Page
CHATFIELD, (cont.)		
Sarah, m. Joseph N. **FRENCH**, Apr. 17, 1783	2	15
Sarah Ann, d. John, m. Aurelius **HYDE**, s. Capt. Abijah, Aug. 5, 1801	2	19
Truman, [s. Isaac & Sarah], b. June 16, 1796	2	54
Zero, [s. Issac & Sarah], b. Dec. [ ], 1798	2	54
CHICKORY, Jeffrey, (colored), [d. 1832], ae. 45	2	111
CHURCH, John, d. [, 1802], ae. 65	2	103
W[illia]m, & w. Lois, had s. [ ], b. Oct. 24, 1800	2	54
W[illia]m, his w. [ ], d. Oct. [ ], [1819], ae. 54; his 3 children, d. Oct. [ ], [1819]	2	110
CLARK, CLARKE, Amos, d. [1824], ae. 48	2	111
Ann, m. John **PARTREE**, Apr. 16, 1845, by Henry Olmstead, Jr.	1	90
Betsey, [d. Abel & Martha], b. Dec. [ ], 1789	2	54
Charles, [s. David & Clary], b. Jan. 22, 1818	2	56
Charles M., m. Delia **THOMPSON**, Dec. 31, 1840, by John D. Smith	1	76
David, [s. Abel & Martha], b. Aug. 19, 1794	2	54
David, [s. David & Clary], b. Jan. 26, 1820	2	56
Elias, m. Susan C. **NEWTON**, Oct. 24, 1805	2	6
Elias, d. [1813], ae. 32	2	107
Elisha, s. George & Lydia, b. Jan. 22, 1799	2	54
Francis A., of Middlebury, m. Ebenezer **RIGGS**, of Oxford, [Mar.] 5, [1846], by Rev. Stephen Topliff	1	92
Irene, m. Bennett **LUM**, Oct. 4, 1840, by John D. Smith	1	73
Jennett, of Oxford, m. William **HINMAN**, of Hudson, N.Y., Jan. 31, 1831, by Samuel Wise, J.P.	1	36
Jos[eph], his w. [, d. 1817], ae. 48	2	109
Joseph, m. Sally **CASTLE**, b. of Oxford, Oct. 8, 1826, by Adonijah French, J.P.	1	24
Martha, w. Abel, d. [1808], ae. 46	2	105
Mary, Mrs. m. David **SANFORD**, of Derby, Apr. 7, 1839, by Rev. John D. Smith, at the house of Ransom Hudson	1	71
Minerva, m. Nathan **DORMAN**, May 11, 1823, by Rev. Stephen Jewett, of Derby, in Woodbridge	1	10
Moses, [d. 1811], ae. 60	2	106
Nancy S., m. Garwood B. **BENHAM**, Feb. 14, 1831, by Rev. Chauncey Prindle	1	36
Patty, [d. Abel & Martha], b. Nov. 9, 1796	2	54
Phineas, Capt. of 1st. Co., in Oxford	2	132
Polly, [d. Abel & Martha], b. Mar. 18, 1792	2	54
Sally, of Southington, m. Garry **RIGGS**, of Oxford, Sept. 19, 1824, by Abel Wheeler, J.P.	1	17
Sam[ue]l & w. Eunice, had s. [ ], b. Nov. 1, 1799	2	54
Sheldon, d. Apr. 10, 1840, ae. 55	2	7

	Vol.	Page
CLARK, CLARKE, (cont.)		
Sherman, d. Apr. [ ], 1822, ae. 39	2	7
Sherman, [d. Apr. [ ], 1822], ae. 38	2	110
Sherman, [d. 1822], ae. 37	2	111
Susan, [d. 1831], ae. 42	2	111
Thomas, Jr., d. [ ], 1797, ae. 33	2	103
Thomas, d. [1811], ae. 82	2	106
COGER, Charles William, s. Jeremiah & Amarettee, b. July 7, 1829	2	54
CONNER, Joseph, of Leesburg, Va., m. Phebe M. **TOMLINSON**, of Oxford, Feb. 8, 1835, by Rev. Charles Smith	1	55
COOKE, George, of Woodbridge, m. Charlotte **SANFORD**, of Oxford, Apr. 3, 1831, by Noah Stone, J.P.	1	36
COOPER, Joseph, s. Chauncey & Anna, b. Aug. 16, 1812	2	54
COREY*, John F., of Humphreysville, m. Betsey M. **CAMP**, of Southbury, Feb. 24, 1845, by Rev. Stephen Topliff		
*(Perhaps "**CASEY**")	1	89
CORNISH, -----, wid., d. [1825], ae. 87	2	111
COUCH, Betsey, [d. Bradley & Aurelia], b. Aug. 23, 1807	2	54
Betsey, m. Charles **MORGAN**, Sept. 2, 1828, by Rev. W[illia]m A. Curtiss, in St. Peters Church	1	30
James, [s. Bradley & Aurelia], b. Oct. 23, 1808	2	54
CRAMER, Everton R., m. Eliza T. **PECK**, June 12, 1849, by Rev. Stephen Topliff	1	112
CURLEY, Eli, of Danbury, m. Laura **HUBBELL**, of Derby, July 3, 1831, by Samuel Wise, J.P.	1	38
CURTISS, Ann, of New York, m. Roswell **HYATT**, of Oxford, Sept. 9, 1838, by Rev. David Miller	1	64
Jason, of Southbury, m. Harriet **BEECHER**, of Oxford, July 25, 1822, by Ephraim G. Swift	1	7
Laura, d. Stephen & Mary, b. Aug. 7, 1790	2	55
Reuben, of Southbury, m. Minerva **McEWEN**, of Oxford, Oct. 11, 1820, by Ephraim G. Swift. Int.Pub.	1	2
[**CUTLER**], **KUTLER**, -----, Dr. 1st English inhabitant of Oxford, about 1715	2	133
DAVIS, Alva, m. Sally **KENNEY**, b. of Derby, Sept. 10, 1833, by John C. Coe, J.P.	1	44
Anson, [s. Capt. John & Mehetable], b. Sept. 5, 1785	2	58
Barrett*, [s. John & Mehetable], b. July 12, 1806		
*(Burritt?)	2	58
Burritt, m. Sarah E. **OSBORN**, b. of Oxford, Dec. 11, 1828, by Rev. W[illia]m A. Curtiss	1	31
Chara, [d. Capt. John & Mehetable], b. Feb. 8, 1794	2	58
Daniel, formerly of Derby, d. Mar. 20, 1822, ae. 74	2	10
Daniel, [d. 1822], ae. 74	2	111
Franklin Lewis, [s. Lewis & Lucinda], b. June 19, 1847	2	58
Henry, s. Lewis & Lucinda, b. Oct. 10, 1830	2	58
Isaac Beecher, s. W[illia]m & Polly, b. May 26, 1798	2	57

	Vol.	Page
DAVIS, (cont.)		
Isaac Beecher, [s. John & Laura], b. Apr. 15, 1817	2	58
John, Capt. m. Mehetable **THOMAS**, Apr. 10, 1782	2	11
John, [s. Capt. John & Mehetable], b. Sept. 8, 1788	2	58
John, d. [1813], ae. 30	2	107
John, Jr., d. Aug. 8, 1844, ae. 56	2	11
John, Capt. of 1st Co., in Oxford	2	132
John Riggs, [s. John & Laura], b. Dec. 20, 1814	2	58
John Riggs, m. Sarah Jenette **WHEELER**, Nov. 7, 1838, by Rev. John D. Smith, of Humphreyville, at the house of Lyman Wheeler	1	71
Joseph, Capt. of 1st. Co., in 1754	2	132
Joseph Wheeler, [s. Capt. John & Mehetable], b. Aug. 13, 1798	2	58
Julia M., m. Ebenezer **RIGGS**, Dec. 9, 1827, by Sayrs Gazley	1	28
Julia Maria, [d. John & Mehetable], b. July 4, 1810	2	58
Lewis, [s. John & Mehetable], b. Jan. 26, 1803	2	58
Lewis, m. Lucinda **PERKINS**, b. of Oxford, Oct. 1, 1829, by Rev. W[illia]m A. Curtiss	1	33
Lewis, Capt. of 1st Co., in Oxford, 1829	2	132
Lucretia, [d. Capt. John & Mehetable], b. Sept. 22, 1790	2	58
Mary, [d. Capt. John & Mehetable], b. May 28, 1792	2	58
Mary, m. Abijah **HYDE**, b. of Oxford, Feb. 12, 1835, by Rev. Charles Smith	1	55
Mary, d. [Lewis & Lucinda], b. Oct. 31, 1840	2	58
Nabby, [twin with Nancy, d. Capt. John & Mehetable], b. Dec. 21, 1795	2	58
Nancy, [twin with Nabby, d. Capt. John & Mehetable], b. Dec. 21, 1795	2	58
Nathan, [d.] Jan. 4, 1823, ae. 69	2	10
Nathan, [d. Feb. [ ], 1823], ae. 69	2	111
Otis, [s. John & Laura], b. Feb. 8, 1825	2	58
Otis, s. John Jr., & Laura, d. Apr. 12, 1842, ae. 18 y.	2	11
Sally, d. Col. J[ ], d. [1808], ae. 24	2	105
Sarah, [d. Capt. John & Mehetable], b. Mar. 31, 1783	2	58
Sheldon, [s. Capt. John & Mehetable], b. Sept. 2, 1800	2	58
Truman, [s. Capt. John & Mehetable], b. Mar. 13, 1787	2	58
William Hart, [s. John & Laura], b. Mar. 10, 1829	2	58
-----, s. Col. [ ], d. [1812], ae. 13	2	107
DEAN, DEANE, Elizabeth, wid. Ichabod D. & [d.] of Wooster **TWITCHEL**, d. Oct. 9, [1823?], ae. 88	2	10
Ichabod, d. [1804], ae. 70	2	104
-----, wid. [d. 1822], ae. 88	2	111
DeFOREST, William, of Salem, m. Lydia Agusta **TOMLINSON**, of Oxford, Oct. 25, 1824, by Rev. Alpheas Geer, of Waterbury	1	17

	Vol.	Page
DICK, Charles L., of Newtown, m. Sarah E. **MEIGS**, of Oxford, Oct. 11, 1847, by Rev. David P. Sanford	1	99
DICKERMAN, -----, his d. [ ], d. Mar. [ ], [1819], ae. 18	2	110
DOLBY, Stephen, m. Anna **LYON**, Nov. 17, 1821, by Beardsley Northrop	1	5
DORMAN, Amos, his w. [ ], d. [1810], ae. 40	2	106
Julia Ritta, m. Asa **SELA**, Mar. 7, 1824, by Adonijah French, J.P.	1	14
Nathan, m. Minerva **CLARK**, May 11, 1823, by Rev. Stephen Jewett, of Derby, in Woodbridge	1	10
DOWNEY, Lois Elizabeth, of Waterbury, m. Alvan Austin **LINES**, of Oxford, May 9, [probably 1824], by Adonijah French, J.P.	1	15
DOWNS, DOWN, Clark B., of Derby, m. Jane M. **FRENCH**, of Oxford, Oct. 20, 1839, by Sam[ue]l Wooster, J.P.	1	68
Joseph, of Woodbridge, m. Mary Adaline **MORRIS**, of Oxford, Sept. 13, 1823, by Abel Wheeler, J.P.	1	11
Thomas M., of Southbury, m. Cynthia C. **WORCESTER**, of Oxford, [Jan.] 1, [1845], by Rev. Stephen Topliff	1	88
DRIVER, James, of Derby, m. Susan **SEELEY**, of Oxford, Aug. 19, 1832, by Wait Bassett, J.P., at the house of John Woodin	1	42
Jane Ennis, d. James, b. Oct. 21, 1828	2	57
DUNHAM, Henry, m. Henrietta **TUCKER**, b. of Oxford, Oct. [ ], 1834, by Rev. Abraham Browne	1	58
DUNN, Anna, w. Eli, d. Oct. 7, [ ], ae. 70	2	102
DURAND, Botsford, [s. Jos[eph] & Pena], b. Dec. 27, 1792; d. Feb. 6, 1795	2	57
Clary, [d. Jos[eph] & Pena], b. July 21, 1799	2	57
Elijah, [s. Jos[eph] & Pena], b. Sept. 6, 1790	2	57
Elijah, d. [1804], ae. 75	2	104
Glover, [s. Jos[eph] & Pena], b. Apr. 25, 1796	2	57
John, [s. Nehemiah & Ruth], b. Mar. 8, 1791	2	57
Joseph, d. [1809], ae. 45	2	105
Naham, his w. [ ], [d. 1816], ae. 57	2	109
Naham, d. [1824], ae. 72	2	111
Polly, [d. Nehemiah & Ruth], b. July 3, 1796	2	57
Sheldon, m. Pamela **CANFIELD**, b. of Derby, May 20, 1831, by Noah Stone, J.P.	1	37
DUTTON, Abigail, d. Apr. [ ], [1824], ae. 92	2	111
Albert Augustus, [s. Thomas A. & Lucinda], b. Feb. 5, 1829	2	57
Almira C., m. Benjamin [ ], Feb. 21, 1810	2	6
Almira Clementin, [d. Hosea & Elizabeth], b. Mar. 15, 1788	2	57
Almira Clementina, d. H[osea] & E[lizabeth], m. Benjamin **BANDS**, s. Capt. Sam[ue]l & Mabel, Feb. 21,		

	Vol.	Page
DUTTON, (cont.)		
1810	1	1
Eliza Maria, [d. Thomas A. & Lucinda], Feb. 23, 1831	2	57
Elizabeth, [d. Hosea & Elizabeth], b. Feb. 14, 1798	2	57
Elizabeth, d. Hosea & Elizabeth, m. Abel Allen **ALLIS**, May 3, 1818	1	1
Elizabeth, m. Abel A. **ALLIS**, May 3, 1818	2	1
Eunice, [d. Hosea & Elizabeth], b. Mar. 2, 1793	2	57
Hosea, physician, s. John & Abigail, of Southington, m. Elizabeth **TROWBRIDGE**, d. Israel & Mary, of Oxford, Jan. 19, 1783	2	11
Hosea, Dr., d. Oct. 9, 1826, ae. about 72 y.	2	11
Huldah, [d. Hosea & Elizabeth], b. Aug. 23, 1786; d. [ ], 1794	2	57
Israel, [s. Hosea & Elizabeth], b. Dec. 29, 1784; d. [ ], 1812	2	57
Israel, s. H[ ], d. Sept. 16, [1812], ae. 27, at New Orleans	2	106
John, [s. Hosea & Elizabeth], b. Nov. 11, 1783	2	57
John, d. [Aug. , 1819], ae. 90	2	110
Lemuel, [s. Hosea & Elizabeth], b. Jan. 23, 1795; d. [ ], 1795	2	57
Maria Sylvia, [d. Hosea & Elizabeth], b. Apr. 10, 1791; d. [ ], 1794	2	57
Philomela, [ch. Hosea & Elizabeth], b. Jan. 22, 1796	2	57
Sabastian, d. [Sept. , 1824], ae. 24	2	111
Sabastian Maria Himenes Patruchia, s. Hosea & Elizabeth, b. Jan. 26, 1801; d. [ ], 1824	2	57
Sophia Charlotte, [d. Hosea & Elizabeth], b. Dec. 11, 1789	2	57
Thomas A., m. Lucinda **SCOTT**, b. of Oxford, Nov. 25, 1827, by Sayrs Gazley	1	28
Thomas Albert Bonnaparte Jefferson, s. [Hosea & Elizabeth], b. Jan. 27, 1802	2	57
EATON, Sam[ue]ll, d. [1814], ae. 47	2	107
EDMUNDS, Milo, m. Lydia Maria **BUNNEL**, b. of Oxford, Nov. 19, 1845, by Rev. G. B. Eastman	1	93
EDWARDS, Julia, m. Isaac B. **CASTLE**, b. of Watertown, Aug. 11, 1823, by Chauncey Prindle	1	11
ELSWORTH, James, of Branchport, N.Y., m. Abigail **HINMAN**, of Oxford, Oct. 8, [1848], by Rev. Charles Steonns, of Humphreyville	1	110
ELTON, Hannah, wid., d. [1815], ae. 80	2	109
ENGLISH, Amos, s. Clement & Sarah, b. Dec. 28, 1798	2	60
Anna, [d. David], b. Apr. 1, 1796	2	60
Dan, s. Clement & Sarah, b. Apr. 24, 1794	2	60
David A., [s. David], b. Dec. 18, 1807	2	60

OXFORD VITAL RECORDS 43

	Vol.	Page

ENGLISH, (cont.)
  Grace, of Derby, m. David **PERRY**, of Oxford, [,
    1834?], by Rev. Abraham Brown. Recorded Nov. 22,
    1834   1   52
  Henry B., of Derby, m. Hannah **WOODING**, of Oxford,
    Apr. 6, 1842, by Rev. Thomas Sparks   1   78
  Joel, s. David & Jerusha, b. Mar. 26, 1799   2   60
  Melissa, d. David, b. Nov. 29, 1793   2   60
  Meneva, [d. David], b. Feb. 1, 1802   2   60
  Sally G., [d. David], b. Oct. 11, 1804   2   60
  Sarah R., d. Clement & Sarah, b. Nov. 26, 1806   2   60
  Stephen Bennett, s. Clement & Sarah, b. Aug. 6, 1801   2   60
EVERETT, Charles, m. Charlotte **BETTS**, [Mar.] 24, [1844], by
  Rev. Stephen Topliff   1   84
FABREGUE, Asa Louison, [s.] W[illia]m L., b. May 9, 1828   2   62
FAIRCHILD, Abial, s. John & Mary, b. Apr. 25, 1800   2   62
  Abial, [d. 1815], ae. 84   2   109
  Boyle, of Newtown, m. Julian **HATCH**, of Oxford, Feb. 14,
    1827, by Rev. Sturgis Gilbert   1   25
  Eben[eze]r, d. [1804], ae. 29   2   104
  Ebenezer, m. Sarah **CANDEE**, b. of Oxford, Oct. 14, 1827,
    by Sayrs Gazley   1   27
  Hanford, s. Eben & Eunice, b. Mar. 7, 1799   2   62
  Hanford, of Oxford, m. Delia E. **TWITCHEL**, of Oxford,
    Jan. 10, 1822, by Beardsley Northrop   1   6
  John L., m. Clary **BUNNELL**, Jan. 26, 1825, by Chauncey
    Prindle   1   20
  Julia, [d. 1831], ae. 36   2   111
  Laura, d. Benj[ami]n, m. Timothy [   ], s. Justus,
    Nov. 11, 1801   2   6
  Lyman, s. [John & Mary], b. Feb. 8, 1803   2   62
  Nathan, d. June 23, 1800, ae. 59   2   102
  Sterne Delos, [s. Hanford & Delia Elvira], b. Feb. 17,
    1828   2   62
  Stiles, s. John & Mary, b. May 6, 1805   2   62
  Stiles, m. Mary **OSBORN**, b. of Oxford, Nov. 17, 1831, by
    Rev. Ashbel Baldwin   1   39
  W[illia]m Augustus, s. Hanford & Delia Elvira, [b.]
    Nov. 6, 1822   2   62
  Zerviah, [d. 1816], ae. 77   2   109
FARNHAM, William H., of Hampton, m. Orvilla **NETTLETON**, of
  Oxford, Sept. 18, 1842, by Rev. John E. Bray   1   80
FERGUSON, FURGUSON, John, of Paisley, Scotland, d. Oct. 25,
  1798, ae. 42, "suicide"   2   102
  John D., d. Nov. 14, 1828, ae. 35 y.   2   15
FLAGG, George A., of New Haven, m. Marietta C. **BEARDSLEE**,
  of Oxford, Jan. 22, 1835, by Rev. Charles Smith   1   54
FOX, Lewis, of Woodbury, m. Charlotte **BROWN**, of Oxford, Dec.

	Vol.	Page
FOX, (cont.)		
1, 1849, by Alfred Harger, J.P.	1	111
FREEMAN, Aaron, m. Pheebean [ ] (colored person), Aug. 28, 1832, by Rev. Chaunc[e]y Prindle	1	41
Harriet, [d. Nath[anie]l & Mary B.], b. Nov. 20, 1810	2	63
Nathaniel, m. Mary B. **FOX**, Nov. 20, 1810	2	15
FRENCH, Abel, of New Stratford, m. Mary **BEECHER**, Apr. 24, 1822, by Ephraim G. Swift	1	7
Bennett, s. Elisha & Ruth, b. July 7, 1800	2	63
David, [s. Joseph N. & Sarah], b. Apr. 16, 1795	2	63
David, m. Elizabeth Ann **WOOSTER**, b. of Oxford, Mar. 8, 1829, by Rev. Nathan D. Benedict	1	32
Harriet, m. Sherman **LINES**, b. of Oxford, Dec. 19, 1824, by Adonijah French, J.P.	1	18
Jane M., of Oxford, m. Clark B. **DOWNS**, of Derby, Oct. 20, 1839, by Sam[ue]l Wooster, J.P.	1	68
John, [s. Joseph N. & Sarah], b. Apr. 27, 1789	2	63
Joseph, [s. Joseph N. & Sarah], b. Feb. 21, 1791	2	63
Jos[eph], [d. 1816], ae. 57	2	109
Joseph N., m. Sarah **CHATFIELD**, Apr. 17, 1783	2	15
Laura A., of Oxford, m. Abraham **BASSETT**, of New Haven, Mar. 20, 1842, by Rev. T. Sparks, Pleasant Vale	1	77
Lucy, [d. Joseph N. & Sarah], b. Feb. 2, 1787	2	63
[Luther], his w. [d. 1825], ae. 54	2	111
Luther, [d. 1825], ae. 50	2	111
Nicholas, s. Joseph, d. [1811], ae. 25	2	106
Nicholas, [s. Joseph N. & Sarah], b. Sept. 4, 1785	2	63
Patty Maria, m. Larren **SMITH**, b. of Oxford, Dec. 15, 1828, by Adonijah French, J.P.	1	31
Philo, [s. Joseph N. & Sarah], b. June 17, 1797	2	63
Philo, [d. Aug. [ ], 1819], ae. 19	2	110
Sally, [d. Joseph N. & Sarah], b. May 11, 1793	2	63
Sarah, w. Dan[ie]l, d. [1814], ae. 60	2	108
Sarah Augusta, d. David & Elizabeth, b. Jan. 7, 1830	2	63
Sheldon, [s. Joseph N. & Sarah], b. Apr. 18, 1784	2	63
-----, wid., d. [1811], ae. 84	2	106
FULLER, George W., of New Haven, m. Sarah E. **RIGGS**, of Oxford, May 28, [1843], by Rev. Stephen Topliff	1	82
Lucius, m. Rhoda **BLACKMAN**, b. of Oxford, Sept. 28, 1835, by Rev. Abraham Browne	1	59
GARRETT, -----, s. Wait, d. Sept. [ ], 1800, ae. 7	2	102
GIBBS, Simeon Martin, s. Gid[eo]n & Eunice, b. Sept. 10, 1811	2	65
GILLETT, Daniel, m. Jennet F. **BRADLEY**, b. of Oxford, Apr. 20, 1836, by Rev. Abraham Browne	1	60
GLOVER, Phebe, m. Sam[ue]l **WHEELER**, Oct. 20, 1795	2	45
GRAHAM, George W., m. Evelina **SMITH**, June 12, 1823, by		

	Vol.	Page
GRAHAM, (cont.)		
Cha[rle]s Bunnell, J.P.	1	10
Matilda, of Oxford, m. Brian G. **BAINBRIDGE**, of Southbury, Feb. 27, 1836, by Rev. Abraham Browne	1	60
Sarah Maria, s. George W[illia]m & Evelina, b. Mar. 4, 1824	2	65
GRIFFIN, Daniel, [s. Jonathan & Lydia], b. [ ]	2	65
Elisha, d. [1814], ae. 82	2	107
John, Lieut. 1st white person, b. in Oxford, 1725, at Quaker Farms; d. [ ], ae. 94	2	133
John, d. [Feb. [ ], 1819], ae. 94	2	110
Mehetable, d. [ ], 1794, ae. 103	2	102
Mehetabel, [d. Jonathan & Lydia], b. July 6, 1798	2	65
William, m. Laura **SPERRY**, Dec. 30, 1839, by Rev. John D. Smith, at the house of Silas Sperry	1	72
GRISWOLD, Marvin, of Litchfield, m. Avis **TOWNER**, of Oxford, [ ], by Rev. Abraham Brown. Recorded Nov. 22, 1834	1	49
GUNN, Abel, Capt. of 1st Co., in Oxford	2	132
Anna, m. Benjamin **BUNNEL**, Oct. 8, 1835, by Rev. Charles Smith	1	56
Mary E., m. William **LUM**, b. of Oxford, June 16, 1847, by Rev. David T. Sanford	1	98
Nancy, of Waterbury, m. George **LUM**, of Oxford, Oct. 29, 1837, by Chauncey M. Hatch, J.P.	1	63
Simeon, his w. [ ], d. Nov. 22, [1802], ae. 30	2	103
Willard S., of Waterbury, m. Catharine M. **BURRITT**, of Bridgeport, Mar. 20, 1844, by Nathan J. Wilcoxson, J.P.	1	84
HAGER, [see also **HARGER**], Bettey, d. Oct. [, 1821], ae. 57	2	110
HAKINS, [see also **HAWKINS**], Mary, of Oxford, m. George T. **STODDARD**, of Southbury, Mar. 8, 1840, by Rev. Josiah Bowen	1	70
HALL, Philo, of New Haven, m. Sarah M. **SKEELS**, of Oxford, Sept. 11, 1836, by Rev. James Sunderland, in Christ Church	1	57
HARD, Carlos, of Huntington, m. Lydia Ann **MUNSON**, of Oxford, Mar. 2, 1831, by Adonijah French, J.P.	1	36
Mary A., of Waterbury, m. Charles **WEBSTER**, of Oxford, Feb. 18, 1838, by Rev. Abraham Brown	1	67
HARGER, HARGAR, HARGIN, [see also **HAGER**], Alfred, m. Ruth **BEARDSLEE**, b. of Oxford, Mar. 13, 1830, by Rev. A. Brown	1	35
Burrett, [d. 1822], ae. 16	2	111
Caroline, d. [Elijah & Sarah], b. Sept. 5, 1802	2	67
Caroline, of Oxford, m. Bennett **LUM**, of Derby, May 19, 1823, by Rev. Abner Smith, of Derby	1	10
Caroline Jane, d. Alfred & Ruth, d. June 25, 1831	2	19

	Vol.	Page
HARGER, HARGAR, HARGIN, (cont.)		
Catharine, [d. 1831], ae. 6 m.	2	111
Catharine Jane, Alfred & Ruth, b. Jan. 1, 1831	2	67
Charles, s. Alfred & Ruth, b. Jan. 23, 1834	2	67
Elijah, d. Mar. 21, 1840, ae. 76 y.	2	19
Henry, s. Alfred & Ruth, b. Apr. 14, 1832	2	67
Lucinda, d. Elijah & Sarah, b. Jan. 5, 1799	2	67
Lucinda, of Oxford, m. Benjamin **HOLBROOK**, of Derby, May 19, [1823], by Rev. Abner Smith, of Derby	1	15
HART, John M., of Boston, Mass., m. Mary **BRADBURY**, of Oxford, Dec. 25, 1833, by Rev. Abraham Brown	1	51
Thomas P., of Watertown, m. Polly **RIGGS**, of Oxford, July 13, 1834, by Rev. Abraham Brown	1	53
HATCH, Benj[ami]n Austin, [s. Sherman & Sarah], b. Oct. 18, 1799	2	68
Catharine, d. Chauncey M., d. June 12, 1827, ae. 15	2	19
Chauncey Miles, s. Cha[rle]s M. & Julia, b. May 24, 1822	2	66
Clarissa, [d. Sherman & Sarah], b. Jan. 13, 1798	2	68
Julia, w. Chauncey M., d. Mar. 19, 1840, ae. 49	2	19
Julian, of Oxford, m. Boyle **FAIRCHILD**, of Newton, Feb. 14, 1827, by Rev. Sturgis Gilbert	1	25
Sally, [d. Sherman & Sarah], b. July [ ], 1795	2	68
Seymour, [s. Sherman & Sarah], b. May 20, 1801	2	68
Sherman, [d. 1818], ae. 67	2	110
Zephaniah, Capt., d. [ ], 1792, ae. 86	2	102
HAWKINS, [see also **HAKINS**], Amos, [s. Isaac & Anna], b. Mar. 29, 1798	2	68
Asa, s. Elijah & Abigail, b. Aug. 18, 1796	2	68
Asa, of Oxford, m. Hannah **WEEDEN**, of Oxford, Aug. 12, 1821, by Beardsley Northrop	1	4
Claraina, m. Benjamin **TWITCHELL**, Feb. 26, 1776	2	42
Eli, s. Silas, d. [1812], ae. 17	2	106
Elijah, d. [1809], ae. 60	2	105
Elizabeth, d. Capt. Zach[ariah], m. John **RIGGS**, s. Joseph & Mabel, of Derby, Dec. 22, 1767	2	36
Elizabeth, m. David **BEECHER**, Mar. 22, 1846, by Samuel Meigs, J.P.	1	96
Elizur, s. Lee & Sarah, b. Jan. 11, 1802	2	68
Harriet, m. Thomas **RILEY**, Feb. 21, 1825, by Rev. Chauncey Prindle	1	20
Isaac, [s. Isaac & Anna], b. Mar. 28, 1796	2	68
John, [d. 1814], ae. 65	2	108
Lewis, 1st ch. Asa, b. Mar. 29, 1822	2	66
Lois, [d. 1814], ae. 65	2	107
Lou, his s. [ ], d. [1823], ae. 22	2	111
Lydia, d. Zachrary & Sally, b. Dec. 7, 1798	2	68
Lydia, d. Aug. 4, [1820], ae. 87	2	110

	Vol.	Page
HAWKINS, (cont.)		
Maria, d. Zachary & Sally, b. Aug. 23, 1800	2	68
Moses, m. Elizabeth **SMITH**, b. of Oxford, Oct. 7,		
1821, by Beardsley Northrop	1	5
Phebe, d. [Elijah & Abigail], b. [ ]	2	68
Russell, [s. Isaac & Anna], b. Apr. 27, 1792	2	68
Russell, m. Betsey **JOHNSON**, Apr. 22, 1822, by		
Ephraim G. Swift	1	7
Sarah, m. Clark **TOMLINSON**, Jan. 24, 1822, by Beardsley		
Northrop	1	6
Silas, his w. [, d. 1820], ae. 58	2	110
Silas, m. Sally **LOCKWOOD**, Feb. 21, 1825, by Sam[ue]l		
Meigs, J.P.	1	21
Zachariah, Capt. of 1st Co., in Oxford, 1754	2	132
Zachariah, Capt., d. [1806], ae. 90	2	104
Zachary, [s. Isaac & Anna], b. Feb. 1, 1794	2	68
HAWLEY, Jared, his w. [, d. 1818], ae. 33	2	110
Jared, his w. [, d. Apr. [ ], 1821], ae.		
24	2	110
Jared, d. Jan. 27, 1822	2	19
Jared, [d. 1822], ae. 40	2	111
HENDRIX, [see also **HENDRYS**], Priscilla, m. Henry **HOYT**, Mar.		
11, 1821, by David Tomlinson, J.P.	1	4
Priscilla, of Oxford, m. Henry **HOYT**, of Danbury, Mar.		
11, 1821, by David Tomlinson, J.P.	1	5
HENDRYS, [see also **HENDRIX**], Olson, m. Mrs. Lucy		
KIMBERLY, b. of Oxford, Apr. 9, 1846, by Rev. G. B.		
Eastman	1	94
HENNEY, Medad, m. Mrs. Sally **SPENCER**, b. of Derby, Jan. 26,		
1827, by Bennett Lum, J.P., at the house of Anson		
Chatfield	1	29
HEWINS, Erastus C., of Alfred, Mass., m. Sabra **WOOSTER**, of		
Oxford, Mar. 17, 1830, by Nathan D. Benedict	1	35
HIGGINS, Sylvester & w. Comfort, had d. [ ], b.		
Aug. 29, 1799	2	68
HINE, HIN, Benet, of Woodbridge, m. Amy C. **PIRSON**, of		
Oxford, June 8, 1829, by Rev. Samuel Potter, of		
Woodbridge & Salem	1	32
Betsey M., of Oxford, m. Clark **BOTSFORD**, of Derby, Aug.		
5, 1821, by Beardsley Northrop	1	4
H[ ], Capt., his w. [ ], d. Nov. 9,		
[ ], ae. 39	2	102
Jehiel, Capt., d. [Dec. [ ], 1823], ae. 62	2	111
Roxana, [d. 1831], ae. 32	2	111
-----, Capt. his w. [ ], d. Feb. [,1819],		
ae. 67	2	110
HINMAN, Abigail, of Oxford, m. James **ELSWORTH**, of		
Branchport, N.Y., Oct. 8, [1848], by Rev. Charles		

	Vol.	Page
HINMAN, (cont.)		
Steonns, of Humphreysville	1	110
Abigail, w. John, d. Oct. 21, [ ], ae. 24	2	102
Betsey Phebe, d. Simeon & Phebe, b. Mar. 14, 1822	2	66
Clary, [d. Philemon & Polly], b. Nov. 2, 1794	2	67
Jennet, [d. 1831], ae. 28	2	111
John d., Dec. [, 1821], ae. 42	2	110
John Wanzer, [s. Simeon & Phebe], b. Nov. 9, 1824	2	66
Laura J., m. Noadiah **WARNER**, [July] 9, [1843], by Rev. Stephen Topliff	1	82
Lyman, s. John & Abigail, b. July 8, 1798	2	67
Nicholas, s. [Simeon & Phebe], b. Oct. 22, 1827	2	66
Phebe, w. Simeon, d. Apr. 29, 1830, ae. 39	2	19
Philemon, [w. Polly, had ch.], b. Sept. 5, 1796	2	67
William, of Hudson, N.Y., m. Jennett **CLARK**, of Oxford, Jan. 31, 1831, by Samuel Wise, J.P.	1	36
William, Capt. of 1st Co., in Oxford, 1833	2	132
HITCHCOCK, George, m. Ruth **JOHNSON**, b. of Oxford, Sept. 15, 1831, by Noah Stone, J.P.	1	39
Harriet E., m. George W. **SMITH**, Feb. 28, 1848, by Rev. Stephen Topliff	1	100
Ruth Ann, Mrs. of Oxford, m. Lyman **ALLEN**, of Woodbridge, [Mar.] 19, 1848, by Rev. Stephen Topliff	1	100
Sam[ue]l, his w. [ ], d. [1813], ae. 56	2	107
Sarah, m. Clarke **WEBSTER**, b. of Derby, Nov. 25, 1833, by Rev. Abraham Brown	1	49
HOLBROOK, Austin, of Derby, m. Betsey Augusta **SPERRY**, of Oxford, Dec. 14, 1825, by Rev. Abner Smith, of Derby	1	22
Benjamin, of Derby, m. Lucinda **HARGIN**, of Oxford, May 19, [1823], by Rev. Abner Smith, of Derby	1	15
Daniel Lum, of Derby, m. Lucy **NICHOLS**, of Oxford, Jan. 28, 1821, by Rev. Abner Smith, of Derby	1	3
Mary, Mrs. of Oxford, m. Ichabod **JOHNSON**, of Newtown, Oct. 26, 1828, by Sayrs Gazley	1	30
Philo, d. [1813], ae. 56	2	107
HORTON, Lucius B., of Waterbury, m. Eunice N. **STONE**, Jan. 14, 1833, by Rev. Abraham Brown	1	48
HOTCHKISS, Almira, m. Lucius L. **OSBORN**, Jan. 13, 1833, by Rev. S. Jewitt of Humphreyville	1	43
Fanny, of Waterbury, m. Horace **BUCKINGHAM**, of Oxford, [Dec.] 13, [1840], by Rev. Stephen Topliff	1	74
Isaac T., of New Haven, m. Eliza C. **TOMLINSON**, of Oxford, Nov. 7, 1827, by Rev. Alpheas Gear, of Waterbury	1	27
Lewis, of Derby, m. Eliza **HULL**, of Oxford, Jan. 18, 1848, by Rev. Charles Dickinson, of Birmingham	1	100

OXFORD VITAL RECORDS

	Vol.	Page
HOTCHKISS, (cont.)		
Louisa A., m. Frederick A. **CANDEE**, b. of Oxford, Oct. 7, 1845, by Rev. G. B. Eastman	1	93
Lucian, m. Maria L. **BLACKMAN**, of Middlebury, Sept. 8, 1841, by Rev. P. L. Hoyt	1	77
William S., of New Haven, m. Mrs. Jennet A. **TOMLINSON**, of Oxford, Dec. 25, 1822, by Rev. Manzies Raynor, of Huntington, Conn.	1	9
HOWARD, Jesse C., m. Jane E. **WHEELER**, Nov. 15, 1840, by John D. Smith	1	76
HOYT, Henry, m. Priscilla **HENDRIX**, Mar. 11, 1821, by David Tomlinson, J.P.	1	4
Henry, of Danbury, m. Priscilla **HENDRIX**, of Oxford, Mar. 11, 1821, by David Tomlinson, J.P.	1	5
HUBBELL, HUBBELS, Almira, [d. Richard & Mercy], b. Aug. 9, 1793	2	68
Augustus, [s. Richard & Mercy], b. Mar. 26, 1795	2	68
Betsey, d. Joseph & Betsey, b. Feb. 5, 1800	2	68
Eph[rai]m, his. w. [, d. 1823], ae. 40	2	111
Everet, of Derby, m. Mrs. Jane **SPERRY**, of Oxford, Nov. 26, 1828, by Bennett Lum, J.P., at the house of Austin Holbrook, Int. Pub.	1	31
Harriet, of Hungtington, m. Amos **WHEELER**, of Southbury, Apr. 15, 1824, by Newton Tuttle	1	14
Harry, [s. Joseph & Betty], b. Nov. 29, 1789	2	68
Joel, [s. Joseph & Betty], b. Mar. [ ], 1795	2	68
Laura, of Derby, m. Eli **CURLEY**, of Danbury, July 3, 1831, by Samuel Wise, J.P.	1	38
Matthew, of Middletown, N.Y., m. Mary **TOWNER**, of Oxford, Oct. 7, 1833, by Rev. Abraham Brown	1	50
Meret, [s. Joseph & Betty], b. June 12, 1793	2	68
Milo, [s. Joseph & Betty], b. Feb. 17, 1798	2	68
Orange J., of Washington, m. Augusta **SMITH**, of Oxford, Sept. 13, 1835, by Rev. Abraham Browne	1	58
Richard, d. [ ], 1796, ae. 45	2	103
Sheldon, of Monroe, m. Mrs. Hannah **BASSETT**, of Oxford, Dec. 19, 1826, by Bennett Lum, J.P., at the house of Edward Bassett. Int.Pub.	1	25
Stephen, of Hamden, m. Martha **STONE**, Oct. 30, 1832, by Rev. Abraham Brown	1	48
HUDSON, Mary B., m. David R. **LUM**, b. of Oxford, Dec. 25, 1836, by Rev. Daniel Burhans	1	61
HULL, Abel, [s. Abel & Abigail], b. June 4, 1794	2	68
Abel & w. Abigail, had ch. b. Jan. 12, 1800	2	68
Abigail, w. Abel, d. [1805], ae. 48	2	104
Amanda, d. Isaac & Diana, b. Apr. 12, 1812	2	66
Bennett, [s. Ezra & Betsey], b. Feb. 1, 1799	2	68
Betty Ann, wid., d. probably Dec. 31, 1839; found on		

	Vol.	Page
HULL, (cont.)		
the farm of Alfred Harger; ae. 67 on Jan. 26, 1840	2	19
Eliza, of Oxford, m. Lewis **HOTCHKISS**, of Derby, Jan. 18, 1848, by Rev. Charles Dickinson, of Birmingham	1	100
Frederic, m. Ruth Ann **SMITH**, b. of Oxford, Feb. 19, 1834, by Rev. Abraham Brown	1	52
Horace, of Waterbury, m. Elizabeth **TWITCHELL**, of Oxford, July 4, 1824, by Levi Candee, J.P.	1	16
Polly, [d. Ezra & Betsey], b. May 30, 1797	2	68
Samuel, [s. Abel & Abigail], b. Dec. 28, 1796	2	68
HUMPHREY, HUMPHREYS, Bernard, [s. Cyrus & Nancy], b. May 31, 1820	2	68
Cyrus, d. Aug. 22, 1826, ae. 29 y.	2	19
Homer, s. [Cyrus & Nancy], d. Aug. 17, 1826, about 18 m.	2	19
Nancy, [d. Cyrus & Nancy], b. Mar. 19, 1822	2	68
Nancy, [w. Cyrus], d. Aug. 25, 1826, ae. 30	2	19
HURLBUTT, Augusta, of Oxford, m. Elam **PIERCE**, of Southbury, Sept. 3, 1834, by Rev. Abraham Brown	1	53
HYATT, Roswell, of Oxford, m. Ann **CURTISS**, of New York, Sept. 9, 1838, by Rev. David Miller	1	64
HYDE, Abijah, Capt., d. July 23, 1801, ae. about 70	2	102
Abijah, m. Sally **CANDEE**, b. of Oxford, Nov. 2, 1820, by Ephraim G. Swift	1	3
Abijah, m. Mary **DAVIS**, b. of Oxford, Feb. 12, 1835, by Rev. Charles Smith	1	55
Abijah, Capt. of 1st Co. in Oxford	2	132
Alanson, [s. John & Betsey], b. July [ ], 1795	2	67
Alva, 1st ch., [Joseph & Anna], b. Jan. 8, 1794	2	66
Asahel, his w. [, d. 1823], ae. 54	2	111
Asahel, d. [1831], ae. 69	2	111
Asahel, Capt. of 1st Co., in Oxford	2	132
Aurelius, s. Capt. Abijah, m. Sarah Ann **CHATFIELD**, d. John, Aug. 5, 1801	2	19
Aurelius, his w. [, d. 1815], ae. 34	2	108
Calvin, [s. Capt. Asahel & Mary], b. Mar. 17, 1796	2	67
Cha[rle]s, d. June 20, [1824], ae. 21	2	111
Clarissa, [d. Joseph & Anna], b. May 24, 1796	2	67
Cynthia, [d. Capt. Asahel & Mary], b. July 11, 1797	2	67
Cyrus, [s. Capt. Asahel & Mary], b. Apr. 6, 1794	2	67
Dan[ie]l, d. [1807], ae. 40	2	105
David, [s. John & Betsey], b. Sept. 28, 1797	2	67
David Ambrose, s. Aurelius & Sarah Ann, b. May 10, 1802	2	67
Duty*, [ch. of Joseph & Anna], b. Apr. 26, 1805 *(Doty?)	2	67
Eunice, [d. Joseph & Anna], b. Mar. 20, 1801	2	67

OXFORD VITAL RECORDS 51

	Vol.	Page
HYDE, (cont.)		
Eunice, of Oxford, m. James **PORTER**, of Cheshire, Aug. 29, 1822, by Rev. John Keys, of Waterbury	1	7
Frederic, [s. Joseph & Anna], b. Aug. 10, 1798	2	67
Garry, [s. Dan[ie]l & Eunice], b. Apr. [ ], 1795	2	67
Garry B., m. Caroline **WOOSTER**, b. of Oxford, July 10, 1831, by Rev. Nathan D. Benedict	1	38
George, [s. Joseph & Anna], b. Feb. 1, 1812	2	66
Hannah, wid., m. Samuel **MEIGS**, b. of Oxford, Nov. 12, 1828, by Rev. W[illia]m A. Curtiss	1	31
Harry, [s. Nathan & Sally], b. June 29, 1794	2	67
Horatio, s. Nathan & Sally, b. [ ], 1800	2	67
Ira, [s. Capt. Asahel & Mary], b. Nov. 17, 1799	2	67
Isaac, [s. Joseph & Anna], b. May 23, 1803	2	67
Jane Janetta, [d. Aurelius & Sarah Ann], b. Dec. 28, 1807	2	67
Jehiel, Capt. of 1st Co., in Oxford	2	132
Larren*, [s.* Nathan & Sally], b. Aug. 21, 1792 (*correction Larren has been crossed out and d. of is handwritten in margin of original manuscript.)	2	67
Laura Jane, d. Abijah & Sally, b. July 28, 1826	2	66
Laura L., of Oxford, m. Samuel N. **WOOD**, of Lowel, Mass., Nov. 29, 1846, by Rev. Stephen Topliff	1	97
Marcus, [s. Capt. Asahel & Mary], b. Oct. 30, 1791	2	67
Marcus, [d. 1814], ae. 23	2	108
Mary, wid. Capt. Abijah, d. Nov. 4, 1822, ae. about 90	2	19
Mary, [d. 1822], ae. 87	2	111
Mary, w. Capt. Asahel, d. [ ], 1823, ae. 54	2	19
Mary Jane, [d. Aurelius & Sarah Ann], b. Oct. 20, 1806	2	67
Meret, [s. Dan[ie]l & Eunice], b. May 12, 1791	2	67
Meret, [s. Dan[ie]l & Eunice], b. Jan. 2, 1794	2	67
Nathan, [s. Nathan & Sally], b. Feb. 8, 1796	2	67
Patience, [d. John & Betsey], b. Jan. 19, 1799	2	67
Rachel, [d. Nathan & Sally], b. Oct. 15, 1797	2	67
Rena, wid. [d. 1817], ae. 82	2	109
Sally Lovilla, [d. Nathan & Sally], b. Apr. 14, 1799	2	67
Sarah Ann, [d. Aurelius & Sarah Ann], b. June 14, 1804	2	67
Sheldon, 7th ch., [Joseph & Anna], b. Aug. 31, 1808	2	66
ISBEL, Robert, E., of Naugatuck, m. Laura A. **CANDEE**, of Oxford, Sept. 13, 1848, by Rev. Stephen Topliff	1	101
IVES, James of Hamden, m. Lucy Ann **CANDEE**, d. Isaiah, of Oxford, Nov. 28, 1838, by Rev. J. Atwater	1	65
JACKSON, Moses, d. Oct. 5, 1837, ae. 34	2	21
JOHNSON, Abigail, d. [1805], ae. 90	2	104
Abner, his d. [ ], [d. 1817], ae. 20	2	109
Alex[ande]r, [d. 1817], ae. 86	2	109
Alvin, [s. Timothy & Olive], b. Sept. 20, 1799	2	69
Amy, [d. Shubel & Chloe], (colored), b. July 22, 1789	2	69

	Vol.	Page
JOHNSON, (cont.)		
Ann S., m. Thomas **JOHNSON**, b. of Oxford, Aug. 21, 1848, by Rve. Stephen Topliff	1	109
Anna, [d. Timothy & Olive], b. May 4, 1797	2	69
Anna, m. Thomas **BUXTON**, b. of Oxford, Dec. 26, 1838, by Chauncey M. Hatch, J.P.	1	66
Arden, m. wid. Irene **OSBORN**, Mar. 6, 1827, by Rev. Chauncey Prindle	1	26
Asa, m. Polly **TWITCHELL**, b. of Oxford, Oct. 14, 1826, by Bennett Lum, J.P., at the house of Ebenezer Twitchell. Int. Pub.	1	24
Benj[amin], of Wallingford, m. Eliza **SHERMAN**, of Oxford, Feb. 23, 1834, by Rev. Abraham Brown	1	52
Betsey, [d. Ezra & Betsey], b. [ ], 1795	2	69
Betsey, [d. Shubel & Chloe], (colored), b. June 5, 1803	2	69
Betsey, m. Russell **HAWKINS**, Apr. 22, 1822, by Ephraim G. Swift	1	7
Betsey, wid., d. Nov. 11, 1841, ae. 72	2	21
Betsey Ann, m. Edwin **SMITH**, Dec. 25, 1839, by Rev. Daniel Burhans	1	69
Bowen, had s., d. Jan. [ ], 1800, ae. under 1	2	102
Bowen, his w. [ ], d. [1810], ae. 36	2	106
Charles, [s. Shubel & Chloe], (colored), b. Oct. 26, 1796	2	69
Charles, [s. Asa & Polly], b. Aug. 15, 1827	2	69
Clarissa, m. Bennett **ALLING**, b. of Oxford, [Nov.] 29, [1843], by Rev. Stephen Topliff	1	84
Clark, m. Mariah **TREAT**, b. of Oxford, Aug. 13, 1820, by Adonijah French, J.P.	1	1
Curtiss, [s. Ezra & Betsey], b. Feb. 27, 1794	2	69
David, d. [1810], ae. 33	2	106
Ebenezer, d. [ ]	2	21
Ebenezer, Jr., d. [ ], 1792, ae. 30	2	102
Ebenezer, d. [ ], 1795, ae. 68	2	102
Elias, of Newtown, m. Hopsey **JUDSON**, of Oxford, Nov. 1, 1820, by Nathan Tuttle	1	2
Eunice, [d. Shubel & Chloe], (colored), b. Oct. 26, 1800	2	69
Hannah, [d. 1815], ae. 45	2	109
Harvey & w. Anne, had ch., b. Aug. 10, 1819; Jan. 25, 1821; Sept. 27, 1822; [ ], 1824	2	69
Henrietta, [d. Shubel & Chloe], (colored), b. June 10, 1794; d. Oct. 15, 1795	2	69
Hiram, m. Polly **TREAT**, b. of Oxford, Apr. 29, 1824, by Adonijah French, J.P.	1	14
Ichabod, of Newtown, m. Mrs. Mary **HOLBROOK**, of Oxford, Oct. 26, 1828, by Sayrs Gazley	1	30

	Vol.	Page
JOHNSON, (cont.)		
Isaac, [s. Shubel & Chloe], (colored), b. Dec. 26, 1787; d. Dec. 30, 1787	2	69
Jeremiah, d. Sept. 8, [ ], ae. 56	2	102
Jerusha, [d. Timothy & Olive], b. Sept. 27, 1792	2	69
Julia, [d. Shubel & Chloe], (colored], b. Aug. 12, 1791	2	69
Lois, [d. 1832], ae. 75	2	111
Mariett, of Oxford, m. Zebulon **LINES**, of Bethany, Dec. 17, 1839, by Calvin Leavenworth, J.P.	1	69
Martha, d. Harvey & Anne, b. Nov. 6, 1826	2	69
Martha, m. James L. **WOOSTER**, [Sept.] 24, [1843], by Rev. Stephen Topliff	1	82
Mary, Mrs., m. Enoch **SOMERS**, b. of Orange, Nov. 19, 1848, by Rev. Stephen Topliff	1	111
Mille, [d. Shubel & Chloe], (colored), b. Nov. 26, 1785	2	69
Nancy, [d. Shubel & Chloe], (colored], b. May 6, 1784	2	69
Nancy, [d. Asa & Polly], b. Jan. 23, 1829	2	69
Phineas, Jr., & w. Lois, had ch., b. July 31, 1797	2	69
Phineas, Jr., & w. Lois, had ch., b. Oct. 15, 1799	2	69
Phineas, d. [Sept. [ ], 1819], ae. 90	2	110
Polly, Mrs., m. Benjamin V. **LINES**, Sept. 4, 1842, by Rev. John D. Smith, of Humphreyville	1	80
Ralph, [s. Ezra & Betsey], b. Aug. 2, 1797	2	69
Ruth, m. George **HITCHCOCK**, b. of Oxford, Sept. 15, 1831, by Noah Stone, J.P.	1	39
Sally E., of Oxford, m. George **BRADLEY**, of Bethany, Aug. 10, 1842, by Rev. Sylvester Smith	1	80
Susanna, d. Phineas & Sarah, b. June 25, 1794	2	69
Thomas, m. Ann S. **JOHNSON**, b. of Oxford, Aug. 21, 1848, by Rev. Stephen Topliff	1	109
Timothy, d. [ ], 1796, ae. 55	2	103
JOLES, Irena, m. Anson **OSBORN**, Dec. 5, 1820, by Rev. Chauncey Prindle	1	3
JONES, Joseph, d. [1806], ae. 84, (pauper)	2	104
Sylvester, m. Ann **BERT**, Oct. 12, 1845, by Rev. Geo[rge] L. Fuller	1	91
Wealthy, d. [1825], ae. 22	2	111
-----, wid., d. [1812], ae. 76	2	106
JORDAN, Curtiss, his w. [, d. 1818], ae. 28	2	110
JOY, Edward, Jr., s. Jesse & Sally, d. Aug. 22, 1826, ae. 2 y.	2	21
Eliza C., m. Orin **SHERWOOD**, b. of Oxford, May 29, 1836, by Rev. Abraham Browne	1	61
Mary P., of Oxford, m. Alanson **CASWELL**, of Bridgeport, June 6, 1839, by Rev. Joseph Scott, of Derby	1	68
JUDD, Asahel S., of Woodbridge, m. Mary **SMITH**, of Oxford,		

	Vol.	Page

JUDD, (cont.)

Sept. 17, 1829, by Rev. W[illia]m A. Curtiss	1	32
Ruth, m. Andrew **SMITH**, July 6, 1790	2	39
Spencer, of Waterbury, m. Caroline **BRISTOL**, of Oxford, Nov. 1, 1835, by Rev. Charles Smith	1	57

JUDSON, Eliza A., m. George A. **TOMLINSON**, b. of Oxford,

Feb. 14, 1830, by Rev. W[illia]m A. Curtiss	1	34
Hopsey, of Oxford, m. Elias **JOHNSON**, of Newtown, Nov. 1, 1820, by Nathan Tuttle	1	2

KANE, Polly, of Oxford, m. H[   ] **TWITCHEL**, of Naugatuck, Nov. 14, 1847, by Rev. David P. Sanford — 1 — 99

KEHOE, Cornelius, m. Electa M. **BUCKINGHAM**, Oct. 29, 1831, by Rev. Chaunc[e]y Prindle — 1 — 39

KELLEY, Matthew, had s. [   ], b. Mar. 3, 1799 — 2 — 71

KENNEY, Sally, m. Alva **DAVIS**, b. of Derby, Sept. 10, 1833, by John C. Coe. J.P. — 1 — 44

KIMBERLEY, KIMBERLY, DeWitt, m. Eliza **LINES**, b. of

Bethany, Nov. 24, 1839, by Rev. John D. Smith, at the house of Sheldon Church	1	71
Eunice, w. Julius, d. Dec. 19, 1826, ae. 36 y.	2	23
Julius, m. Eunice **WEEDEN**, b. of Oxford, Apr. 30, 1821, by Ephraim G. Swift	1	4
Julius, m. Lucy **WOOSTER**, b. of Oxford, June 10, 1827, by Nathan D. Benedict	1	27
Lorenda, d. [1813], ae. 25	2	107
Lucy, Mrs., m. Olson **HENDRYS**, b. of Oxford, Apr. 9, 1846, by Rev. G. B. Eastman	1	94

KINGSLEY, Eurania, of Oxford, m. Harvey **CARPENTER**, of Derby, Dec. 20, 1829, by Rev. W[illia]m A. Curtiss — 1 — 34

KNOW----, Woster, w. of Thomas, 2d white person b. in Oxford — 2 — 133

KUTLER, [see under **CUTLER**]

LAKE, [see also **LEEK**], Anna Augusta, [d. Walker & Anna],

b. Jan. 1, 1814	2	73
Eliza, [d. Walker & Anna], b. May 21, 1803	2	73
Elnathan, d. [1814], ae. 75	2	107
Elnathan, his wid., d. [1815], ae. 74	2	109
Isaac, [s. Walker & Anna], b. Aug. 7, 1801	2	73
Lucius, [s. Walker & Anna], b. June 8, 1807	2	73
Mary, [d. Walker & Anna], b. May 22, 1805	2	73
Sally, [d. Walker & Anna], b. Apr. 11, 1809	2	73
Sally, m. Arad **SHULES**, [ ]	2	39
Victory, of Huntington, m. Caroline Augusta **BRADLEY**, of Oxford, Sept. 14, 1823, by Rev. Mezies Raynor, of Huntington	1	12

LAMB, Jane, of Oxford, m. Henry C. **ATWOOD**, of Woodbury, Oct. 6, 1822, by Ephraim G. Swift — 1 — 8

LARABEE, Willis E., of Cheshire, m. Eunice **SMITH**, of Oxford,

	Vol.	Page
LARABEE, (cont.)		
[Feb.] 8, [1845], by Rev. Stephen Topliff	1	89
LARKIN, Peter, [d. 1821], ae. 64	2	110
LEAVENWORTH, Betsey, [d. Dorman & Lucy], b. Oct. 19, 1796	2	73
Calvin, m. Ester **BEECHER**, Oct. 4, 1840, by John D. Smith	1	74
Edmund, m. Mrs. Amy **TOMLINSON**, of Oxford, Oct. 26, [1823], by Rev. Menzies Raynor, of Huntington	1	12
Mark, [s. Dorman & Lucy], b. Sept. 28, 1798	2	73
Oscar, of Woodbury, m. Sarah M. **OSBORN**, of Oxford, Sept. 4, 1842, by Rev. Abel Nichols	1	85
Sophia, w. Calvin, d. Sept. 20, 1839	2	24
LEEK*, [see also **LAKE**], Alonzo, m. Lucinda **CABLE**, July [ ], 1843, by Rev. Abel Nichols *(Perhaps "**LAKE**")	1	87
LEWIS, Agur, m. Eliza **BEEBE**, Nov. 5, 1838, by Samuel Meigs, J.P.	1	95
Betsey, m. Philo **SMITH**, b. of Oxford, Mar. 26, 1826, by Rev. David Bennett	1	22
Eleazer, [d. 1815], ae. 84	2	109
Glover, of South East, N.Y., m. Althea **BASSETT**, of Southbury, [Feb.] 10, [1828], by Noah Smith	1	29
Hepzibah, [d. Silas & Mary], b. Nov. 22, 1791	2	73
John Nichols, of Waterbury, m. Jane **TOMLINSON**, of Derby, Sept. 23, 1838, by Rev. John D. Smith, Humphreyville, at the house of Samuel Lake	1	64
Nancy, [d. Silas & Mary], b. Sept. 1, 1793	2	73
Samuel, m. Polly **WHEELER**, Sept. 8, 1841, by Samuel Meigs, J.P.	1	95
Sarah, w. W[illia]m, Jr., d. [1808], ae. 45	2	105
W[illia]m, d. [1807], ae. 86	2	105
LIMBURNER, Harriet, [d. John & Fanny], b. Oct. 29, 1818	2	72
James Wallace, [s. John & Fanny], b. Feb. 9, 1814	2	72
Jane, [d. John & Fanny], b. May 12, 1808	2	72
Janette, [d. John & Fanny], b. July 5, 1802	2	72
Janette, 2nd, [d. John & Fanny], b. Sept. 17, 1816	2	72
Jennet, of Oxford, m. Henry **WOODING**, of Bethany, [Oct.] 22, [1843], by Rev. Stephen Topliff	1	83
John, d. [1808], ae. 80	2	105
John, [s. John & Fanny], b. Mar. 20, 1810	2	72
John, Jr., m. Lucy **OVIATT**, b. of Milford, Aug. 14, 1832, by Noah Stone, J.P.	1	41
Lydia, [d. John & Fanny], b. Feb. 18, 1812	2	72
Mary, [d. John & Fanny], b. May 8, 1806	2	72
Mary, d. of John, m. John **WOOSTER**, b. of Oxford, Jan. 7, 1828, by Sayres Gazley	1	29
Robert Bruce, [s. John & Fanny], b. Mar. 21, 1821	2	72
LINES. Alvan Austin, of Oxford, m. Lois Elizabeth **DOWNEY**, of Waterbury, May 9, [probably 1824], by Adonijah		

	Vol.	Page
LINES, (cont.)		
French, J.P.	1	15
Benjamin V., m. Mrs. Polly **JOHNSON**, Sept. 4, 1842, by Rev. John D. Smith, of Humphreyville	1	80
Eliza, m. DeWitt **KIMBERLEY**, b. of Bethany, Nov. 24, 1839, by Rev. John D. Smith, at the house of Sheldon Church	1	71
Erastus, his w. [, d. Nov. [ ], 1815], ae. 67	2	109
Erastus, [d. Nov. 15, 1815], ae. 64.	2	109
Joseph, d. [1804], ae. 45	2	104
Sherman, s. Zebulon & Lois, b. Nov. 12, 1798	2	73
Sherman, m. Harriet **FRENCH**, b. of Oxford, Dec. 19, 1824, by Adonijah French, J.P.	1	18
Thirza, d. Zebul & Lois, b. Oct. 3, 1800	2	73
Thirza, of Oxford, m. Elijah Johnson **WILLIAMS**, of Cheshire, Mar. 3, 1824, by Rev. Laban Clark	1	13
Zebulon, of Bethany, m. Mariett **JOHNSON**, of Oxford, Dec. 17, 1839, by Calvin Leavenworth, J.P.	1	69
LITTLE, Anson, [s. W[illia]m & Martha], b. Sept. 18, 1794	2	73
Lewis, [s. W[illia]m & Martha], b. June 27, 1792	2	73
LOCKWOOD, Sally, m. Silas **HAWKINS**, Feb. 21, 1825, by Sam[ue]l Meigs, J.P.	1	21
LORD, Mariah, m. William **MANVILLE**, Aug. 1, 1831, by Rev. Chauncey Prindle	1	38
LOUNSBURY, Fanny, m. Byram **TUCKER**, Mar. 14, 1841, by John D. Smith	1	76
Joseph, of Danbury, m. Lois **CANDEE**, of Oxford, Mar. 27, 1827, by Rev. Mark Mead	1	26
LOVELAND, Abijah, [s. Benj[amin] & Hannah], b. Nov. 11, 1797	2	74
Alfred, [s. Benj[ami]n & Hannah], b. [ ]	2	74
Asa, [s. Benj[amin] & Hannah], b. Dec. 23, 1799	2	74
Betsey A., w. Miles, d. July 13, 1827, ae. 49 y.	2	24
Clark, his w. [ ], d. [1810], ae. 38	2	106
Jos[eph], Capt. [d. 1816], ae. 79	2	109
Miles, m. Marilda **SCOTT**, Dec. [ ], 1831, by Rev. A. Browne	1	40
Miles, m. Marilda **SCOTT**, b. of Oxford, [1831], by Rev. Abraham Brown. Recorded Nov. 22, 1834	1	46
LUKE, Samuel, m. Grace **TOMLINSON**, b. of Derby, Oct. 3, 1829, by W[illia]m A. Curtiss	1	33
LUM, Bennett, of Derby, m. Caroline **HARGAR**, of Oxford, May 19, 1823, by Rev. Abner Smith, of Derby	1	10
Bennett, m. Irene **CLARK**, Oct. 4, 1840, by John D. Smith	1	73
Billy, [d. 1820], ae. 42	2	110
David R., m. Mary B. **HUDSON**, b. of Oxford, Dec. 25, 1836, by Rev. Daniel Burhans	1	61
Elizabeth, of Derby, wid. Lieut. [ ], d. [1810], ae. 97	2	106

	Vol.	Page
LUM, (cont.)		
Enos, [s. Billy & Diadomia], b. Nov. 21, 1801	2	73
Enos, m. Lois **OSBORN**, Dec. 29, 1824, by Rev. Chauncey Prindle	1	19
George, [s. Billy & Diadomia], b. Jan. 20, 1809	2	73
George, of Oxford, m. Nancy **GUNN**, of Waterbury, Oct. 29, 1837, by Chauncey M. Hatch, J.P.	1	63
Henry, of Derby, m. Mrs. Ann **BUXTON**, of Oxford, [Nov.] 25, [1843], by Rev. Stephen Topliff	1	83
Jane, [d. Billy & Diadomia], b. Jan. 29, 1804	2	73
John, Capt. of 1st Co., in Oxford	2	132
Jonathan, Lieut. of Derby, d. [, 1802], ae. 90	2	103
Lydia, d. Jonathan, m. Amos **BATES**, s. Elihu, Jan. 29, 1802	2	3
Lydia, w. Jonathan, d. [1808], ae. 50	2	105
Polly Maria, d. David & Polly, b. [ ], 1802	2	73
Sally, d. Billy & Diadim, b. Oct. 16, 1799	2	73
William, m. Mary E. **GUNN**, b. of Oxford, June 16, 1847, by Rev. David T. Sanford	1	98
LYON, Anna, m. Stephen **DOLBY**, Nov. 17, 1821, by Beardsley Northrop	1	5
-----, d. [1823], ae. 45	2	111
McEWEN, Dwight F., [s. David & Francis], b. May 12, 1838	2	77
Emily C., [d. David & Francis], b. Aug. 19, 1843	2	77
Hannah, m. Joel **BUCKINGHAM**, b. of Oxford, June 5, 1837, by Rev. Abraham Browne	1	66
James, [s. David & Sally], b. July 6, 1798	2	77
Jane E., [d. David & Francis], b. May 13, 1833	2	77
Louisa M., [d. David & Francis], b. Aug. 13, 1830	2	77
Mary, of Oxford, m. Joseph **WHEELER**, of Southbury, Oct. 11, 1820, by Eph[rai][m G. Swift. Int. Pub.	1	1
Minerva, d. David & Sally, b. May 19, 1802	2	77
Minerva, of Oxford, m. Reuben **CURTISS**, of Southbury, Oct. 11, 1820, by Ephraim G. Swift. Int. Pub.	1	2
Polly, d. [David & Sally], b. Oct. 31, 1799	2	77
Virgil H., [s. David & Francis], b. Apr. 26, 1835	2	77
Wilbur, [s. David & Francis], b. Aug. 1, 1848	2	77
Wooster B., [s. David & Francis], b. Mar. 26, 1841	2	77
McGUIRE, Ellen, [d. 1831], ae. 3	2	111
McNEIL, -----, wid. [d. Mar. [ ], 1821], ae. 78	2	110
MALLORY, Ruth, w. David, d. [1810], ae. 62	2	106
MANDEVILLE, Lois, m. Jehiel **PEET**, Jan. 12, 1791	2	32
MANSFIELD, D----, d. [1820], ae. 97	2	131
Sally, of Oxford, m. Hezekiah J.* **UPSON**, of Southington, Nov. 15, 1825, by Rev. Newton Tuttle (*correction J. has been crossed out and Todd has been handwritten in at the end of this entry)	1	25

	Vol.	Page
MANTER, Lucy, of Oxford, m. Nelson **BASSETT**, of Derby, Jan. 13, 1841, by Elias Scott, J.P.	1	75
MANTON, Grapter, of Martha's Vineyard, Mass., m. Lucy **ANDREWS**, of Oxford, Feb. 15, 1825, by Abel Wheeler, J.P.	1	20
MANVILLE, William, m. Mariah **LORD**, Aug. 1, 1831, by Rev. Chauncey Prindle	1	38
MARVIN, Rosalind, m. Noah **STONE**, Oct. 1, 1810	2	39
MASON, Caroline H., of Lowell, Mass., m. Ja[me]s S. **BIDWELL**, of Oxford, May 1, 1842, by Rev. Tho[ma]s Sparks	1	78
MEIGS, Benj[ami]n Clark, [s. Samuel & Lorena], b. Aug. 14, 1820	2	77
Benj[ami]n Clark, s. Samuel & Laura, d. Apr. 21, 1821, ae. 8 m.	2	27
David Tomlinson, [s. Samuel & Lorena], b. Feb. 21, 1822	2	77
Jane Caroline, [d. Samuel & Lorena], b. Apr. 14, 1818	2	77
Samuel, m. wid. Hannah **HYDE**, b. of Oxford, Nov. 12, 1828, by Rev. W[illia]m A. Curtiss	1	31
Sarah E., of Oxford, m. Charles L. **DICK**, of Newtown, Oct. 11, 1847, by Rev. David P. Sanford	1	99
Sarah Elizabeth, [d. Samuel & Lorena], b. May 16, 1816	2	77
MERRIAM, Erastus, m. Sarah Maria **WATTLES**, Sept. 26, 1830, by Rev. A. Brown	1	35
MINOT, Betsey, d. Lewis & Anna, b. Nov. 27, 1797	2	77
Eliz[abeth], wid. [d. 1816], ae. 57	2	109
Lewis, d. [1814], ae. 70	2	107
MITCHELL, MITCHEL, Whiting, his w. [d. Jan. [ ], 1821], ae. 50	2	110
Whiting, m. Sarah **BALDWIN**, b. of Oxford, Nov. 15, 1821, by Rev. Abner Smith, of Derby	1	6
MONSON, Laura, m. Clarke **PHELPS**, b. of Oxford, Nov. 17, 1833, by Rev. Eli Bennett	2	32
MORGAN, Charles, m. Betsey **COUCH**, Sept. 2, 1828, by Rev. W[illia]m A., Curtiss, in St. Peters Church	1	30
MOORE, Polly, [m.] Josiah **TUCKER**, [ ]	2	42
MORRIS, Adaline, [d. W[illia]m & Betsey], b. Oct. 9, 1806	2	77
Betsey, w. W[illia]m, d. [1808], ae. 38	2	105
Elliot, [s. W[illia]m & Betsey], b. Apr. 9, 1803	2	77
Jason, [s. W[illia]m & Betsey], b. May 3, 1805	2	77
Jason, m. Cynthia **BUCKINGHAM**, b. of Oxford, Apr. 18, 1838, by Rev. Abraham Browne	1	67
Levi, m. Juliette **SMITH**, Mar. 24, 1841, by Samuel Meigs, J.P.	1	95
Lucretia A., of Oxford, m. Edward J. **SUTTON**, of St. George, Vt., May 24, 1840, by Rev. Stephen Topliff	1	73
Mary Adaline, of Oxford, m. Joseph **DOWN**, of Woodbridge, Sept. 13, 1823, by Abel Wheeler, J.P.	1	11
Maryatt, m. Jeremiah **THOMAS**, Feb. 15, 1822, by		

	Vol.	Page
MORRIS, (cont.)		
Beardsley Northrop	1	6
Sheldon, [s. W[illia]m & Betsey], b. Apr. 8, 1801	2	77
Vira, d. [1814], ae. 17	2	107
William, s. W[illia]m & Betsey, b. May 6, 1799	2	77
MUNN, MUN, Diodate, m. Selena **BATEMAN**, Nov. 22, 1807	2	27
Marcus S., of Southbury, m. Louisa R. **BEARDSLEY**, of Oxford, [Oct.] 11, [1846], by Rev. Stephen Topliff	1	96
Rhoda, [d. Deodate & Selina], b. June 14, 1809	2	77
Seduski, [ch. of Deodate & Selina], b. Mar. 24, 1811	2	77
MUNSON, Betsey, [d. Charles & Serane], b. Feb. 15, 1810	2	77
Eliza, [d. Charles & Serane], b. Apr. 10, 1806	2	77
Isaac, [s. Charles & Serane], b. Apr. 23, 1808	2	77
Janette, d. Charles & Serane, b. May 5, 1800	2	77
Laura, m. Clarke **PHELPS**, b. of Oxford, Nov. 17, 1833, by Rev. Eli Bennett	1	45
Lydia Ann, of Oxford, m. Carlos **HARD**, of Huntington, Mar. 2, 1831, by Adonijah French, J.P.	1	36
Vanderbilt, [s. Charles & Serane], b. Feb. 17, 1804	2	77
VanTuyl Barbara, s. [Charles & Serane], b. Apr. 19, 1802	2	77
NETTLETON, Ashley, m. Maria **STODDARD**, Sept. 13, 1841, by Rev. P.L. Hoyt	1	77
Orvilla, of Oxford, m. William H. **FARNHAM**, of Hampton, Sept. 18, 1842, by Rev. John E. Bray	1	80
NEWTON, Jere, m. Esther **RIGGS**, Jan. 21, 1823, by Jason Allen	1	8
Lester Miles, of Waterbury, m. Caroline Augusta **RIGGS**, of Oxford, Dec. 15, 1830, by Rev. Jason Atwater	1	35
Susan C., m. Elias **CLARKE**, Oct. 24, 1805	2	6
NICHOLS, Abigail, wid., d. Mar. [, 1825], ae. 78	2	111
Benj[ami]n, [s. Russell & Abigail], b. Apr. 10, 1817	2	81
Charles B., of Bridgeport, m. Elizabeth S. **CHATFIELD**, of Oxford, Apr. 19, 1843, by Rev. Abel Nichols	1	87
Isaac, d. [1806], ae. 56	2	104
Isaac, [s. Russell & Abigail], b. Oct. 26, 1809	2	81
Isaac, d. Dec. 23, 1826, ae. 56 y.	2	29
Lucy, [d. Russell & Abigail], b. May 23, 1802	2	81
Lucy, of Oxford, m. Daniel Lum **HOLBROOK**, of Derby, Jan. 28, 1821, by Rev. Abner Smith, of Derby	1	3
Lyman, [d. 1821], ae. 49	2	110
Maria, m. Nelson **SMITH**, Sept. 2, 1824, by Rev. Chauncey Prindle	1	16
Polly, d. Lewis & Betsey, b. July 3, 1796	2	81
Riggs, [s. Russell & Abigail], b. Nov. 30, 1799	2	81
Riggs, of Oxford, m. Sally **OATMAN**, of Oxford, Sept. 9, 1826, by Levi Candee, J.P.	1	24
NOBLE, David, of Southbury, m. Lois E. **TOWNER**, of Oxford,		

	Vol.	Page
NOBLE, (cont.)		
Apr. 7, 1841, by W. H. Whittemore	1	75
NORTON, Eunice, m. Justus **CANDEE**, Dec. 21, 1778	2	6
NOYES, William, his w. [ ], d. [July [ ], 1819], ae. 45	2	110
OATMAN, Charles, [s. David & Sarah], b. Nov. 4, 1799	2	85
Charles, m. Sally **STODDARD**, b. of Oxford, Jan. 14, 1821, by Ephraim G. Swift	1	3
David, [s. David & Sarah], b. Jan. 19, 1797	2	85
George, s. Charles & Sally, b. May 2, 1822	2	85
Polly, [d. David & Sarah], b. Jan. 25, 1794	2	85
Sally, of Oxford, m. Riggs **NICHOLS**, of Oxford, Sept. 9, 1826, by Levi Candee, J.P.	1	24
O'CAIN, Hiram, m. Thirza **TREAT**, July 8, 1832, by Wait Bassett, J.P., at the house of William O.Cain	1	41
-----, wid., d. [1822], ae. 70	2	111
OSBORN, Abigail, formerly wid.[ ] Lyman, d. [ ], 1791, ae. 69	2	102
Amanda, [d. Ambrose & Rebecca], b. Oct. 13, 1826	2	85
Amanda, of Oxford, m. Charles S. **WELLON**, of Humphreyville, [Apr.] 8, [1846], by Rev. Stephen Topliff	1	92
Ambrose, m. Rebeckah **WOODEN**, b. of Oxford, Feb. 8, 1824, by Abel Wheeler, J.P.	1	13
Ambrose, m. Avis **CANDEE**, b. of Oxford, Dec. 19, 1832, by Rev. Abraham Brown	1	46
Ambrose, d. May 22, 1840, ae. 55 y.	2	31
Anson, m. Irena **JOLES**, Dec. 5, 1820, by Rev. Chauncey Prindle	1	3
Clarissa, (**TOWNER**), w. Rev. Joseph, d. Oct. 19, 1832, ae. 54 y.	2	42
Daniel, [s. Naboth & Susanna], b. Oct. [ ], 1801	2	85
Eletas, [ch. of Naboth & Susanna], b. Dec. [ ], 1813	2	85
Esther, [d. Ransom & Sarah], b. July 8, 1822	2	85
Eunice, d. Ambrose & Rebecca, b. Feb. 17, 1825	2	85
Gilbert, d. July [, 1825], ae. 43	2	111
Henry, s. Tho[ma]s L. & Eunice, d. Sept. 20, 1828, ae. 2 y.	2	31
Irene, wid., m. Arden **JOHNSON**, Mar. 6, 1827, by Rev. Chauncey Prindle	1	26
Jane C., m. Jeremiah **SACKETT**, Dec. 4, 1842, by Rev. Abel Nichols	1	86
Joel, m. Catharine S. **WASHBAND**, b. of Oxford, June 11, 1846, by Rev. G. B. Eastman	1	94
Joseph, d. [ ], 1794], ae. 46	2	102
Joseph, Capt. d. [ ], 1797, ae. 79	2	103
Joseph, Capt. of 1st Co., in Oxford	2	132
Joseph Miles, [s. Ransom & Sarah], b. Oct. 25, 1824	2	85
Laura, [d. 1817], ae. 27	2	109

OXFORD VITAL RECORDS 61

	Vol.	Page
OSBORN, (cont.)		
Leman Stone, [s. Naboth & Susanna], b. June 4, 1793	2	85
Lewis, [s. Naboth & Susanna], b. Jan. 2, 1791	2	85
Lois, m. Enos **LUM**, Dec. 29, 1824, by Rev. Chauncey Prindle	1	19
Lucius L., m. Almira **HOTCHKISS**, Jan. 13, 1833, by Rev. S. Jewitt of Humphreyville	1	43
Luthena, [ch. of Naboth & Susanna], b. Nov. [ ], 1795	2	85
Major E., of Waterbuiry, m. Mary **PRICHARD**, of Middlebury, [Aug.] 8, 1820, by Rev. Chaunc[e]y Prindle	1	1
Margaret 2nd w. Jared, d. [1811], ae. 55	2	106
Martha Candee, d. Ambrose & Avis, b. June 13, 1834	2	85
Martha Caroline, [d. Ransom & Sarah], b. May 31, 1829	2	85
Mary, m. Stiles **FAIRCHILD**, b. of Oxford, Nov. 17, 1831, by Rev. Ashbel Baldwin	1	39
Noah Ambrose, s. [Ambrose & Rebecca], b. May 25, 1829	2	85
Ransom, s. Joseph & Sarah, b. Apr. 5, 1790	2	85
Rosalind Mary, [d. Ransom & Sarah], b. May 17, 1827	2	85
Ruth Ann, [d. Ransom & Sarah], b. July [ ], 1818	2	85
Sally, [d. Naboth & Susanna], b. Apr. [ ], 1798	2	85
Sarah, [d. Ransom & Sarah], b. Sept. 2, 1816	2	85
Sarah E., m. Burritt **DAVIS**, b. of Oxford, Dec. 11, 1828, by Rev. W[illia]m A. Curtiss	1	31
Sarah M., of Oxford, m. Oscar **LEAVENWORTH**, of Woodbury, Sept. 4, 1842, by Rev. Abel Nichols	1	85
Sarah Rebecca, d. [Ambrose & Rebecca], b. July 23, 1830	2	85
Solomon, Capt. of 1st Co., in Oxford, 1821	2	132
Thomas, d. [1807], ae. 90	2	105
Tho[ma]s, his wid., d. [1814], ae. 64	2	108
Tho[ma]s C., m. Nancy R. **SMITH**, Dec. 20, 1828, by Rev. Chauncey Prindle	1	32
Thomas L., of Oxford, m. Eunice **RIGGS**, of Oxford, June 30, 1824, by Levi Candee, J.P.	1	15
W[illia]m, Capt. of 1st Co., in Oxford	2	132
OVIATT, Lucy, m. John **LIMBURNER**, Jr., b. of Milford, Aug. 14, 1832, by Noah Stone, J.P.	1	41
PANGMAN, Betsey Elizabeth, of Oxford, m. Lewis Burton **CANDEE**, of Woodbury, [Mar.] 30, [1835], by Rev. Charles Smith	1	55
Prue, w. James, d. [1807], ae. 76	2	105
-----, wid. [d. 1820], ae. 53	2	110
PARDEE, William L., of Madison, m. Sarah E. **SACKET**, of Oxford, Jan. 19, 1843, by Rev. Sylvester Smith	1	81
PARKS, Phebe, [d. 1822], ae. 71	2	111
[**PARSON**], [see under **PIRSON**]		
PARTREE, John, m. Ann **CLARK**, Apr. 16, 1845, by Henry Olmstead, Jr.	1	90

	Vol.	Page
PECK, Almira E., of Oxford, m. Henry W. **RICHARDS**, of Woodbury, Dec. 30, 1849, by Rev. Stephen Topliff	1	112
David, d. May 3, 1841, ae. 80 y.	2	32
Eliza T., m. Everton R. **CRAMER**, June 12, 1849, by Rev. Stephen Topliff	1	112
John Austin, of Southbury, m. Eunice **CANDEE**, of Oxford, Jan. 1, 1840, by Rev. John D. Smith, at the house of Enos Candee	1	72
----- & 3 children, d. [1805]	2	104
PEET, Betsey, [d. Jehiel & Lois], b. Oct. 13, 1794	2	86
Eunice, [d. Jehiel & Lois], b. Sept. 10, 1799	2	86
Jehiel, m. Lois **MANDEVILLE**, Jan. 12, 1791	2	32
Lois, [d. Jehiel & Lois], b. Jan. 1, 1804	2	86
Lois, m. Warner **TOWNER**, b. of Oxford, [Mar.] 18, [1845], by Rev. Stephen Topliff	1	89
Lydia, [d. Jehiel & Lois], b. Dec. 2, 1809	2	86
Mana, [d. 1820], ae. 22	2	110
Minerva, [d. Jehiel & Lois], b. Oct. 5, 1801	2	86
Minerva, of Oxford, m. Charles Y. **SEXTON**, of New York, Oct. 23, 1831, by Rev. A. Browne	1	40
Nancy, [d. Jehiel & Lois], b. Nov. 1, 1792	2	86
Sally, [d. Jehiel & Lois], b. July 30, 1807	2	86
PENDLETON, William, of Westville, m. Ruth Ann **CANDEE**, of Oxford, June 27, 1848, by Rev. David P. Sanford	1	101
PERCY, Clement, of Roxbury, m. Louisa **WOOSTER**, of Oxford, Mar. 20, 1833, by Rev. Nathan D. Benedict	1	43
PERKINS, Adoniram, [ch. of Roger & Betsey], b. Nov. 25, 1799	2	86
Agnes, [d. Roger & Betsey], b. [ ], 1795	2	86
Atta, d. Joseph & Sarah, b. Apr. 25, 1797	2	86
Candee, [s. Roger & Betsey], b. May 26, 1794	2	86
Charles, [s. Roger & Betsey], b. Sept. 26, 1796	2	86
David & W. Abigail, had ch., b. Dec. 3, 1796; Jan. 21, 1799; Nov. 1, 1800	2	86
David, [d. 1831], ae. 64	2	111
Fairy, [d. Roger & Betsey], b. July 28, 1792	2	86
Hannah, [d. David & Abigail], b. Mar. [ ], 1795	2	86
Lodema, of Watertown, m. Orrin **SKEELS**, of Oxford, Nov. 22, 1829, by Rev. W[illia]m A. Curtiss	1	33
Lucinda, m. Lewis **DAVIS**. b. of Oxford, Oct. 1, 1829, by Rev. W[illia]m A. Curtiss	1	33
Lucy, [d. Roswell & Eunice], b. Mar. 20, 1826	2	86
Lucy, [d. Roswell & Eunice], d. Mar. 2, 1822 or 1832, ae. 5 y.	2	32
Lucy, [d. 1832], ae. 5	2	111
Mark, s. Roswell & Eunice, b. Jan. 23, 1822	2	86
Mark, s. Roswell & Eunice, d. [ ], ae. 1 m.	2	32
Polly Ann, [d. David & Abigail], b. June 15, 1790	2	86
Ralph, [s. Roger & Betsey], b. June 12, 1798	2	86

OXFORD VITAL RECORDS

	Vol.	Page
PERKINS, (cont.)		
Rebeckah, [d. David & Abigail], b. Mar. 24, 1793	2	86
Roswell, his w. [ ], d. [1816], ae. 21	2	109
Sally, [d. Roswell & Eunice], b. [ ]	2	86
Sally C., m. Philo B. **BUCKINGHAM**, [Oct.] 12, [1842], by Rev. Stephen Topliff	1	81
Sally Caroline, d. Roswell & Eunice, b. Jan. 1, 1823	2	87
PERRY, Aurinda, had s. Manvil, b. Oct. 24, 1797	2	77
Benjamin, [s. Caleb], b. July 18, 1792	2	86
Bennett, s. [Joel & Bettey], b. Jan. 31, 1794	2	86
Betsey, [d. Joel & Bettey], b. June 28, 1792	2	86
Caleb, [s. Caleb], b. July 18, 1794	2	86
Caleb, d. [ ], 1796, ae. 42	2	103
Comfort, w. Gideon, d. Nov. 4, 1798, ae. 45	2	102
David, [s. Joel & Bettey], b. Mar. 10, 1800	2	86
David, of Oxford, m. Grace **ENGLISH**, of Derby, [, 1834?], by Rev. Abraham Brown. Recorded Nov. 22, 1834	1	52
Elizabeth Jane, d. James & Lois, b. Mar. 12, 1825	2	87
Emily Amelia, [d. George & Betsey Ann], b. Apr. 12, 1838	2	87
Eunice, [d. Joel & Bettey], b. Apr. 13, 1815	2	86
Ezekiel, d. [1811], ae. 76	2	106
George, [s. Joel & Bettey], b. Sept. 9, 1809	2	86
George, Capt. of 1st Co., in Oxford	2	132
George Albert, [s. George & Betsey Ann], b. Mar. 6, 1835	2	87
Gideon, d. [1814], ae. 82	2	107
Harriet, [d. Joel & Bettey], b. Sept. 10, 1803	2	86
Harriet, m. Marcus **SANFORD**, Dec. 11, 1825, by Rev. Edw[ar]d J. Ives	1	23
Israel M., of Woodbridge, m. Mary **WOOSTER**, of Oxford, Apr. 5, 1840, by Rev. James Mallory, of Newtown	1	72
James, his w., d. [1815], ae. 77	2	108
James, [d. 1820], ae. 95	2	110
James, his w. [, d. Sept. [ ], 1821], ae. 35	2	110
James, m. Lois **CHATFIELD**, b. of Oxford, Nov. 1, 1823, by Levi Candee, J.P.	1	12
Jane, d. Cyrus, b. Oct. 29, 1822	2	87
John D., of Oxford, m. Emily E. **THOMPSON**, of Branford, Jan. 26, 1846, by Rev. Stephen Topliff	1	91
John Dutton, s. James & Mary, b. Aug. 31, 1821	2	87
John Riggs, [s. Joel & Bettey], b. Jan. 20, 1791	2	86
Joseph, Dr. of Woodbury, b. 1727; d. 1793; 3rd white person b. in Oxford	2	133
Joshua, d. [1823], ae. 87	2	111
Joshua, his w. [ ], d. Apr. [, 1823], ae. 85	2	111

	Vol.	Page
PERRY, (cont.)		
Josiah, d. [ ], 1790, ae. 90 1/2	2	102
Lucy, m. Samuel **CANDEE**, Jr., of Southbury, [1834(?)], by Rev. Abraham Brown. Recorded Nov. 22, 1834	1	48
Lucy, [d. Joel & Bettey], b. Jan. 10, 1796	2	86
Manvil, s. Aurinda, b. Oct. 24, 1797	2	77
Nathan, [s. Joel & Betsey], b. Apr. 17, 1806	2	86
Salena, [d. George & Betsey Ann], b. July 7, 1832	2	87
Thirza, [d. Joel & Bettey], b. Feb. 15, 1798	2	86
Thirza, m. Lewis **CHATFIELD**, b. of Oxford, Feb. 8, 1823, by Beardsley Northrop	1	9
Yelverton, [d. 1821], ae. 83	2	110
Yelveston, his w. [ ], d. [1823], ae. 7[ ]	2	111
-----, wid., d. [1823], ae. 35	2	111
PHELPS, Clarke, m. Laura **MONSON**, b. of Oxford, Nov. 17, 1833, by Rev. Eli Bennett	2	32
Clarke, m. Laura **MUNSON**, b. of Oxford, Nov. 17, 1833, by Rev. Eli Bennett	1	45
PIERCE, Elam, of Southbury, m. Augusta **HURLBUTT**, of Oxford, Sept. 3, 1834, by Rev. Abraham Brown	1	53
Noble, m. Mrs. Polly **PIERCE**. Jan. 17, 1825, by Sam[ue]l Meigs, J.P.	1	19
Polly, Mrs., m. Noble **PIERCE**, Jan. 17, 1825, by Sam[ue]l Meigs, J.P.	1	19
PIERSON, [see also **PIRSON**], David, Capt. of 1st Co. in Oxford	2	132
Eli, [s. Lewis & Esther], b. Mar. 17, 1799	2	86
Elijah, [s. Lewis & Esther], b. Nov. 23, 1797	2	86
PIRSON, [see also Pierson], Amy C., of Oxford, m. Benet **HINE**, of Woodbridge, June 8, 1829, by Rev. Samuel Potter, of Woodbridge & Salem	1	32
PLUMB, Charity, m. Nath[anie]l **WOOSTER**, Feb. 5, 1789	2	45
POOL, Betsey Mariah, of Oxford, m. William Henry **TOMLINSON**, of Derby, Nov. 23, 1824, by Stephen Jewitt	1	18
POPE, Andrew, of Monroe, m. Sally **SMITH**, of Oxford, Oct. 11, 1824, by Ashbel Baldwin, minister	1	17
PORTER, James, of Cheshire, m. Eunice **HYDE**, of Oxford, Aug. 29, 1822, by Rev. John Keys, of Waterbury	1	7
POWE, Lucius, of Derby, m. Harriet **BLACKMAN**, of Oxford, Sept. 16, 1844, by Rev. Abel Nichols	1	87
PRICHARD, Mary, of Middlebury, m. Major E. **OSBORN**, of Waterbury, [Aug.] 8, 1820, by Rev. Chaunc[e]y Prindle	1	1
PRINDLE, Eb[ezeze]r, d. [1814], ae. 81	2	107
Maria, d. Jabez & Susanna, b. June 9, 1801	2	87
-----, Mr., d. [1812], ae. 70	2	106
RANSOM, Elizabeth, m. Harvey W. **UPSON**, b. of Oxford, Oct.		

OXFORD VITAL RECORDS 65

	Vol.	Page
RANSOM, (cont.)		
23, 1836, by Rev. Abraham Browne	1	61
RICHARDS, Henry W., of Woodbury, m. Almira E. **PECK**, of Oxford, Dec. 30, 1849, by Rev. Stephen Topliff	1	112
RIGGS, Ann Maria, m. Sheldon **SANFORD**, Apr. 7, 1841, by John D. Smith	1	76
Anna, [d. John & Elizabeth], b. June 20, 1784	2	90
Anna, [twin with Elizabeth, d. Samuel & Chary], b. Aug. 2, 1801	2	90
Anna, w. Capt. E[ ], d. [1812], ae. 59	2	106
Anson, [s. Samuel & Chary], b. Apr. 19, 1807	2	90
Betsey, [d. John & Elizabeth], b. Aug. 15, 1768	2	90
Betsey, d. Sam[ue]l, d. [1818], ae. 17	2	110
Caroline Augusta, of Oxford, m. Lester Miles **NEWTON**, of Waterbury, Dec. 15, 1830, by Rev. Jason Atwater	1	35
Charles, of New Haven, m. Augusta **SMITH**, of Oxford, June 22, 1848, by Rev. David P. Sanford	1	101
Charles Pierpoint, s. [Leman & Sina], b. Nov. 30, 1827	2	90
Chary, [d. Samuel & Chary], b. Apr. 9, 1805	2	90
David, d. Mar. 26, 1822, ae. 56	2	36
David, [d. 1822], ae. 57	2	111
Eben[eze]r, Capt. of 1st Co., in Oxford, 1781	2	132
Eben[eze]r, Jr., d. [1808], ae. 24	2	105
Ebenezer, m. Julia M. **DAVIS**, Dec. 9, 1827, by Sayrs Gazley	1	28
Ebenezer, Capt. of 1st. Co., in Oxford, 1832	2	132
Ebenezer, of Oxford, m. Francis A. **CLARK**, of Middlebury, [Mar.] 5, [1846], by Rev. Stephen Topliff	1	92
Edward, d. July 27, 1821, ae. 59 1/2 y.	2	36
Edward, [d. July [ ], 1821], ae. 60	2	110
Elizabeth, w. of John, b. Jan. 10, 1746	2	90
Elizabeth, [twin with Anna, d. Samuel & Chary], b. Aug. 2, 1801	2	90
Esther, m. Jere **NEWTON**, Jan. 21, 1823, by Jason Allen	1	8
Eunice, b. July 25, 1771	2	99
Eunice, m. Abel **WHEELER**, Oct. 1, 1786	2	45
Eunice, [d. Samuel & Chary], b. June 27, 1797	2	90
Eunice, of Oxford, m. Thomas L. **OSBORN**, of Oxford, June 30, 1824, by Levi Candee, J.P.	1	15
Garry, of Oxford, m. Sally **CLARK**, of Southington, Sept. 19, 1824, by Abel Wheeler, J.P.	1	17
Gideon, [s. John & Elizabeth], b. Jan. 30, 1782	2	90
Gideon, Capt. of 1st Co., in Oxford	2	132
Jane, [d. Samuel & Chary], b. Nov. 14, 1809	2	90
John, b. Apr. 10, 1743	2	90
John, s. Joseph & Mabel, of Derby, m. Elizabeth **HAWKINS**, d. Capt. Zach[ariah], Dec. 22, 1767	2	36

	Vol.	Page
RIGGS, (cont.)		
John, [s. John & Elizabeth], b. Dec. 22, 1771	2	90
John, Capt. of 1st Co. in Oxford, 1779	2	132
John, d. [1814], ae. 71	2	107
John, d. June 18, [1814], ae. 71	2	108
John, his w. [ ], d. [1823], ae. 85	2	111
Joseph, [s. John & Elizabeth], b. Oct. 11, 1775	2	90
Julia, w. Ebenezer, d. Aug. 9, 1844, ae. 34	2	36
Leman, [s. Samuel & Chary], b. July 19, 1799	2	90
Leman, s. Sam[ue]l & Charity, b. July 19, 1799	2	90
Leman, m. Lucina **CANDEE**, b. of Oxford, Mar. 27, 1821, by Ephraim G. Swift	1	4
Leverett, [s. John & Elizabeth], b. July 16, 1788	2	90
Leverett, his w. [ ], d. [1816], ae. 25	2	109
Lucy, [d. John & Elizabeth], b. Jan. 17, 1787	2	90
Mary, [d. John & Elizabeth], b. Nov. 20, 1773	2	90
Mary Jane, d. Leman & Sina, b. Apr. 19, 1823	2	90
Mary Jane, m. Samuel C. **WILLIAMS**, b. of Oxford, [Jan.] 29, [1845], by Rev. Stephen Topliff	1	88
Milessa, m. Isaiah [ ], Oct. 25, 1807	2	6
Minerva, m. Woodruff **CANDEE**, Feb. 13, 1822, by Ephraim G. Swift	1	6
Moses, his w. [ ], d. [Mar. [ ], 1819], ae. 55	2	110
Nabby, [d. John & Elizabeth], b. Apr. 2, 1779	2	90
Nancy, Mrs. m. Noyes **BRADLEY**, b. of Oxford, Mar. 1, 1827, by Nathaniel G. Huntington	1	26
Oliver, s. David & Hannah, b. Sept. 14, 1797	2	90
Pat, his w. [ ], d. [1810], ae. 16	2	106
Pierpoint, [s. Samuel & Chary], b. May 18, 1803	2	90
Pierpoint, d. Oct. [, 1825], ae. 22	2	111
Polly, of Oxford, m. Thomas P. **HART**, of Watertown, July 13, 1834, by Rev. Abraham Brown	1	53
Sam[ue]l, [s. John & Elizabeth], b. Aug. 7, 1770	2	90
Sam[ue]l & w. Betsey, had s. [ ], b. Nov. 18, 1800	2	90
Samuel, [s. Samuel & Chary], b. Apr. 29, 1818	2	90
Sam[ue]l, his d. [ ], d. Nov. [, 1819], ae. 15	2	110
Samuel, his d. [d. 1820], ae. 11	2	110
Samuel, d. Nov. 18, 1835, ae. 65 y.	2	36
Sarah E., of Oxford, m. George W. **FULLER**, of New Haven, May 28, [1843], by Rev. Stephen Topliff	1	82
Zerviah, d. [1813], ae. 20	2	107
-----, wid. [d. 1815], ae. 69	2	109
RILEY, Thomas, m. Harriet **HAWKINS**, Feb. 21, 1825, by Rev. Chauncey Prindle	1	20
ROBINSON, Lester, of Middletown, m. Nancy **TWITCHELL**, Oxford, May 26, 1833, by Rev. Abraham Brown	1	50

	Vol.	Page
ROCKWELL, Benjamin Franklin, s. Jacob & Hannah R., b.		
Oct. 20, 1824	2	91
-----, [d. 1832], ae. 2	2	111
ROOT, Lemuel, m. Clarissa **SANFORD**, Dec. 28, 1825, by Rev.		
Chauncey Prindle	1	21
Olive, of Oxford, m. Eber **BENHAM**, of Southbury, Apr.		
5, 1827, by Tho[ma]s L. Shipman	1	28
ROWE, Frederic Wesley, s. [Frederic & Hepsibah], b. Jan.		
27, 1828	2	91
Georgeana, d. Frederic & Hepsibah, b. Sept. 10, 1822	2	91
Hepzibah Minerva, [d. Frederic & Hepsibah], b. May		
9, 1824	2	91
SACKETT, SACKET, Jeremiah, m. Jane C. **OSBORN**, Dec. 4,		
1842, by Rev. Abel Nichols	1	86
Sarah E., of Oxford, m. William L. **PARDEE**, of Madison,		
Jan. 19, 1843, by Rev. Sylvester Smith	1	81
William Washington, m. Sally **WOODING**, b. of Oxford,		
Feb. 15, 1823, by Adonijah French, J.P.	1	9
SANFORD, Alma, m. Clark **SELA**, b. of Oxford, Sept. 16, 1827,		
by Adonijah French, J.P.	1	27
Charlotte, of Oxford, m. George **COOKE**, of Woodbridge,		
Apr. 3, 1831, by Noah Stone, J.P.	1	36
Clarissa, m. Lemuel **ROOT**, Dec. 28, 1825, by Rev.		
Chauncey Prindle	1	21
David, of Derby, m. Mrs. Mary **CLARK**, Apr. 7, 1839, by		
Rev. John D. Smith, at the house of Ransom Hudson	1	71
Jane, d. Harris & Emeline, d. Mar. [ ], 1836, ae. [ ]	2	41
John, d. Nov. 16, 1826, ae. 51 y.	2	41
Laura, d. Moses, d. Apr. 16, 1822, ae. 22 y.	2	41
Marcus, m. Harriet **PERRY**, Dec. 11, 1825, by Rev.		
Edw[ar]d J. Ives	1	23
Maria, of Wolcott, m. David H. **BUCKINGHAM**, of Oxford,		
Dec. 17, 1828, by Sayrs Gazley, V.D.M.	1	31
Marvin R., m. Harriet **TREAT**, May 10, 1831, by Samuel		
Meigs, J.P.	1	37
Merit, m. Charey **STORES**, b. of Oxford, June 24, 1824,		
by Adonijah French, J.P.	1	15
Sam[ue]l, Dr. of Derby, d. [ ], 1803, ae. 36	2	103
Sheldon, m. Ann Maria **RIGGS**, Apr. 7, 1841, by John D.		
Smith	1	76
Zadoc, his wid. [ ], d. [1813], ae. 62	2	107
-----, wid. [d. 1814], ae. about 60	2	108
SCOTT, Ann Jennett, m. Leonard **SPERRY**, Apr. 8, 1826, by Rev.		
Chauncey Prindle	1	23
Asahel Lewis, [s. Elias & Eunice], b. May 25, 1811	2	94
David, [s. Jesse & Mary], b. July 15, 1801	2	93
David, his w. [, d. 1823], ae. 24	2	111
David, m. Eliza **BEARDSLEY**, b. of Oxford, Jan. 7, 1824,		

	Vol.	Page
SCOTT, (cont.)		
by Abel Wheeler, J.P.	1	12
Eunice Maria, [d. Elias & Eunice], b. Dec. 18, 1814	2	94
Gibson, d. [1805], ae. 30	2	104
Harvey, [s. Jesse & Mary], b. May 1, 1796	2	93
Julian, s. Ransom & Nabby, b. Apr. 23, 1827	2	94
Juliann, d. Oct. 6, 1828, ae. 1 y. 6 m.	2	39
Laura E., m. Nathaniel **WALKER**, b. of Oxford, Oct. 8, 1837, by Rev. Abraham Brown	1	67
Lucinda, w. Elias, d. [1804], ae. 17	2	104
Lucinda, [d. Elias & Eunice], b. Aug. 2, 1809	2	94
Lucinda, m. Thomas A. **DUTTON**, b. of Oxford, Nov. 25, 1827, by Sayrs Gazley	1	28
Lyman, d. [1831], ae. 54	2	111
Marilda, m. Miles **LOVELAND**, Dec. [ ], 1831, by Rev. A. Browne	1	40
Marilda, m. Miles **LOVELAND**, b. of Oxford, [, 1831 (?)], by Rev. Abraham Brown. Recorded Nov. 22, 1834	1	46
Merit Beecher, s. Lyman, b. Dec. 26, 1827	2	92
Ransom, d. Sept. 6, 1828, ae. 41 y.	2	39
Samuel T., m. Edna J. **TYLER**, b. of Oxford, [June] 16, [1847], by Rev. Stephen Topliff	1	98
Thomas, s. David C. & Eliza, d. Mar. 6, 1832, ae. 7 m.	2	39
Thomas, [d. 1832], ae. 7 m.	2	111
William, [s. Jesse & Mary], b. July 5, 1798	2	93
-----, w. Uri, d. Apr. 11, 1840, ae. 81	2	40
SCOVILL, Bennett, m. Lucinda **SPERRY**, [July] 3, 1842, by Rev. Stephen Topliff	1	79
David, [d. 1820], ae. 24	2	110
T----, his w. [ ], d. July [, 1819], ae. 52	2	110
SEELEY, SELEY, Augusta, m. Enos **TYLER**, b. of Oxford, June 6, 1848, by Rev. Stephen Topliff	1	101
J----, [d. 1831], ae. 2	2	111
Olive, of Oxford, m. Benjamin **TOMLINSON**, of Derby, Sept. 27, 1824, by Abel Wheeler, J.P.	1	16
Sarah, m. Nathan T. **BASSETT**, Nov. 3, 1842, by Rev. Abel Nichols	1	86
Susan, of Oxford, m. James **DRIVER**, of Derby, Aug. 19, 1832, by Wait Bassett, J.P., at the house of John Woodin	1	42
W[illia]m & w. Olive, had s. [ ], b. Mar. 28, 1800	2	93
W[illia]m, d. [1823], ae. 74	2	111
SELA, Asa, m. Julia Ritta **DORMAN**, Mar. 7, 1824, by Adonijah French, J.P.	1	14
Clark, m. Alma **SANFORD**, b. of Oxford, Sept. 16, 1827, by Adonijah French, J.P.	1	27

OXFORD VITAL RECORDS

	Vol.	Page
SEXTON, Charles Y., of New York, m. Minerva **PEET**, of Oxford, Oct. 23, 1831, by Rev. A. Browne	1	40
SHARP, Abia, [d. 1817], ae. 24	2	109
SHERMAN, Cynthia, d. [ ] & Lucy, now of Newtown, b. June 14, 1810	2	94
Eliza, of Oxford, m. Benj[amin] **JOHNSON**, of Wallingford, Feb. 23, 1834, by Rev. Abraham Brown	1	52
Flora, of Oxford, m. James **SHERWOOD**, of Redding, May 29, 1842, by Henry Hine, J.P.	1	79
Ira Elijah, [s. Ira & Hannah], b. June 12, 1826	2	93
Sarah, d. Ira & Hannah, b. Nov. 11, 1815	2	93
Sarah, m. Charles **BETTS**, Nov. 11, 1834, by Matthew Batchelor	1	47
SHERWOOD, James, of Redding, m. Flora **SHERMAN**, of Oxford, May 29, 1842, by Henry Hine, J.P.	1	79
Orin, m. Eliza C. **JOY**, b. of Oxford, May 29, 1836, by Rev. Abraham Browne	1	61
Orrin, d. Mar. 31, 1840, ae. 29	2	40
SHULES, [see under **SKEELS**]		
SKILTON, Avery J. Dr., of Troy, N.Y., m. Mary A. **CANDEE**, of Oxford, Mar. 2, 1828, by Rev. Daniel Wooster	1	29
SKEELS, SKULE, SHULES, Aaron, [s. Arad & Sally], b. [ ]	2	94
Arad, m. Sally **LAKE**, [ ]	2	39
Bennett, [s. Arad & Sally], b. [ ], 18[ ]	2	94
Burritt, m. Sally **BRADLEY**, b. of Oxford, May 4, 1828, by Nathan D. Benedict	1	29
Delia, m. George **TOMLINSON**, Oct. 18, 1835, by Rev. Charles Smith, in Christ Church	1	56
Jason, [s. Arad & Sally], b. Dec. 31, 1802	2	94
Orrin, of Oxford, m. Lodema **PERKINS**, of Watertown, Nov. 22, 1829, by Rev. W[illia]m A. Curtiss	1	33
Sally, w. Arad, d. [1810], ae. 33	2	106
Sally Minerva, [d. Arad & Sally], b. Feb. 2, 1812	2	94
Sarah M., of Oxford, m. Philo **HALL**, of New Haven, Sept. 11, 1836, by Rev. James Sunderland, in Christ Church	1	57
SKULE, [see under **SKEELS**]		
SMITH, [Abel], [& w. Damaries, had ch., b. Dec. 19, 1798]	2	93
Abraham E., m. Caroline **CANDEE**, b. of Oxford, Nov. 25, 1833, by Rev. Abraham Brown	1	51
Andrew, m. Ruth **JUDD**, July 6, 1790	2	39
Andrew, d. [1813], ae. 47	2	107
Andrew Harley, [s.] Andrew & Ruth, b. Nov. 23, 1800	2	93
Anna, m. James A. **BUCKINGHAM**, Jan. 29, 1832, by Rev. A. Browne	1	40
Anthony L., of Oxford, m. Obedience **WHITING**, of		

SMITH, (cont.)

	Vol.	Page
of Hamden, [May] 19, [1844], by Rev. Stephen Topliff	1	85
Augusta, of Oxford, m. Orange J. **HUBBELL**, of Washington, Sept. 13, 1835, by Rev. Abraham Browne	1	58
Augusta, of Oxford, m. Charles **RIGGS**, of New Haven, June 22, 1848, by Rev. David P. Sanford	1	101
Bennett, s. Ab[raha]m E. & Emma Marie, b. Aug. 4, 1820	2	94
Betsey, [d. David, 4th & Eliza], b. Nov. 20, 1797	2	93
Chester, his w. [ ], d. [1817], ae. 44	2	109
David & w. Eliza, had ch., b. Feb. 23, 1800	2	93
David, his w. [ ], d. [1813], ae. 46	2	107
Edwin, m. Betsey Ann **JOHNSON**, Dec. 25, 1839, by Rev. Daniel Burhans	1	69
Elijah, his wid., d. [1815], ae. 76	2	108
Elizabeth, m. Moses **HAWKINS**, b. of Oxford, Oct. 7, 1821, by Beardsley Northrop	1	5
Esther, of Southbury, m. Charles H. **TOMLINSON**, of Oxford, Nov. 15, 1835, by Rev. Abraham Browne	1	60
Eunice, of Oxford, m. Willis E. **LARABEE**, of Cheshire, [Feb.] 8, [1845], by Rev. Stephen Topliff	1	89
Eunice, d. [Willis & Olive], b. [ ]	2	92
Evalina, [d. Andrew & Ruth], b. Oct. 24, 1796	2	93
Evelina, m. George W. **GRAHAM**, June 12, 1823, by Cha[rle]s Bunnell, J.P.	1	10
Genette E., of Oxford, m. Samuel L. **TUTTLE**, of Southbury, Nov. 28, 1844, by Rev. O. B. Butterfield, of South Britain	1	88
George W., m. Harriet E. **HITCHCOCK**, Feb. 28, 1848, by Rev. Stephen Topliff	1	100
Hepzibah, [d. David & Polly], b. Oct. 26, 1797	2	93
Ira Barns, s. Willis & Olive, b. Jan. 3, 1829	2	92
Ira K., m. Jennet **WOODING**, May 23, 1827, by Rev. Chauncey Prindle	1	27
Ira K., m. Jenette **SMITH**, b. of Oxford, May 15, 1842, by Rev. Tho[ma]s Sparks	1	78
Isaac, [s. Andrew & Ruth], b. May 10, 1803	2	93
Jenette, m. Ira K. **SMITH**, b. of Oxford, May 15, 1842, by Rev. Tho[ma]s Sparks	1	78
Jesse, [d. 1831], ae. 74	2	111
John, [d. Jan. [ ], 1821], ae. 60	2	110
Jonas, [s. Abel & Damaries], b. [ ], 1795	2	93
Josiah, [s. Isaac & Sarah], b. Sept. 23, 1803	2	94
Juliette, m. Levi **MORRIS**, Mar. 24, 1841, by Samuel Meigs, J.P.	1	95
Lampson, of Kinderhook, N.Y., m. Mehitable **BEARDSLEY**, of Oxford, May 22, 1826, by Eph[rai]m Swift	1	23

	Vol.	Page

SMITH, (cont.)

	Vol.	Page
Larren, m. Patty Maria **FRENCH**, b. of Oxford, Dec. 15, 1828, by Adonijah French, J.P.	1	31
Lucinda, [d. Abel & Damaries], b. May 2, 1793	2	93
Mary, w. David, d. Oct. 28, 1822, ae. 62	2	40
Mary, [d. 1822], ae. 62	2	111
Mary, of Oxford, m. Asahel S. **JUDD**, of Woodbridge, Sept. 17, 1829, by Rev. W[illia]m A. Curtiss	1	32
Mary Antonette, of Oxford, m. Harry **SUTTON**, of Derby May 9, 1833, by Stephen Jewitt	1	43
Nancy R. m. Tho[ma]s C. **OSBORN**, Dec. 20, 1828, by Rev. Chauncey Prindle	1	32
Nelson, m. Maria **NICHOLS**, Sept. 2, 1824, by Rev. Chauncey Prindle	1	16
Philo, m. Betsey **LEWIS**, b. of Oxford, Mar. 26, 1826, by Rev. David Bennett	1	22
Philo, [s. Isaac & Sarah], b. [ ]	2	94
Polly, [d. David & Obedience], b. Dec. 24, 1799	2	93
Polly, of Oxford, m. Bennett **TWITCHELL**, of Waterbury, Aug. 3, 1831, by Rev. W[illia]m A. Curtiss, of Woodbridge	1	38
Richard, d. [, 1803], ae. 72	2	103
Ruth Ann, m. Frederick **HULL**, b. of Oxford, Feb. 19, 1834, by Rev. Abraham Brown	1	52
Sally, of Oxford, m. Andrew **POPE**, of Monroe, Oct. 11, 1824, by Rev. Ashbel Baldwin	1	17
Sally, [d. Isaac & Sarah], b. [ ]	2	94
Samuel, s. Harvey & Susan, b. Jan. 27, 1824	2	94
Samuel C., of Derby, m. Amanda H. **CHATFIELD**, of Oxford, Nov. 28, 1838, by Rv. Daniel Miller	1	65
Sarah, [d. Isaac & Sarah], b. Feb. 16, 1801	2	94
Sheldon, s. David & Polly, b. Mar. 7, 1792	2	93
Stephen, of Derby, m. Ruth Ann **SUMMERS**, of Milford, Apr. 12, 1843, by Samuel Wise, J.P.	1	81
Stiles, s. Chester & Kezia, b. Aug. 20, 1798	2	93
Susan, wid., Rev. Dil, d. Nov. 27, [ ], ae. 67	2	102
Susan, [d. Isaac & Sarah], b. [ ]	2	94
Sylvia, [d. Isaac & Sarah], b. [ ]	2	94
Ursula, [d. David & Obedience], b. Aug. 5, 1797	2	93
Willard, [s. Andrew & Ruth], b. Jan. 7, 1794	2	93
William, s. John & Lucy, b. June 20, 1796	2	93
William, 3rd, m. Laura **BASSETT**, Sept. 27, 1840, by Rev. John D. Smith	1	73
Willis Jude, [s. Andrew & Ruth], b. June 12, 1791	2	93
Wyllys, s. Chester & Kezia, b. June 17, 1796	2	93
-----, wid., [d. Sept. [ ], 1821], ae. 54	2	110

SOMERS, Enoch, m. Mrs. Mary **JOHNSON**, b. of Orange, Nov. 19, 1848, by Rev. Stephen Topliff — 1, 111

	Vol.	Page
SPENCER, Caleb, [d. 1817], ae. 30	2	109
Sally, Mrs. m. Medad **HENNEY**, b. of Derby, Jan. 26, 1827, by Bennett Lum, J.P., at the house of Anson Chatfield	1	29
SPERRY, Betsey Augusta, of Oxford, m. Austin **HOLBROOK**, of Derby, Dec. 14, 1825, by Rev. Abner Smith, of Derby	1	22
Eleazer, d. [1808], ae. 64	2	105
George, of Bethlem, m. Mary Ann **CABLE**, of Oxford, Nov. 19, 1845, by Rev. G. B. Eastman	1	94
Jane, Mrs. of Oxford, m. Everet **HUBBELL**, of Derby, Nov. 26, 1828, by Bennett Lum, J.P., at the house of Austin Holbrook. Int. Pub.	1	31
Laura, m. William **GRIFFIN**, Dec. 30, 1839, by Rev. John D. Smith, at the house of Silas Sperry	1	72
Leonard, m. Ann Jennett **SCOTT**, Apr. 8, 1826, by Rev. Chauncey Prindle	1	23
Lucinda, m. Bennett **SCOVIL**, [July] 3, 1842, by Rev. Stephen Topliff	1	79
Moses, m. Polly **WEAPER**, Mar. 2, 1824, by Chauncey Prindle	1	13
SPRING, Charles Isaac, s. Sam[ue]l Isa[a]c & Nabby], b. Oct. 29, 1823	2	93
George Alonzo, [s. Sam[ue]l & Isa[a]c & Nabby], b. Apr. 20, 1821	2	93
Maryann, d. [Sam[ue]l Isa[a]c & Nabby], b. June 27, 1826	2	93
Moses, his w. [ ], d. [1823], ae. 38	2	111
Sam[ue]l, d. Apr. 13, 1828, ae. 35 y.	2	40
STACY, Caroline Bunnell, [d. 1831], ae. 22	2	111
STEVENS, Barzillar, m. Minerva T. **ADAMS**, b. of Waterbury, Sept. 13, 1835, by Rev. Abraham Browne	1	58
STILES, David, s. Garwood & Nancy, b. Sept. 22, 1824	2	93
Nancy, m. Thomas **WORTHINGTON**, Oct. 15, 1832, by Noah Stone, J.P.	1	42
Simeon, d. [1810], ae. 25	2	106
STODDARD, George T., of Southbury. m. Mary **HAKINS**, of Oxford, Mar. 8, 1840, by Rev. Josiah Bowen	1	70
Maria, m. Ashley **NETTLETON**, Sept. 13, 1841, by Rev. P.L. Hoyt	1	77
Merab, d. Sept. 15, 1828, ae. 28 y.	2	40
Sally, m. Charles **OATMAN**, b. of Oxford, Jan. 14, 1821, by Ephraim G. Swift	1	3
STONE, Andrew, [s. Noah & Rosalind], b. Nov. 25, 1815	2	93
Chester, of [Middlebury], m. Minerva **WELTON**, of Oxford, [June] 11, 1823, by Rev. Mark Mead	1	10
David, [s. Noah & Rosalind,], b. Dec. 23, 1817	2	93
Eunice, [d. Noah & Rosalind], b. Nov. 12, 1812	2	93

OXFORD VITAL RECORDS 73

	Vol.	Page
STONE, (cont.)		
Eunice N., m. Lucius B. **HORTON**, of Waterbury, Jan. 14, 1833, by Rev. Abraham Brown	1	48
Martha, [d. Noah & Rosalind], b. May 15, 1814	2	93
Martha, m. Stephen **HUBBELL**, of Hamden, Oct. 30, 1832, by Rev. Abraham Brown	1	48
Mary E., d. Nov. 9, 1814, ae. 3 y 4 m.	2	39
Mary Elizabeth, [d. Noah & Rosalind], b. July 9, 1811	2	93
Mary Elizabeth, d. Noah & Rosalind, d. Nov. 9, 1814	2	107
Noah, m. Rosalind **MARVIN**, Oct. 1, 1810	2	39
STORES, Charey, m. Merit **SANFORD**, b. of Oxford, June 24, 1824, by Adonijah French, J.P.	1	15
STRONG, Eli, of Southbury, m. Mary **BUCKINGHAM**, of Oxford, [, 1820?], by Ephraim G. Swift. Int. Pub.	1	2
SUMMERS, Isaac, of Otis, Mass, m. Polly **TYREL**, of Woodbridge, Conn., May 21, 1832, by Wait Bassett, J.P., at the house of Elijah Johnson	1	41
Ruth Ann, of Milford, m. Stephen **SMITH**, of Derby, Apr. 12, 1843, by Samuel Wise, J.P.	1	81
SUTTON, Edward J., of St. George, Vt., m. Lucretia A. **MORRIS**, of Oxford, May 24, 1840, by Rev. Stephen Topliff	1	73
Harry, of Derby, m. Mary Antonette **SMITH**, of Oxford, May 9, 1833, by Stephen Jewitt	1	43
John, d. [1813], ae. 30	2	107
SWIFT, W[illia]m, [d. Dec. [ ], 1821], ae. 26	2	110
TALMADGE, Jacob, of Middlebury, m. Sally **WHITE**, of Waterbury, Feb. 6, 1850, by Rev. Stephen Topliff	1	109
TERRILL, TERRELL, TERRIL, Mary C., of Bethany, m. Stephen **TREAT**, of Oxford, Oct. 16, 1833, by Rev. Abraham Brown	1	50
Phineas, [d. 1822], ae. 74	2	111
Rebecca, of Bethany, m. William B. **WATSON**, of Oxford, Jan. 19, 1840, by Rev. Sylvester Smith	1	69
-----, wid. [d. 1816], ae. 86	2	109
THOMAS, Jeremiah, m. Maryatt **MORRIS**, Feb. 15, 1822, by Beardsley Northrop	1	6
Mehetable, m. Capt. John **DAVIS**, Apr. 10, 1782	2	11
THOMPSON, Amelia, m. Samuel N. **ANDREW**, Oct. 26, 1846, by Rev. John D. Smith	1	97
Betsey, m. Bristol **TRUMAN**, Dec. 18, 1801	2	3
Delia, m. Charles M. **CLARK**, Dec. 31, 1840, by John D. Smith	1	76
Emily E., of Branford, m. John D. **PERRY**, of Oxford, Jan. 26, 1846, by Rev. Stephen Topliff	1	91
Nathan L., m. Hannah M. **WOOSTER**, [Oct.] 5, [1837], by Rev. H. Wooster, of Deep River	1	62
TOLLES, Horace, of Bethany, m. Caroline **WOOSTER**, of Oxford,		

	Vol.	Page
TOLLES, (cont.)		
June 18, 1837, by John D. Smith	1	62
TOMLINSON, Amy, Mrs. of Oxford, m. Edmund **LEAVENWORTH**, Oct. 26, [1823], by Rev. Menzies Raynor, of Huntington	1	12
Balson, d. [1824], ae. 21	2	111
Benjamin, of Derby, m. Olive **SELEY**, of Oxford, Sept. 27, 1824, by Abel Wheeler, J.P.	1	16
Bennett, [s. W[illia]m Clark & Amey], b. May 1, 1811	2	96
Bennett, [d. 1822], ae. 23	2	111
Bennett Benedict, [s. David & Lorena], b. May 5, 1799	2	96
Burke, m. Juliet **CANDEE**, Jan. 4, 1840, by Rev. Daniel Burhans	1	70
Burton, [s. W[illia]m Clark & Amey], b. Jan. 1, 1805	2	96
Center, [ch. of W[illia]m Clark & Amey], b. Feb. 3, 1798	2	96
Charles, [s. David & Lorena], b. June 19, 1785	2	96
Charles, [s. W[illia]m Clark & Amey], b. July 6, 1809	2	96
Charles H., of Oxford, m. Esther **SMITH**, of Southbury, Nov. 15, 1835, by Rev. Abraham Browne	1	60
Clark, [s. W[illia]m Clark & Amey], b. May 30, 1799	2	96
Clark, m. Sarah **HAWKINS**, Jan. 24, 1822, by Beardsley Northrop	1	6
Clark, m. Manerva **BROWN**, Dec. 28, 1838, by Bennett Lum, J.P.	1	63
D[ ], [d. 1822], ae. 60	2	111
David, [s. David & Lorena], b. July 11, 1787	2	96
David, s. David & Lorena, d. Mar. 4, 1788	2	103
David, [s. David & Lorena], b. Aug. 1, 1791	2	96
David, Jr., [d. 1814], ae. 23	2	108
David, Senator, d. Mar. 23, 1822, ae. 60	2	43
Eliza, [d. David & Lorena], b. May 29, 1805	2	96
Eliza C., of Oxford, m. Isaac T. **HOTCHKISS**, of New Haven, Nov. 7, 1827, by Rev. Alpheas Gear, of Waterbury	1	27
George, m. Delia **SKEELS**, Oct. 18, 1835, by Rev. Charles Smith, in Christ Church	1	56
George A., m. Eliza A. **JUDSON**, b. of Oxford, Feb. 14, 1830, by Rev. W[illia]m A. Curtiss	1	34
George Albert, [twin with Janet Adeline, s. David & Lorena], b. July 6, 1803	2	96
Grace, m. Samuel **LUKE**, b. of Derby, Oct. 3, 1829, by W[illia]m A. Curtiss	1	33
Harry, [s. W[illia]m Clark & Amey], b. Mar. 17, 1801	2	96
Henrietta, [d. David & Lorena], b. Sept. 13, 1807	2	96
Henrietta L., d. David & Lorena, d. Aug. 14, 1829, in her 22nd year	2	43

	Vol.	Page
TOMLINSON, (cont.)		
Jane, of Derby, m. John Nichols **LEWIS**, of Waterbury, Sept. 23, 1838, by Rev. John D. Smith, of Humphreyville, at the house of Samuel Lake	1	64
Jane Caroline, [d. David & Lorena], b. June 30, 1797	2	96
Janet Adeline, [twin with George Albert, d. David & Lorena], b. July 6, 1803	2	96
Jennet A., Mrs. of Oxford, m. William S. **HOTCHKISS**, of New Haven, Dec. 25, 1822, by Rev. Manzies Raynor, of Huntington, Conn.	1	9
Locky, d. Caleb & Abigail, b. June 26, 1797	2	95
Lorena, [d. David & Lorena], b. Aug. 4, 1793	2	96
Lydia Augusta, [d. David & Lorena], b. Sept. 25, 1795	2	96
Lydia A[u]gusta, of Oxford, m. William **DeFOREST**, of Salem, Oct. 25, 1824, by Rev. Alpheas Geer, of Waterbury	1	17
Maria Theresa, [d. David & Lorena], b. Aug. 17, 1789	2	96
Mary Ann, [d. David & Lorena], b. Mar. 10, 1801	2	96
Mary Ann, [d. 1832], ae. 31	2	111
Noah, d. [ ], 1794, ae. 67	2	102
Noah, Jr., d. [ ], [1803], ae. 46	2	103
Pat, his wid. [d. 1820], ae. 54	2	110
Phebe M., of Oxford, m. Joseph **CONNER**, of Leesburg, Va., Feb. 8, 1835, by Rev. Charles Smith	1	55
Russell, [s. W[illia]m Clark & Amey], b. Apr. 5, 1807	2	96
Russell, of Derby, d. [1809], ae. 54	2	105
Sally, d. Noah & Mary, b. May 10, 1794	2	95
Sally, [d. W[illia]m Clark & Amey], b. Oct. 2, 1796	2	96
Sally, d. Caleb & Abigail, b. Dec. 28, 1798	2	95
Sally, 2nd, d. Caleb, d. Apr. 7, 1800, ae. 1	2	102
Sally, d. Caleb & Abigail, b. [ ], 1806	2	95
Sarah A., m. George **BUNNEL**, b. of Oxford, Feb. 13, 1848, by Rev. David P. Sanford	1	100
Stephen, [s. W[illia]m Clark & Amey], b. July 29, 1803	2	96
William, [s. W[illia]m Clark & Amey], b. Feb. 1, 1813	2	96
W[illia]m, [d. Nov. [ ], 1819], ae. 47	2	110
W[illia]m Augustus, [s. David & Lorena], b. Sept. 15, 1809	2	96
William Henry, of Derby, m. Betsey Mariah **POOL**, of Oxford, Nov. 23, 1824, by Stephen Jewitt	1	18
Zalmon, d. [1807], ae. 32	2	105
-----, had negro, Philip, [d. 1818], ae. 36	2	110
TOMPKINS, TOMKINS, Francis & w. Mary, had s. [ ], b. Nov. [ ], 1800	2	95
Hall, s. Francis & Mary, b. Dec. 22, 1798	2	95
TOWNER, Albert Bronson, [s. Asahel & Abigail], b. June 23, 1824	2	95

	Vol.	Page
TOWNER, (cont.)		
Amey, d. Apr. 27, [1802], ae. 17	2	103
Avis, of Oxford, m. Marvin **GRISWOLD**, of Litchfield, [ ], by Rev. Abraham Brown. Recorded Nov. 23, 1834	1	49
Betsey, [d. 1825], ae. 40	2	111
Clarissa, w. Rev. Joseph **OSBORN**, d. Oct. 19, 1832, ae. 54 y.	2	42
David, d. July 4, [1823], ae. 43	2	111
Emeline T., of Oxford, m. Matthias **WILSEY**, of Onondago, N.Y., [July] 7, [1830], by Tho[ma]s L. Shipman	1	44
Enos, d. Jan. [ ], [1819], ae. 40	2	110
Enos, s. Asael & Abigail, d. Feb. 27, 1832, ae. 2 y.	2	42
Enos, [d. 1832], ae. 2	2	111
Enos Warner, [s. Asahel & Abigail], b. June 27, 1830	2	95
Isaac, his w. [d. 1818], ae. 30	2	110
John, of Southbury, d. [1805], ae. 90	2	104
John, d. [1810], ae. 60	2	106
John, his wid. [d. 1815], ae. 67	2	108
Joseph, d. [ ], 1790, ae. 79	2	102
Joseph, d. [1806], ae. 50	2	104
Lois, d. [July [ ], 1819], ae. 32	2	110
Lois E., of Oxford, m. David **NOBLE**, of Southbury, Apr. 7, 1841, by W. H. Whittemore	1	75
Martha, [d. Asahel & Abigail], b. July 8, 1826	2	95
Mary, wid. Joseph, d. June 24, 1822, ae. 67	2	43
Mary, wid., [d. 1822], ae. 67	2	111
Mary, of Oxford, m. Matthew **HUBBELL**, of Middletown, N.Y., Oct. 7, 1833, by Rev. Abraham Brown	1	50
Polly, w. David, d. [1814], ae. 30	2	107
Rachel, d. [1824], ae. 81	2	111
Simeon, m. Sally **CAMP**, b. of Oxford, [, 1834 (?)], by Rev. Abraham Browne	1	54
Truman Hurlburt, [s. Asahel & Abigail], b. Oct. 21, 1822	2	95
Warner, m. Lois **PEET**, b. of Oxford, [Mar.] 18, [1845], by Rev. Stephen Topliff	1	89
TRASSELL, Phineas & w. Rachel, had s. [ ], b. Dec. 9, 1800	2	95
TREAT, Harriet, m. Marvin R. **SANFORD**, May 10, 1831, by Samuel Meigs, J.P.	1	37
Harvey, s. Daniel & Betsey, b. May 15, 1797	2	95
Maria, d. Elijah & Esther, b. Dec. 22, 1799	2	95
Mariah, m. Clark **JOHNSON**, b. of Oxford, Aug. 13, 1820, by Adonijah French, J.P.	1	1
Polly, m. Hiram **JOHNSON**, b. of Oxford, Apr. 29, 1824, by Adonijah French, J.P.	1	14

	Vol.	Page

TREAT, (cont.)
   Stephen, of Oxford, m. Mary C. **TERRIL**, of Bethany, Oct.
      16, 1833, by Rev. Abraham Brown   1   50
   Thirza, m. Hiram O. **CAIN**, July 8, 1832, by Wait
      Bassett, J.P., at the house of William O. **CAIN**   1   41
TROWBRIDGE, Elizabeth, d. Israel & Mary, of Oxford, m.
   Hosea **DUTTON**, physician, s. John & Abigail, of
   Southington, Jan. 19, 1783   2   11
TRUMAN, Bristol, m. Betsey **THOMPSON**, Dec. 18, 1801   2   3
TRUMBULL, Eliz[abeth], pauper, d. [1806], ae. 70   2   104
   Emily, d. Thomas, b. Apr. 30, 1820   2   96
TUCKER, Betsey, m. John **WOODIN**, Jr., b. of Oxford, Feb.
   22, 1831, by Rev. Charles Thompson, of Humphrey-
   ville   1   37
   Burton, [d. Nov. [ ], 1819], ae. 33   2   110
   Byram, m. Fanny **LOUNSBURY**, Mar. 14, 1841, by John D.
   Smith   1   76
   Ellen Jane, m. Moodey M. **BROWNE**, b. of Oxford, Aug.
   10, 1834, by Rev. Abraham Browne   1   53
   Eunice, m. John C. **BOOTH**, Feb. 19, 1840, by Rev.
   John E. Bray   1   70
   George, [s. Josiah & Betty], b. July 17, 1812   2   95
   Gideon, [d. 1815], ae. 70   2   109
   Harry, s. Josiah, d. Nov. 14, 1799, ae. 2   2   102
   Harry, [d. Josiah & Betty], b. Feb. 22, 1810   2   95
   Henrietta, d. Dan & Laura, b. May 21, 1811   2   96
   Henrietta, m. Henry **DUNHAM**, b. of Oxford, Oct. [ ],
   [1834], by Rev. Abraham Browne   1   58
   Josiah, [m.] Polly **MOORE**, [   ]   2   42
   Josiah, m. Betty **WHEELER**, Mar. 12, 1808   2   42
   Josiah, his w. [, d. 1817], ae. 42   2   109
   Laura, d. Josiah & Polly, b. Oct. 29, 1800   2   95
   Lucy, of Oxford, m. Simeon L. **BRISTOL**, of Milford,
   Sept. 4, 1845, by Rev. Stephen Topliff   1   90
   Maria, m. Joseph **BEEBE**, b. of Oxford, [,
   1834 (?)], by Rev. Abraham Brown. Recorded Nov.
   22, 1834   1   54
   Mary Ann, m. James **CARY**, b. of Oxford, Sept. 30, 1821,
   by Eph[rai]m G. Swift   1   5
   Mary L., [d. Josiah & Betty], b. Sept. 1, 1808   2   95
   Nancy, d. Josiah & Polly, b. Oct. 12, 1798   2   95
   Polly, w. Josiah, d. [, 1803], ae. 33   2   103
   Samuel, d. [1810], ae. 78   2   106
   Sam[ue]l, his w. [   ], d. Aug. [, 1825],
   ae. 69   2   111
   Sarah, wid. Sam[ue]l, d. [1812], ae. 75   2   106
   Sarah, [d. Josiah & Betty], b. Sept. 11, 1814   2   95
TURNER, Julia Ann, m. Beach **BEARDSLEE**, Apr. 12, [1835], by

	Vol.	Page
TURNER, (cont.)		
Rev. Matthew Batchelor	1	56
Ruth A., m. Bennett **CHATFIELD**, b. of Oxford, [Apr.] 27, [1835], by Rev. Matthew Batchelor	1	56
TUTTLE, Samuel L., of Southbury, m. Genette E. **SMITH**, of Oxford, Nov. 28, 1844, by Rev. O.B. Butterfield, of South Britain	1	88
TWITCHELL, TWITCHEL, Abijah, d. [1811], ae. 35	2	106
Anson, s. David & Margaret, b. Mar. 10, 1790	2	95
Benjamin, m. Claraina **HAWKINS**, Feb. 26, 1776	2	42
Benjamin, d. Oct. 6, 1805, ae. 6	2	104
Bennett, of Waterbury, m. Polly **SMITH**, of Oxford, Aug. 3, 1831, by Rev. W[illia]m A. Curtiss, of Woodbridge	1	38
David, s. John, d. [ ]. 1796, ae. 43	2	102
Delana, of Oxford, m. Samuel **BRONSON**, of Southbury, Apr. 11, 1827, by Tho[ma]s L. Shipman	1	28
Delia E., m. Hanford **FAIRCHILD**, b. of Oxford, Jan. 10, 1822, by Beardsley Northrop	1	6
Edwin, s. Shelden & Mary, b. Oct. 16, 1827	2	95
Elizabeth, see Elizabeth **DEAN**	2	10
Elizabeth, of Oxford, m. Horace **HULL**, of Waterbury, July 4, 1824, by Levi Candee, J.P.	1	16
Enoch, d. Oct. [, 1802], ae. 49	2	103
Esther, [d. Benj[ami]n & Clarana], b. July 15, 1781	2	95
Gilbert, his w. [, d. 1822], ae. 40	2	111
Grace, [d. Benj[ami]n & Clarana], b. July 26, 1785	2	95
H[ ], of Naugatuck, m. Polly **KANE**, of Oxford, Nov. 14, 1847, by Rev. David P. Sanford	1	99
Hannah, [d. Benj[ami]n & Clarana], b. Oct. [ ], 1792	2	95
Jabez, d. Jan. [ ], 1789, ae. 40; "was first buried in the Church yard"	2	103
Jerusha, w. Capt. **GILBERT**, d. June 9, 1822	2	43
John, [s. Benj[ami]n & Clarana], b. July 21, 1779	2	95
John, d. Jan. [ ], 1789, ae. 40; first to be buried in the church yard	2	133
John, d. [1804], ae. 90	2	104
Joseph, d. [ ], 1797, ae. 80	2	103
Laura E., of Oxford, m. Bennett R. **BEECHER**, of Waterbury, [ ], by Rev. Abraham Brown. Recorded Nov. 22, 1834	1	51
Lusanna, [ch. of Benj[ami]n & Clarana], b. Aug. 20, 1783	2	95
Marilla, wid. David, d. [1812], ae. 57	2	106
Mary, ae. 27, m. Benj[amin] **BUNNELL**, ae. 24, Nov. 22, 1786	2	3
Nancy, of Oxford, m. Lester **ROBINSON**, of Middletown, May 26, 1833, by Rev. Abraham Brown	1	50

	Vol.	Page
TWITCHELL, TWITCHEL, (cont.)		
Polly, d. Eben[eze]r & Jerusha, b. Mar. 8, 1800	2	95
Polly, m. Asa **JOHNSON**, b. of Oxford, Oct. 14, 1826, by Bennett Lum, J.P., at the house of Ebenezer Twitchell. Int. Pub.	1	24
Robert, [s. Benj[ami]n & Clarana], b. Jan. 9, 1777	2	95
Robert & W. Anna, had s. [ ], b. Dec. 15, 1800	2	95
Robert Starr, [s. Benj[ami]n & Clarana], b. Feb. 27, 1798	2	95
Ruth M., d. Nov. 10, 1805, ae. 6	2	104
Ruthia, [d. Benj[ami]n & Clarana], b. Apr. 1, 1790	2	95
Sam[ue]l, [d. 1808], ae. 30	2	105
Sarah, [d. Mar. [ ], 1821], ae. 85	2	110
TYLER, Edna J., m. Samuel T. **SCOTT**, b. of Oxford, [June] 16, [1847], by Rev. Stephen Topliff	1	98
Enos, m. Augusta **SEELEY**, b. of Oxford, June 6, 1848, by Rev. Stephen Topliff	1	101
TYRRELL, TYREL, Phinehas, formerly, of Woodbridge, Nov. 27, 1822, ae. 74	2	43
Polly, of Woodbridge, Conn., m. Isaac **SUMMERS**, of Otis, Mass., May 21, 1832, by Wait Bassett, J.P.	1	41
UPSON, Harvey W., m. Elizabeth **RANSOM**, b. of Oxford, Oct. 23, 1836, by Rev. Abraham Browne	1	61
Hezekiah J.*, of Southington, m. Sally **MANSFIELD**, of Oxford, Nov. 15, 1826, by Rev. Newton Tuttle (*correction J. is crossed out and Todd is handwritten at the end of the entry)	1	25
VON*, Nathan, d. [Mar. [ ], 1819], ae. 47 *(**VOSS**?)	2	110
VOSS, Mary Ann, of Oxford, m. Smith **BENNETT**, of Monroe, Jan. 28, 1827, by Rev. David Bennett	1	25
WALES, Catharine, [d. Isaac Miles & Lois], b. Jan. 9, 1807, at New Haven	2	99
John Heaton, [s. Isaac Miles & Lois], b. June 12, 1800, at New Haven	2	99
Sam[ue]l Albert, [s. Isaac Miles & Lois], b. May 10, 1802, at New Haven	2	99
-----, female, d. [1813], ae. 30	2	107
WALKER, Nathaniel, m. Laura E. **SCOTT**, b. of Oxford, Oct. 8, 1837, by Rev. Abraham Brown	1	67
Nathaniel, Capt. of 1st Co., in Oxford	2	132
WALLACE, John, d. May 30, 1840, ae. 52	2	45
Juliana, w. John, d. June 13, 1840, ae. 51 y.	2	45
WARNER, James, m. Eunice A. **BRADLEY**, b. of New Haven, June 4, 1837, by Rev. Abraham Browne	1	66
Noadiah, m. Laura J. **HINMAN**, [July] 9, [1843], by Rev. Stephen Topliff	1	82
WARRIMER, William C., of Springfield, Mass., m. Julia S.		

	Vol.	Page
WARRIMER, (cont.)		
BLACKMAN, of Oxford, July 24, 1831, by Rev.		
Charles Thompson, of Hymphreyville	1	37
WASHBAND, [see also **WASHBURN**], Bowen, [d. 1817], ae. 73	2	109
Bowen, his wid., d. [1823], ae. 67	2	111
Cathareine S., m. Joel **OSBORN**, b. of Oxford, June 11,		
1846, by Rev. G. B. Eastman	1	94
Geo[rge Washington, [s. Josiah & Keturah], b. Jan. 30,		
1803	2	99
Josiah, d. [1810], ae. 75	2	106
Josiah Smith, [s. Josiah & Keturah], b. July 31, 1793	2	99
Julia Laminta, d. Josiah, Jr. & Keturah, b. Apr. 6,		
1797	2	98
Jelia Laminta, [d. Josiah & Keturah], b. Apr. 6, 1797	2	99
Seth Perkins Staples, [s. Josiah & Keturah], b. Feb.		
15, 1810	2	99
Smith, d. May [, 1823], ae. 29	2	111
Stan Sterling, [s. Josiah & Keturah], b. Feb. 12, 1807	2	99
WASHBURN*, [see also **WASHBAND**], Josiah Smith, m. Sally		
Marin **WHEELER**, b. of Oxford, Nov. 28, 1822, by		
Stephen Jewet *(**WASHBAND**(?)	1	8
WATERS, WATTERS, Abel, his s. [d. 1825], ae. 20	2	111
Augusta, of Oxford, m. Curtiss **BLACKMAN**, of Huntington,		
Jan. 1, 1843, by Rev. Abel Nichols	1	86
Betsey [d. Abel & Ruth], b. June 1, 1798	2	98
Betsey Ann, of Oxford, m. Enos **BENHAM**, of Woodbury,		
Jan. 24, 1848, by Rev. David P. Sanford	1	100
Laura, [d. Abel & Ruth], b. July 28, 1793	2	98
Russell, [s. Abel & Ruth], b. July 3, 1796	2	98
Sarah, m. Frederic A. **BRADLEY**, b. of Oxford, Apr. 30,		
1845, by Rev. A. Nichols	1	90
WATSON, William B., of Oxford, m. Rebecca **TERRILL**, of		
Bethany, Jan. 19, 1840, by Rev. Sylvester Smith	1	69
WATTLES, Anna, [d. 1821], ae. 21	2	110
Sarah Maria, m. Erastus **MERRIAM**, Sept. 26, 1830, by		
Rev. A. Brown	1	35
W[illia]m, s. Joseph, b. Oct. 10, 1820	2	99
WEAPER, Polly, m. Moses **SPERRY**, Mar. 2, 1824, by Chauncey		
Prindle	1	13
WEBSTER, Charles, of Oxford, m. Mary A. **HARD**, of Waterbury,		
Feb. 18, 1838, by Rev. Abraham Brown	1	67
Clarke, m. Sarah **HITCHCOCK**, b. of Derby, Nov. 25, 1833,		
by Rev. Abraham Brown	1	49
Joel F., of Waterbury, m. Laura L. **BUCKINGHAM**, of		
Oxford, Nov. 2, 1835, by Rev. Abraham Browne	1	59
WEEDEN, David, d. [ ], 1797, ae. 60	2	103
Eunice, m. Julius **KIMBERLEY**, b. of Oxford, Apr. 30,		
1821, by Ephraim G. Swift	1	4

	Vol.	Page
WEEDEN, (cont.)		
Hannah, m. Asa **HAWKINS**, b. of Oxford, Aug. 12, 1821, by Beardsley Northrop	1	4
William, d. [ ], 1792, ae. 76	2	102
WELLON, Charles S., of Humphreyville, m. Amanda **OSBORN**, of Oxford, [Apr.] 8, [1846], by Rev. Stephen Topliff	1	92
WELLS, Ari Bennett, [s. Gesham & Hannah], b. Apr. 8, 1812	2	99
Herman Perry, [s. Gesham & Hannah], b. Jan. 15, 1806	2	99
WELTON, Minerva, of Oxford, m. Chester **STONE**, of [Middlebury], [June] 11, 1823, by Rev. Mark Mead	1	10
WHEELER, Abel, [s. Sam[ue]l, Jr. & Lois], b. Dec. 18, 1765	2	99
Abel, m. Eunice **RIGGS**, Oct. 1, 1786	2	45
Abel, d. Oct. 27, 1830, ae. 65 y.	2	45
Amos, of Southbury, m. Harriet **HUBBELL**, of Huntington, Apr. 15, 1824, by Newton Tuttle	1	14
Betsey, [d. Samuel & Phebe], b. June 10, 1803	2	98
Betsey, m. Orlando **CABLE**, b. of Oxford, Nov. 9, 1825, by Rev. Menzies Raynor, of Huntington	1	21
Betsey Ann S.E., [d. Robert & Julia Laminta], b. Oct. 30, 1820	2	100
Betsey Ann Sarah Elizabeth, d. Robert & Julia Laminta, b. Oct. 30, 1821	2	100
Betty, [m.] Josiah **TUCKER**, Mar. 12, 1808	2	42
Birdsey Glover, [s. Samuel & Phebe], b. Aug. 12, 1807	2	98
Daniel, d. Oct. 1, 1821, ae. 39	2	45
Dan[ie]l, [d. 1821], ae. 40	2	110
Elisha, [s. Robert & Julia Laminta], b. Oct. 31, 1836	2	100
Elisha, [s. Robert & Ruth], b. Jan. 29, 1771	2	99
Eunice, w. Abel, b. July 25, 1771	2	99
Ezra, d. Apr. 4, 1840	2	45
George, [s. Robert & Julia Laminta], b. Feb. 3, 1823	2	100
James, s. Robert, d. [1805], ae. 26	2	104
James, [twin with Joseph, s. Robert & Ruth], d. [ ]	2	99
Jane E., m. Jesse C. **HOWARD**, Nov. 15, 1840, by John D. Smith	1	76
Joseph, of Southbury, m. Mary **McEWEN**, of Oxford, Oct. 11, 1820, by Eph[rai]m G. Swift. Int. Pub.	1	1
Joseph, [twin with James, s. Robert & Ruth], d. [ ]	2	99
Julia Ann, [d. Robert & Julia Laminta], b. Nov. 26, 1840	2	100
Lois, d. [1805], ae. 67	2	104
Moses, [s. Robert & Ruth], b. Mar. 6, 1773	2	99
Moses, d. [1823], ae. 73	2	111
Moses, his w. [ ], d. June [,1823], ae. 74	2	111
Polly, m. Samuel **LEWIS**, Sept. 8, 1841, by Samuel Meigs, J.P.	1	95

	Vol.	Page
WHEELER, (cont.)		
Robert, d. [ ], 1781	2	103
Robert, Jr., [s. Robert & Julia Laminta], b. Mar. 23, 1828	2	100
Ruth, d. [1825], ae. 36	2	111
Sally Maria, d. Samuel & Phebe, b. Nov. 7, 1797	2	98
Sally Maria, m. Josiah Smith **WASHBURN**, b. of Oxford, Nov. 28, 1822, by Stephen Jewet	1	8
Sam[ue]l, [s. Robert & Ruth], b. July 2, 1769	2	99
Sam[ue]l, m. Phebe **GLOVER**, Oct. 20, 1795	2	45
Sam[ue]l, Lieut., d. Dec. 24, 1799, ae. 81	2	102
Sarah, [d. Robert & Ruth], b. July 26, 1775	2	99
Sarah, wid. Capt. J[ame]s, d. [1812], ae. 92	2	106
Sarah Jenette, m. John Riggs **DAVIS**, Nov. 7, 1838, by Rev. John D. Smith, of Humphreyville, at the house of Lyman Wheeler	1	71
Smith, [s. Robert & Julia Laminta], b. Jan. 30, 1826	2	100
WHITE, Ambrose, m. Nancy **WOOSTER**, Mar. 20, 1832, by Rev. Chauncey Prindle	1	40
Sally, of Waterbury, m. Jacob **TALMADGE**, of Middlebury, Feb. 6, 1850, by Rev. Stephen Topliff	1	109
WHITFORD, Charles, of Amenia, m. Jane **BRIANT**, of Oxford, Nov. 21, 1838, by Rev. Daniel Miller	1	65
WHITING, Obedience, of Hamden, m. Anthony L. **SMITH**, of Oxford, [May] 19, [1844], by Rev. Stephen Topliff	1	85
WHITMAN, Sarah, d. [1812], ae. 80	2	106
WILCOXSON, Frances Ann, d. N.J. & Ann, b. July 26, 1831	2	100
WILLIAMS, Elijah Johnson, of Cheshire, m. Thirza Lines, of Oxford, Mar. 3, 1824, by Rev. Laban Clark	1	13
Priscilla, m. Frederic H. **CHATFIELD**, b. of Oxford, Nov. 29, 1840, by Rev. Sylvester Smith	1	74
Reuben L., m. Elizabeth Ann **BALDWIN**, Oct. 18, 1840, by John D. Smith	1	75
Sabrina, d. May 20, 1825, ae. 28	2	45
Sabrina, d. [1825], ae. about 30	2	111
Samuel C., m. Mary Jane **RIGGS**, b. of Oxford, [Jan.] 29, [1845], by Rev. Stephen Topliff	1	88
WILMOT, Eliza, [d. Wilkin & Polly], b. Aug. 7, 1811	2	99
Jane, [d. Wilkin & Polly], b. July 26, 1813	2	99
Joanna, wid., [d. Oct. [ ], 1821], ae. 85	2	110
John, [s. Wilkin & Polly], b. Feb. 11, 1809	2	99
Julia Ann, [d. Wilkin & Polly], b. May 20, 1817	2	99
Mellecent, w. Walker, d. [, 1803], ae. 36	2	103
Sally, [d. Wilkin & Mellecent], b. May 4, 1800	2	99
WILSEY, Matthias, of Onondago, N.Y., m. Emeline T. **TOWNER**, of Oxford, [July] 7, [1830], by Tho[ma]s L. Shipman	1	44
WISE, Nancy, d. Aug. 23, 1827, ae. 42 y.	2	45
WOOD, Samuel N., of Lowel, Mass., m. Laura L. **HYDE**, of		

OXFORD VITAL RECORDS 83

	Vol.	Page

WOOD, (cont.)
    Oxford, Nov. 29, 1846, by Rev. Stephen Topliff   1   97
WOODING, WOODIN, WOODEN, Hannah, d. W[illia]m, b. Oct.
    7, 1797   2   98
  Hannah, of Oxford, m. Henry B. **ENGLISH**, of Derby,
    Apr. 6, 1842, by Rev. Thomas Sparks   1   78
  Henry, of Bethany, m. Jennet **LIMBURNER**, of Oxford,
    [Oct.] 22, [1843], by Rev. Stephen Topliff   1   83
  Jennet, m. Ira K. **SMITH**, May 23, 1827, by Rev.
    Chauncey Prindle   1   27
  John, Jr., of Oxford, m. Betsey **TUCKER**, of Oxford,
    Feb. 22, 1831, by Rev. Charles Thompson, of
    Humphreyville   1   37
  Rebeckah, m. Ambrose **OSBORN**, b. of Oxford, Feb. 8,
    1824, by Abel Wheeler, J.P.   1   13
  Sally, m. William Washington **SACKET**, b. of Oxford,
    Feb. 15, 1823, by Adonijah French, J.P.   1   9
  Susanna, d. Charles & Eliza, b. Aug. 30, 1798   2   98
  Sybel, m. [   ], May 5, 1811   2   39
WOODRUFF, Maria, [d. Nathan & Charity], b. Nov. 15, 1797   2   98
  Nathan & w. Charity, had ch., b. Aug. 30, 1799   2   98
  Olive, m. Eben **BUCKINGHAM**, Oct. 28, 1792   2   3
WOOSTER, WOOSLEE, WOOSTI, WORCESTER, Abijah, [d.
    1815], ae. 44   2   109
  Abr[aha]m, "a pauper", d. Mar. 1, 1800, ae. 81   2   102
  Anna Riggs, [d. Nath[anie]l & Charity], b. Nov. 13,
    1793; d. Oct. 29, 1794   2   98
  Arthur, his w. [   ], d. [   ], 1796   2   103
  Arthur, d. [   ], 1796, ae. 84   2   103
  Austin, s. Jos[eph], Jr. & Eliz[a] Ann, b. Feb. 2, 1797   2   98
  Bennett, [s. Nath[anie]l & Charity], b. Oct. [ ], 1795   2   98
  Bennett, m. Sally **BASSETT**, b. of Oxford, Mar. 16, 1823,
    by Beardsley Northrop   1   9
  Caroline, m. Garry B. **HYDE**, b. of Oxford, July 10,
    1831, by Rev. Nathan D. Benedict   1   38
  Caroline, of Oxford, m. Horace **TOLLES**, of Bethany, June
    18, 1837, by John D. Smith   1   62
  Charity, w. Nath[anie]l, b. July 26, 1767   2   98
  Clarissa, [d. Nath[anie]l & Charity], b. Mar. 4, 1798   2   98
  Cynthia C., of Oxford, m. Thomas M. **DOWNS**, of South-
    bury, [Jan.] 1, [1845], by Rev. Stephen Topliff   1   88
  Cynthia Cordelia, [d. Russell & Avis], b. Dec. 21, 1824   2   98
  Ebenezer, Town Clerk, d. Mar. 30, 1800, ae. 50
    "suicide"   2   102
  Elisha, d. [   ], 1797, ae. 67   2   103
  Elizabeth Ann, m. David **FRENCH**, b. of Oxford, Mar. 8,
    1829, by Rev. Nathan D. Benedict   1   32
  Enos, s. Jonas & Marian, b. Nov. 17, 1794   2   98

WOOSTER, WOOSLEE, WOOSTI, WORCESTER, (cont.)

	Vol.	Page
Eunice, w. John, d. Apr. 18, 1799, ae. 72	2	102
Grace, [d. Nath[anie]l & Charity], b. Feb. 9, 1791	2	98
Hannah, [d. Joseph & Hannah], b. July 7, 1794	2	98
Hannah M., m. Nathan L. **THOMPSON**, [Oct.] 5, [1837], by Rev. H. Wooster, of Deep River	1	62
Henry, d. [1824], ae. 50	2	111
James L., m. Martha **JOHNSON**, [Sept.] 24, [1843], by Rev. Stephen Topliff	1	82
Jane, [d. 1831], ae. 5	2	111
John, d. [, 1803], ae. 80	2	103
John, m. Mary **LIMBURNER**, d. John, b. of Oxford, Jan. 7, 1828, by Sayres Gazley	1	29
John, Capt. of 1st Co., in Oxford	2	132
Jos[eph], his w. [ ], d. [1814], ae. 31	2	107
Jos[eph], [d. Dec. [ ], 1819], ae. 76	2	110
Jos[eph], Jr., d. May [, 1819], ae. 57	2	110
Larman, [d. 1817], ae. 21	2	109
Lois, wid. Thomas, d. Aug. 29, 1822, ae 94	2	45
Lois, [d. 1822], ae. 94	2	111
Louisa, of Oxford, m. Clement **PERCY**, of Roxbury, Mar. 20, 1833, by Rev. Nathan D. Benedict	1	43
Lucinda, of Oxford, m. Henry **BUXTEN**, of Danbury, Oct. 31, 1831, by Samuel Wise, J.P.	1	40
Lucy, [d. Joseph, Jr. & Eliza Ann], b. Nov. 16, 1799	2	98
Lucy, m. Julius **KIMBERLEY**, b. of Oxford, June 10, 1827, by Nathan D. Benedict	1	27
Mamre, [d. Nath[anie]l & Charity], b. Sept. 23, 1789	2	98
Mary, d. Samuel, d. Feb. 13, 1823, ae 84	2	45
Mary, wid. [d. Feb. 13, 1823], ae. 84	2	111
Mary, of Oxford, m. Israel M. **PERRY**, of Woodbridge, Apr. 5, 1840, by Rev. James Mallory, of Newtown	1	72
Melissa, [d. Joseph, Jr. & Eliza Ann], b. Nov. 26, 1800	2	98
Meret, d. [ ]	2	45
Moses, "a pauper", d. Sept. [ ], 1799, ae. 50	2	102
Nancy, m. Ambrose **WHITE**, Mar. 20, 1832, by Rev. Chauncey Prindle	1	40
Nathan, A. M., [d. 1808], ae. 48	2	105
Nath[anie]l, b. Nov. 25, 1766	2	98
Nath[aniel], m. Charity **PLUMB**, Feb. 5, 1789	2	45
Nath[anie]l Ransom, [s. Nath[anie]l & Charity], b. Nov. 18, 1809	2	98
Newton, [s. Joseph, Jr. & Eliza Ann], b. Feb. 28, 1798	2	98
Russell, [s. Joseph & Hannah], b. Apr. 26, 1791	2	98
Sabra, of Oxford, m. Erastus C. **HEWINS**, of Alfred, Mass., Mar. 17, 1830, by Nathan D. Benedict	1	35
Sally, [d. Joseph & Hannah], b. Aug. 5, 1792	2	98
Samuel, s. Sam[ue]l, decd. & Betsey **PERRY**, b. Dec. 31,		

	Vol.	Page
WOOSTER, WOOSLEE, WOOSTI, WORCESTER, (cont.)		
1790	2	98
Sam[ue]l, d. [1805], ae. 67	2	104
Samuel Russell, [s. Russell & Avis], b. Apr. 22, 1829	2	98
Seth Madison, [s. Sheldon & Sally], b. Feb. 23, 1812	2	98
Sheldon, his w. [, d. 1818], ae. 33	2	110
Thomas, d. Dec. 9, 1798, ae. 74	2	102
Thomas, d. June 28, 1800, ae. 42	2	102
William Burr, [s. Russell & Avis], b. Aug. 22, 1821	2	98
WORCHESTER, [see under **WOOSTER**]		
WORTHINGTON, Thomas, m. Nancy **STILES**, Oct. 15, 1832, by Noah Stone, J.P.	1	42
WYETT, Mary, of Birmingham, Eng. m. John **BROOKS**, of Yorkshire, Eng., Nov. 6, 1834, by Samuel Wise, J.P.	1	47
YATES, W[illia]m, [d. 1817], ae. 35	2	109
NO SURNAME		
Benjamin, m. Almira C. **DUTTON**, Feb. 21, 1810	2	6
Catharine S., d. Josiah S. & Maria, b. Aug. 25, 1823	2	99
Chloe, negress, d. [1813], ae. 50	2	107
David, s. David, now of Harwinton, m. Hannah **CATLIN**, d. Abijah, of Harwinton, Nov. 14, 1808	2	6
Isaiah, m. Milessa **RIGGS**, Oct. 25, 1807	2	6
Phebe, w. Park, d. Nov. [ ], 1822, ae. 67	2	32
Pheebean, m. Aaron **FREEMAN** (colored persons), Aug. 28, 1832, by Rev. Chauncey Prindle	1	41
Philo, negro, d. [1813]	2	107
Timothy, s. Justus, m. Laura **FAIRCHILD**, d. Benj[ami]n, Nov. 11, 1801	2	6

PLAINFIELD VITAL RECORDS
1699 - 1852

	Vol.	Page
ABBE, Sarah, m. John **WELCH**, Apr. 11, 1729	2	22
ABBETT, Huldah, m. Benjamin **BRIGGS**, June 24, 1847, by Peleg Peckham, Elder	3	44
ABEL, Andrew, of Lisbon, m. Maria **FRY**, of Plainfield, Nov. 28, 1844, by V.R. Osborn, V.D.M.	3	26
ADAMS, Azeriah, s. Micaijah & Elizabeth, b. Nov. 13, 1751	2	15
Ednah, of Plainfield, m. Sidney **OLCOTT**, of Manchester, Jan. 9, 1824, by Orin Fowler, V.D.M.	2	193
Eliphalet, s. Micaijah & Elizabeth, b. Mar. 27, 1753	2	23
Eliphalett, s. Micaijah, d. Nov. 10, 1757, ae. 4 y. 7 m. 13 d.	2	44
Eliphalet, s. Micajah & Elizabeth, b. Feb. 8, 1761	2	49
Eunice, d. Micaijah & Elizabeth, b. Dec. 8, 1754	2	31
Gamaleel Ripley, s. John & Elizabeth, d. Apr. 29, 1802, ae. 1 y. 2 m.	2	108
Jabez, of Canterbury, m. Jane L. **LESTER**, of Plainfield, Dec. 8, 1851, by Rev. George J. Tillotson, of Brooklyn, Conn.	3	73
Jerad, m. Harriet **PHILLIPS**, Apr. 1, 1821, by Rev. Nathaniel Cole	2	134
Jerusha, d. Benjamin & Jerusha, b. Nov. 29, 1751	2	22
Jerusha, w. Benjamin, d. July 28, 1752	2	22
John, s. John & Elizabeth, b. Mar. 20, 1802	2	108
John G., m. Abby O.E. **GIBSON**, b. of Sterling, Sept. 3, 1848, by Peleg Peckham, Elder	3	58
Jonathan Sabin, s. Joshua & Abigail, b. Sept. 22, 1802	2	108
Mary May, d. Joshua & Abigail, b. Apr. 4, 1804	2	110
Micaijah, m. Elizabeth **DEAN**, Nov. 7, 1750	2	15
Micaijah, s. Micaijah & Elizabeth, b. Dec. 23, 1756	2	15
Oliver, s. Micaijah & Elizabeth, b. Mar. 28, 1759	2	44
Salome, m. William W. **HOPKINS**, b. of Plainfield, Dec. 9, 1824, by Orin Fowler, V.D.M.	2	197
Simeon, s. Micaijah & Elizabeth, b. Dec. 26, 1762	2	54
William, s. of the w. of Major **FITCH**, d. Aug. 12, 1700. He was 16 y. old the 17th of Dec. before his death	1	3
William K., of Providence, R.I., m. Elizabeth **ALMY**, of Tiverton, R.I., Nov. 15, 1847, by Rev. J. Mather	3	47
ALBRO, Samuel, m. Hannah W. **GREENWOOD**, of Warwick, R.I., May 4, 1834, by Rev. Samuel Rockwell	2	218
ALDRICH, Henry, Dr., of South Kingston, R.I., m. Betsy		

	Vol.	Page

ALDRICH, (cont.)
    TILLINGHAST, of Voluntown, June 23, 1830, by Rev.
        Orin Fowler   2   211
    Henry L, of Worcester, Mass., m. Anna **TALBOT**, of
        Plainfield, Apr. 22, 1850, by Rev. J. O. Knapp   3   64
    Henry L., merchant, ae. 24, b. Plainfield, res.
        Worcester, Mass., m. Annie W. **TALBOT**, ae. 25, b. N.
        Bridge, Mass., res. Plainfield, Apr. 22, 1850, by
        Rev. J.O. Knapp   4   6
ALEXANDER, Benjamin M., m. Ann E. **SHELDON**, b. of
    Warwick, R.I., Apr. 26, 1847, by Rev. James M.
    Mather   3   44
    Sarah D., m. Gershom P. **DOUGLASS**, b. of Voluntown,
        July 21, 1850, by Rev. Henry Robinson   3   65
ALIOT*, Lucinda, m. William G. **SHORT**, b. of Providence,
    R.I., Nov. 20, 1848, by Rev. George W. Brewster
    (***ELIOT**?)   3   57
ALLEN, [see also **ALLYN** and **ALLING**], Horace, m. Harriet
    MITCHELL, b. of Killingly, Sept. 21, 1845, by
    James Smither, Elder   3   34
    Horace, of Canterbury, m. Emily **HERRICK**, of Plainfield,
        Nov. 25, 1845, by Rev. C.C. Barnes   3   33
    James G., of Providence, R.I., m. Nancy F.C. **CONGDON**,
        of Plainfield, Aug. 2, 1854, by Rev. Peter S.
        Marther   3   85
    John R., m. Mary E. **CRANDALL**, b. of Coventry, R.I.,
        Feb. 2, 1848, by Rev. J. Mather   3   51
    Lois, m. Isaac **WHE[E]LER**, Jr., June 3, 1755   2   40
    Weltha, of Sterling, m. John **WHITMAN**, Jr., of Griswold,
        May 21, 1821, by Jonathan Gallup, J.P.   2   133
ALLERTON, Sarah, d. Isaac & Lucy, b. Feb. 12, 1770   2   72
ALLING, [see also **ALLEN** and **ALLYN**], Eliot, m. Sarah A.
    CAHOON, b. of Plainfield, Feb. 24, 1850, by Rev.
    Joseph P. Brown   3   63
ALLYN, [see also **ALLEN** and **ALLING**], Jabez, m. Elizabeth
    RUMBALL, Dec. 29, 1736   1   68
    Thomas, s. Joseph & Mercy, b. Feb. 20, 1779   2   90
ALMY, Annah, d. Nov. 23, [1847], ae. 5 w.   4   61
    Elizabeth, of Tiverton, R.I., m. William K. **ADAMS**, of
        Providence, R.I., Nov. 15, 1847, by Rev. J. Mather   3   47
    Elizabeth H., m. Harry **PECKHAM**, b. of Middletown, R.I.,
        residing in Plainfield, Nov. 18, 1838, by Peleg
        Peckham, Elder   2   238
    Frederick, s. Samson, manufacturer, ae. 55, & Eliza,
        ae. 42, b. Nov. 10, 1849   4   29
    Frederick, d. May 19, 1850, ae. 8 m.   4   64
    Martha, d. Samson, manufacturer, ae. 53, & Alice Talbot
        ALMY, ae. 40, b. Oct. 19, 1847   4   23

	Vol.	Page
ALMY, (cont.)		
Mason, s. William, wool sorter, ae. 29, & Mary, ae. 28, b. Jan. 1, 1849	4	27
Mason, d. Aug. 17, 1850, ae. 8 m.	4	64
AMES, Edwin, m. Mehitable C. **TYLER**, b. of Plainfield, Feb. 28, 1843, by Rev. A. Dunning	3	18
Israel, m. Louisa **GREEN**, b. of Plainfield, Aug. 9, 1853, by Rev. Alfred Gates	3	79
John, m. Fanny E. **BENNETT**, Oct. 2, 1849, by William Dyer, J.P.	3	60
John, carpenter, ae. 23, b. New London, Ct., res. Plainfield, m. Henry (sic) E. **BENNETT**, ae. 18, of Plainfield, Oct. 5, 1849, by W[illia]m Dyer, Esq.	4	5
John, carpenter, ae. 21, b. Lyme, Ct., res. Plainfield, m. Fanney E. **BENNETT**, domestic, ae. 17, of Plainfield, Oct. 2, 1849, by William Dyer, Esq.	4	6
John B., of Providence, R.I., m. Harriet T. **BURGESS**, of Plainfield, May 13, 1840, by Rev. Samuel Rockwell	3	4
Julia Ann, of Plainfield, m. Orrin P. **GILBERT**, of Pomfret, June 5, 1834, by Rev. Samuel Rockwell	2	219
Mary J., m. Amos **WITTER**, Apr. 13, 1828, by Rev. Orin Fowler	2	205
Rhoby M., of Plainfield, m. Zuriel **POTTER**, of Cranston, Feb. 2, 1832, by Rev. Dennis Platt	2	215
Samuel, carpenter, ae. 24, b. Lyme, Ct., res. Plainfield m. Abigail T. **BENNETT**, domestic, ae. 22, of Plainfield, Sept. 9, 1849, by Rev. S. W. Coggeshall	4	6
Sarah, m. John F. **CAULKINS**, b. of Waterford, Sept. 7, 1852, by Rev. Henry Robinson	3	76
William B., m. Lucy A. **GALLUP**, b. of Plainfield, Apr. 21, 1839, by Rev. Samuel Rockwell	2	241
ANDERSON, Mary, m. Abel **SPAULDING**, Nov. 23, 1749	2	48
ANDREW, ANDREWS [see also Andros], George R., of Plainfield, m. Olive **BENNET**, of Canterbury, Oct. 20, 1822, by Jonathan Gallup, J.P., Canterbury	2	189
Huldah, of Plainfield, m. George **SMITH**, of Salem, July 21, 1823, by John Dunlap, J.P.	2	192
Jane, m. Hazard **RODMAN**, b. of Plainfield, Apr. 20, 1824, by Rev. Nathaniel Cole	2	194
Rebecca, m. Jason **PRAY** b. of Plainfield, Feb. 10, 1822, by John Dunlap, J.P.	2	187
Robert, m. Susan A. **WHALEY**, b. of Coventry, R.I., Nov. 29, 1847, by Rev. J. Mather	3	47
ANDROS, ANDRAS, ANDRUS, [see also **ANDREW**], Abel Averell, s. Benjamin & Sally b. Jan. 27, 1819	2	136
Anna, of Plainfield, m. Jonathan **CARD**, of New York, Feb. 16, 1785	2	91

	Vol.	Page
ANDROS, ANDRAS, ANDRUS, (cont.)		
Benjamin, s. Abel & Bridget, b. Oct. 20, 1777	2	105
Benjamin, of Plainfield, m. Sally **AVERELL**, of Preston, Mar. 16, 1803	2	136
Benjamin, Dea., d. Jan. 28, ae. 82 y. 3 m. 8 d.	2	136
James Sanford, s. Benjamin & Sally, b. Oct. 18, 1808	2	136
Milton, s. Thomas & Abigail, b. Apr. 16, 1786	2	92
Thomas, m. Abigail **CUTLER**, May 18, 1784	2	92
William, s. Abel & Bridget, b. Nov. 3, 1780	2	105
William Noice, s. Benjamin & Sally, b. May 26, 1806	2	136
ANGEL, ANGELL, Adda A., d. Sept. 14, 1849, ae. 14 m.	4	64
Clarissa D., of Scituate, R.I., m. Calvin F. **WICKS**, of Providence, R.I., Nov. 14, 1844, b. A. Dunning	3	25
Daniel, of Plainfield, m. Sarah B. **DODGE**, of New Shoreham, R.I., Sept. 12, 1836, by Rev. Samuel Rockwell	2	227
Eliza, of Scituate, m. James B. **YEAW**, of R.I., residing in Sterling, Dec. 2, 1838, by Peleg Peckham, Elder	2	238
Ellen, d. Henry, farmer, ae. 56, & Rebecca, ae. 43, b. Dec. 17, 1848	4	24
Harriet, of Plainfield, m. Lewis **POND**, of Clinton, N.Y., June 3, 1821, by Orin Fowler, V.D.M.	2	133
Israel, m. Nancy **PRAY**, b. of Plainfield, Oct. 14, [1826], by Elder George W. Appleton, Sterling	2	200
Job F., of Providence, R.I., m. Julian **LESTER**, of Plainfield, Sept. 3, 1826, by Rev. Orin Fowler	2	199
Julia, d. Daniel, farmer, ae. 40, & Lucy, ae. 28, b. July 14, 1848	4	24
Prudy, m. Nathaniel **MEDBERY**, Jr., b. of Plainfield, Feb. 29, 1824, by Rev. Nathaniel Cole	2	194
Thomas, farmer, d. Apr. 29, 1850, ae. 55	4	64
ANTRAM, ANTRIM, Jeremiah, s. Francis & Eunice, b. Sept. 13, 1790	2	116
Thomas, s. Francis & Eunice, b. Dec. 7, 1781	2	105
Waterman, s. Francis & Eunice, b. Sept. 3, 1786	2	114
William, Jr., of Providence, m. Sarah **DEAN**, of Plainfield, Apr. 9, 1750, by Rev. David Rowland	2	11
ARNOLD, Abner, laborer, res. Mass., m. Lucy Ann **PARKHURST**, cotton operator, res. Mass., June 9, [1850?]	4	7
Ann E., b. Canterbury, res. S. Killingly, d. May 12, 1848, ae. 21	4	61
Ann R., of Plainfield, m. John A.P. **FAIRMAN**, of Killingly, Sept. 6, 1852, by Rev. Joseph P. Brown	3	75
Benjamin M., of Sterling, m. Mary **KITTLE**, of Plainfield, Aug. 19, 1849, by Peleg Peckham, Elder	3	59
Georgianna, d. Ira W., tailor, ae. 25, & Harriet, ae. 27, b. Oct. 23, 1848	4	27

	Vol.	Page

ARNOLD, (cont.)
Georgianna Sears, m. Stephen **SHELDON**, b. of Warwick,
   R.I., Aug. 11, 1846, by Peleg Peckham, Elder   3   38
Harriet N., d. Ira W., tailor, ae. 27, & Harriet, ae.
   22, b. Apr. 7, 1850   4   30
Ira, m. Harriet **SNELL**, b. of Plainfield, Jan. 13, 1845,
   by James Smither, Elder   3   29
Jeremiah, of Warwick, R.I., m. Elvira A. **SMITH**, of
   Warwick, R.I., Sept. 17, 1848, by Rev. Geo[rge] W.
   Brewster   3   56
Josiah Lynden, of St. Jansbury, Vt., m. Susanna
   PERKINS, of Plainfield, Feb. 8, 1795, by W[illia]m
   Robinson, Clerk   2   101
Lucian E., d. Brainard C., shoemaker, ae. 23, & Ann E.,
   ae. 21, b. May 12, 1848   4   21
Mary A., m. James R. **TURNER**, b. of Warwick, R.I., Nov.
   25, 1847, by Rev. Frederic Charlton   3   50
Nathaniel, m. Alice Ann **SNELL**, July 1, 1847, by Rev.
   Fred[eri]c Charlton   3   49
Susanna, of Plainfield, m. Charles **MARSH**, of Woodstock,
   Vt., June 3, 1798   2   103
Warnare M., of Sterling, m. Abby **DERBY**, of Plainfield,
   Jan. 18, 1829, by Rev. Orin Fowler   2   208
ARYE, Hannah, of Plainfield, m. Simon **DAVIS**, of Thompson,
   Aug. 3, 1831, by Rev. Otis Lane, of Sterling &
   Voluntown   2   214
AUSTIN, Abby B., of East Greenwich, R.I., m. Enos **LAPHAM**, of
   Scituate, R.I., Apr. 23, 1843, by Rev. Erastus
   Benten   3   19
William R., m. Mary L. **BAKER**, b. of Plainfield, May 2,
   1852, by Rev. Henry Robinson   3   75
AVERELL, Harmony, m. Aaron **CRARY**, Apr. 17, 1794   2   120
Sally, of Preston, m. Benjamin **ANDROS**, of Plainfield,
   Mar. 16, 1803   2   136
AVERY, Abby T., of Plainfield, m. Henry **BENNET**, of Hartford,
   Ohio, Sept. 17, 1838, by Rev. Samuel Rockwell   2   236
Anna, d. John & Elizabeth, b. May 7, 1792   2   102
Erasmus D., of Groton, m. Sarah **HINCKLEY**, of Plain-
   field, Aug. 7, 1844, by A. Dunning   3   24
Gilbert, s. John & Elizabeth, b. Mar. 10, 1794   2   102
John, Jr., s. John & Elizabeth, b. Feb. 26, 1790   2   102
Thankful, m. John **RUSSEL[L]**, b. of Killingly, Jan. 12,
   1844, by James Smither, Elder   3   28
William W., of Preston, m. Dorcas **FISK**, of Plainfield,
   Dec. 4, 1823, by Nathaniel Cole, Elder   2   192
Zepporah, d. John & Elizabeth, b. Nov. 2, 1787   2   102
AYRE, [see under **ARYE**]
BABCOCK, Elizabeth, m. Ebenezer **GALLUP**, Nov. 26, 1797   2   103

	Vol.	Page
BABCOCK, (cont.)		
Hannah, of Hopkinton, m. John **HARRIS**, of Plainfield, June 2, 1770, by Joseph Davis, Elder, Hopkinton	2	72
Justus, m. Martha **STARKWEATHER**, Apr. 13, 1806	2	117
Lois, d. Timothy & Esther, b. Apr. 4, 1774	2	78
Lois, of Sterling, m. George W. **CROSS**, of Charlestown, R.I., Mar. 11, 1849, by Peleg Peckham, Elder	3	58
Sarah A., d. John, whipper tender, & Sarah, b. Aug. 27, 1848	4	25
Welcom[e], m. Mary Ann **WOOD**, Apr. 6, 1842, by Rev. John Read	3	14
BACHELOR, BASHELLER, Nancy, of Woonsocket, R.I., m. Moses **LEWIS**, of Plainfield, Oct. 7, 1841, by John Dunlap, J.P.	3	11
Naoma, cotton operator, ae. 20, b. Sterling, m. Otis **GILLSON**, cotton operator, ae. 25, b. Sterling, Apr. [1849?]	4	6
BACK, George, m. Hannah **RUSSEL[L]**, Dec. 17, 1761	2	63
BACKUS, Andrew, m. Lois **PEIRCE**, Feb. 8, 1759	2	40
Eunice, d. Andrew & Lois, b. June 14, 1770	2	71
Lucy, d. Andrew & Lois, b. Mar. 14, 1777	2	82
Lydia, d. Thomas & Lydia, b. Mar. 28, 1795	2	103
Mary, m. John **LESTER**, Aug. 7, 1796	2	122
Phebe, m. Jonathan **SPAULDING**, Mar. 20, 1765	2	59
Polly, d. Andrew & Lois, b. Jan. 7, 1773	2	78
Sabra, m. William **KNIGHT**, Sept. 14, 1806	2	120
Silvanus, s. Andrew & Lois, b. June 3, 1768	2	51
Simon, s. Andrew & Lois, b. Apr. 12, 1765	2	51
Simon, s. Major Andrew & Lois, d. Sept. 19, 1788	2	97
Stephen, s. Andrew & Lois, b. Nov. 27, 1759	2	40
Thomas, s. Andrew & Lois, b. May 19, 1762	2	51
Thomas, Dr., of Plainfield, m. Lydia **LATHROP**, of Norwich, Nov. 6, 1793	2	103
Thimoty J., of Ashford, m. Sally **WILSON**, of Plainfield, July 15, 1838, by William Dyer, J.P.	2	235
BACON, Amos, s. Jacob & Sarah, b. Jan. 18, 1786	2	90
Asa[h]el, s. Jacob & Sarah, b. July 5, 1784	2	90
Benjamin, Jr., m. Joanna **KINSMAN**, b. of Plainfield, Sept. 15, 1824, by Orin Fowler, V.D.M.	2	195
Horace, s. Benjamin & Irena, b. Sept. 4, 1800	2	109
Maria, ae. 22, b. Canterbury, Ct., res. Plainfield, m. Mason **WOOD**, rag bleacher, ae. 21, b. Foster, R.I., res. Plainfield, Sept. 12, 1849, by Rev. Leonard	4	5
Rebeckah, m. Josiah **SHEPHARD**, Nov. 1, 1753	2	26
BAGGS, Russel[l], of Richmond, R.I., m. Clarissa **DAVIS**, of Plainfield, Feb. 12, 1828, by Rev. Orin Fowler	2	205
BAILEY, Amanda, d. Silas, Jr. & Anna, b. Mar. 15, 1810;		

	Vol.	Page
BAILEY, (cont.)		
d. Sept. 29, 1811	2	139
Caroline, d. Silas, Jr. & Anna, b. July 29, 1815	2	139
Caroline E., of Plainfield, m. James **CADY**, of Thompson, June 6, 1842, by Andrew Dunning	3	16
Mary Ann, d. Silas, Jr. & Anna, b. Mar. 29, 1820	2	139
Nancy Louisa, d. Silas, Jr., & Polly, b. Mar. 14, 1807	2	139
Polly, w. Silas, Jr., d. Apr. 26, 1807	2	139
Roswell W., of Bolton, m. Betsey **STOWELL**, of Plainfield, Mar. 19, 1826, by Orin Fowler, V.D.M.	2	198
Serel O., m. Mary Ann **PHILLIPS**, b. of Providence, R.I., Oct. 30, 1847, by Rev. J. Mather	3	46
Silas, Jr., m. Anna **HALL**, Nov. 13, 1808, by Rev. Nathaniel Cole	2	196
Silas Martin, s. Silas & Anny, b. Aug. 13, 1826	2	139
BAKER, Abby P., of Warwick, R.I., m. William H. **COLE**, of Providence, R.I., Oct. 25, 1846, by Rev. J. Mather	3	39
Albert W., of Mobile, m. Melessent F. **BRUCE**, of Plainfield, Nov. 28, 1852, by Rev. William Turkington	3	77
Balanea, of Thompson, m. Sybel **BUTLER***, of Canterbury, Oct. 20, 1839, by Rev. Tubal Wakefield (*correction Butler has been crossed out and Button handwritten in original manuscript)	2	248
Balenea, of Plainfield, m. Sybel **BUTTON**, of Canterbury, Oct. 20, 1839, by Rev. Tubal Wakefield	3	1
Clista, m. John **THOMAS**, b. of Plainfield, Nov. 20, 1831, by Peleg Peckham, Elder	2	214
Elizabeth, m. Jonathan **SHEPHARD**, Mar. 29, 1729	2	21
Elisabeth, m. Jonathan **SHEPARD**, Mar. 29, 1731	1	57
Elizabeth C., of Plainfield, m. Silas **SISSON**, of Seekank, Mass., July 23, 1826, by Orin Fowler, V.D.M.	2	199
Emma Victoria, d. Reuben, carpenter, ae. 35, & Lucy, ae. 30, b. May 17, 1849	4	25
Frank, of Brooklyn, m. Lucy A. **KENYON**, of Plainfield, Nov. 21, 1849, by Rev. Henry Robinson	3	61
Frank E., farmer, ae. 27, of Brooklyn, m. Lucy A. **KENYON**, ae. 21, of Plainfield, Nov. 21, 1849, by Henry Robinson	4	5
Frank E., of Brooklyn, m. Ruth M. **KENYON**, of Plainfield, Oct. 29, 1851, by Rev. Henry Robinson	3	72
Hannah, of Plainfield, m. Gilbert P. **PERKINS**, of Ledyard, Dec. 31, 1837, by Rev. Tubal Wakefield	2	233
Jane, d. Belerma, laborer, ae. 44, & Sibbel, ae. 28, b. May 19, 1850	4	29

BARBOUR COLLECTION

	Vol.	Page
BAKER, (cont.)		
John M., of Brooklyn, m. Sarah **FRENCH**, of Plainfield, Feb. 15, 1848, by Rev. Henry Robinson	3	52
John M., carriage maker, ae. 27, of Brooklyn, m. Sarah **FRENCH**, ae. 23, b. Plainfield, Feb. 16, 1848, by Rev. Henry Robinson	4	1
Levi A., s. Belamy, laborer, ae. 43, & Sybell, ae. 27, b. Oct. 27, 1848	4	26
Marcus, shoemaker, b. Brooklyn, res. Plainfield, d. Feb. [ ], 1850, ae. 30	4	66
Marcus, farmer, b. Brooklyn, res. Plainfield, d. Feb. [ ], 1850, ae. 50	4	66
Marcus T., d. [ ], 1850, ae. 1	4	66
Marcus T., d. Feb. [ ], 1850, ae. 1	4	66
Marcus T., s. Marcus, boot & shoemaker, & Polly M., b. May 30, 1850	4	28
Mary L., m. William R. **AUSTIN**, b. of Plainfield, May 2, 1852, by Rev. Henry Robinson	3	75
Polly, m. John **KINNE**, Dec. 26, 1813, by Thomas Backus, J.P.	2	125
Reuben W., m. Sibel Ann **CORY**, b. of Plainfield, Dec. 21, 1837, by Amos Witter, J.P.	2	233
W[illia]m, of Cranston, R.I., m. Elvia **MATHEWSON**, of Providence, R.I., Dec. 8, 1845, by Joseph S. Gladding, J.P.; Intention recorded.	3	33
BALDWIN, Henry, s. Elijah, Jr., physician, ae. 29, & Sarah, ae. 24, b. July 24, 1850	4	29
Jane P., of Canterbury, m. Lucius **GALLUP**, of Norwich, Jan. 2, 1854, by Rev. Alfred Gates	3	83
Lovell W., of Dalton, Mass., m. Mary Ann **STARK-WEATHER**, of Plainfield, Nov. 25, 1839, by Rev. Samuel Rockwell	2	249
Lovell W., of Dalton, Mass., m. Mary Ann **STARK-WEATHER**, of Plainfield, Nov. 25, 1839, by Rev. Samuel Rockwell	3	2
Mary, b. Lisbon, Ct., res. Plainfield, d. Sept. 23, 1849, ae. 1	4	64
Permilla S., m. John B. **FARNHAM**, b. of Canterbury, Apr. 15, 1838, by Rev. Tubal Wakefield, Packersville	2	234
-----, child of Lovell W., farmer, & Mary, b. Dec. [1847]. (Entered under the surname of **"BARDIN"** in the Arnold Copy)	4	23
BALLARD, Inoch, m. Hester **LAWRENCE**, Sept. 25, 1734 (Enoch)	2	15
Enoch, s. Enoch & Hester, b. Oct. 8, 1737	2	15
Hannah, d. Peleg & Bethiah, b. Aug. 20, 1726	1	53
Hester, d. Inoch & Hester, b. July 3, 1735	2	15

	Vol.	Page
BALLARD, (cont.)		
John, s. Peleg & Bethiah, b. Feb. 24, 1730/31	1	53
Peleg, m. Bethiah **BUMP**, Aug. 23, 1721	1	53
Peleg, s. Peleg & Bethiah, b. Dec. 6, 1728	1	53
William, s. Peleg & Bethiah, b. Nov. 29, 1722	1	53
BALLOU, Jane E.C., m. Edward W. **FISK**, b. of Coventry, R.I., May 28, 1854, by Peleg Peckham, Elder	3	83
BANNAH, Chloe, m. Prince D. **BROWN**, b. of Plainfield, Oct. 20, 1839, by Amos Witter, J.P.	2	249
BARBER, Betsey, of Canterbury, m. George **HICKS**, of Plainfield, Jan. 1, 1849, by Rev. Henry Robinson	3	56
Betsey, b. Plainfield, res. Canterbury, m. George **HICKS**, laborer, b. Pomfret, Ct., res. Canterbury, Jan. 1, 1849, by Rev. Henry Robinson	4	3
Joseph T., m. Rebecca Jane **SAYLES**, b. of Plainfield, Nov. 19, 1854, by Rev. Joseph P. Brown	3	87
Lucy, of Plainfield, m. Alexander **GREEN**, of Griswold, Mar. 10, 1839, by Rev. Tubal Wakefield	2	240
BARDIN, [see under **BALDWIN**]		
BARMAN*, Martha, m. Joseph **WARREN**, Jan. 2, 1722/3 (*correction **BARMAN** crossed out and **BATEMAN** handwritten in margin of original manuscript.)	1	29
BARNEY, Thomas J., of Plainfield, m. Frances **ROSS**, of Griswold, Mar. 28, 1824, by Orin Fowler, V.D.M.	2	194
BARRETT, BARRET, BARIT, BARET, Abigaiel, d. Eleazer & Cathren, b. June 27, 1733	1	59
Bartholeme, s. Eleazer & Cathren, b. May 5, 1736	1	65
Cha[u]ncey L, s. Elisha M., mason, ae. 43, & Matilda S., ae. 38, b. Oct. 16, 1813	4	29
Ebenezer, s. Ele[a]ser & Catharine, b. Oct. 6, 1731	1	54
Eleazer, m. Catharine **WILLIAMS**, Dec. 25, 1730	1	54
Elisha, laborer, b. Canterbury, res. Plainfield, d. Oct. 9, 1847, ae. 12	4	61
Elisha M., m. Matilda S. **MOORE**, Dec. 21, 1834, by Calvin Philo, Elder	2	242
Ellen, d. Aug. 10, [18]49, ae. 2	4	62
Ellen M., b. Lisbon, Ct., res. Plainfield, d. Aug. 19, 1849, ae. 2	4	64
Hildreth, s. Eleazer & Cathren, b. Mar. 28, 1741	1	96
Mathew, d. Moses & Mary, b. Aug. 6, 1750	2	12
Sarah, m. Nathaniel **JUEL**, Jan. 9, 1732/3	1	69
Sarah, d. Eleazer & Cathren, b. Nov. 17, 1738	1	96
William, d. May 4, 1848, ae. 3	4	61
BARROWS, Charles H., of Griswold, m. Susan M. **GREY**, of Plainfield, Dec. 8, 1850, by Rev. J. B. Guild	3	68
Charles H., overseer in weaver looms, ae. 23, b. Griswold, res. Jewett City, m. Susan M. **GRAY**, weaver, ae. 22, b. Plainfield, res. Jewett City, Dec. 8.		

	Vol.	Page
BARROWS, (cont.)		
1850, by J.B. Guile	4	7
Esther, of Killingly, m. Daniel **GALLUP**, of West Greenwich, R.I., now of Plainfield, July 7, 1834, by William Dyer, J.P.	2	219
BARSTOW, BARSTO, [see also **BASTON**], Ira, m. Delilah **WHITFORD**, b. of Sterling, Apr. 28, 1833, by Peleg Peckham, Elder	2	217
Olive, of Canterbury, m. Levi **ROBINSON**, of Plainfield, Sept. 25, 1797	2	103
BARTLETT, Abby E., m. Samuel **BULLOCK**, b. of Providence, R.I., Sept. 30, 1839, by Rev. Tubal Wakefield	2	248
Abby E., m. Samuel **BULLOCK**, b. of Providence, R.I., Sept. 30, 1839, by Rev. Tubal Wakefield	3	1
Jane, m. David **HILL**, b. of Plainfield, Dec. 18, 1853, by Rev. Joseph P. Brown	3	81
BASHELLER, [see under **BACHELOR**]		
BASS, [see also **BOSS**], Sanford, of Olneyville, R.I., m. Lydia [ ], of Foster, R.I., May 8, 1836, by Rev. Tubael Wakefield	2	226
BASSETT, Emma Elizabeth, d. Mason & Lydia G., b. Apr. 17, 1827	2	246
BASTON, [see also **BARSTOW**], G. Forrester, m. Mary T. **COGSWELL**, b. of Plainfield, June 23, 1853, by Rev. Henry Robinson	3	79
BATEMAN, [see under **BARMAN**]* (*Correction this entire entry handwritten in original manuscript.)		
BATES, George, m. Ann Maria **LIPPITT**, b. of Cranston, R.I., Feb. 24, 1848, by Rev. J. Mather	3	53
BATTEY, Mary R., d. of James, of West Greenwich, R.I., m. Horace B. **MATHEWSON**, s. of Wanton, late of Coventry, now residing in Plainfield, May 3, 1840, by Pardon Tillinghast, Elder	3	7
BAXTER, Thomas A., of Brooklyn, m. Catharine H. **KENYON**, of Plainfield, Nov. 21, 1849, by Rev. Henry Robinson	3	61
Thomas R., wagon maker, ae. 40, of Brooklyn, m. Catharine H. **KENYON**, ae. 34, of Plainfield, Nov. 21, 1849, by Henry Robinson	4	5
BEACH, Lucius, of Hartford, m. Abby B. **PHILLIPS**, of Preston, Mar. 15, 1829, by Rev. Orin Fowler	2	208
BELCHER, Gideon, of South Kingstown, R.I., m. Eunice **GEERS**, of Plainfield, Nov. 24, 1825, by Orin Fowler, V.D.M.	2	198
BELL, Anna, m. Daniel **BUTTON**, Oct. 1, 1716	1	25
BELLUS(?), Roxianna, of Quardon, Vt., m. Henry **HARRIS**, of Plainfield, Apr. 25, 1847, by Rev. Fred[eri]c Charlton	3	48
BEMIS, Adeline, m. Samuel T. **DOW**, b. of Sterling, Oct. 27,		

	Vol.	Page
BEMIS, (cont.)		
1827*, by Rev. Henry Robinson (*Probably 1850)	3	66
Adeline, of Sterling, m. Samuel T. **LOW**, of Sterling, Oct. 27, 1850, by H. Robinson	4	7
BENCHLEY, John S.R., of Windham, m. Caroline S. **PHILLIPS**, of Plainfield, Nov. 27, 1834, by Peleg Peckham, Elder	2	220
BENEDICT, Anna, d. Rev. Joel & Sarah, b. July 25, 1783, at North Salem, N.Y.	2	113
Elizabeth, [twin with William Mackown], d. Rev. Joel & Sarah, b. May 20, 1788	2	113
Joel, Rev., d. Feb. 13, 1816, in the 72nd y. of his age & 32nd y. of his Ministry in Plainfield, 1st Society	2	128
Joel, Rev., d. Feb. 13, 1816, in the 72nd y. of his age & 32nd y. of his Ministry in Plainfield	2	129
Louisa Kirtland, d. Rev. Joel & Sarah, b. Nov. 1, 1795	2	113
Margaret, d. Rev. Joel & Sarah, b. Sept. 17, 1791	2	113
Mary, d. Rev. Joel & Sarah, b. July 21, 1778, at Norwich, Newent Society	2	113
Richard Hutson, s. Rev. Joel & Sarah, b. Dec. 5, 1780, at Norwich, Newent Society	2	113
Robert, s. Rev. Joel & Sarah, b. July 11, 1776, at Norwich, Newent Society	2	113
Sarah, d. Rev. Joel & Sarah, b. Aug. 29, 1774, at Norwich, Newent Society; m. Rev. Eliphalet **NOTT**, [ ]; d. Mar. 9, 1804, at Balls Town, N.Y.	2	112
Susanna, d. Rev. Joel & Sarah, b. Feb. 16, 1786	2	113
William, s. Rev. Joel & Sarah, b. Sept. 22, 1772, at Norwich, Newent Society; d. May 15, 1774	2	112
William A., m. Eliza A. **EATON**, b. of Plainfield, Feb. 4, 1850, by Rev. Henry Robinson	3	63
William Mackown, [twin with Elizabeth], s. Rev. Joel & Sarah, b. May 20, 1788	2	113
BENJAMIN, BENJAMINS, Annah, m. Ebenezer **HARRIS**, Oct. 29, 1751	2	14
Anna, w. Simeon, d. Dec. 13, 1793	2	99
Elizabeth, m. Oliver **WILBOUR**, Oct. 23, 1777	2	85
Simeon, d. Dec. 20, 1792	2	99
BENNETT, BENNET, Abby A.S., m. Oliver K. **KENYON**, b. of Johnston, R.I., Dec. 30, 1848, by Caleb Bennet, J.P.	3	55
Abby B., m. Solomon **ROOD**, Jr., b. of Plainfield, Aug. 6, 1854, by Rev. Alfred Gates	3	87
Abby S., m. Solomon **RUDE**, b. of Plainfield, Aug. 6, 1854, by Rev. Alfred Gates	3	85

	Vol.	Page

BENNETT, BENNET, (cont.)
Abigail T., domestic, ae. 22, of Plainfield, m.
   Samuel **AMES**, carpenter, ae. 24, b. Lyme, Ct.,
   res. Plainfield, Sept. 9, 1849, by Rev. S. W.
   Coggeshall   4   6
Alfred, s. Ephraim & Artemissa, b. June 25, 1825   2   246
Alfred A., farmer, ae. 23, b. Plainfield, res.
   Canterbury, m. Maria P. **SMITH**, ae. 22, b.
   Sheffield, Mass., res. Canterbury, Apr. 12, 1848,
   by Rev. Mr. Bradford   4   1
Alice, d. Ebenezer & Grace, b. Jan. 14, 1772   2   75
Amos, Jr., m. Phebe E. **PHILLIPS**, b. of Plainfield,
   Feb. 6, 1837, by Chester Tilden   2   231
Amos, d. Dec. 22, 1849, ae. 4   4   63
Basheba T., of Brooklyn, m. Edwin **HARRIS**, of Plain-
   field, Sept. 4, 1854, by Levi Meech, Elder   3   85
Betsey, m. Abner **FRENCH**, Feb. 1, 1821, by Rev.
   Nathaniel Cole   2   133
Caleb, m. Lovina **HALL**, b. of Plainfield, July 12,
   1829, by Nathaniel Cole, Elder   2   209
Caleb, of Plainfield, m. Elmira **LITTLEFIELD**, of
   Brooklyn, Apr. 16, 1837, by Chester Tilden   2   231
Chloe, m. Prince D. **BROWN**, b. of Plainfield, Oct. 20,
   1839, by Amos Witter, J.P.   3   2
Daniel, s. Ephraim & Artemissa, b. Mar. 15, 1823   2   246
Daniel, m. Fanny **GARDINER**, b. of Plainfield, Aug. 16,
   1827, by Rev. Orin Fowler   2   202
Daniel Colton, b. Mar. 18, 1834   2   246
Dorkis, d. John & Dorkas, b. June 25, 1768   2   66
Dorkis, w. John & d. John & Elizabeth **SPAULDING**, d.
   July 24, 1768, in the 22d y. of her age   2   66
Dorkis, [d. John & Dorkas], d. Jan. 29, 1769   2   66
Ebenezer, m. Grace **ENSWORTH**, Nov. 17, 1768   2   68
Edwin, of Sterling, m. Susan A. **FREEMAN**, of Plainfield,
   May 30, 1852, by Peleg Peckham, Elder   3   75
Electa, d. Aug. 19, 1849, ae. 2   4   62
Electa, d. Aug. 19, 1849, ae. 1   4   64
Elisha, s. Ephraim, farmer, ae. 51, & Artemissa, ae.
   45, of Plainfield, b. Nov. 16, 1847   4   21
Elizabeth H., m. Horace A. **SMITH**, b. of Sterling, May
   21, 1854, by Peleg Peckham, Elder   3   83
Ellen, d. Stephen, farmer, ae. 55, & Emily, ae. 38, b.
   Apr. 21, 1849   4   25
Europa, m. William T. **BUDLONG**, b. of Warwick, R.I.,
   Feb. 2, 1848, by Rev. J. Mather   3   51
Fanny E., m. John **AMES**, Oct. 2, 1849, by William Dyer,
   J.P.   3   60
Fanney E., domestic, ae. 17, of Plainfield, m. John

	Vol.	Page

BENNETT, BENNET, (cont.)
  AMES, carpenter, ae. 21, b. Lyme, Ct., res.
    Plainfield, Oct. 2, 1849, by William Dyer, Esq.   4   6
  George, b. Oct. 11, 1837   2   246
  George W., m. Eliza A. **GALLUP**, Apr. 10, 1842, by
    Lawton Cady, Elder   3   14
  Grafton, of Plainfield, m. Hannah **STODDARD**, of
    Canterbury, June 12, 1828, by Rev. James K.
    Wheelock, of Canterbury   2   206
  Harriet, m. Rawson **PARKIS**, b. of Plainfield, Oct.
    24, 1841, by John Read, Elder   3   11
  Henry, of Hartford, Ohio, m. Abby T. **AVERY**, of Plain-
    field, Sept. 17, 1838, by Rev. Samuel Rockwell   2   236
  Henry (sic) E., ae. 18, of Plainfield, m. John **AMES**,
    carpenter, ae. 23, b. New London, Ct., res.
    Plainfield, Oct. 5, 1849, by W[illia]m Dyer, Esq.
    (Should be "Fanny")   4   5
  Henry H., m. Rebecca T. **PALMER**, b. of Plainfield, May
    11, 1840, by Rev. Samuel Rockwell   3   4
  Hiram, of Plainfield, m. Maryetta **WHEELER**, of Canter-
    bury, Aug. 4, 1833, by Jonathan Goff, J.P.   2   218
  Hiram, m. Sarah **READ**, b. of Plainfield, Feb. 14, 1836,
    by Rev. Samuel Rockwell   2   225
  Isaac Hide, s. Nathan & Lydia, b. Oct. 24, 1778   2   85
  Israel, miller, b. Foster, R.I., res. Plainfield, d.
    Aug. 17, [18]49, ae. 69   4   62
  Israel, farmer, b. Sterling, Ct., res. Plainfield, d.
    Aug. 18, 1849, ae. 69   4   64
  Jacob, laborer, ae. 28, b. Foster, R.I., res. Plain-
    field, m. Lidea **WILSON**, ae. 19, July 20, 1849, by
    [   ]   4   3
  John, m. Dorcas **SPAULDING**, Jan. 22, 1767   2   66
  Jonah H., m. Mary L. **PALMER**, b. of Plainfield, Oct. 9,
    1842, by Peleg Peckham, Elder   3   17
  Joseph, d. Oct. 5, [18]47, ae. 4 y.   4   61
  Joshua, m. Mary **MITCHELL**, b. of Plainfield, Nov. 20,
    1851, by Rev. Joseph P. Brown   3   72
  Leonard R., m. Naomi **MEDBERY**, b. of Plainfield, June
    18, 1854, by Rev. Peter S. Mather   3   84
  Louisa, m. William W. **CADY**, b. of Plainfield, Feb. 20,
    1848, by Rev. Frederic Charlton   3   55
  Louisa, ae. 18, m. William **CADY**, carpenter, ae. 21, b.
    Plainfield, res. Norwich, Feb. 20, 1848, by Rev.
    Frederick Charlton   4   2
  Marcas F., of Sterling, m. Azubah D. **TILLINGHAST**, of
    West Greenwich, R.I., Oct. 12, 1851, by Peleg
    Peckham, Elder   3   72
  Mary, m. Ebenezer **ROBINSON**, Nov. 14, 1749   2   12

	Vol.	Page
BENNETT, BENNET, (cont.)		
Mercy, m. Simon **STEVENS**, June 20, 1751	2	56
Naomy, m. Stephen **HALL**, 3d, Oct. 9, 1783	2	93
Napoleon, s. Josiah H., tavern keeper, ae. 35, & Mary L. Palmer **BENNETT**, ae. 28, b. July 26, 1848	4	23
Nathan, m. Lydia **HIDE**, Mar. 1, 1778	2	82
Olive, of Canterbury, m. George R. **ANDREW**, of Plainfield, Oct. 20, 1822, by Jonathan Gallup, J.P., Canterbury	2	189
Sarah, b. Canterbury, res. Plainfield, d. July 31, [18]48, ae. 58	4	61
Silvester H., m. Martha **COOPER**, Oct. 5, 1834, by Peleg Peckman, Elder	2	219
Stephen, Jr., of Plainfield, m. Emily **MORGAN**, of Lisbon, Aug. 7, 1831, by J. Gordon, J.P.	2	214
Stephen Napoleon, b. Mar. 19, 1832	2	246
Waterman, s. Ebenezer & Grace, b. May 21, 1775	2	81
W[illia]m D., of Plainfield, m. Eliza M. **GRISWOLD**, of Griswold, Oct. 2, 1850, by Rev. Joseph P. Brown	3	67
W[illia]m D., farmer, ae. 21, of Plainfield, m. Eliza M. **GRISWOLD**, cotton mill, ae. 20, of Plainfield, Oct. 20, 1850, by Rev. Joseph P. Brown	4	7
-----, child of Daniel, woolen tender, ae. 26, & Ann Day **BENNETT**, ae. 24, b. July 6, 1848	4	23
-----, d. Jeriah H., hotel keeper, ae. 37, & Louisa, ae. 30, b. July 7, 1850	4	30
BENSON, Susan S., m. Jared **HALL**, b. of Plainfild, Nov. 12, 1854, by Rev. Joseph P. Brown	3	87
BENTLEY, Gardiner, m. Mary M. **DENISON**, b. of Plainfield, Jan. 7, 1852, by Rev. Sidney Dean	3	73
BETTY, Sarah Ann, m. Jonathan **SALISBURY**, b. of Scituate, R.I., Sept. 24, 1854, by Benjamin Bacon, J.P.	3	86
BILL, Benjamin J., s. Jeptha, farmer, ae. 27, & Prudence L., ae. 30, b. Aug. 24, 1850	4	31
BILLINGS, Anne, m. Simon **SPAULDING**, June 1, 1737	2	9
Debra, m. Isaiah **WILLIAMS**, Aug. 8, 1725	1	56
BINGHAM, Eliphalet, m. Sarah **UNDERWOOD**, Nov. 25, 1761	2	52
Gurdon, m. Lucy **HOVEY**, Mar. 20, 1788	2	98
Mary, d. Eliphalet & Sarah, b. May 1, 1762	2	52
BISHOP, Cyrus, of Canterbury, m. Eliza D. **LEWIS**, of Plainfield, Jan. 2, 1851, by Rev. Henry Robinson	3	68
Cyrus, of N.Y., m. Eliza D. **LEWIS**, Jan. 2, 1851, by H. Robinson	4	7
BISSELL, Harriet M., m. William H.R. **WHITMORE**, b. of Warwick, R.I., Feb. 2, 1848, by Rev. J. Mather	3	51
BLAKE, Anna, m. William **ROBINSON**, May 13, 1762	2	60
BLIVEN, Sarah, m. John Dalton **PETER**, Feb. 5, 1804	2	109

PLAINFIELD VITAL RECORDS 101

	Vol.	Page
BLODGETT, BLOGGET, BLOGGETT, Alden W., of Stafford, m. Lucinday C. **HAWKINS**, of Sterling, Sept. 2, 1844, by Peleg Peckham, Elder	3	24
Ama, m. Joshua **WHITNEY**, Jr., about the 8th of Apr., 1743	2	5
Ame, d. William & Sarah, b. Feb. 16, 1723/4	1	29
Benjamin, s. William & Sarah, b. May 17, 1717	1	17
Esther, m. Ezekiel **PIERCE**, Jr., July 8, 1749	2	20
Hester, d. William & Sarah, b. June 2, 1730	1	51
Hester, d. William & Sarah, b. June 2, 1730	1	58
Mary, d. William & Sarah, b. June 13, 1721	1	24
Sarah, w. Dr. William, d. Jan. 14, 1735/6	1	64
Tace, d. William & Sarah, b. June 9, 1727	1	45
William, m. Sarah **SPAULDING**, wid. of Benjamin, Jr., Aug. 18, 1714	1	14
William, s. William & Sarah, b. May 20, 1715	1	14
William, m. Mehetable **STEEVENS***, Mar. 31, 1737 (*Note at bottom of page of original manuscript states: "Wm. Blodgett's widow is referred to as widow of Samuel **STERRY** in probate files of Blodgett estate")	1	68
BLUNT, Andres, s. John & Neomey, b. June 6, 1738	1	97
Ezakiel, s. Sam[ue]ll & Elizabeth, b. July 29, 1727	1	42
John, m. Neomey **LOVEJOYE**, May 1, 1734	1	64
John, s. John & Neomey, b. Nov. 13, 1734	1	64
John, s. John & Neomey, b. Oct. 6, 1736	1	66
Lidah, d. Samuel & Elisabeth, b. June 8, 1724	1	30
Mary, d. Sam[ue]ll & Elisabeth, b. Oct. 14, 1721	1	25
Samuel, s. Sam[ue]ll & Elisabeth, b. Oct. 9, 1716	1	16
Sarah, d. Samuell & Elisabeth, b. Oct. 29, 1718	1	19
BOESSELLE, Nicholas, m. Julia **MURPHY**, b. of Plainfield, Aug. 13, 1854, by Rev. Henry Robinson	3	84
BOMAN, [see also **BOOMAN**], Phebe, m. James **MAXWELL**, Dec. 18, 1799	2	117
BOOKER, -----, d. Isaac, laborer, b. June 26, 1851	4	31
BOOMAN, [see also **BOMAN**], Rosella, m. Ephraim **SAFFORD**, b. of Canterbury, Dec. 19, 1839, by Rev. Tubal Wakefield	3	3
BOSS, [see also **BASS**], John, of West Greenwich, R.I., m. Edelia G. **SPRAGUE**, of Plainfield, Jan. 30, 1825, by Orin Fowler, V.D.M.	2	197
Sarah, d. Fenner L., cotton manufacturer, of Plainfield, b. Aug. 25, 1850	4	32
BOSTON, BOSTEN, Nanney, d. Ceazer & Dorcas, b. Jan. 27, 1789	2	99
Ruth, d. Ceazer & Dorcas, b. Sept. 27, 1795	2	103
BOSWORTH, Sanford, of Ashford, m. M. **BUGBEE**, of Plainfield,		

	Vol.	Page
BOSWORTH, (cont.)		
Oct. 8, 1839, by Rev. Tubal Wakefield, Packersville	2	248
Sanford, of Ashford, m. Mary **BUGBEE**, of Plainfield, Oct. 4, 1839, by Rev. Tubal Wakefield	3	1
BOTTOM, BOTTUM, John, m. Fanny **HOPKINS**, June 14, 1801	2	109
Rebecca, m. as 2d w., Oliver **SPAULDING**, May 9, 1784	2	94
Rebecca, m. William **SWANSBROUGH**, June 26, 1794	2	100
William Davis, s. John & Fanny, b. Apr. 2, 1802	2	109
BOVEY*, John, farmer, b. Ireland, d. Oct. 4, 1849, ae. 20 (*Perhaps **ROONEY**)	4	63
BOWEN, Alfred, manufacturer, res. Griswold, m. Mary A. **NORTH[R]UP**, b. Griswold, res. Plainfield, Nov. [ ], 1848, by Frederick Charlton	4	4
Rebecca, of Warwick, m. Allen E. **KEECH**, May 19, 1845, by James Smither, Elder	3	30
Sarah V., teacher, d. Oct. 17, 1848, ae. 22	4	62
BOWMAN,[see under **BOMAN** and **BOOMAN**]		
BOYD, BOYDE, BOID, Abraham, s. William & Jane, b. Dec. 25, 1739	2	62
Abraham, m. Mercy **HALL**, Dec. 11, 1761	2	62
Elizabeth, d. William & Jane, b. Sept. 11, 1743	2	62
Elizabeth, d. Abraham & Mercy, b. Oct. 5, 1762	2	62
James, s. Joseph & Katharine, b. May 8, 1751	2	6
Jean, d. William & Jane, b. Feb. 20, 1745	2	62
Jenne, m. Timothy **CORY**, Mar. 6, 1764	2	64
John, s. Joseph & Caite, b. Nov. 10, 1748	2	6
Joseph, s. Mary, b. Nov. 5, 1760	2	90
Katharine, m. William **TURNER**, Feb. 7, 1759	2	42
Mary, d. William & Jane, b. Jan. 22, 1735	2	62
Mary had s. Joseph **STUART**, b. Feb. 10, 1760	2	62
Meriam, d. William & Jane, b. Mar. 17, 1741	2	62
Phebe, d. Joseph & Catharine, b. Jan. 6, 1754	2	23
Robert, s. William & Jane, b. Oct. 25, 1737	2	62
Robert, s. William & Jane, d. Feb. 20, 1759	2	62
BOYDEN, Henry, m. Amey **SIMMONS**, Sept. 14, 1806	2	114
BOYLE, Hannah, m. Thomas **GIST**, b. of Plainfield, Sept. 27, 1852, by Rev. Henry Robinson	3	76
BRADFORD, Edward Anthony, s. Henry & Lois, b. Sept. 27, 1813	2	138
Geo[rge] P., b. New Orleans, res. Plainfield, d. June 27, 1851, ae. 5 m.	4	66
George Partridge, s. Henry & Lois, b. Apr. 2, 1809	2	138
Hannah, m. Willard **SPAULDING**, Feb. 20, 1745	2	13
Henry, m. Lois **EATON**, b. of Plainfield, Nov. 3, 1805, by Rev. Joel Benedict	2	197
James Thomas, s. Henry & Lois, b. Oct. 13, 1806	2	138

	Vol.	Page
BRADFORD, (cont.)		
Olive Douglass, d. Henry & Lois, b. Nov. 29, 1819	2	139
Sarah E., of Plainfield, m. T. Willis **PRATT**, of Norwich, June 4, 1840, by Rev. Samuel Rockwell	3	6
Sarah Eaton, d. Henry & Lois, b. July 2, 1816	2	139
William Douglass, s. Henry & Lois, b. Sept. 3, 1811	2	138
BRADHURST, Hannah, d. Ralph & Hannah, of Old Roxbury, m. Timothy **PEARCE**, Oct. 12, 1709	1	8
BRAINARD, Pamalie M., m. Jesse **ROOD**, b. of Killingly, [probably Sept.] 21, 1842, by Rev. A.B. Wheeler	3	17
William, of Killingly, m. Mary Jane **WHIPPLE**, of Cumberland, R.I., June 25, 1854, by Rev. E. Loomis	3	83
BRAMIN, Amelia, of Plainfield, m. Giles H. **PEABODY**, of Stonington, May 10, 1841, by Rev. Thomas Barber	3	10
BRANCH, Amos, s. Capt. Moses & Abigail, b. Oct. 13, 1776	2	89
Elisha, m. Rebecca **DOUGLASS**, Sept. 4, 1791	2	98
Stephen, b. R.I., res. R.I., d. May 27, 1851, ae. 62	4	66
Temperance, of Preston, m. William **PHILLIPS**, of Plainfield, Feb. 4, 1748/9, by Hezekiah Lord, Clerk	2	8
BRAND, Edward, s. John, laborer, b. June [ ], 1851	4	31
BRAYTON, Caleb F., of Cranston, R.I., m. Marian **PAINE**, of Plainfield, July 8, 1838, by Rev. Samuel Rockwell	2	235
William W., of Scituate, R.I., m. Amanda M.F. **DAWLEY**, of Coventry, R.I., Nov. 3, 1852, by Peleg Peckham, Elder	3	76
BREN[N]ON, Martin, of Ross County of Ross Commons, Ireland, m. Lucinda **KEMP**, of Plainfield, May 22, 1838, by Rev. Samuel Rockwell	2	234
BREWER, Charles H., of Norwich, m. Martha L. **WITTER**, of Plainfield, Sept. 30, 1847, by Rev. Henry Robinson	3	45
BRICE, -----, s. David, laborer, ae. 30, & Maria, ae. 26, b. Aug. 17, 1848	4	27
BRIGGS, BRIGS, Almira C., of Coventry, R.I., m. Edwin T. **BRIGGS**, of Scituate, R.I., Sept. 30, 1849, by Rev. Joseph P. Brown	3	60
Asher, of Plainfield, m. Eliza **PARKS**, of Sterling, Feb. 8, 1835, by Peleg Peckham, Elder	2	220
Benjamin, m. Huldah **ABBETT**, June 24, 1847, by Peleg Peckham, Elder	3	44
Caroline, of Sterling, m. Nelson **FRENCH**, of Plainfield, Sept. 6, 1852, by Rev. Henry Robinson	3	76
Clarrissa, m. Robert **KENNEDY**, b. of Plainfield, Mar. 29, 1843, by Rev. A. Dunning	3	18
Daniel, farmer, ae. 42, of Voluntown, Ct., m. 2d w. Lucretia **PARKIS**, domestic, ae. 36, b. Canterbury, res. Plainfield, July 4, 1850, by Rev. John Lovejoy	4	6

	Vol.	Page
BRIGGS, BRIGS, (cont.)		
Edwin T., of Scituate, R.I., m. Almira C. **BRIGGS**, of Coventry, R.I., Sept. 30, 1849, by Rev. Joseph P. Brown	3	60
Emma, of Plainfield, m. Andrew M. **DORRANCE**, of New York, Dec. 23, 1844, by V. R. Osborn, V.D.M.	3	26
Emma, d. William, farmer, ae. 34, & Ruth, ae. 23, b. June 21, 1848	4	22
George, merchant, d. Dec. 1, 1848, ae. 31	4	63
Harriet N., m. John T. **CAPRON**, b. of Warwick, R.I., Dec. 14, 1845, by Rev. Tho[ma]s Dowling, of N. Lyme	3	33
Martin, carpenter, b. Griswold, res. Plainfield, d. June 20, [18]48, ae. 19	4	61
Mary Ann, ae. 25, of Sterling, m. Albert **FRINK**, farmer, ae. 29, b. Plainfield, Ct., res. Sterling, Nov. 8, 1848, by Rev. Allen	4	3
Silvester H., m. Fanny **WILLIAMS**, b. of Plainfield, Apr. 1, 1832, by Peleg Peckham, Elder	2	215
BRISHNELL, Esther S., ae. 25, b. Stafford, res. Plainfield, m. William **WILCOX**, manufacturer, ae. 26, b. Lisbon, res. Norwich, Feb. [ ], 1848, by Rev. Benton	4	1
BROCKWAY, Ebenezer D., of Lyme, m. Mary C. **ROBINSON**, of Plainfield, July 14, 1840, by Rev. Samuel Rockwell	3	6
BROWN, Albert, m. Rachel **TRUESDELL**, b. of Killingly, Nov. 10, 1844, by James Smither, Elder	3	28
Barbara, m. Christopher M. **GREEN**, b. of Plainfield, Nov. 23, 1823, by Orin Fowler, V.D.M.	2	192
Charles, bank clerk, ae. 25, of Norwich, m. Martha L. **WITTER**, ae. 18, b. Plainfield, Sept. 30, 1847, by Rev. Henry Robinson	4	1
Cha[rle]s Frederic, s. Prince, black, laborer, ae. 43, & C[h]loe, black, ae. 33, b. May 13, 1849	4	25
Dorcas C., m. William H. **BUTLER**, Sept. 27, 1847, by Peleg Peckham, Elder	3	53
Eleazer, m. Sarah **GURDON**, Oct. 10, 1728	1	48
Eliza, m. Joseph **WYLIE**, b. of Plainfield, May 18, 1845, by James Smither, Elder	3	29
Elizabeth, of Plainfield, m. Walter **WILSON**, of Providence, R.I., Sept. 5, 1848, by Rev. Frederic Charlton	3	55
Elizabeth, ae. 21, b. Plainfield, res. Providence, R.I., m. Walter **WILSON**, butcher, ae. 26, b. Plainfield, res. Providence, R.I., Sept. 17, 1848, by Rev. Frederic Charlton	4	3
Gurdon P., m. Esther **DEAN**, b. of Plainfield, June 16, 1822, by Orin Fowler, V.D.M.	2	187
John, s. Zebulon & Tabatha, b. Dec. 5, 1745	2	58

	Vol.	Page
BROWN, (cont.)		
Judah, m. Ebenezer **WILLIAMS**, May 14, 1723	1	29
Leonard A., of Killingly, m. Roba **GRIFFIN**, of Sterling, May 4, 1848, by Peleg Peckham, Elder	3	51
Louisa, ae. 24, b. Chester, Mass, res. Plainfield, m. Albert C. **GREEN**, farmer, ae. 26, by W. Greenwich, R.I., res. Plainfield, Aug. 1, 1849, by Rev. H. Robinson	4	3
Lowes, d. Ebenezer & Sarah, b. July 20, 1729	1	48
Lucinda, m. Caleb **HERRINGTON**, b. of Killingly, Apr. 17, 1836, by Chester Tilden	2	226
Lydia, m. Daniel **HEFFERLOW**, Nov. 28, 1841, by Rev. John Read	3	12
Martha R., m. Pashal P. **TIDD**, July 14, 1844, by William Dyer, J.P.	3	24
Mary Louisa, ae. 16, b. Lisbon, res. Plainfield, m. Charles **WEAVER**, laborer, ae. 24, b. Plainfield, June 10, 1849, by Amos Witter, Esq.	4	3
Millard S., d. Frederick S., farmer, ae. 46, & Lydia, ae. 36, of Canterbury, b. Sept. 29, 1850	4	31
Orilla, m. William **OLIN**, Jr., b. of Plainfield, Feb. 18, 1839, by Rev. Tubal Wakefield	2	239
Phebe, b. Stonington, res. Plainfield, d. Mar. 6, 1850, ae. 84	4	64
Prince D., m. Chloe **BANNAH**, b. of Plainfield, Oct. 20, 1839, by Amos Witter, J.P.	2	249
Prince D., m. Chloe **BENNET**, b. of Plainfield, Oct. 20, 1839, by Amos Witter, J.P.	3	2
Rhoda Ann, m. Asa **PHILLIPS**, b. of Plainfield, Dec. 13, 1846, by Rev. A. Dunning	3	41
Roba, m. Obed **DAVIS**, b. of Plainfield, Mar. 20, 1823, by Rev. Orin Fowler	2	190
Robert, 2d, Capt., m. Ann Maria **NOYES**, b. of Westerly, R.I., Apr. 4, 1831, by Rev. Orin Fowler	2	213
Ruth, d. Zebulon & Tabatha, b. June 5, 1743	2	58
Susan, cotton weaver, ae. 56, b. Ireland, res. Plainfield, m. 2d h. Abner **FRENCH**, farmer, ae. 59, of Plainfield, Dec. 14, 1850, by Rev. Joseph P. Brown	4	7
Susan, m. Abner **FRENCH**, b. of Plainfield, Dec. 15, 1850, by Rev. Joseph P. Brown	3	68
Tabatha, m. Jonas **WHEELER**, Mar. 12, 1756	2	44
Tabatha, m. Jonas **WHELER**, [ ]	2	43
BROWNELL, Phebe, of Smithfield, R.I., m. Horace **COLVIN**, of Warwick, R.I., Oct. 5, 1847, by Rev. J. Mather	3	46
BROWNING, Emily, cotton weaver, b. Ireland, res. Plainfield, d. Aug. 30, 1847, ae. 23	4	61
BROWNLEE, Frederick, s. Robert Prescilla, b. Mar. 15, 1752	2	20

	Vol.	Page
BROWNLEE, (cont.)		
Priscilla, d. Robert & Priscilla, b. July 27, 1755	2	30
Robert, m. Prescilla **MARSH**, Jan. 5, 1752	2	20
William, s. Robert & Prescilla, b. Sept. 3, 1753	2	23
BRUCE, Artemas S., of Pomfret, m. Freelove M. **KENYON**, of Plainfield, Mar. 28, 1848, by Rev. James Mather	3	54
David, m. Agnis **PON**, b. of Plainfield, Nov. 27, 1853, by Rev. William Turkington	3	81
Arastus S., of Pomfret, m. Amey A. **FRENCH**, of Plainfield, Nov. 18, 1850, by Rev. Joseph P. Brown (Erastus)	3	67
Erastus L., farmer, ae. 32, of Pomfret, m. Amy A. **FRENCH**, woolen weaver, ae. 27, of Plainfield, Nov. 18, 1850, by Rev. Joseph P. Brown	4	7
Melessent F., of Plainfield, m. Albert W. **BAKER**, of Mobile, Nov. 28, 1852, by Rev. William Turkington	3	77
BRUMLEY, Calista C., d. Amos G., farmer, ae. 41, & Eliza A., ae. 29, b. Nov. 2, 1850	4	31
BRYAN, Patrick, gate tender, b. Ireland, res. Plainfield, d. Aug. 12, [18]48, ae. 55	4	61
BRYANT, Reuben, farmer, d. Nov. [ ], 1850, ae. 90	4	66
BUCK, Emiline E., m. Albert **GODFREE**, b. of Plainfield, Feb. 28, 1837, by Rev. Samuel Rockwell	2	230
BUCKLIN, Alpha M., m. Jeremiah E. **FULLER**, b. of Sterling, Dec. 8, 1835, by Peleg Peckham, Elder	2	224
BUDLONG, William T., m. Europa **BENNETT**, b. of Warwick, R.I., Feb. 2, 1848, by Rev. J. Mather	3	51
BUGBEE, Alonzo Comerral, s. Chester & Phebe, b. Aug. 7, 1822	2	164
Caroline, m. John G. **KNOX**, b. of Plainfield, Aug. 27, 1848, by Rev. Frederic Charlton	3	55
Danforth Cemerrold*, s. Chester & Phebe, b. June 12, 1830 (*correction Cemarral handwritten in margin of original manuscript)	2	246
George Edgar, s. Chester & Phebe, b. June 4, 1826	2	246
Lucetta Ellen, d. Chester & Phebe, b. Sept. 14, 1824	2	164
M. of Plainfield, m. Sanford **BOSWORTH**, of Ashford, Oct. 8, 1839, by Rev. Tubal Wakefield, Packersville	2	248
Mary, of Plainfield, m. Sanford **BOSWORTH**, of Ashford, Oct. 4, 1839, by Rev. Tubal Wakefield	3	1
William Pitt, s. Chester & Phebe, b. Mar. 27, 1828	2	246
BULLOCK, Samuel, m. Abby E. **BARTLETT**, b. of Providence, R.I., Sept. 30, 1839, by Rev. Tubal Wakefield	2	248
Samuel, m. Abby E. **BARTLETT**, b. of Providence, R.I., Sept. 30, 1839, by Rev. Tubal Wakefield	3	1
BUMP, Bethiah, m. Peleg **BALLARD**, Aug. 23, 1721	1	53
Jemimah, d. Philip, of Plainfield, m. Thomas **SMITH**, May 9, 1706	1	4

	Vol.	Page
BUMP, (cont.)		
Phillip, d. Jan. 20, 1724/5	1	34
William, s. Phillip & Marcy, b. Oct. 26, 1723	1	34
BURDEN, BURDIN, Betsey, m. Geo[rge] **WEAVER**, b. of Plainfield, Oct. 31, 1847, by Rev. Fred[eri]c Charlton	3	49
Innocent, d. Joseph & Bethany, b. July 23, 1781	2	89
Israel, s. Joseph & Bethany, b. Feb. 18, 1786	2	97
Nancy, d. Joseph & Bethany, b. Nov. 28, 1784	2	89
BURDICK, Betsey, ae. 19, b. Brooklyn, res. Plainfield, m. George **WEAVER**, laborer, ae. 21, b. Dudley, Mass., res. Providence, Oct. 30, [18]48, by Rev. Frederic Charlton	4	1
Caroline, cotton operator, ae. 17, b. Sterling, res. R.I., m. Flavell **RANDALL**, laborer, ae. 22, b. Sterling, res. R.I., Apr. [1849?]	4	6
Geroge W., m. Minerva **HILL**, b. of Griswold, [ ] 24, 1853, by Rev. Alfred Gates	3	77
Joel, m. Mary A. **TILLINGHAST**, Feb. 19, 1847, by Rev. Fred[eri]c Charlton	3	48
Joel, of Griswold, m. Marcelia **LYON**, of Plainfield, Jan. 6, 1850, by Rev. W. Emerson	3	63
Joel, master weaver, ae. 25, b. Voluntown, res. Griswold, m. Marcelia **LYON**, cotton weaver, ae. 21, b. [S]cituate, res. Griswold, Jan. 6, 1850, by Rev. Warren Emerson	4	6
Lucy, d. Thomas & Molly, b. July 31, 1815	2	138
Matilda, of Plainfield, m. Thomas J. **PRENTICE**, of Gardner, Mass., Jan 19, 1852, by Rev. Henry Robinson	3	73
Polly, m. Thomas Dow **GALLUP**, of Plainfield, Feb. 28, 1816, by Joseph Easton, J.P.	2	131
Sarah, of Plainfield, m. Jeremiah **STONE**, of West Killingly, Jan. 16, 1848, by Rev. James Mather	3	50
Sarah J., b. Killingly, m. Jeremiah **STONE**, mechanic, of Killingly, Feb. [ ], 1848, by Rev. James Mathew	4	2
Susan, d. Thomas & Molly, b. July 1, 1813	2	138
BURGESS, BURGES, Ase, s. Joseph & Mehetibell, b. Dec. 10, 1756	2	35
Charles, s. Joseph & Mehetibell, b. Nov. 7, 1760	2	35
Daniel, s. Nathan & Sally, b. June 25, 1803	2	124
Daniel, of Hartford, m. Paulina L. **DEAN**, of Plainfield, Mar. 12, 1827, by Orin Fowler, V.D.M.	2	201
Harriet Frances, d. Morey & Martha, b. Feb. 14, 1818	2	139
Harriet T., of Plainfield, m. John B. **AMES**, of Providence, R.I., May 13, 1840, by Rev. Samuel Rockwell	3	4
Harry, s. Nathan & Sally, b. Apr. 30, 1801	2	124

	Vol.	Page
BURGESS, BURGES, (cont.)		
Horace, s. Morey & Martha, b. May 14, 1824	2	139
Janette, m. [ ] **FULLER**, apothecary, of Hartford, June [ ], 1848, by Rev. Frederic Charlton	4	2
Janett, m. William J. **FULLER**, b. of Hartford, May 1, 1848, by Rev. Frederic Charlton	3	55
Jared W., of Plainfield, m. Mary E. **ROBINSON**, of Sterling, Oct. 13, 1852, by Peleg Peckham, Elder	3	76
Jesse, s. Joseph & Mehetibell, b. Dec. 22, 1758	2	35
John, s. Morey & Martha, b. Nov. 28, 1820	2	139
Joseph, m. Mehetabell **SHEPHARD**, Mar. 21, 1756	2	35
Julia, d. Nathan & Sally, b. Mar. 16, 1808	2	124
Lydia, d. Joseph & Mehetabell, b. Dec. 27, 1762	2	52
Lydia, of Plainfield, m. Orin D. **KING**, of Scituate, R.I., Sept. 29, 1828, by Rev. Orin Fowler	2	207
Matilda, m. Hyram W. **POTTER**, of Scituate, R.I., May 19, 1828, by Rev. Orin Fowler	2	205
Nathan, of Plainfield, m. Sophia **SCOTT**, of Coventry, R.I., Sept. 19, 1824, by John Dunlap, J.P.	2	196
Nathan, Capt., d. Aug. 10, 1825, ae. 45 y.	2	139
Nathan G., s. Nathan & Sally, b. Oct. 26, 1813	2	138
Sally, w. Capt. Nathan, d. Apr. 26, 1824	2	139
Sally G., d. Nathan & Sally, b. Mar. 24, 1824	2	139
Sarah, m. Erastus L. **PRIOR**, Feb. 6, 1841, by Rev. John Read	3	13
Sarah, of Plainfield, m. Zebulon **WHIPPLE**, of Providence, R.I., June 1, 1852, by Rev. Joseph P. Brown	3	75
Susan G., m. William **DYER**, b. of Plainfield, Oct. 19, 1835, by Rev. Otis G. Whiton, of Canterbury, Canterbury	2	222
Susan Green, d. Morey & Martha, b. Sept. 29, 1816	2	139
Thankfull, m. Jacob **SPAULDING**, Nov. 27, 1760	2	45
BURIL, Sarah Ann, dressmaker, black, b. Clayville, R.I., res. Plainfield, d. July 9, [18]49, ae. 21	4	62
BURLEIGH, Charles Collister, s. Rinaldo & Lydia, b. Nov. 3, 1810	2	138
Cyrus Moses, s. Rinaldo & Lydia, b. Feb. 8, 1820	2	138
Frances Mary Bradford, d. Rinaldo & Lydia, b. Apr. 7, 1807	2	138
George, s. Rinoldo & Lydia, b. Mar. 26, 1821	2	138
John Oscar, s. Rinaldo & Lydia, b. June 8, 1809	2	138
Lucian, s. Rinaldo & Lydia, b. Dec. 3, 1817	2	138
Theresa W., d. Charles C., lecturer, & Gertrude R., b. July 9, 1851	4	31
William Henry, s. Rinaldo & Lydia, b. Feb. 2, 1812, at Woodstock, Conn.	2	138
-----, child of Lucian, farmer, & Elizabeth, b. July		

	Vol.	Page
BURLEIGH, (cont.)		
28, 1848	4	21
BURLESON, Allen J., m. Harriet A. **WESTCOTT**, b. of Plainfield, May 23, 1836, by Chester Tilden	2	226
Clarrissa C., of Plainfield, m. William **HOLT**, of Oxford, Mass., July 15, 1839, by Rev. Thomas Barber	2	243
Oliver, d. Feb. [ ], 1850, ae. 65	4	66
BURLINGAME, George W., of Warwick, R.I., m. Miranda **HENRY**, of Coventry, Mar. 13, 1845, by James Smither, Elder	3	29
Harriet, d. Thomas, painter, ae. 34, & Hannah, ae. 33, b. Sept. 16, 1850	4	31
James P., of Worcester, Mass., m. Hannah **HOOD**, of Plainfield, Mar. 2, 1845, by V.R. Osborn, V.D.M.	3	27
Mary E., m. Frances **CAMPBELL**, b. of Plainfield, Sept. 12, 1848, by Rev. George W. Brewster	3	56
BURNET, John, of Windham, m. Abigail **HARRINGTON**, of Plainfield, Feb. 29, 1824, by Rev. Roswell Whitmore	2	193
BURNS, Joseph E., s. Joseph, mule spinner, ae. 33, & Mary, ae. 32, b. May 13, 1850	4	30
BURR, Elvira T., d. Thomas, weaver, & Lucinda, b. Feb. 1, 1849	4	25
BURRILL, [see under **BURIL**]		
BURTON, Elizabeth, of Preston, m. John **DOW**, Mar. 8, 1764	2	60
Elizabeth, m. John **DOW**, Jr., b. of Plainfield, Dec. 12, 1802, by Anthony Bradford, J.P.	2	111
BUSHNELL, Susan, Mrs., domestic, b. Sterling, res. Plainfield, d. July 9, 1850, ae. 69	4	64
BUTCHER, Joseph, of England, now residing in Plainfield, m. Polly **WHEELER**, of Plainfield, Mar. 21, 1833, by Peleg Peckham, Elder	2	217
Martha, wid., m. William **PHILLIPS**, b. of Plainfield, Mar. 31, 1833, by Rev. Benjamin Paine	2	216
BUTLER, Caroline H., of Plainfield, m. Edward **BUTLER**, of Boston, Mass., Sept. 22, 1822, by Orin Fowler, V.D.M.	2	188
Desire, d. Zacheas & Content, b. June 13, 1764	2	51
Edward, of Boston, Mass., m. Caroline H. **BUTLER**, of Plainfield, Sept. 22, 1822, by Orin Fowler, V.D.M.	2	188
Hannah, s. Nathaniel & Christoble, b. Apr. 22, 1762	2	58
Nathaniel, m. Christable **PARKE**, Oct. 1, 1761	2	58
Sarah, d. Nathaniel & Christoble, b. Mar. 20, 1764	2	58
Sybel*, of Canterbury, m. Balanea **BAKER**, of Thompson, Oct. 20, 1839, by Rev. Tubal Wakefield (*Correction **BUTTON** written in original manuscript)	2	248
William H., m. Dorcas C. **BROWN**, Sept. 27, 1847, by Peleg Peckham, Elder	3	53
BUTTERFIELD, Pheby, d. Samuell, of Chelmsford, m. John		

	Vol.	Page
BUTTERFIELD, (cont.)		
HOW[E], Apr. 13, 1709	1	9
BUTTON, Abegel, d. Matthias, m. Felix **POWEL**, Apr. [ ], 1724	1	30
Berredell, d. Daniel & Anna, b. Sept. 25, 1721	1	26
Biall, d. Matthias & Han[n]ah, b. Mar. 22, 1718/19	1	21
Daniel, m. Anna **BELL**, Oct. 1, 1716	1	25
Deliverance, s. Peter & Hannah, b. Oct. 7, 1734	1	67
Elias, s. Daniel & Anna, b. Apr. 27, 1720	1	25
Han[n]ah, d. Matthias & Han[n]ah, b. Sept. 24, 1717	1	21
John, s. Matthias & Mary, b. June 22, 1698; d. Apr. 29, 1700	1	1
John, s. Daniel & Anna, b. Nov. 7, 1717	1	25
Matthias, s. Peter & Hannah, b. July 29, 1730	1	67
Peter, m. Hannah **CLEAVELAND**, Oct. 11, 1729	1	67
Sarah, d. Matthias & Mary, b. Apr. 8, 1695	1	1
Sarah, d. of Matthias, m. William **MARSH**, s. of William, Mar. 2, 1712/13	1	14
Sarah J., m. Elijah **GREEN**, b. of Canterbury, Nov. 24, 1853, by Rev. Alfred Gates	3	82
Sybel, of Canterbury, m. Balenea **BAKER**, of Plainfield, Oct. 20, 1839, by Rev. Tubal Wakefield (*"also 248" handwritten in margin of original manuscript)	3	1*
William, s. Peter & Hannah, b. Feb. 8, 1732/3	1	67
Zerviah, d. Matthias & Mary, b. Sept. 13, 1708	1	6
BUTTS, Hollis, of Canterbury, m. Rebecca **HOPKINS**, of Plainfield, Aug. 31, 1828, by Nathaniel Cole, Elder	2	206
Polly, of Plainfield, m. [ ] **HIDE**, of Sterling, June 11, 1831, by Peleg Peckham, Elder	2	213
CADY, Abigail, d. Elijah & Dinah, b. May 14, 1749	2	46
Abijah, m. Allice **NICHOLS**, Aug. 24, 1749, by Samuel Dorrance, M.	2	11
Abijah, m. Meriam **WILLSON**, May 24, 1763	2	54
Adeline, d. Sept. 17, 1850, ae. 4 y.	4	66
Alexander, s. George A., farmer, ae. 30, & Lydia E., ae. 32, b. June 18, 1848	4	24
Alexander, d. Sept. 19, 1850, ae. 2	4	66
Bennajah, m. Mary **NICHOLS**, Jan. 11, 1747/8	2	6
Charles Tillinghast Johnson, s. John & Susan J., b. July 11, 1830, at West Greenwich, R.I.	2	140
Curtis, s. Elijah & Dinah, b. June 30, 1755	2	46
Edwin, of Brooklyn, m. Roby **CASE**, of Plainfield, Oct. 9, 1823, by Nathaniel Cole, Elder	2	192
Edwin, of Brooklyn, m. Lydia **COLE**, of Plainfield, Apr. 9, 1827, by Nathaniel Cole, Elder	2	201
Eleazer, m. Keziah **SPAULDING**, Oct. 28, 1739	2	36
Elias, s. Elijah & Dinah, b. Mar. 21, 1743	2	46
Elijah, s. Elijah & Dinah, b. Nov. 1, 1747	2	46

PLAINFIELD VITAL RECORDS

	Vol.	Page
CADY, (cont.)		
Ellis, d. A[a]ron & Annah, b. June 16, 1752	2	21
Else, w. Abijah, d. Nov. 7, 1751	2	34
Emor J., d. George, farmer, b. Mar. 9, 1851	4	32
Frances Maria, d. John & Susan, b. Nov. 11, 1828, at West Greenwich, R.I.	2	140
George, s. Squire & Thankful, b. Jan. 24, 1795	2	106
George A., m. Lydia E. **KENYON**, b. of Plainfield, Apr. 3, 1842, by Peleg Peckham, Elder	3	14
Gideon, m. Mary E. **WHITING**, May 11, 1851, by John J. Penrose, J.P.	3	69
Harriet, d. Sept. 25, 1850, ae. 6	4	66
James, of Thompson, m. Caroline E. **BAILEY**, of Plainfield, June 6, 1842, by Andrew Dunning	3	16
Jere, s. Jeremiah & Abigail, b. Apr. 12, 1761	2	56
Jeremiah, s. William & Phebe, b. Oct. 17, 1731	1	55
Jeremiah, m. Abigail **LAWRENCE**, Jan. 8, 1755	2	32
Joanne, m. Timothy **PARKHURST**, Jr., Mar. 25, 1757	2	64
John, s. Eleazer & Keziah, b. May 16, 1744	2	36
John, s. Jeremiah & Abigail, b. Feb. 2, 1765	2	56
John, s. Abijah & Meriam, b. Sept. 6, 1765	2	54
John, s. Squire & Thankful, b. Oct. 30, 1792	2	106
John, of West Greenwich, R.I., m. Susan J. **CADY**, of Providence, R.I., Oct. 31, 1827, b. [ ] Kent, Elder, in Providence	2	213
Joseph, school teacher, d. Sept. 19, 1850, ae. 26	4	66
Lucey, d. Eleazer & Keziah, b. Apr. 11, 1742	2	36
Lucy, d. Squire & Thankful, b. Dec. 3, 1790	2	106
Lucy, of Plainfield, m. William Shaw **EDDY**, of Middleborough, Mass., Dec. 19, 1819, by Rev. Roswell Whitmore	2	188
Lydia, m. William **WILLIAMS**, b. of Plainfield, Apr. 8, 1764, by Alex[ande]r Miller, V.D.M.	2	54
Lydia, d. Jeremiah & Abigail, b. Oct. 31, 1767	2	56
Maria, d. Squire & Abiah, b. July 16, 1808	2	117
Maria, of Plainfield, m. Otis T. **COBB**, of Amhurst, Mass., Sept. 16, 1833, by Rev. Samuel Rockwell	2	218
Maria, of Plainfield, m. Otis T. **COBB**, of Amhurst, Mass., Sept. 16, 1833, by Rev. Samuel Rockwell	3	35
Mary, w. Benajah, d. Jan. 2, 1750/51	2	6
May, m. Isaac **PARKHURST**, Nov. 19, 1762	2	68
Nichols, s. Benajah & Mary, b. Nov. 4, 1748	2	6
Noah, s. Elijah & Dinah, b. May 15, 1760	2	46
Pamelia L., m. Pasco **HANES**, Jr., b. of Providence, R.I., June 27, 1847, by Rev. James Mather	3	43
Phebe, d. William & Phebe, b. Sept. 31, 1733 (sic)	1	59
Phebe, m. David **SHEPHERD**, Mar. 3, 1757	2	57
Phinehas, s. Jeremiah & Abigail, b. Feb. 15, 1759	2	56

	Vol.	Page
CADY, (cont.)		
Priscella, d. Elijah & Dinah, b. Jan. 30, 1752	2	46
Robert, s. Abijah & Meriam, b. Aug. 11, 1768	2	65
Ruth, m. Becket **CHAPMAN**, Mar. 22, 1772	2	74
Sally Ann, m. Samuel B. **CARTER**, b. of Warwick, R.I., Apr. 25, 1847, by Rev. James Mather	3	43
Sarah, d. Elijah & Dinah, b. Nov. 29, 1757	2	46
Squier, s. Eleazer & Keziah, b. Oct. 28, 1754	2	31
Squire, m. Thankful **CUTLER**, Apr. 18, 1790	2	106
Squire, m. Abiah **SPAULDING**, May 29, 1799	2	106
Squire, d. June 3, 1841	2	163
Squire, d. June 3, [ ]	2	137
Stephen, s. Abijah & Els, b. Sept. 12, 1750	2	34
Susan, m. Joseph S. **SPAULDING**, b. of Plainfield, Apr. 23, 1817, by Rev. Daniel Dow, Thompson	2	130
Susan J., of Providence, R.I., m. John **CADY**, of West Greenwich, R.I., Oct. 31, 1827, by [ ] Kent, Elder, in Providence	2	213
Susanna, d. Squire & Thankful, b. Mar. 10, 1798	2	106
Thankful, w. Squire, d. Jan. 23, 1799	2	106
Warren, s. Jeremiah & Abigail, b. Dec. 25, 1762	2	56
William, s. William & Phebe, b. June 8, 1729	1	55
William, m. Phebe **KINGSBURY**, Nov. 11, 1729	1	55
William, s. Jeremiah & Abigail, b. Oct. 20, 1756	2	56
William, s. Squir[e] & Abiah, b. Feb. 4, 1811	2	119
William, s. Squier & Abiah, d. Mar. 4, 1814, ae. 3 y. 1 m.	2	125
William, carpenter, ae. 21, b. Plainfield, res. Norwich, m. Louisa **BENNETT**, ae. 18, Feb. 20, 1848, by Rev. Frederick Charlton	4	2
William C., Rev., of Sterling, m. Mary E. **PHILLIPS**, of Plainfield, Mar. 5, 1848, by Rev. James Mather	3	53
William O., minister, ae. 26, b. Willington, res. Sterling, m. Mary E. **PHILLIPS**, ae. 24, Mar. 5, [18]48, by Rev. Mathews	4	1
William W., m. Louisa **BENNETT**, b. of Plainfield, Feb. 20, 1848, by Rev. Frederic Charlton	3	55
CAHOON, CAHOONE, Gorton, of Coventry, R.I., m. Sally C. **KENYON**, of Sterling, Dec. 10, 1838, by Peleg Peckham, Elder	2	238
Sarah, m. Eliot **ALLING**, b. of Plainfield, Feb. 24, 1850, by Rev. Joseph P. Brown	3	63
Thomas G., of Coventry, m. Nancy B. **KENYON**, of Sterling, Sept. 13, 1841, by Peleg Peckham, Elder	3	11
-----, m. Almira **SCRANTON**, ae. 18, b. of Plainfield, Sept. 10, 1849, by Joseph P. Brown	4	6
CALL, Charles C., of Sterling, m. Emily H. **KENYON**, of Plainfield, July 4, 1850, by Peleg Peckham, Elder	3	65

	Vol.	Page

CALL, (cont.)
Cha[rle]s C., harness & trunk maker, ae. 21, of
    Sterling, m. Emily H. **KENYON**, ae. 20, of Plain-
    field, July 4, 1850, by Rev. Peleg Peckham   4   5
Hannah J., d. Charles, farmer, & Emily, b. Nov. [ ],
    1850   4   31
Hannah J., d. Charles, & Emily, b. Nov. [ ], 1850   4   32
CAMP, Henry, Jr., of Brooklyn, m. Ruth Fidelia **SHIPPEY**, of
    Canterbury, Nov. 10, 1850, by Rev. Henry Robinson   3   66
CAMPBELL, Frances, m. Mary E. **BURLINGAME**, b. of
    Plainfield, Sept. 12, 1848, by Rev. George W.
    Brewster   3   56
George, s. James, cotton manufacturer, of Thompson, b.
    Apr. 21, 1851   4   32
Geo[rge] M., s. James, cotton operator, b. Apr. 11,
    [1850]   4   30
William H., physician, b. Voluntown, res. Plainfield,
    d. Mar. 4, 1850, ae. 52   4   65
CAPRON, John T., m. Harriet N. **BRIGGS**, b. of Warwick, R.I.,
    Dec. 14, 1845, by Rev. Tho[ma]s Dowling, of N. Lyme   3   33
CARA, Albert, m. Lucy **COZSENS**, b. of Plainfield, Oct. 6,
    1839, by Rev. Samuel Rockwell (Probably Albert
    CARD)   2   247
Albert, m. Lucy **COZZENS**, b. of Plainfield, Oct. 6,
    1839, by Rev. Samuel Rockwell (Probably Albert
    CARD)   3   1
CARD, Alvan, m. Betsey P. **KENYON**, b. of Sterling, Dec. 4,
    1837, by Peleg Peckham, Elder   2   233
Betsey, m. Edwin B. **SHELDON**, b. of Sterling, Nov. 15,
    1846, by Peleg Peckham, Elder   3   40
Christopher, wheelwright, b. Sterling, res. Plainfield,
    d. June 8, [18]48, ae. 68   4   61
Jonathan, of New York, m. Anna **ANDRAS**, of Plainfield,
    Feb. 16, 1785   2   91
Jonathan, Jr., s. Jonathan & Anna, b. Jan. 24, 1786   2   93
Joshua P., of Killingly, m. Betsey **PHILLIPS**, of Plain-
    field, Jan. 5, 1823, by John Dunlap, J.P.   2   189
Judah H., m. Daniel **HOLLAND**, b. of Sterling, June 28,
    1846, by Peleg Peckham, Elder   3   38
Lucinda, d. Dec. [ ], 1849, ae. 15   4   64
Mary, of Sterling, m. Solomon T. **ELLIS**, of Plainfield,
    Feb. 6, 1837, by Rev. Samuel Rockwell   3   6
Mary Elizabeth, d. Albert, wagon maker, ae. 34, & Lucy
    C., ae. 34, b. Mar. 30, 1849   4   26
Silas P., of Brooklyn, Conn., m. Nancy **MILLER**, of
    Plainfield, May 2, 1853, by Rev. William Turkington   3   78
Welcome, of Charlestown, R.I., m. Lois **FRINK**, of
    Sterling, Mar. 3, 1851, by Peleg Peckham, Elder   3   69

	Vol.	Page
CAREW, John A., of Norwich, m. Mary **HOPKINS**, of Plainfield, Oct. 10, 1824, by Rev. Nathaniel Cole	2	196
CAREY, CARY, [see also **CORY**], Abegill, of Windham, m. Jacob **WARREN**, Mar. 12, 1723	1	28
Abigaiel, m. Elijah **DEAN**, May 15, 1733	1	65
Freelove, of Providence, R.I., m. William C. **SWEET**, of Smithfield, R.I., Nov. 28, 1846, by Rev. J. Mather	3	40
CARPENTER, Abby E., m. Joseph A. **PEIRCE**, Nov. 22, 1846, by Benjamin Bacon, J.P.	3	39
George B., of Warwick, R.I., m. Mary E. **NOYES**, of Warwick, R.I., Feb. 14, 1847, by Rev. J. Mather	3	42
Sally Ann, m. Samuel D. **MILLET**, b. of Plainfield, Oct. 7, 1833, by Peleg Peckham, Elder	2	218
Susan R., of Plainfield, m. George **PICKET**, of Killingly, Oct. 16, 1853, by Rev. William Turkinton	3	80
Thomas P., m. Olive **HILL**, b. of Plainfield, Mar. 20, 1837, by Rev. Samuel Rockwell	2	229
CARR, Daniel, s. Robert & Prudence, b. Oct. 25, 1766	2	61
Mary, d. Robert & Prudence, b. Feb. 24, 1770	2	72
Robert, m. Prudence **WHE[E]LER**, Dec. 31, 1765	2	61
Samuel, s. Robert & Prudence, b. May 12, 1768	2	72
CARTER, Asaph, s. John & Mary, b. Nov. 2, 1757	2	43
Mary, d. John & Mary, b. Sept. 2, 1759	2	43
Samuel B., m. Sally Ann **CADY**, b. of Warwick, R.I., Apr. 25, 1847, by Rev. James Mather	3	43
Sarah E., m. Anderson E. **PARKER**, b. of Saco, Me., Nov. 16, 1849, by Rev. Joseph P. Brown. Witnesses: Caleb Bennett, A. S. Brown	3	89
Sarah E., m. Andrew E. **PARKER**, b. of Maine, Nov. 16, 1849, by Rev. Joseph P. Brown (Written"**CARTEY**")	3	62
CASE, Abby Ann, d. Aug. 16, [18]48, ae. 1 y. 10 m.	4	62
Lucinda, m. Lewis K. **SMALL**, Sept. 5, 1842, by John Read, Elder	3	16
Roby, of Plainfield, m. Edwin **CADY**, of Brooklyn, Oct. 9, 1823, by Nathaniel Cole, Elder	2	192
Sarah, m. Thomas C. **LOVE**, Dec. 6, 1842, by Rev. John Reed	3	17
W[illia]m Henry, m. Mary **JONES**, b. of Plainfield, Apr. 20, 1845, by V.R. Osborn, V.D.M.	3	27
CASEY, Thankful, m. Ebenezer **HALL**, b. of Plainfield, Oct. 21, 1827, by Peleg Peckham, Elder	2	203
CASWELL, Robert, of Warwick, R.I., m. Lucinda S. **WELLS**, of East Greenwich, R.I., Sept. 7, 1846, by Rev. James Mather	3	40
CATLAIN, Lydiah, w. Daniel, d. Apr. 4, 1748	1	48
CAULKINS, John F., m. Sarah **AMES**, b. of Waterford, Sept. 7, 1852, by Rev. Henry Robinson	3	76

	Vol.	Page
CHAFFEE, Lucy, m. William **HAIR**, b. of Woodstock, May 2, 1853, by Rev. William Turkington	3	78
CHAMPIN, [see also **CHAMPLAIN**], Parnel, m. Phillip **SPAULDING**, May 1, 1750	2	41
CHAMPLAIN, [see also **CHAMPIN**], Abby, m. Joseph A. WALKER, b. of Plainfield, June 21, 1852, by William Turkington	3	75
Caroline, of Plainfield, m. Asa W. **GRAVES**, of Killingly, Sept. 18, 1854, by Peleg Peckham, Elder	3	85
Elias, s. Paul & Anne, b. July 15, 1783	2	106
Gideon, s. Paul & Anne, b. Sept. 16, 1791	2	106
Hallam, s. Paul & Anne, b. June 27, 1794	2	106
Lucy, of Plainfield, m. Hugh **HOUGH**, of Lisbon, Aug. 23, 1846, by Rev. J. Mather	3	39
Lydia, m. Ephraim **PICKET**, Aug. 1, 1853, by Rev. Alfred Gates	3	79
Mary M., m. Thomas **WESTCOTT**, b. of Plainfield, Nov. 6, 1853, by Rev. W[illia]m Turkington	3	80
Nancy, d. Paul & Anne, b. June 21, 1777	2	106
Prudence, d. Paul & Anne, b. July 2, 1778	2	106
Silas, s. Paul & Anne, b. May 2, 1786	2	106
Susan, m. William **DEAN**, b. of Plainfield, Nov. 26, 1843, by Rev. Daniel Dorchester	3	23
CHANDLER, Joseph, m. Zeanah **VAUGHAN**, b. of Plainfield, Sept. 14, 1824, by Rev. Nathaniel Cole	2	196
CHAPMAN, Abby Jane, of Plainfield, m. George H. **GARDINER**, of South Kingston, R.I., Sept. 21, 1851, by Rev. Thomas O. Rice	3	71
Abby Jane, of Plainfield, m. George H. **GARDINER**, of Wakefield, R.I., Sept. 21, 1851, by Rev. Thomas O. Rice	3	72
Alieyuse (?), b. Westerly, R.I., res Plainfield, d. Feb. 26, [18]49, ae. 55	4	62
Amos, s. Josiah F., pedler, & Harriet, b. May 1, 1851	4	31
Becket, m. Ruth **CADY**, Mar. 22, 1772	2	74
Chester, s. Benjamin & Jemima, b. Dec. 30, 1762	2	58
Cyrus, s. Benjamin & Jemima, d. Feb. 26, 1763	2	58
Erastus, s. Becket & Ruth, b. Jan. 25, 1773	2	76
Rebecca, d. Becket & Ruth, b. Sept. 30, 1774	2	78
CHAPPELL, Nathan C., of Norwich, m. Mary A. **GALLUP**, of Plainfield, Aug. 9, 1853, by Rev. C. A. Tracy	3	79
CHARLTON, Frederic, Jr., s. Frederick & Julia M., b. Dec. 24, 1847	3	50
Frederic, Jr., s. Frederick, Baptist minister, ae. 25, & Juliaette Wells, ae. 23, b. Dec. 24, 1847	4	23
[CHESEBROUGH], CHESSBROUG, CHEASBOROUGH, Hannah E., of Sterling, m. Albert **HYDE**, of Plainfield, Oct. 18, 1841, by Peleg Peckham, Elder	3	11

	Vol.	Page
[CHESEBROUGH], CHESSBROUG, CHEASBOROUGH, (cont.)		
Mary, m. Asa **PHILLIPS**, Nov. 27, 1760	2	50
CHILD, CHILDS, Susannah, m. Ezekiel **FOX**, Oct. 10, 1791	2	101
Thomas D., m. Keziah **VIOL**, b. of Plainfield, June 8, 1828, by Rev. Orin Fowler	2	205
CHILSON, Gardiner, of Providence, m. Mary **SNELL**, of Sterling, Oct. 8, 1826, by Rev. Orin Fowler	2	199
CHURCH, Clarrissa, of Plainfield, m. Henry **HOLDEN**, of Canterbury, Oct. 28, 1838, by Francis B. Johnson, J.P.	2	237
Elizabeth, d. Samuel, m. Thomas **HARRIS**, s. Ebenezer, Feb. 11, 1713/14	1	24
Johnathan, s. Samuel & Mary, b. July 17, 1714		
Rebeckah, d. Samu[e]ll & Mary, b. Jan. 15,	1	14
1717/18	1	18
Sarah, m. Daniel **CONGDON**, b. of Plainfield, Aug. 5, 1838, by Rev. Samuel Rockwell	2	236
Thomas, s. Sam[ue]ll & Mary, b. Jan. 3, 1712/13	1	12
CLAPP, Charlotte, w. Seth, of Pomfret, d. July 12, 1833, ae. 71 y.	2	141
Ebenezer, m. Deborah **SPAULDING**, Sept. 15, 1773	2	226
CLARK, CLARKE, CLERK, Abby Jane, of Lebanon, m. Albert G. **HEATH**, of Providence, R.I., Oct. 2, 1843, by Rev. A. Latham	3	20
Abigail, m. Phinehas **DEAN**, Dec. 17, 1742	2	41
Amos, s. Daniel & Anna, b. Apr. 30, 1774	2	83
Anne, d. Daniel & Anne, b. July 10, 1761	2	48
Apphia, m. Lyman **SPAULDING**, Apr. 24, 1823, by Rev. Orin Fowler	2	191
Asa, s. Nathaniel & Thankfull, b. June 23, 1753	2	23
Benjamin, s. Silas & Gerusha, b. Aug. 22, 1758	2	80
Daniel, s. James & Thankfull, b. July 22, 1736	1	66
Daniel, m. Anne **DOWNING**, Aug. 29, 1759	2	48
Daniel, s. Daniel & Anne, b. Dec. 25, 1768	2	68
Daniel, Capt., d. Sept. 22, 1777, in the Battle of Stillwater	2	83
David, s. Daniel & Anne, b. Nov. 4, 1770	2	71
David, of Killingly, m. Mary **COLE**, of Plainfield, Jan. 27, 1825, by Rev. Nathaniel Cole	2	197
David, of Brooklyn, m. Emma **EATON**, of Plainfield, May 4, 1840, by Rev. Samuel Rockwell	3	4
Edward, m. Olive **WHEELER**, b. of Plainfield, Feb. 24, 1839, by Rev. Samuel Rockwell	2	239
Elisha, s. Nathaniel & Thankfull, b. Dec. 17, 1755	2	34
Elizabeth, m. Isaac **PARK**, Sept. 22, 1725	1	43
Eunice, m. Stephen **TRACY**, Oct. 13, 1768, by Isaac Coit, Esq.	2	74
George H., of Ashford, m. Zilphia **WILSON**, of Plain-		

PLAINFIELD VITAL RECORDS

	Vol.	Page
CLARK, CLARKE, CLERK, (cont.)		
field, Apr. 16, 1845, by Peleg Peckham, Elder	3	31
George Washington, s. Daniel & Anna, b. Mar. 18, 1776	2	83
Hannah, d. Daniel & Anne, b. Nov. 25, 1766	2	61
Hester, d. Daniel & Anna, b. Feb. 1, 1763	2	54
James, s. Nathaniel & Thankfull, b. Oct. 10, 1754	2	34
James, s. Daniel & Anna, b. July 24, 1772	2	74
Jeremiah, s. James & Thankfull, b. July 18, 1734	1	66
Gerusha, d. Silas & Gerusha, b. Oct. 21, 1758 (sic)	2	80
Gerusha, w. Silas, d. June 14, 1759	2	79
Jesse, s. Silas & Gerisha, b. Jan. 6, 1753; d. Feb. 10, 1753	2	80
Jesse, s. Silas & Zipporah, b. Dec. 8, 1769	2	80
Mary, d. Silas & Jerusha, b. Mar. 22, 1754	2	34
Mary, d. Daniel & Anna, b. Apr. 30, 1778	2	83
Mary, of Canterbury, m. Hiram **TARBOX**, 2d, of Lisbon, Dec. 1, 1839, by Rev. Tubal Wakefield	2	249
Mary, of Canterbury, m. Hiram **TARBOX**, 2d, of Lisbon, Dec. 1, 1839, by Rev. Tubal Wakefield	3	2
Mary Ann, m. Albert **HOTH**, b. of Canterbury, July 28, 1839, by Rev. Tubal Wakefield	2	243
Mary E., ae. 18, b. Coventry, R.I., m. Richmond L. **POTTER**, harness maker, ae. 24, b. Coventry, R.I., res. Plainfield, May 1, 1848, by James Thomas	4	1
Mercy, d. Silas & Zipporah, b. Mar. 30, 1764; d. June 8, 1776	2	80
Oliver, m. Lydia **GREENMAN**, b. of Plainfield, Nov. 17, 1845, by Rev. C. C. Barnes	3	33
Perry, m. Sarah **PHILLIPS**, Nov. 22, 1743	2	2
Perry, m. Lydia **LESTER**, Nov. 4, 1747	2	2
Robert, manufacturer, b. Ireland, res. Plainfield, d. Oct. 19, 1849, ae. 23	4	63
Ruth, d. Daniel & Anne, b. Feb. 15, 1765	2	57
Sabra, of Exeter, R.I., m. Davis **COLVIN**, of Plainfield, May 17, 1829, by Peleg Peckham, Elder	2	209
Sarah, w. Perry, d. Apr. 5, 1746	2	2
Sarah, m. Isaac **STEVENS**, Sept. 19, 1758	2	40
Sarah, d. Silas & Zipporah, b. June 30, 1773	2	80
Silas, Jr., s. Silas & Zipporah, b. June 24, 1776	2	80
Stephen, s. Perry & Sarah, b. Mar. 3, 1745	2	2
Thankfull, d. Daniel & Anne, b. Jan. 8, 1760	2	48
Zipporah, d. Silas & Zipporah, b. Sept. 22, 1761	2	80
CLERK, [see under **CLARK**]		
CLEVELAND, CLEAVELAND, Ann, d. Issac & Elisabeth, m. Phillip **SPAULDING**, Aug. 10, 1721	1	27
Bethabia, d. Apr. 15, 1835, ae. 71 y. at Ware Village, Mass.	2	141

	Vol.	Page

CLEVELAND, CLEAVELAND, (cont.)
    Darkhorse, m. Samuel **WILLIAMS**, of Plainfield, Apr.
      11, 1739   1   97
    Dorkas, m. Samuel **WILLIAMS**, Apr. 11, 1739   2   18
    Hannah, m. Peter **BUTTON**, Oct. 11, 1729   1   67
    Hiram, m. Esther **ROBINSON**, b. of Plainfield, Sept.
      12, 1824, by Orin Fowler, Minister   2   195
    John, s. Josiah & Mary, b. June 28, 1698   1   4
    Jonathan, s. Josiah & Mary, b. [   ] 1, 1697/8; d.
      Apr. 5, 1698   1   4
    Kezia, m. Lot **MORGAN**, Aug. 11, 1791   2   99
    Louisa, of Plainfield, m. James H. **ISAACSON**, of
      Hartford, Sept. 1, 1835, by Rev. Otis C. Whiton,
      of Canterbury   2   221
    Luther, m. Lydia C. **WOODWORD**, b. of Plainfield, Oct.
      15, 1834, by Rev. Samuel Rockwell   2   219
    Mary, m. Nelson **PALMER**, b. of Plainfield, Oct. 17,
      1824, by Rev. Orin Fowler   2   196
    Persie, w. Samuell, d. Feb. 22, 1697/8, about 39th y.
      of her age   1   4
COATS, Elias Franklin, s. Elias & Mariah, b. Aug. 21, 1821   2   132
    John N., of Sterling, m. Lucinda A. **JOHNSON**, of Plain-
      field, Apr. 22, 1832, by Rev. Samuel Rockwell   2   215
    John N., m. Sarah B. **DOUGLASS**, b. of Sterling, Oct. 12,
      1841, by Peleg Peckham, Elder   3   11
COBB, [see also **COPP**], Frances Maria, d. Otis T. **COBB** &
    Maria, b. May 4, 1836, at Barre, Mass.   2   141
    Frances Maria, d. Otis T. & Maria, b. May 4, 1836, in
      Barre, Mass.   3   36
    Joseph Sherman Gladding, s. Otis T. & Maria, b. July
      28, 1839   3   36
    Lois, m. Ebenezer **EATON**, Apr. 15, 1770   2   77
    Otis T., of Amhurst, Mass., m. Maria **CADY**, of Plain-
      field, Sept. 16, 1833, by Rev. Samuel Rockwell   2   218
    Otis T., of Amhurst, Mass., m. Maria **CADY**, of Plain-
      field, Sept. 16, 1833, by Rev. Samuel Rockwell   3   35
    Sally, of Scituate, R.I., m. Stillman W. **ELLIS**, of
      Providence, R.I., Dec. 6, 1847, by Rev. James
      Mather   3   47
    Susan Adeline, d. Otis T. & Maria, b. May 28, 1842, in
      Rockaway, N.J.   3   36
    William Eddy, s. Otis T. & Maria, b. July 10, 1844   3   36
COFFREY, James, dresser tender, ae. 22, b. Ireland, res.
    Plainfield, m. Eliza M. **HARVEY**, ae. 20, May 1,
    [18]48, by Michael Tume   4   2
COGSWELL, Daniel, of Brooklyn, m. Sylva **HOPKINS**, of Plain-
    field, June 20, 1831, by Nathaniel Cole, Elder   2   214
    Manah A., of Warwick, R.I., m. Robert M. **PERKINS**, of

	Vol.	Page
COGSWELL, (cont.)		
Washington, N.C., Sept. 21, 1840, by Rev. John Read	3	6
Mary T., m. G. Forrester **BASTON**, b. of Plainfield, June 23, 1853, by Rev. Henry Robinson	3	79
COIT, COITE, Benjamin, s. Sam[ue]ll & Sarah, b. Mar. 28, 1731	1	63
Betsey Pomeroy, d. Roger & Frances, b. Jan. 30, 1827	2	141
Catharine, d. Roger & Frances, b. Dec. 4, 1811, at Griswold	2	140
Daniel, s. Rev. Joseph, d. Apr. 19, 1762	2	49
Daniel Roger, s. Roger & Frances, b. Aug. 23, 1829	2	141
Elizabeth, d. Joseph & Experience, b. Feb. 19, 1706/7	1	5
Ephraim, s. Joseph, 2d, & Experience, b. Nov. 27, 1720	1	99
Frances, d. Roger & Frances, b. June 9, 1816	2	140
Frances, m. Jeremiah S. **WEBB**, b. of Plainfield, Apr. 30, 1840, by Rev. Samuel Rockwell	3	4
Harriet Gordon, d. Roger & Frances, b. Oct. 12, 1825	2	141
Henry Robinson, s. Roger & Frances, b. Oct. 5, 1820	2	141
Isaac, s. Joseph & Experience, b. Dec. 6, 1714	1	14
James Mason, s. Roger & Frances, b. Feb. 15, 1813, at Griswold	2	140
Jane, d. Roger & Frances, b. Jan. 6, 1818	2	140
John, s. Roger & Frances, b. Aug. 28, 1809, at Griswold	2	140
John, m. Pamala L. **FULLER**, b. of Plainfield, Mar. 10, 1836, by Rev. Samuel Rockwell	2	225
Joseph, m. Experience **WHEELER**, d. Isaac, of Stoningtown, Sept. 18, 1705	1	5
Joseph, Rev., d. July 1, 1750, in the 77th y. of his age. Minister for 44 y. in Christ Church, Plainfield	2	49
Lydia, of Plainfield, m. Philip C. **SPOONER**, of Lawrenceburgh, Ind., Sept. 11, 1839, by Rev. Samuel Rockwell	2	247
Lydia Lord, d. Roger & Frances, b. Aug. 9, 1814, at Griswold	2	140
Olive Tyler, d. Roger & Frances, b. Nov. 17, 1823	2	141
Pamela L., of Plainfield, m. Thomas L. **SHIPMAN**, of Jewett City, May 1, 1844, by A. Dunning	3	23
Ruth Harwood, d. Roger & Frances, b. Jan. 18, 1822	2	141
Sam[ue]ll, m. Sary **SPAULDING**, d. Benjamin, Jr., Mar. 30, 1730	1	63
Samuel, s. Sam[ue]ll & Sarah, b. July 23, 1733	1	63
Samuel, s. Roger & Frances, b. Feb. 17, 1819	2	141
Samuel, of Hartford, m. Mary E. **GLADDING**, of Plainfield, Sept. 27, 1842, by A. Dunning	3	16
Susan, d. Roger & Frances, b. Oct. 8, 1810, at Griswold	2	140

	Vol.	Page
COIT, COITE, (cont.)		
Susan, of Plainfield, m. Daniel **PARKER**, Jr. of Hawkinsville, Ga., Sept. 21, 1831, by Rev. Levi Kneeland, of Canterbury	2	214
Will[ia]m, s. Sam[ue]ll & Sarah, b. Feb. 13, 1735	1	63
COLBURN, Royal S., of Brooklyn, m. Lydia S. **STARKWEATHER**, of Plainfield, Jan. 24, 1850, by Rev. Henry Robinson	3	64
Royal S., carpenter, ae. 40, b. Windham, Ct., res. Plainfield, m. 2d w. Lydia S. **STARKWEATHER**, ae. 38, b. Plainfield, res. Plainfield, June 24, 1850, by Henry Robinson	4	6
COLE, Allis, d. Ebenezer & Elizabeth, b. July 30, 1756	2	25
Amey C., m. Esek **HALL**, b. of Plainfield, Mar. 7, 1853, by Rev. Joseph P. Brown	3	77
Asa, s. Eben[eze]r & Elizabeth, b. June 20, 1772	2	74
Barnet, m. Susanna **HALL**, May 6, 1796	2	103
Benj[ami]n, s. Ebenezer & Elizabeth, b. Feb. 18, 1761	2	33
Caleb, m. Hannah **CRANDALL**, b. of Plainfield, Mar. 30, 1826, by Rev. Nathaniel Cole	2	199
Daniel, s. Hezeciah & Sarah, b. Oct. 24, 1728	1	46
Daniel, s. Ebenezer & Elizabeth, b. Sept. 19, 1759	2	33
Ebenezer, s. Hezeciah & Sarah, b. Aug. 21, 1726	1	44
Ebenezer, m. Elizabeth **WHE[E]LER**, Apr. 23, 1751	2	14
Ebenezer, s. Ebenezer & Elizabeth, b. Dec. 17, 1765	2	54
Elizabeth, d. Ebenezer & Elizabeth, b. Feb. 12, 1768	2	55
Elizabeth, d. Ebenezer & Elizabeth, d. Aug. 14, 1773	2	76
Eunice, m. George **POPPLE**, b. of Plainfield, Aug. 2, 1846, by Rev. Chauncy Wilcox	3	38
Hannah, m. Benjamin P. **WATSON**, b. of Plainfield, Sept. 4, 1843, by Rev. Daniel Dorchester	3	22
Hezeciah, m. Sarah **MAINE**, Dec. 29, 1725	1	37
Hezekiah, s. Hezekiah & Sarah, b. Feb. 22, 1748	2	25
Jeremiah, s. Barnet & Susanna, b. Jan. 6, 1797	2	103
John, s. Ebenezer & Elizabeth, b. Sept. 1, 1752	2	23
Lucinda, m. Elisha **POPPLE**, b. of Plainfield, Mar. 28, 1842, by Peleg Peckman, Elder	3	14
Lydia, of Plainfield, m. Edwin **CADY**, of Brooklyn, Apr. 9, 1827, by Nathaniel Cole, Elder	2	201
Marinda, m. Isaac **PARKIS**, b. of Plainfield, Oct. 3, 1853, by Rev. Joseph P. Brown	3	80
Mary, d. Hezekiah & Sary, b. Dec. 27, 1731	1	95
Mary, of Plainfield, m. David **CLARK**, of Killingly, Jan. 27, 1825, by Rev. Nathaniel Cole	2	197
Olive, d. Spencer & Zilpha, b. June 3, 1811	2	124
Olive, m. Thomas **WEAVER**, b. of Plainfield, Sept. 8, 1828, by Peleg Peckham, Elder	2	207
Ruth, d. Hezekiah & Sarah, b. Dec. 29, 1734	1	95

	Vol.	Page
COLE, (cont.)		
Samuel, s. Hezekiah & Sarah, b. Mar. 18, 1738	1	95
Samuel, s. Ebenezer & Elizabeth, b. July 8, 1754	2	25
Sarah, d. Hezekiah & Sarah, b. Mar. 4, 1737	1	95
Sarah, m. Jonas **WHE[E]LER**, Oct. 12, 1757	2	44
Sarah, d. Ebenezer & Elizabeth, b. Feb. 12, 1770	2	55
Stephen, s. Hezekiah & Sarah, b. Sept. 18, 1744	2	25
Stephen, s. Ebenezer & Elizabeth, b. Nov. 10, 1763	2	53
William H., of Providence, R.I., m. Abby P. **BAKER**, of Warwick, R.I., Oct. 25, 1846, by Rev. J. Mather	3	39
Zilpha, d. Spencer & Zilpha, b. Nov. 22, 1802	2	124
Zilpha, m. Ira K. **CRANDALL**, b. of Plainfield, Jan. 28, 1827, by Nathaniel Cole, Elder	2	201
COLEGROVE, Benjamin, s. Jonathan & Gemima, b. June 10, 1787	2	109
Esther, d. Jonathan & Gemima, b. Jan. 10, 1778	2	108
Esther, of Plainfield, m. Dr. Elijah **GIBS**, of Coventry, R.I., Feb. 10, 1800, by Rev. Joel Benedict	2	104
Gemima, d. Jonathan & Gemima, b. Dec. 12, 1782	2	109
Jonathan, Jr., s. Jonathan & Gemima, b. July 25, 1781	2	108
Olive, d. Jonathan & Gemima, b. May 1, 1774	2	108
Parke, s. Jonathan & Gemima, b. Dec. 27, 1779	2	108
Phebe, d. Jonathan & Gemima, b. Nov. 7, 1776	2	108
Polly, d. Jonathan & Gemima, b. Mar. 5, 1792	2	109
COLLINS, COLINS, Lydia M., m. Seabury **MACUMBER**, b. of Plainfield, Mar. 9, 1829, by Rev. Orin Fowler	2	208
Mary A., d. Patrick & Sarah, b. July 21, 1850	4	31
Mary Ann, d. James, farmer, & Patience, b. Feb. 1, 1849	4	27
Noel, m. Elizabeth **JURDON**, now residing in Plainfield, but belonging in the State of R.I., Sept. 22, 1822, by Jonathan Gallup, J.P.	2	188
Rufus, of Columbia, m. Olive **POTTER**, of Sterling, Dec. 19, 1830, by Peleg Peckham, Elder	2	212
Sarah, m. Isaac P. **FARMAN**, b. of Plainfield, Nov. 21, 1821, by Nathaniel Cole, Elder	2	134
Willard W., m. Abby E. **KENYON**, b. of Hopkinton, R.I., Nov. 16, 1845, by Peleg Peckham, Elder	3	32
COLVIN, Amanda, ae. 46, b. Chaplain, Ct., res. Plainfield, m. Marvin **STARKWEATHER**, laborer, ae. 40, of Plainfield, Nov. 30, 1848, by Amos Witter, Esq.	4	3
Davis, of Plainfield, m. Sabra **CLARKE**, of Exeter, R.I., May 27, 1829, by Peleg Peckman, Elder	2	209
Fernando C., of Abington, Penn., m. Zuba **LOVE**, of Coventry, R.I., Mar. 21, 1847, by Rev. J. Mather	3	44
Henry A., m. Harriet **PRATT**, b. of Smithfield, R.I., Sept. 21, 1846, by Mowry Burgess, J.P.	3	42
Horace, of Warwick, R.I., m. Phebe **BROWNELL**, of		

	Vol.	Page
COLVIN, (cont.)		
Smithfield, R.I., Oct. 5, 1847, by Rev. J. Mather	3	46
Lydia, m. Nathan **MATHEWS**, b. of Plainfield, Sept. 19, 1847, by Rev. J. Mather	3	45
Lydia, ae. 39, b. Plainfield, m. Nathan **MATHER**, corder, ae. 46, b. Killingly, res. Canterbury, Sept. 26, [18]48, by Rev. James Mather	4	1
COMSTOCK, Elizabeth R., m. Edward P. **HALL**, b. of Plainfield, Mar. 28, 1852, by Rev. Henry Robinson	3	74
CONGDON, Daniel, m. Sarah **CHURCH**, b. of Plainfield, Aug. 5, 1838, by Rev. Samuel Rockwell	2	236
Daniel, of Plainfield, m. Betsey **PELOM**, of Griswold, Sept. 6, 1843, by Rev. A. Dunning	3	20
Eliza, m. Daniel **SMITH**, b. of Plainfield, Sept. 10, 1837, by Rev. Samuel Rockwell	2	232
Eliza G., m. Horace P. **YOUNG**, b. of Griswold, Oct. 19, 1851, by [ ]. Witness: John Paine	3	71
Eunice, illeg. d. Mary A., ae. 26, b. July 1, 1851	4	32
Jerusha, m. William H. **WEST**, b. of Plainfield, Dec. 25, 1842, at Mr. Thomas Haris's, by Rev. Lawton Cady	3	89
Jesse, m. Catharine A. **GARDINER**, b. of Plainfield, Mar. 8, 1835, by Rev. Samuel Rockwell	2	220
Joseph, of West Greenwich, R.I., m. Polly **MATTHEWSON**, of Plainfield, Nov. 27, 1823, by Orin Fowler, V.D.M.	2	192
Joseph J.H., of Exeter, R.I., m. Julia Ann **ELDREDGE**, of Plainfield, Sept. 14, 1850, by Rev. S. W. Coggeshall, Killingly	3	65
Louisa, m. Joseph **WILLIAMS**, b. of Plainfield, Aug. 13, 1850, by Rev. Warren Emerson	3	65
Martha, b. Griswold, Ct., res. Plainfield, d. Sept. 2, [18]48, ae. 13	4	62
Mary, housework, black, ae. 16, of Plainfield, m. Samuel K. **EDWARDS**, farmer, black, ae. 20, of Plainfield, Feb. 18, 1851, by Rev. Joseph P. Brown	4	7
Nancy F.C., of Plainfield, m. James G. **ALLEN**, of Providence, R.I., Aug. 2, 1854, by Rev. Peter S. Marther	3	85
Nancy Jane, of Exeter, R.I., m. Samuel H. **ELDREDGE**, of Plainfield, Feb. 18, 1851, by Rev. Joseph P. Brown	3	69
Nubury, m. Susan **CONGDON**, b. of Plainfield, Nov. 12, 1845, by Rev. Charles C. Barnes	3	33
Sepona, child of Sarah, black, b. Mar. 18, 1848	4	22
Susan, m. Nubury **CONGDON**, b. of Plainfield, Nov. 12, 1845, by Rev. Charles C. Barnes	3	33
CONSTANTINE, Thomas, m. Susan F. **SCOTT**, b. of Plainfield, Dec, 24, 1854, by Rev. P.S. Mather	3	88
COOK, Leah, d. Samuel & Eunice, b. Jan. 26, 1758	2	38

	Vol.	Page
COOK, (cont.)		
Samuel, d. Apr. 9, 1758, in Newtown, Mass., Bay	2	38
Zerviah, of Preston, m. Vincent **HINCKLEY**, of Plainfield, Dec. 31, 1807, by Rev. Levi Hart	2	121
COOLEY, Thomas, of Hartford, m. Nancy **COREY**, of Plainfield, June 4, 1839, by Frances B. Johnson, J.P.	2	241
COON, Sylvester C., of Canterbury, m. Almira **SCRANTON**, of Plainfield, Sept. 10, 1849, by Rev. Joseph P. Brown	3	60
COONEY, John J., s. Samuel, farmer, ae. 48, & Olive C., ae. 40, b. Dec. 2, 1848	4	26
COOPER, Clarrissa, m. Luther **KEECH**, Mar. 10, 1844, by Archibald Douglass, J.P.	3	22
Elizabeth, of Scituate, m. Jacob **WARREN**, Jr., of Plainfield, Dec. 27, 1739	1	98
Joseph, s. Samuel & Martha, b. Sept. 3, 1777	2	82
Lucy Ann, m. John Willson **KENNEDY**, June 25, 1831	2	264
Martha, m. Silvester H. **BENNET**, Oct. 5, 1834, by Peleg Peckham, Elder	2	219
Phebe, m. John **KENNEDY**, b. of Plainfield, Feb. 10, 1828, by Rev. Orin Fowler	2	204
Samuel, Jr., s. Samuel & Martha, b. Feb. 9, 1775	2	82
Samuel, m. Clarry **PHILLIPS**, b. of Plainfield, Sept. 7, 1835, by Peleg Peckham, Elder	2	222
COPP, [see also **COBB**], Ebenezer, Capt., d. Mar. 1, 1835, ae. 88 y.	2	141
CORBIN, Almanda, m. Marvin **STARKWEATHER**, b. of Plainfield, Nov. 30, 1848, by Amos Witter, J.P.	3	56
Amasa, of Canterbury, m. Mary Ann **LARKIN**, of Plainfield, Dec. 13, 1840, by Rev. Tubal Wakefield	3	8
Lucy, m. William T. **HITCHCOCK**, b. of Plainfield, Dec. 13, 1840, by Rev. Samuel Rockwell	3	8
CORNELL, Anna Elizabeth, d. Mason & Philena, b. Mar. 3, 1830	2	141
Eunice, m. Cornell **MUNRO**, Sept. 17, 1826, by Samuel L. Hough, J.P.	2	200
Frances, d. Mason & Philena, b. Feb. 5, 1831	2	141
Frances C., of Plainfield, m. John S. **SMITH**, of Canterbury, Mar. 27, 1854, by Rev. James Bates	3	86
Mason, s. Mason & Philena, b. May 28, 1838	3	15
Mason, Sr., d. July 19, 1841, ae. 39 y. 5 m. 4 d.	3	15
Ruth, m. Hiram **MADISON**, b. of Sterling, June 13, 1842, by Peleg Peckham, Elder	3	16
William, m. Huldah **KINNE**, Dec. 5, 1793	2	100
William, s. Mason & Philena, b. July 7, 1832	2	141
CORY, COREY, COERY, [see also **CAREY**], Benjamin, s. Joseph & Freelove, b. Apr. 9, 1761, at Groton	2	47
Catharine, of Plainfield, m. Spencer **WEEVER**, of		

	Vol.	Page
CORY, COREY, COERY, (cont.)		
Coventry, R.I., Sept. 26, 1824, by Orin Fowler, V.D.M.	2	195
Elizabeth, m. Benedick **SATERLY**, Jan. 16, 1738/9	2	4
Elizabeth, d. Joseph & Freelove, b. Dec. 7, 1755	2	34
Enis, d. Joseph & Jerusha, b. June 9, 1738	1	71
Eunice, m. James **FAIRMAN**, Jan. 4, 1759	2	40
Hannah, d. Joseph & Jerush[a], b. Jan. 29, 1730	1	71
Hannah, m. Oliver **KINGSBURY**, Sept. 17, 1754	2	30
Harriet, of Sterling, m. Samuel W. **GREEN**, of Warwick, R.I., Aug. 25, 1845, by James Smither, Elder	3	34
Isaac, s. Isaac & Hannah, b. Sept. 22, 1708	1	6
Isaac, s. Joseph & Freelove, b. June 28, 1748	2	2
James Arnold, s. Joseph & Apphia, b. June 30, 1822	2	140
Jane, of Coventry, R.I., m. Stephen **DEXTER**, 2d, of Cumberland, R.I., May 31, [probably 1846], by Rev. James Mather	3	37
Jerusha, w. Joseph, d. Oct. 14, 1739	1	95
Joseph, s. Isaac & Hannah, b. Feb. 22, 1709/10	1	8
Joseph, s. Isaac & Han[n]ah, b. Apr. 12, 1713	1	13
Joseph, m. Jerusheah **NIFF**, June 5, 1733	1	61
Joseph, m. Freelove **JOYE***, Feb. 5, 1739/40 (*Arnold Copy says "**JOYE** should be **LOVEJOY**")	1	94
Joseph, m. Freelove **LOVEJOY**, Feb. 5, 1739/40	1	95
Joseph, s. Josiah & Sarah, b. June 2, 1770	2	70
Joseph, of Tivertown, m. Aphia **LITTLE**, of Little Comton, R.I., Aug. 30, 1821, by Rev. Nathaniel Cole	2	134
Josiah, s. Joseph & Jerusheah, b. Feb. 22, 1733/4	1	61
Josiah, m. Sarah **KILE**, Jan. 4, 1758	2	70
Josiah, s. Josiah & Sarah, b. Apr. 19, 1762	2	70
Manser, s. Joseph & Freelove, b. Aug. 11, 1763	2	54
Nancy, of Plainfield, m. Thomas **COOLEY**, of Hartford, June 4, 1839, by Frances B. Johnson, J.P.	2	241
Olive, m. John L. **SMITH**, Jan. 1, 1845, by V.R. Osborn, V.D.M.	3	26
Phillip, s. Timothy & Jenne, b. Oct. 22, 1764	2	64
Polly, w. Asa, d. Aug. 16, 1861, ae. 67 y. 5 m.	2	143
Priscilla, d. Joseph & Freelove, b. Mar. 13, 1743	1	2X
Rachel, d. Josiah & Freelove, b. June 7, 1758	2	38
Rachel, d. Joseph & Freelove, d. Aug. 29, 1760, ae. 2 y. and a half	2	47
Robert, s. Timothy & Jenne, b. Apr. 23, 1766	2	64
Ruth, d. Joseph & Freelove, b. May 30, 1753	2	24
Sarah, d. Isaac, Jr. & Sarah, b. May 27, 1740	1	97
Sibel Ann, m. Reuben W. **BAKER**, b. of Plainfield, Dec. 21, 1837, by Amos Witter, J.P.	2	233
Simeon, s. Joseph & Freelove, b. July 30, 1743	1	101

	Vol.	Page
CORY, COREY, COERY, (cont.)		
Timothy, s. Joseph & Freelove, b. Dec. 17, 1740	1	96
Timothy, m. Jenne **BOYDE**, Mar. 6, 1764	2	64
William G., m. Mary C. **NICHOLS**, May 20, 1843, by Peleg Peckham, Elder	3	19
Ziprah, d. Josiah & Sarah, b. Apr. 4, 1764	2	70
COZZENS, COZSENS, George Brown, s. John, Jr. & Betsey, b. Nov. 9, 1818	2	140
George Brown, s. John, Jr. & Betsey, d. Aug. 27, 1822	2	140
James Rogers, s. John, Jr. & Betsey, b. July 4, 1811	2	127
Lucy, d. John, Jr. & Betsey, b. June 12, 1815	2	127
Lucy, m. Albert **CARA***, b. of Plainfield, Oct. 6, 1839, by Rev. Samuel Rockwell *(Probably "**CARD**")	2	247
Lucy, m. Albert **CARA***, b. of Plainfield, Oct. 6, 1839, by Rev. Samuel Rockwell *(Probably "**CARD**")	3	1
Sallena, d. John, Jr. & Betsey, b. July 2, 1813	2	127
Silence, of Plainfield, m. Stephen **WHITEHORN**, of South Kingstown, R.I., Oct. 22, 1837, by Rev. Samuel Rockwell	2	233
CRAIN, Georgiana, d. Oct. 14, 1849, ae. 1 y.	4	64
CRANDALL, Hannah, m. Caleb **COLE**, b. of Plainfield, Mar. 30, 1826, by Rev. Nathaniel Cole	2	199
Ira K., m. Zilpha **COLE**, b. of Plainfield, Jan. 28, 1827, by Nathaniel Cole, Elder	2	201
Joseph, of Exeter, R.I., m. Hannah **KENYON**, of Richmond, R.I., Feb. 18, 1829, by Peleg Peckham, Elder	2	208
Mary E., m. John R. **ALLEN**, b. of Coventry, R.I., Feb. 2, 1848, by Rev. J. Mather	3	51
CRANE, [see under **CRAIN**]		
CRAPE, Patience, m. John **LAWSON**, Sept. 9, 1827, by Rev. Erastus Ripley	2	202
CRARY, CRERY, Aaron, s. Benjamin & Amey, b. Mar. 2, 1769	2	76
Aaron, m. Harmony **AVERELL**, Apr. 17, 1794	2	120
Aaron Averell, s. Aaron & Harmony, b. July 27, 1803	2	121
Abigail, w. Benjamin, d. Jan. 30, 1822	2	140
Ann, d. John & Prudence, b. Dec. 12, 1723	1	50
Anna, w. John, d. Sept. 21, 1754, in the 62d y. of her age	2	26
Benjamin, s. Aaron & Harmony, b. Aug. 5, 1797	2	120
Benjamin, m. Nancy **PALMER**, b. of Plainfield, Nov. 14, 1824, by Orin Fowler, V.D.M.	2	196
Christobel, m. Nathaniel **MARSH**, Aug. 21, 1751	2	16
Desire, m. Nathan **GLOVER**, Sept. 27, 1786	2	94
Elizabeth, d. John & Prudence, b. Dec. 26, 1717	1	49
Elizabeth, d. John, Jr. & Mary, b. Aug. 6, 1751	2	23
Hannah, d. John & Prudence, b. Dec. 20, 1719	1	49
Harmony, w. Capt. Aaron, d. Sept. 13, 1812, ae. 40 y. 6 m. 7 d.	2	121

	Vol.	Page
CRARY, CRERY, (cont.)		
James, s. Aaron & Harmony, b. July 8, 1799	2	121
Jane E., d. Aaron A., farmer, ae. 48, & Nancy, b. Dec. 4, 1850	4	32
John*, m. Prudence **WHIT**, Oct. 12, 1715 (*correction added to bottom of page of original manuscript, as follows: "**CRARY**, John, m. Prudence **WHITE**, Oct. 12, 1715, in Concord, Mass. (Cf. "Concord Recs. of Births, Marriages, & Deaths", pg. 87. Mar. also recorded in V.R. of Plainfield, Conn.) Info. by Neil Crawford of Buffalo, N.Y., Nov. 15, 1941.")	1	16
John, s. John & Prudence, b. Aug. 13, 1716	1	16
John, m. Mary **RAYMENT**, May 20, 1750	2	23
John, s. John, Jr. & Mary, b. Mar. 9, 1753	2	23
John, Esq. The executor of his will was Benjamin Spaulding, Jr.	2	52
Luce, d. John & Prudence, b. Aug. [ ], 1728; d. Dec. 15, 1728	1	50
Lucy, d. Aaron & Harmony, b. Sept. 16, 1795	2	120
Mary, d. John & Prudence, b. May [ ], 1726	1	50
Prudence, d. John & Prudence, b. Feb. 6, 1722	1	49
Rachel, d. John & Prudence, b. Jan. 9, 1730	1	50
Rachel, m. Benjamin **SPAULDING**, Jan. 29, 1756	2	33
Samuel, s. Aaron & Harmony, b. June 3, 1801	2	121
Samuel, farmer, d. May 10, 1851, ae. 49	4	66
Stephen, s. Aaron & Harmony, b. June 6, 1808	2	121
William Peirce, s. Aaron & Harmony, b. Apr. 29, 1806	2	121
CRAWFORD, Susan, of Coventry, R.I., m. Charles **WILSON**, Apr. 16, 1847, by Rev. Fred[eri]c Charlton	3	48
CROSS, Ann, black, ae. 20, of Griswold, m. Daniel **FROST**, laborer, black, ae 27, of Griswold, Nov. 10, [1850?], by Benjamin Bacon	4	7
George W., of Charlestown, R.I., m. Lois **BABCOCK**, of Sterling, Mar. 11, 1849, by Peleg Peckham, Elder	3	58
CULLING, Cynthia, b. Sterling, res. Plainfield, d. Mar. 2, [1849?], ae. 4	4	63
CUNDALL, Clarrissa, of Plainfield, m. Lucius **FULLER**, of Hartford, Nov. 27, 1844, by James Smither, Elder	3	29
Harriet, of Plainfield, m. Gideon **SEGAR**, of Killingly, Jan. 25, 1844, by James Smither, Elder	3	28
CURTIS, Eunice K., m. Henry A. **HARRIS**, b. of Fairfield, Sept. 1, 1842, by Rev. A. B. Wheeler	3	17
Mary A., of Plainfield, m. Seth A. **WILSON**, of Killingly, Dec. 5, 1849, by Rev. Joseph P. Brown	3	62
CUTLER, Abigail, d. William & Susannah, b. Apr. 28, 1763	2	65
Abigail, m. Thomas **ANDRAS**, May 18, 1784	2	92
Andrew, s. Simon & Betsey, b. Feb. 8, 1799	2	107

	Vol.	Page
CUTLER, (cont.)		
Benjamin L., s. Benjamin, farmer, ae. 25, & Nancy, ae. 22, b. Dec. [ ], 1850	4	31
Benjamin L., s. Benjamin, farmer, & Nancy, b. Dec. [ ], 1850	4	32
Eunice, d. Will[ia]m & Susanah, b. Dec. 15, 1759	2	49
Hogges, s. Beach & Abigail, b. July 27, 1752	2	20
Isaac K., of Plainfield, m. Mary Elizabeth **GORDON**, of Sterling, Nov. 3, 1828, by Rev. Orin Fowler	2	207
Isaac Theodalet, s. Simon & Betsey, b. July 15, 1805	2	115
Job Herrick, s. Simon & Betsey, b. June 3, 1807	2	115
John, s. Simon & Betsey, b. Nov. 5, 1813	2	128
Jonathan, s. William & Susanah, b. Jan. 24, 1762	2	49
Joseph, s. William & Susanah, b. Apr. 14, 1755	2	29
Marcy E., of Plainfield, m. John C. **JACOBI**, of New Orleans, Sept. 17, 1850, by Rev. J. O. Knapp	3	66
Mary, d. Simon & Betsey, b. Nov. 14, 1815	2	128
Molle, d. William & Susanah, b. Mar. 21, 1753	2	24
Simon, s. William & Susanah, b. Sept. 6, 1766	2	65
Simon, m. Betsey **HERRICK**, Dec. 17, 1797	2	107
Simon, Jr., s. Simon & Betsey, b. May 15, 1811	2	128
Susan, m. Rufus W. **KENNEDY**, b. of Plainfield, Dec. 20, 1829, by Rev. Orin Fowler	2	210
Susannah, d. Simon & Betsey, b. June 26, 1800	2	107
Thankfull, d. William & Susanah, b. Aug. 17, 1757	2	36
Thankful, m. Squire **CADY**, Apr. 18, 1790	2	106
Willard, s. William & Susanah, b. Sept. 3, 1751	2	24
William, m. Susanah **SHEPHARD**, Nov. 7, 1750	2	24
William, s. Simon & Betsey, b. Oct. 9, 1802	2	115
William H., of Plainfield, m. Sarah E. **THOMPSON**, of New Haven, June 16, 1851, by Rev. Henry Robinson	3	70
William H., merchant, ae. 21, b. Conn., res. Plainfield, m. Sarah E. **THOMPSON**, school teacher, ae. 22, b. Conn., June 16, 1851, by Rev. Robinson	4	7
DADD, Orin, m. Philena **TILLOTSON**, b. of Griswold, June 13, 1841, by Peleg Peckham, Elder (See also **LADD**)	3	10
DAGGETT, George H., m. Melinda J. **EBBINS**, b. of Taunton, Mass., Apr. 26, 1847, by Rev. James Mather	3	44
DANIELSON, Elisha, of Killingly. m. Eliza **LESTER**, of Plainfield, Apr. 4, 1821, by Rev. Orin Fowler	2	132
DARBESHER, [see under **DARBY**]		
DARBY, DARBE, Elizabeth, d. William, Jr. & Elisabeth, b. Apr. 26, 1719	1	22
John, s. William & Elisabeth, b. Feb. 6, 1722/3	1	28
Mary, d. William & Elisabeth, b. Apr. 26, 1721	1	28
DART, Seabury, of Lyme, m. Hope Grafton **ROBINSON**, of Plainfield, June 19, 1826, by Orin Fowler, V.D.M.	2	199

	Vol.	Page
DAVENPORT, Waightstill, m. Nathan **WILLIAMS**, Aug. 26, 1755	2	35
DAVIS, Clarissa, of Plainfield, m. Russel[l] **BAGGS**, of Richmond, R.I., Feb. 12, 1828, by Rev. Orin Fowler	2	205
Eben[ezer] P., of Newbury, Mass., m. R[h]oda A. **THA[T]CHER**, of Plainfield, Sept. 17, 1844, by J.R. Osborn, V.D.M.	3	25
John W., of Coventry, R.I., m. Lois B. **LESTER**, of Plainfield, Mar. 27, 1837, by Rev. Samuel Rockwell	2	229
Jonathan, m. Alared **WOOD**, b. of Plainfield, June 19, 1837, by Chester Tilden	2	231
Juliette, b. Killingly, res. Plainfield, d. Feb. 14, 1850, ae. 3	4	64
Noah, of Norwich, m. Emeline Eliza **ROBINSON**, of Plainfield, Nov. 25, 1833, by Rev. Samuel Rockwell	2	218
Obed, m. Roba **BROWN**, b. of Plainfield, Mar. 20, 1823, by Rev. Orin Fowler	2	190
Simon, of Thompson, m. Hannah **ARYE**, of Plainfield, Aug. 3, 1831, by Rev. Otis Lane, of Sterling & Voluntown	2	214
Thankful, of Preston, m. Elisha **DOW**, of Plainfield, Mar. 21, 1811, by John Tyler, J.P., Preston	2	125
DAWLEY, Amanda M.F., of Coventry, R.I., m. William W. **BRAYTON**, of Scituate, R.I., Nov. 3, 1852, by Peleg Peckham, Elder	3	76
Frances, w. of Merchant, d. Feb. 13, 1849, ae. 26	4	62
Lydia H., of Coventry, R.I., m. Josiah **SLADE**, of Sterling, Nov. 3, 1852, by Peleg Peckham, Elder	3	76
Richard, of R.I., m. Mercy M. **KENYON**, of Sterling, Oct. 17, 1841, by Peleg Peckham, Elder	3	11
Warren, of Griswold, m. Naomi Ann **WINDSOR**, of Sterling, Mar. 6, 1837, by Peleg Peckham, Elder	2	230
William F., of Norwich, m. Frances H. **HARRIS**, of Plainfield, Nov. 16, 1841, by Rev. Roswell Whitmore	3	14
William G., of Coventry, R.I., m. Fanny H. **JOHNSON**, of Sterling, Feb. 3, 1845, by Peleg Peckham, Elder	3	26
DAY, Calvin, s. Benjamin & Deborough, b. Aug. 21, 1804	2	118
Patience, m. Josiah **HOW[E]**, Nov. 20, 1741	2	1
DEAN, Abigaiel, d. Elijah & Abigaiel, b. Dec. 20, 1738	1	94
Abigail, d. Phinehas & Abigail, b. Mar. 2, 1746	2	41
Abigail, w. Phinehas, d. Apr. 20, 1766, ae. 43 y. 3 m. 14 d.	2	72
Abigail, w. Phinehas, d. Apr. 21, 1766, in the 44th y. of her age	2	61
Abigail, d. Josiah & Meriam, b. Feb. 11, 1773	2	84
Abigail, m. Zadock **HARRIS**, May 30, 1793	2	101
Abijah, s. William & Sarah, b. Oct. 7, 1707	1	8
Amy, d. Seth & Mercy, b. Dec. 26, 1744/5; d. Nov. 27, 1745, ae. 11 m.	2	7

PLAINFIELD VITAL RECORDS

	Vol.	Page
DEAN, (cont.)		
Amy, d. Seth & Mercy, b. Feb. 18, 1746	2	7
Annah, d. Joseph A. & Anna, b. June 15, 1839	3	5
Anne, d. Phinehas & Abigail, b. May 8, 1752	2	42
Anne, d. Seth & Mercy, b. Sept. 15, 1757	2	8
Benjamin, s. William, Jr. & Elizabeth, b. Sept. 14, 1738	1	71
Christofee, s. William, Jr. & Elizabeth, b. Apr. 30, 1737	1	68
Christopher, s. William, Jr. & Elizabeth, d. Feb. 11, 1739	1	99
Christopher, s. James & Mary, b. Oct. 2, 1751	2	19
Christopher, d. Sept. 6, 1821, ae. 70 y.	2	142
Delight, d. Jonathan & Sarah, b. Mar. 8, 1733	1	60
Delight, d. Jonathan & Sarah, b. Mar. 3, 1733	1	64
Delight, d. Lemuel & Mary, b. Nov. 11, 1751	2	1
Desire, d. Phinehas & Abigail, b. Feb. 12, 1744	2	41
Elias, farmer, d. Dec. [ ], 1850, ae. 73	4	65
Elijah, s. William & Sarah, b. May 27, 1709	1	8
Elijah, m. Abigaiel **CARY**, May 15, 1733	1	65
Elifelett, s. Jonathan & Sarah, b. Nov. 27, 1723	1	29
Eliflet, s. Jonathan & Sarah, d. Mar. 9, 1724/5	1	33
Elisabeth, d. Jonathan & Sarah, b. June 3, 1731	1	60
Elisabeth, d. Jonathan & Sarah, b. June 5, 1731	1	54
Elizabeth, m. William **DEAN**, Jr., Dec. 25, 1735	1	68
Elizabeth, m. Micaijah **ADAMS**, Nov. 7, 1750	2	15
Elizabeth, m. William **STORES**, b. of Plainfield, Feb. 26, 1823, by Orin Fowler, V.D.M.	2	190
Easter, d. William & Sarah, b. Feb. 7, 1710/11	1	8
Esther, d. Seth & Mercy, b. Aug. 5, 1755	2	8
Esther, d. Josiah & Meriam, b. Nov. 27, 1775	2	84
Esther, m. Gurdon P. **BROWN**, b. of Plainfield, June 16, 1822, by Orin Fowler, V.D.M.	2	187
[E]unice, d. James & Mary, b. Oct. 10, 1750; d. Oct. 15, 1851	2	19
Ezra, s. Jonathan & Sarah, b. Nov. 18, 1718	1	23
Ezra, s. Phinehas & Abigail, b. Feb. 7, 1749	2	41
Ezra, s. Phinehas & Abigail, d. Feb. 7, 1771, in the 22nd y. of his age wanting 13 d. He died at Parke Avery's, Groton	2	72
Francis, s. James & Sarah, d. Aug. 9, 1700, ae. 17 y. 11 m. 1 d.	1	3
Hannah, d. Jonathan & Sarah, b. Mar. 24, 1722	1	29
Hannah, m. Thomas **GALLUP**, Aug. 11, 1748	2	11
Hannah, d. Phinehas & Abigail, b. Nov. 4, 1754	2	42
Hester, d. Elijah & Abigaiel, b. July 8, 1734	1	65
James, d. May 29, 1725	1	34
James, s. Abijah & Rachel, b. Aug. 10, 1729	1	49

	Vol.	Page
DEAN, (cont.)		
James, s. Abija[h] & Rachel, d. Apr. 15, 1733	1	58
John, s. Seth & Mercy, b. Dec. 18, 1747	2	7
Jonathan, m. Sarah **DOUGLAS**, Jan. 17, 1715/16	1	64
Jonathan, d. May 18, 1763	2	72
Joseph A., of Taunton, Mass., m. Ann M. **TYLER**, of Plainfield, July 2, 1838, by Rev. Samuel Rockwell	2	235
Joseph A., carpenter, ae. 33, b. Taunton, res. Plainfield, m. 2d w. Catharine S. **HALL**, ae. 30, b. Plainfield, Feb. 22, 1848, by Rev. Henry Robinson	4	1
Joseph A., m. Catharine L. **HALL**, b. of Plainfield, Mar. 2, 1848, by Rev. Henry Robinson	3	52
Josiah, s. Lemuel & Mary, b. Jan. 10, 1747/8	2	1
Josiah, m. Marian **TRACY**, Feb. 12, 1769	2	66
Josiah, m. Meriam **TRACY**, Feb. 12, 1769	2	84
Lamira, m. Amarick **STORY**, b. of Plainfield, Sept. 17, 1832, by Rev. Samuel Rockwell	2	215
Leah, d. Abija[h] & Rachal, b. Feb. 2, 1733; d. Feb. 3, [1733]	1	57
Lemuel, s. Jonathan & Sarah, b. Nov. 15, 1725	1	49
Lemuel, m. Marah **LAWRANCE**, June 26, 1746	2	1
Lois, d. Josiah & Meriam, b. Feb. 24, 1778; d. Apr. 10, 1778	2	84
Louisa, d. Phinehas & Abigail, b. Aug. 16, 1747; d. Nov. 1, 1756, in the 10th y. of her age	2	41
Lovisa, d. Phinehas & Abigail, b. Mar. 20, 1761	2	61
Lucy, w. Nathaniel, d. Apr. 14, 1752	2	20
Luce, d. Phinehas & Abigail, b. Apr. 27, 1756	2	42
Lucy, m. Jenckes **HAWKINS**, of Brooklyn, Jan. 23, 1837, by Chester Tilden	2	229
Lydiah, d. Abijah & Rach[el], b. Aug. 9, 1731	1	55
Lydia, d. Lemuel & Mary, b. Apr. 17, 1756	2	34
Mary, d. Jonathan & Sarah, b. Jan. 10, 1716/17	1	18
Mary, d. Lemuel & Mary, b. Oct. 28, 1749	2	11
Mary, m. John **WILLIAMS**, Nov. 4, 1762	2	70
Mary, d. Josiah & Meriam, b. Mar. 31, 1770	2	84
Mary, m. Abijah **PARKE**, Mar. 25, 1772	2	73
Mary, of Plainfield, m. Ephraim **PRENTICE**, of Preston, Feb. 9, 1797	2	104
Mary, b. Charlton, N.J., res. Norwich, d. Oct. 10, 1847, ae. 36	4	61
Mehetable, d. Nathaniel & Susanah, b. Jan. 9, 1720/21	1	25
Mercy, d. Seth & Mercy, b. June 14, 1749	2	7
Meriam, d. Josiah & Miriam, b. Sept. 9, 1779	2	86
Parniel, d. Nathaniel & Luce, b. Feb. 3, 1750	2	12
Paulina L., of Plainfield, m. Daniel **BURGESS**, of Hartford, Mar. 12, 1827, by Orin Fowler, V.D.M.	2	201

	Vol.	Page
DEAN, (cont.)		
Peace, d. Phinehas & Abigail, b. Feb. 10, 1745	2	41
Phinehas, s. Jonathan & Sarah, b. July 19, 1720	1	23
Phinehas, m. Abigail **CLERK**, Dec. 17, 1742	2	41
Phinehas, s. Phinehas & Abigail, b. Sept. 21, 1750; d. Feb. 21, 1752, in the 2nd y. of his age	2	41
Phinehas, s. Phinehas & Abigail, b. Jan. 24, 1758	2	42
Rebecka, d. Lemuel & Mary, b. Aug. 13, 1758	2	38
Ruth, of Plainfield, m. William **GREAVES**, of Killingly, Jan. 9, 1823, by John Dunlap, J.P.	2	191
Samuel, s. Nathaniel & Johanah, b. May 8, 1723	1	30
Sarah, d. Apr. 26, 1726	1	34
Sarah, d. Francis & Hester, b. Dec. 8, 1731	1	69
Sarah, d. Elijah & Abigail, b. Dec. 25, 1740	2	3
Sarah, w. William, d. Dec. 21, 1746	2	5
Sarah, of Plainfield, m. William **ANTRAM**, Jr., of Providence, Apr. 9, 1750, by Rev. David Rowland	2	11
Sarah, d. Seth & Mercy, b. Nov. 3, 1752 O.S.	2	8
Sarah, d. Lemuel & Mary, b. May 7, 1754	2	1
Seth, s. William & Sarah, b. Aug. 7, 1715	1	15
Seth, of Plainfield, m. Mercy **FFENNER**, d. of the late John, of Providence, Oct. 6, 1743, by Richard Ffenner, Asst.	2	7
Seth, s. Seth & Mercy, b. Oct. 9, 1750	2	7
Sibel, d. Elijah & Abigail, b. Aug. 11, 1735; d. Dec. 1, 1739	1	94
Sidney, Rev., of South Windsor, m. Betsey **HERRICK**, of Plainfield, Sept. 13, 1846, by Rev. J. Mather	3	40
Silas, s. John & Lydia, b. Sept. 14, 1709	1	10
Sybil, [see under Sibel]		
Thankfull, d. Abiah & Rachal, b. Aug. 3, 1735	1	69
Thankfull, d. William, Jr. & Elizabeth, b. June 12, 1742	1	99
Tisdell, s. Jonathan & Sarah, b. Nov. 25, 1729	1	50
Violette, d. Phinehas & Abigail, b. Oct. 12, 1762	2	61
William, s. William & Sarah, b. Mar. 1, 1712/13	1	13
William, Jr., m. Elizabeth **DEAN**, Dec. 25, 1735	1	68
William, s. William, Jr. & Elizabeth, b. Aug. 23, 1739	1	99
William, m. Susan **CHAMPLAIN**, b. of Plainfield, Nov. 26, 1843, by Rev. Daniel Dorchester	3	23
William, s. William, Jr. & Elizabeth, b. Nov. 4 [ ]	1	2X
Wilson F., of Eastport, m. Ellen M. **GOODELL**, of Plainfield, May 15, 1853, by Rev. Alfred Gates	3	79
DENISON, Esther S., of Plainfield, m. Archibald A. **WALKER**, of Newton, Mass., Mar. 29, 1846, by Rev. Andrew Dunning	3	37
Mary, d. William, 3d, of Stonington & Priscilla, b. Dec. 12, 1750	2	29

	Vol.	Page

DENISON, (cont.)

	Vol.	Page
Mary M. m. Gardiner **BENTLEY**, b. of Plainfield, Jan. 7, 1852, by Rev. Sidney Dean	3	73
Sarah G., of Plainfield, m. John **MEDBERY**, Jr., of Smithfield, R.I., July 29, 1844, by A. Dunning	3	24
Susan M., m. George **MONTGOMERY**, b. of Plainfield, Mar. 23, 1845, by A. Dunning	3	28
-----, child of Nathan, mechanic, ae. 56, & Sally, ae. 36, b. Oct. 31, 1847	4	22
-----, d. Oct. [1847]	4	61
-----, s. George M., wagon maker, & Lucinda, b. Mar. 1, 1849	4	25
-----, s. Nathan, miller, & Sally, b. Mar. 31, 1849	4	25

DERBY, Abby, of Plainfield, m. Warnare M. **ARNOLD**, of Sterling, Jan. 18, 1829, by Rev. Orin Fowler — 2, 208

DEXTER, Jenckes, of Pomfret, m. Caroline **DOW**, of Plainfield, Mar. 30, 1825, by Orin Fowler, V.D.M. — 2, 197

Stephen, 2d, of Cumberland, R.I., m. Jane **CORY**, of Coventry, R.I., May 31, [probably 1846], by Rev. James Mather — 3, 37

DIBAL, Abigail, m. John **WELCH**, Sept. 11, 1722 — 1, 32

DICKEREY, James, of Griswold, m. Mary **SHAY**, of Plainfield, July 6, 1845, by Amos Witter, J.P. — 3, 32

DILL, Mary, m. Ephraim **FELLOWS**, Jr., Nov. 10, 1737 — 1, 94

DITCHFIELD, Esther, m. Remington **WEAVER**, Feb. 16, 1812, by John Parish, Esq., Brooklyn — 3, 12

DIXON, Arnold, m. Caroline **STUELL**, b. of Plainfield, Nov. 27, 1836, by Chester Tilden — 2, 228

	Vol.	Page
Erastus E., m. Cynthia **HALL**, formerly **GOODSPEED**, b. of Sterling, Jan. 13, 1848, by Peleg Peckham, Elder	3	50
George, s. Thomas & Ruth, b. May 6, 1804	3	5
George, m. Harriet **MONTGOMERY**, b. of Plainfield, Mar. 1, 1835, by Rev. Samuel Rockwell	2	220
Harriet, d. Thomas & Ruth, b. Dec. 18, 1810	3	5
Harriet E., of Plainfield, m. George W. **GORDON**, of Dedham, Mass., Dec. 17, 1839, by Rev. Samuel Rockwell	3	3
Helen Manson, d. George & Harriet, b. Sept. 16, 1839	3	5
James, s. Thomas & Lydia, b. June 11, 1760	2	45
Lewis E., of Plainfield, m. Martha R. **HILL**, of Sterling, Oct. 10, 1854, by Rev. Joseph P. Brown	3	87
Maria B., of Sterling, m. George **UPTON**, of Chaplin, Jan. 30, 1843, by Rev. A. B. Wheeler	3	18
Nathan Fellows, s. William & Prescilla, b. Dec. 13, 1774	2	82
Robert, s. Thomas & Ruth, b. Jan. 28, 1820	3	5

Robert H., of Sterling, m. Hannah B. **KEN[N]EDY**, of

	Vol.	Page
DIXON, (cont.)		
Voluntown, Oct. 16, 1849, by Peleg Peckham, Elder	3	61
Rufus E., s. Thomas & Ruth, b. Mar. 15, 1816	3	5
Ruth Sheperd, d. George & Harriet, b. [ ]	3	5
Samuel, s. Thomas & Ruth, b. Mar. 27 1807	3	5
Sarah Susanna, d. George & Harriet, b. [ ]	3	5
Shepard, of Killingly, m. Betsey **MONTGOMERY**, of Plainfield, Oct. 22, 1838, by Peleg Peckham, Elder	2	237
Wheaton, s. Thomas & Ruth, b. Jan. 20, 1813; d. [ ]	3	5
William Denison, s. William & Priscilla, b. Nov. 6, 1780	2	108
William P., m. Mary A. **JAQ[U]ES**, b. of Sterling, Oct. 15, [1850], by Peleg Peckham, Elder	3	66
DODGE, Olney, of Smithfield, R.I., m. Susan H. **SHEPARD**, of Plainfield, July 31, 1854, by Rev. Henry Robinson	3	84
Sarah B., of New Shoreham, R.I., m. Daniel **ANGELL**, of Plainfield, Sept. 12, 1836, by Rev. Samuel Rockwell	2	227
DOOLEY, Alice M., of Plainfield, m. Edward **VAUGHAN**, of Brooklyn, Nov. 18, 1849, by Rev. J. O. Knapp	3	61
DORING, Topsye, of Killingly, m. Samuel R. **TIFT**, of Foster, R.I., both now residing in Plainfield, June 24, 1827, by Rev. Nathaniel Cole	2	202
DORRANCE, Almiry E., m. Andrew J. **HOPKINS**, July 20, 1840, by Rev. Samuel Rockwell	3	6
Andrew M., of New York, m. Emma **BRIGGS**, of Plainfield, Dec. 23, 1844, by V.R. Osborn, V.D.M.	3	26
DOUGLAS, DOUGLASS, DOWDGLAS, Abiah, d. William & Sarah, b. Feb. 26, 1702/3	1	2
Abiath, m. Henry **HOLLAND**, May 3, 1720	1	24
Alvin, of Killingly, m. Matilda **GALLUP**, of Plainfield, Feb. 28, 1842, by Peleg Peckham, Elder	3	13
Asa, s. William & Sarah, b. Dec. 11, 1715	1	15
Asubah C., m. John **LADD**, b. of Plainfield, July 15, 1839, by Rev. Samuel Rockwell	2	243
Benajah, s. William & Sarah, b. Sept. [ ]	1	7
Benjamin, s. John & Olive, b. July 27, 1741	2	25
Dolly, of Voluntown, m. Edward **MEDBERY**, Jr. of Plainfield, Dec. 26, 1811	2	196
Edward L., s. Robert & Amey, b. Apr. 11, 1828	3	76
Gershom P., m. Sarah D. **ALEXANDER**, b. of Voluntown, July 21, 1850, by Rev. Henry Robinson	3	65
Hannah, d. William & Sarah, b. Sept. 7, 1696	1	2
Han[n]ah, d. William, m. Thomas **WILLIAMS**, s. of Thomas, Feb. 9, 1713/14	1	13
Hannah, d. Asa & Rebecah, b. Jan. 17, 1744/5	2	2
Henry, of Sterling, m. Delia A. **POTTER**, of Plainfield,		

DOUGLAS, DOUGLASS, DOWDGLAS, (cont.)

	Vol.	Page
Oct. 16, 1832, by Rev. Benjamin Paine	2	216
Horatio N., m. Happy C. **KENYON**, b. of Sterling, Jan. 2, 1848, by Peleg Peckham, Elder	3	50
James, s. William & Sarah, b. May 20, 1711	1	10
James, m. Rachel **MARSH**, Sept. 4, 1733	1	58
James, m. Elizabeth [ ], Oct. 7, 1782	3	3
James, of Lebanon, m. Olive **PRIOR**, of Plainfield, Apr. 19, 1834, by Peleg Peckham, Elder	2	218
Jeruse, m. John **FELLOWS**, Jr., Oct. 22, 1728	1	52
John, m. Olief **SPAULDING**, Jan. 13, 1724/5	1	32
John, s. John & Olive, b. Apr. 9, 1734	2	25
John, s. John & Alice, b. Apr. 12, 1734	1	63
Margaret Elizabeth, d. Robert & Amey, b. Dec. 7, 1830	3	76
Mary, d. William, Jr. & Mary, b. Jan. 15, 1717/18	1	18
Mary, w. William, Jr., d. Jan. 20, 1717/18	1	18
Matilda, m. John W. **JAMES**, b. of Plainfield, Nov. 29, 1852, by Rev. Joseph P. Brown	3	77
Olive, d. John & Alice, b. Nov. 4, 1731	1	63
Olive, d. John & Olive, b. Oct. 14, 1749; d. Sept. 17, 1752	2	25
Olive, w. John, d. Feb. 21, 1752	2	25
Pamela, m. Joseph **EATON**, b. of Plainfield, Nov. 11, 1827, by Rev. Orin Fowler	2	203
Prusha, d. William & Sarah, b. Apr. 26, 1706	1	4
Rebecah, d. Asa & Rebecah, b. Jan. 3, 1741/2	2	2
Rebecca, m. Elisha **BRANCH**, Sept. 4, 1791	2	98
Robert, of Sterling, m. Amey **PLACE**, of Plainfield, Feb. 4, 1827, by Nathaniel Cole, Elder	2	201
Samuel, s. William & Sarah, b. Apr. 13, 1699; d. about Jan. 1703	1	2
Samuell, 2d, s. William & Sarah, b. Dec. 3, 1707	1	8
Sarah, d. William & Sarah, b. Dec. 7, 1704	1	2
Sarah, d. Samuell & Sarah, b. Apr. 6, 1715	1	18
Sarah, m. Jonathan **DEAN**, Jan. 17, 1715/16	1	64
Sarah, d. John & Olive, b. Apr. 1, 1744	2	25
Sarah, m. Elisha **PERKINS**, Sept. 23, 1762	2	53
Sarah, m. Eldridge G. **HILL**, b. of Plainfield, Dec. 26, 1830, by Rev. Orin Fowler	2	212
Sarah B., m. John N. **COATS**, b. of Sterling, Oct. 12, 1841, by Peleg Peckham, Elder	3	11
Sibbel, m. Nehemiah **PARKS**, Nov. 16, 1757	2	38
Suesanna, d. James & Rachel, b. June 24, 1733(?) (Date conflicts with the date of marriage of parents)	1	58
Thomas, s. William & Sarah, b. Nov. 26, 1712	1	10
William, s. William & Sarah, b. Feb. 19, 1698	1	2
William, Jr., m. Mary **HANNOUR**, d. of Greenfield, of		

	Vol.	Page

DOUGLAS, DOUGLASS, DOWDGLAS, (cont.)

	Vol.	Page
Tanton, Mar. 26, 1716	1	18
William, Jr., d. Sept. 13, 1719	1	18
William, s. John & Alice, b. Apr. 26, 1729	1	47
William, s. James & Rachel, b. June 24, 1735	1	64
William, s. John & Olive, b. Jan. 27, 1742	2	25
William, s. Asa & Rebecah, b. Aug. 22, 1743	2	2
William, of Voluntown, m. Betsey **JAMES**, of Plainfield, Apr. 11, 1821, by Rev. Orin Fowler	2	133
-----, s. William & Sarah, b. July 28, 1703	1	2
DOW, Asa, s. Henry & Rebecca, b. Jan. 27, 1792	2	98
Asa, s. Henry & Rebecca, d. Feb. 6, 1795	2	107
Asa, s. Henry & Rebecca, b. May 8, 1803	2	114
Asa, s. Henry & Rebecca, [ ]	2	113
Benjamin, s. Henry & Rebecca, b. Feb. 16, 1797	2	107
Caroline, of Plainfield, m. Jenckes **DEXTER**, of Pomfret, Mar. 30, 1825, by Orin Fowler, V.D.M.	2	197
Daniel, m. Elizabeth **MARSH**, July 4, 1751	2	15
Elisha, s. Henry & Rebecca, b. Feb. 25, 1790	2	98
Elisha, of Plainfield, m. Thankful **DAVIS**, of Preston, Mar. 21, 1811, by John Tyler, J.P., Preston	2	125
Elizabeth, d. John & Elizabeth, b. May 23, 1770	2	71
Elizabeth, d. John & Elizabeth, b. May 23, 1770	2	76
Elizabeth, m. Jonathan **GALLUP**, Jan. 3, 1788	2	97
Henry, s. John & Elizabeth, b. June 1, 1766	2	60
Henry, m. Rebecca [ ], Dec. 6, 1787	2	95
Henry, Jr., s. Henry & Rebecca, b. May 13, 1794	2	107
Henry, Jr., m. Marcy **KINNE**, b. of Plainfield, Oct. 2, 1814, by Thomas Backus, J.P.	2	127
Jeremiah Kinne, s. Thomas & Anna, b. July 6, 1796	2	103
John, m. Elizabeth **BURTON**, of Preston, Mar. 8, 1764	2	60
John, Jr., s. John & Elizabeth, b. May 6, 1768	2	71
John, 3d, s. Henry & Rebecca, b. Apr. 15, 1799	2	107
John, Jr., m. Elizabeth **BURTON**, b. of Plainfield, Dec. 12, 1802, by Anthony Bradford, J.P.	2	111
John, d. Dec. 5, 1825, ae. 88 y.	2	142
John, Dr., d. Mar. 7, 1851, ae. 83	4	66
Lydia, d. John & Elizabeth, b. June 9, 1783	2	93
Lydia, of Plainfield, m. Aaron **PRESTON**, of Lisbon, Dec. 15, 1806, by William Dixon, J.P.	2	115
Mary, d. John & Elizabeth, b. Mar. 18, 1776	2	93
Nathan, s. Henry & Rebecca, b. June 24, 1801	2	107
Olive Smith, d. Elisha & Thankful, b. Nov. 22, 1813	2	125
Penelope Davis, d. Elisha & Thankful, b. Feb. 23, 1815	2	127
Phebe A., of Franklin, m. Henry **LEONARD**, of Plainfield, Mar. 18, 1824, by Rev. Levi Nelson, of Lisbon	2	193
Polly, d. Henry & Rebecca, b. Sept. 8, 1788	2	95

	Vol.	Page
DOW, (cont.)		
Rebecca, m. Nehemiah **STEVENS**, Dec. 24, 1747	2	6
Rebecca, s. Henry & Rebecca, b. Aug. 19, 1805	2	114
Samuel T., m. Adeline **BEMIS**, b. of Sterling, Oct. 27, 1827, by Rev. Henry Robinson	3	66
Susanna, m. Cyrus **MARSH**, Apr. 25, 1757	2	37
Susanna, d. John, Jr. & Elizabeth, b. Mar. 26, 1803	2	111
Thomas, s. John & Elizabeth, b. Sept. 19, 1772	2	76
Thomas, m. Anna **KINNE**, Dec. 11, 1795	2	101
Thomas, s. John, Jr. & Elizabeth, b. Feb. 2, 1805	2	111
Thomas, m. Prudence **PRESTON**, Jan. 8, 1839, by Rev. Charles S. Weaver, of Voluntown	2	239
Thomas, d. Sept. 13, 1844, in the 40th y. of his age	3	25
DOWNER, Elisha, m. Lois **PEIRCE**, Sept. 10, 1772	2	76
George Dorrance, s. Elisha & Lois, b. Feb. 20, 1778	2	82
Molle, d. Elisha & Lois, b. June 28, 1774	2	77
DOWNING, Anne, m. Daniel **CLERK**, Aug. 29, 1759	2	48
Mary, d. David & Ann, b. Nov. 5, 1738	1	98
DRAEN, Royal S., of Rehobath, Mass., m. Lydia J. **MASON**, of Sterling, Sept. 1, 1844, by Peleg Peckham, Elder	3	24
DRAPER, Francis T., m. Elizabeth **NEWCOMB**, b. of Plainfield, Apr. 15, 1838, by Frances B. Johnson, J.P.	2	234
DUNHAM, Celinda, m. Peter **JASPER**, Nov. 3, 1799, by Calvin, Goddard, J.P.	2	114
DUNLAP, DUNLOP, Betsey, d. Mar. 22, 1850, ae. 71	4	65
Charles L., s. John & Betsey, b. Dec. 29, 1806	2	142
Edwin, s. John & Betsey, b. Mar. 29, 1804	2	142
Eliza, d. John & Betsey, b. Mar. 7, 1802	2	142
Eliza, of Plainfield, m. Ambrose **MORSE**, of Coventry, Mar. 15, 1829, by Rev. Orin Fowler	2	208
Frances M., of Plainfield, m. George G. **LYON**, of Fall River, Mass., Dec. 15, 1846, by Rev. Jared C. Knapp, Central Village	3	41
Frances Maria, d. John & Betsey, b. Feb. 27, 1817	2	142
George, s. John & Betsey, b. June 1, 1811	2	142
George, m. Nancy **MEDBERY**, b. of Plainfield, Sept. 23, 1839, by Rev. Samuel Rockwell	2	247
Harriet, d. John & Betsey, b. July 11, 1813	2	142
Horace, s. John & Betsey, b. Jan. 20, 1800	2	142
John, d. June 17, [18]48, ae. 73	4	61
Sarah Jane, d. George & Nancy, b. Nov. 20, 1840	3	13
Timothy L., s. John & Betsey, b. Mar. 15, 1809	2	142
DYER, DYAR, Elizabeth had s. Jonathan **SPAULDING**, b. May 1, 1738	2	10
Susan G.B., d. May 5, 1837, ae. 20	2	142
William, m. Susan G. **BURGESS**, b. of Plainfield, Oct. 19, 1835, by Rev. Otis C. Whiton, of Canterbury.		

PLAINFIELD VITAL RECORDS 137

	Vol.	Page
DYER, DYAR, (cont.)		
Dated in Canterbury.	2	222
William, m. Olivia **SESSIONS**, b. of Plainfield, Oct. 15, 1850, by Rev. J. O. Knapp	3	66
William Burgess, s. W[illia]m & Susan G., b. Jan. 14, 1837	2	142
EARLY, -----, s. Patrick, wool spinner, & Bridget, b. Aug. 16, 1850	4	32
EATON, Anne, m. Joseph **WARREN**, June 6, 1759	2	43
Benjamin Smith, s. Col. Elkanah C. & Mary, b. Dec. 20, 1823	2	145
Dolle, d. Ebenezer & Lois, b. Dec. 27, 1777	2	83
Ebenezer, Capt., d. Nov. 29, 1825, ae. 75	2	145
Ebenezer, m. Lois **COBB**, Apr. 15, 1770	2	77
Ebenezer, Jr., s. Ebenezer & Lois, b. July 21, 1782	2	89
Edwin, s. Ebenezer, Jr., & Sibyl, b. July 19, 1817	2	144
Eliza, d. Ebenezer, Jr., & Sibyl, b. Oct. 3, 1820	2	145
Eliza A., m. William A. **BENEDICT**, b. of Plainfield, Feb. 4, 1850, by Rev. Henry Robinson	3	63
Elizabeth, d. Elkanah C. & Mary, b. Aug. 12, 1819	2	132
Elizabeth, m. Samuel **ROCKWELL**, b. of Plainfield, May 5, 1840, by Rev. William Wight, of Jewett City, Griswold	3	4
Elkanah, s. Ebenezer & Lois, b. May 16, 1780	2	83
Elkanah Cobb, m. Mary **SMITH**, Apr. 19, 1812	2	123
Elkanah Cobb, Jr., s. Elkanah Cobb & Mary, b. Sept. 28, 1815	2	130
Ellen M., of Plainfield, m. Seth **PEIRCE**, of Locksport, N.Y., Apr. 19, 1853, by Rev. Henry Robinson	3	78
Ellen P., twin with William P., d. Joseph & Margaret W., b. Apr. 23, 1817	2	144
Emma, d. Ebenezer, Jr. & Sibyl, b. Mar. 5, 1819	2	144
Emma, of Plainfield, m. David **CLARK**, of Brooklyn, May 4, 1840, by Rev. Samuel Rockwell	3	4
Esther, d. Ebenezer & Lois, b. Sept. 6, 1788	2	107
Esther, m. Henry **SABIN**, b. of Plainfield, Feb. 20, 1828, by Rev. Orin Fowler	2	205
Esther P., d. Joseph & Margaret W., b. July 28, 1819; d. Mar. 6, 1821	2	144
Esther P., of Plainfield, m. John M. **FULLER**, of Wrentham, Mass., Sept. 27, 1848, by Rev. Henry Robinson	3	53
Esther Peirce, d. Ebenezer, Jr. & Sibyl, b. Oct. 19, 1820	2	145
Esther Peirce, ae. 28, b. Plainfield, Ct., res. Wrentham, m. John M. **FULLER**, farmer, ae. 23, of Wrentham, Mass., Sept. 30, 1848, by Rev. H. Robinson	4	3

	Vol.	Page
EATON, (cont.)		
Giles M., s. Joseph & Margaret W., b. Dec. 2, 1815	2	144
Hannah, m. Ezra **SPAULDING**, Mar. 10, 1781	2	87
Hannah, d. Col. Elkanah C. & Mary, b. July 20, 1821	2	144
Harriet Ensworth, twin with Henry Bradford, d. Ebenezer, Jr. & Sibyl, b. Nov. 31, 1825	2	145
Henry Bradford, twin with Harriet Ensworth, s. Ebenezer, Jr. & Sibyl, b. Nov. 29, 1825	2	145
Horace, s. Ebenezer, Jr. & Sibyl, b. Nov. 25, 1808	2	144
Joseph, Jr., s. Ebenezer & Lois, b. July 9, 1775	2	79
Joseph, s. Ebenezer, Jr. & Sibyl, b. June 12, 1812	2	144
Joseph, of Plainfield, m. Margaret Wright **MARDENBOROUGH**, of St. Christophers, Nov. 3, 1814, at Newport, R.I.	2	144
Joseph, m. Pamela **DOUGLASS**, b. of Plainfield, Nov. 11, 1827, by Rev. Orin Fowler	2	203
Lois, d. Ebenezer & Lois, b. Sept. 26, 1784	2	89
Lois, m. Henry **BRADFORD**, b. of Plainfield, Nov. 3, 1805, by Rev. Joel Benedict	2	197
Lois, d. Ebenezer, Jr. & Sibyl, b. Feb. 24, 1814	2	144
Lois, of Plainfield, m. Frederick **JONES**, of Nassau, N.Y., Oct. 17, 1849, by Rev. Henry Robinson	3	61
Lucy, d. Ebenezer & Lois, b. Jan. 22, 1791	2	107
Lucy Wilson, d. Ebenezer, Jr. & Sibyl, b. Nov. 11, 1815	2	144
Luther Smith, s. Elkanah Cobb & Mary, b. Mar. 6, 1813	2	123
Luther Smith, s. Elkanah C., Jr. & Eliza W., b. Nov. 26, 1844	3	43
Margaret Elizabeth, d. Elkanah C., Jr. & Eliza W., b. Jan. 6, 1845	3	26
Mary S., d. Elkanah Cobb & Mary, b. July 20, 1817	2	130
Nehemiah, s. Ebenezer & Lois, b. Apr. 19, 1771	2	77
Nehemiah, s. Ebenezer & Lois, d. Apr. 23, 1771	2	77
Sally, d. Ebenezer, Jr. & Sibyl, b. Mar. 19, 1810	2	144
Samuel Ensworth, s. Ebenezer, Jr. & Sibyl, b. May 3, 1823	2	145
Sarah, d. Ebenezer & Lois, b. Apr. 26, 1773	2	77
Susanah, m. Jedeiah **PEIRCE**, Apr. 11, 1764	2	58
W[illia]m H., s. Elkanah, Jr., farmer, & Eliza, b. Sept. 13, 1850	4	31
William P., twin with Ellen P., s. Joseph & Margaret W., b. Apr. 23, 1817	2	144
William Peirce, s. Ebenezer & Lois, b. May 11, 1795	2	107
EBBINS, Melinda J., m. George H. **DAGGETT**, b. of Taunton, Mass., Apr. 26, 1847, by Rev. James Mather	3	44
EDDY, George W., of Cranston, R.I., m. Maria **HALL**, of Plainfield, June 20, 1824, by Orin Fowler, V.D.M.	2	195

	Vol.	Page
EDDY, (cont.)		
Jesse, of Northbridge, Mass., m. Sarah **PAINE**, of Plainfield, Feb. 22, 1824, by Orin Fowler, V.D.M.	2	193
William Cady, s. William Shaw & Lucy, b. May 12, 1821, at Middleborough, Mass.	2	144
William Shaw, of Middleborough, Mass., m. Lucy **CADY**, of Plainfield, Dec. 19, 1819, by Rev. Roswell Whitmore	2	188
EDMOND, Andrew, of Griswold, m. Mary E. **TYLER**, of Plainfield, Mar. 20, 1845, by A. Dunning	3	27
EDWARDS, Lewis, of Warwick, R.I., m. Lucy **UPTON**, of Plainfield, Dec. 2, 1850, by Rev. Joseph P. Brown	3	68
Lucius*, farmer, ae. 25, b. Norwich, res. Plainfield, m. Lucy **UPTON**, cotton weaver, ae. 23, b. Chaplin, res. Plainfield, Dec. 2, 1850, by Rev. Joseph P. Brown (*correction Levias handwritten in margin of original manuscript.)	4	7
Murand, m. George **HILL**, b. of Plainfield, Oct. 23, 1853, by Rev. Joseph P. Brown	3	80
Perry, b. Voluntown, res. Plainfield, d. July 21, 1848, ae. 44	4	61
Samuel K., farmer, black, ae. 20, of Plainfield, m. Mary **CONGDON**, black, housework, ae. 16, of Plainfield, Feb. 18, 1851, by Rev. Joseph P. Brown	4	7
ELDREDGE, George W., of Warwick, R.I., m. Sarah A. **INGRAHAM**, of Coventry, R.I., Sept. 26, 1847, by Rev. James Mather	3	45
Julia Ann, of Plainfield, m. Joseph J.H. **CONGDON**, of Exeter, R.I., Sept. 14, 1850, by Rev. S. W. Coggeshall, Killingly	3	65
Samuel H., of Plainfield, m. Nancy Jane **CONGDON**, of Exeter, R.I., Feb. 18, 1851, by Rev. Joseph P. Brown	3	69
ELLIOT, [see under **ALIOT**]		
ELLIS, Atlucy(?), of West Greenwich, R.I., m. Bowen **VAUGHAN**, of East Greenwich, R.I., Aug. 23, 1841, by Peleg Peckham, Elder	3	10
Mary, b. Sterling, res. Plainfield, d. Oct. [ ], 1848, ae. 33	4	63
Solomon T., of Plainfield, m. Mary **CARD**, of Sterling, Feb. 6, 1837, by Rev. Samuel Rockwell	3	6
Solomon T., of Plainfield, m. Ursula **MILLER**, of Westfield, Vt., Sept. 6, 1851, by Peleg Peckham, Elder	3	71
Stillman W., of Providence, R.I., m. Sally **COBB**, of Scituate, R.I., Dec. 6, 1847, by Rev. James Mather	3	47
-----, child of Solomon, agriculturist, ae. 42, & Mary P. **CARD ELLIS**, ae. 33, b. Aug. 11, 1848	4	23
-----, d. Solomon, wool spinner, & Mary, b. Oct. [ ],		

	Vol.	Page
ELLIS, (cont.)		
1848	4	27
ENSWORTH, Grace, m. Ebenezer **BENNET**, Nov. 17, 1768	2	68
ESLECK, Mary, d. Isaac & Martha, b. May 12, 1782	2	89
EVANS, EVENS, Andrew, s. Edward & Mary, b. May 13, 1753	2	26
Cathren, d. Edward & Jean, b. May 8, 1737	1	70
Edward, s. William & Jannet, b. Mar. 3, 1750	2	37
Edward, m. Mary **PRATT**, Dec. 3, 1751	2	16
Hannah, d. John & Hannah, b. Aug. 15, 1744	2	38
Isaac, s. Edward & Mary, b. Sept. 17, 1756	2	37
John, s. Edward & Mary, b. Nov. 17, 1754	2	26
Margeret, d. William & Jen[n]y, b. Feb. 8, 1748	2	9
Ma[r]tha, d. William & Jennet, b. Apr. 30, 1754	2	37
Mary, s. Edward & Jane, b. Oct. 6, 1732	1	59
Mary, d. William & Jennet, b. Apr. 12, 1756	2	37
William, s. Edward & Jane, b. Oct. 10, 1731	1	59
William, m. Jen[n]y [ ], July 9, 1747, by Rev. Thomas Stevens	2	9
William, s. William & Jannet, b. Jan. 31, 1752	2	37
FAGINS, Ichabod, of Killingly, m. Lucinda **HENLY**, of Plainfield, June 27, 1835, by John Dunlap, J.P.	2	221
FAIRBANKS, Abel, s. Eleazer & Prudence, b. May 12, 1754	2	26
Bette, d. Eleazer & Prudence, b. Feb. 1, 1750	2	18
Eleazer, s. Eleazer & Prudence, b. May 10, 1752	2	18
James, farmer, d. Oct. 5, 1848, ae. 66	4	63
Sarah, d. Eleazer & Prudence, b. Mar. 20, 1757	2	36
FAIRMAN, FARMAN, FAREMAN, Isaac P., m. Sarah **COLLINS**, b. of Plainfield, Nov. 21, 1821, by Nathaniel Cole, Elder	2	134
James, of Killingly, m. Almira M. **LYON**, of Plainfield, Jan. 6, 1850, by Rev. W. Emerson	3	63
James, m. Eunice **CORY**, Jan. 4, 1759	2	40
James, farmer, ae. 19, of Killingly, m. Almira M. **LYON**, ae. 19, cotton weaver, b. Scituate, res. Killingly, Jan. 6, 1850, by Rev. Warren Emerson	4	6
Jane E., m. Anthony B. **KENYON**, Nov. 29, 1849, by Peleg Peckham, Elder	3	62
Jane E., ae. 18, of Plainfield, m. Anthony B. **KENYON**, farmer, ae. 24, of Plainfield, Nov. 29, 1849, by Peleg Peckham	4	5
John A.P., of Killingly, m. Ann R. **ARNOLD**, of Plainfield, Sept. 6, 1852, by Rev. Joseph P. Brown	3	75
Mary Ann, of Plainfield, m. Godfrey W. **FOWLER**, of Canterbury, Jan. 14, 1850, by Peleg Peckham, Elder	3	63
Mary Ann, ae. 25, of Plainfield, m. Godfrey **FOWLER**, farmer, ae. 35, of Canterbury, Jan. 19, 1850, by Peleg Peckham	4	5

	Vol.	Page
FAIRMAN, FARMAN, FAREMAN, (cont.)		
Susan, m. Ichabod **POTTER**, b. of Plainfield, Jan. 12, 1823, by Rev. Nathaniel Cole	2	190
FANNING, Ann G., m. Jabez C. **GATES**, b. of Plainfield, July 2, 1849, by Rev. Henry Robinson	3	57
Anna P., ae. 17, b. Lisbon, res. Plainfield, m. Jabez C. **GATES**, "capter", ae. 23, b. Voluntown, res. Plainfield, July 3, [1849?], by Rev. Henry Robinson	4	3
FARLAN, Hutchinson, m. Lydia **JOHNSON**, b. of Plainfield, June 4, 1809, by Rev. Joel Benedict	2	120
FARNUM, FARNHAM, John B., m. Permilla S. **BALDWIN**, b. of Canterbury, Apr. 15, 1838, by Rev. Tubal Wakefield, Packersville	2	234
Lucy, m. Robert **WASHBURN**, Feb. 9, 1764	2	59
Nathaniel, s. Stephen & Olive, b. Mar. 7, 1769	2	66
Peter, of Philadelphia, Pa., m. Caroline **SPAULDING**, of Plainfield, Jan. 26, 1852, by Rev. Joseph P. Brown	3	73
Stephen, m. Olive **WHE[E]LER**, Mar. 10, 1768	2	66
FAR[R]EL, Emeline, m. Thomas D. **RHODES**, b. of Plainfield, Apr. 10, 1848, by Rev. Frederic Charlton	3	55
FELLOWS, FFELLOWS, Abial, s. Ephraim & Mary, b. Oct. 29, 1734	1	62
Abigail, d. John & Rachal, b. May 13, 1701	1	2
Abegall, d. Sergt. John, m. Samuel **HALL**, Jan. 4, 1720/21	1	25
Amos, s. Isaac & Abigaiel, b. Apr. 21, 1729	1	48
Amy, m. Thomas **STEEVENS**, Jr., Nov. 8, 1716	1	17
Crarry *, s. John & Rachall, b. Mar. 25, 1694 (*Should be "Varney". See Ipswich Records)	1	2
David, s. Ephraim, Jr. & Mary, b. Nov. 23, 1738	1	94
Elizabeth, d. Ephraim, m. Henry **STEEVENS**, Mar. 2, 1708/9	1	7
Elizabeth, d. Isaac & Abigail, b. Apr. 28, 1722	1	45
Elizabeth, m. Wait **HER[R]ICK**, June 26, 1739	1	101
Ephraim, m. Mary [ ], Dec. 3, 1711	1	11
Ephraim, s. Ephraim & Mary, b. June 12, 1715	1	15
Ephraim, Jr., m. Mary **DILL**, Nov. 10, 1737	1	94
Ezra, s. John, Jr. & Jeresha, b. Apr. 9, 1730	1	52
Isaac, s. John & Rachall, b. Sept. 1, 1696	1	2
Isaac, s. Isaac & Abigaiel, b. Jan. 8, 1732/3	1	63
Joanah, d. Ephraim & Mary, b. Nov. 12, 1717	1	18
John, s. John & Rachall, b. Mar. 3, 1703/4	1	1
John, Jr., m. Jeruse **DOUGLASS**, Oct. 22, 1728	1	52
John, s. Nathan & Priscilla, b. June 24, 1732; d. July 28, 1754	2	26
John, s. John & Jerusha, b. July 7, 1735	1	69
Jonathan, s. Ephraim & Mary, b. Dec. 11, 1728	1	46

	Vol.	Page
FELLOWS, FFELLOWS, (cont.)		
Joseph, s. Ephraim & Mary, b. Mar. 23, 1760	1	56
Mary, d. Ephraim & Mary, b. Sept. 27, 1712	1	11
Mary, d. Ephraim & Mary, b. Oct. 30, 1740	1	96
Merian, d. Ephraim & Marah, b. Apr. 2, 1726	1	36
Nathan, m. Priscilla **WARREN**, Jan. 29, 1750	2	26
Nathan, d. Sept. 24, 1754	2	26
Prescilla, d. Nathan & Priscilla, b. Aug. 25, 1730; d. Oct. 18, 1754	2	26
Rachall, d. John & Rachall, b. Oct. 22, 1698	1	2
Rachel, d. John & Jerusha, b. Jan. 31, 1732	1	56
Sarah, d. John, Jr. & Jerusha, b. Sept. 28, 1733	1	59
Thomas, s. Ephraim & Mercy, b. Mar. 13, 1723	1	27
Varney*, s. John & Rachall, b. Mar. 25, 1694 (*See Ipswich Records. Arnold Copy has "Crarry")	1	2
Varney, s. Isaac & Abigaiel, b. July 11, 1724	1	45
William, s. Ephraim & Mary, b. Nov. 29, 1720	1	23
FENNER, FFENNER, Amey, m. Christopher A. **TILLINGHAST**, b. of Sterling, Nov. 6, 1836, by Peleg Peckham, Elder	2	228
Harden H., merchant, ae. 21, b. Foster, R.I., res. Sterling, m. Nancy A. **HOPKINS**, ae. 19, of Plainfield, Mar. 25, 1850, by Peleg Peckham	4	5
Harden W., of Sterling, m. Nancy H. **HOPKINS**, of Plainfield, Mar. 25, 1850, by Peleg Peckham, Elder	3	64
John O., m. Elizabeth **JACQUES**, b. of R.I., Jan. 3, 1847, by Mowry Burgess, J.P.	3	42
John O., of Johnson, R.I., m. Elizabeth **JACQUES**, of Providence, R.I., Jan. 3, 1847, by M. Burgess, J.P.	3	44
Joshua, of Canterbury, m. Mary A. **OLIN**, of Plainfield, Apr. 24, 1853, by Rev. Henry Robinson	3	79
Mary M., of Sterling, m. James **FRANKLIN**, of Killingly, July 6, 1845, by Peleg Peckham, Elder	3	31
Mercy, d. of the late John, of Providence, m. Seth **DEAN**, of Plainfield, Oct. 6, 1743, by Richard Ffenner, Asst.	2	7
Sarah E., of Sterling, m. George J. **ROSS**, of Franklin, Oct. 18, 1840, by Peleg Peckham, Elder	3	7
FERENSIDE, John, m. Theda E. **JACOBS**, Sept. 17, 1854, by Rev. Alfred Gates	3	86
FERNALD, James, m. Adaline W. **POTTER**, b. of Coventry, R.I., Dec. 3, 1843, by A. Dunning	3	21
FIELDS, FIELD, Charles, farmer, b. Smithfield, R.I., res. Plainfield, d. May 15, 1847, ae. 73	4	63
Mary, m. John J. **HALL**, b. of Plainfield, Dec. 31, [probably 1852], by Rev. William Turkington	3	77
FISH, Darius A., m. Mary **TILLINGHAST**, b. of Sterling, Sept.		

PLAINFIELD VITAL RECORDS 143

	Vol.	Page
FISH, (cont.)		
4, 1843, by Peleg Peckham, Elder	3	20
Desire, m. Elihu **WILLIAMS**, Nov. 17, 1747	2	22
Eliza, m. Alfred B. **MADISON**, b. of Sterling, July 20, 1851, by Peleg Peckham, Elder	3	70
Eunice, of Stonington, m. Timothy **PEIRCE**, of Plainfield, Aug. 8, 1754	2	29
Patience, of Plainfield, m. John **NILES**, of Windham, Jan. 25, 1852, by Rev. Henry Robinson	3	73
FISHER, Anna, d. Donald & Susanna, b. Feb. 13, 1797, at Freetown, Mass.	2	115
Arrabella, d. Donald & Susanna, b. May 26, 1803, in Killingly	2	115
Donald, s. Donald & Susanna, b. May 2, 1805	2	110
John, s. Donald & Susanna, b. Mar. 11, 1795, at St. John, Province of New Brunswick	2	115
Mary, d. Donald & Susanna, b. Feb. 3, 1799, at Glocester, R.I.	2	115
Sally, d. Donald & Susanna, b. Sept. 2, 1807	2	115
Sally, of Plainfield, m. Elisha R. **SYDLEMAN**, of Canterbury, May 9, 1841, by Rev. John Read	3	9
Susanna, d. Donald & Susanna, b. Apr. 14, 1801, in Glocester, R.I.	2	115
William, m. Speedy **YORK**, b. of Plainfield, Mar. 17, 1839, by Rev. Samuel Rockwell	2	240
FISK, Dolly, of Plainfield, m. Joseph **JOHNSON**, of Griswold, July 22, 1837, by Daniel Hill, J.P.	2	231
Dorcas, of Plainfield, m. William W. **AVERY**, of Preston, Dec. 4, 1823, by Nathaniel Cole, Elder	2	192
Edward W., m. Jane E. C. **BALLOU**, b. of Coventry, R.I., May 28, 1854, by Peleg Peckham, Elder	3	83
Hopkins, of Plainfield, m. Aurelia **STEWELL**, of Bolton, Sept. 3, 1827, by Enoch Burt, Manchester	2	203
FITCH, Stanton, of Norwich, m. Lydia **ROOD**, of Killingly, Oct. 15, 1844, by James Smither, Elder	3	28
FOGG, Lydia E., of Boston, Mass., m. Levi W. **FOWLE**, of Worcester, Mass., July 3, 1847, by Rev. J. Mather	3	43
FORD, Jane, m. Edward **McDONALD**, b. of Sterling, Sept. 18, 1850, by John J. Penrose, J.P.	3	88
Lucy, m. Edward **McDONALD**, Sept. 18, 1850, by John J. Penrose, J.P.	3	65
FORTUNE, Dick, m. Dinah **THAYER**, Nov. 19, 1795	2	102
FOSTER, Alfred, of Leicester, Mass., m. Susan **WEST**, of Plainfield, May 23, 1841, by Rev. John Read	3	10
Arnold K., m. Lucy **PRIOR**, b. of Plainfield, [probably Aug.] 29, 1842, by Rev. A.B. Wheeler	3	17
Frances M., of Plainfield, m. Alva **NIYLIE**, of Apalachercola, Florida, [ ], by Rev.		

	Vol.	Page
FOSTER, (cont.)		
Samuel Rockwell	2	243
Waty, m. John **JOSLIN**, Jr., Nov. 5, 1820, by Nathaniel Cole, Elder	2	133
Weaver, m. Lydia **GRAVES**, Dec. 6, 1821, by Nathaniel Cole, Elder	2	134
FOWLE, Levi W., of Worcester, Mass., m. Lydia E. **FOGG**, of Boston, Mass., July 3, 1847, by Rev. J. Mather	3	43
FOWLER, Godfrey, farmer, ae. 35, of Canterbury, m. Mary Ann **FAIRMAN**, ae. 25, of Plainfield, Jan. 19, 1850, by Peleg Peckham	4	5
Godfrey W., of Canterbury, m. Mary Ann **FAIRMAN**, of Plainfield, Jan. 14, 1850, by Peleg Peckham, Elder	3	63
Mary Moseley, d. Rev. Orin & Amaryllis, b. July 13, 1822; d. Nov. 7, 1827, ae. 5 y. 4 m.	2	146
Mary Moseley, d. Rev. Orin & Amaryllis, d. Nov. 7, 1827, ae. 5 y. 4 m.	2	146
Peggy, m. David **WARREN**, Oct. 18, 1790	2	98
FOX, Elijah, m. Polly **PARK**, Feb. 28, 1788	2	97
Ezekiel, m. Susannah **CHILD**, Oct. 10, 1791	2	101
Lucy, d. Elijah & Polly, b. Jan. 10, 1794	2	103
Otis, s. Elijah & Polly, b. June 6, 1797	2	103
Rachel Wright, d. Ezekiel & Susanna, b. Jan. 1, 1793	2	101
Samuel, Jr., [twin with Sibbel], s. Elijah & Polly, b. Apr. 5, 1789	2	97
Sibbel, [twin with Samuel, Jr.], d. Elijah & Polly, b. Apr. 5, 1789	2	97
FRANKLIN, Eliza, of Plainfield, m. Mason **SALSBURY**, of R.I. Sept. 19, 1824, by J. Gordon, J.P.	2	195
James, of Killingly, m. Mary M. **FENNER**, of Sterling, July 6, 1845, by Peleg Peckham, Elder	3	31
Lucinda, of Plainfield, m. Henry M. **SAILS**, of Sterling, June 14, 1846, by Peleg Peckham, Elder	3	38
FRAZIER, Thomas M., of Norwich, m. Maria B. **WOOD**, of Plainfield, Apr. 2, 1843, by Rev. A.B. Wheeler	3	18
FREEMAN, Charles D., s. George, farmer, black, & Lucy, black, b. May 9, 1848	4	21
Gethan G., m. Albert **WILBUR**, b. of Sterling, Oct. 3, 1847, by Peleg Peckham, Elder	3	53
Samuel, Capt., m. Olive A. **MATHEWSON**, b. of Providence, R.I., Oct. 4, 1839, by Rev. Tubal Wakefield, Packersville	2	248
Samuel, m. Alice A. **MATHEWSON**, b. of Providence, R.I., Oct. 4, 1839, by Rev. Tubal Wakefield	3	1
Susan A., of Plainfield, m. Edwin **BENNETT**, of Sterling, May 30, 1852, by Peleg Peckham, Elder	3	75
FRENCH, Abner, m. Betsey **BENNETT**, Feb. 1, 1821, by Rev. Nathaniel Cole	2	133

	Vol.	Page
FRENCH, (cont.)		
Abner, farmer, ae. 59, of Plainfield, m. 2d w. Susan **BROWN**, cotton weaver, ae. 56, b. Ireland, res. Plainfield, Dec. 14, 1850, by Rev. Joseph P. Brown	4	7
Abner, m. Susan **BROWN**, b. of Plainfield, Dec. 15, 1850, by Rev. Joseph P. Brown	3	68
Amey A., of Plainfield, m. Arastus L. **BRUCE**, of Pomfret, Nov. 18, 1850, by Rev. Joseph P. Brown	3	67
Amy A., woolen weaver, ae. 27, of Plainfield, m. Erastus L. **BRUCE**, farmer, ae. 32, of Pomfret, Nov. 18, 1850, by Rev. Joseph P. Brown	4	7
Betsey, d. Oct. 19, 1849, ae. 50	4	64
Delight, d. Hezekiah & Olive, b. Apr. 11, 1824	3	15
Edwin, s. Hezekiah & Olive, b. Nov. 27, 1833	3	15
Edwin, farmer, d. Oct. 25, 1849, ae. 17	4	64
Elizabeth, d. John S., farmer, ae. 32, & Jane, ae. 30, b. Sept. 5, 1848	4	25
Emeline Elizabeth, d. Hezekiah & Olive, b. May 8, 1817	3	15
Henry, s. Hezekiah & Olive, b. Nov. 6, 1818	3	15
Henry H., s. John S. & Jane, b. July 4, 1840	3	8
Hezekiah, s. Nathaniel & Sarah, b. Sept. 1, 1744	2	39
Hezekiah, m. Olive F. **HALL**, Apr. 28, 1816	3	15
Hezekiah, s. Hezekiah & Olive, b. Feb. 28, 1831	3	15
Hezekiah, m. Eliza A. **WELLS**, Oct. 3, 1853, by Rev. W[illia]m Turkington	3	80
Isaac, s. Nathaniel & Sarah, b. May 5, 1750	2	39
John, s. Nathaniel & Sarah, b. Oct. 26, 1747	2	32
John, s. Nathaniel & Sarah, b. Oct. 26, 1747	2	39
John S., of Plainfield, m. Jane H. **LATHROP**, of [Norwich], Oct. 22, 1839, by Rev. Henry Dyon, Norwich	3	8
John Spaulding, s. Nathaniel & Rachel, b. May 25, 1819	2	146
Jonas, m. Asenath **HALL**, b. of Plainfield, May 17, 1814, by Rev. Joel Benedict	2	200
Jonas, d. Oct. 11, 1820, ae. 33	2	146
Louisa, m. Daniel **STARKWEATHER**, b. of Plainfield, Feb. 19, 1846, by Rev. A. Dunning	3	35
Lucy, d. Nathaniel & Rachel, b. Nov. 24, 1813	2	146
Lucy E., d. Feb. 21, 1851, ae. 2	4	66
Lydia, d. Nathaniel & Sarah, b. Dec. 14, 1742	2	39
Lydia, of Plainfield, m. Colonel **VAUGHN**, of Bennington, Vt., Sept. 16, 1827, by Elder George W. Appleton, Sterling	2	203
Mary Jane, d. Hezekiah & Olive, b. Jan. 16, 1835	3	15
Mehetabel, d. Nathaniel & Sarah, b. Sept. 14, 1746	2	39
Mehetibel, d. Nathaniel & Sarah, b. Sept. 14, 1746	2	49
Nelson, of Plainfield, m. Caroline **BRIGGS**, of Sterling, Sept. 6, 1852, by Rev. Henry Robinson	3	76

	Vol.	Page
FRENCH, (cont.)		
Olive, d. Hezekiah & Olive, b. May 16, 1828	3	15
Olive, of Plainfield, m. Warren **WILLIAMS**, of Brooklyn, Nov. 25, 1847, by Rev. Henry Robinson	3	47
Olive, ae. 20, b. Plainfield, m. Warren **WILLIAMS**, farmer, ae. 23, of Brooklyn, Nov. 25, [18]47, by Rev. Henry Robinson	4	1
Ruby P., tailoress, d. July 13, 1847, ae. 21	4	61
Ruth H., d. Jonas & Asenath, b. July 9, 1816	2	146
Sally, d. Hezekiah & Olive, b. Sept. 6, 1820	3	15
Sarah, wid. Nath[anie]l, m. Jonathan **PARKER**, Dec. 29, 1757	2	40
Sarah, wid. Nathaniel, m. Jonathan **PARKER**, b. of Plainfield, Dec. 29, 1757, by John Crery, J.P.	2	52
Sarah, of Plainfield, m. John M. **BAKER**, of Brooklyn, Feb. 15, 1848, by Rev. Henry Robinson	3	52
Sarah, ae. 23, b. Plainfield, m. John M. **BAKER**, carriage maker, ae. 27, of Brooklyn, Feb. 16, 1848, by Rev. Henry Robinson	4	1
Stephen John, s. Hezekiah & Olive, b. Apr. 21, 1822	3	15
Susan, d. Hezekiah & Olive, b. Feb. 11, 1826	3	15
Thomas J., m. Adah **HOPKINS**, b. of Sterling, Sept. 8, 1845, by Peleg Peckham, Elder	3	32
William, m. Abby R. **GIBSON**, b. of Sterling, May 13, 1844, by Peleg Peckham, Elder	3	23
FRINK, Albert, farmer, ae. 29, b. Plainfield, Ct., res. Sterling, m. Mary Ann **BRIGGS**, ae. 25, of Sterling, Nov. 8, 1848, by Rev. Allen	4	3
Amarilla, of Plainfield, m. John R. **GALLUP**, of Sterling, Nov. 16, 1851, by Rev. Henry Robinson	3	72
Ambrose, of Sterling, m. Amelia **SPAULDING**, of Plainfield, Mar. 3, 1822, by John Dunlap, J.P.	2	187
Bridget, m. Joseph **SPAULDING**, b. of Plainfield, Nov. 16, 1809, by Rev. Joel Benedict	2	118
Esther, of Plainfield, m. Manuel **KINNIE**, of Voluntown, June 3, 1822, by Orin Fowler, V.D.M.	2	187
Lois, of Sterling, m. Welcome **CARD**, of Charlestown, R.I., Mar. 3, 1851, by Peleg Peckham, Elder	3	69
Samuel, b. Sterling, res. Plainfield, d. Aug. 14, 1850, ae. 85	4	66
FROST, Daniel, laborer, black, ae. 27, of Griswold, m. Ann **CROSS**, black, ae. 20, of Griswold, Nov. 10, [1850?], by Benjamin Bacon	4	7
David, m. Nancy Anna **PETERSON**, Nov. 17, 1850, by Benjamin Bacon, J.P.	3	67
FRY, Henry, m. Mary E. **GIBSON**, b. of Plainfield, May 23, 1833, by Rev. Samuel Rockwell	2	217

	Vol.	Page

FRY, (cont.)
   Maria, of Plainfield, m. Andrew **ABEL**, of Lisbon,
      Nov. 28, 1844, by V.R. Osborn, V.D.M.   3   26
   Mary H., of Plainfield, m. Henry F. **STEWARD**, of
      Norwich, Mar. 4, 1852, by Rev. Joseph P. Brown   3   74
   Nancy, m. Joseph **PRESTON**, b. of Plainfield, Mar. 10,
      1833, by Rev. Samuel Rockwell   2   216
   Rhoda, of Plainfield, m. Jason **STONE**, of Sterling,
      Sept. 18, 1837, by Chester Tilden   2   232
   -----, s. Harry, overseer in woolen mill, & Mary,
      b. May 24, 1851   4   32
FULLER, Asaph, s. Rev. John & Lodema, b. July 24, 1776   2   110
   Cha[u]nc[e]y, b. Killingly, res. Plainfield, d.
      Feb. [ ], 1851, ae. 11 1/2 y.   4   66
   Frank, s. Elisha L., farmer, & Sophia, b. May 12,
      1851   4   31
   Frank, d. July [1851], ae. 3 m.   4   66
   Harriet B., ae. 19, b. Thompson, Ct., res. Plainfield,
      m. Edwin M. **TANNER**, tailor, ae. 21, b. R.I., res.
      Plainfield, July 1, 1849, by Frederic Coe   4   3
   James A., of Worcester, Mass., m. Mary E. **KENYON**, of
      Exeter, Oct. 28, 1847, by Peleg Peckham, Elder   3   53
   Jeremiah E., m. Alpha M. **BUCKLIN**, b. of Sterling,
      Dec. 8, 1835, by Peleg Peckham, Elder   2   224
   John M., of Wrenthan, Mass., m. Esther P. **EATON**, of
      Plainfield, Sept. 27, 1848, by Rev. Henry
      Robinson   3   53
   John M., farmer, ae. 23, of Wrentham, Mass., m. Esther
      Peirce **EATON**, ae. 28, b. Plainfield, Ct., res.
      Wrentham, Sept. 30, 1848, by Rev. H. Robinson   4   3
   John M., of Hanover, m. Hannah Ann **WILCOX**, of Norwich,
      Jan. 31, 1854, by Rev. William Turkington   3   82
   Lucius, of Hartford, m. Clarrissa **CUNDALL**, of Plain-
      field, Nov. 27, 1844, by James Smither, Elder   3   29
   Pamala L., m. John **COIT**, b. of Plainfield, Mar. 10,
      1836, by Rev. Samuel Rockwell   2   225
   Parker H., m. Sophia **RHODES**, b. of Sterling, July 25,
      1842, by Peleg Peckham, Elder   3   16
   William J., m. Janett **BURGES**, b. of Hartford, May 1,
      1848, by Rev. Frederic Charlton   3   55
   -----, apothecary, of Hartford, m. 2d w. Janette
      BURGESS, June [ ], 1848, by Rev. Frederic Charlton   4   2
GAIL, Jerusha, m. Thomas **WILSON**, June 27, 1749   2   8
GAIN[E]S, Tecunsah, school boy, black, b. Arkansas, res.
   Plainfield, d. Jan. 7, 1851, ae. 18   4   66
GALLANDET, GALLENEDETT, Peter Wallace, of West Spring-
   field, Mass., m. Margaret E. **ROBINSON**, of Plain-
   field, June 20, 1849, by Rev. Henry Robinson

	Vol.	Page
GALLANDET, GALLENEDETT, (cont.)		
(GALLAUDET?)	3	57
Peter Wallace, mechanic, ae. 23, b. Hartford, res. W. Springfield, m. Marg[a]ret Elizabeth **ROBINSON**, ae. 19, June 20, 1849, by Rev. H. Robinson	4	3
GALLUP, Abigail, w. Ebenezer, d. Sept. 10, 1797, in the 70th year of her age	2	102
Almira, of Sterling, m. Daniel **KINNE**, of Plainfield, Dec. 1, 1844, by Peleg Peckham, Elder	3	25
Alvan, of West Greenwich, R.I., m. Sarah **SPAULDING**, of Plainfield, Feb. 4, 1839, by Rev. Samuel Rockwell	2	239
Anne, d. Thomas & Hannah, b. July 17, 1754	2	25
Asa, s. Thomas & Hannah, b. June 22, 1752	2	18
Asa, s. Benj[ami]n & Martha, b. Feb. 2, 1785	2	90
Avery, s. Thomas Dow & Polly, b. Sept. 14, 1823	2	149
Benjamin, s. Thomas & Hannah, b. June 17, 1758	2	38
Benjamin, m. Martha [ ], Dec. 6, 1781	2	90
Benjamin, s. Benjamin & Martha, b. May 12, 1790	2	105
Benjamin, m. Sally **PARK**, Mar. 15, 1801	2	149
Brigget, d. John & Brigget, b. Dec. 31, 1752	2	23
Bridget, d. John & Bridget, d. Mar. 29, 1765, in the 13th y. of her age	2	58
Daniel, of West Greenwich, R.I., now of Plainfield, m. Esther **BARROWS**, of Killingly, July 7, 1834, by William Dyer, J.P.	2	219
Daniel, of Sterling, m. Julia Ann **WOODWARD**, of Plainfield, Oct. 14, 1835, by Rev. Geo[rge] Perkins, of Griswold	2	223
David, s. John & Brigget, b. Oct. 17, 1754	2	26
David, s. Jonathan & Elizabeth, b. May 26, 1790	2	99
Denison G., of Voluntown, m. Ruby A. **PERKINS**, of Sterling, Feb. 18, 1849, by Peleg Peckham, Elder	3	58
Ebenezer, m. Abigail **SPAULDING**, Mar. 27, 1755	2	44
Ebenezer, s. Ebenezer & Abigail, b. Oct. 8, 1762; d. Oct. 11, 1762	2	50
Ebenezer, m. Elizabeth **BABCOCK**, Nov. 26, 1797	2	103
Edward Parks, s. Moses, tin manufacturer, & Talatha, b. Dec. 25, 1847	4	22
Eliza A., m. George W. **BENNET**, Apr. 10, 1842, by Lawton Cady, Elder	3	14
Elizabeth, m. Attwood **WILLIAMS**, Aug. 3, 1749	2	50
Elizabeth, d. Dec. 16, 1850, ae. 80	4	64
Fanny, m. Sessions **LESTER**, b. of Plainfield, Apr. 3, 1814	2	158
Hannah, of Voluntown, m. Levi **KINNE**, of Plainfield, Jan. 4, 1787, by Rev. Micaiah **PORTER**, of the 1st Soc. in Voluntown	2	112
Hannah, d. Benjamin & Martha, b. June 19, 1788	2	105

PLAINFIELD VITAL RECORDS

	Vol.	Page
GALLUP, (cont.)		
Hannah, m. Rodman **JAMES**, b. of Plainfield, Mar. 7, 1830, by Rev. Orin Fowler	2	211
Hester, d. John & Brigget, b. May 23, 1759	2	41
Horace, s. Thomas Dow & Polly, b. Feb. 24, 1821	2	148
Isaac, s. Benjamin & Martha, b. June 20, 1794	2	105
Jerusha, d. John & Brigget, b. Dec. 22, 1748	2	7
John, m. Brigget **PALMER**, Nov. 5, 1747	2	7
John, s. John & Brigget, b. Oct. 13, 1750	2	12
John, 3rd, s. Jonathan & Elizabeth, b. Jan. 4, 1789	2	97
John, 3rd, s. Jonathan & Elizabeth, d. Sept. 6, 1793	2	148
John, s. Benjamin & Martha, b. Jan. 13, 1797	2	105
John R., of Sterling, m. Amarilla **FRINK**, of Plainfield, Nov. 16, 1851, by Rev. Henry Robinson	3	72
Jonathan, s. John & Briggit, b. July 14, 1756	2	26
Jonathan, m. Elizabeth **DOW**, Jan. 3, 1788	2	97
Jonathan, d. Aug. 26, 1828, ae. 72 y.	2	149
Judeth, of Plainfield, m. Henry **HALL**, of Pomfret, Mar. 23, 1845, by Peleg Peckham, Elder	3	26
Julia Ella, d. David & Julia, b. Jan. 5, 1847	3	60
Julyett, d. Thomas Dow & Polly, b. Mar. 3, 1828	2	149
Lucius, of Norwich, m. Jane P. **BALDWIN**, of Canterbury, Jan. 2, 1854, by Rev. Alfred Gates	3	83
Lucy, d. Benj[ami]n & Martha, b. May 1, 1786	2	105
Lucy A., m. William B. **AMES**, b. of Plainfield, Apr. 21, 1839, by Rev. Samuel Rockwell	2	241
Lucy Ann, d. Thomas Dow & Polly, b. Aug. 11, 1816	2	131
Lucy E., of Sterling, m. Charles G. **WILLIAMS**, of Brooklyn, Feb. 25, 1846, by Peleg Peckham, Elder	3	36
Lydia, of Plainfield, m. Smith **OLNEY**, of North Providence, R.I., Mar. 31, 1822, by Orin Fowler, V.D.M.	2	187
Margeret, d. Thomas & Hannah, b. Oct. 1, 1756	2	25
Margaret, d. John & Bridget, b. Aug. 29, 1764	2	58
Margaret, d. Benjamin & Martha, b. Jan. 13, 1799	2	105
Margaret, of Sterling, m. Joseph **MOORE**, of Plainfield, Jan. 9, 1837, by Rev. Samuel Rockwell	2	229
Martha, d. Benjamin & Martha, b. Mar. 19, 1792	2	105
Martha, w. Benjamin, d. Jan. 23, 1799	2	105
Mary A., of Plainfield, m. Nathan C. **CHAPPELL**, of Norwich, Aug. 9, 1853, by Rev. C.A. Tracy	3	79
Matilda, d. Thomas Dow & Polly, b. Mar. 7, 1818	2	131
Matilda, of Plainfield, m. Alvin **DOUGLASS**, of Killingly, Feb. 28, 1842, by Peleg Peckham, Elder	3	13
Mathew, d.* Thomas & Hannah, b. July 5, 1761 (*Son?)	2	46
Mehetabell, m. Zebulon **WHIPPLE**, Mar. 1, 1759	2	40
Mercy, m. Ezra **STARKWEATHER**, June 8, 1797	2	102
Moses, s. Benjamin & Sally, b. July 27, 1809	2	149

	Vol.	Page

GALLUP, (cont.)
    Orra E., of Sterling, m. Elisha **PARK**, of Plainfield,
        Oct. 6, 1851, by Peleg Peckham, Elder — 3 — 71
    Rebecca, d. Benjamin & Sally, b. Apr. 16, 1803 — 2 — 149
    Sabra, m. Horace W. **WINSOR**, b. of Sterling, Apr. 7,
        1845, by Peleg Peckham, Elder — 3 — 27
    Sally, w. Benjamin, d. Aug. 28, 1828, ae. 53 — 2 — 149
    Samuel, of Sterling, m. Maria **PARK**, of Plainfield,
        Nov. 20, 1823, by Orin Fowler, V.D.M. — 2 — 192
    Sarah, m. Jeremiah **GREEN**, b. of Plainfield, Mar. 19,
        1854, by Rev. Henry Robinson — 3 — 83
    Simon, s. Jonathan & Elizabeth, b. Sept. 27, 1793 — 2 — 107
    Susan, d. Thomas Dow & Polly, b. Aug. 28, 1819 — 2 — 148
    Susan, m. John F. **KENNEDY**, b. of Plainfield, Feb. 24,
        1840, by Rev. Samuel Rockwell — 3 — 4
    Thomas, m. Hannah **DEAN**, Aug. 11, 1748 — 2 — 11
    Thomas, s. Thomas & Hannah, b. May 23, 1750 — 2 — 11
    Thomas, s. Benj[ami]n & Martha, b. Sept. 4, 1782 — 2 — 90
    Thomas Dow, s. Jonathan & Elizabeth, b. May 12, 1792 — 2 — 107
    Thomas Dow, m. Polly **BURDICK**, b. of Plainfield, Feb.
        28, 1816, by Joseph Eaton, J.P. — 2 — 131
    William, s. Benjamin & Sally, b. Aug. 13, 1805 — 2 — 149
    W[illia]m L., s. David, farmer, ae. 42, & Julia, ae.
        36, b. Oct. 15, 1849 — 4 — 29

GARDER, Mary, black, b. Plainfield, res. Killingly, d. Sept.
    5, 1850, ae. 18 — 4 — 64

GARDINER, Catharine A., m. Jesse **CONGDON**, b. of Plainfield,
    Mar. 8, 1835, by Rev. Samuel Rockwell — 2 — 220
    Eliza, m. Wanton **ROUSE**, Oct. 7, 1839, by Charles S.
        Weaver, Elder — 2 — 249
    Eliza, m. Wanton **ROUSE**, b. of Plainfield, Oct. 7, 1839,
        by Charles S. Weaver, Elder — 3 — 2
    Fanny, m. Daniel **BENNET**, b. of Plainfield, Aug. 16,
        1827, by Rev. Orin Fowler — 2 — 202
    George H., of South Kingston, R.I., m. Abby Jane
        CHAPMAN, of Plainfield, Sept. 21, 1851, by Rev.
        Thomas O. Rice — 3 — 71
    George H., of Wakefield, R.I., m. Abby Jane **CHAPMAN**,
        of Plainfield, Sept. 21, 1851, by Rev. Thomas O.
        Rice — 3 — 72
    Henry, s. William, carpenter, ae. 30, & Thirza, ae. 29,
        b. July 17, 1850 — 4 — 29
    Hiram, black, of Killingly, d. Oct. 10, 1850, ae. 4 — 4 — 64
    John, m. Mary **PARKIS**, b. of Plainfield, Sept. 19, 1830,
        by Rev. Orin Fowler — 2 — 211

GARY, Alice, m. Jonathan **HALL**, Apr. 15, 1772 — 2 — 102

GASKILL, George B., of Sterling, m. We[a]lthy **WILLIAMS**, of
    Woodstock, Feb. 22, 1854, by Peleg Peckham, Elder — 3 — 82

	Vol.	Page
GATES, Abigail, m. Charles **SPAULDING**, Dec. 25, 1764	2	59
Anna, of Griswold, m. Clark **HERRINGTON**, of Lisbon, Feb. 9, 1823, by Orin Fowler, V.D.M.	2	190
Hannah, m. Walter **PALMER**, Apr. 22, 1784	2	95
Jabez C., m. Ann G. **FANNING**, b. of Plainfield, July 2, 1849, by Rev. Henry Robinson	3	57
Jabez C., "capter", ae. 23, b. Voluntown, res. Plainfield, m. Anna P. **FANNING**, ae. 17, b. Lisbon, res. Plainfield, July 3, [1849?], by Rev. Henry Robinson	4	3
GEASON, [see also **GLEASON**], Andrew E., m. Abby T. **MATHEWSON**, b. of Plainfield, Dec. 2, 1849, by Rev. Joseph P. Brown	3	62
GEER, GEERS, Eunice, of Plainfield, m. Gideon **BELCHER**, of South Kingstown, R.I., Nov. 24, 1825, by Orin Fowler, V.D.M.	2	198
Kezia, m. Caleb **HALL**, Jr., Jan. 13, 1780	2	92
GERAULD, GEROULD, JERAULD, JEARAULD, Dupe. s. James & Ruth, b. Apr. 15, 1742	2	18
James, s. James & Ruth, b. Apr. 22, 1740	2	18
Mathew, d. James & Ruth, b. Oct. 12, 1735	2	18
Mathew, m. Jacob **SPAULDING**, May 1, 1753	2	26
Mathew, m. Jacob **SPAULDING**, May 2, 1753	2	12
Mathew, d. Reuben & Johannah, b. Aug. 22, 1759	2	51
Molle, d. James & Ruth, b. June 8, 1744	2	18
Molly, m. Azariah **SPAULDING**, Sept. 7, 1744	2	16
Molle, d. Reuben & Johannah, b. Sept. 22, 1761	2	51
R[e]uben, s. James & Ruth, b. Nov. 7, 1733	2	18
Reuben, m. Joannah **SPAULDING**, Jan. 1, 1757	2	39
Sila, d. Reuben & Joannah, b. Jan. 19, 1758	2	39
GIBBS, GIBS, Andrew, m. Dolly **PALMER**, b. of Plainfield, Dec. 31, 1812, by Rev. Joel Benedict	2	121
Caleb, s. Caleb & Eunice, b. July 31, 1774	2	86
Elijah, Dr., of Coventry, R.I., m. Esther **COLEGROVE**, of Plainfield, Feb. 10, 1800, by Rev. Joel Benedict	2	104
Mary Ann, d. Andrew & Dolly, b. May 5, 1817	2	130
Samuel Stanton, s. Andrew & Dolly, b. Nov. 26, 1815	2	128
GIBSON, Abby O.E., m. John G. **ADAMS**, b. of Sterling, Sept. 3, 1848, by Peleg Peckham, Elder	3	58
Abby R., m. William **FRENCH**, b. of Sterling, May 13, 1844, by Peleg Peckham, Elder	3	23
Charles H., d. Oct. [ ], 1848, ae. 10 m.	4	62
George, m. Hannah **PHILLIPS**, Sept. 24, 1854, by Rev. Alfred Gates	3	85
George S., m. Lydia **JOHNSON**, b. of Plainfield, Nov. 17, 1842, by Peleg Peckham, Elder	3	17
Lydia Ann, d. George A., laborer, & Lydia Ann, b. Dec.		

	Vol.	Page
GIBSON, (cont.)		
25, 1847	4	22
Mary E., m. Henry **FRY**, b. of Plainfield, May 23, 1833, by Rev. Samuel Rockwell	2	217
GILBERT, GILBARD, Lewis E., b. Fall River, Mass., res. Plainfield, d. Aug. 21, 1848, ae. 13 m.	4	62
Mary, m. Isaac **MARSH**, June 16, 1742	1	99
Orrin P., of Pomfret, m. Julia Ann **AMES**, of Plainfield, June 5, 1834, by Rev. Samuel Rockwell	2	219
GILES, Abbee, s. Samuel & Mary, b. Jan. 12, 1806	2	114
Elizabeth, d. Samuel & Mary, b. May 10, 1793	2	108
Samuel, Jr., s. Samuel & Mary, b. Sept. 7, 1789	2	108
GILKEY, Hannah, m. Timothy **PEIRCE**, Feb. 28, 1765	2	71
GILLSON, Otis, cotton operator, ae. 25, b. Sterling, m. Naoma **BACHELOR**, cotton operator, ae. 20, b. Sterling, Apr. [ ], [1849?]	4	6
GIST, Thomas, m. Hannah **BOYLE**, b. of Plainfield, Sept. 27, 1852, by Rev. Henry Robinson	3	76
GLADDING, Mary E., of Plainfield, m. Samuel **COIT**, of Hartford, Sept. 27, 1842, by A. Dunning	3	16
Mary Elizabeth, d. Joseph S. & Susan, b. Feb. 16, 1819	2	148
Nathaniel, s. Joseph S. & Susan, b. Feb. 28, 1827; d. Mar. 1, 1827	2	149
Phebe A., m. Zebulon **WHIPPLE**, b. of Plainfield, May 11, 1846, by A. Dunning	3	37
Phebe Ann, d. Joseph S. & Susan, b. June 30, 1823	2	149
Sarah R., b. Hardwick, Mass., res. Plainfield, d. June 22, 1851, ae. 30	4	66
Susan Cady, d. Joseph S. & Susan, b. Dec. 2, 1820	2	148
Susan Cady, d. Joseph S. & Susan, d. Dec. 10, 1822, ae. 2 y. 8 d.	2	148
Susan Cady, 2d, d. Joseph S. & Susan, d. Jan. 16, 1831	2	149
GLEASON, GLEZEN, [see also **GEASON**], Andrew, brood finisher, ae. 23, b. Pomfret, Ct., res. N. Kingston, R.I., m. Abby **MATHEWSON**, ae. 23, b. R.I., res. Plainfield, Dec. 3, 1849, by Joseph P. Brown	4	6
Arthur, farmer, b. Pomfret, res. Plainfield, d. May 22, 1851, ae. 56	4	66
Susan P., of Plainfield, m. Jared M. **ROOT**, of Binghampton, N.Y., Oct. 27, 1834, by Rev. Otis C. Whiton, of Canterbury	2	221
GLOVER, Abigail, d. Nathan & Desire, b. May 4, 1790	2	100
Benjamin, s. Nathan & Desire, b. Dec. 2, 1791	2	100
Mary, d. Nathan & Desire, b. Aug. 22, 1787	2	94
Nathan, m. Desire **CRARY**, Sept. 27, 1786	2	94
GODDARD, Calvin, m. Alice Cogswell **HART**, Nov. 27, 1794	2	101
Charles Backus, s. Calvin & Alice Cogswell, b. Oct. 5,		

	Vol.	Page

GODDARD, (cont.)
    1796 — 2 — 106
    George Calvin, s. Calvin & Alice Cogswell, b. Nov.
        28, 1798 — 2 — 106
GODFREY, GODFREE, Albert, m. Emeline E. **BUCK**, b. of
    Plainfield, Feb. 28, 1837, by Rev. Samuel Rockwell — 2 — 230
    Dennis, of Pawtucket, m. Lusina **HALL**, of Providence,
        Oct. 18, 1843, by Peleg Peckham, Elder — 3 — 21
GOFF, Anna, d. Sept. 29, 1849, ae. 62 — 4 — 64
GOODELL, Ellen M., of Plainfield, m. Wilson F. **DEAN**, of
    Eastport, May 15, 1853, by Rev. Alfred Gates — 3 — 79
    Mary E., m. George W. **LEWIS**, b. of Plainfield, Nov.
        27, 1853, by Rev. Joseph P. Brown — 3 — 81
GOODSPEED, Cynthia, see Cynthis **HALL** — 3 — 50
GOODWILL, Elizabeth, m. John **HARRIS**, June 15, 1760, by
    Lawton Palmer, J.P., Hopkinton, [R.I.] — 2 — 50
GORDON, [see also **GORTON** and **GURDON**], Albert H., s.
    Albert & Emeline, b. June 10, 1845 — 3 — 87
    Alexander Hamilton, s. James, Jr. & Katharine, b. Feb.
        8, 1813 — 2 — 148
    Charles T., s. Albert & Emeline, b. Aug. 7, 1847 — 3 — 87
    Charles T., s. Albert, tailor, ae. 38, & Emeline, ae.
        31, b. Aug. 10, 1847 — 4 — 22
    George W., of Dedham, Mass., m. Harriet E. **DIXON**, of
        Plainfield, Dec. 17, 1839, by Rev. Samuel Rockwell — 3 — 3
    Harriet Elizabeth, d. Albert & Emeline, b. Feb. 7,
        1842 — 3 — 16
    James, Gen., d. Sept. 27, 1822 — 2 — 148
    James, b. Sterling, res. Plainfield, d. Aug. 12,
        [18]49, ae. 2 — 4 — 62
    James Wright, s. James, Jr. & Katharine, b. Mar. 30,
        1809 — 2 — 148
    John, of Voluntown, m. Abby **HALL**, of Plainfield, July
        2, 1826, by Rev. Orin Fowler — 2 — 199
    Mary, domestic, black, b. Sterling, res. Killingly,
        d. July 20, [18]49, ae. 17 — 4 — 62
    Mary Elizabeth, of Sterling, m. Isaac K. **CUTLER**, of
        Plainfield, Nov. 3, 1828, by Rev. Orin Fowler — 2 — 207
    Rebecca, w. Gen. James, d. Oct. 1, 1822 — 2 — 148
    Sarah, factory operative, b. Sterling, res. Plainfield,
        d. Aug. 8, [18]49, ae. 7 — 4 — 62
GORTON, [see also **GORDON** and **GURDON**], Jonathan, m.
    Susan A. **PHILLIPS**, b. of Plainfield, Jan. 20, 1851,
        by Rev. W. Emerson — 3 — 68
    Jonathan, merchant, ae. 30, b. R.I., res. Plainfield,
        m. Susan A. **PHILLIPS**, ae. 24, [1850 or 1851],
        by Rev. Emerson — 4 — 7
    Jonathan, s. Jonathan, merchant, ae. 30, & Susan A.,

	Vol.	Page
GORTON, (cont.)		
ae. 24, b. Feb. 27, 1851	4	31
Susan A., b. Foster, R.I., res. Plainfield, d. Mar. 8, 1851, ae. 24	4	66
GOULD, Sarah, m. Ebenezer **STEEVENS**, Feb. 28, 1740	1	96
GRANT, Edwin L., of Tolland, m. Sarah E. **LADD**, of Sterling, Nov. 2, 1846, by Peleg Peckham, Elder	3	40
GRAVES, GREAVES, [see also **GROVES**], Asa W., of Killingly, m. Caroline **CHAMPLAIN**, of Plainfield, Sept. 18, 1854, by Peleg Peckham, Elder	3	85
Lydia, m. Weaver **FOSTER**, Dec. 6, 1821, by Nathaniel Cole, Elder	2	134
William, of Killingly, m. Ruth **DEAN**, of Plainfield, Jan. 9, 1823, by John Dunlap, J.P.	2	191
GRAY, GREY, Frederick, farmer, b. Voluntown, res. Plainfield, d. Mar. 3, 1850, ae. 82	4	64
Julia, d. William, tailor, ae. 27, & Frances A., ae. 20, b. Mar. 20, 1848	4	24
Julia, d. Mar. 21, [18]48, ae. 1 d.	4	61
Susan M., of Plainfield, m. Charles H. **BARROWS**, of Griswold, Dec. 8, 1850, by Rev. J.B. Guild	3	68
Susan M., weaver, ae. 22, b. Plainfield, res. Jewett City, m. Charles H. **BARROWS**, overseer in weaver looms, ae. 23, b. Griswold, res. Jewett City, Dec. 8, 1850, by J.B. Guile	4	7
-----, m. Denison **RICHMOND**, b. of Plainfield, June 12, 1853, by Rev. Alfred Gates	3	79
GREEN, GREENE, Albert C., farmer, ae. 26, b. W. Greenwich, R.I., res. Plainfield, m. Louisa **BROWN**, ae. 24, b. Chester, Mass., res. Plainfield, Aug. 1, 1849, by Rev. H. Robinson	4	3
Alexander, of Griswold, m. Lucy **BARBER**, of Plainfield, Mar. 10, 1839, by Rev. Tubal Wakefield	2	240
Alme C., of Sterling, m. Newman C. **PERKINS**, of Tolland, Sept. 21, 1835, by Rev. Ziba Loveland. Witnesses: Allen M. Perkins, Huldah Perkins, Huldah Loveland	2	222
Almira, of Plainfield, m. Jason **WOOD**, of Sterling, Dec. 22, 1839, by Peleg Peckham, Elder	2	250
Almira, of Plainfield, m. Jason **WOOD**, of Sterling, Dec. 22, 1839, by Peleg Peckham, Elder	3	2
Andra Ann, of Plainfield, m. Stephen B. **SWEET**, of Sterling, Nov. 30, 1843, by Peleg Peckham, Elder	3	21
Benjamin S., of Providence, R.I., m. Dorcas C. **NOYES**, of Warwick, R.I., Feb. 14, 1847, by Rev. J. Mather	3	42
Caroline, ae. 22, b. Foster, R.I., m. Simon **MATHEWSON**, woolen dresser, ae. 24, of Plainfield, Oct. 31, [18]47, by R. F. Charlton	4	2
Christopher M., m. Barbara **BROWN**, of Plainfield, Nov.		

	Vol.	Page
GREEN, GREENE, (cont.)		
23, 1823, by Orin Fowler, V.D.M.	2	192
Cordelia, m. Simon **MATTESON**, b. of Plainfield, Sept. 26, 1847, by Rev. Fred[eri]c Charlton	3	49
Duty, m. Amey R.**KINYON**, b. of Plainfield, Sept. 7, 1835, by Peleg Peckham, Elder	2	222
Edward H., m. Mary E. **TUCKERMAN**, b. of Sterling, Oct. 26, 1845, by Peleg Peckham, Elder	3	32
Elijah, m. Sarah J. **BUTTON**, b. of Canterbury, Nov. 24, 1853, by Rev. Alfred Gates	3	82
Elvia, m. Charles **MATHEWSON**, b. of Cranston, R.I., June 30, 1845, by Rev. Daniel Dorchester	3	31
Emely, of Plainfield, m. Joseph **TAYLER**, of Scituate, R.I., Jan. 1, 1822, by Rev. Orin Fowler	2	134
Freelove C., m. Henry C. **PALMER**, b. of Plainfield, Sept. 23, 1839, by Rev. Samuel Rockwell	2	247
Jeremiah, m. Sarah **GALLUP**, b. of Plainfield, Mar. 19, 1854, by Rev. Henry Robinson	3	83
Jonathan H., m. Fan[n]y **MADISON**, b. of Plainfield, Sept. 20, 1840, by Rev. Hezekiah Thacher	3	7
Lois, of Plainfield, m. Handson **KENYON**, of Sterling, Feb. 26, 1843, by Peleg Peckham, Elder	3	18
Louisa, m. Israel **AMES**, b. of Plainfield, Aug. 9, 1853, by Rev. Alfred Gates	3	79
Mary A., of Warwick, R.I., m. Rowland C. **JOHNSON**, of Coventry, R.I., Nov. 28, 1849, by Rev. Joseph P. Brown	3	62
Michael, of New York, m. Abby **PICKET**, of Plainfield, Nov. 18, 1846, by Rev. J.C. Knapp, Central Village	3	41
Nancy, m. Pierce **HANDELL**, b. of Plainfield, Mar. 18, 1833, by Rev. Samuel Rockwell	2	216
Samuel, of Charlestown, R.I., m. Ele[a]nor **PECKHAM**, of Plainfield, Oct. 21, 1839, by Peleg Peckham, Elder	2	249
Samuel, of Charlestown, R.I., m. Eleanor **PECKHAM**, of Plainfield, Oct. 21, 1839, by Peleg Peckham, Elder	3	1
Samuel W., of Warwick, R.I., m. Harriet **COREY**, of Sterling, Aug. 25, 1845, by James Smither, Elder	3	34
Susan A., of Coventry, R.I., m. Cullen L. **POTTER**, of Sterling, Feb. 28, 1848, by Peleg Peckham, Elder	3	52
Tepputt E., of Lisbon, m. George W. **OLIR**, of Plainfield, Mar. 31, 1839, by Francis B. Johnson, J.P.	2	240
-----, illeg. s. Julia, washwoman, ae. 32, b. June 3, 1849	4	26
-----, s. Charles T., laborer, ae. 25, b. May 24, 1850	4	28
GREENMAN, Joan C., m. John **WESTCOTT**, b. of Plainfield, Oct. 21, 1850, by Rev. Joseph P. Brown	3	67
Lydia, m. Oliver **CLARK**, b. of Plainfield, Nov. 17,		

	Vol.	Page
GREENMAN, (cont.)		
1845, by Rev. C.C. Barnes	3	33
Mary Ann, m. Bowen H. **MATTEWSON**, b. of Plainfield, Mar. 28, 1839, by Rev. Tubal Wakefield	2	240
GREENWOOD, Hannah W., m. Samuel **ALBRO**, b. of Warwick, R.I., May 4, 1834, by Rev. Samuel Rockwell	2	218
GRIFFIN, Roba, of Sterling, m. Leonard A. **BROWN**, of Killingly, May 4, 1848, by Peleg Peckham, Elder	3	51
[**GRIFFITH**], **GREFFETH, GRIFFIS**, George, Jr., m. Hannah A. **REYNOLDS**, b. of Sterling, Oct. 13, 1850, by Peleg Peckham, Elder	3	66
Roxana, of Foster, R.I., m. Charles **JONES**, of Plainfield, May 10, 1835, by Jonathan Goff, J.P.	2	221
GRINMAN, Joanna, cotton mill, ae. 21, of Plainfield, m. John **WESTCOTT**, cotton mill, ae. 30, b. Sterling, res. Plainfield, Nov. [ ], 1850, by Joseph P. Brown	4	7
GRISWOLD, Eliza M., of Griswold, m. W[illia]m D. **BENNETT**, of Plainfield, Oct. 2, 1850, by Rev. Joseph P. Brown	3	67
Eliza M., cotton mill, ae. 20, of Plainfield, m. W[illia]m D. **BENNETT**, farmer, ae. 21, of Plainfield, Oct. 20, 1850, by Rev. Joseph P. Brown	4	7
Jane M., m. Daniel V. **LAD[D]**, b. of Franklin, Aug. 11, 1840, by Rev. Nicholas Branch, of Killingly	3	6
GROVER, Alvah, of Killingly, m. Polly **WOOD**, of Plainfield, Dec. 23, 1827, by Rev. Roswell Whitmore	2	204
Hannah, of Killingly, m. Josiah **SPAULDING**, of Plainfield, May 18, 1738	1	95
GROVES, [see also **GRAVES**], Peleg, m. Frances **RANDALL**, Oct. 9, 1842, by Rev. John Read, Thompson	3	16
GUILE, Asa C., m. Harriet **STOWELL**, b. of Plainfield, Aug. 24, 1835, by Peleg Peckham, Elder	2	222
William D., of Plainfield, m. Robey **HARRIS**, of Sterling, Mar. 16, 1829, by Peleg Peckham, Elder	2	208
GURDON, [see also **GORDON** and **GORTON**], Sarah, m. Eleazer **BROWN**, Oct. 10, 1728	1	48
HACKINS, Hannah, d. July 27, [18]48, ae. 87	4	61
HAINES, HANES, Abigail, d. of Samuell, of Haverell, m. Jacob **WARREN**, Jr., Jan. 11, 1714/15	1	15
Elizabeth, of Haverell, m. Isaac **SPAULDING**, Feb. 2, 1712/13	1	13
Judeth, m. Jacob **JOHNSON**, May 8, 1734	1	47
Pasco, Jr., m. Pamelia L. **CADY**, b. of Providence, R.I., June 27, 1847, by Rev. James Mather	3	43
HAIR, Benjamin, of Glocester, R.I., m. Phebe A. **KEECH**, of Plainfield, Feb. 21, 1842, by Peleg Peckham, Elder	3	13
William, m. Lucy **CHAFFEE**, b. of Woodstock, May 2,		

PLAINFIELD VITAL RECORDS 157

	Vol.	Page
HAIR, (cont.)		
1853, by Rev. William Turkington	3	78
HALE, Elisha P., m. Abby A. **HILL**, b. of Plainfield, Jan.		
19, 1852, by Rev. Joseph P. Brown	3	73
Eunice, of Sterling, m. Philo **PHILLIPS**, of Plainfield,		
May 8, 1848, by Rev. Geo[rge] W. Brewster	3	52
Lydia A., m. Daniel **HUBBARD**, Jan. 12, 1847, by Rev.		
Fred[eri]c Charlton	3	48
-----, st. b. child of Orrin, laborer, b. May [ ],		
1851	4	31
HALL, Abby, of Plainfield, m. John **GORDON**, of Voluntown,		
July 2, 1826, by Rev. Orin Fowler	2	199
Abigaiel, d. Sept. 24, 1727, in the 26th y. of her		
age	1	42
Abigaiel, d. Sam[ue]ll & Elisabeth, b. July 3, 1730	1	64
Abigail, d. Joshua & Susanah, b. June 11, 1761	2	67
Abigail, d. Sam[ue]l, Jr. & Abigail, b. Aug. 14, 1769	2	73
Alice, d. Jonathan & Alice, b. Feb. 27, 1773	2	102
Alpheas, s. John & Jemima, b. Jan. 10, 1757	2	37
Anna, m. Silas **BAILEY**, Jr., Nov. 13, 1808, by Rev.		
Nathaniel Cole	2	196
Asa, s. John & Jemima, b. Mar. 20, 1752	2	37
Asenath, d. John, Jr. & Ruth, b. May 22, 1793	2	101
Asenath, m. Jonas **FRENCH**, b. of Plainfield, May 17,		
1814, by Rev. Joel Benedict	2	200
Asher, s. Stephen, 3rd, & Naomy, b. Oct. 29, 1787	2	93
Betsey, m. Benjamin **TIBBETTS**, b. of Plainfield, Apr.		
1, 1827, by Rev. Roswell Whitmore	2	201
Caleb, Jr., m. Kezia **GEER**, Jan. 13, 1780	2	92
Calvin, m. Louisa **ROUSE**, b. of Plainfield, Dec. 30,		
1827, by Orin Fowler, V.D.M.	2	204
Catharine L, m. Joseph A. **DEAN**, b. of Plainfield,		
Mar. 2, 1848, by Rev. Henry Robinson	3	52
Catharine Lucretia, d. William & Ruth, b. Apr. 1, 1812	2	151
Catharine Luenetice (?), d. William & Ruth, b. Aug.		
28, 1814	2	151
Catharine S., ae. 30, b. Plainfield, m. Joseph A. **DEAN**,		
carpenter, ae. 33, b. Taunton, res. Plainfield,		
Feb. 22, 1848, by Rev. Henry Robinson	4	1
Ceazer, negro, [s.] Phillis, b. Aug. 1, 1788	2	100
Charles, s. Stephen, teacher, ae. 31, & Mary, ae. 20,		
b. Aug. 10, 1847	4	22
Cynthia, formerly **GOODSPEED**, m. Erastus E. **DIXON**, b.		
of Sterling, Jan. 13, 1848, by Peleg Peckham, Elder	3	50
David, s. Elisha & Phillippa, b. July 23, 1717	1	19
David, s. Joshua & Susannah, b. July 20, 1766	2	67
Ebenezer, m. Thankful **CASEY**, b. of Plainfield, Oct. 21,		
1827, by Peleg Peckham, Elder	2	203

	Vol.	Page
HALL, (cont.)		
Edward P., m. Elizabeth R. **COMSTOCK**, b. of Plainfield, Mar. 28, 1852, by Rev. Henry Robinson	3	74
Edward Perry, s. William & Ruth, b. Oct. 23, 1812	2	151
Edward Perry, s. W[illia]m & Ruth, b. Oct. 13, 1813	2	151
Elias, s. John & Jemima, b. Oct. 2, 1754	2	37
Elizabeth, d. Stephen, m. Edward **SPAULDING**, Oct. 21, 1708	1	6
Elizabeth, w. Joshua, d. Sept. 6, 1789	2	100
Esek, m. Amey C. **COLE**, b. of Plainfield, Mar. 7, 1853, by Rev. Joseph P. Brown	3	77
Esther, of Plainfield, m. James **WILSON**, of Griswold, Feb. 21, 1830, by Orin Fowler, V.D.M.	2	210
Eunice, d. Sam[ue]l, Jr. & Abigail, b. Apr. 22, 1763	2	73
Ezekiel, s. Caleb, Jr. & Keziah, b. Feb. 20, 1785	2	92
Fanny, d. John, Jr. & Ruth, b. Feb. 17, 1789	2	98
George, s. William & Ruth, b. July 30, 1811	2	151
Hannah Ritta, d. Squir[e] & Polly, b. May 4, 1794, at Sterling	2	119
Henry, s. William & Ruth, b. July 7, 1816	2	151
Henry, s. William & Ruth, b. Apr. 19, 1818	2	151
Henry, of Pomfret, m. Judeth **GALLUP**, of Plainfield, Mar. 23, 1845, by Peleg Peckham, Elder	3	26
Hester, d. Stephen & Hester, b. Nov. 3, 1757	2	37
Israel, s. Stephen, 3rd, & Naomy, b. Dec. 13, 1784	2	93
Israel Barney, s. Squire & Polly, b. Mar. 19, 1798, at Sterling	2	119
Jared, m. Susan S. **BENSON**, b. of Plainfield, Nov. 12, 1854, by Rev. Joseph P. Brown	3	87
Gemima, d. Caleb, Jr. & Keziah, b. Dec. 2, 1786	2	92
Jeremiah, s. John, Jr. & Ruth, b. June 3, 1791	2	101
John, s. John d. Feb. 24, 1713/14	1	13
John, s. Samuel & Abigail, b. May 27, 1723	1	29
John, m. Olive **SPAULDING**, June 23, 1744	1	2X
John, s. John & Olive, b. July 3, 1747	2	11
John, of Plainfield, m. Jemima **READ**, of Norwich, June 6, 1749, by Rev. Daniel Kirtland, Newent, Norwich	2	7
John, m. Hannah **WILLIAMS**, Feb. 25, 1762	2	77
John, s. John & Hannah, b. July 21, 1764	2	77
John, Jr., m. Ruth **KENNEDY**, Nov. 8, 1787	2	98
John J., m. Mary **FIELD**, b. of Plainfield, Dec. 31, [probably 1852], by Rev. William Turkington	3	77
Jonathan, s. Elisha & Phillippe, b. July 10, 1712	1	10
Jonathan, s. Samuell & Abigaiel, b. Sept. 21, 1727	1	42
Jonathan, m. Alice **GARY**, Apr. 15, 1772	2	102
Joshewa, s. Joshewa & Susanah, b. Sept. 15, 1759	2	45
Joshua, d. Mar. 8, 1791	2	100
Joshua, farmer, d. Dec. 23, 1849, ae. 45	4	64

PLAINFIELD VITAL RECORDS 159

	Vol.	Page
HALL, (cont.)		
Judya, of Plainfield, m. Martin **PEIRCE**, of Pomfret, Sept. 29, 1826, by Nathaniel Cole, Elder	2	200
Lois, d. Sam[ue]l, Jr., & Abigail, b. Apr. 20, 1761	2	73
Lovina, m. Caleb **BENNET**, b. of Plainfield, July 12, 1829, by Nathaniel Cole, Elder	2	209
Lucindal, of Plainfield, m. Earl P. **WHOOD**, of Coventry, R.I., Jan. 7, 1827, by Nathaniel Cole, Elder	2	200
Lucy, d. Stephen & Hester, b. Nov. 18, 1750	2	12
Lucy, d. Samuel, Jr. & Abigail, b. May 29, 1765	2	73
Lusina, of Providence, m. Dennis **GODFREY**, of Pawtucket, Oct. 18, 1843, by Peleg Peckham, Elder	3	21
Lydia, m. Warren **SHEPERD**, b. of Plainfield, Oct. 3, 1819	2	191
Lydia P., of Plainfield, m. Edwin D. **PELLET**, of Canterbury, May 12, 1839, by Jonathan Goff, J.P.	2	242
Maria, of Plainfield, m. George W. **EDDY**, of Cranston, R.I., June 20, 1824, by Orin Fowler, V.D.M.	2	195
Mary, d. Stephen, m. Thomas **STEEVENS**, Jr., May 26, 1702	1	3
Mary, w. John, d. Oct. 17, 1710, in the 19th y. of her age	1	6
Mary, d. Elisha & Fillipe, b. Sept. 30, 1714	1	14
Mary, d. Sam[ue]ll, Jr. & Abigail, b. Jan. 18, 1759	2	73
Mary, m. Nathan **HARRIS**, b. of Plainfield, Nov. 28, 1842, by Ephraim Browning, J.P., Canterbury	3	19
Mercy, m. Abraham **BOYD**, Dec. 11, 1761	2	62
Noah, m. Catharine A. **SHIPPEE**, b. of Killingly, July 11, 1837, by Peleg Peckham, Elder	2	231
Olive, d. John & Olive, b. May 22, 1745	1	2X
Olive, w. John, d. Aug. 30, 1748	2	11
Olive, m. Samuel **WHE[E]LER**, Dec. 26, 1765	2	63
Olive F., m. Hezekiah **FRENCH**, Apr. 28, 1816	3	15
Peleg Peck, s. Squire & Polly, b. Oct. 10, 1796, at Sterling	2	119
Phillip Davis, s. William & Ruth, b. Aug. 19, 1820	2	151
Phillip Davis, s. William & Ruth, b. June 8, 1822	2	151
Polly, d. Jonathan & Alice, b. May 20, 1775	2	102
Ruth, w. Stephen, d. June 6, 1715	1	15
Ruth, d. Samuel & Abigail, b. Feb. 25, 1757	2	38
Ruth, d. Caleb, Jr. & Keziah, b. Nov. 2, 1780	2	92
Samuel, m. Abegall **FFELLOWS**, d. Sergt. John, Jan. 4, 1720/21	1	25
Sam[ue]ll, s. Sam[ue]ll & Abiga[i]l, b. July 10, 1725	1	36
Sam[ue]ll, s. Sam[ue]ll & Abigaiel, d. Mar. 7, 1728/9	1	47
Sam[ue]ll, m. Elizabeth **STEVENS**, Aug. 27, 1729	1	48
Sam[ue]ll, s. Sam[ue]ll & Elisabeth, b. Mar. 28, 1735	1	64
Samuel, m. Abigail **SPAULDING**, May 19, 1756	2	38

	Vol.	Page
HALL, (cont.)		
Samuel, 3d, s. Samuel, Jr. & Abigail, b. July 9, 1767	2	73
Samuel, d. Nov. 5, 1770, ae. 78	2	73
Sapphira, d. Jonathan & Alice, b. Aug. 22, 1789	2	102
Sarah, d. Stephen, m. Benjamin **SPAULDING**, Jr., Oct. 21, 170[ ]	1	7
Sarah, d. Stephen & Hester, b. Jan. 8, 1756	2	12
Sela, d. John, Jr. & Ruth, b. Mar. 27, 1795	2	101
Silus, s. John & Jemima, b. May 19, 1750	2	37
Squire, s. John & Hannah, b. Apr. 30, 1769	2	77
Stephen, s. Sam[ue]ll & Abegall, b. Sept. 4, 1721	1	26
Stephen, s. Samuel & Abegall, b. Oct. 30, 1721	1	29
Stephen, d. Oct. 1, 1724, in the 87th y. of his age	1	31
Stephen, m. Hester **LENNARD**, Mar. [ ], 1748	2	10
Stephen, s. Steven & Hester, b. July 6, 1749	2	10
Stephen, 3d, m. Naomy **BENNET**, Oct. 9, 1783	2	93
Stephen, s. William & Ruth, b. Aug. 15, 1814	2	151
Stephen, s. William & Ruth, b. Feb. 23, 1816	2	151
Stephen, m. Mary **WESTCOTT**, Apr. 20, 1847, by Rev. Fred[eri]c Charlton	3	48
Susannah, d. Stephen, m. John **SMITH**, June 25, 169[ ]	1	1
Susannah, d. Joshua, Jr. & Susannah, b. July 28, 1771	2	91
Susanna, m. Barnet **COLE**, May 6, 1796	2	103
William, s. John & Hannah, b. Sept. 16, 1778	2	100
William, Jr., s. William & Ruth, b. June 4, 1815	2	151
William F., s. William & Ruth, b. Mar. 13, 1820	2	151
William F., m. Abby J. **SHEPARD**, b. of Plainfield, Mar. 28, 1852, by Rev. Henry Robinson	3	74
Zadock, s. Sam[ue]l, Jr. & Abigail, b. Oct. 24, 1771	2	73
----, s. Stephen, school teacher, b. May 18, [1850]	4	30
HAMMETT, Augustus, clerk in store, ae. 21, of Plainfield, m. Lucy **WESTCOTT**, woolen finisher, ae. 20, of Plainfield, Apr. 7, 1851, by Rev. Joseph P. Brown	4	7
Augustus J., m. Lucy N. **WESTCOTT**, b. of Plainfield, Apr. 13, 1851, by Rev. Joseph P. Brown	3	69
HANDELL, HANDALL, Lucinda, b. Killingly, res. Plainfield, d. Aug. 5, 1849, ae. 40	4	62
Pierce, m. Nancy **GREEN**, b. of Plainfield, Mar. 18, 1833, by Rev. Samuel Rockwell	2	216
HANN, Hannah, w. Jonathan, d. Nov. 24, 1774	2	78
Jonathan, m. Hannah **SPAULDING**, July 7, 1774	2	78
HANNOUR, Mary, d. of Greenfield, of Tanton, m. William **DOUGLASS**, Jr., Mar. 26, 1716	1	18
HANSEY, HANSY, Andrew*, s. Andrew & Sarah, b. Nov. 20, 1787 (*The name "**HARPER**[sic]" follows this name)	2	96
Polly, d. Andrew & Sarah, b. June 17, 1785	2	90
HARD, Amey, d. Thomas & Lydia, b. Oct. 3, 1735	1	93
Bethiah, d. Thomas & Lydiah, b. June 18, 1720	1	93

PLAINFIELD VITAL RECORDS 161

	Vol.	Page
HARD, (cont.)		
Jacob, s. Thomas & Lydiah, b. Feb. 7, 1729	1	93
John, [twin with Thomas], s. Thomas & Lydiah, b. Oct. 10, 1724	1	93
Josiah, s. Thomas & Lydiah, b. Sept. 23, 1726	1	93
Mary, d. Thomas & Lydiah, b. Jan. 20, 1731	1	93
Sarah, d. Thomas & Lydiah, b. Mar. 23, 1722	1	93
Thomas, [twin with John], s. Thomas & Lydiah, b. Oct. 10, 1724	1	93
HARPER, [see under **HANSEY**]		
HARRINGTON, [see also **HERRINGTON**], Abigail, of Plainfield, m. John **BURNET**, of Windham, Feb. 29, 1824, by Rev. Roswell Whitmore	2	193
Angenette A., d. John, manufacturer, ae. 23, & Amey E. ae. 21, b. July 28, 1848	4	24
Bettice D., of Plainfield, m. William **LESTER**, Jr. of Norwich, Feb. 14, 1836, by Rev. O.C. Whiton, of Canterbury	2	224
Waitey, ae. 22, b. Foster, R.I., res. Plainfield, m. Leroy W. **KENYON**, harness maker, ae. 23, b. Sterling, Ct., res. Plainfield, Mar. 12, 1850, by Rev. Brown	4	5
Waitey A., m. Leroy M. **KENYON**, b. of Plainfield, Mar. 12, 1850, by Rev. Joseph P. Brown	3	63
HARRIS, Adaline, m. Aaron **STARKWEATHER**, b. of Plainfield, Mar. 10, 1840, by Rev. Tubal Wakefield	3	4
Allen, m. Almira **VAUGHN**, b. of Plainfield, Sept. 21, 1827, by Orin Fowler, Clericus	2	202
An[n], d. Ebenezer & C[h]ristable, b. Oct. 23, 1714	1	23
Ann, d. Ebenezer & [Sarah]*, b. Dec. 2, 1738 (*Supplied by L.B.B.)	1	2X
Ann, d. Nathan & Susannah, b. Jan. 31, 1751	2	14
Anna, of Oxford, m. Jonathan **WOODWARD**, Jan. 15, 1752	2	20
Anne, d. Daniel & Ann, b. Mar. 26, 1746	2	10
Azariah, s. Ebenezer, Jr. & Sarah, b. Aug. 13, 1733	1	65
Azeriah, d. Apr. 13, 1751	2	14
Caroline, m. William H. **RANDALL**, b. of Sterling, Oct. 26, 1845, by Peleg Peckham, Elder	3	32
Cathrain, d. Thomas & Sarah, b. June 3, 1722	1	96
Charles, m. Fanny **SMITH**, b. of Plainfield, Nov. 30, 1820, by Rev. Orin Fowler	2	132
Christoble, d. Ebennezer & Christople, b. Mar. 22, 1703/4; d. Apr. 1, 170[ ]	1	1
Christoble, d. Ebenezer & Christoble, b. Nov. [ ], 1710	1	8
C[h]ristable, m. William **PARKE**, Jr., Nov. 5, 1729	1	52
Christobel, d. Daniel & Ann, b. June 6, 1747	2	10
Daniel, s. Ebenezer & C[h]ristable, b. Apr. 23,		

	Vol.	Page
HARRIS, (cont.)		
1712	1	23
Daniel, m. Ann **WELCH**, May 25, 1749 (Date conflicts with dates of birth of children)	2	10
Daniel, s. Daniel & Ann, b. Aug. 25, 1749	2	10
Ebenezer, s. Ebenezer & Christobel, b. July 6, 1705	1	3
Ebenezer, Jr., m. Sarah **TRACY**, June 5, 1732	1	60
Ebenezer, s. Ebenezer, Jr. & Sarah, b. Sept. 6, 1736	1	65
Ebenezer, d. Apr. 14, 1751	2	14
Ebenezer, m. Annah **BENJAMINS**, Oct. 29, 1751	2	14
Ebenezer, s. Daniel & Ann, b. [ ], 1751	2	10
Ebenezer, s. Ebenezer & Annor, b. Feb. 16, 1756	2	34
Edwin, of Plainfield, m. Basheba T. **BENNETT**, of Brooklyn, Sept. 4, 1854, by Levi Meech, Elder	3	85
Elijah Dyer, s. Jeptha & Sarah, b. June 27, 1795	2	104
Elisabeth, d. Ebenezer & Christable, b. Jan. 16, 1708	1	23
Elisabeth, d. Thomas & Elisabeth, b. Jan. 20, 1716/17	1	24
Experience, m. Ephraim **WHE[E]LER**, Jr., Apr. 16, 1761	2	57
Frances H., of Plainfield, m. William F. **DAWLEY**, of Norwich, Nov. 16, 1841, by Rev. Roswell Whitmore	3	14
Frances Harriet, d. Charles & Fanny, b. June 5, 1823	2	150
Geo[rge] W., of German Flatts, N.Y., m. Caroline F. **WALLS**, of Plainfield, [ ], by Rev. John F. Sheffield	3	71
Henry, of Plainfield, m. Roxianna **BELLUS**, of Quardon, Vt., Apr. 25, 1847, by Rev. Fred[eri]c Charlton	3	48
Henry A., m. Eunice K. **CURTIS**, b. of Fairfield, Sept. 1, 1842, by Rev. A.B. Wheeler	3	17
Hester, d. Thomas, Jr. & Elizabeth, b. Apr. 9, 1727	1	92
Jeremiah, s. Jeptha & Sarah, b. Nov. 30, 1796	2	104
John, m. Elizabeth **GOODWILL**, June 15, 1760, by Lawton Palmer, J.P. Hopkinton, [R.I.]	2	50
John, of Plainfield, m. Hannah **BABCOCK**, of Hopkinton, June 2, 1770, by Joseph Davis, Elder, Hopkinton	2	72
John, m. Elizabeth G. **PERKINS**, b. of Sterling, Nov. 8, 1841, by Peleg Peckham, Elder	3	12
Lydia, m. William A. **LESTER**, Apr. 28, 1841, by Roswell Whitmore	3	9
Lydia C., d. Charles & Fanny, b. Aug. 8, 1821	2	150
Martha, d. Ebennezer & Rebeckah, b. Nov. 26, 1696	1	1
Martha, d. Thomas & Elisabeth, b. Mar. 1, 1718/19	1	24
Mary, d. Ebenezer & C[h]ristable, b. Mar. 3, 1718/19	1	23
Nathan, s. Ebenezer & Christable, b. Dec. 18, 1721	1	26
Nathan, m. Susannah **ROOD**, July 5, 1749	2	14
Nathan, s. Nathan & Susanah, b. Feb. 8, 1750	2	14
Nathan, m. Mary **HALL**, b. of Plainfield, Nov. 28, 1842, by Ephraim Browning, J.P. Canterbury	3	19
Peter, s. Ebenezer & C[h]ristable, b. Mar. 17, 1716/17	1	23

	Vol.	Page
HARRIS, (cont.)		
Peter, s. Peter & Mary, b. June 25, 1744	1	2X
Rebeckah, w. Ebennezer, d. June 16, 1699	1	1
Rebecka, d. Thomas & Elisabeth, b. Sept. 26, 1714	1	24
Robey, of Sterling, m. William D. **GUILE**, of Plainfield, Mar. 16, 1829, by Peleg Peckham, Elder	2	208
Ruth, d. Thomas, Jr. & Elizabeth, b. July 27, 1730	1	92
Sarah, d. Ebennezer & Christoble, b. Aug. 10, 1702	1	1
Sarah, d. Thomas & Sarah, b. Mar. 3, 1716/17	1	96
Sarah, d. Thomas, Jr. & Elizabeth, b. May 18, 1722	1	92
Sarah, w. Ebenezer, d. Mar. 29, 1751	2	14
Sarah, d. Ebenezer & Annah, b. Sept. 23, 1752	2	14
Sarah, d. Ebenezer & Annor, d. Jan. 16, 1754, ae. 15 m. 18 d.	2	16
Sarah, d. Ebenezer & Annor, b. May 16, 1754	2	34
Solomon, s. Jeptha & Sarah, b. Aug. 8, 1798	2	104
Sophia, m. Otis H. **SLADE**, b. of Plainfield, Nov. 26, 1827, by Orin Fowler, V.D.M.	2	204
Stephen, s. Stephen & Sarah, b. Feb. 15, 1738	2	8
Stephen, d. Apr. 26, 1749	2	8
Stephen, m. Mary **WINTWORTH**, Mar. 17, 1761	2	45
Thankfull, d. Daniel & Ann, b. Jan. 6, 1753	2	19
Thomas, s. Ebenezer, m. Elisabeth **CHURCH**, d. Samuel, Feb. 11, 1713/14	1	24
Thomas, 3rd, s. Thomas & Sarah, b. Apr. 29, 1715	1	94
Thomas, s. Thomas, Jr. & Elizabeth, b. Sept. 27, 1725	1	92
Thomas, s. Peter & Mary, b. Mar. 20, 1743	1	2X
Zadock, m. Abigail **DEAN**, May 30, 1793	2	101
-----, d. Henry, merchant*, ae. 41, & Eliza, ae. 31, b. July 29, 1850 (*Perhaps machinist)	4	28
HARRISON, John, m. Jemima [ ], Oct. 10, 1813, by Thomas Backus, J.P.	2	124
HART, Alice Cogswell, m. Calvin **GODDARD**, Nov. 27, 1794	2	101
HARTSHORN, Chloe, d. Samuel & Sarah, b. Apr. 14, 1798, at Pomfrett, Conn.	2	110
Lucretia, d. Samuel & Sarah, b. Apr. 10, 1796, at Otsego, N.Y.	2	110
Mary Ann, d. Samuel & Sarah, b. May 19, 1801	2	110
Sally Trowbridge, d. Samuel & Sarah, b. Aug. 2, 1794, at Otsego, N.Y.	2	110
HARVEY, Eliza M., ae. 20, m. James **COFFREY**, dresser tender, ae. 22, b. Ireland, res. Plainfield, May 1, [18]48, by Michael Tume	4	2
HARWOOD, Ruth, m. Luther **SMITH**, Jan. 6, 1780	2	93
HATCH, Sally Richards, d. Alpheas & Mehetabel, b. May 13, 1792	2	119
Sarah, d. John & [ ], b. Dec. 9, 1765	2	65
HAVENS, Prudence, m. Jeduthan **STEVENS**, Mar. 8, 1766	1	104

	Vol.	Page
HAWKINS, Frank b. Brooklyn, res. Plainfield, d. July 30, 1847, ae. 12	4	63
Frank, m. Susan F. **ROOD**, b. of Plainfield, July 4, 1858, by Rev. Mason B. Hopkins	3	88
Frank, saloon keeper, of Plainfield, m. Susan F. **ROOD**, of Plainfield, July 4, 1858, in Foster, R.I., by Mason B. Hopkins	4	4
Hiram, of Plainfield, m. Susan A. **SMITH**, of Sterling, Jan. 1, 1852, by Rev. Henry Robinson	3	73
Jenckes, of Brooklyn, m. Lucy **DEAN**, Jan. 23, 1837, by Chester Tilden	2	229
Joseph, of Sterling, m. Rachel **SPAULDING**, of Plainfield, June 29, 1828, by John Dunlap, J.P.	3	3
Lucinday C., of Sterling, m. Alden W. **BLODGETT**, of Stafford, Sept. 2, 1844, by Peleg Peckham, Elder	3	24
Lydia W., of Sterling, m. Stuteley K. **KENYON**, of Plainfield, Jan. 1, 1829, by Rev. Orin Fowler	2	207
Mary Jane, d. George, butcher, ae. 39, & Mary, ae. 34, b. Dec. 28, 1849	4	28
Ralph, d. Nov. 18, [18]47, ae. 3	4	61
Robiah B., of Sterling, m. Zadock J. **STEERE**, of Plainfield, Aug. 20, 1837, by Peleg Peckham, Elder	2	232
Susan F., m. Nathaniel **MEDBERY**, Jr., b. of Plainfield, Mar. 12, 1854, by Rev. William Turkington	3	82
HAYWARD, Lemuel, of Pomfret, m. Ruth **ROBINSON**, of Plainfield, Jan. 30, 1826, by Orin Fowler, V.D.M.	2	198
HAZARD, HASARD, Lydia, m. Simon **SHEPHARD**, May 17, 1843, by Amos Witter, J.P.	3	19
Oliver S., of Coventry, R.I., m. Julia E. **SHOLES**, of Warwick, R.I., Nov. 1, 1849, by Rev. Joseph P. Brown	3	61
HEALEY, Eliza A., m. George W. **MOREDOCK**, b. of Plainfield, Aug. 16, 1841, by Rev. Thomas Barber	3	10
HEATH, Albert G., of Providence, R.I., m. Abby Jane **CLARKE**, of Lebanon, Oct. 2, 1843, by Rev. A. Latham	3	20
HEBARD, [see also **HUBBARD**], George W., of Willimantic, m. Mehetable **WILBOUR**, of Plainfield, May 8, 1833, by Rev. Samuel Rockwell	2	217
HEFFERLOW, Daniel, m. Lydia **BROWN**, Nov. 28, 1841, by Rev. John Read	3	12
HEFLIN, Betsey, d. Aug. 1, 1847, ae. 64	4	63
Julia Ann, d. Aug. 1, 1847, ae. 2	4	63
Lydia, d. Daniel, laborer, ae. 35, & Lydia, ae. 35, b. Apr. 7, 1850	4	28
HENLY, Lucinda, of Plainfield, m. Ichabod **FAGINS**, of Killingly, June 27, 1835, by John Dunlap, J.P.	2	221
HENRY, Eliza, of Plainfield, m. Christopher H. **TAYLOR**, of Mass., Nov. 1, 1841, by Peleg Peckham, Elder	3	12

PLAINFIELD VITAL RECORDS 165

	Vol.	Page
HENRY, (cont.)		
Ellen, d. John, mule spinner, & Amanda, b. Sept. 24, 1847	4	23
George R., of Plainfield, m. Emeline E. **WOOD**, of Brookfield, Mass., Sept. 8, 1851, by Rev. Henry Robinson	3	70
Ichabod, m. Mehetable **MORDOCK**, Jan. 1, 1815, by Thomas Backas, J.P.	2	126
Miranda, of Coventry, m. George W. **BURLINGAME**, of Warwick, R.I., Mar. 13, 1845, by James Smither, Elder	3	29
HENST, Mahlon F., of Naihes, Miss., m. Luthmia **LATHROP**, of Plainfield, Sept. 3, 1839, by Rev. Samuel Rockwell	2	247
HERRICK, HERICK, HERRECK, Betsey, m. Simon **CUTLER**, Dec. 17, 1797	2	107
Betsey, of Plainfield, m. Rev. Sidney **DEAN**, of South Windsor, Sept. 13, 1846, by Rev. J. Mather	3	40
Cha[rle]s, s. Hyrum, manufacturer, ae. 39, & Marius, ae. 35, b. Nov. 4, 1848	4	25
Elizabeth, d. Ebenezer, b. [ ]	1	2X
Emily, of Plainfield, m. Horace **ALLEN**, of Canterbury, Nov. 25, 1845, by Rev. C.C. Barnes	3	33
Isaac, s. Wait & Elizabeth, b. Mar. 8, 1743	1	101
Lucy, A., b. Richmond, R.I., res. Plainfield, d. Aug. 3, 1851, ae. 40	4	66
Maria, b. Griswold, res. Plainfield, d. Sept. 14, 1850, ae. 31	4	66
Reuben, b. Canterbury, res. Plainfield, d. May 12, 1848, ae. 3	4	61
Reuben, d. Nov. 4, 1848, ae. 2	4	62
Septimus, m. Isabel R. **POTTER**, b. of Plainfield, Oct. 12, 1831, by Peleg Peckham, Elder	2	214
Wait, m. Elizabeth **FELLOWS**, June 26, 1739	1	101
William, of Griswold, m. Sally **PHILLIPS**, of Plainfield, Feb. 23, 1840, by Rev. Thomas Barber	3	3
-----, d. Wait & Elizabeth, b. Aug. 8, 1740	1	101
HERRINGTON, [see also **HARRINGTON**], Anne, d. Timothy & Anne, b. July 6, 1767	2	68
Caleb, m. Lucinda **BROWN**, b. of Killingly, Apr. 17, 1836, by Chester Tilden	2	226
Clark, of Lisbon, m. Anna **GATES**, of Griswold, Feb. 9, 1823, by Orin Fowler, V.D.M.	2	190
Daniel, s. Timothy & Anne, b. Apr. 27, 1764	2	68
Hannah, d. Katharine **TURNER**, b. Oct. 27, 1762	2	64
Mehetable, m. Anthony **PARKIS**, Feb. 27, 1820	2	189
Olive, d. Timothy & Anne, b. Feb. 16, 1765	2	68
Sally, of Canterbury, m. John O. **PICKET**, of Plainfield, Nov. 5, 1815, by Daniel Frost, Jr., J.P., Canterbury	2	127

	Vol.	Page
HERRINGTON, (cont.)		
Susan W., m. Thomas **WILSON**, b. of Plainfield, Sept. 9, 1838, by Peleg Peckham, Elder	2	237
HEWETT, HUET, HUETT, Elisabeth, m. John **WARREN**, Apr. 29, 1734	1	64
Ephraim, s. Thomas & Perces, b. Jan. 4, 1728/9	1	47
Lydiah, m. Isaac **LAWRANCE**, Dec. 19, 1727	1	55
Prudence, m. Benjamin **WHEELER**, Jan. 29, 1729/30	1	62
Thankfull, d. Thomas & Perses, b. Aug. 20, 1722	1	27
HEWLET, [see under **HULET** and **HOWLET**]		
HIBBARD, [see under **HEBARD**]		
HICKS, [see under **HIX**]		
HIDE, [see under **HYDE**]		
HIFLIN, [see also **HEFLIN**], Esther, d. Daniel B., laborer, ae. 36, & Lydia, ae. 32, b. July 7, 1848	4	21
HILL, Abby A., m. Elisha P. **HALE**, b. of Plainfield, Jan. 19, 1852, by Rev. Joseph P. Brown	3	73
Alcy Ann, d. Feb. 14, 1848, ae. 20	4	61
Alexander, m. Ruth A. **HILL**, b. of Plainfield, Jan. 20, 1844, by James Smither, Elder	3	28
Caroline, manufacturer, d. Jan. 22, 1850, ae. 28	4	64
Daniel, m. Deborah **WOOD**, b. of Plainfield, Dec. 11, 1814, by Rev. Nath[anie]l Cole	2	132
David, m. Jane **BARTLETT**, b. of Plainfield, Dec. 18, 1853, by Rev. Joseph P. Brown	3	81
Edward E., m. Caroline **POTTER**, b. of Plainfield, May 19, 1845, by James Smither, Elder	3	29
Eldridge G., m. Sarah **DOUGLASS**, b. of Plainfield, Dec. 26, 1830, by Rev. Orin Fowler	2	212
George, m. Murand **EDWARDS**, b. of Plainfield, Oct. 23, 1853, by Rev. Joseph P. Brown	3	80
George T., of Plainfield, m. Lydia **ROBERTS**, of Coventry, R.I., Sept. 19, 1847, by Rev. Fred[eri]c Charlton	3	49
Henry W., m. Ruth **MILLER**, b. of Plainfield, Sept. 17, 1838, by Rev. Samuel Rockwell	2	236
Jeremiah, m. Louisa **YOUNG**, b. of Sterling, Nov. 10, 1844, by Peleg Peckham, Elder	3	25
Jeremiah, m. Freelove M. **POTTER**, Feb. 14, 1848, by Rev. Isaac C. Day	3	56
Juliett, of Sterling, m. Clark D. **VAUGHAN**, of Killingly, May 18, 1846, by Peleg Peckham, Elder	3	37
Laury A., of Griswold, m. William P. **YOUNG**, Jr., of Sterling, Nov. 25, 1851, by Rev. Joseph P. Brown	3	72
Martha R., of Sterling, m. Lewis E. **DIXON**, of Plainfield, Oct. 10, 1854, by Rev. Joseph P. Brown	3	87
Mary, m. Stephen G. **YOUNG**, b. of Sterling, Dec. 8, 1835, by Peleg Peckham, Elder	2	224

	Vol.	Page
HILL. (cont.)		
Mary S., m. Gardiner **ROUSE**, b. of Plainfield, Jan. 21, 1831, by Benjamin R. Allen, Elder	2	213
Minerva, m. George W. **BURDICK**, b. of Griswold, [ ] 24, 1853, by Rev. Alfred Gates	3	77
Olive, m. Thomas P. **CARPENTER**, b. of Plainfield, Mar. 20, 1837, by Rev. Samuel Rockwell	2	229
Rachel A., m. William E. **KENNEDY**, b. of Foster, R.I., Dec. 6, 1846, by Peleg Peckham, Elder	3	41
Rocinda C., d. Jonathan, carpenter, ae. 36, & Rocinda, ae. 38, b. Feb. 24, 1848	4	22
Ruth A., m. Alexander **HILL**, b. of Plainfield, Jan. 20, 1844, by James Smither, Elder	3	28
Sarah A., of Plainfield, m. Andrew E. **MURFEY**, of Norwich, Dec. 18, 1853, by Rev. Joseph P. Brown	3	81
Solomon, s. Solomon & Mercy, b. Aug. 27, 1718	1	19
----, s. Joseph, laborer, b. Nov. 10, [1850]	4	30
HILLIS, John, m. Bridget **TUNO**, b. of Plainfield, Mar. 31, 1839, by Rev. Samuel Rockwell	2	240
HINKLEY, Albert, s. Vincent & Zerviah, b. May 9, 1810	2	122
Charles, s. Vincent & Surviah, b. Dec. 5, 1814	2	130
Maria, d. Vincent & Surviah, b. June 2, 1820	2	134
Nancy, d. Vincent & Zerviah, b. Apr. 5, 1809	2	122
Nancy, d. Vincent & Surviah, d. June 25, 1814	2	130
Sarah, d. Vincent & Surviah, b. Feb. 13, 1817	2	130
Sarah, of Plainfield, m. Erasmus D. **AVERY**, of Groton, Aug. 7, 1844, by A. Dunning	3	24
Vincent, of Plainfield, m. Zerviah **COOK**, of Preston, Dec. 31, 1807, by Rev. Levi Hart	2	121
HITCHCOCK, William T., m. Lucy **CORBIN**, b. of Plainfield, Dec. 13, 1840, by Rev. Samuel Rockwell	3	8
HIX, HICKS, Cynthia, m. Comfort **LOVE**, b. of Plainfield, [ ] 28, [ ], by Rev. Samuel Rockwell	2	224
George, of Plainfield, m. Betsey **BARBER**, of Canterbury, Jan. 1, 1849, by Rev. Henry Robinson	3	56
George, laborer, b. Pomfret, Ct., res. Canterbury, m. Betsey **BARBER**, b. Plainfield, res. Canterbury, Jan. 1, 1849, by Rev. Henry Robinson	4	3
HOARD, Anne, d. Thomas & Keziah, b. May 27, 1754	2	36
Jacob, m. Amy **WELCH**, Aug. 18, 1750	2	32
John, m. Jemima **HUNTER**, of Norwich, May 12, 1757	2	36
Lydia, d. Jacob & Amy, b. Mar. 19, 1751	2	32
Thomas, m. Keziah **RICHARDSON**, Oct. 27, 1752	2	36
Zadock, s. Thomas & Keziah, b. Feb. 23, 1757	2	36
HOLDEN, Clark, m. Susan **PATTISON**, b. of Coventry, R.I., June 21, 1847, by Rev. Fred[eri]c Charlton	3	49
Henry, of Canterbury, m. Clarrissa **CHURCH**, of Plain-		

168   BARBOUR COLLECTION

	Vol.	Page
HOLDEN, (cont.)		
field, Oct. 28, 1838, by Francis B. Johnson, J.P.	2	237
Henry J., of Warwick, R.I., m. Setilice D. **WHITFORD**, of West Greenwich, R.I., Aug. 2, 1846, by A. Dunning	3	38
HOLLAND, HOLAND, Daniel, m. Judah H. **CARD**, b. of Sterling, June 28, 1846, by Peleg Peckham, Elder	3	38
Edward, s. Henry & Abiah, b. Apr. 15, 1726	1	46
Henry, m. Abiath **DOUGLASS**, May 3, 1720	1	24
Henry, s. Henry & Abiah, b. Feb. 5, 1727/8	1	46
Mary, d. Henry & Abiah, b. Oct. 3, 1722	1	46
Sarah, d. Henry & Abiath, b. Feb. 8, 1720/21	1	24
HOLLEY, Elizabeth B., m. George T. **WELLS**, b. of Plainfield, Dec. 4, 1854, by Rev. Joseph P. Brown	3	88
HOLLOWAY, William F., m. Emily S. **PHILLIPS**, b. of Plainfield, Mar. 20, 1854, by Rev. Henry Robinson	3	83
HOLT, George H., s. William, manufacturer, ae. 40, & Clarrissa B., ae. 35, b. Sept. 25, 1848	4	23
William, of Oxford, Mass., m. Clarrissa C. **BURLESON**, of Plainfield, July 15, 1839, by Rev. Thomas Barber	2	243
HOLWAY, Esther, of West Greenwich, R.I., m. William **SMITH**, of Plainfield, Apr. 4, 1841, by Rev. Hezekiah Thatcher	3	9
HOOD, Hannah, of Plainfield, m. James P. **BURLINGAME**, of Worcester, Mass., Mar. 2, 1845, by V.R. Osborn, V.D.M.	3	27
HOPKINS, Adah, m. Thomas J. **FRENCH**, b. of Sterling, Sept. 8, 1845, by Peleg Peckham, Elder	3	32
Amhurst, m. Hannah **ROGERS**, b. of Warwick, R.I., Dec. 19, 1847, by Rev. J. Mather	3	47
Andrew, m. Abigail R. **INGRAHAM**, b. of Foster, R.I., Oct. 20, 1847, by Rev. J. Mather	3	46
Andrew J., m. Almiry E. **DORRANCE**, July 20, 1840, by Rev. Samuel Rockwell	3	6
Andrew Jackson, s. William & Sally, b. Feb. 24, 1820	2	150
Betsey Northup, s.* William & Sally, b. Mar. 21, 1808 (*Probably a daughter)	2	125
David, s. William & Sally, b. July 10, 1806	2	125
Emeline, m. William **PEIRCE**, Jr., b. of Foster, R.I., Mar. 19, 1848, by Rev. James Mather	3	54
Fanny, m. John **BOTTUM**, June 14, 1801	2	109
Happy Ann, d. William & Sally, b. July 25, 1811	2	126
James Munroe, s. William & Sally, b. Oct. 7, 1821	2	150
James W., of Plainfield, m. Nancy E. **PARKHURST**, of Rutland, Mass., Sept. 23, 1845, by James Smither, Elder	3	34
John, s. William & Sally, b. Feb. 14, 1805	2	125

	Vol.	Page
HOPKINS, (cont.)		
Joseph, s. William & Sally, b. Oct. 26, 1823	2	150
Julia A., d. Feb. [ ], 1851, ae. 5	4	66
Latem, m. Julia Ann Keziah **JOHNSON**, b. of Plainfield, Mar. 25, 1827, by Rev. Orin Fowler	2	201
Martha Emeline, d. William & Sally, b. Apr. 9, 1817	2	150
Mary, of Plainfield, m. John A. **CAREW**, of Norwich, Oct. 10, 1824, by Rev. Nathaniel Cole	2	196
Nancy A., ae. 19, of Plainfield, m. Harden H. **FENNER**, merchant, ae. 21, b. Foster, R.I., res. Sterling, Mar. 25, 1850, by Peleg Peckham	4	5
Nancy H., of Plainfield, m. Harden W. **FENNER**, of Sterling, Mar. 25, 1850, by Peleg Peckham, Elder	3	64
Peggy Loisa, d. William & Sally, b. June 28, 1818	2	150
Rebecca, of Plainfield, m. Hollis **BUTTS**, of Canterbury, Aug. 31, 1828, by Nathaniel Cole, Elder	2	206
Sally Phebe, d. William & Sally, b. Mar. 2, 1813	2	126
Samuel Slater, s. William & Sally, b. Nov. 16, 1825	2	150
Sophia Caroline, d. William & Sally, b. Apr. 14, 1815	2	150
Susan M., m. David A. **KENYON**, b. of Plainfield, Mar. 1, 1854, by Rev. Joseph P. Brown	3	82
Sylva, of Plainfield, m. Daniel **COGSWELL**, of Brooklyn, June 20, 1831, by Nathaniel Cole, Elder	2	214
Tramtrum, s. William & Sally, b. Nov. 23, 1809	2	125
William, m. Sally **TRANTUM**, May 6, 1804	2	125
William B., of R.I., now residing in Sterling, m. Cyfuantus(?) B. **TAYLOR**, of Sterling, Apr. 28, 1844, by Peleg Peckham, Elder	3	23
William S., m. Asenath M. **JOHNSON**, b. of Plainfield, Feb. 21, 1830, by Orin Fowler, V.D.M.	2	210
William W., m. Salome **ADAMS**, b. of Plainfield, Dec. 9, 1824, by Orin Fowler, V.D.M.	2	197
HORTON, James S., m. Elmira **STARKWEATHER**, b. of Plainfield, Jan. 6, 1828, by Orin Fowler, V.D.M.	2	204
HOTH, Albert, m. Mary Ann **CLARK**, b. of Canterbury, July 28, 1839, by Rev. Tubal Wakefield	2	243
HOUGH, Hugh, of Lisbon, m. Lucy **CHAMPLAIN**, of Plainfield, Aug. 23, 1846, by Rev. J. Mather	3	39
HOVEY, Lucy, m. Gurdon **BINGHAM**, Mar. 20, 1788	2	98
Marius M., farmer, ae. 33, b. Sutton, Mass., res. Sutton, m. Louisa L. **SABIN**, ae. 33, b. Sterling, Ct., res. Sutton, June 8, 1851, by H. Robinson	4	7
Marious M., of Sutton, Mass., m. Louisa L. **SABIN**, of Plainfield, June 18, 1851, by Rev. Henry Robinson	3	70
HOWARD, Elizabeth, m. Augustus **LEWIS**, b. of Coventry, R.I., Nov. 30, 1848, by Rev. George W. Brewster	3	57
George F., of Griswold, m. Mary F. **PHILLIPS**, of Plainfield, Aug. 27, 1849	3	59

	Vol.	Page

HOWARD, (cont.)

	Vol.	Page
Mary J., m. Albert L. **SMITH**, b. of Scituate, Apr. 10, 1845, by James Smither, Elder	3	29

HOWE, HOW, HOWES, Abegall, d. Samuel, Jr. & Sarah, b.

	Vol.	Page
Mar. 26, 1718	1	20
Anna, d. John & Mary, b. Nov. 24, 1756	2	35
Azubah, d. Tho[ma]s & Perces, b. Feb. 6, 1717/18	1	19
Damaris, d. John & Mary, b. July 7, 1758	2	44
Dressor, s. Josiah & Patience, b. June 21, 1749	2	8
Dresser, s. Josiah & Patience, d. Oct. 20, 1754, ae. 5	2	28
Hannah, d. Jonas & Sarah, b. Mar. 26, 1756	2	35
James, s. John & Febe, b. Oct. 7, 1715	1	20
James, m. Johannah **SPAULDING**, Feb. 3, 1742	2	17
James, s. Jonas & Sarah, b. Oct. 18, 1754	2	28
James, s. Jonas & Sarah, d. Dec. 20, 1755, ae. 2 m. 2 d.	2	28
James, Jr., m. Abigail **WARREN**, May 15, 1774	2	78
Johanah, d. Joseph & Merabah, b. Apr. 2, 1741	2	16
Johannah, m. Sampson **HOW[E]**, Mar. 1, 1756	2	44
John, m. Pheby **BUTTERFIELD**, d. Samuell, of Chelmsford, Apr. 13, 1709	1	9
John, s. John & Phebe, b. Aug. 6, 1712	1	11
John, d. Aug. 27, [1727], in the 40th y. of his age	1	42
John, s. Thomas & Abigaiel, b. Dec. 17, 1729; d. Dec. [31], 1729	1	62
John, s. Samuel & Mathew*, b. Oct. 27, 1744 (*Martha?)	2	2
John, m. Mary **WHE[E]LER**, Dec. 25, 1755	2	44
John, s. John & Jemime, b. Oct. 12, 1759	2	44
Jonas, s. John & Phebe, b. June 13, 1726	1	37
Jonas, m. Sarah **WHE[E]LER**, Jan. 24, 1750/51	2	12
Jonas, d. May 9, 1776	2	79
Jonathan, s. John & Phebe, b. Apr. 3, 1724; d. Apr. 13, 1724	1	29
Jonathan, s. Josiah & Patience, b. Oct. 20, 1742	2	1
Joseph, s. Samuel & Sarah, b. Apr. 18, 1720	1	23
Joseph, m. Merabah **KEE**, Apr. 2, 1740	2	16
Joseph, s. Joseph & Merabah, b. Apr. 24, 1747	2	16
Joseph, d. July 7, 1751	2	16
Josiah, s. John & Pheby, b. Mar. 22, 1710/11	1	8
Josiah, of Plainfield, m. Patience **MARSH**, of Killingly, Nov. 19, 1741	1	101
Josiah, m. Patience **DAY**, Nov. 20, 1741	2	1
Josiah, d. Nov. 1, 1759, at Crown Point	2	58
Lemuel, s. Joseph & Merabah, b. Feb. 19, 1745	2	16
Luce, m. Thomas **WHEELER**, [ ]	1	71
Luissee, d. John & Feebe, b. May 8, 1714	1	13
Martha, d. James, Jr. & Abigail, b. May 2, 1775	2	78

	Vol.	Page
HOWE, HOW, HOWES, (cont.)		
Mary, d. Samuell & Sarah, b. Mar. 1, 1714/15	1	14
Mary, d. Sept. 1, 1727	1	34
Mary, d. Thomas & Abigaiel, b. Aug. 13, 1732	1	62
Mirabah, d. Joseph & Merabah, b. Apr. 20, 1743	2	16
Nathan, s. Josiah & Patience, b. Nov. [ ], 1742	1	101
Noah, s. John & Mary, b. Apr. 30, 1760	2	51
Olive, d. James, Jr. & Abigail, b. Dec. 29, 1776	2	83
Phebe, d. Sam[ue]ll, Jr. & Ma[r]tha, b. Aug. 12, 1741	1	100
Phebe, wid., d. Dec. 3, 1758	2	44
Phebe, d. Jonas & Sarah, b. Jan. 19, 1760	2	42
Robert, s. Josiah & Patience, b. Feb. 11, 1745/46	2	1
Samson, s. Thomas & Abigaiel, b. July 28, 1734	1	62
Sampson, m. Johannah **HOW[E]**, Mar. 1, 1756	2	44
Samuel, s. John & Ffebe, b. June 24, 1716	1	16
Samuel, d. Dec. 29, 1724	1	34
Samuel, Jr., m. Ma[r]tha **SPAULDING**, Oct. 30, 1740	1	100
Samuel, s. Jonathan, b. June 8, 1788	2	103
Sarah, d. Joseph & Merabah, b. May 5, 1749	2	16
Sarah, w. Sam[ue]ll, d. Aug. 31, 1755	2	31
Sealah, d. John & Mary, b. Apr. 27, 1762	2	51
Silas, s. Samuel & Mathew*, b. Apr. 15, 1747 (*Martha?)	2	2
Simeon, s. Josiah & Patience, b. Mar. 6, 1744	2	1
Squire, s. Jonas & Sarah, b. Nov. 2, 1752	2	22
Stephen, s. Samuel & Mathew*, b. Nov. 23, 1748 (*Martha?)	2	8
Thomas, s. Samuell, Jr. & Sarah, b. Oct. 17, 1708	1	7
Thomas, m. Abigaiel **WHEELER**, May 28, 1729	1	62
HOWLAND, Charles W., m. Lucy W. **SPAULDING**, b. of Plainfield, Mar. 27, 1837, by Rev. Samuel Rockwell	2	229
HOWLET, [see also **HEWLET** and **HULET**], A[a]ron, s. Nathaniel & Susanah, b. Jan. 23, 1755	2	34
Nathaniel, s. Nathaniel & Susannah, b. Dec. 3, 1751	2	19
HOWORTH, Lucetta W., of Exeter, R.I., m. Alvin **TUCKER**, of South Kingstown, R.I., Sept. 17, 1848, by Rev. Geo[rge] W. Brewster	3	56
HOXSIE, Nathan G., of Richmond, R.I., m. Susan A. **PECKHAM**, of Plainfield, July 8, 1850, by Peleg Peckham, Elder	3	65
HUBBARD, [see also **HUBET** and **HEBARD**], Daniel, m. Lydia A. **HALE**, Jan. 12, 1847, by Rev. Fred[eri]c Charlton	3	48
Frances Mehitable, b. Aug. 27, 1834; d. Feb. 14, 1836; Willimantic Village, Windham, birthplace	2	232
HUBET, Eunis, d. Elip]ha]let & Sarah, b. Mar. 5, 1745/6 (**HULET**?)	1	2X
HUDSON, Alfred S., of Providence, R.I., m. Laury A.		

	Vol.	Page

HUDSON, (cont.)
    WILLIAMS, of Plainfield, May 1, 1853, by Rev.
        Joseph P. Brown   3   78
    Emeline A., d. Nathaniel, teacher, ae. 31, & Cordelia,
        ae. 28, bf Bangor, Me., b. Feb. 11, 1849   4   27
HUETT, [see under **HEWETT**]
HULET, [see also **HEWLET, HOWLET** and **HUBET**], Dinah, d.
    Nathaniel & Susanah, b. Aug. 25, 1747; d. Jan. 16,
    1747/8   2   7
    Eunis, d. Elip[ha]let & Sarah, b. Mar. 5, 1745/6
        (Arnold Copy has the name "**HUBET**")   1   2X
    Experience, m. Ebenezer **KINGSBURY**, Feb. 23, 1743/4   1   2
    Rachel, m. Elisha **REYNOLDS**, July 27, 1769   2   75
    Susan[n]ah, d. Nathaniel & Susan[n]ah, b. Dec. 16,
    1748   2   7
HULL, Tamar, farmer, b. Conn., res. Plainfield, d. July 10,
    1849, ae. 84   4   62
    -----, twins, s. & d. Eleazer, farmer, ae. 45, &
        Hannah, ae. 40, b. Aug. 17, 1848   4   26
HUMES, Edmund, of Griswold, m. Sarah **POTTER**, of Plainfield,
    July 10, 1836, by Chester Tilden   2   227
    Julia A., of Plainfield, m. John S. **SMITH**, of Slaters-
    ville, R.I., May 15, 1851, by Rev. John F.
    Sheffield   3   70
    Mary, Mrs., domestic, b. Warwick, R.I., res. Plainfield,
        d. Mar. 4, 1850, ae. 52   4   64
HUNT, Peleg, of Worcester, Mass., m. Jane **STERRY**, of
    Norwich, Mar. 25, 1823, by Rev. Orin Fowler   2   191
HUNTER, Jemima, of Norwich, m. John **HOARD**, May 12, 1757   2   36
    Mary, m. Oliver **SPAULDING**, June 17, 1762, in the 23rd
        y. of his age   2   83
    William, s. William & Mary, b. Mar. 6, 1749   2   28
HUNTINGTON, Mary Ann, m. Gilbert **POTTER**, b. of Sterling,
    Nov. 27, 1834, by Peleg Peckham, Elder   2   220
HUTCHINS, HUTCHINGS, HUTCHING, HUCHENS,
    HUCHINGS, HUCHINS, HUTCHENS, Anne, d. John
    & Mary, b. Apr. 16, 1712   1   10
    Eunice, of Plainfield, m. Ebenezer **SANGER**, of Brooklyn,
        June 2, 1824, by Rev. Thomas J. Mordock, Canterbury   2   194
    Ezrah, s. John & Mary, b. Oct. 11, 1714   1   14
    Joseph, s. John & Mary, b. Dec. 31, 1709   1   8
    Joshua, s. Benjamin & Prudence, b. Feb. 24, 174[ ]   1   2X
    Keziah, d. John & Mary, b. Dec. 11, 1708   1   7
    Mary, d. John & Mary, b. Mar. 19, 1715/16   1   15
    Mary, m. Samuel **PARKHURST**, Feb. 24, 1742/3   2   2
    Rachel, m. Benjamin **PRIOR**, Nov. 10, 1771   2   75
    Ruth, d. John & Mary, b. Nov. 22, 1710   1   8
    Silass, s. John & Mary, b. Oct. 7, 1717   1   18

	Vol.	Page
HUTCHINS, HUTCHINGS, HUTCHING, HUCHENS, HUCHINGS, HUCHINS, HUTCHENS, (cont.)		
Wyman, s. John & Mary, b. June 7, 1713	1	12
-----, st. b. s. Joseph, farmer, age 29, & Lucy R., ae. 28, by June 25, 1849	4	26
HUTCHINSON, Ann G., d. Moses, carpenter, & Mary, b. Mar. 19, 1848	4	21
Elizabeth D. of Plainfield, m. Lewis **YO[U]NG**, of Killingly, Aug. 7, 1842, by Andrew Dunning	3	16
Lucretia, b. Griswold, res. Plainfield, d. Apr. 26, [18]49, ae. 87	4	62
Margaret, d. Ralph & Eliza, b. Dec. 22, 1828	2	150
Moses Dwight, s. Ralph & Eliza, b. Apr. 28, 1823	2	150
Ralph Peboddy, s. Ralph & Eliza, b. Mar. 6, 1825	2	150
HUTTON, Austis, d. William Carr & Acsah, b. Jan. 18, 1788	2	99
Charles, s. William C. & Acsah, b. July 7, 1795	2	102
Charles Stewart, s. William C. & Axsah, b. Apr. 17, 1801	2	111
James s. William Carr & Acsah, b. Feb. 4, 1793	2	100
Jean, d. William Carr & Acsah, b. July 18, 1790	2	99
William Carr, m. Acsah, **SMART**, July 20, 1787	2	99
HYDE, HIDE, Albert, of Plainfield, m. Hannah E. **CHEAS-BOROUGH**, of Sterling, Oct. 18, 1841, by Peleg Peckham, Elder	3	11
Charles H. s. Ira, farmer, ae. 45, & Olive, ae. 34, b. February 18, 1848	4	24
Edmund, s. Abner & Sally, b. Feb. 8, 1806	2	118
Eliza, d. Abner & Sally, b. Mar. 19, 1804	2	118
Emily, d. Abner & Sally, b. July 6, 1810	2	118
Eunis, m. Joseph **WARREN**, May 29, 1754	2	53
George, farmer, d. Apr. 6, 1850, ae. 17	4	64
George B., m. Asenath **ROUNDS**, b. of Sterling, July 2, 1843, by Peleg Peckham, Elder	3	19
Henry, d. Nov. 22, [1848], ae. 2	4	62
Henry A., s. Albert, laborer, ae. 27, & Hannah E., ae. 25, b. Dec. 25, 1847	4	21
Ira, m. Olive **WILSON**, b. of Plainfield, Oct. 24, 1841, by John Read, Elder	3	11
Lydia, m. Nathan **BENNET**, Mar. 1, 1778	2	82
Mary E., of Canterbury, m. Christopher **PLACE**, of Foster, R.I., Oct. 8, 1844, by James Smither, Elder	3	28
Prudence, m. James **PHILLIPS**, b. of Sterling, Oct. 5, 1845, by Peleg Peckham, Elder	3	32
Sally, d. Abner & Sally, b. July 12, 1808	2	118
Samuel, m. Jane **MARPLES**, Sept. 13, 1846, by John J. Penrose, J.P.	3	39
Squire, farmer, b. Killingly, res. Plainfield, d. Dec. 28, [18]47, ae. 80	4	61

	Vol.	Page
HYDE, HIDE, (cont.)		
William J., m. Sarah M. **POTTER**, b. of Plainfield, Nov. 14, 1853, by Rev. Joseph P. Brown	3	81
-----, of Sterling, m. Polly **BUTTS**, of Plainfield, June 11, 1831, by Peleg Peckham, Elder	2	213
INGALS, Sophia, m. Gardiner **ROUSE**, b. of Plainfield, May 5, 1843, by Rev. A. B. Wheeler	3	20
INGRAHAM, Abigail R., m. Andrew **HOPKINS**, b. of Foster, R.I., Oct. 20, 1847, by Rev. J. Mather	3	46
Sarah A., of Coventry, R.I., m. George W. **ELDREDGE**, of Warwick, R.I., Sept. 26, 1847, by Rev. James Mather	3	45
ISAACSON, James H., of Hartford, m. Louisa **CLEVELAND**, of Plainfield, Sept. 1, 1835, by Rev. Otis C. Whiton, of Canterbury	2	221
JACKSON, David, m. Clarissa **MOODY**, b. of Plainfield, July 15, 1838, by Rev. Samuel Rockwell	2	235
JACOBI, John C., of New Orleans, m. Marcy E. **CUTLER**, of Plainfield, Sept. 17, 1850, by Rev. J. O. Knapp	3	66
JACOBS, Jane G., m. Isaac N. **WHILDEN**, b. of Lisbon, Sept. 3, 1854, by Rev. Alfred Gates	3	86
Theda E., m. John **FERENSIDE**, Sept. 17, 1854, by Rev. Alfred Gates	3	86
JACOY, William H., of Warwick, R.I., m. Hepsbeth B. **SWEET**, of West Greenwich, R.I., May 8, 1846, by Rev. James Mather	3	37
JACQUES, JAQES, Elizabeth, m. John O. **FENNER**, b. of R.I., Jan. 3, 1847, by Mowry Burgess, J.P.	3	42
Elizabeth, of Providence, R.I., m. John O. **FENNER**, of Johnson, R.I., Jan. 3, 1847, by M. Burgess, J.P.	3	44
Mary A., m. William P. **DIXON**, b. of Sterling, Oct. 15, [1850], by Peleg Peckham, Elder	3	66
JAMES, Betsey, of Plainfield, m. William **DOUGLASS**, of Voluntown, Apr. 11, 1821, by Rev. Orin Fowler	2	133
Eunice L., d. Rodmon & Margaret, b. May 18, 1822	2	152
Hannah C., d. Rodmon & Margaret, b. Dec. 21, 1818	2	152
Hannah C., of Plainfield, m. Benjamin **LEWIS**, of Worcester, Mass., Jan. 7, 1850, by Rev. Jared O. Knapp	3	63
James W., s. Rodmon & Margaret, b. Oct. 25, 1810	2	152
John W., m. Matilda **DOUGLASS**, b. of Plainfield, Nov. 29, 1852, by Rev. Joseph P. Brown	3	77
Joseph, farmer, d. July 14, 1850, ae. 45	4	64
Joseph W., s. Rodmon & Margaret, b. May 27, 1805	2	152
Lucy A., d. Rodmon & Margaret, b. Sept. 30, 1817	2	152
Lydia M., d. Rodmon & Margaret, b. July 20, 1808	2	152
Mary A., d. Rodmon & Margaret, b. Aug. 4, 1813	2	152
Rodman, m. Margaret **STRINGER**, b. of Plainfield, Nov. 25, 1802, by Rev. Joel Benedict	2	190

	Vol.	Page
JAMES, (cont.)		
Rodman, m. Hannah **GALLUP**, b. of Plainfield, Mar. 7, 1830, by Rev. Orin Fowler	2	211
Sarah S., d. Rodmon & Margaret, b. Dec. 4, 1803	2	152
JASPER, Peter, m. Celinda **DUNHAM**, Nov. 3, 1799, by Calvin Goddard, J.P.	2	114
JENNINGS, Maria, of Franklin, m. Ebenezer **JEWETT**, of Thompson, Sept. 12, 1824, by Orin Fowler	2	195
JENSON, Judeth, m. Joseph **PARKHURST**, Aug. 12, 1741	1	100
JERAULD, [see under **GERAULD**]		
JEWELL, JUEL, JEWEL, Abegal, d. Nathaniel & Sarah, b. Nov. 3, 1719	1	20
Abigaiel, d. Nathaniel & Sarah, b. Mar. 27, 1739	1	99
Archable, s. Joseph & Mary, b. Apr. 8, 1716	1	17
Ebenezer, s. Nathaniel & Sarah, b. Jan. 25, 1736/7	1	69
Han[n]ah, m. Daniel **LAWRANCE**, Nov. 5, 1712	1	11
Han[n]ah, d. Nathaniel & Sarah, b. Dec. 6, 1720	1	23
Martha, d. Joseph & Mary, b. Mar. 12, 1717/18	1	19
Nathaniel, Jr., m. Sarah **WHITNEY**, d. Joshua, of Grotton, July 11, 1704	1	9
Nathaniel, m. Sarah **WHITNEY**, d. Joshua, of Grotton, July 11, 1704	1	10
Nathaniel, m. Sarah **BAR[R]ET**, Jan. 9, 1732/3	1	69
Nathaniel, s. Nathaniel & Sarah, b. Oct. 28, 1733; d. Dec. 10, 1733	1	69
Nathaniel, s. Nathaniel & Sarah, b. Jan. 27, 1734/5	1	69
Nathaniel, s. Nathaniel & Sarah, b. Oct. 8, [ ]	1	5
Nathaniel, s. Nathaniel & Sarah, b. [ ]	1	2
Sarah, d. Nathaniel & Sarah, b. July 11, 1711	1	10
Sarah, d. Nathaniel & Sarah, b. July 24, 1711	1	9
JEWETT, Ebenezer, of Thompson, m. Maria **JENNINGS**, of Franklin, Sept. 12, 1824, by Orin Fowler	2	195
JOHNSON, JONSON, Abadiah Elderkin, s. Jacob & Abigail, b. Jan. 15, 1783	2	118
Abadiah Nelson, s. Abadiah Elderkin & Lucy, b. Sept. 20, 1810	2	120
Abigail, d. Joseph & Elizabeth, b. Apr. 17, 1699; d. May 7, 1700	1	3
Abegell, m. Sylvan **STEVANS**, b. of Plainfield, May 1, 1723	1	28
Alfred, s. Jacob & Abigail, b. July 27, 1766	2	67
Anson, s. Jacob & Abigail, b. Oct. 13, 1768; d. July 27, 1769, ae. 9 m. & 1/2	2	67
Asenath M., m. William S. **HOPKINS**, b. of Plainfield, Feb. 21, 1830, by Orin Fowler, V.D.M.	2	210
Benjamin W., of Lisbon, m. Lucinda **KENNEDY**, bf Plainfield, Oct. 31, 1830, by Rev. Orin Fowler	2	212
Caroline Elizabeth, d. Anson & Huldah, b. Apr. 4, 1818	2	152

JOHNSON, JONSON, (cont.)

	Vol.	Page
Ebenezer Murray, s. Jacob & Abigail, b. Nov. 19, 1786	2	120
Elderkin Roger, s. Anson & Huldah, b. June 4, 1813	2	152
Elizabeth, d. Joseph & Elizabeth, b. Jan. 12, 1705/6	1	3
Elizabeth, d. Ebenezer Murray & Elizabeth, b. Feb. 16, 1824	2	153
Fanny H., of Sterling, m. William G. **DAWLEY**, of Coventry, R.I., Feb. 3, 1845, by Peleg Peckham, Elder	3	26
Hannah, of Warwick, R.I., m. Oliver **PHILLIPS**, of Coventry, R.I., Nov. 6, 1848, by Rev. Geo[rge] W. Brewster	3	52
Horatio Huntington, s. Anson & Huldah, b. Dec. 10, 1808	2	118
Isaac G., s. W[illia]m M., blacksmith, ae. 34, & Elizabeth M., ae. 30, b. Apr. 28, 1850	4	29
Isaac G., d. June 1, 1851, ae. 1 y. 21 d.	4	66
Jacob, m. Judeth **HAINES**, May 8, 1734	1	47
Jacob, d. Jan. 29, 1738/9	1	92
John, m. Olive **MORGAN**, Aug. 26, 1786	2	97
John Morgan, s. John & Olive, b. Nov. 29, 1787	2	97
Jonathan, of Plainfield, m. Abby **WILCOX**, of Voluntown, Nov. 8, 1840, by Amos Witter	3	8
Joseph, of Griswold, m. Dolly **FISK**, of Plainfield, July 22, 1837, by Daniel Hill, J.P.	2	231
Julia Ann Keziah, m. Latem **HOPKINS**, b. of Plainfield, Mar. 25, 1827, by Rev. Orin Fowler	2	201
Louisa Abigail, d. Jacob & Abigail, b. June 14, 1764	2	67
Lucinda A., of Plainfield, m. John N. **COATS**, of Sterling, Apr. 22, 1832, by Rev. Samuel Rockwell	2	215
Lydia, m. Hutchinson **FARLAN**, b. of Plainfield, June 4, 1809, by Rev. Joel Benedict	2	120
Lydia, m. George S. **GIBSON**, b. of Plainfield, Nov. 17, 1842, by Peleg Peckham, Elder	3	17
Lydia, of Coventry, R.I., m. Christopher R. **PEIRCE**, July 9, 1854, by Rev. Alfred Gates	3	84
Mary, d. Jacob & Judeth, b. Nov. 17, 1735	1	92
Nancy M., of Sterling, m. Dwight A. **YENCKES**, of Coventry, R.I., Mar. 1, 1846, by Peleg Peckham, Elder	3	36
Rebec[c]a, d. Jacob & Judeth, b. Oct. 9, 1738	1	92
Rowland C., of Coventry, R.I., m. Mary A. **GREEN**, of Warwick, R.I., Nov. 28, 1849, by Rev. Joseph P. Brown	3	62
Susan W., of Plainfield, m. George **PENDLETON**, of Camden, Me., Sept. 28, 1831, by Rev. Dennis Platt, of Canterbury	2	214
Susannah Welthan, d. Anson & Huldah, b. Dec. 15, 1810, at Brooklyn	2	152

	Vol.	Page
JOHNSON, JONSON, (cont.)		
William M., of Killingly, m. Elizabeth M. **SHEPHARD**, of Plainfield, Apr. 28, 1841, by Rev. Tubal Wakefield	3	9
JONES, JOANS, Charles, of Plainfield, m. Roxana **GREFFETH**, of Foster, R.I., May 10, 1835, by Jonathan Goff, J.P.	2	221
Elisabeth, d. Joseph & Elisabeth, b. Dec. 25, 1731	1	55
Frederick, of Nassau, N.Y., m. Lois **EATON**, of Plainfield, Oct. 17, 1849, by Rev. Henry Robinson	3	61
Mary, m. W[illia]m Henry **CASE**, b. of Plainfield, Apr. 20, 1845, by V.R. Osborn, V.D.M.	3	27
Simeon, of Plainfield, m. Abby **PRENTICE**, of Griswold, Apr. 15, 1829, by Rev. Orin Fowler	2	209
Susan M., m. William S. **PRIOR**, Apr. 27, 1841, by Rev. George J. Tillotson	3	10
JORDAN, JORDON, JOURDON, JURDON, [see also **GURDON**], Deborah, of Coventry, R.I., m. Stephen C. **RANDALL**, of Providence, R.I., Aug. 30, 1847, by Rev. James Mather	3	45
Elizabeth, now residing in Plainfield, but belonging in the State of R.I., m. Noel **COLLINS**, Sept. 22, 1822, by Jonathan Gallup, J.P.	2	188
Esek, m. Sally **POTTER**, Mar. 27, 1842, by Rev. John Read	3	14
Sarah A., of Plainfield, m. George N. **PHILLIPS**, of Cranston, R.I., Nov. 11, 1849, by Rev. Joseph P. Brown	3	62
Susan, of Canterbury, m. William H. **MINER**, of Blandford, Mass., Nov. 30, 1848, by Rev. J. B. Guild, Packerville	3	54
Susan, b. Canterbury, res. Blanford, m. W[illia]m H. **MAINE**, laborer or farmer, b. Blanford, Mass., res. Blanford, Nov. 30, 1848, by Rev. J.B. Guild	4	3
JOSLIN, JOSHLIN, John, Jr., m. Waty **FOSTER**, Nov. 5, 1820, by Nathaniel Cole, Elder	2	133
William V., m. Amanda M. **PEIRCE**, Nov. 22, 1846, by Benjamin Bacon, J.P.	3	39
JOYE, Freelove, m. Joseph **CORY**, Feb. 5, 1739/40 (Arnold Copy says "**JOYE**" should be "**LOVEJOY**")	1	94
KEE, Joanna, m. Samuel **SPAULDING**, June 11, 1771	2	91
Merabah, m. Joseph **HOW[E]**, Apr. 2, 1740	2	16
KEECH, KEACH, Allen E., m. Rebecca **BOWEN**, of Warwick, May 19, 1845, by James Smither, Elder	3	30
Daniel D., m. Sarah A. **KENYON**, b. of Plainfield, Mar. 23, 1835, by Peleg Peckham, Elder	2	220
George, m. Jane **SWEET**, b. of Brooklyn, Feb. 10, 1850, by Rev. W. Emerson	3	63

	Vol.	Page
KEECH, KEACH, (cont.)		
Luther, m. Clarrissa **COOPER**, Mar. 10, 1844, by Archibald Douglass, J.P.	3	22
Phebe A., of Plainfield, m. Benjamin **HAIR**, of Glocester, R.I., Feb. 21, 1842, by Peleg Peckham, Elder	3	13
KEIGWIN, Gardiner, s. Amos & Thankfull, b. July 29, 1782	2	88
KELLOGG, Austin, of Granby, N.Y., m. Frances M. **MOORE**, of Plainfield, Nov. 10, 1836, by Rev. Tubal Wakefield, (Packersville)	2	228
KEMP, Henry, Jr., of Brooklyn, Ct., m. Fidelia **SHIPPEE**, Nov. 10, 1850, by H. Robinson	4	7
Lucinda, of Plainfield, m. Martin **BRENON**, of Ross County of Ross Commons, Ireland, May 22, 1838, by Rev. Samuel Rockwell	2	234
KENDAL, Jedediah, s. Phinehas & Olive, b. June 27, 1783	2	90
Lydia, d. Phinehas & Olive, b. Feb. 16, 1785	2	109
Olive, d. Phinehas & Olive, b. Feb. 17, 1783	2	109
Susannah, d. Peter & Susannah, b. Apr. 4, 1797	2	104
KENNEDY, KENEDY, KENADY, Abel, twin with Robert, s. Robert & Magdalene, b. Sept. 7, 1805	2	116
Albert, s. Joshua & Clarrissa, b. Feb. 11, 1815	2	157
Alice, d. John & Jane, b. Feb. 2, 1808	2	157
Alice, d. John & Jane, d. Feb. 15, 1823	2	264
Caroline, d. Oct. 16, [18]47, ae. 4	4	61
Clarinda Ann, d. Joseph & Clarina, b. May 16, 1821	2	157
Clarrissa, m. William C. **MARPLE**, b. of Plainfield, Mar. 12, 1844, by A. Dunning	3	22
David Henry, s. John Willson & Lucy Ann, b. May 12, 1832	2	264
Elizabeth, d. Robert, manufacturer, ae. 41, & Clarrissa, ae. 30, b. May 8, 1848	4	24
Elizabeth, d. Kimball, manufacturer, ae. 45, & Elizabeth, ae. 36, b. Apr. 22, 1850	4	28
Emily, d. Robert & Magdalene, b. Aug. 7, 1809	2	118
George Burt, s. John W. & Lucy Ann, b. May 19, 1834	2	264
Gordon C., d. Aug. 25, [18]48, ae. 4 y.	4	61
Hannah B., of Voluntown, m. Robert H. **DIXON**, of Sterling, Oct. 16, 1849, by Peleg Peckham, Elder	3	61
Horace, s. Robert & Clarrissa, b. Mar. 25, 1844	3	31
Jane, w. John, d. Feb. 24, 1819, in the 49th y. of her age	2	264
John, m. Marcy **SKILLION**, Nov. 3, 1763	2	53
John, Jr., s. John & Mary, b. Apr. 19, 1774	2	77
John, m. Jane **WILSON**, Apr. 6, 1797	2	221
John, s. Joshua & Clarinda, b. Feb. 28, 1811	2	156
John, m. Mary **SHEPERD**, b. of Plainfield, Dec. 31, 1820, by Rev. Orin Fowler	2	132

PLAINFIELD VITAL RECORDS

	Vol.	Page
KENNEDY, KENEDY, KENADY, (cont.)		
John, m. Phebe **COOPER**, b. of Plainfield, Feb. 10, 1828, by Rev. Orin Fowler	2	204
John F., m. Susan **GALLUP**, b. of Plainfield, Feb. 24, 1840, by Rev. Samuel Rockwell	3	4
John Wilson, s. John & Jane, b. Oct. 1, 1810	2	264
John Willson, m. Lucy Ann **COOPER**, June 25, 1831	2	264
Joshua Shepard, s. Joshua & Clarissa, b. Dec. 6, 1823	2	157
Kimbal, s. Robert & Magdalene, b. Jan. 8, 1803	2	116
Lois, d. John & Jane, b. Mar. 11, 1804	2	157
Lois, d. John & Jane, d. Oct. 20, 1806	2	264
Lucinda, of Plainfield, m. Benjamin W. **JOHNSON**, of Lisbon, Oct. 31, 1830, by Rev. Orin Fowler	2	212
Lucy Ann, w. John W., d. June 29, 1834	2	264
Magdalene, w. Robert, d. Dec. 11, 1827, ae. 57	2	157
Maria T., b. Woodstock, res. Plainfield, d. July 8, [18]48, ae. 1	4	61
Martha, d. John & Jane, b. Feb. 25, 1798	2	157
Martha, of Plainfield, m. Jeremiah B. **SMITH**, of Canterbury, Sept. 19, 1824, by Rev. James Porter, of Pomfret	2	195
Mary, d. Joshua & Clarinda, b. Aug. 29, 1812	2	156
Mary, 2d w. of John, d. Sept. 18, 1827	2	264
Mary Ann, m. Dean **WEST**, b. of Plainfield, Aug. 29, 1837, by Chester Tilden	2	232
Menerva T., m. Royal A. **NEY**, b. of Providence, R.I., Mar. 28, 1847, by Rev. J. Mather	3	44
Nancy D., of Voluntown, m. Albert M. **PERKINS**, of Sterling, Oct. 6, 1850, by Peleg Peckham, Elder	3	66
Robert, s. John & Mercy, b. Dec. 10, 1764	2	58
Robert, m. Magdalene **SMITH**, Feb. 9, 1797	2	116
Robert, twin with Abel, s. Robert & Magdalene, b. Sept. 7, 1805	2	116
Robert, m. Clarrissa **BRIGGS**, b. of Plainfield, Mar. 29, 1843, by Rev. A. Dunning	3	18
Roxana, d. John & Jane, b. June 17, 1802	2	157
Roxana, d. John & Jane, d. Dec. 17, 1817	2	264
Rufus, s. Robert & Magdalene, b. May 7, 1799	2	116
Rufus W., m. Susan **CUTLER**, b. of Plainfield, Dec. 20, 1829, by Rev. Orin Fowler	2	210
Ruth, d. John & Mercy, b. Oct. 9, 1766	2	67
Ruth, d. John & Mercy, b. Oct. 9, 1767	2	68
Ruth, m. John **HALL**, Jr., Nov. 8, 1787	2	98
Ruth, d. John & Jane, b. Oct. 6, 1799	2	157
Ruth Smith, d. John & Jane, d. Oct. 6, 1823	2	264
Theodore P., m. Sally M. **ROUNDS**, b. of Foster, Feb. 8, 1846, by Peleg Peckham, Elder	3	36

	Vol.	Page
KENNEDY, KENEDY, KENADY, (cont.)		
William E., m. Rachel A. **HILL**, b. of Foster, R.I., Dec. 6, 1846, by Peleg Peckham, Elder	3	41
-----, John F., farmer, ae. 38, & Susan, ae. 29, b. Aug. 22, 1848	4	25
KENT, -----, d. Alvin, laborer, ae. 30, & Catharine, ae. 28, b. June 20, 1848	4	25
KENYON, KINYON, Abby E., m. Willard W. **COLLINS**, b. of Hopkinton, R.I., Nov. 16, 1845, by Peleg Peckham, Elder	3	32
Amey A., of Sterling, m. Allen M. **SHELDON**, of Coventry, R.I., Jan. 9, 1843, by Peleg Peckham, Elder	3	18
Amey R., m. Duty **GREEN**, b. of Plainfield, Sept. 7, 1835, by Peleg Peckham	2	222
Anthony B., m. Jane E. **FAIRMAN**, Nov. 29, 1849, by Peleg Peckham, Elder	3	62
Anthony B., farmer, ae. 24, of Plainfield, m. Jane E. **FAIRMAN**, ae. 18, of Plainfield, Nov. 29, 1849, by Peleg Peckham	4	5
Anthony Bradford, s. Thomas & Mary P., b. Apr. 12, 1825	2	156
Benjamin L., m. Mary S. **KENYON**, b. of Sterling, Nov. 5, 1838, by Peleg Peckham, Elder	2	237
Betsey P., m. Alvan **CARD**, b. of Sterling, Dec. 4, 1837, by Peleg Peckham, Elder	2	233
Caroline, d. George & Freelove, b. Apr. 2, 1823	2	156
Catharine H., of Plainfield, m. Thomas A. **BAXTER**, of Brooklyn, Nov. 21, 1849, by Rev. Henry Robinson	3	61
Catharine H., ae. 34, of Plainfield, m. Thomas R. **BAXTER**, wagon maker, ae. 40, of Brooklyn, Nov. 21, 1849, by Henry Robinson	4	5
Daniel S., m. Almira M. **REED**, b. of Plainfield, Dec. 19, 1842, by Peleg Peckham, Elder	3	18
David A., m. Susan M. **HOPKINS**, b. of Plainfield, Mar. 1, 1854, by Rev. Joseph P. Brown	3	82
Edmund P., s. George & Freelove, b. Sept. 14, 1821	2	156
Edward W[illia]m, s. William & Hannah, b. May 17, 1838	3	31
Emily H., of Plainfield, m. Charles C. **CALL**, of Sterling, July 4, 1850, by Peleg Peckham, Elder	3	65
Emily H., ae. 20, of Plainfield, m. Cha[rle]s C. **CALL**, harness & trunk maker, ae. 21, of Sterling, July 4, 1850, by Rev. Peleg Peckham	4	5
Esther, m. Sessions **LESTER**, b. of Plainfield, Feb. 14, 1802	2	158
Esther, d. Thomas & Mary, b. July 13, 1833	2	157
Freelove M., d. George & Freelove, b. May 25, 1820	2	156
Freelove M., d. George & [Freelove], b. May 25, 1820	2	180
Freelove M., of Plainfield, m. Artemas S. **BRUCE**, of		

KENYON, KINYON, (cont.)

	Vol.	Page
Pomfret, Mar. 28, 1848, by Rev. James Mather	3	54
Handson, of Sterling, m. Lois **GREEN**, of Plainfield, Feb. 26, 1843, by Peleg Peckham, Elder	3	18
Hannah, of Richmond, R.I., m. Joseph **CRANDALL**, of Exeter, R.I., Feb. 18, 1829, by Peleg Peckham, Elder	2	208
Hannah, of Sterling, m. Thomas S. **SLADE**, of Woodstock, Sept. 29, 1839, by Peleg Peckham, Elder	2	248
Hannah, of Sterling, m. Thomas S. **SLADE**, of Woodstock, Sept. 29, 1839, by Peleg Peckham, Elder	3	1
Hannah, shoemaker, b. Sterling, res. Plainfield, d. Dec. [ ], 1850, ae. 49	4	66
Hannah, housekeeper, b. Voluntown, res. Plainfield, d. Dec. [ ], 1850, ae. 49	4	66
Hannah, m. Edward B. **PERRY**, b. of South Kingstown, R.I., Oct. 3, 1854, b. Rev. Peter L. Mather	3	87
Hannah Emily, d. William & Hannah, b. Jan. 12, 1830	2	157
Hannah M., of Sterling, m. Edwin B. **SHELDON**, of Coventry, R.I., Dec. 13, 1840, by Peleg Peckham, Elder	3	9
Happy C., m. Horatio N. **DOUGLASS**, b. of Sterling, Jan. 2, 1848, by Peleg Peckham, Elder	3	50
Julia Ann, d. William & Hannah, b. June 24, 1833	2	157
Leroy M., m. Waitey A. **HARRINGTON**, b. of Plainfield, Mar. 12, 1850, by Rev. Joseph P. Brown	3	63
Leroy W., harness maker, ae. 23, b. Sterling, Ct., res. Plainfield, m. Waitey **HARRINGTON**, ae. 22, b. Foster, R.I., res. Plainfield, Mar. 12, 1850, by Rev. Brown	4	5
Lucy A., of Plainfield, m. Frank **BAKER**, of Brooklyn, Nov. 21, 1849, by Rev. Henry Robinson	3	61
Lucy A., ae. 21, of Plainfield, m. Frank E. **BAKER**, farmer, ae. 27, of Brooklyn, Nov. 21, 1849, by Henry Robinson	4	5
Lucy A., b. Plainfield, res. Brooklyn, d. July 14, 1850, ae. 22	4	64
Lucy Angeline, d. William & Hannah, b. June 19, 1842	3	31
Lydia E., m. George A. **CADY**, b. of Plainfield, Apr. 3, 1842, by Peleg Peckham, Elder	3	14
Mary E., of Exeter, m. James A. **FULLER**, of Worcester, Mass., Oct. 28, 1847, by Peleg Peckham, Elder	3	53
Mary Esther, d. William & Hannah, b. Aug. 13, 1835	3	31
Mary S., m. Benjamin L. **KENYON**, b. of Sterling, Nov. 5, 1838, by Peleg Peckham, Elder	2	237
Mercy M., of Sterling, m. Richard **DAWLEY**, of R.I., Oct. 17, 1841, by Peleg Peckham, Elder	3	11
Nancy, m. Hiram **PARKIS**, b. of Plainfield, Oct. 27,		

	Vol.	Page
KENYON, KINYON, (cont.)		
1822, by Rev. Nathaniel Cole	2	189
Nancy B., of Sterling, m. Thomas G. **CAHOON**, of Coventry, Sept. 13, 1841, by Peleg Peckham, Elder	3	11
Nancy G., of Plainfield, m. George B. **WHEELER**, of Mantua, O., Sept. 19, 1854, by Rev. James Bates	3	86
Olive D., d. Thomas & Mary, b. May 21, 1829	2	157
Oliver K., m. Abby A.S. **BENNETT**, b. of Johnston, R.I., Dec. 30, 1848, by Caleb Bennet, J.P.	3	55
Rhoda, d. George & Freelove, b. May 19, 1818	2	156
Rhoda, d. George & Freelove, b. May 19, 1818	2	180
Ruth M., of Plainfield, m. Frank E. **BAKER**, of Brooklyn, Oct. 29, 1851, by Rev. Henry Robinson	3	72
Sally C., of Sterling, m. Gorton **CAHOONE**, of Coventry, R.I., Dec. 10, 1838, by Peleg Peckham, Elder	2	238
Sarah A., m. Daniel D. **KEECH**, b. of Plainfield, Mar. 23, 1835, by Peleg Peckham, Elder	2	220
Shepard, of Sterling, m. Eleanor **LAWTON**, of Plainfield, Sept. 3, 1829, by Rev. Orin Fowler	2	210
Sprague, m. Hannah **REYNOLDS**, b. of Richmond, R.I., Sept. 8, 1850, by Rev. Joseph P. Brown	3	65
Stuteley K., of Plainfield, m. Lydia W. **HAWKINS**, of Sterling, Jan. 1, 1829, by Rev. Orin Fowler	2	207
William, m. Louisa **SPAULDING**, b. of Plainfield, [ ], by Rev. Joseph P. Brown	3	77
William P., m. Martha **SMITH**, June 27, 1847, by Peleg Peckham, Elder	3	45
KETTLE, Ruth, ae. 27, b. Norwich, res. Plainfield, m. Henry **SHELDON**, farmer, ae. 30, b. Norwich, res. Plainfield, June 3, 1849, by Peleg Peckham (See also Ruth **KITTLE**)	4	4
KIBBE, Hannah, d. Joshua & Mary, m. Samuel **KINGSBURY**, Nov. 26, 1714	1	15
KIES, Joseph, s. Nathaniel & Johannah, b. Mar. 1, 1769	2	126
Juda, w. Joseph, b. May 18, 1762, in Killingly	2	126
Mereba, d. Joseph & Juda, b. Jan. 2, 1811	2	126
Phila, d. Joseph & Juda, b. Sept. 13, 1807	2	126
Uriah, d. Feb. 28, 1825	2	156
William, s. James W., shoemaker, ae. 35, & Elatheen, ae. 38, b. July 5, 1848	4	24
KILE, Anne, d. Ephraim & Phebe, b. Dec. 6, 1758	2	39
Ephraim, m. Phebe **NICHOLS**, Jan. 18, 1758	2	39
Sarah, m. Josiah **CORY**, Jan. 4, 1758	2	70
William, s. Ephraim & Phebe, b. Nov. 5, 1760	2	48
KILLUM, Hiphzabah, m. Nehemiah **STEVENS**, Jan. 24, 1766	2	61
KIMBALL, Abigail, m. Ebenezer **WILLIAMS**, May 17, 1756	2	38
Eliphalet, m. Elizabeth **WOODWARD**, May 10, 1759	2	47

PLAINFIELD VITAL RECORDS 183

	Vol.	Page
KIMBALL, (cont.)		
James M., of Rockland, N.Y., m. Caroline **WOLCOTT**, of Plainfield, Feb. 17, 1847, by Rev. Jared C. Knapp, Central Village	3	42
John Lovel, s. Eliphalet & Elizabeth, b. Jan. 21, 1762	2	47
Mary, m. Jesse **SPAULDING**, Feb. 28, 1757	2	48
Tammerson, d. Eliphalet & Elizabeth, b. Mar. 8, 1760	2	47
KING, Amanda M., m. John W. **SPAULDING**, b. of Plainfield, Feb. 2, 1851, by Rev. W. Emerson	3	68
Arnold, of Foster, R.I., m. Sally **SIMMONS**, of Plainfield, Nov. 16, 1823, by Nathaniel Cole, Elder	2	192
Nathan, of West Greenwich, R.I., m. Mary **SMITH**, of Canterbury, May 9, 1830, by Francis B. Johnson, J.P.	2	211
Orin D., of Scituate, R.I., m. Lydia **BURGESS**, of Plainfield, Sept. 29, 1828, by Rev. Orin Fowler	2	207
Sarah, of Foster, R.I., m. Robert **KNIGHT**, of Scituate, R.I., Apr. 7, 1825, by Orin Fowler, V.D.M.	2	197
KINGSBURY, KINGSBERY, Abigail, m. Ele[a]zer **SPAULDING**, Nov. 14, 1712	1	32
Abigail, d. James. m. Eleazar **SPAULDING**, Nov. 17, 1712	1	11
Abiga[i]l, d. Samuel & Hannah, b. Mar. 3, 1721/2	1	28
Asa, s. Ephraim, Jr. & Lydia, b. Mar. 29, 1722	1	35
Asa, m. Elizabeth **PEIRCE**, Sept. 5, 1748	2	24
David, s. Sam[ue]ll & Hannah, b. May 29, 1731	1	54
Ebenezer, s. Samuel & Han[n]ah, b. Feb. 25, 1717/18	1	22
Ebenezer, m. Experience **HULET**, Feb. 23, 1743/4	1	2X
Ephraim, s. Ephraim & Phebe, b. Oct. 15, 1702	1	5
[E]unice, d. Samuel & Dorkis, b. Mar. 5, 1735	2	17
Jacob, s. Stephen & Sarah, b. Jan. 21, 1761	2	52
James, s. Samuel & Han[n]ah, b. Apr. 27, 1716	1	17
Jeremiah, s. Samuell & Hannah, d. June 3, 1725	1	37
Jeremiah, s. Ephraim, Jr. & Lydiah, b. Feb. 4, 1729	1	49
Jeremiah, s. Asa & Elizabeth, b. June 18, 1754	2	24
John, s. Ephraim & Phebe, b. June 19, 1713	1	16
John, s. Stephen & Sarah, b. July 3, 1757	2	37
John, s. Jonathan & Susannah, b. Feb. 11, 1767	2	62
Jonathan, m. Susanah **WOODWARD**, Nov. 14, 1764	2	57
Joseph, s. Oliver & Hannah, b. Aug. 5, 1760	2	54
Joseph, s. Oliver & Hannah, b. Aug. 5, 1760	2	67
Joseph, s. Stephen & Sarah, b. Mar. 20, 1768	2	68
Lydiah, d. Ephraim & Lydiah, b. Apr. 7, 1736	1	69
Lidya, m. Josiah **RUSSEL[L]**, Mar. 8, 1758	2	39
Mary, d. Samuel & Han[n]ah, b. Feb. 29, 1719/20	1	22

KINGSBURY, KINGSBERY, (cont.)

	Vol.	Page
Molley, d. Stephen & Sarah, b. Nov. 3, 1765	2	52
Nathaniel, s. Samuel & Hannah, b. Feb. 1, 1728	1	53
Nehemiah, s. Samuel & Hannah, b. June 2, 1724	1	32
Oliver, s. Sam[ue]ll & Hannah, b. Sept. 2, 1733	1	60
Oliver, m. Hannah **CORY**, Sept. 17, 1754	2	30
Oliver, s. Oliver & Hannah, b. Aug. 28, 1755	2	32
Oliver, d. Nov. 27, 1760	2	54
Oliver, d. Nov. 27, 1760, returning home from the Campaign in 1760	2	67
Patience, d. Sam[ue]ll & Hannah, b. Aug. 25, 1737	1	92
Phebe, d. Ephraim & Phebe, b. Jan. 8, 1703/4	1	5
Phebe, m. William **CADY**, Nov. 11, 1729	1	55
Phebe, d. Ephraim, Jr. & Lydiah, b. Mar. 29, 1731	1	62
Phebe, m. David **PARKHURST**, Dec. 28, 1750	2	40
Rachall, d. Ephraim & Phebe, b. Apr. [ ], 1706	1	5
Rachel, m. Daniel **LAWRANCE**, Jr., May 31, 1725	1	34
Rachel, d. Ephraim, Jr. & Lydiah, b. Mar. 29, 1731	1	62
Razel, s. Asa, d. Mar. 14, 1754	2	24
Ruth, d. Ephraim & Lydia, b. Jan. 15, 1723/4	1	35
Ruth, m. Edward **SPAULDING**, July 9, 1744	2	15
Ruth, d. Jonathan & Susan[n]ah, b. July 8, 1765	2	57
Samuel, m. Hannah **KIBBE**, d. Joshua & Mary, Nov. 26, 1714	1	15
Samuel, m. Dorkis **SPAULDING**, May 12, 1730	2	17
Samuel, d. Aug. 21, 1739	2	17
Samuel, s. Oliver & Hannah, b. May 30, 1758	2	67
Sarah, d. Samu[e]ll & Hannah, b. Aug. 5, 1726	1	39
Sarah, d. Samuel & Dorkis, b. Feb. 23, 1732	2	17
Stephen, m. Sarah **SPAULDING**, Dec. 10, 1755	2	37
Stephen, s. Stephen & Sarah, b. Mar. 25, 1763	2	52
Tarbel, s. Stephen & Sarah, b. Feb. 10, 1759; d. Feb. 29, 1760	2	52
Thomas, d. June 11, 1720	1	22
Thomas, s. Samuel & Dorkis, b. Nov. 4, 1730	2	17
William, s. Asa, d. May 15, 1753	2	24
Zip[p]orah, d. Asa & Elizabeth, b. May 6, 1749	2	24
KINGSLEY, Elias, s. Joseph & Sarah, b. Oct. 31, 1756	2	36
KINNE, KINNIE, KINNEY, KINNEE, Almira, of Plainfield, m. Thomas **KINNIE**, of Thompson, N.Y., Oct. 25, 1826, by Rev. Thomas J. Mordock, Canterbury	2	202
Amey, d. Levi & Hannah, b. June 18, 1788	2	112
Anna, m. Thomas **DOW**, Dec. 11, 1795	2	101
Daniel, of Plainfield, m. Almira **GALLUP**, of Sterling, Dec. 1, 1844, by Peleg Peckham, Elder	3	25
George Whitefield, s. Joseph & Gemima, b. Apr. 14, 1771	2	81
Huldah, m. William **CORNELL**, Dec. 5, 1793	2	100

	Vol.	Page
KINNE, KINNIE, KINNEY, KINNEE, (cont.)		
John, s. Levi & Hannah, b. Feb. 13, 1793	2	112
John, m. Polly **BAKER**, Dec. 26, 1813, by Thomas Backus, J.P.	2	125
Laura, of Voluntown, m. Thomas S. **TILLINGHAST**, of Plainfield, Feb. 26, 1843, by Peleg Peckham, Elder	3	18
Levi, of Plainfield, m. Hannah **GALLUP**, of Voluntown, Jan. 4, 1787, by Rev. Micaiah **PORTER**, of the First Society in Voluntown	2	112
Louisa, b. Griswold, res. Plainfield, d. Oct. 30, 1850, ae. 36	4	64
Manuel, s. Levi & Hannah, b. Sept. 26, 1796	2	112
Manuel, of Voluntown, m. Esther **FRINK**, of Plainfield, June 3, 1822, by Orin Fowler, V.D.M.	2	187
Marcy, m. Henry **DOW**, Jr., b. of Plainfield, Oct. 2, 1814, by Thomas Backus, J.P.	2	127
Mary E., m. Erastus L. **PRIOR**, b. of Plainfield, Mar. 7, 1836, by Peleg Peckham, Elder	2	225
Mercy, d. Levi & Hannah, b. June 24, 1791	2	112
Robert, m. Clarissa **WILSON**, b. of Plainfield, Mar. 14, 1824, by Orin Fowler, V.D.M.	2	193
Thomas, of Thompson, N.Y., m. Almira **KINNIE**, of Plainfield, Oct. 25, 1826, by Rev. Thomas J. Mordock, Canterbury	2	202
We[a]lthy, d. Joseph & Gemima, b. Apr. 11, 1773	2	81
-----, cotton operative, d. July [ ], 1850, ae. 34	4	65
KINSMAN, Joanna, m. Benjamin **BACON**, Jr., b. of Plainfield, Sept. 15, 1824, by Orin Fowler, V.D.M.	2	195
Marg[a]ret, of Norwich, m. Cyrus **MARSH**, of Plainfield, May 29, 1740	1	96
KITTLE [see also **KETTLE**], Mary, of Plainfield, m. Benjamin M. **ARNOLD**, of Sterling, Aug. 19, 1849, by Peleg Peckham, Elder	3	59
Ruth, m. Henry S. **SHELDON**, b. of Plainfield, June 3, 1849, by Peleg Peckham, Elder	3	59
KNAPING, Mary, of Plainfield, m. Jesse **PARSON**, of Cold Spring, N.Y., Dec. 5, 1841, by Amos Witter, J.P.	3	12
KNIGHT, Ambrose, m. Sarah **MERRICE**, b. of Plainfield, Aug. 27, 1843, by Peleg Peckham, Elder	3	20
Charles Francis, s. William & Sabra, b. Feb. 12, 1822	2	156
David, s. Benjamin & Grace, b. Dec. 22, 1740	1	97
Edward Clark, s. William & Sabra, b. Nov. 18, 1819, at Sterling	2	156
Elizabeth, m. Ezekiel **WHITNEY**, Mar. 7, 1757	2	35
Elizabeth Clark, d. William & Sabra, b. Oct. 11, 1817	2	156
J. Whitney, of Westerly, R.I., m. Mary Ann **PERKINS**, of Sterling, Nov. 26, 1838, by Peleg Peckham, Elder	2	238

BARBOUR COLLECTION

	Vol.	Page
KNIGHT, (cont.)		
John, m. Catharine **McKINGLY**, b. of Plainfield, Jan. 29, 1854, by Rev. William Turkington	3	82
Margaret Whitney, d. William & Sabra, b. Jan. 31, 1809	2	120
Phebe Green, d. Isaac, b. Oct. 5, 1840	3	60
Rhuame, d. John & Susan[n]ah, d. Dec. 31, 1754, in the 20th y. of her age	2	28
Robert, of Scituate, R.I., m. Sarah **KING**, of Foster, R.I., Apr. 7, 1825, by Orin Fowler, V.D.M.	2	197
William, m. Sabra **BACKUS**, Sept. 14, 1806	2	120
William Tracy, s. William & Sabra, b. Sept. 29, 1813, in Canterbury	2	156
KNOX, John G., m. Caroline **BUGBEE**, b. of Plainfield, Aug. 27, 1848, by Rev. Frederic Charlton	3	55
Lamira, m. Jesse H. **MEDBERY**, b. of Plainfield, July 30, 1838, by Rev. Hezekiah Thecker (Thatcher?)	2	236
LADD, LAD, Daniel V., m. Jane M. **GRISWOLD**, b. of Franklin, Aug. 11, 1840, by Rev. Nicholas Branch, Killingly	3	6
John, m. Asubah C. **DOUGLASS**, b. of Plainfield, July 15, 1839, by Rev. Samuel Rockwell	2	243
Luther, laborer, b. Coventry, R.I., m. Emeline **MUNRO**, b. Plainfield, Apr. 30, 1850, by Elder Emerson	4	5
Martin L., m. Emeline C. **MUNROE**, b. of Plainfield, Apr. 30, 1850, by Rev. W. Emerson	3	64
Sarah E., of Sterling, m. Edwin L. **GRANT**, of Tolland, Nov. 2, 1846, by Peleg Peckham, Elder	3	40
Thrsa, m. Joseph **VAUGHN**, b. of Sterling, Oct. 10, 1836, by Peleg Peckham, Elder	2	227
LAMB, Prudence, of Plainfield, m. William **WHIPPLE**, of Groton, Sept. 5, 1822, by Jonathan Gallup, J.P.	2	188
LAMPHERE, Nancy, of Plainfield, m. Samuel **MUNRO**, of Canterbury, Aug. 4, 1833, by Francis B. Johnson, J.P.	2	217
LANE, Cyrus, s. Hezekiah & Deborah, b. Apr. 24, 1785	2	91
Job, s. Hezekiah & Deborah, b. Apr. 22, 1787	2	93
Lydia, d. Hezekiah & Deborah, b. June 30, 1778	2	91
Nathan, s. Hezekiah & Deborah, b. July 11, 1781	2	91
Polly, d. Hezekiah & Deborah, b. July 29, 1783	2	91
LANGWORTHY, Andrew, s. Andrew & Ruth, b. June 21, 1765	2	65
Anne, d. Joseph & Azubah, b. Apr. 23, 1764	2	49
Elizabeth, d. Joseph & Azuba, b. July 26, 1761	2	48
Evengalles, s. Andrew & Ruth, b. May 15, 1767	2	65
Willard, s. Andrew & Ruth, b. Apr. 16, 1769	2	68
LAPHAM, Enos, of Scituate, R.I., m. Abby B. **AUSTIN**, of East Greenwich, R.I., Apr. 23, 1843, by Rev. Erastus Benten	3	19
LARKHANA, Lot, of Voluntown, m. Sarah **PHILLIPS**, of Plainfield, Apr. 6, 1835, by Peleg Peckham, Elder	2	221

	Vol.	Page
LARKIN, Mary Ann, of Plainfield, m. Amasa **CORBIN**, of Canterbury, Dec. 13, 1840, by Rev. Tubal Wakefield	3	8
LARRABEE, John, m. Mary **SPAULDING**, Dec. 16, 1762	2	55
John Spaulding, s. John & Mary, b. July 22, 1766	2	55
Sarah, d. John & Mary, b. Apr. 5, 1768	2	55
Timothy, s. John & Mary, b. July 6, 1763	2	55
LATHROP, Caroline Elizabeth, d. Samuel B. & Emma, b. Mar. 28, 1822	2	158
Dixwell, m. Esther **SHEPHERD**, b. of Plainfield, Nov. 17, 1823, by Orin Fowler, V.D.M.	2	192
Elizabeth, of Norwich, m. John **PROFIT**, of Colchester, Oct. 25, 1841, by John Read, Elder	3	12
George, s. Joseph & Mehetabel, b. Oct. 8, 1814	2	159
Jane H., of [Norwich], m. John S. **FRENCH**, of Plainfield, Oct. 22, 1839, by Rev. Henry Dyon, Norwich	3	8
Joseph, m. Lydia **SHEPERD**, b. of Plainfield, July 25, 1823, by Rev. Orin Fowler	2	191
Julia Burkett, d. George & Marion, b. Mar. 5, 1838	2	159
Luthena, d. Samuel B. & Emma, b. May 22, 1820	2	134
Luthmia, of Plainfield, m. Mahlon F. **HENST**, of Naihes, Miss., Sept. 3, 1839, by Rev. Samuel Rockwell	2	247
Lydia, of Norwich, m. Thomas **BACKUS**, of Plainfield, Nov. 6, 1793	2	103
Mary M., of Plainfield, m. Dudley A. **SUMMERS**, of Hartford, July 7, 1834, by Rev. Samuel Rockwell	2	219
LAW, Martha, d. Samuel & Martha, d. Nov. 19, 1714	1	14
Samuel, s. Samuel & Marthah, b. Nov. 15, 1714	1	14
LAWRENCE, LAWRANCE, LAWRANS, Abigail, m. Jeremiah **CADY**, Jan. 8, 1755	2	32
Amie, d. Daniel & Sarah, b. Aug. 22, 1727; d. Dec. 9, 1728	1	46
Amie, d. Daniel & Sarah, b. Aug. 22, 1727	1	47
Amy, d. Isaac & Lydiah, b. Dec. 8, 1734	1	63
Asa, s. Samuel & Sarah, b. June 1, 1738	1	92
Azubah, see under Esubah		
Daniel, m. Han[n]ah **JEWELL**, Nov. 5, 1712	1	11
Daniel, m. Sarah **WILLIAMS**, Mar. 4, 1724/5	1	32
Daniel, Jr., m. Rachel **KINGSBURY**, May 31, 1725	1	34
Daniel, d. Dec. 9, 1728	1	47
David, twin with Jonathan, s. Jeremiah & Olive, b. Oct. 7, 1732	2	12
Deborah, d. Gideon & Eunis, b. Feb. 11, 1749/50	2	12
Eles, d. Daniel & Sarah, b. Apr. 19, 1731	1	53
Eliza, d. Daniel & Sarah, b. Jan. 6, 1725/6	1	47
Elisabeth, d. Daniel & Sarah, b. Jan. 6, 1725/6	1	36
Elizabeth, d. Daniel & Sarah, b. Jan. 6, 1725/6	1	46

	Vol.	Page
LAWRENCE, LAWRANCE, LAWRANS, (cont.)		
Esubah, d. Isaac & Lydiah, b. Dec. 8, 1730	1	55
Eunis, d. Daniel & Sarah, b. Mar. 20, 1733; d. [Mar.] 29, [1733]	1	58
[E]unis, d. Gid[e]on & [E]unis, b. Feb. 12, 1741	1	97
Experience, m. Joseph **WILLIAMS**, Mar. 6, 1758	2	45
Experience, m. Joseph **WILLIAMS**, Apr. 5, 1758	2	39
Gideon, s. Daniel & Han[n]ah, b. Mar. 15, 1716/17	1	17
Gid[e]on, s. Daniel, Jr. & Rachiel, b. Nov. 21, 1727	1	42
Gid[e]on, m. [E]unis **PARKHURST**, Aug. 1, 1738	1	97
Gideon, s. Gideon & Eunis, b. Mar. 16, 1746	2	12
Han[n]a[h], d. Daniel & Han[n]a[h], b. Sept. 22, 1718	1	20
Hannah, d. Daniel & Hannah, d. May 18, 1733	1	58
Hannah, d. Gid[e]on & [E]unis, b. Sept. 18, 1739; d. Dec. 13, 1739	1	97
Hester, d. Daniel & Sarah, b. Feb. 10, 1728/9	1	52
Hester, m. Inoch **BALLARD**, Sept. 25, 1734	2	15
Isaac, m. Lydiah **HUET**, Dec. 19, 1727	1	55
Isaac, s. Isaac & Lydiah, b. Mar. 5, 1737	1	70
Jeremiah, m. Olive **WHEELER**, Feb. 2, 1729	1	37
John, s. Daniel & Sarah, b. Jan. 2, 1735/6	1	65
Jonas, s. Isaac & Lydiah, b. Dec. 1, 1728	1	55
Jonathan, twin with Davis, s. Jeremiah & Olive, b. Oct. 7, 1732	2	12
Joseph, s. Thomas & Sarah, b. Oct. 2, 1745	1	2X
Josiah, s. Josiah & Sarah, b. Mar. 22, 1733	1	61
Josiah, m. Releif **LAWRENCE**, Jan. 25, 1758	2	38
Marah, m. Lemuel **DEAN**, June 26, 1746	2	1
Mary, d. Daniel, b. July 22, 1713	1	12
Mary, d. Joseph & Mary, b. Jan. 27, 1727/28	1	44
Mary, d. Gideon & Eunis, b. Apr. 5, 1748	2	12
Nathaniel, s. Daniel & Han[n]h[h], b. Oct. 28, 1714	1	20
Nathaniel, s. Daniel & Hannah, d. June 2, 1733	1	58
Nathaniel, s. Daniel, Jr. & Rachel, b. June 21, 1733	1	60
Nathaniel, s. Gideon & Eunis, b. Sept. 23, 1743	2	12
Nehemiah, s. Jeremiah & Olive, b. Mar. 18, 1730	1	54
Rachel, d. Daniel, Jr. & Rachel, b. Apr. 26, 1726	1	42
Rachiel, d. Daniel, Jr. & Rachiel, d. Sept. 8, 1729	1	56
Releif, m. Josiah **LAWRENCE**, Jan. 25, 1758	2	38
Ruefus, s. Daniel, Jr. & Rachal, b. Aug. 3, 1735	1	68
Ruth, d. Daniel & Han[n]ah, b. July 11, 1720	1	23
Sarah, d. Daniell & Sarah, b. Oct. 7, 1709	1	10
Sarah, w. Danil, d. Jan. 26, 1711/12	1	10
Sarah, m. Joseph **PARKHURST**, Jan. 20, 1730/31	1	54
Sarah, d. Daniel, Jr. & Rachel, b. Apr. 15, 1731	1	55
Sarah, d. Daniel & Sarah, b. May 26, 1741	1	98
Steven, s. Isaac & Lydiah, b. Oct. 26, 1732; d. Jan. 1, 1733/4	1	62

	Vol.	Page

LAWRENCE, LAWRANCE, LAWRANS, (cont.)
Susannah, d. Peleg, of Grotton, m. Joseph **WILLIAMS**,
Oct. 13, 1710 — 1, 9
Sibel, d. Daniel, Jr. & Rachel, b. Sept. 6, 1729 — 1, 55
Thomas, s. Joseph & Mary, b. Feb. 1, 1714/15 — 1, 14
-----, s. Thomas & Sarah, b. [   ] — 2, 10

LAWSON, John, m. Patience **CRAPE**, Sept. 9, 1827, by Rev.
Erastus Ripley — 2, 202
Mary, m. Edward **SMITH**, b. of Plainfield, Oct. 7,
1827, by Orin Fowler, V.D.M. — 2, 203

LAWTON, Ann, m. Simon **MILLER**, b. of Plainfield, Apr. 18,
1836, by Chester Tilden — 2, 225
Benjamin J., m. Sabina B. **VENNER**, b. of Notich, R.I.,
Apr. 25, 1847, by Rev. J. Mather — 3, 43
Eleanor, of Plainfield, m. Shepard **KINYON**, of Sterling,
Sept. 3, 1829, by Rev. Orin Fowler — 2, 210

LEE, Anna, d. Benjamin & Ruth, b. Sept. 3, 1753 — 2, 4
Beman, Capt., m. Ruth **STEVENS**, July 8, 1746 — 1, 2X
Benjamin, m. Ruth **STEAVENS**, July 8, 1746 — 2, 4
Elias, s. Benj[ami]n & Ruth, b. Apr. 5, 1757 — 2, 4
Jonathan, s. Benjamin & Ruth, b. July 15, 1750 — 2, 4
Lucy, d. Benjamin & Ruth, b. Feb. 11, 1748/9 — 2, 4
Thomas, s. Benjamin & Ruth, b. Apr. 22, 1747 — 2, 4
Thomas, s. William, weaver, b. Nov. 10, 1850 — 4, 32
Thomas, d. Jan. 14, 1851, ae. 2 m. — 4, 66

LEFFINGWELL, Eunice, d. Jeremiah & Sarah, b. July 8, 1778 — 2, 109
Eunice, d. Jeremiah & Sarah, d. Dec. 16, 1793 — 2, 109
Molle, d. Jeremiah & Sarah, b. Apr. 16, 1773 — 2, 109
Olive, d. Jeremiah & Sarah, b. Dec. 22, 1780 — 2, 109
Prosper, s. Jeremiah & Sarah, b. July 23, 1770 — 2, 109
Rebecca, d. Jeremiah & Sarah, b. Nov. 12, 1775 — 2, 109

LEONARD, LENNARD, Betsey, of Plainfield, m. Benjamin
TUCKERMAN, of Sterling, Jan. 18, 1824, by Orin
Fowler, V.D.M. — 2, 193
Cynthia, m. Wilson **POTTER**, b. of Plainfield, Apr. 4,
1827, by Orin Fowler, V.D.M. — 2, 202
Elizabeth, m. Jacob **STEVENS**, May 26, 1757 — 2, 37
Henry, of Plainfield, m. Phebe A. **DOW**, of Franklin,
Mar. 18, 1824, by Rev. Levi Nelson, of Lisbon — 2, 193
Hester, m. Stephen **HALL**, Mar. [ ], 1748 — 2, 10
Lucinda J., d. Mary Ann, ae. 30, of Charlestown, R.I.,
b. Dec. 18, 1849 — 4, 29

LESTER, Albert, s. Sessions & Fanny, b. Nov. 28, 1822 — 2, 159
Albert G., m. Maria A. **STORRS**, b. of Plainfield, Sept.
1, 1846, by A. Dunning — 3, 38
Andrew Clark, s. Sessions & Fanny, b. Mar. 8, 1820 — 2, 159
Betsey, 2d w. Timothy, d. Apr. 24, 1820, ae. 65 — 2, 158
Charles, s. Sessions & Esher, b. July 27, 1807 — 2, 158

BARBOUR COLLECTION

	Vol.	Page
LESTER, (cont.)		
Darius Sessions, s. Timothy & Elizabeth, b. Sept. 29, 1774	2	81
Eliza, of Plainfield, m. Elisha **DANIELSON**, of Killingly, Apr. 4, 1821, by Rev. Orin Fowler	2	132
Elizabeth, w. Timothy, d. Oct. 29, 1795, ae. 47	2	158
Elizabeth, d. Erastus & Betsey, b. Dec. 6, 1818	2	158
Elizabeth, ae. 30, b. Plainfield, res. Brooklyn, Ct., m. Rev. W[illia]m **TILLOTSON**, pastor, Cong. Church, ae. 45, res. Brooklyn, Ct., Nov. 12, 1848, by Rev. J.C. Knapp	4	3
Elizabeth H., of Plainfield, m. Rev. George J. **TILLOTSON**, of Brooklyn, Nov. 15, 1848, by Rev. Jared O. Knapp, Central Village	3	54
Elizabeth Kinne, d. John & Mary, b. Jan. 19, 1798	2	122
Emily, d. Sessions & Esther, b. May 20, 1812	2	158
Erastus, Col., s. Timothy & Betsey, d. Aug. 14, 1861, ae. 73	2	159
Esther, w. Sessions, d. Sept. 22, 1813	2	158
Eunice, of Plainfield, m. Simon **McGREGER**, of Sterling, Apr. 4, 1821, by Rev. Orin Fowler	2	132
Eunice Backus, d. John & Mary, b. Aug. 20, 1799	2	122
Fanny, d. Sessions & Fanny, b. May 27, 1817	2	159
Frances Mary, d. John & Mary, b. Mar. 4, 1806	2	122
George Barkus, s. John & Mary, b. Apr. 12, 1833	3	5
James, s. Sessions & Esther, b. Feb. 1, 1810	2	158
Jane, d. Sessions & Fanny, b. Nov. 16, 1824	2	159
Jane L., of Plainfield, m. Jabez **ADAM**, of Canterbury, Dec. 8, 1851, by Rev. George J. Tillotson, of Brooklyn, Conn.	3	73
John, m. Mary **BACKUS**, Aug. 7, 1796	2	122
John, s. John & Mary, b. July 11, 1810	2	122
John Gallup, s. Sessions & Fanny, b. Apr. 1, 1815	2	159
Julian, d. Sessions & Esther, b. June 17, 1804	2	158
Julian, of Plainfield, m. Job F. **ANGELL**, of Providence, R.I., Sept. 3, 1826, by Rev. Orin Fowler	2	199
Julian, of Plainfield, m. Silas **RICHFORD**, of Providence, R.I., [ ], by Rev. Orin Fowler	2	209
Lois, d. John & Mary, b. Nov. 21, 1803	2	122
Lois B., of Plainfield, m. John W. **DAVIS**, of Coventry, R.I., Mar. 27, 1837, by Rev. Samuel Rockwell	2	229
Sarah M., ae. 25, of Plainfield, m. Henry **WILCOX**, mechanic, ae. 26, b. Georgia, res. New Haven, Sept. 10, 1850, by Rev. Jared O. Knapp	4	5
Sarah Maria, m. Henry A. **WILCOX**, of New Haven, Apr. 10, 1850, by Rev. Jared O. Knapp	3	64
Sessions, m. Esther **KINYON**, b. of Plainfield, Feb. 14, 1802	2	158

	Vol.	Page
LESTER, (cont.)		
Sessions, m. Fanny **GALLUP**, b. of Plainfield, Apr. 3, 1814	2	158
Simon Backus, s. John & Mary, b. Feb. 12, 1809	2	122
Susan, d. John & Mary, b. July 19, 1801	2	122
Susan, of Plainfield, m. Ezekiel **MORSE**, of Coventry, R.I., Aug. 31, 1828, by Rev. Orin Fowler	2	206
Timothy, Jr., s. Erastus & Betsey, b. Apr. 10, 1812	2	158
Timothy, d. Oct. 10, 1820, ae. 72	2	158
Timothy, of Hartford, m. Harriet **SHEPARD**, of Plainfield, June 5, 1831, by Rev. S.D. Jewett	2	213
William, Jr., of Norwich, m. Bettice D. **HARRINGTON**, of Plainfield, Feb. 14, 1836, by Rev. O.C. Whiton, of Canterbury	2	224
William A., m. Lydia **HARRIS**, Apr. 28, 1841, by Roswell Whitmore	3	9
William Andros, s. Erastus & Betsey, b. Feb. 13, 1816	2	158
LEVALLEY, Stephen, m. Harriet **MASON**, b. of Plainfield, Jan. 1, 1823, by Rev. Orin Fowler	2	189
LEWIS, Augustus, m. Elizabeth **HOWARD**, b. of Coventry, R.I., Nov. 30, 1848, by Rev. George W. Brewster	3	57
Benjamin, of Worcester, Mass., m. Hannah C. **JAMES**, of Plainfield, Jan. 7, 1850, by Rev. Jared O. Knapp	3	63
Deborah E., of Scituate, R.I., m. James **WHITE**, of Cranston, R.I., Mar. 19, 1848, by Rev. James Mather	3	54
Eliza D., of Plainfield, m. Cyrus **BISHOP**, of Canterbury, Jan. 2, 1851, by Rev. Henry Robinson	3	68
Eliza D., m. Cyrus **BISHOP**, of N.Y., Jan. 2, 1851, by H. Robinson	4	7
Eliza E., m. Arnold **ROUND**, b. of Sterling, Mar. 9, 1851, by Peleg Peckham, Elder	3	69
George W., m. Mary E. **GODDELL**, b. of Plainfield, Nov. 27, 1853, by Rev. Joseph P. Brown	3	81
Lucy, d. Samuel, merchant, ae. 30, & Sarah, ae. 31, b. June 14, 1848	4	24
Marinda, d. Robert & Clarissa, b. Nov. 28, 1838	2	241
Moses, of Plainfield, m. Nancy **BASHELLER**, of Woonsocket, R.I., Oct. 7, 1841, by John Dunlap, J.P.	3	11
Robert, s. Joseph & Sarah, b. Nov. 12, 1813, in Sterling	2	241
Robert, of Plainfield, m. Clarissa A. **PALMER**, of Killingly, Apr. 17, 1837, by Chester Tilden	2	231
LILLIBRIDGE, John S., of Exeter, R.I., m. Dulinda **NICHOLS**, of Coventry, R.I., Dec. 24, 1848, by Rev. George W. Brewster	3	57
LIPPITT, Ann Maria, m. George **BATES**, b. of Cranston, R.I., Feb. 24, 1848, by Rev. J. Mather	3	53

	Vol.	Page
LITTLE, Aphia, of Little Comton, R.I., m. Joseph **CORY**, of Tivertown, Aug. 30, 1821, by Rev. Nathaniel Cole	2	134
Linas, s. Quash & Comfort, Dec. 17, 1783	2	98
LITTLEFIELD, Elmira, of Brooklyn, m. Caleb **BENNETT**, of Plainfield, Apr. 16, 1837, by Chester Tilden	2	231
LOGIN, Robert, [twin with Samuel], s. John & Marg[a]ret, b. July 12, 1739	1	97
Samuel, [twin with Robert], s. John & Marg[a]ret, b. July 12, 1739	1	97
LORD, Harriet, m. Charles **MONDAY**, Jan. 1, 1811, by Nathaniel Cole, Elder	2	133
LOVE, Comfort, m. Cynthia **HIX**, b. of Plainfield, [ ] 28, [ ], by Rev. Samuel Rockwell	2	224
Cynthia A., m. Charles H. **PALMER**, b. of Sterling, Apr. 10, 1842, by Peleg Peckham, Elder	3	14
Thomas C., m. Sarah **CASE**, Dec. 6, 1842, by Rev. John Reed	3	17
Zuba, of Coventry, R.I., m. Fernando C. **COLVIN**, of Abington, Penn., Mar. 21, 1847, by Rev. J. Mather	3	44
LOVEGROVE, Jemima F., m. William **SPENCER**, b. of Plainfield, June 27, 1831, by Rev. Benjamin R. Allen	2	213
Lydia, m. Asa **RUSSEL[L]**, b. of Plainfield, Jan. 1, 1823, by Rev. Orin Fowler	2	189
LOVEJOY, Freelove, d. John & Barsheba, b. Feb. 16, 1719/20	1	21
Freelove, m. Joseph **CORY**, Feb. 5, 1739/40 (Written "Freelove **JOYE**" and corrected by Mr. Arnold)	1	94
Freelove, m. Joseph **CORY**, Feb. 5, 1739/40	1	95
Naomy, d. John & Barsheba, b. Oct. 19, 1717	1	18
Neomey, m. John **BLUNT**, May 1, 1734	1	64
Timothy, s. John & Bathshebath, b. Oct. 13, 1716; d. Oct. 28, 1716	1	16
LOW, LOWS, Rachel S., of Johnston, R.I., m. William **PARKHURST**, of Providence, R.I., Dec. 15, 1846, by Rev. J. Mather	3	41
Samuel T., of Sterling, m. Adeline **BEMIS**, of Sterling, Oct. 27, 1850, by H. Robinson	4	7
LOWELL, Henry S., m. Sally Maria **SUMNER**, b. of Plainfield, Nov. 24, 1846, by Rev. Jared C. Knapp, Central Village	3	41
LOWS, [see under **LOW**]		
LYMAN, Ann, of Providence, R.I., m. Josiah **MATTHEWSON**, of Plainfield, Dec. 18, 1823, by Orin Fowler, V.D.M.	2	193
LYON, Almira M., of Plainfield, m. James **FAIRMAN**, of Killingly, Jan. 6, 1850, by Rev. W. Emerson	3	63
George G., of Fall River, Mass., m. Frances M. **DUNLAP**, of Plainfield, Dec. 15, 1846, by Rev. Jared C. Knapp, Central Village	3	41

PLAINFIELD VITAL RECORDS 193

	Vol.	Page
LYON, (cont.)		
Marcelia, of Plainfield, m. Joel **BURDICK**, of Griswold, Jan. 6, 1850, by Rev. W. Emerson	3	63
Marcelia, cotton weaver, ae. 21, b. [S]cituate, res. Griswold, m. Joel **BURDICK**, master weaver, ae. 25, b. Voluntown, res. Griswold, Jan. 6, 1850, by Rev. Warren Emerson	4	6
Mary A., m. William J. **POTTER**, b. of Plainfield, Jan. 9, 1850, by Rev. W. Emerson	3	64
Mary A., cotton weaver, ae. 23, b. Foster, R.I., res. Plainfield, m. William J. **POTTER**, mule spinner, ae. 24, of Plainfield, June 9, 1850, by Rev. Warren Emerson	4	6
Rachel, m. Cyprian **STEVENS**, Aug. 9, 1748	2	24
MACOMBER, MACUMBER, Seabury, m. Lydia M. **COL[L]INS**, b. of Plainfield, Mar. 9, 1829, by Rev. Orin Fowler	2	208
Susan, m. Jonathan **MATHEWSON**, Jan. 3, 1847, by Rev. Frederic Charlton	3	48
MADISON, Alfred B., m. Eliza **FISH**, b. of Sterling, July 20, 1851, by Peleg Peckham, Elder	3	70
Fan[n]y, m. Jonathan H. **GREEN**, b. of Plainfield, Sept. 20, 1840, by Rev. Hezekiah Thacher	3	7
Hiram, m. Ruth **CORNELL**, b. of Sterling, June 13, 1842, by Peleg Peckham, Elder	3	16
MAIN, MAINE, Annah, [w. Nath[anie]l], d. Apr. 19, 1738	1	70
Anna, d. Nathaniel & Johanna, b. Mar. 24, 1742	1	100
Annor, d. Nathaniel & Johannah, b. Mar. 24, 1742	2	17
Eunice, d. Nathaniel & Johannah, b. Mar. 3, 1757	2	36
Floy Judson, s. David O., machinist, ae. 30, & Permelia, ae. 23, b. Mar. 7, 1848	4	21
George K., s. Ira, cotton dresser tender, ae. 38, & Martha H., ae. 31, b. June 15, 1848	4	23
Hester, d. Nathaniel & Johannah, b. Apr. 2, 1748	2	16
Isaac, s. Nathaniel & Johannah, b. Oct. 8, 1749	2	16
Johannah, d. Nathaniel & Johannah, b. Apr. 15, 1754	2	16
Judah Billings, d. of Han[n]a[h], m. Jonathan **SPAULDING**, Apr. 22, 1714	1	20
Lydia, ae. 31, b. N. Stonington, m. Perry **POPPLE**, blacksmith, ae. 25, b. Killingly, res. Plainfield, Sept. 12, [18]47, by Rev. Mather.	4	2
Lydia, b. Sterling, res. Plainfield, d. Sept. 15, 1847, ae. 54	4	61
Lydia, ae. 32, b. Voluntown, res. Plainfield, m. Perry **POPPLE**, blacksmith, ae. 25, b. N. Stonington, res. Plainfield, Sept. 28, 1847, by Rev. Mathew	4	1
Lydia A., m. Perry **POPPLE**, b. of Plainfield, Sept. 12, 1847, by Rev. J. Mathew	3	45
Nath[anie]l, of Stonington, m. Annah **SPAULDING**, Jan.		

	Vol.	Page
MAIN, MAINE, (cont.)		
10, 1737/8	1	70
Nathaniel, m. Johannah **PARKHURST**, Apr. 13, 1741	1	96
Nathaniel, m. Johanah **PARKHURST**, Apr. 13, 1741	2	16
Nathaniel, s. Nathaniel & Johannah, b. Sept. 27, 1750	2	16
Noah, s. Nathaniel & Johannah, b. Aug. 31, 1761	2	47
Sarah, m. Hezeciah **COLE**, Dec. 29, 1725	1	37
W[illia]m H., laborer or farmer, b. Blanford, Mass., res. Blanford, m. Susan **JORDAN**, b. Canterbury, res. Blanford, Nov. 30, 1848, by Rev. J. B. Guild	4	3
Zadock, s. Nathaniel & Johannah, b. July 18, 1766	2	64
MANSFIELD, Daniel, Jr., s. Daniel & Eunice, b. Oct. 31, 1770	2	76
Jacob, s. Daniel & Eunice, b. Nov. 11, 1772	2	76
MAPLE, [see also **MARPLES**], Richard, s. W[illia]m C., tailor, ae. 34, & Olevilpa (?), ae. 30, b. May 14, 1851	4	31
MARDENBOROUGH, Margaret Wright, of St. Christophers, m. Joseph **EATON**, of Plainfield, Nov. 3, 1814, at Newport, R.I.	2	144
MARDOCK, MAREDOCK, [see under **MURDOCK**]		
MARPLES, MARPLE, [see also **MAPLE**], Jane, m. Samuel **HYDE**, Sept. 13, 1846, by John J. Penrose, J.P.	3	39
William C., m. Clarrissa **KENNEDY**, b. of Plainfield, Mar. 12, 1844, by A. Dunning	3	22
MARSH, Charles, of Woodstock, Vt., m. Susanna **ARNOLD**, of Plainfield, June 3, 1798	2	103
Siras, s. William & Sarah, b. Mar. 14, 1718/19 (Cyrus)	1	21
Cyrus, of Plainfield, m. Margaret **KINSMAN**, of Norwich, May 29, 1740	1	96
Cyrus, m. Susanna **DOW**, Apr. 25, 1757	2	37
Desier, d. William & Sarah, b. Mar. 10, 1737/8	1	94
Elias, s. James & Hannah, b. Nov. 26, 1736	1	66
Elihy, s. Thomas & Eunis, b. July 18, 1719	1	53
Elisha, s. Tho[ma]s & Uness, b. July 17, 1716	1	16
Elisabeth, d. Will[ia]m & Sarah, b. Aug. 16, 1729	1	51
Elizabeth, m. Daniel **DOW**, July 4, 1751	2	15
Easther, d. William, Jr. & Sarah, b. Mar. 21, 1724	1	30
Eunis, d. Thomas & Eunice, b. Feb. 17, 1724	1	48
Eunis, d. Thomas & Eunis, b. Feb. 17, 1724	1	53
Eunes, [twin with Lydiah], b. James & Hannah, b. Apr. 14, 1726	1	36
Euniss, d. Isaac & Mary, b. Jan. 6, 1749	2	14
Experience, d. William & Sarah, b. June 5, 1735	1	65
Hester, d. William & Sarah, d. Jan. 8, 1724/5	1	31
Isaac, s. James & Hannah, b. Sept. 20, 1719	1	99
Isaac, m. Mary **GILBARD**, June 16, 1742	1	99

	Vol.	Page
MARSH, (cont.)		
James, m. Han[n]ah **SHEPARD**, Dec. 3, 1711	1	11
James, s. James & Han[n]ah, b. Oct. 28, 1712	1	11
James, s. James & Hannah, b. Jan. 7, 1729	1	66
James, d. Apr. 6, 1749	2	6
Joel, s. Isaac & Mary, b. Jan. 6, 1746	2	14
John, s. Tho[ma]s & Uness, b. Dec. 11, 1714	1	16
John, s. Thomas & Eunis, b. Dec. 11, 1715	1	53
Joseph, s. Thomas & Eunis, b. Apr. 6, 1721	1	53
Joseph, s. Thomas & Eunis, b. Apr. 9, 1721	1	48
Lydiah, [twin with Eunes], d. James & Hannah, b. Apr. 14, 1726	1	36
Lydia, d. Isaac & Mary, b. May 27, 1748	2	14
Moses, s. Jonas & Mary, b. Oct. 29, 1735	1	93
Nathaniel, s. James & Han[n]ah, b. July 28, 1715	1	16
Nathaniel, s. James & Han[n]ah, b. July 28, 1715	1	15
Nathaniel, s. Isaac & Mary, b. Sept. 6, 1745	2	14
Nathaniel, m. Christobel **CRARY**, Aug. 21, 1751	2	16
Patience, of Killin[g]ly, m. Josiah **HOW[E]**, of Plainfield, Nov. 19, 1741	1	101
Persiler, d. Will[ia]m & Sarah, b. Oct. 20, 1726	1	40
Prescilla, m. Robert **BROWNLEE**, Jan. 5, 1752	2	20
Rachell, d. James & Han[nah], b. Oct. 7, 1717	1	19
Rachel, m. James **DOUGLASS**, Sept. 4, 1733	1	58
Rufas, s. Jonas & Mary, b. June 13, 1738	1	93
Sarah, d. William & Sarah, b. Aug. 11, 1714	1	14
Sarah, d. June 4, 1729, by being burned	1	47
Sarah, d. Will[ia]m & Sarah, d. June 4, 1729	1	51
Sarah, d. James & Hannah, b. Apr. 29, 1731	1	66
Sarah, d. William & Sarah, b. June 20, 1732	1	57
Sarah, w. William, d. Feb. 21, 1739/40	1	94
Sarah, d. Cyrus & Marg[a]ret, b. Feb. 19, 1741	1	97
Susannah, w. Cyrus, d. June 19, 1759, in the 29th y. of her age	2	37
Thomas, m. [E]uness **PARKHOUSE**, Feb. 4, 1711/12	1	11
Thomas, s. Thomas & [E]uness, b. Jan. 25, 1712/13	1	11
William, s. of William, m. Sarah **BUTTON**, d. of Matthias, Mar. 2, 1712/13	1	14
William, s. William & Sarah, b. Apr. 1, 1716	1	17
William, s. William & Sarah, d. Dec. 30, 1724	1	31
William, s. Thomas & Eunice, b. Dec. 23, 1725	1	48
William, s. Thomas & Eunice, b. Dec. 23, 1725	1	53
William, s. Cyrus & Susanna, b. Dec. 25, 1757	2	37
William, d. Jan. 23, 1759, in the 74th y. of his age	2	38
MARSHALL, Israel, m. Elizabeth **MORRIS**, b. of Plainfield, Nov. 27, 1842, by Benjamin Bacon, J.P.	3	17
MARTIN, Emily, m. Wheeton **SALISBURY**, b. of Killingly, Dec. 9, 1844, by James Smither, Elder	3	29

	Vol.	Page
MARTIN, (cont.)		
Lucretia, m. William **MATTISON**, Feb. 14, 1770	2	74
MASON, Harriet, m. Stephen **LEVALLEY**, b. of Plainfield, Jan. 1, 1823, by Rev. Orin Fowler	2	189
Lydia J., of Sterling, m. Royal S. **DRAEN**, of Rehobath, Mass., Sept. 1, 1844, by Peleg Peckham, Elder	3	24
Mary, m. Joshua **STRANAHAN**, of Killingly, Nov. 18, 1821, by Nathaniel Cole, Elder	2	134
Mary E., of Plainfield, m. William H. **WILSON**, of Dartmouth, Mass., Sept. 25, [ ], by Rev. A.B. Wheeler	3	17
Mehetibell, d. Andrew & Mary, b. Mar. 25, 1755	2	29
MATHER, Nathan, corder, ae. 46, b. Killingly, res. Canterbury, m. 4th w. Lydia **COLVIN**, ae. 39, b. Plainfield, Sept. 26, [18]48, by Rev. James Mather	4	1
[**MATHEWS**], **MATHEWS**, Jenne, m. Ezekiel **SPAULDING**, Mar. 26, 1754	2	24
John, s. Col. & Catharine, b. June 29, 1743	2	23
Mary, d. Col. & Catharine, b. June 3, 1745	2	23
Nathan, m. Lydia **COLVIN**, b. of Plainfield, Sept. 19, 1847, by Rev. J. Mather	3	45
Ruth, d. Col. & Catharine, b. Sept. 4, 1753	2	23
MATTHEWSON, MATTEWSON, MATHEWSON, Abby, ae. 23, b. R.I., res. Plainfield, m. Andrew **GLEASON**, brood finisher, ae. 23, b. Pomfret, Ct., res. N. Kingston, R.I., Dec. 3, 1849, by Joseph P. Brown	4	6
Abby T., m. Andrew E. **GEASON**, b. of Plainfield, Dec. 2, 1849, by Rev. Joseph P. Brown	3	62
Alice A., m. Samuel **FREEMAN**, b. of Providence, R.I., Oct. 4, 1839, by Rev. Tubal Wakefield	3	1
Bowen H., m. Mary Ann **GREENMAN**, b. of Plainfield, Mar. 28, 1839, by Rev. Tubal Wakefield	2	240
Charles, m. Elvia **GREEN**, b. of Cranston, R.I., June 30, 1845, by Rev. Daniel Dorchester	3	31
Elvia, of Providence, R.I., m. W[illia]m **BAKER**, of Cranston, R.I., Dec. 8, 1845, by Joseph S. Gladding, J.P. Intention recorded.	3	33
George, m. Louisa **WILSON**, b. of Sterling, July 30, 1854, by Peleg Peckham, Elder	3	85
Horace B., s. Wanton, late of Coventry, now residing in Plainfield, m. Mary R. **BATTEY**, d. James, of West Greenwich, R.I., May 3, 1840, by Pardon Tillinghast, Elder	3	7
Jonathan, m. Susan **MACOMBER**, Jan. 3, 1847, by Rev. Frederic Charlton	3	48
Josiah, of Plainfield, m. Ann **LYMAN**, of Providence, R.I., Dec. 18, 1823, by Orin Fowler, V.D.M.	2	193

	Vol.	Page

MATTHEWSON, MATTEWSON, MATHEWSON, (cont.)

	Vol.	Page
Olive A., m. Capt. Samuel **FREEMAN**, b. of Providence, R.I., Oct. 4, 1839, by Rev. Tubal Wakefield, Packersville	2	248
Polly, of Plainfield, m. Joseph **CONGDON**, of West Greenwich, R.I., Nov. 27, 1823, by Orin Fowler, V.D.M.	2	192
Simon, woolen dresser, ae. 24, of Plainfield, m. Caroline **GREENE**, ae. 22, b. Foster, R.I., Oct. 31, [18]47, by R. F. Charlton	4	2
-----, child of Jonathan, carpenter, ae. 26, & Susan M., ae. 19, b. Feb. 4, 1848	4	23

MATTISON, MATTESON, Edmond, m. Charlotte **SWEET**, b. of

	Vol.	Page
R.I., Feb. 15, 1830, by Peleg Peckham, Elder	2	210
Ira C., m. Phebe D. **STRAIGHT**, Jan. 3, 1841, by Sam[ue]l D. Hough, J.P.	3	9
Loaden, [twin with Simon], s. William & Lucretia, b. July 12, 1771	2	74
Nancy, m. William **WISE**, Dec. 13, 1840, by Solomon Payne, J.P.	3	8
Obed, m. Louisa **WILSON**, Nov. 8, 1840, by Samuel L. Hough, J.P.	3	8
Simon, [twin with Loaden], s. William & Lucretia, b. July 12, 1771	2	74
Simon, m. Cordelia **GREEN**, b. of Plainfield, Sept. 26, 1847, by Rev. Fred[eri]c Charlton	3	49
William, m. Lucretia **MARTIN**, Feb. 14, 1770	2	74

MAXFIELD, James, s. Joshua & Mary, b. July 26, 1742 (Perhaps

	Vol.	Page
"**MAXWELL**")	1	100
Joshua, m. Mary **PHIPS**, Oct. 12, 1741 (Perhaps "**MAXWELL**")	1	100
Joshua, s. Joseph & Mary, b. Jan. 6, 1745/6 (Perhaps "**MAXWELL**")	1	2X

MAXWELL, Alexander, s. James & Hannah, b. Mar. 9, 1771

	Vol.	Page
Alexander, s. James & Hannah, b. Mar. 9, 1771	2	96
Asa, s. James & Hannah, b. June 16, 1781	2	96
Christopher, s. James & Hannah, b. Apr. 3, 1779	2	96
Hannah, w. James, d. May 29, 1799	2	117
James, s. Joshua & Mary, whose maiden name was Mary **PHIPS**, b. July 26, 1742 (See under **MAXFIELD**)	2	43
James, m. Hannah **PHILLIPS**, Oct. 1, 1762	2	96
James, Jr., s. James & Hannah, b. Apr. 12, 1769	2	96
James, m. Phebe **BOMAN**, Dec. 18, 1799	2	117
John Douglass, s. James & Hannah, b. Apr. 28, 1767	2	96
John Douglass, s. James & Hannah, d. Aug. 18, 1786	2	96
Joshua, s. James & Hannah, b. May 6, 1773	2	96
Meriam, d. James & Hannah, b. Jan. 4, 1765	2	96
Olive, d. James & Hannah, b. Mar. 26, 1786	2	96
Phillip, s. James & Hannah, b. May 21, 1777	2	96

	Vol.	Page
MAXWELL, (cont.)		
Sarah, d. James & Hannah, b. Mar. 31, 1775	2	96
McAMS, Daniel, s. Daniel & Jean, b. Mar. 24, 1727	1	43
McCARTER, Mary, d. William & Elizabeth, b. Apr. 25, 1725	1	43
Rozanna, d. Will[ia]m & Elizabeth, b. Dec. 1, 1727	1	43
McDANIEL, McDANIELS, James, laborer, b. Ireland, res. Plainfield, d. Aug. 17, [18]49, ae. 75	4	62
James, laborer, b. Ireland, res. Plainfield, d. Aug. 18, 1849, ae. 70	4	64
McDONALD, Edward, m. Lucy **FORD**, Sept. 18, 1850, by John J. Penrose, J.P.	3	65
Edward, m. Jane **FORD**, b. of Sterling, Sept. 18, 1850, by John J. Penrose, J.P.	3	88
McGREGER, Simon, of Sterling, m. Eunice **LESTER**, of Plainfield, Apr. 4, 1821, by Rev. Orin Fowler	2	132
McKAY, -----, st. b. child of Edward, laborer, ae. 32, & Rosamond, ae. 26, b. Apr. 8, 1849	4	26
McKINGLY, Catharine, m. John **KNIGHT**, b. of Plainfield, Jan. 29, 1854, by Rev. William Turkington	3	82
McLEAN, Allen, Rev., of Simsbury, m. Nancy **MORGAN**, of Plainfield, Jan. 28, 1833, by Rev. Dennis Platt	2	216
MEDBERY, MEDBURY, Anna, w. Edward, d. Mar. 7, 1829, ae. 81	2	160
Archibald, m. Mary [ ], Oct. 14, 1839; d. Apr. 18, 1842, ae. 28	3	88
Archibold D., s. Edward, Jr. & Dolly, b. Oct. 13, 1824 (Entry crossed out)	2	160
Archibald D., s. Edward, Jr. & Dolly, b. Oct. 13, 1814	2	160
Archibald D., s. Edward & Dolly, b. Oct. 13, 1814	3	88
Archibald D., m. Mary **PRESTON**, b. of Plainfield, Oct. 14, 1839, by Rev. Samuel Rockwell	2	248
Archibald D., m. Mary **PRESTON**, b. of Plainfield, Oct. 14, 1839, by Rev. Samuel Rockwell	3	1
Daniel, s. John & Rachel, b. May 27, 1811	3	84
Daniel, s. John & Rachel, d. June 27, 1814, ae. 3 y. 1 m.	3	84
Dinah, m. Daniel **SPAULDING**, b. of Plainfield, Apr. 7, 1822, by Rev. Nathaniel Cole	2	187
Dolly, w. Edward, b. Oct. 7, 1792; d. July 1, 1854, ae. 62	3	88
Edward, b. May 18, 1788	3	88
Edward, Jr., of Plainfield, m. Dolly **DOUGLASS**, of Voluntown, Dec. 26, 1811	2	196
Edward, m. Dolly [ ], Dec. 26, 1811	3	88
Edward, s. John & Rachel, b. Sept. 6, 1815	3	84
Edward, d. Dec. 25, 1828, ae. 80 y.	2	160
George, s. John & Rachel, b. May 27, 1827	3	84
Jesse H., m. Lamira **KNOX**, b. of Plainfield, July 30,		

	Vol.	Page
MEDBERY, MEDBURY, (cont.)		
1838, by Rev. Hezekiah Thecker	2	236
John, b. July 20, 1785	3	84
John, m. Rachel **PRIOR**, June 24, 1810. Certified from family record	3	83
John, s. John & Rachel, b. Aug. 25, 1817	3	84
John, Jr., of Smithfield, R.I., m. Sarah G. **DENISON**, of Plainfield, July 29, 1844, by A. Dunning	3	24
Joseph, s. John & Rachel, b. Oct. 16, 1821	3	84
Lucy H., d. Ephraim & Betsey, b. Sept. 28, 1812	2	160
Lucy H., of Plainfield, m. Oliver C. **TURNER**, of Providence, R.I., May 22, 1843, by Rev. A.B. Wheeler	3	19
Mary, w. Archibald, b. Mar. 24, 1818	3	88
Mary Ann, d. Ephraim & Betsey, b. Apr. 3, 1811	2	160
Mary Ann, m. Jonathan S. **PARKIS**, b. of Plainfield, Apr. 1, 1832, by Peleg Peckham, Elder	2	215
Nancy, d. John & Rachel, b. Aug. 5, 1813	3	84
Nancy, m. George **DUNLAP**, b. of Plainfield, Sept. 23, 1839, by Rev. Samuel Rockwell	2	247
Naomi, m. Leonard R. **BENNETT**, b. of Plainfield, June 18, 1854, by Rev. Peter S. Mather	3	84
Nathaniel, Jr., m. Prudy **ANGELL**, b. of Plainfield, Feb. 29, 1824, by Rev. Nathaniel Cole	2	194
Nathaniel, Jr., m. Susan F. **HAWKINS**, b. of Plainfield, Mar. 12, 1854, by Rev. William Turkington	3	82
Rachel, w. John, d. Aug. 31, 1853, in the 69th y. of her age	3	84
Rachel **PRIOR**, w. John, b. Mar. 18, 1785	3	84
Sarah, d. Edward, d. Nov. 8, 1821, ae. 42	2	160
MEECHAM, Lydiah, m. David **SHEPARD**, Dec. 3, 1735	1	67
MERRICE, Sarah, m. Ambrose **KNIGHT**, b. of Plainfield, Aug. 27, 1843, by Peleg Peckham, Elder	3	20
MIDDLETON, Abby, of Plainfield, m. Egbert **WALDO**, of Norwich, Feb. 19, 1828, by Rev. Orin Fowler	2	205
Mary P., m. Samuel R. **TRACY**, b. of Plainfield, Apr. 19, 1824, by Orin Fowler, V.D.M.	2	194
MIGAN, John, laborer, b. Ireland, res. Plainfield, d. Aug. 23, 1849, ae. 25	4	64
Mary A., d. John, laborer, ae. 27, & Ann, ae. 20, b. Sept. 17, 1849	4	30
MILLER, Daniel, s. Daniel & Jean, d. Nov. 11, 1757	2	45
Hannah P., of Plainfield, m. Charles R. **WEBSTER**, of Harwinton, Conn., Feb. 3, 1841, by Rev. Thomas Barber	3	9
James, m. Lois **PARKHURST**, Apr. 27, 1780	2	95
James, s. James, farmer, ae. 42, & Susan, ae. 35, b. July 20, 1849	4	27
Lydia, d. James & Lois, b. May 13, 1781	2	95

	Vol.	Page
MILLER, (cont.)		
Mercy, m. Oliver **PEIRCE**, Apr. 21, 1768	2	67
Nancy, of Plainfield, m. Silas P. **CARD**, of Brooklyn, Conn., May 2, 1852, by Rev. William Turkington	3	78
Ruth, m. Daniel **WHEELER**, b. of Plainfield, Aug. 19, 1801, by Rev. Joel Benedict	2	190
Ruth, m. Henry W. **HILL**, b. of Plainfield, Sept. 17, 1838, by Rev. Samuel Rockwell	2	236
Samuel, s. James & Lois, b. June 29, 1784	2	95
Sarah H., m. Cyrus **TITUS**, b. of Plainfield, Dec. 30, 1832, by Peleg Peckham, Elder	2	216
Simon, m. Ann **LAWTON**, b. of Plainfield, Apr. 18, 1836, by Chester Tilden	2	225
Ursula, of Westfield, Vt., m. Solomon T. **ELLIS**, of Plainfield, Sept. 6, 1851, by Peleg Peckham, Elder	3	71
MILLET, Samuel D., m. Sally Ann **CARPENTER**, b. of Plainfield, Oct. 7, 1833, by Peleg Peckham, Elder	2	218
MINER, William H., of Blandford, Mass., m. Susan **JORDON**, of Canterbury, Nov. 30, 1848, by Rev. J.B. Guild, Packerville	3	54
MITCHELL, Cyrus, m. Julian **WOOD**, b. of Killingly, Sept. 21, 1845, by James Smither, Elder	3	34
Harriet, m. Horace **ALLEN**, b. of Killingly, Sept. 21, 1845, by James Smither, Elder	3	34
Mary, m. Joshua **BENNETT**, b. of Plainfield, Nov. 20, 1851, by Rev. Joseph P. Brown	3	72
MONDAY, Charles, m. Harriet **LORD**, Jan. 1, 1811, by Nathaniel Cole, Elder	2	133
MONTGOMERY, Betsey, of Plainfield, m. Shepard **DIXON**, of Killingly, Oct. 22, 1838, by Peleg Peckham, Elder	2	237
Charles N., s. George, manufacturer, & Susan, b. Aug. 20, 1850	4	32
Electa C., m. William **RAYMAN**, of Canterbury, May 1, 1844, by Peleg Peckham, Elder	3	23
George, of Sterling, m. Mary B. **STOWELL**, of Plainfield, Sept. 20, 1830, by Benj[ami]n R. Allen, Elder	2	211
George, of Sterling, m. Mary B. **STOWELL**, of Plainfield, Sept. 20, 1830, by Benj[ami]n R. Allen, Elder	2	212
George, m. Susan M. **DENISON**, b. of Plainfield, Mar. 23, 1845, by A. Dunning	3	28
Harriet, m. George **DIXON**, b. of Plainfield, Mar. 1, 1835, by Rev. Samuel Rockwell	2	220
John, m. Susan **PRINTICE**, b. of Plainfield, Mar. 24, 1845, by Peleg Peckham, Elder	3	27
Mary A., ae. 18, b. Sterling, res. Plainfield, m. James **SAUNDERS**, wheelwright, ae. 23, b. Voluntown, res.		

	Vol.	Page

MONTGOMERY, (cont.)
    Griswold, Oct. 6, 1849, by Rev. Joseph P. Brown   4   6
    Mary A., of Plainfield, m. James P. **SAUNDERS**, of
      Griswold, Oct. 7, 1849, by Rev. Joseph P. Brown   3   60
    ----, child of George, machinist, ae. 41, & Susan
      DENISON MONTGOMERY, ae. 31, b. Aug. 13, 1848   4   23
MOODY, Clarissa, m. David **JACKSON**, b. of Plainfield, July
    15, 1838, by Rev. Samuel Rockwell   2   235
MOORE, Frances M., of Plainfield, m. Austin **KELLOGG**, of
    Granby, N.Y., Nov. 10, 1836, by Rev. Tubal Wake-
    field, (Packersville)   2   228
    Joseph, of Plainfield, m. Margaret **GALLUP**, of Sterling,
      Jan. 9, 1837, by Rev. Samuel Rockwell   2   229
    Matilda S., m. Elisha M. **BARRETT**, Dec. 21, 1834, by
      Calvin Philo, Elder   2   242
    William B., of Charleston, S.C., m. Sarah A. **WHEELER**,
      of Plainfield, Jan. 6, 1828, by Orin Fowler,
      V.D.M.   2   204
MORDOCK, [see under **MURDOCK**]
MORGAN, Calesta, d. Lot & Kezia, b. Mar. 18, 1792   2   99
    Charles, s. Isaac & Polly, b. Dec. 8, 1800   2   106
    Deborah, d. Isaac & Allis, b. Mar. 13, 1760; d. Dec. 9,
      1763, ae. 3 y. 9 m.   2   43
    Dwelle, s. Isaac & Allis, b. Oct. 26, 1764   2   43
    Elisha, s. Rev. Solomon & Eunice, b. June 7, 1782   2   87
    Elisha Abbe, s. Capt. Lot & Keziah, b. Sept. 2, 1805   2   111
    Elizabeth Kellogg, d. George D. & Mary, b. Aug. 17,
      183[9]   2   249
    Elizabeth Kellogg, d. George D. & Mary, b. Aug. 17,
      1839   3   1
    Elizabeth R., w. George D., d. Apr. 4, 1837, ae. 29   2   231
    Emily, of Lisbon, m. Stephen **BENNET**, Jr., of Plain-
      field, Aug. 7, 1831, by J. Gordon, J.P.   2   214
    Eunice Elizabeth, d. Capt. Lot & Keziah, b. Aug. 4,
      1816   2   129
    George Dunworth, s. Capt. Lot & Kezia, b. Sept. 14,
      1802   2   110
    Isaac, m. Allis **SPAULDING**, Mar. 26, 1759   2   43
    John Adams, s. Isaac & Polly, b. Dec. 18, 1798   2   104
    Joseph Luce, s. Capt. Lot & Keziah, b. Feb. 22, 1810   2   129
    Lott, s. Isaac & Allis, b. July 22, 1762   2   43
    Lot, m. Kezia **CLEAVELAND**, Aug. 11, 1791   2   99
    Nancy, of Plainfield, m. Rev. Allen **McLEAN**, of Sims-
      bury, Jan. 28, 1833, by Rev. Dennis Platt   2   216
    Olive, m. John **JOHNSON**, Aug. 26, 1786   2   97
    Shubael Cleaveland, s. Capt. Lot & Kezia, b. Aug. 25,
      1793   2   101
MORRIS, Elizabeth, m. Israel **MARSHALL**, b. of Plainfield,

	Vol.	Page
MORRIS, (cont.)		
Nov. 27, 1842, by Benjamin Bacon, J.P.	3	17
MORSE, Ambrose, of Coventry, R.I., m. Eliza **DUNLAP**, of		
Plainfield, Mar. 15, 1829, by Rev. Orin Fowler	2	208
Charles D., m. Almy F. **WESTCOTT**, b. of Plainfield,		
Jan. 29, 1854, by Rev. William Turkington	3	81
Elizabeth H., d. Ambrose & Eliza, b. Jan. 9, 1830	3	5
Eugene H., s. [ ] Potter & Lydia A. Morse,		
b. Sept. [ ], 1847	4	23
Ezekiel, of Coventry, R.I., m. Susan **LESTER**, of		
Plainfield, Aug. 31, 1828, by Rev. Orin Fowler	2	206
Lowell A., s. Ambrose & Eliza, b. Nov. 20, 1831	3	5
Susan, m. Jordan **SPOONER**, May 22, 1842, by Lawton		
Cady, Elder	3	14
MOWRY, MORY, Eliza, m. Henry **WESTCOTT**, b. of Sterling,		
July 2, 1838, by Peleg Peckham, Elder	2	235
Mary, m. Godfrey **STONE**, b. of Killingly, July 17, 1823,		
by Orin Fowler, V.D.M.	2	191
MUNROE, MUNRO, Abby Ann, d. Cornell & Eunice, b. [Dec.] 12,		
1831	3	30
Abel C., s. Job & Phebe, b. Nov. 11, 1819	2	160
Abigail, d. Samuel & Sarah, b. [May] 17, 1835	2	181
Cornell, m. Eunice **CORNELL**, Sept. 17, 1826, by Samuel		
L. Hough, J.P.	2	200
Cornell, d. [Oct.] 8, [ ], ae. 54	3	30
Emeline, b. Plainfield, m. Luther **LADD**, laborer, b.		
Coventry, R.I., Apr. 30, 1850, by Elder Emerson	4	5
Emeline C., m. Martin L. **LADD**, b. of Plainfield, Apr.		
30, 1850, by Rev. W. Emerson	3	64
Emeline Church, d. Cornell & Eunice, b. Nov. 12, 1826	3	30
George, s. Cornell & Eunice, b. [May] 10, 1838	3	30
Harriet Jenette, d. Cornell & Eunice, b. [May] 20,		
1840	3	30
James W., s. Job & Phebe, b. [July] 13, 1821	2	160
John, d. Feb. 18, 1829, ae. 85	2	161
John, s. Samuel & Sarah, b. [Apr.] 5, 1833, in Pomfret	2	161
John Edward, s. Cornell & Eunice, b. [Sept.] 20, 1833;		
d. [Jan.] 8, 1835	3	30
Mary, of Seekonk, Mass., m. Joseph **SPAULDING**, of Plain-		
field, May 18, 1823	2	170
Mary, of Seekonk, Mass., m. Joseph **SPAULDING**, of Plain-		
field, May 18, 1823	3	22
Mary Cogswell, d. Cornell & Eunice, b. [Feb.] 19, 1830	3	30
Mary E., d. Job & Phebe, b. [Aug.] 21, 1824, at North		
Stonington	2	160
Nancy, d. Samuel & Sarah, b. [Oct.] 18, 1831, in		
Killingly	2	161
Nancy Maria, d. Cornell & Eunice, b. [Sept.] 24, 1835	3	30

	Vol.	Page
MUNROE, MUNRO, (cont.)		
Parthenia, d. Nov. 4, 1834, ae. 74	2	161
Philena Antenia, d. John & Parthenia, b. Nov. 30, 1796	2	129
Samuel, Jr., s. Samuel & Sarah, b. [Nov.] 4, 1828, at Pawtucket, Mass.	2	161
Samuel, of Canterbury, m. Nancy **LAMPHERE**, of Plainfield, Aug. 4, 1833, by Francis B. Johnson, J.P.	2	217
Sarah Ann, d. Samuel & Sarah, b. [Feb.] 22, 1830, at Foster, R.I.	2	161
Thomas E., s. Job & Phebe, b. [Apr.] 26, 1828	2	160
William Cornell, s. Cornell & Eunice, [Apr.] 3, 1828 (Birth)	3	30
MURDOCK, MORDOCK, MAREDOCK, MARDOCK, Charles M., m. Cindarilla **POTTER**, b. of Plainfield, Oct. 26, 1835, by Rev. Ziba Loveland, Central Village	2	223
Daniel, m. Hannah **POTTER**, b. of Plainfield, Jan. 2, 1831, by Benjamin R. Allen, Elder	2	212
George W., m. Eliza A. **HEALEY**, b. of Plainfield, Aug. 16, 1841, by Rev. Thomas Barber	3	10
Mary Ann, b. R.I., res. Plainfield, d. Jan. [ ], 1851, ae. 41	4	66
Mehetable, m. Ichabod **HENRY**, Jan. 1, 1815, by Thomas Backas, J.P.	2	126
Susan Jane, d. George W. & Elvia H., b. July 27, 1842	3	35
William, m. Mary Ann **POTTER**, b. of Plainfield, Nov. 2, 1828, by Peleg Peckham, Elder	2	207
MURPHY, MURFEY, Andrew E., of Norwich, m. Sarah A. **HILL**, of Plainfield, Dec. 18, 1853, by Rev. Joseph P. Brown	3	81
Julia, m. Nicholas **BOESSELLE**, b. of Plainfield, Aug. 13, 1854, by Rev. Henry Robinson	3	84
MYERS, Ellery, b. W. Greenwich, R.I., res. Plainfield, d. Mar. 27, 1849, ae. 88	4	62
NEEDY, Hannah, m. Samuel **WELLS**, Apr. 9, 1730	1	65
NEWBURY, Silas, school boy, black, b. Arkansas, res. Plainfield, d. Apr. 15, 1851, ae. 18	4	66
NEWCOMB, Elizabeth, m. Francis T. **DRAPER**, b. of Plainfield, Apr. 15, 1838, by Francis B. Johnson, J.P.	2	234
NEY, George, m. Rosilla **SPAULDING**, b. of Plainfield, Feb. 1, 1832, by Nathaniel Cole, Elder	2	215
Royal A., of Providence, R.I., m. Menerva T. **KENNEDY**, of Providence, R.I., Mar. 28, 1847, by Rev. J. Mather	3	44
NICHOLS, Allice, m. Abijah **CADY**, Aug. 24, 1749, by Samuel Dorrance, M.	2	11
Ambrose S., of West Greenwich, R.I., m. Hannah A. **SCOTT**, of Coventry, R.I., Oct. 3, 1847, by Rev. Ja[me]s Mather	3	46

	Vol.	Page

NICHOLS, (cont.)
  Amey A., of West Greenwich, R.I., m. William R.
    TAYLER, of Scituate, R.I., Nov. 15, 1846, by Rev.
    J. Mather   3   40
  Anne, d. Joseph & Anne, b. Aug. 10, 1760   2   38
  Dulinda, of Coventry, R.I., m. John S. **LILLIBRIDGE**,
    of Exeter, R.I., Dec. 24, 1848, by Rev. George
    W. Brewster   3   57
  Joseph, m. Anna **RATHBURN**, Jan. 13, 1757   2   38
  Luke, farmer, b. Hopkinton, res. Plainfield, d. Mar.
    17, [18]48, ae. 64   4   61
  Mary, m. Bennajah **CADY**, Jan. 11, 1747/8   2   6
  Mary C., m. William G. **CORY**, May 20, 1843, by Peleg
    Peckham, Elder   3   19
  Phebe, m. Ephraim **KILE**, Jan. 18, 1758   2   39
  Sarah, d. Joseph & Anna, b. June 27, 1758   2   38
NIFF, Jerusheah, m. Joseph **CORY**, June 5, 1733   1   61
NILES, George N., m. Elvira **WEAVER**, b. of Warwick, R.I.,
    Feb. 2, 1848, by Rev. J. Mather   3   51
  John, of Windham, m. Patience **FISH**, of Plainfield,
    Jan. 25, 1852, by Rev. Henry Robinson   3   73
NIYLIE, Alva, of Apalachercola, Florida, m. Frances M.
    FOSTER, of Plainfield, [   ], by Rev.
    Samuel Rockwell   2   243
NORTH[R]UP, Mary A., b. Griswold, res. Plainfield, m. Alfred
    BOWEN, manufacturer, res. Griswold, Nov. [ ],
    1848, by Frederick Charlton   4   4
NOTT, Eliphalet, m. Sarah **BENEDICT**, d. Rev. Joel & Sarah
    BENEDICT   2   112
  Sarah, w. Rev. Eliphalet & d. of Rev. Joel **BENEDICT** &
    Sarah, d. Mar. 9, 1804, at Balls Town, N.Y.   2   112
NOYES, Ann Maria, m. Capt. Robert **BROWN**, 2d, b. of Westerly,
    R.I., Apr. 4, 1831, by Rev. Orin Fowler   2   213
  Dorcas C., of Warwick, R.I., m. Benjamin S. **GREEN**, of
    Providence, R.I., Feb. 14, 1847, by Rev. J. Mather   3   42
  Mary E., m. George B. **CARPENTER**, b. of Warwick, R.I.,
    Feb. 14, 1847, by Rev. J. Mather   3   42
OLCOTT, Sidney, of Manchester, m. Ednah **ADAMS**, of Plainfield,
    Jan. 9, 1824, by Orin Fowler, V.D.M.   2   193
OLIN, Henrietta, d. Giles, farmer, ae. 23, & Jane, ae. 25,
    b. Mar. 20, 1848   4   24
  James, farmer, b. Canterbury, res. Plainfield, d. June
    14, [18]48, ae. 25   4   61
  John F., s. George W., railroad agent, & Y.E., b. Sept.
    8, 1847   4   21
  John F., d. Mar. 10, 1849, ae. 1 y. 6 m.   4   62
  Mary A., of Plainfield, m. Joshua **FENNER**, of Canter-
    bury, Apr. 24, 1853, by Rev. Henry Robinson   3   79

	Vol.	Page

OLIN, (cont.)
Sarah Frances, d. Giles, laborer, ae. 25, & Jane, ae.
    27, b. Feb. 17, 1850 — 4, 28
William, Jr., m. Orilla **BROWN**, b. of Plainfield, Feb.
    18, 1839, by Rev. Tubal Wakefield — 2, 239
W[illia]m, b. Griswold, res. Plainfield, d. Feb. [ ],
    1851, ae. 48 — 4, 66

OLIR, George W., of Plainfield, m. Tepputt E. **GREEN**, of
    Lisbon, Mar. 31, 1839, by Francis B. Johnson, J.P.
    (Oliver?) — 2, 240

OLIVER, [see also **OLIR**], Julia Ann, d. George W., depot agt.
    N. & W. R.R., ae. 33, & Teppett E., ae. 31, b. Apr.
    11, 1849 — 4, 27

OLNEY, Smith, of North Providence, R.I., m. Lydia **GALLUP**, of
    Plainfield, Mar. 31, 1822, by Orin Fowler, V.D.M. — 2, 187

ORBOLD, Tracy, b. Killingly, res. Plainfield, d. Aug. 17,
    1849, ae. 2 — 4, 62

PAINE, PAIN, Elisha, m. Elizabeth **SPAULDING**, May 20, 1762,
    by Rev. Alex[ande]r Miller, in the Second Society — 2, 51
Hester, d. John & Sarah, b. Apr. 2, 1736 — 1, 65
Jane, black, ae. 17, b. Griswold, res. Plainfield, m.
    Horace **SIMONS**, laborer, black, ae. 20, b. Griswold,
    res. Plainfield, [1850], by Joseph
    Hutchins — 4, 5
John*, m. Zeviah **SPAULDING**, Dec. 24, 1750 (*correction
    PIERCE(?) handwritten in margin of original
    manuscript) — 2, 24
John, 2nd s. Elisha & Elizabeth, b. Mar. 5, 1765 — 2, 58
Marian, of Plainfield, m. Caleb F. **BRAYTON**, of
    Cranston, R.I., July 8, 1838, by Rev. Samuel
    Rockwell — 2, 235
Prescilla, m. Josiah **SPAULDING**, Dec. 24, 1755 — 2, 36
Ruth, d. Elisha & Elizabeth, b. July 9, 1769 — 2, 68
Sarah, d. Ic[h]abod & Hannah, b. Nov. 4, 1749 — 2, 17
Sarah, of Plainfield, m. Jesse **EDDY**, of Northbridge,
    Mass., Feb. 22, 1824, by Orin Fowler, V.D.M. — 2, 193
Smith, s. Samuel & Lydia, b. Oct. 13, 1748 — 2, 8
Squier, s. Ic[h]abod & Hannah, b. July 24, 1751; d.
    Feb. 6, 1752 — 2, 17
William, s. Elisha & Elizabeth, b. Sept. 17, 1772 — 2, 76
Zenas, 3rd, s. Elisha & Elizabeth, b. Jan. 5, 1767 — 2, 63
-----, s. Christopher, farmer, ae. 35, & Marada, ae.
    37, of Killingly, b. Jan. 19, 1850 — 4, 28

PALMER, Brigget, m. John **GALLUP**, Nov. 5, 1747 — 2, 7
Brigget, d. Walter & Margaret, b. Feb. 14, 1767 — 2, 67
Charles H., m. Cynthia A. **LOVE**, b. of Sterling, Apr.
    10, 1842, by Peleg Peckham, Elder — 3, 14
Clarissa A., of Killingly, m. Robert **LEWIS**, of Plain-

	Vol.	Page
PALMER, (cont.)		
field, Apr. 17, 1837, by Chester Tilden	2	231
Dolly, m. Andrew **GIBBS**, b. of Plainfield, Dec. 31, 1812, by Rev. Joel Benedict	2	121
Elizabeth, d. Vose & Scillinda, b. Nov. 24, 1787	2	93
Francis S., of Lownesbow, Ala., m. Mary Ann **WHITTER**, of Plainfield, Feb. 4, 1846, by Rev. A. Dunning	3	35
George H., m. Prudence **PHILLIPS**, b. of Plainfield, Sept. 3, 1854, by Rev. Henry Robinson	3	86
Henry C., m. Freelove C. **GREEN**, b. of Plainfield, Sept. 23, 1839, by Rev. Samuel Rockwell	2	247
Isaac, s. Walter & Margaret, b. Aug. 17, 1769	2	67
Lucinda, d. Wa[l]ter & Mary, b. Sept. 5, 1779	2	87
Lucy R., of Plainfield, m. Isaac P. **STUTSON**, of Lysbon, Aug. 4, 1844, by Rev. Daniel Lyon, Packerville	3	25
Lydiah, d. George & Hannah, b. June 15, 1746	1	2X
Lydia, d. Azariah & Mary, b. June 7, 1776	2	81
Mary Elizabeth, m. John W. **SPAULDING**, b. of Plainfield, Apr. 12, 1846, by Rev. Andrew Dunning	3	37
Mary L., m. Jonah H. **BENNET**, b. of Plainfield, Oct. 9, 1842, by Peleg Peckham, Elder	3	17
Nancy, m. Benjamin **CRARY**, b. of Plainfield, Nov. 14, 1824, by Orin Fowler, V.D.M.	2	196
Nelson, m. Mary **CLEAVELAND**, b. of Plainfield, Oct. 17, 1824, by Rev. Orin Fowler	2	196
Polly, d. Walter & Hannah, b. Apr. 13, 1785	2	95
Rebecca T., m. Henry H. **BENNET**, b. of Plainfield, May 11, 1840, by Rev. Samuel Rockwell	3	4
Samuel, farmer, ae. 25, of Plainfield, m. Lucy **SHEPARD**, milliner, ae. 28, b. Brooklyn, res. Plainfield, Nov. 27, 1850, by Rev. Samuel Robinson	4	7
Samuel, Jr., m. Lucy G. **SHEPARD**, b. of Plainfield, Nov. 28, 1850, by Rev. Henry Robinson	3	67
Walter, m. Hannah **GATES**, Apr. 22, 1784	2	95
Walter, Jr., s. Walter & Hannah, b. Aug. 23, 1787	2	95
Walter, m. Hannah **SHEPHARD**, b. of Plainfield, Feb. 20, 1848, by Rev. Henry Robinson	3	52
Walter, farmer, ae. 24, of Plainfield, m. Hannah **SHEPARD**, ae. 22, b. Brooklyn, Mar. 5, [18]48, by Rev. Henry Robinson	4	1
William, s. Walter & Mary, b. Apr. 27, 1782	2	87
PARK, PARKE, PARKS, [see also **PARKIS**], Abijah, m. Mary **DEAN**, Mar. 25, 1772	2	73
Allice, d. William & Christoble, b. June 12, 1754	2	59
Alice, d. William & Christoble, d. Dec. 21, 1778	2	86

Vol.   Page

PARK, PARKE, PARKS, (cont.)
Andrew, farmer, b. Plainfield, res. Killingly, d.
   May 31, [1847], ae. 82   4   61
Anne, d. Nehemiah & Sibel, b. Aug. 17, 1760   2   47
Asa, s. Will[ia]m & Christobel, b. Jan. 6, 1733   1   93
Asa, s. William, Jr. & Sarah, b. Oct. 14, 1759   2   53
Asa, s. Elias & Lucretia, b. Dec. 15, 1776   2   86
Christable, m. Nathaniel **BUTLER**, Oct. 1, 1761   2   58
Cynthia, d. William & Christoble, b. Apr. 22,
   1749   2   58
Syntha, d. William & Christobel, b. Apr. 25, 1749   2   17
Douglass, s. Nehemiah & Sibbel, b. Mar. 21, 1766   2   71
Elias, s. William & Christobel, b. Sept. 25, 1746   2   17
Elias, s. William & Christoble, b. Sept. 25, 1746   2   58
Elias, m. Lucretia **TRACY**, Feb. 29, 1776   2   86
Elias, s. Elias & Lucretia, b. July 10, 1778   2   86
Elias, d. Oct. 11, 1778, in the 33rd y. of his age   2   86
Elisha, s. Nehemiah & Sibbel, b. Sept. 17, 1771   2   85
Elisha, of Plainfield, m. Orra E. **GALLUP**, of Sterling,
   Oct. 6, 1851, by Peleg Peckham, Elder   3   71
Eliza, m. Stephen H. **PARKS**, b. of Plainfield, Feb. 3,
   1831, by Benjamin R. Allen, Elder   2   213
Eliza, of Sterling, m. Asher **BRIG[G]S**, of Plainfield,
   Feb. 8, 1835, by Peleg Peckham, Elder   2   220
Elizabeth, d. William, Jr. & Sarah, b. May 24, 1762   2   53
Han[n]ah, d. William, m. Richard **RICHESON**, Feb. 18,
   1721/2   1   24
Isaac, m. Elizabeth **CLARK**, Sept. 22, 1725   1   43
Isaac, s. Isaac & Elizabeth, b. May 5, 1726; d. Aug.
   20, 1727   1   43
Jemima, d. Robert & Tamson, b. Mar. 5, 1716/7   1   17
Joseph B., of Norwich, m. Lucy Ann **POTTER**, of Plain-
   field, May 14, 1848, by Peleg Peckham, Elder   3   51
Joseph B., carpenter, ae. 23, b. Milltown, res.
   Sterling, m. Sally Ann **POTTER**, ae. 20, May 14,
   [18]48, by Rev. Peleg Peckham   4   1
Lucy, d. Nehemiah & Sibbel, b. Sept. 16, 1758   2   38
Mara, d. William & Jane, b. May 15, 1716   1   17
Maria, of Plainfield, m. Samuel **GALLUP**, of Sterling,
   Nov. 20, 1823, by Orin Fowler, V.D.M.   2   192
Mary, d. Nehemiah & Sibbel, b. Jan. 25, 1764   2   71
Moses, s. Nehemiah & Sibbel, b. Dec. [ ], 1777   2   85
Nathaniel, d. Sept. 7, 1751   2   17
Nathaniel, s. Nehemiah & Sibbel, b. Jan. 26, 1768   2   71
Nehemiah, s. William & Christobel, b. Jan. 7, 1735   1   93
Nehemiah, m. Sibbel **DOUGLASS**, Nov. 16, 1757   2   38
Polly, m. Elijah **FOX**, Feb. 28, 1788   2   97

	Vol.	Page
PARK, PARKE, PARKS, (cont.)		
Rachall, d. William & Jane, b. Nov. 14, 1713	1	13
Rachel, d. William, Jr. & C[h]ristable, b. Oct. 5, 1730	1	52
Rachel, m. Lieut. Benedick **SATTERLEE**, May 16, 1758	2	39
Rebecka, twin with Simon, d. Nehemiah & Sibbel, b. Nov. 10, 1769	2	71
Sally, m. Benjamin **GALLUP**, Mar. 15, 1801	2	149
Samuel, s. William & Christobel, b. Jan. 4, 1744	2	17
Samuel, s. Nehemiah & Sibbel, d. Jan. 30, 1779	2	85
Sarah, d. Nehemiah & Sibbel, b. Nov. 21, 1775	2	85
Sibbel, d. Nehemiah & Sibbel, b. Nov. 10, 1773	2	85
Simon, twin with Rebecka, s. Nehemiah & Sibbel, b. Nov. 10, 1769	2	71
Stephen H., m. Eliza **PARK**, b. of Plainfield, Feb. 3, 1831, by Benjamin R. Allen, Elder	2	213
Thankfull, d. Will[ia]m & Jane, b. June 27, 1717	1	20
Thankfull, m. Enoch **WHITNEY**, Dec. 21, 1732	1	67
Theoda, d. William & Jane, b. Aug. 4, 1719	1	22
William, Jr., m. C[h]ristable **HARRIS**, Nov. 5, 1729	1	52
William, s. William & Christobel, b. July 9, 1737	1	93
William, d. Feb. 18, 1750	2	17
William, Jr., m. Sarah **WILLIAMS**, Dec. 28, 1758	2	39
William, Jr., m. Sarah **WILLIAMS**, Dec. 28, 1758	2	53
William, s. Nehemiah & Sibbel, b. Mar. 29, 1780	2	85
William, d. Feb. 6, 1781	2	86
Zerviah, d. William & Joan, b. Feb. 19, 1721/2	1	36
PARKER, Abby Ann, of Coventry, R.I., m. Harris H. **STONE**, of Cranston, R.I., Oct. 6, 1846, by Rev. J. Mather	3	39
Anderson E., m. Sarah E. **CARTER**, b. of Saco, Me., Nov. 16, 1849, by Rev. Joseph P. Brown. Witnesses: Caleb Bennett, A.S. Brown	3	89
Andrew E., m. Sarah E. **CARTEY**, b. of Maine, Nov. 16, 1849, by Rev. Joseph P. Brown	3	62
Daniel, Jr., of Hawkinsville, Ga., m. Susan **COIT**, of Plainfield, Sept. 21, 1831, by Rev. Levi Kneeland, of Canterbury	2	214
Jonathan, m. Sarah **FRENCH**, wid. of Nath[anie]l, Dec. 29, 1757	2	40
Jonathan, m. Sarah **FRENCH**, wid. Nathaniel, b. of Plainfield, Dec. 29, 1757, by John Crery, J.P.	2	52
Martin, of Killingly, m. Levina E. **POTTER**, of Scituate, R.I., Nov. 27, 1836, by Chester Tilden	2	229
Mary F., m. John F. **WILSON**, b. of Plainfield, Sept. 2, 1845, by Peleg Peckham, Elder	3	32
PARKHOUSE, [see also **PARKHURST**], Uness, m. Thomas **MARSH**, Feb. 4, 1711/12	1	11

	Vol.	Page
PARKHURST, [see also **PARKHOUSE** and **PARKIS**], Andrew,		
s. Jonathan & Judah, b. Oct. 14, 1766	2	69
Anne, d. Timothy, Jr. & Joanne, b. Dec. 27, 1758	2	64
Azel, s. Lemuel & Hannah, b. July 29, 1761	2	49
Benjamin, s. Joseph, Jr. & Mary, b. Nov. 29, 1745	2	39
Betty, d. Isaac & Mary, b. Sept. 26, 1767	2	69
Calvin, s. Joseph & Judah, b. June 12, 1753	2	76
David, m. Phebe **KINGSBURY**, Dec. 28, 1750	2	40
David, twin with Jonathan, s. Timothy & Joanne, b. Sept. 19, 1768	2	69
Dinah, d. Isaac & Mary, b. Oct. 22, 1769	2	69
Ebenezer, s. Joseph & Judah, b. May 8, 1746	2	79
Elias, s. Isaac & Mary, b. May 30, 1764	2	68
Esther, w. Samuel, d. Nov. 4, 1740	2	2
[E]unis, m. Gid[e]on **LAWRANCE**, Aug. 1, 1738	1	97
Eunis, wid., d. Jan. 19, 1743/4, in the 83rd y. of her age	1	100
Eunice, d. Samuel & Mary, b. Nov. 24, 1754	2	34
Eunice, d. Samuel & Mary, b. May 18, 1758	2	43
Eunice, d. Timothy, Jr. & Joanne, b. July 12, 1766	2	64
George W[illia]m Frederick, s. John, Jr. & Phebe, b. Dec. 16, 1761	2	54
Hannah, d. John & Abigaiel, b. Aug. 25, 1724	1	44
Hannah, d. Joseph & Judah, b. Mar. 14, 1748	2	79
Hannah, d. John & Phebe, b. Oct. 24, 1753	2	25
Hannah, d. Sept. 16, 1758, in the 5th y. of her age	2	42
Hannah, d. Jonathan & Judah, b. July 30, 1762	2	69
Hannah, w. Lemuel, d. Feb. 29, 1764	2	54
Isaac, m. May **CADY**, Nov. 19, 1762	2	68
Jabes, s. Joseph & Sarah, b. Nov. 12, 1734	1	63
Jabez, s. John & Phebe, b. Apr. 13, 1759	2	42
James, s. Jonathan & Judah, b. Aug. 12, 1764	2	69
Job, s. Samuel & Mary, b. Apr. 19, 1749	2	15
Johannah, m. Nathaniel **MAINE**, Apr. 13, 1741	1	96
Johanah, m. Nathaniel **MAIN**, Apr. 13, 1741	2	16
John, s. John & Abigaiel, b. May 13, 1730	1	50
John, s. Joseph & Mary, b. Sept. 4, 1749	2	8
John, m. Phebe **PEIRCE**, Dec. 6, 1749	2	14
Jonathan, s. David & Phebe, b. Mar. 13, 1757	2	40
Jonathan, m. Judah **WILLSON**, May 12, 1761	2	69
Jonathan, twin with David, s. Timothy & Joanna, b. Sept. 19, 1768	2	69
Joseph, d. Dec. 11, 1720, in the 57th y. of his age	1	23
Joseph, s. John & Abegall, b. June 25, 1721	1	26
Joseph, m. Sarah **LAWRANCE**, Jan. 20, 1730/31	1	54
Joseph, m. Judeth **JENSON**, Aug. 12, 1741	1	100
Joseph, s. Joseph & Mary, b. Aug. 9, 1747	1	1X
Joseph, s. Joseph, Jr. & Mary, b. Aug. 9, 1747	2	40

	Vol.	Page
PARKHURST, (cont.)		
Joseph, Jr., s. Joseph & Judah, b. Mar. 1, 1750	2	79
Josiah, s. John, Jr. & Phebe, b. Dec. 19, 1763	2	54
Lemeuel, s. Sam[ue]ll & Hester, b. Feb. 17, 1732	1	60
Lemuel, m. Hannah **PEIRCE**, Nov. 14, 1753	2	25
Lemuel, m. Hannah **PEIRCE**, Nov. 14, 1753	2	104
Lemuel, s. Lemuel & Hannah, b. Aug. 16, 1754	2	25
Lemuel, s. Lemuel & Hannah, b. Aug. 16, 1754	2	104
Lois, d. David & Phebe, b. June 14, 1753	2	40
Lois, m. James **MILLER**, Apr. 27, 1780	2	95
Lucy Ann, cotton operator, res. Mass, m. Abner **ARNOLD**, laborer, res. Mass., June 9, [1850?]	4	7
Marah, d. Samuel & Mary, d. Nov. 27, 1743	2	3
Mary, d. Joseph & Unis, b. Nov. 18, 1702	1	1
Mary, d. John & Abigaiel, b. Mar. 2, 1726	1	44
Mary, [twin with Sarah], d. Samuel & Mary, b. Nov. 10, 1743	2	2
Mary, d. Samuel & Mary, b. Dec. 30, 1751	2	15
Nancy E., of Rutland, Mass., m. James W. **HOPKINS**, of Plainfield, Sept. 23, 1845, by James Smither, Elder	3	34
Oliver, s. Isaac & Mary, b. Mar. 6, 1763	2	68
Phinehas, s. John & Abegal, b. Apr. 28, 1716	1	16
Phinehas, s. Joseph, Jr. & Mary, b. Nov. 21, 1743	2	39
Peirce, s. Lemuel & Hannah, b. Nov. 26, 1756	2	36
Peirce, s. Lemuel & Hannah, b. Nov. 25, 1757	2	104
Peirley, s. Timothy, Jr. & Joanne, b. July 30, 1762	2	64
R[e]uben, s. Joseph, Jr. & Mary, b. May 1, 1753	2	23
Ruth, d. Samuel & Mary, b. Oct. 7, 1746	2	3
Ruth, d. Oct. 10, 1849, ae. 70	4	64
Sally, d. Timothy, Jr. & Joanne, b. Apr. 10, 1764	2	64
Sam[ue]ll, m. Hester **SPAULDING**, Jan. 20, 1731	1	60
Samuel, s. Samuel & Hester, b. Sept. 3, 1734	1	67
Samuel, m. Mary **HUCHENS**, Feb. 24, 1742/3	2	2
Samuel, 3rd, s. Lemuel & Hannah, b. Jan. 29, 1764	2	104
Samuel, 3rd, s. Lemuel & Hannah, b. Feb. 29, 1764	2	54
Sarah, w. Joseph, d. Nov. 20, 1738	1	92
Sarah, d. Joseph & Judeth, b. Oct. 3, 1742	1	100
Sarah, [twin with Mary], d. Samuel & Mary, b. Nov. 10, 1743; d. Nov. 25, 1743	2	2
Sarah, d. John & Phebe, b. Nov. 19, 1756	2	36
Sarah, d. Sept. 17, 1758, in the 2d y. of her age	2	42
Sarah, d. Joseph, Jr. & Mary, b. Apr. 23, 1760	2	43
Silas, s. Isaac & Mary, b. Sept. 7, 1766	2	68
Silas, s. Isaac & Mary, d. Oct. 11, 1766	2	69
Simeon, s. John & Phebe, b. Sept. 16, 1751	2	14
Susan[n]ah, d. Joseph & Sarah, b. Aug. 28, 1735	1	69
Suesannah, d. Joseph & Sarah, d. Aug. 3, 1738	1	92

	Vol.	Page

PARKHURST, (cont.)

Tille, s. Joseph & Sarah, b. Oct. 10, 1732	1	56
Timothy, Jr., m. Joanne **CADY**, Mar. 25, 1757	2	64
Timothy, s. Jonathan & Judah, b. Jan. 6, 1769	2	69
Timothy, d. Mar. 3, 1770, in the 82nd y. of his age	2	70
Willard, s. Samuel & Mary, b. Oct. 17, 1744	2	3
Willard, m. Alice **THOMAS**, Feb. 9, 1773	2	77
William, of Providence, R.I., m. Rachal S. **LOWS**, of Johnston, R.I., Dec. 15, 1846, by Rev. J. Mather	3	41

PARKIS, [see also **PARK, PARKHOUSE** and **PARKHURST**],

Andrew, s. Peirce & Hannah, b. Mar. 2, 1794	2	123
Anthony, m. Mehetable **HERRINGTON**, Feb. 27, 1820	2	189
Betsey, m. William H. **POTTER**, Nov. 4, 1839, by Rev. Hezekiah Thatcher	2	252
Betsey, m. William H. **POTTER**, b. of Plainfield, Nov. 4, 1839, by Rev. Hezekiah Thacher	3	2
Elias, Jr., m. Hannah B. **PERRY**, b. of Plainfield, Aug. 18, 1833, by Rev. Daniel G. Sprague	2	217
Freelove, d. Anthony & Mehetable, b. May 20, 1821	2	166
George, m. Mary Ann **WILBOUR**, b. of Plainfield, Apr. 3, 1837, by Rev. Samuel Rockwell	2	230
Hannah, d. Peirce & Hannah, b. Nov. 28, 1789	2	123
Hannah, w. Peirce, d. Dec. 29, 1832, ae. 70	2	166
Hiram, m. Nancy **KINYON**, b. of Plainfield, Oct. 27, 1822, by Rev. Nathaniel Cole	2	189
Isaac, m. Marinda **COLE**, b. of Plainfield, Oct. 3, 1853, by Rev. Joseph P. Brown	3	80
Jonathan, s. Peirce & Hannah, b. Nov. 29, 1784	2	123
Jonathan S., m. Mary Ann **MEDBERY**, b. of Plainfield, Apr. 1, 1832, by Peleg Peckham, Elder	2	215
Judeth, d. Peirce & Hannah, b. Nov. 25, 1801	2	123
Lemuel, s. Peirce & Hannah, b. Feb. 2, 1787; d. Feb. 26, 1788	2	123
Lois, d. Peirce & Hannah, b. May 13, 1807	2	123
Louisa, domestic, d. Apr. 27, 1849, ae. 78	4	62
Lucretia, domestic, ae. 36, b. Canterbury, res. Plainfield, m. 2d h. Daniel **BRIGGS**, farmer, ae. 42, of Voluntown, July 4, 1850, by Rev. John Lovejoy	4	6
Mary, m. John **GARDINER**, b. of Plainfield, Sept. 19, 1830, by Rev. Orin Fowler	2	211
Peirce, m. Hannah [ ], Feb. 12, 1784	2	123
Peirce, s. Peirce & Hannah, b. July 28, 1791	2	123
Peirce, d. Jan. 6, 1833, ae. 75	2	166
Peirce, m. Susan **PARKIS**, b. of Plainfield, Jan. 25, 1852, by Rev. John F. Sheffield	3	74
Rawson, m. Harriet **BENNET**, b. of Plainfield, Oct. 24, 1841, by John Read, Elder	3	11
Susan, m. Peirce **PARKIS**, b. of Plainfield, Jan. 25,		

	Vol.	Page
PARKIS, (cont.)		
1852, by Rev. John F. Sheffield	3	74
PARRISH, PARISH, Abigail, d. Ebenezer & Susannah, b.		
July 30, 1764	2	57
Ebenezer, m. Susannah **WILLIAMS**, Feb. 13, 1752	2	23
Ebenezer, s. Ebenezer & Susannah, b. Jan. 29, 1760	2	57
Hester, d. Ebenezer & Susan[n]ah, b. Dec. 13, 1755	2	32
Hester, d. Ebenezer & Susannah, d. Oct. 20, 1760	2	57
Nathan, s. Ebenezer & Susannah, b. Dec. 8, 1757	2	57
Pallatiah, s. Ebenezer & Susannah, b. Jan. 2, 1754	2	23
Pelletiah, s. Ebenezer & Susan[n]ah, d. Mar. 1, 1755	2	32
Pallatiah, s. Ebenezer & Susannah, d. Mar. 7, 1755	2	57
Preserved, s. Ebenezer & Susannah, b. Apr. 15, 1762	2	57
PARSON, Jesse, of Cold Spring, N.Y., m. Mary **KNAP[P]ING**,		
of Plainfield, Dec. 5, 1841, by Amos Witter, J.P.	3	12
PARTRICK, John, s. Mat[t]hew & Elizabeth, b. Feb. 6, 1730	1	49
Mat[t]hew, m. Elizabeth **ROGERS**, Nov. 20, 1726	1	49
Mat[t]hew, s. Matthew & Elizabeth, b. Aug. 28, 1727	1	42
Mat[t]hew, s. Mat[t]hew & Elizabeth, b. Aug. 28, 1727	1	49
PATTISON, Susan, m. Clark **HOLDEN**, b. of Coventry, R.I.,		
June 21, 1847, by Rev. Fred[eri]c Charlton	3	49
PEABODY, Giles H., of Stonington, m. Amelia **BRAMIN**, of		
Plainfield, May 10, 1841, by Rev. Thomas Barber	3	10
PECK, William, of Coventry, R.I., m. Mary **WALKER**, of		
Killingly, Sept. 9, 1822, by Rev. Nathaniel Cole	2	189
PECKHAM, Caroline, m. Joseph A. **TILLINGHAST**, b. of Plain-		
field, Sept. 17, 1837, by Peleg Peckham, Elder	2	232
Ele[a]nor, of Plainfield, m. Samuel **GREEN**, of Charles-		
town, R.I., Oct. 21, 1839, by Peleg Peckham, Elder	2	249
Eleanor, of Plainfield, m. Samuel **GREEN**, of Charles-		
town, R.I., Oct. 21, 1839, by Peleg Peckham, Elder	3	1
Harry, m. Elizabeth H. **ALMY**, b. of Middletown, R.I.,		
residing in Plainfield, Nov. 18, 1838, by Peleg		
Peckham, Elder	2	238
Susan, w. Howland, d. Jan. 24, 1822	2	166
Susan A., of Plainfield, m. Nathan G. **HOXSIE**, of		
Richmond, R.I., July 8, 1850, by Peleg Peckham,		
Elder	3	65
PELLET, Edwin D., of Canterbury, m. Lydia P. **HALL**, of Plain-		
field, May 12, 1839, by Jonathan Goff, J.P.	2	242
PELOM, Betsey, of Griswold, m. Daniel **CONGDON**, of Plain-		
field, Sept. 6, 1843, by Rev. A. Dunning	3	20
PENDLETON, George, of Camden, Me., m. Susan W. **JOHNSON**,		
of Plainfield, Sept. 28, 1831, by Rev. Dennis		
Platt, of Canterbury	2	214
PERKINS, PURKINS, Albert M., of Sterling, m. Nancy D.		
KENNEDY, of Voluntown, Oct. 6, 1850, by Peleg		
Peckham, Elder	3	66

	Vol.	Page
PERKINS, PURKINS, (cont.)		
Benjamin, s. Dr. Elisha & Sarah, b. June 24, 1774	2	78
Elisha, m. Sarah **DOUGLASS**, Sept. 23, 1762	2	53
Elisha, s. Elisha & Sarah, b. July 18, 1763	2	53
Elizabeth, d. Dr. Elisha & Sarah, b. Nov. 6, 1778	2	85
Elizabeth G., m. John **HARRIS**, b. of Sterling, Nov. 8, 1841, by Peleg Peckham, Elder	3	12
George, s. Elisha & Sarah, b. Oct. 19, 1783	2	89
Gilbert P., of Ledyard, m. Hannah **BAKER**, of Plainfield, Dec. 31, 1837, by Rev. Tubal Wakefield	2	233
Hannah D., of Sterling, m. Penn **TUCKERMAN**, of New York, Sept. 14, 1840, by Peleg Peckham, Elder	3	7
Henry, s. Elisha & Sarah, b. Apr. 20, 1781	2	86
Jane F., of Sterling, m. Dr. Nathan S. **PIKE**, of Plainfield, Apr. 28, 1853, by Peleg Peckham, Elder	3	78
John Douglass, s. E[l]isha & Sarah, b. Feb. 3, 1769	2	65
Joshua, of Lisbon, m. Amey **SHEPERD**, of Plainfield, July 10, 1826, by Rev. Orin Fowler	2	199
Lydiah, d. Joseph & Lydiah, b. Dec. 19, 1729, in Norwich	1	48
Lydiah, w. Joseph, d. Jan. 7, 1730	1	48
Mary Ann, of Sterling, m. J. Whitney **KNIGHT**, of Westerly, R.I., Nov. 26, 1838, by Peleg Peckham, Elder	2	238
Newman C., of Tolland, m. Alme C. **GREEN**, of Sterling, Sept. 21, 1835, by Rev. Ziba Loveland. Witnesses: Allen M. Perkins, Huldah Perkins, Huldah Loveland	2	222
Norah, d. Elisha & Sarah, b. Aug. 12, 1765	2	59
Olive, d. Elisha & Sarah, b. Mar. 13, 1786	2	91
Prentice, farmer, d. May 5, 1849, ae. 51	4	62
Robert M., of Washington, N.C., m. Manah A. **COGSWELL**, of Warwick, R.I., Sept. 21, 1840, by Rev. John Read	3	6
Ruby A., of Sterling, m. Denison G. **GALLUP**, of Voluntown, Feb. 18, 1849, by Peleg Peckham, Elder	3	58
Sarah, d. Dr. Elisha & Sarah, b. Oct. 27, 1771	2	74
Susa, d. Elisha & Sarah, b. Oct. 9, 1776	2	82
Susanna, of Plainfield, m. Josiah Lynden **ARNOLD**, of St. Jansbury, Vt., Feb. 8, 1795, by W[illia]m Robinson, Clerk	2	101
PERRY, Edward B., m. Hannah **KENYON**, b. of South Kingstown, R.I., Oct. 3, 1854, by Rev. Peter L. Mather	3	87
Hannah B., m. Elias **PARKIS**, Jr., b. of Plainfield, Aug. 18, 1833, by Rev. Daniel G. Sprague	2	217
PETERS, PETER, Anna, m. Jonathan **WHIPPLE**, Apr. 15, 1781	2	86
John Dalton, m. Sarah **BLIVEN**, Feb. 5, 1804	2	109
-----, d. Ann, housework, black, ae. 23, of Griswold, Ct., b. July 9, 1850	4	29

	Vol.	Page
PETERSON, Nancy Anna, m. David **FROST**, Nov. 17, 1850, by Benjamin Bacon, J.P.	3	67
PHILLIPS, PHILIPS, Abby B., of Preston, m. Lucius **BEACH**, of Hartford, Mar. 15, 1829, by Rev. Orin Fowler	2	208
Alvin, s. Arthur & Asenath, b. Apr. 10, 1822	2	166
Alvin, s. Arthur & Asenath, b. [ ]	2	166
Arthur, s. Daniel & Olive, b. Oct. 8, 1793	2	101
Asa, m. Mary **CHESSBROUG**, Nov. 27, 1760	2	50
Asa, m. Rhoda Ann **BROWN**, b. of Plainfield, Dec. 13, 1846, by Rev. A. Dunning	3	41
Ayer, d. May 31, 1799	2	105
Bathsheba, d. Asa & Mary, b. Feb. 28, 1762	2	50
Betsey, of Plainfield, m. Joshua P. **CARD**, of Killingly, Jan. 5, 1823, by John Dunlap, J.P.	2	189
Caroline S., of Plainfield, m. John S. R. **BENCHLEY**, of Windham, Nov. 27, 1834, by Peleg Peckham, Elder	2	220
Clarry, m. Samuel **COOPER**, b. of Plainfield, Sept. 7, 1835, by Peleg Peckham, Elder	2	222
Darius, s. Asa & Mary, b. Oct. 28, 1764	2	50
Ebenezer, b. Sterling, res. Plainfield, d. Aug. [ ], 1849, ae. 1	4	63
Ellen S., of Plainfield, m. George F. **SANDS**, of Springfield, Mass., Apr. 8, 1849, by Rev. Joseph P. Brown	3	57
Emily S., m. William F. **HOLLOWAY**, b. of Plainfield, Mar. 20, 1854, by Rev. Henry Robinson	3	83
George, s. Ichabod, cotton dresser tender, ae. 27, & Mary W., ae. 26, b. Apr. 7, 1848	4	23
George N., of Cranston, R.I., m. Sarah A. **JOURDON**, of Plainfield, Nov. 11, 1849, by Rev. Joseph P. Brown	3	62
Hannah, m. James **MAXWELL**, Oct. 1, 1762	2	96
Hannah, m. George **GIBSON**, Sept. 24, 1854, by Rev. Alfred Gates	3	85
Harriet, m. Jerad **ADAMS**, Apr. 1, 1821, by Rev. Nathaniel Cole	2	134
Henry, s. Arthur & Asenath, b. May 10, 1825	2	166
Henry, m. Mary **WHEELER**, b. of Plainfield, Jan. 15, 1835, by Rev. Samuel Rockwell	2	220
Huldah, d. Daniel & Olive, b. Jan. 19, 1797	2	102
James, m. Prudence **HYDE**, b. of Sterling, Oct. 5, 1845, by Peleg Peckham, Elder	3	32
Job, s. William & Temperance, b. Aug. 5, 1763	2	60
Job, d. Nov. 23, 1834, ae. 71	2	167
John, s. Joseph & Mary, b. Jan. 12, 1735	1	98
Joseph, s. Arthur & Asenath, b. Dec. 2, 1819	2	166
Juliette, d. Ichabod, mule spinner, b. July 3, [1850]	4	30
Loah, d. William & Temperance, b. Aug. 26, 1761	2	8
Lois, d. Joseph & Mary, b. Oct. 14, 1757	2	37

	Vol.	Page
PHILLIPS, PHILIPS, (cont.)		
Martha B., m. Phillip Orton **ROBERTS**, Dec. 24, 1843, by Rev. W. Clark, Canterbury	3	21
Mary, d. Joseph & Mary, b. Dec. 26, 1738	1	98
Mary, d. William & Temperance, b. July 28, 1765	2	60
Mary, d. Asa & Mary, b. Sept. 22, 1767	2	50
Mary, d. Arthur & Asenath, b. Aug. 7, 1818	2	166
Mary, m. Jared **STARKWEATHER**, b. of Plainfield, Jan. 15, 1854, by Rev. William Turkington	3	81
Mary A., d. [ ], 1850, ae. 5	4	66
Mary A., d. [ ], 1851, ae. 5	4	66
Mary Ann, m. Serel O. **BAILEY**, b. of Providence, R.I., Oct. 30, 1847, by Rev. J. Mather	3	46
Mary E., of Plainfield, m. William C. **CADY**, Minister, of Sterling, Mar. 5, 1848, by Rev. James Mather	3	53
Mary E., ae. 24, m. William O. **CADY**, minister, ae. 26, b. Willington, res. Sterling, Mar. 5, [18]48, by Rev. Mathews	4	1
Mary F., of Plainfield, m. George F. **HOWARD**, of Griswold, Aug. 27, 1849	3	59
Olive, d. Daniel & Olive, b. Jan. 28, 1795	2	101
Oliver, of Coventry, R.I., m. Hannah **JOHNSON**, of Warwick, R.I., Nov. 6, 1848, by Rev. Geo[rge] W. Brewster	3	52
Orin F., s. Arthur & Asenath, b. Dec. 19, 1820	2	166
Patty, of Plainfield, m. Russel[l] **TANNER**, of Voluntown, Nov. 10, 1851, by Rev. Henry Robinson	3	72
Phebe E., m. Amos **BENNETT**, Jr., b. of Plainfield, Feb. 6, 1837, by Chester Tilden	2	231
Philo, of Plainfield, m. Eunice **HALE**, of Sterling, May 8, 1848, by Rev. Geo[rge] W. Brewster	3	52
Prudence, domestic, b. Sterling, res. Plainfield, d. Apr. 3, 1850, ae. 23	4	64
Prudence, m. George H. **PALMER**, b. of Plainfield, Sept. 3, 1854, by Rev. Henry Robinson	3	86
Sabrina, d. William & Temperance, b. May 5, 1767	2	63
Sally, of Plainfield, m. William **HERRICK**, of Griswold, Feb. 23, 1840, by Rev. Thomas Barber	3	3
Sarah, m. Perry **CLARK**, Nov. 22, 1743	2	2
Sarah, m. William **UNDERWOOD**, Apr. 3, 1763	2	59
Sarah, d. Daniel & Olive, b. Jan. 1, 1799	2	105
Sarah, of Plainfield, m. Lot **LARKHANA**, of Voluntown, Apr. 6, 1835, by Peleg Peckham, Elder	2	221
Sarah Ann, of Plainfield, m. Lucius **TUCKER**, of Pomfret, Mar. 4, 1845, by Peleg Peckham, Elder	3	27
Sarah B., of Plainfield, m. Brownell **WILKMAN**, of Watertown, N.Y., May 4, 1829, by Peleg Peckham, Elder	2	209
Simon, laborer, black, d. Sept. 25, [18]48, ae. 65	4	63

	Vol.	Page
PHILLIPS, PHILIPS, (cont.)		
Susan A., m. Jonathan **GORTON**, b. of Plainfield, Jan. 20, 1851, by Rev. W. Emerson	3	68
Susan A., ae. 24, m. Jonathan **GORTON**, merchant, ae. 30, b. R.I., res. Plainfield, [1850 or 1851], by Rev. Emerson	4	7
William, of Plainfield, m. Temperance **BRANCH**, of Preston, Feb. 4, 1748/9, by Hezekiah Lord, Clerk	2	8
William, m. Wid. Martha **BUTCHER**, b. of Plainfield, Mar. 31, 1833, by Rev. Benjamin Paine	2	216
-----, child of Charles, laborer, ae. 43, & Hannah, ae. 38, b. Mary 7, 1848	4	21
-----, s. Charles, laborer, ae. 46, & Hannah G., ae. 41, b. May 28, 1851	4	31
PHIPS, Mary, m. Joshua **MAXFIELD**, Oct. 12, 1741	1	100
Mary, see under James **MAXWELL** and James **MAXFIELD**		
PICKET, Abby, of Plainfield, m. Michael **GREEN**, of New York, Nov. 18, 1846, by Rev. J.C. Knapp, Central Village	3	41
Ephraim, m. Lydia **CHAMPLAIN**, Aug. 1, 1853, by Rev. Alfred Gates	3	79
George, of Killingly, m. Susan R. **CARPENTER**, of Plainfield, Oct. 16, 1853, by Rev. William Turkington	3	80
John O., of Plainfield, m. Sally **HERRINGTON**, of Canterbury, Nov. 5, 1815, by Daniel Frost, Jr., J.P., Canterbury	2	127
Leonard O., s. John O. & Eunice, b. June 4, 1798	2	126
Maria H., d. Rachel, b. Feb. 24, 1834	2	167
Rachel, m. Clark **STANTON**, b. of Plainfield, Sept. 25, 1836, by Chester Tilden	2	227
Thomas, s. Sarah, b. Mar. 22, 1817	2	167
PIERCE, PEIRCE, PEARCE, PARCE, Abell, s. Timothy & Han[n]ah, b. June 17, 1720	1	26
Abel, d. Sept. 4, 1736	1	65
Abel, s. Ezekiel & Lois, b. Dec. 15, 1736	1	101
Abel, s. Ezekiel & Lois, b. Dec. 15, 1736	2	5
Alis, d. Ezekiel & Lois, b. Nov. 17, 1738	1	101
Allis, d. Ezekiel & Lois, b. Nov. 17, 1738	2	5
Amanda M., m. William V. **JOSHLIN**, Nov. 22, 1846, by Benjamin Bacon, J.P.	3	39
Amase, s. Thomas & Mary, b. Aug. 3, 1702	1	1
Andrew Alanson, s. James & Betsey, b. July 14, 1823	2	166
Ann Elizabeth, d. James & Betsey, b. Aug. 26, 1825	2	166
Benjamin, s. Timothy & Hannah, b. July 17, 1710	1	8
Betty, d. Samuel & Ruth, b. Mar. 4, 1798	2	105
Christopher R., m. Lydia **JOHNSON**, of Coventry, R.I., July 9, 1854, by Rev. Alfred Gates	3	84
Daniel, s. Ezekiel & Lois, b. Jan. 30, 1740	1	101

PLAINFIELD VITAL RECORDS 217

	Vol.	Page
PIERCE, PEIRCE, PEARCE, PARCE, (cont.)		
Daniel, s. Ezekiel & Lois, b. Jan. 30, 1740	2	5
David, s. Nathaniel & Lydiah, b. Jan. 24, 1760	2	40
Eaton, [s. Jedediah & Susannah], b. Apr. 22, 1781	2	92
Ebenezer, s. Thomas & Mary, b. Sept. 10, 1698	1	2
Ebenezer, [twin with Lucy], s. Jedediah & Susanna, b. Dec. 9, 1776	2	81
Elisha, s. Jedediah & Susanna, b. Nov. 27, 1774	2	79
Elizabeth, d. Thomas & Mary, b. July 23, 1700	1	2
Elizabeth, d. Thomas & Mary, d. July 5, 1704	1	1
Elizabeth, d. Nathaniel & Elizabeth, b. Nov. 26, 1736	1	68
Elizabeth, w. Nathaniel, d. July 13, 1748	2	1
Elizabeth, m. Asa **KINGSBURY**, Sept. 5, 1748	2	24
Elizabeth, d. Nathaniel, Jr. & Priscilla, b. May 14, 1756	2	46
Easter, d. Thomas & Mary, b. Oct. 17, 1740; d. Nov. 16, 1746	1	1X
Esther, d. John & Zeriah, b. Apr. 1, 1755	2	30
[E]unice, d. Thomas & Mary, b. Jan. 30, 1744	1	1X
Ezekiel, s. Nathaniel & Elizabeth, b. Dec. 18, 1730	1	67
Ezekiel, m. Lois **STEVENS**, Feb. 11, 1736	1	101
Ezekiel, m. Lois **STEVENS**, Feb. 11, 1736	2	5
Ezekiel, Jr., m. Esther **BLOGGET**, July 8, 1749	2	20
Ezekiel, d. Sept. 11, 1751	2	20
Ezekiel, s. Ezekiel & Esther, b. Feb. 17, 1752	2	20
Ezekiell, s. Timothy & Han[n]ah, b. Jan. 8, 17[ ]	1	11
Han[n]ah, d. Timothy & Han[n]ah, b. May 8, 1717	1	17
Hannah, d. Timo[thy] & Hannah, d. Sept. 13, 1727, in the 11th y. of her age	1	41
Hannah, d. Timo[thy], Jr. & Mary, b. Sept. 8, 1730	1	52
Hannah, w. Timo[thy], d. Apr. 2, 1747	1	2X
Hannah, w. Timo[thy], d. Apr. 2, 1747, in the 61st y. of her age	2	1
Hannah, d. Ezekiel & Lois, b. Jan. 25, 1749	2	5
Hannah, m. Lemuel **PARKHURST**, Nov. 14, 1753	2	25
Hannah, m. Lemuel **PARKHURST**, Nov. 14, 1753	2	104
Hannah, d. Nathaniel & Lydia, b. May 10, 1766	2	60
Hannah, d. Timothy & Hannah, b. Aug. 26, 1768	2	71
Hester, d. Jedediah & Susanah, b. Nov. 22, 1766	2	62
Isaac Knight, s. James & Betsey, b. Apr. 23, 1819	2	166
Jabez, m. Susanna **SHEPARD**, b. of Plainfield, June 27, 1748, by Thomas Stevens, J.P.	2	7
Jedediah, s. Timothy & Lydia, b. Feb. 23, 1703/4	1	3
Jedediah, s. Nathaniel & Elizabeth, b. Feb. 22, 1740	2	39
Jed[ed]iah, d. Feb. 2, 1746	1	2X
Jedediah, m. Susan[n]ah **EATON**, Apr. 11, 1764	2	58

	Vol.	Page
PIERCE, PEIRCE, PEARCE, PARCE, (cont.)		
Jedediah, Jr., s. Jedediah & Susannah, b. Feb. 4, 1779	2	92
John, s. Thomas & Mary, b. Feb. 10, 1723	1	29
John, s. Ezekiel & Lois, b. Mar. 10, 1745	2	5
John, s. John & Zeviah, b. Aug. 19, 1753	2	24
John, m. Elizabeth [ ], Dec. 9, 1779	2	87
John, Jr., s. John & Elizabeth, b. Sept. 14, 1780	2	87
Joseph, s. Jedediah & Susan[n]ah, b. Aug. 19, 1765	2	58
Joseph A., m. Abby E. **CARPENTER**, Nov. 22, 1846, by Benjamin Bacon, J.P.	3	39
Lemeuel, s. Ebenezer & Lydiah, b. Nov. 16, 1730	1	52
Lemuel, m. Dorcas **SPAULDING**, Feb. 10, 1756	2	35
Lowis, d. Thomas & Mary, b. May 19, 1732	1	57
Lois, d. Thomas & Mary, b. Aug. 14, 1732	1	1X
Lois, d. Ezekiel & Lois, b. May 6, 1753	2	5
Lois, m. Andrew **BACKUS**, Feb. 8, 1759	2	40
Lois, w. Ezekiel, d. June 25, 1762, ae. 44 y. 9 m. 7 d.	2	1
Lois, d. Jedediah & Susannah, b. Sept. 14, 1772	2	74
Lewcreshe, d. Ebenezer & Lydiah, b. Apr. 7, 1734	1	62
Lucy, d. Nathaniel, Jr. & Priscilla, b. Dec. 28, 1764	2	59
Lucy, [twin with Ebenezer], d. Jedediah & Susanna, b. Dec. 9, 1776	2	81
Lydia, d. Timothy & Lydia, b. Mar. 10, 1705/6	1	3
Lydia, w. Timothy, d. Mar. 23, 1705/6	1	3
Lyd[i]ah, d. Timo[thy] & Marah, b. Nov. 1, 1724	1	37
Lydiah, d. Ebenez[er] & Lydiah, b. July 27, 1732	1	56
Lydiah, d. Ebenezer & Lydiah, d. Aug. 17, 1737	1	68
Lydiah, m. Thomas **STEEVENS**, Jr., Oct. [ ], 1742	1	2X
Lydiá, m. Thomas **STEVENS**, Oct. [ ], 1742	2	15
Lydiah, d. Ezekiel & Lois, b. Feb. 11, 1743	1	101
Lydia, d. Ezekiel & Lois, b. Feb. 17, 1743	2	5
Lydia, d. Jabez & Susannah, b. July 23, 1749	2	14
Maria Matilda, d. James & Betsey, b. Oct. 29, 1821	2	166
Martha, d. Nathaniel, Jr. & Priscilla, b. Mar. 1, 1758	2	46
Martin, of Pomfret, m. Judya **HALL**, of Plainfield, Sept. 29, 1826, by Nathaniel Cole, Elder	2	200
Mary, d. Timo[thy], Jr. & Mary, b. Nov. 15, 1728	1	45
Mary, d. Thomas & Mary, b. Dec. 6, 1735	1	1X
Mary, [d.] Thomas & Mary, b. Dec. 7, 1735	1	67
Mary, m. R[e]uben **SPAULDING**, Oct. 1, 1747	2	7
Mary, d. John & Zeviah, b. Apr. 5, 1757	2	33
Mary, d. Jedediah & Susannah, b. Feb. 16, 1787	2	92
Nathaniell, s. Timothy & Lydia, b. Jan. 3, 1701/2	1	3
Nathaniel, m. Elisabeth **STEVENS**, Feb. 20, 1723	1	38
Nathaniel, s. Nathaniel & Elizabeth, b. Mar. 19, 1728	1	67

	Vol.	Page
PIERCE, PEIRCE, PEARCE, PARCE, (cont.)		
Nathaniel, m. Prescilla **SHEPHARD**, Sept. 24, 1754	2	29
Nehemiah, m. Lydiah **SHEPHERD**, May 3, 1759	2	40
Olive, d. Lemuel & Darkis, b. Apr. 9, 1760	2	46
Oliver, m. Mercy **MILLER**, Apr. 21, 1768	2	67
Palmer, s. Timothy & Eunice, b. Oct. 8, 1761	2	55
Parnel, d. Lemuel & Darkis, b. Apr. 17, 1758	2	46
Parnel, d. Lemuel & Dorcas, d. Sept. 27, 1761	2	49
Feebee, d. Lieut. Timothy & Han[n]ah, b. Feb. 14, 1714/15	1	14
Phebe, d. Timothy, Jr. & Mary, b. May 27, 1732	1	56
Phebe, d. Nathaniel & Elizabeth, b. Feb. 5, 1732	1	67
Phebe, m. John **SMITH**, Nov. 24, 1736	1	66
Phebe, m. John **PARKHURST**, Dec. 6, 1749	2	14
Phebe, d. Nathaniel, d. Apr. 13, 1751	2	20
Phebe, d. Ezekiel & Lois, b. Sept. 5, 1755	2	5
Phebe, d. Nathaniel, Jr. & Priscilla, b. Jan. 13, 1760	2	46
Phinehas, s. Thomas & Mary, b. Sept. 28, 1725	1	57
Phinehas, s. Ezekiel & Lois, b. Jan. 17, 1751	2	5
Pheenehas, s. Thomas & Mary, d. May 9, 1751	2	31
Phinehas, s. John & Zeviah, b. Jan. 15, 1759	2	33
Priscilla, d. John & Zeviah, b. Apr. 24, 1761	2	33
Ruth, d. Nathaniel & Elisabeth, b. Nov. 27, 1725	1	38
Ruth, d. Jedediah & Susan[n]ah, b. Aug. 23, 1768	2	62
Sarah, d. Ezekiel & Esther, b. Feb. 6, 1750	2	20
Sarah, m. Squire **SHEPHARD**, Dec. 26, 1758	2	45
Seth, of Locksport, N.Y., m. Ellen M. **EATON**, of Plainfield, Apr. 19, 1853, by Rev. Henry Robinson	3	78
Spaulding, s. John & Zeniah, b. Feb. 29, 1768 (Zeviah?)	2	66
Stephen, s. Thomas & Mary, b. Oct. 31, 1727	1	57
Stephen, s. Thomas & Mary, d. May 12, 1751	2	31
Stephen, s. Jabez & Susan[n]ah, b. Nov. 19, 1751	2	14
Stephen, s. John & Zeviah, b. June 2, 1765	2	33
Susan[n]ah, d. Thomas & Mary, b. May 19, 1730	1	1X
Su[s]annah, d. Thomas & Mary, b. May 19, 1730	1	57
Susannah, d. Thomas & Mary, d. May 9, 1751	2	31
Susan[n]ah, d. John & Zeviah, b. Nov. 3, 1751	2	24
Susannah, Jr., [d. Jedediah & Susannah], b. Mar. 29, 1783	2	92
Temperance, d. Ebenezer & Lydiah, b. July 23, 1736	1	65
Thomas, d. Jan. 18, 1762	2	33
Thomas, s. John & Zeviah, b. Apr. 8, 1763	2	33
Timothy, m. Lydia **SPALDING**, d. Joseph, May 27, 1696	1	3
Timothy, s. Timothy & Lydia, b. Oct. 7, 1698	1	3
Timothy, m. Hannah **BRADHURST**, d. Ralph & Hannah, bf Old Roxbury, Oct. 12, 1709	1	8

	Vol.	Page
PIERCE, PEIRCE, PEARCE, PARCE, (cont.)		
Timo[thy], Jr., m. Mary **WHEELER**, June 12, 1723	1	37
Timothy, s. Timothy, Jr. & Mary, b. May 22, 1734	1	62
Timothy, s. Ezekiel & Lois, b. Jan. 23, 1747	2	5
Timo[thy], Col., d. May 25, 1748, in the 74th y. of his age	2	1
Timothy, of Plainfield, m. Eunice **FISH**, of Stonington, Aug. 8, 1754	2	29
Timothy, s. Timothy & Eunice, b. Sept. 13, 1756	2	35
Timothy, m. Hannah **GILKEY**, Feb. 28, 1765	2	71
Willard, s. Nathaniel & Elizabeth, b. Mar. 6, 1743	2	39
Willard, s. Nathaniel, Jr. & Priscilla, b. Jan. 28, 1762	2	51
William, s. Jedediah & Susan[n]ah, b. Sept. 5, 1770	2	73
William, of Troy, N.Y., m. Lydia **STEVENS**, of Plainfield, Oct. 5, 1800	2	106
William, Jr., m. Emeline **HOPKINS**, b. of Foster, R.I., Mar. 19, 1848, by Rev. James Mather	3	54
-----, illeg. s. Maria, ae. 38, b. Dec. 10, 1850	4	31
PIKE, Nathan S., Dr., of Plainfield, m. Jane F. **PERKINS**, of Sterling, Apr. 28, 1853, by Peleg Peckham, Elder	3	78
PINK, Cleonna, m. Daniel **SPAULDING**, b. of Plainfield, Apr. 19, 1821, by Rev. Orin Fowler	2	133
PINKNODDLE, Robert, s. George & Genney, b. Dec. 10, 1775	2	88
PLACE, Amey, of Plainfield, m. Robert **DOUGLASS**, of Sterling, Feb. 4, 1827, by Nathaniel Cole, Elder	2	201
Christopher, of Foster, R.I., m. Mary E. **HYDE**, of Canterbury, Oct. 8, 1844, by James Smither, Elder	3	28
Jane F., cotton weaver, b. Norwich, res. Plainfield, d. July 11, 1850, ae. 17	4	64
Olive L., of Foster, m. Edward Henry **VALENTINE**, of Sterling, Sept. 2, 1843, by Peleg Peckham, Elder	3	20
Sarah A., of Foster, R.I., m. Russel[l] **VAUGHAN**, of Sterling, Apr. 22, 1849, by Peleg Peckham, Elder	3	58
PLIMPTON, Bette, d. Jeremiah & Elisabeth, b. Sept. 25, 1720	1	24
POLLARD, Oliver W., m. Ann E. **THURSTON**, b. of East Greenwich, R.I., Jan. 10, 1854, by Rev. Joseph P. Brown	3	82
PON, Agnis, m. David **BRUCE**, b. of Plainfield, Nov. 27, 1853, by Rev. William Turkington	3	81
POND, Lewis, of Clinton, N.Y., m. Harriet **ANGELL**, of Plainfield, June 3, 1821, by Orin Fowler, V.D.M.	2	133
POPPLE, Elisha, m. Lucinda **COLE**, b. of Plainfield, Mar. 28, 1842, by Peleg Peckham, Elder	3	14
George, m. Eunice **COLE**, b. of Plainfield, Aug. 2, 1846, by Rev. Chauncey Wilcox	3	38
George, s. Elisha, manufacturer, ae. 28, & Lucinda, ae. 30, b. July 7, 1848	4	24

	Vol.	Page

POPPLE, (cont.)
Perry, blacksmith, ae. 25, b. Killingly, res. Plainfield, m. Lydia **MAINE**, ae. 31, b. N. Stonington, Sept. 12, [18]47, b. Rev. Mather — 4 — 2
Perry, m. Lydia A. **MAINE**, b. of Plainfield, Sept. 12, 1847, by Rev. J. Mather — 3 — 45
Perry, blacksmith, ae. 25, b. N. Stonington, res. Plainfield, m. Lydia **MAINE**, ae. 32, b. Voluntown, res. Plainfield, Sept. 28, 1847, by Rev. Mathew — 4 — 1
Perry A., m. Sally M. **TAYLOR**, b. of Sterling, Nov. 15, 1847, by Peleg Peckham, Elder — 3 — 47

POTTER, Adaline W., m. James **FERNALD**, b. of Coventry, R.I., Dec. 3, 1843, by A. Dunning — 3 — 21
Caroline, m. Edward E. **HILL**, b. of Plainfield, May 19, 1845, by James Smither, Elder — 3 — 29
Charles H., s. Warren, manufacturer, ae. 28, & Harriet, ae. 28, b. Nov. 1, 1850 — 4 — 31
Cindarilla, m. Charles M. **MAREDOCK**, b. of Plainfield, Oct. 26, 1835, by Rev. Ziba Loveland, Central Village — 2 — 223
Cullen L., of Sterling, m. Susan A. **GREEN**, of Coventry, R.I., Feb. 28, 1848, by Peleg Peckham, Elder — 3 — 52
Delia L., of Plainfield, m. Henry **DOUGLASS**, of Sterling, Oct. 16, 1832, by Rev. Benjamin Paine — 2 — 216
Elipha, of Plainfield, m. Nathan **STONE**, of Sterling, Nov. 24, 1839, by Rev. Hezekiah Thatcher — 2 — 252
Elipha, of Plainfield, m. Nathan **STONE**, of Sterling, Nov. 24, 1839, by Rev. Hezekiah Thacher — 3 — 2
Elisha L., of Griswold, m. Mariah **SABIN**, of Plainfield, Aug. 30, 1853, by Rev. Henry Robinson — 3 — 80
Eugene H., see under Eugene H. **MORSE** — 4 — 23
Eunice A., of Plainfield, m. William H. **ROBINSON**, of Thompson, May 2, 1841, by Rev. Tubal Wakefield — 3 — 9
Freelove M., m. Jeremiah **HILL**, Feb. 14, 1848, by Rev. Isaac C. Day — 3 — 56
Gilbert, m. Mary Ann **HUNTINGTON**, b. of Sterling, Nov. 27, 1834, by Peleg Peckham, Elder — 2 — 220
Hannah, m. Daniel **MURDOCK**, b. of Plainfield, Jan. 2, 1831, by Benjamin R. Allen, Elder — 2 — 212
Hyram W., of Scituate, R.I., m. Matilda **BURGESS**, May 19, 1828, by Rev. Orin Fowler — 2 — 205
Ichabod, m. Susan **FAREMAN**, b. of Plainfield, Jan. 12, 1823, by Rev. Nathaniel Cole — 2 — 190
Isabel R., m. Septimus **HERRECK**, b. of Plainfield, Oct. 12, 1831, by Peleg Peckham, Elder — 2 — 214
James F., laborer, ae. 25, res. Killingly, m. Caroline **PRINCE**, ae. 23, Apr. 11, [18]48, by Rev. Peleg Peckham — 4 — 1

POTTER, (cont.)

	Vol.	Page
Jason J., m. Frances P. **YOUNG**, Oct. 1, 1837, by Peleg Peckham, Elder	2	233
Jonathan Nicholas, of Sterling, m. Polly **PRINCE**, of Plainfield, Nov. 20, 1840, by Rev. Hezekiah Thatcher	3	7
Julia E., b. Coventry, R.I., res. Plainfield, d. May 25, 1848, ae. 1	4	61
Levina E., of Scituate, R.I., m. Martin **PARKER**, of Killingly, Nov. 27, 1836, by Chester Tilden	2	229
Lucy Ann, of Plainfield, m. Joseph B. **PARKS**, of Norwich, May 14, 1848, by Peleg Peckham, Elder	3	51
Mary Ann, of Plainfield, m. Thomas **TYLER**, of Manchester, Sept. 30, 1827, by Orin Fowler, V.D.M.	2	203
Mary Ann, m. William **MURDOCK**, b. of Plainfield, Nov. 2, 1828, by Peleg Peckham, Elder	2	207
Mesheck, m. Ricksea **PRAY**, Apr. 22, 1821, by Rev. Nathaniel Cole	2	134
Olive, of Sterling, m. Rufus **COLLINS**, of Columbia, Dec. 19, 1830, by Peleg Peckham, Elder	2	212
Phebe A., d. William H., ae. 31, manufacturer, & Betsey D., ae. 31, b. Nov. 18, 1850	4	31
Richmond L., harness maker, ae. 24, b. Coventry, R.I., res. Plainfield, m. Mary E. **CLARK**, ae. 18, b. Coventry, R.I., May 1, 1848, by James Thomas	4	1
Sally, m. Esek **JORDAN**, Mar. 27, 1842, by Rev. John Read	3	14
Sally Ann, ae. 20, m. Joseph B. **PARK**, carpenter, ae. 23, b. Milltown, res. Sterling, May 14, [18]48, by Rev. Peleg Peckham	4	1
Sarah, of Plainfield, m. Edmund **HUMES**, of Griswold, July 10, 1836, by Chester Tilden	2	227
Sarah M., m. William J. **HIDE**, b. of Plainfield, Nov. 14, 1853, by Rev. Joseph P. Brown	3	81
William, of Norwich, m. Martha M. **SHEPARD**, of Plainfield, Sept. 14, 1851, by Rev. Henry Robinson	3	71
William H., m. Betsey **PARKIS**, Nov. 4, 1839, by Rev. Hezekiah Thatcher	2	252
William H., m. Betsey **PARKIS**, b. of Plainfield, Nov. 4, 1839, by Rev. Hezekiah Thacher	3	2
William J., m. Mary A. **LYON**, b. of Plainfield, Jan. 9, 1850, by Rev. W. Emerson	3	64
William J., mule spinner, ae. 24, of Plainfield, m. Mary A. **LYON**, cotton weaver, ae. 23, b. Foster, R.I., res. Plainfield, June 9, 1850, by Rev. Warren Emerson	4	6
Wilson, m. Cynthia **LEONARD**, b. of Plainfield, Apr. 4, 1827, by Orin Fowler, V.D.M.	2	202
Zuriel, of Cranston, R.I., m. Rhoby M. **AMES**, of Plain-		

	Vol.	Page
POTTER, (cont.)		
field, Feb. 2, 1832, by Rev. Dennis Platt	2	215
-----, d. Mesheck, miller, ae. 60, & Alithea, ae. 34, b. July 4, 1849	4	26
-----, s. Richmond L., grocer, ae. 25, & Mary C., ae. 20, b. July 7, 1850	4	30
POWEL, Felix, m. Abegel **BUTTON**, d. Matthias, Apr. [ ], 1724	1	30
William, s. Felix & Abigall, b. Nov. 20, 1724; d. Nov. 25, 1724	1	31
PRATT, Harriet, m. Henry A. **COLVIN**, b. of Smithfield, R.I., Sept. 21, 1846, by Mowry Burgess, J.P.	3	42
Mary, m. Edward **EVENS**, Dec. 3, 1751	2	16
T. Willis, of Norwich, m. Sarah E. **BRADFORD**, of Plainfield, June 4, 1840, by Rev. Samuel Rockwell	3	6
PRAY, Jason, m. Rebecca **ANDREW**, b. of Plainfield, Feb. 10, 1822, by John Dunlap, J.P.	2	187
Jason, m. Sophia Maria Fanning **WESTCOTT**, b. of Plainfield, July 27, 1828, by Rev. Orin Fowler	2	206
Nancy, m. Israel **ANGELL**, b. of Plainfield, Oct. 14, [1826], by Elder George W. Appleton, Sterling	2	200
Ricksea, m. Mesheck **POTTER**, Apr. 22, 1821, by Rev. Nathaniel Cole	2	134
PRENTICE, PRINTICE, Abby, of Griswold, m. Simeon **JONES**, of Plainfield, Apr. 15, 1829, by Rev. Orin Fowler	2	209
A. Leroy, of Lisbon, m. Eunice W. **SPAULDING**, of Plainfield, June 9, 1844, by Rev. D. Dorchester	3	24
Charles, b. Killingly, res. Plainfield, d. July 16, [18]48, ae. 16	4	61
David, m. Freelove Ann **STANTON**, Nov. 18, 1824, by Rev. John Hyde, Preston	2	196
Dorothy, m. Isaac **SHEPHARD**, Nov. 24, 1743	2	33
Ephraim, of Preston, m. Mary **DEAN**, of Plainfield, Feb. 9, 1797	2	104
Ephraim, m. Rachel **WILSON**, b. of Plainfield, June 30, 1845, by Peleg Peckham, Elder	3	31
Susan, m. John **MONTGOMERY**, b. of Plainfield, Mar. 24, 1845, by Peleg Peckham, Elder	3	27
Thomas J., of Gardner, Mass., m. Matilda **BURDICK**, of Plainfield, Jan. 19, 1852, by Rev. Henry Robinson	3	73
PRESTON, Aaron, of Lisbon, m. Lydia **DOW**, of Plainfield, Dec. 15, 1806, by William Dixon, J.P.	2	115
Elizabeth, d. Aaron & Lydia, b. Dec. 26, 1812	2	123
Joseph, s. Aaron & Lydia, b. June 3, 1810	2	118
Joseph, m. Nancy **FRY**, b. of Plainfield, Mar. 10, 1833, by Rev. Samuel Rockwell	2	216
Mary, d. Aaron & Lydia, b. Mar. 24, 1818	2	131
Mary, m. Archibald D. **MEDBERY**, b. of Plainfield, Oct.		

	Vol.	Page
PRESTON, (cont.)		
14, 1839, by Rev. Samuel Rockwell	2	248
Mary, m. Archibald D. **MEDBERY**, b. of Plainfield, Oct. 14, 1839, by Rev. Samuel Rockwell	3	1
Prudence, m. Thomas **DOW**, Jan. 8, 1839, by Rev. Charles S. Weaver, of Voluntown	2	239
Rebecca, d. Aaron & Lydia, b. Mar. 17, 1816	2	129
Rebecca, d. Aaron & Lydia, b. Mary 17, 1816	2	131
PRINCE, Aparna, b. Lebanon, Ct., res. Plainfield, d. Mar. 3, [18]47, ae. 71	4	62
Caroline, ae. 23, m. James F. **POTTER**, laborer, ae. 25, res. Killingly, Apr. 11, [18]48, by Rev. Peleg Peckham	4	1
Polly, of Plainfield, m. Jonathan Nicholas **POTTER**, of Sterling, Nov. 20, 1840, by Rev. Hezekiah Thatcher	3	7
PRIOR, Anna, d. John & Ruth, b. Dec. 24, 1805	2	129
Augustus, m. Olive B. **ROBINSON**, b. of Plainfield, Apr. 19, 1824, by Orin Fowler, V.D.M.	2	194
Benjamin, m. Rachel **HUTCHENS**, Nov. 10, 1771	2	75
Edward M., m. Emily **THURSTON**, b. of Plainfield, Oct. 13, 1847, by Rev. James Mather	3	46
Erastus L., m. Mary E. **KINNIE**, b. of Plainfield, Mar. 7, 1836, by Peleg Peckham, Elder	2	225
Erastus L., m. Sarah **BURGESS**, Feb. 6, 1841, by Rev. John Read	3	13
Eunice, d. Benjamin & Rachel, b. May 24, 1774	2	78
Fanny, d. John & Ruth, b. Oct. 24, 1807	2	129
Frederick W., s. Edward M., farmer, ae. 26, & Emily, ae. 23, b. July 1, 1849	4	25
Henry, s. John & Ruth, b. Aug. 7, 1815	2	129
Henry, [s. John & Ruth], d. Jan. 18, 1816	2	130
Joseph, Jr., s. John & Ruth, b. Jan. 11, 1811	2	129
Lucy, m. Samuel K. **SPAULDING**, May 1, 1816	2	172
Lucy, m. Arnold K. **FOSTER**, b. of Plainfield, [probably Aug.] 29, 1842, by Rev. A.B. Wheeler	3	17
Olive, d. Benjamin & Rachel, b. Nov. 1, 1777	2	82
Olive, d. John & Ruth, b. Feb. 10, 1813	2	129
Olive, of Plainfield, m. James **DOUGLASS**, of Lebanon, Apr. 19, 1834, by Peleg Peckham, Elder	2	218
Rachel, w. John **MEDBERY**, b. Mar. 18, 1785	3	84
Rachel, m. John **MEDBERY**, June 24, 1810. Certified from family record	3	83
William, s. John & Ruth, b. Jan. 4, 1817	2	130
William J., s. Erastus L., laborer, b. Jan. [ ], 1851	4	31
William S., m. Susan M. **JONES**, Apr. 27, 1841, by Rev. George J. Tillotson	3	10

	Vol.	Page
PROFIT, John, of Colchester, m. Elizabeth **LATHROP**, of Norwich, Oct. 25, 1841, by John Read, Elder	3	12
PULLMAN, Nathaniel, of West Greenwich, R.I., m. Rhody **SWEET**, of Plainfield, Jan. 31, 1822, by Rev. Nathaniel Cole	2	187
RAGE, Daniel, s. Mat[t]hew & Marg[a]ret, b. Feb. 4, 1730/31	1	92
RANDALL, Charles, s. William, dress tender, & Caroline, b. Dec. 12, 1847	4	23
Flavell, laborer, ae. 22, b. Sterling, res. R.I., m. Caroline **BURDICK**, cotton operator, ae. 17, b. Sterling, res. R.I., Apr. [1849?]	4	6
Frances, m. Peleg **GROVES**, Oct. 9, 1842, by Rev. John Read, Thompson	3	16
Levi, m. Phebe Ann **WESTCOTT**, b. of Plainfield, Nov. 25, 1830, by Benj[ami]n R. Allen, Elder	2	212
Mary S., of Foster, R.I., m. George **WASHINGTON**, of Providence, Nov. 27, 1845, by Peleg Peckham, Elder	3	34
Stephen C., of Providence, R.I., m. Deborah **JORDAN**, of Coventry, R.I., Aug. 30, 1847, by Rev. James Mather	3	45
William H., m. Caroline **HARRIS**, b. of Sterling, Oct. 26, 1845, by Peleg Peckham, Elder	3	32
RATHBURN, Anna, m. Joseph **NICHOLS**, Jan. 13, 1757	2	38
Hannah L., formerly of Plainfield, m. Arnold **ROUNDS**, Jan. 5, 1846, by Peleg Peckham, Elder	3	34
RAY, Dinah, d. William & Mary, b. Feb. 14, 1747	2	8
James, s. William & Mary, b. May 27, 1746	2	8
James E., s. Moses, cotton dresser tender, ae. 34, & Orpha, ae. 34, b. Apr. 3, 1850	4	29
Moses, m. Opha **SHERMAN**, b. of Plainfield, Nov. 25, 1839, by Rev. Hezekiah Thacher	3	3
William, d. June 20, 1750	2	13
William, s. William & Mary, b. Jan. 14, 1750/51	2	13
RAYMAN, William, of Canterbury, m. Electa C. **MONTGOMERY**, May 1, 1844, by Peleg Peckham, Elder	3	23
RAYMENT, Jonathan, s. John & Sarah, b. Sept. 25, 1772	2	77
Mary, m. John **CRARY**, May 20, 1750	2	23
READ, REED, Almira M., m. Daniel S. **KENYON**, b. of Plainfield, Dec. 19, 1842, by Peleg Peckham, Elder	3	18
Horace, m. Mary R. **SWEET**, b. of Warwick, R.I., Sept. 28, 1847, by Rev. J. Mather	3	46
Jemima, of Norwich, m. John **HALL**, of Plainfield, June 6, 1749, by Rev. Daniel Kirtland, Newent, Norwich	2	7
Sarah, m. Hiram **BENNET**, b. of Plainfield, Feb. 14, 1836, by Rev. Samuel Rockwell	2	225
REYNOLDS, Betsey M., of Sterling, m. John W. **STONE**, of West Greenwich, Nov. 13, 1843, by Peleg Peckham, Elder	3	21
David, of Coventry, R.I., m. Prudence **SPAULDING**, b.		

	Vol.	Page
REYNOLDS, (cont.)		
residing in Plainfield, Oct. 19, 1828, by Peleg Peckham, Elder	2	207
Elisha, m. Rachel **HEWLET**, July 27, 1769	2	75
Ezekiel, m. Albina **WEAVER**, b. of Warwick, R.I., Dec. 16, 1846, by Rev. J. Mather	3	42
Hannah, m. Sprague **KENYON**, b. of Richmond, R.I., Sept. 8, 1850, by Rev. Joseph P. Brown	3	65
Hannah A., m. George **GRIFFIS**, Jr., b. of Sterling, Oct. 13, 1850, by Peleg Peckham, Elder	3	66
John, s. Elisha & Rachel, b. Mar. 29, 1774	2	79
Patience, d. Elisha & Rachel, b. Feb. 20, 1770	2	75
Susanna, d. Elisha & Rachel, b. July 24, 1771	2	75
RHODES, Sophia, m. Parker H. **FULLER**, b. of Sterling, July 25, 1842, by Peleg Peckham, Elder	3	16
Thomas, farmer, ae. 30, b. Sterling, res. Vermont, m. Emeline **SWEET**, ae. 23, Mar. 27, [18]48, by Rev. Frederick Charlton	4	2
Thomas D., m. Emeline **FAR[R]EL**, b. of Plainfield, Apr. 10, 1848, by Rev. Frederic Charlton	3	55
RICHARDSON, RICHERDSON, RICHESON, Elizabeth, d. Hannah, b. Aug. 19, 1726	1	56
Kesiah, d. Hannah, b. June 10, 1731	1	56
Keziah, m. Thomas **HOARD**, Oct. 27, 1752	2	36
Mary, m. Stephen **ROODE**, Dec. 2, 1755	2	32
Richard, m. Han[n]ah **PARK**, d. William, Feb. 18, 1721/2	1	24
Thomas, s. Hannah, b. Sept. 6, 1728	1	56
RICHFORD, Silas, of Providence, R.I., m. Julian **LESTER**, of Plainfield, [1829], by Rev. Orin Fowler	2	209
RICHMOND, Denison, m. [ ] **GRAY**, b. of Plainfield, June 12, 1853, by Rev. Alfred Gates	3	79
RIGBE*, Suesanna, d. Jonathan & Hannah, d. May 8, 1729, in the 5th y. of her age (*Should be "**RIGHT**". L.B.B.)	1	50
RIGHT, [see under **WRIGHT**]		
RILEY, Daniel, d. Aug. 22, 1849, ae. 11 m.	4	64
Emily, Mrs., housekeeper, b. Ireland, res. Plainfield, d. [1847], ae. 25	4	61
Mary A., d. Philip, laborer in woolen mill, & Mary, b. Nov. 3, 1850	4	32
RISLEY, Timothy, of Manchester, m. Eliza A. **WEAVER**, of Plainfield, May 2, 1853, by Rev. William Turkington	3	78
RITCHY, David, of Saratoga, N.Y., m. Elizabeth **STEWARD**, of Plainfield, July 18, 1852, by Rev. Joseph P. Brown	3	75
ROANA, Paulina, m. Joseph **TENNANT**, b. of Plainfield, Dec. 7, 1835, by Rev. Samuel Rockwell	2	223
ROBERTS, Lydia, of Coventry, R.I., m. George T. **HILL**, of Plainfield, Sept. 19, 1847, by Rev. Fred[eri]c Charlton	3	49

	Vol.	Page

ROBERTS, (cont.)
Phillip Orton, m. Martha B. **PHILLIPS**, Dec. 24, 1843,
   by Rev. W. Clark, Canterbury — 3 — 21
ROBINSON, Abby A., m. Jared N. **WILBOUR**, b. of Sterling,
   May 26, 1850, by Peleg Peckham, Elder — 3 — 64
Ann Adelia, twin with William Erasmus, d. Levi &
   Olive, b. July 31, 1809 — 2 — 117
Charles Barstow, s. Levi & Olive, b. Sept. 1, 1798 — 2 — 103
Charles Barstow, s. Levi & Olive, d. May 25, 1820, at
   Havannah, in the 22nd y. of his age — 2 — 170
Deborah, m. Jacob **SHEPHARD**, Nov. 3, 1762 — 2 — 56
Deliverance, s. Ebenezer & Mary, b. May 26, 1753; d.
   Nov. 9, 1754 — 2 — 29
Ebenezer, m. Mary **BENNET**, Nov. 14, 1749 — 2 — 12
Ebenezer, s. Levi & Olive, b. June 25, 1817 — 2 — 170
Emmeline Eliza, d. Levi & Olive, b. Aug. 30, 1805, at
   Stonington — 2 — 117
Emeline Eliza, of Plainfield, m. Noah **DAVIS**, of Nor-
   wich, Nov. 25, 1833, by Rev. Samuel Rockwell — 2 — 218
Esther, m. Hiram **CLEVELAND**, b. of Plainfield, Sept. 12,
   1824, by Orin Fowler, Minister — 2 — 195
Harvey, s. William & Anne, b. Nov. 10, 1769 — 2 — 63
Hope Grafton, of Plainfield, m. Seabury **DART**, of Lyme,
   June 19, 1826, by Orin Fowler, V.D.M. — 2 — 199
James, s. Levi & Olive, b. Nov. 22, 1811 — 2 — 170
Josiah, s. Ebenezer & Mary, b. Nov. 10, 1750 — 2 — 12
Levi, s. William & Anne, b. Nov. 22, 1767 — 2 — 63
Levi, of Plainfield, m. Olive **BARSTOW**, of Canterbury,
   Sept. 25, 1797 — 2 — 103
Levi, Jr., s. Levi & Olive, b. Mar. 14, 1819 — 2 — 170
Margaret E., of Plainfield, m. Peter Wallace **GALLANDET**,
   of West Springfield, Mass., June 20, 1849, by Rev.
   Henry Robinson — 3 — 57
Marg[a]ret Elizabeth, ae. 19, m. Peter Wallace
   GALLENEDETT, mechanic, ae. 23, b. Hartford, res.
   W. Springfield, June 20, 1849, by Rev. H. Robinson — 4 — 3
Mary C., of Plainfield, m. Ebenezer D. **BROCKWAY**, of
   Lyme, July 14, 1840, by Rev. Samuel Rockwell — 3 — 6
Mary Cleveland, d. Levi & Olive, b. Feb. 14, 1814 — 2 — 170
Mary E., of Sterling, m. Jared W. **BURGESS**, of Plain-
   field, Oct. 13, 1852, by Peleg Peckham, Elder — 3 — 76
Moses Bradford, s. Levi & Olive, d. Aug. 26, 1809 — 2 — 117
Olive B., m. Augustus **PRIOR**, b. of Plainfield, Apr. 19,
   1824, by Orin Fowler, V.D.M. — 2 — 194
Ruth, of Plainfield, m. Lemuel **HAYWARD**, of Pomfret,
   Jan. 30, 1826, by Orin Fowler, V.D.M. — 2 — 198
Sarah C., b. Killingly, res. Plainfield, d. June 2,
   1848, ae. 6 — 4 — 61

	Vol.	Page
ROBINSON, (cont.)		
William, m. Anna **BLAKE**, May 13, 1762	2	60
William, s. Will[ia]m & Anna, b. Oct. 25, 1764	2	60
William had negro Dinah who d. May 5, 1766	2	54
William Erasmus, twin with Ann Adelia, s. Levi & Olive, b. July 31, 1809	2	117
William H., of Thompson, m. Eunice A. **POTTER**, of Plainfield, May 2, 1841, by Rev. Tubal Wakefield	3	9
ROBSON, Elisabeth, d. Joseph & Martha Walch, b. Aug. 26, 1730	1	54
ROCKWELL, Samuel, m. Elizabeth **EATON**, b. of Plainfield, May 5, 1840, by William Wight, of Jewett City, Griswold	3	4
RODMAN, Hazard, m. Jane **ANDREWS**, b. of Plainfield, Apr. 20, 1824, by Rev. Nathaniel Cole	2	194
ROGERS, Caleb B., of Montville, m. Harriet S. **WEBB**, of Plainfield, May 10, 1830, by Benjamin R. Allen, Elder	2	211
Elizabeth, m. Mat[t]hew **PARTRICK**, Nov. 20, 1726	1	49
Hannah, m. Amhurst **HOPKINS**, b. of Warwick, R.I., Dec. 19, 1847, by Rev. J. Mather	3	47
ROLINS, Gilbert C., m. Lucy A. **TRIPP**, b. of Plainfield, Nov. 18, 1838, by Rev. Samuel Rockwell	2	237
ROOD, [see under **RUDE**]		
ROONEY, John, farmer, b. Ireland, res. Plainfield, d. Oct. 4, 1849, ae. 20	4	63
ROOT, Jared M., of Binghampton, N.Y., m. Susan P. **GLEZEN**, of Plainfield, Oct. 27, 1834, by Rev. Otis C. Whiton, of Canterbury	2	221
ROSS, Frances, of Griswold, m. Thomas J. **BARNEY**, of Plainfield, Mar. 28, 1824, by Orin Fowler, V.D.M.	2	194
George J., of Franklin, m. Sarah E. **FENNER**, of Sterling, Oct. 18, 1840, by Peleg Peckham, Elder	3	7
ROTH, Albert, of Norwich, m. E. **WOOD**, of Plainfield, Apr. 19, 1852, by Rev. Joseph P. Brown	3	74
ROUNDS, ROUND, Alfred, of Foster, m. Lucinda **SMITH**, of Plainfield, July 2, 1843, by Peleg Peckham, Elder	3	19
Arnold, m. Hannah L. **RATHBURN**, formerly of Plainfield, Jan. 5, 1846, by Peleg Peckham, Elder	3	34
Arnold, m. Eliza E. **LEWIS**, b. of Sterling, Mar. 9, 1851, by Peleg Peckham, Elder	3	69
Asenath, m. George B. **HYDE**, b. of Sterling, July 2, 1843, by Peleg Peckham, Elder	3	19
Hannah, b. Voluntown, res. Plainfield, d. May 25, 1850, ae. 23	4	64
Sally M., m. Theodore P. **KENNEDY**, b. of Foster, Feb. 8, 1846, by Peleg Peckham, Elder	3	36

	Vol.	Page
ROUSE, Delilah, m. Albert **WELLS**, b. of Plainfield, Jan. 28, 1852, by Rev. Joseph P. Brown	3	74
Gardiner, m. Mary S. **HILL**, b. of Plainfield, Jan. 21, 1831, by Benjamin R. Allen, Elder	2	213
Gardiner, m. Sophia **INGALS**, b. of Plainfield, May 5, 1843, by Rev. A.B. Wheeler	3	20
Louisa, m. Calvin **HALL**, b. of Plainfield, Dec. 30, 1827, by Orin Fowler, V.D.M.	2	204
Wanton, m. Eliza **GARDINER**, Oct. 7, 1839, by Charles S. Weaver, Elder	2	249
Wanton, m. Eliza **GARDINER**, b. of Plainfield, Oct. 7, 1839, by Charles S. Weaver, Elder	3	2
ROWLAND, Alethina Gratia, d. Rev. David & Mary, b. Sept. 15, 1755	2	34
David, Rev., m. Mary **SPAULDING**, Feb. 20, 1754	2	29
Frederick Will[ia]m, [s. Rev. David & Mary], b. May 26, 1761	2	43
Sherman, [s. Rev. David & Mary], b. July 6, 1759	2	43
Thea, d. Rev. David & Mary, b. July 19, 1757	2	43
RUDE, ROOD, ROODE, Abigail, d. Benjamin & Mary, b. Apr. 3, 1695	1	2
Isaac, s. Stephen & Mary, b. Apr. 8, 1754	2	28
Isaac, s. Stephen & Mary, d. Oct. 24, 1754	2	28
Isaac, s. Stephen & Mary, b. May 30, 1756	2	36
Jesse, m. Pamalie M. **BRAINARD**, b. of Killingly, [probably Sept.] 21, 1842, by Rev. A.B. Wheeler	3	17
Joanna, d. Stephen & Mary, b. July 9, 1749	2	20
Joanna, d. Stephen & Mary, d. Oct. 1, 1754	2	28
Job, s. Stephen & Elizabeth, b. Feb. 13, 1776	2	98
Lydia, of Killingly, m. Stanton **FITCH**, of Norwich, Oct. 15, 1844, by James Smither, Elder	3	28
Mary, d. Benjamin & Mary, b. July 7, 1698	1	2
Mary, d. Stephen & Mary, d. Oct. 16, 1754	2	28
Mary, w. Stephen, d. Nov. 11, 1754	2	28
Solomon, m. Abby S. **BENNETT**, b. of Plainfield, Aug. 6, 1854, by Rev. Alfred Gates	3	85
Solomon, Jr., m. Abby B. **BENNETT**, b. of Plainfield, Aug. 6, 1854, by Rev. Alfred Gates	3	87
Stephen, s. Steven & Mary, b. Apr. 25, 1746	1	2X
Stephen, m. Mary **RICHARDSON**, Dec. 2, 1755	2	32
Stephen, s. Stephen & Elizabeth, b. June 20, 1783	2	89
Susan F., of Plainfield, m. Frank **HAWKINS**, saloon keeper, of Plainfield, July 4, 1858*, in Foster, R.I., by Mason B. Hopkins (*1848?)	4	4
Susan F., m. Frank **HAWKINS**, b. of Plainfield, July 4, 1858, by Rev. Mason B. Hopkins	3	88
Susannah, m. Nathan **HARRIS**, July 5, 1749	2	14
RUMBALL, Elizabeth, m. Jabez **ALLYN**, Dec. 29, 1736	1	68

	Vol.	Page
RUSSELL, RUSSEL, RUSEL, Asa, m. Lydia **LOVEGROVE**, b. of Plainfield, Jan. 1, 1823, by Orin Fowler, Minister	2	189
Azubah, d. Josiah & Marcy, b. Mar. 10, 1741, in Lexington, Mass. Bay	2	19
Delight, d. Josiah & Marcy, b. Apr. 4, 1750	2	19
Este, d. Josiah & Marcy, b. Oct. 10, 1752	2	19
Hannah, d. Josiah & Marcy, b. July 25, 1745, in Lexington, Mass. Bay	2	19
Hannah, m. George **BACK**, Dec. 17, 1761	2	63
Job, of Providence, R.I., m. Martha **SIMMONS**, of Plainfield, Mar. 9, 1823, by John Dunlap, J.P.	2	191
John, m. Thankful **AVERY**, b. of Killingly, Jan. 12, 1844, by James Smither, Elder	3	28
Josiah, s. Josiah & Marcy, b. Mar. 19, 1735, in Westborough, Mass. Bay	2	19
Josiah, m. Lidya **KINGSBURY**, Mar. 8, 1758	2	39
Josiah, s. Josiah & Lidya, b. Mar. 19, 1759	2	39
Lucy, d. Josiah & Marcy, b. Aug. 10, 1743, in Lexington, Mass. Bay	2	19
Marcy, d. Josiah & Marcy, b. Mar. 25, 1748, in Lexington, Mass. Bay	2	19
Mary, d. Josiah & Marcy, b. May 12, 1737, in Westborough, Mass. Bay	2	19
Thomas, s. Josiah & Marcy, b. Mar. 19, 1739, in Lexington, Mass. Bay	2	19
RYEN, Walter, late of Great Britain, m. Betsey **SIMMONS**, of Plainfield, Sept. 22, 1822, by Orin Fowler, V.D.M.	2	188
SABIN, Deborah, d. Sept. 8, 1850, ae. 89	4	64
Frances Maria, d. Henry & Harriet, b. Aug. 19, 1825; d. Aug. 19, 1825	3	3
Harriet, w. Henry, d. Nov. 4, 1825	3	3
Harriet Caroline, d. Henry & Harriet, d. Oct. 5, 1843	3	21
Henry, m. Esther **EATON**, b. of Plainfield, Feb. 20, 1828, by Rev. Orin Fowler	2	205
Louisa L., ae. 33, b. Sterling, Ct., res. Sutton, m. Marius M. **HOVEY**, farmer, ae. 33, b. Sutton, Mass., res. Sutton, June 8, 1851, by H. Robinson	4	7
Louisa L., of Plainfield, m. Marvious M. **HOVEY**, of Sutton, Mass., June 18, 1851, by Rev. Henry Robinson	3	70
Maria, d. Henry & Esther, b. Feb. 18, 1830	3	3
Mariah, of Plainfield, m. Elisha L. **POTTER**, of Griswold, Aug. 30, 1853, by Rev. Henry Robinson	3	80
Martha, m. Cyril **SPAULDING**, Feb. 14, 1809	2	173
Mary Ann, of Plainfield, m. Hiram A. **TRACY**, of Sutton, Mass., June 24, 1835, by Rev. Samuel Rockwell	2	221
Sylvester, s. Nathaniel & Deborah, b. Jan. 29, 1787	2	110

PLAINFIELD VITAL RECORDS 231

	Vol.	Page
SABIN, (cont.)		
We[a]lthy Welh(?), d. Henry & Harriet, b. Oct. 14, 1821	3	3
SAFFORD, Ephraim, m. Rosella **BOOMAN**, b. of Canterbury, Dec. 19, 1839, by Rev. Tubal Wakefield	3	3
SAILS, [see under **SAYLES**]		
SALISBURY, SALSBURY, Jonathan, m. Sarah Ann **BETTY**, b. of Scituate, R.I., Sept. 24, 1854, by Benjamin Bacon, J.P.	3	86
Mason, of R.I., m. Eliza **FRANKLIN**, of Plainfield, Sept. 19, 1824, by J. Gordon, J.P.	2	195
Wheeton, m. Emily **MARTIN**, b. of Killingly, Dec. 9, 1844, by James Smither, Elder	3	29
SAMPSON, SAMSON, Betsey, d. James & Mary Ann, b. June 6, 1813	2	127
Elinder, d. James & Mary, b. Apr. 2, 1820	2	173
James Glane, s. James & Mary Ann, b. May 21, 1815	2	127
Squire, s. James & Maryann, b. Dec. 18, 1817	2	131
SANDS, George F., of Springfield, Mass., m. Ellen S. **PHILLIPS**, of Plainfield, Apr. 8, 1849, by Rev. Joseph P. Brown	3	57
SANFORD, Ephraim, m. Rachel **STEVENS**, b. of Plainfield, Apr. 1, 1838, by William Dyer, J.P.	2	234
SANGER, Ebenezer, of Brooklyn, m. Eunice **HUTCHINS**, of Plainfield, June 2, 1824, by Rev. Thomas J. Mordock, Canterbury	2	194
Elizabeth, m. John **SPAULDING**, Jan. 22, 1744	2	30
Lewis Cass, s. Luther, farmer, ae. 30, & Harriet F., ae. 28, b. Dec. 29, 1847	4	22
Sarah A., d. Luther, farmer, of Brooklyn, Ct., & Harriet, of Griswold, Ct., b. Apr. 21, 1850	4	29
SATTERLEE, SATERLY, SATTERLY, Anne, d. Benedick & Elizabeth, b. Jan. 20, 1747/8	2	4
Belle, d. Benedick & Rachel, b. June 1, 1762	2	55
Benedick, m. Elizabeth **COERY**, Jan. 16, 1738/9	2	4
Benedick, Lieut., m. Rachel **PARKS**, May 16, 1758	2	39
Bette, d. Benedick & Rachel, b. June 1, 1762	2	49
Daniel, s. Benedick & Rachel, b. Feb. 19, 1771	2	72
Elias, s. Benedick & Rachel, b. June 11, 1768	2	55
Elisha, s. Benedick & Rachel, b. May 12, 1760	2	44
Elisha, s. Benedick & Rachel, b. May 12, 1760	2	55
John, s. Benedick & Elizabeth, b. May 10, 1742	2	4
John, s. Lieut. Benedick & Rachel, b. Oct. 28, 1758	2	39
Nathaniel, s. Benedick & Elizabeth, b. Mar. 4, 1746	2	4
Prudence, d. Benedick & Elizabeth, b. July 28, 1739	2	4
Rachel, d. Benedick & Rachel, b. May 17, 1764	2	55
Samuel, s. Benedick & Elizabeth, b. Mar. 2, 1744	2	4
Sibbel, d. Nathaniel & Deborah, b. Oct. 2, 1769	2	69

	Vol.	Page

SATTERLEE, SATERLY, SATTERLY, (cont.)
    William, s. Benedick & Elizabeth, b. Jan. 10, 1740 — 2, 4

SAUNDERS, James, wheelwright, ae. 23, b. Voluntown, res. Griswold, m. Mary A. **MONTGOMERY**, ae. 18, b. Sterling, res. Plainfield, Oct. 6, 1849, by Rev. Joseph P. Brown — 4, 6

    James P., of Griswold, m. Mary A. **MONTGOMERY**, of Plainfield, Oct. 7, 1849, by Rev. Joseph P. Brown — 3, 60

SAYLES, SAILS, Clarrissa, b. Sterling, res. Plainfield, d. Sept. 3, 1850, ae. 58 — 4, 65

    Henry M., of Sterling, m. Lucinda **FRANKLIN**, of Plainfield, June 14, 1846, by Peleg Peckham, Elder — 3, 38

    Rebecca Jane, m. Joseph T. **BARBER**, b. of Plainfield, Nov. 19, 1854, by Rev. Joseph P. Brown — 3, 87

SCOTT, Charles P., s. Wanton & Lois, b. Jan. 20, 1818 — 2, 172

    George A., s. Wanton & Lois, b. Mar. 5, 1820 — 2, 172

    Hannah A., of Coventry, R.I., m. Ambrose S. **NICHOLS**, of West Greenwich, R.I., Oct. 3, 1847, by Rev. Ja[me]s Mather — 3, 46

    John C., s. Wanton & Lois, b. June 3, 1816 — 2, 172

    Sophia, of Coventry, R.I., m. Nathan **BURGES[S]**, of Plainfield, Sept. 19, 1824, by John Dunlap, J.P. — 2, 196

    Susan F., m. Thomas **CONSTANTINE**, b. of Plainfield, Dec. 24, 1854, by Rev. P.S. Mather — 3, 88

    Wanton of Worcester, Mass., m. Mary **WATTS**, of Plainfield, Aug. 29, 1836, by Chester Tilden — 2, 227

    William A., s. Wanton & Lois, b. July 18, 1814 — 2, 172

SCRANTON, Almira, of Plainfield, m. Sylvester C. **COON**, of Canterbury, Sept. 10, 1849, by Rev. Joseph P. Brown — 3, 60

    Almira, ae. 18 m. [ ] **CAHOONE**, b. of Plainfield, Sept. 10, 1849, by Joseph P. Brown — 4, 6

SCRIPTURE, John, formerly of Grotton, now of Plainfield, m. Abigail **UTLY**, d. Samuell, of Stoningtown, May 15, 1712 — 1, 10

SEAMANS, Layton E., m. Mary **WICKES**, b. of Coventry, R.I., Apr. 21, 1851, by Rev. Joseph P. Brown — 3, 69

    Layton E., physician, b. R.I., res. Plainfield, m. Mary **WICKES**, b. R.I., res. Plainfield, Apr. 21, 1851, by Rev. Joseph P. Brown — 4, 7

SEGAR, Gideon, of Killingly, m. Harriet **CUNDALL**, of Plainfield, Jan. 25, 1844, by James Smither, Elder — 3, 28

SESSIONS, Olivia, m. William **DYER**, b. of Plainfield, Oct. 15, 1850, by Rev. J.O. Knapp — 3, 66

    Theon, b. Thompson, res. Plainfield, d. May 10, 1847, ae. 10 — 4, 63

SHATDOW(?), Eliza, ae. 31, m. David **TUMA**, laborer, ae. 25,

PLAINFIELD VITAL RECORDS 233

	Vol.	Page
SHATDOW, (cont.)		
b. Ireland, res. Plainfield, June 20, 1849	4	3
SHAY, SHAYS, John, s. James, farmer, & Lucy, b. May 26,		
1850	4	28
John, d. July 3, 1850, ae. 2 m.	4	64
Laura, d. Dec. 22, 1850, ae. 1	4	64
Laura A., d. James, farmer, ae. 23, & Lucy A., ae. 22,		
b. Nov. 20, 1848	4	26
Lydia, d. July 24, 1850, ae. about 40	4	64
Mary, of Plainfield, m. James **DICKEREY**, of Griswold,		
July 6, 1845, by Amos Witter, J.P.	3	32
SHELDON, Allen M., of Coventry, R.I., m. Amey A. **KENYON**, of		
Sterling, Jan. 9, 1843, by Peleg Peckham, Elder	3	18
Ann E., m. Benjamin M. **ALEXANDER**, b. of Warwick, R.I.,		
Apr. 26, 1847, by Rev. James M. Mather	3	44
Edwin B., of Coventry, R.I., m. Hannah M. **KENYON**, of		
Sterling, Dec. 13, 1840, by Peleg Peckham, Elder	3	9
Edwin B., m. Betsey **CARD**, b. of Sterling, Nov. 15,		
1846, by Peleg Peckham, Elder	3	40
Henry, farmer, ae. 30, b. Norwich, res. Plainfield, m.		
Ruth **KETTLE**, ae. 27, b. Norwich, res. Plainfield,		
June 3, 1849, by Peleg Peckham	4	4
Henry S., m. Ruth **KITTLE**, b. of Plainfield, June 3,		
1849, by Peleg Peckham, Elder	3	59
Stephen, m. Georgianna Sears **ARNOLD**, b. of Warwick,		
R.I., Aug. 11, 1846, by Peleg Peckham, Elder	3	38
SHEPARD, SHEPHARD, SHEPHERD, SHEPERD, Abby J., m.		
William F. **HALL**, b. of Plainfield, Mar. 28, 1852,		
by Rev. Henry Robinson	3	74
Abigail, d. Isaac & Han[n]ah, b. Dec. 7, 1705 (Date		
conflicts with birth of Joseph)	1	9
Abega[i]l, d. Samuel & Elloner, b. Dec. 6, 1713	1	13
Abega[i]ll, d. Samuel & Ellenor, d. Aug. 12, 1720	1	22
Abigail, d. David & Lydiah, b. Aug. 1, 1746	2	21
Abigail, d. Isaac & Dorothy, b. Aug. 11, 1747	2	33
Abraham, s. Isaac, Jr. & Mary, b. May 27, 1739	1	94
Abraham, s. Squire & Sarah, b. Aug. 27, 1759	2	45
Abram, m. Hannah **WEBB**, b. of Plainfield, June 16, 1828,		
by Rev. Orin Fowler	2	206
Amey, d. Simon & Rachel, b. Apr. 11, 1766	2	85
Amey, of Plainfield, m. Joshua **PERKINS**, of Lisbon, July		
10, 1826, by Rev. Orin Fowler	2	199
Ann, Mrs., d. [1848?]	4	61
Ann Williams, d. Jerem[i]ah, manufacturer, ae. 44, b.		
Jan. 10, 1849	4	27
Anne, d. Reuben & Rebecca, b. Dec. 28, 1764	2	75
Asa, s. David & Lydiah, b. Aug. 17, 1742	2	21
Asa, s. Josiah & Rebeckah, b. Sept. 10, 1754	2	26

	Vol.	Page
SHEPARD, SHEPHARD, SHEPHERD, SHEPERD, (cont.)		
Asa, m. Hannah [ ], Nov. 25, 1778	2	87
Benjamin, s. Samuel & Eleanor, b. Feb. 21, 1722/3	1	28
Benjamin, s. David & Lydiah, b. July 4, 1740	2	21
Bette, m. Curtis **SPAULDING**, Dec. 26, 1753	2	25
Bette, d. Simon & Rachel, b. June 6, 1757	2	53
Caleb, s. Jonas & Mary, d. Nov. 12, 1762, in the 21st y. of his age	2	52
Caleb, s. Jacob & Deborah, b. Nov. 22, 1766	2	61
Daniel, s. Jonathan & Elizabeth, b. Apr. 7, 1742	2	22
David, s. David & Mephebel, b. Jan. 10, 1732	1	57
David, m. Mephebal **SPAULDING**, May 8, 1732	1	57
David, s. David & Mehetable, b. Jan. 10, 1733	2	21
David, m. Lydiah **MEECHAM**, Dec. 3, 1735	1	67
David, d. Nov. 10, 1752	2	21
David, m. Phebe **CADY**, Mar. 3, 1757	2	57
David, s. David & Phebe, b. Apr. 24, 1763	2	57
David, Jr., s. David & Phebe, b. Apr. 24, 1763	2	88
Dorothy, d. Isaac & Dorothy, b. July 26, 1745	2	33
Ebenezer, s. Asa & Hannah, b. Oct. 28, 1782	2	87
Eleanor, d. Samuell & Eleanor, b. Mar. 6, 1701/2	1	5
Ele[a]nor, d. Nathan & Susan[n]ah, b. Apr. 20, 1745	2	4
Elisha, s. Reuben & Rebecca, b. July 17, 1776	2	95
Elizabeth, d. Jesse & Sarah, b. Sept. 24, 1767	2	64
Elizabeth M., of Plainfield, m. William M. **JOHNSON**, of Killingly, Apr. 28, 1841, by Rev. Tubal Wakefield	3	9
Esther, d. Isaac & Dorithy, b. Sept. 5, 1744	2	33
Esther, d. Josiah & Rebeckah, b. Sept. 17, 1756	2	65
Esther, m. Dixwell **LATHROP**, b. of Plainfield, Nov. 17, 1823, by Orin Fowler, V.D.M.	2	192
Esther, ae. 26, b. Brooklyn, m. George **WILBOUR**, manufacturer, ae. 26, of Plainfield, Dec. 26, 1847, by W[illia]m Shepard, Esq.	4	1
Eunice, d. Simon & Rachel, b. Oct. 28, 1752	2	28
Eunice, d. Reuben & Rebecca, b. July 7, 1782	2	95
Hannah, d. Isaac & Hannah, b. Nov. 13, 1695	1	8
Han[n]ah, m. James **MARSH**, Dec. 3, 1711	1	11
Hannah, d. Jonas & Mary, b. Nov. 2, 1730	1	52
Hannah, m. Curtis **SPAULDING**, Dec. 19, 1750	2	18
Hannah, d. Isaac & Dorothy, b. Feb. 23, 1754	2	33
Hannah, d. Josiah & Rebeckah, b. Mar. 29, 1759	2	65
Hannah, d. Josiah & Rebeckah, b. Apr. 29, 1759	2	40
Hannah, d. Jacob & Deborah, b. Feb. 10, 1765	2	56
Hannah, m. Walter **PALMER**, b. of Plainfield, Feb. 20, 1848, by Rev. Henry Robinson	3	52
Hannah, ae. 22, b. Brooklyn, m. Walter **PALMER**, farmer, ae. 24, of Plainfield, Mar. 5, [18]48, by Rev.		

	Vol.	Page
SHEPARD, SHEPHARD, SHEPHERD, SHEPERD, (cont.)		
Henry Robinson	4	1
Harriet, of Plainfield, m. Timothy **LESTER**, of Hartford, June 5, 1831, by Rev. S.D. Jewett	2	213
Hazael, s. Jonas & Mary, b. Oct. 10, 1748	2	27
Hester, d. Sam[ue]ll & Mary, b. Mar. 22, 1737	1	68
Hester, d. Josiah & Rebeckah, b. Sept. [ ], probably 1757	2	40
Isaac, s. Isaac & Hannah, b. Sept. 14, 1700	1	8
Isaac, s. Isaac, Jr. & Mary, b. Feb. 15, 1723	1	48
Isaac, m. Dorothy **PRENTICE**, Nov. 24, 1743	2	33
Isaac, s. Jonas & Mary, b. Dec. 27, 1748	2	52
Israel, s. Jonathan & Elizabeth, b. Mar. 21, 1746	2	22
Jacob, s. Jonas & Mary, b. Feb. 26, 1738/9	1	94
Jacob, m. Deborah **ROBINSON**, Nov. 3, 1762	2	56
Jere, s. David & Phebe, b. Sept. 27, 1767	2	88
Jeremiah, m. Orilla **WILSON**, b. of Plainfield, Dec. 31, 1826, by Elder George W. Appleton, of Sterling	2	200
Jesse, s. David & Lydiah, b. July 6, 1744	2	21
Jesse, m. Sarah **WIGHT**, Sept. 24, 1766	2	64
Jobe, s. Isaac & Dorothy, b. May 29, 1756	2	33
John, s. Isaac, Jr. & Mary, b. Apr. 25, 1728	1	49
John, B.A., d. Dec. 9, 1749	2	10
John, s. David & Lydiah, b. May 5, 1751	2	21
John, s. Reuben & Rebeckah, b. June 22, 1761	2	47
John, s. Reuben & Rebecca, b. June 22, 1761; d. May 11, 1764	2	75
John, s. Jesse & Sarah, b. May 24, 1771	2	73
Jonas, s. Isaac & Hannah, b. May 12, 1698	1	8
Jonas, of Plainfield, m. Susan[n]a **SMITH**, of Volluntown, May 29, 1722	1	26
Jonas, s. Jonas & Susan[n]a, b. May 29, 1722* (*correction "(should be 1723)" handwritten in original manuscript)	1	26
Jonas, m. Mary **WARREN**, June 1, 1727	1	52
Jonas, m. Mary **WHITMORE**, d. Samuel, Nov. 5, 1747	1	IX
Jonas, m. Mary **WHITMORE**, Nov. 5, 1747	2	27
Jonathan, s. Samuel & Eleanor, b. Mar. 3, 1707/8	1	5
Jonathan, m. Elizabeth **BAKER**, Mar. 29, 1729	2	21
Jonathan, m. Elisabeth **BAKER**, Mar. 29, 1731	1	57
Jonathan, s. Jonathan & Elisabeth, b. Aug. 2, 1734	1	65
Jonathan, s. Jonathan & Elizabeth, b. Aug. 9, 1734	2	22
Joseph, s. Isaac & Han[n]ah, b. Sept. 11, 1705	1	9
Joseph, s. Isaac, Jr. & Mary, b. Apr. 3, 1733	1	63
Josiah, s. Sam[ue]ll & Mary, b. Dec. 1, 1731	1	59
Josiah, m. Rebeckah **BACON**, Nov. 1, 1753	2	26
Keziah, d. Jonas & Mary, b. Oct. 17, 1754	2	27

	Vol.	Page
SHEPARD, SHEPHARD, SHEPHERD, SHEPERD, (cont.)		
Lerenze, d. Simon & Rachel, b. Sept. 20, 1759	2	53
Lois, d. David & Phebe, b. Mar. 24, 1758	2	57
Lois, d. David & Phebe, b. Mar. 24, 1758	2	88
Lussee, d. Samuel & Ele[a]ner, b. Nov. 14, 1718	1	20
Luci, d. Sam[ue]ll & Mary, b. Apr. 20, 1733, stillborn	1	59
Lucy, d. David & Phebe, b. Dec. 19, 1761	2	57
Lucy, d. David & Phebe, b. Dec. 19, 1761	2	88
Lucy, milliner, ae. 28, b. Brooklyn, res. Plainfield, m. Samuel **PALMER**, farmer, ae. 25, of Plainfield, Nov. 27, 1850, by Rev. Samuel Robinson	4	7
Lucy G., m. Samuel **PALMER**, Jr., b. of Plainfield, Nov. 28, 1850, by Rev. Henry Robinson	3	67
Lydia, d. Isaac & Han[n]ah, b. May 20, 1708	1	9
Lydiah, d. Isaac, Jr. & Mary, b. Sept. 3, 1730	1	63
Lydiah, d. David & Lydia, b. Sept. 13, 1737	2	21
Lydia, d. Isaac & Dorothy, b. Aug. 3, 1749	2	33
Lydiah, m. Nehemiah **PEIRCE**, May 3, 1759	2	40
Lydia, d. Jesse & Sarah, b. May 28, 1769	2	73
Lydia, m. Joseph **LATHROP**, b. of Plainfield, July 25, 1823, by Rev. Orin Fowler	2	191
Lidiah, m. Boaz **STEVENS***, Nov. 18, [1725*] (*correction **STEVENS** crossed out and **STEARNS** handwritten in margin of original manuscript; *correction 1725 handwritten inside brackets of original manuscript)	1	35
Ma[r]tha, d. Jonas & Mary, b. Jan. 15, 1737	1	94
Martha M., of Plainfield, m. William **POTTER**, of Norwich, Sept. 14, 1851, by Rev. Henry Robinson	3	71
Mary, d. Samuell & Eleanor, b. Aug. 11, 1703	1	5
Mary, d. Isaac, Jr. & Mary, b. Apr. 23, 1726	1	48
Mary, d. Jonas & Mary, b. Sept. 23, 1740	1	96
Mary, d. Nathan & Susan[n]ah, b. May 7, 1743	2	4
Mary, m. Timothy **WHE[E]LER**, June 18, 1751	2	14
Mary, d. Isaac & Dorothy, b. Nov. 9, 1751	2	33
Mary, w. Jonas, Jr., d. Sept. 30, 1756	2	27
Mary, m. John **KENNEDY**, b. of Plainfield, Dec. 31, 1820, by Rev. Orin Fowler	2	132
Mary E., ae. 21, b. Brooklyn, m. George **WILBOUR**, woolen finisher, ae. 24, of Plainfield, Dec. 24, [18]47, by William Shepard, Esq.	4	2
Mehetable, d. David & Lydiah, b. Sept. 4, 1735	1	67
Mehetable, d. David & Lydia, b. Sept. 11, 1735	2	21
Mehetabell, m. Joseph **BURGESS**, Mar. 21, 1756	2	35
Mehetabel, d. Jacob & Deborah, b. Sept. 26, 1763	2	56
Molle, d. Josiah & Rebeckah, b. Apr. 15, 1763	2	65

	Vol.	Page
SHEPARD, SHEPHARD, SHEPHERD, SHEPERD, (cont.)		
Moses, s. Jonas & Mary, b. Feb. 28, 1744	2	52
Moses, m. Lydia **STEVENS**, Oct. 15, 1765	2	62
Nathan, s. Samuel & Ellener, b. June 15, 1720	1	22
Nathan, m. Susan[n]ah **WHE[E]LER**, Feb. 15, 1743	2	4
Noah, s. Reuben & Rebecca, b. Dec. 29, 1778	2	95
Olive, d. Nathan & Susannah, b. Feb. 23, 1748	2	3
Olive, d. David & Phebe, b. June 15, 1765	2	88
Phillemon, s. David & Phebe, b. May 14, 1759	2	57
Philemon, s. David & Phebe, b. May 14, 1759	2	88
Persila, d. James* & Mary, b. Oct. 9, 1734		
(*correction Jonas handwritten above James in original manuscript)	1	65
Prescilla, m. Nathaniel **PEIRCE**, Sept. 24, 1754	2	29
Rachel, d. Simon & Rachel, b. Sept. 10, 1761	2	85
Rachel, d. Simon & Rachel, b. Oct. 18, 1761	2	53
Rebeckah, d. Josiah & Rebeckah, b. July 18, 1765	2	65
Rebecca, d. Reuben & Rebecca, b. Mar. 2, 1772	2	75
R[e]uben, s. Isaac & Mary, b. May 14, 1736	1	68
Reuben, m. Rebeckah **SPAULDING**, Feb. 27, 1760	2	47
Reuben, m. Rebeckah **SPAULDING**, Feb. 27, 1760	2	75
Reubin, s. Reubin & Rebecca, b. Dec. 4, 1766; d. July 26, 1769	2	75
Reubin, Jr., s. Reubin & Rebecca, b. Oct. 16, 1769	2	75
Rufus, s. Jonas & Mary, b. June 18, 1752	2	27
Ruth, d. James & Susannah, b. Aug. 29, 1724; d. same day	1	31
Ruth, m. Simon **SPAULDING**, Apr. 15, 1761	2	73
Ruth, d. Reuben & Rebecca, b. May 5, 1774	2	95
Samuell, s. Samuell & Eleanor, b. Sept. 31, [sic], 1705	1	5
Samuell, s. Isaac & Han[n]ah, b. Apr. 2, 1711	1	9
Sam[ue]ll, m. Mary **SPAULDING**, Jan. 20, 1731	1	59
Samuell, s. Jonathan & Elizabeth, b. Jan. 29, 1732/3	1	57
Samuel, s. Jonathan & Elizabeth, b. Jan. 29, 1733	2	21
Sam[ue]ll, s. Sam[ue]ll & Mary, b. Aug. 23, 1741	1	98
Samuel, s. Josiah & Rebeckah, b. Feb. 24, 1761	2	65
Sarah, d. Samu[e]ll & Elena, b. June 28, 1716	1	17
Sarah, d. James & Mary, b. Oct. 7, 1732	1	65
Sarah, d. David & Lydiah, b. Jan. 16, 1749	2	21
Sarah, m. Elias **STEAVENS**, Feb. 27, 1754	2	24
Sarah, d. Simon & Rachal, b. Nov. 1, 1754	2	28
Simon, m. Rachal **SPAULDING**, Dec. 25, 1751	2	28
Simon, Jr., s. Simon & Rachel, b. May 16, 1764	2	85
Simon, s. David & Phebe, b. Feb. 14, 1770	2	88
Simon, m. Lydia **HAZARD**, May 17, 1843, by Amos Witter, J.P.	3	19
Simon, farmer, d. Aug. 2, [18]48, ae. 83	4	61

	Vol.	Page
SHEPARD, SHEPHARD, SHEPHERD, SHEPERD, (cont.)		
Squire, s. Sam[ue]ll & Mary, b. Feb. 20, 1735	1	68
Squire, m. Sarah **PEIRCE**, Dec. 26, 1758	2	45
Susan H., of Plainfield, m. Olney **DODGE**, of Smithfield, R.I., July 31, 1854, by Rev. Henry Robinson	3	84
Susannah, w. James, d. Aug. 30, 1724	1	31
Susannah, d. Jonas & Mary, b. Mar. 30, 1729	1	52
Susanna, m. Jabez **PEIRCE**, b. of Plainfield, June 27, 1748, by Thomas Stevens, J.P.	2	7
Susannah, d. Nathan & Susannah, b. Jan. 10, 1749/50	2	12
Susan[n]ah, d. Jonas & Mary, b. June 2, 1750	2	27
Susan[n]ah, m. William **CUTLER**, Nov. 7, 1750	2	24
Susannah, d. Moses & Lydia, b. July 25, 1766	2	62
Timothy, s. Jonathan & Elizabeth, b. Nov. 20, 1743	2	22
Warren, m. Lydia **HALL**, Oct. 3, 1819, b. of Plainfield	2	191
Warren, Jr., s. Warren & Lydia, b. July 11, 1820	2	173
Warren, d. July 9, 1821	2	173
William, s. Jonathan & Elizabeth, b. Oct. 12, 1737	2	22
William, s. David & Phebe, b. June 14, 1773; d. Oct. 12, 1773	2	88
SHERMAN, Opha, m. Moses **RAY**, b. of Plainfield, Nov. 25, 1839, by Rev. Hezekiah Tha[t]cher	3	3
SHIPMAN, Thomas L., of Jewett City, m. Pamela L. **COIT**, of Plainfield, May 1, 1844, by A. Dunning	3	23
SHIPPEY, SHIPPEE, Catharine A., m. Noah **HALL**, b. of Killingly, July 11, 1837, by Peleg Peckham, Elder	2	231
Fidelia, m. Henry **KEMP**, Jr., of Brooklyn, Ct., Nov. 10, 1850, by H. Robinson	4	7
Ruth Fidelia, of Canterbury, m. Henry **CAMP**, Jr., of Brooklyn, Nov. 10, 1850, by Rev. Henry Robinson	3	66
SHOLES, Julia E., of Warwick, R.I., m. Oliver S. **HASARD**, of Coventry, R.I., Nov. 1, 1849, by Rev. Joseph P. Brown	3	61
SHORT, William G., of Providence, R.I., m. Lucinda **ALIOT***, of Providence, R.I., Nov. 20, 1848, by Rev. George W. Brewster (*Perhaps "**ELIOT**")	3	57
SIMMONS, [see also **SIMONS**], Allen S., d. Aug. 29, 1847, ae. 1 y.	4	61
Amey, m. Henry **BOYDEN**, Sept. 14, 1806	2	114
Betsey, of Plainfield, m. Walter **RYEN**, late of Great Britain, Sept. 22, 1822, by Orin Fowler, V.D.M.	2	188
Chester L., s. Davenport, carriage worker, b. Aug. 19, 1850	4	32
Martha, of Plainfield, m. Job **RUSSEL[L]**, of Providence, R.I., Mar. 9, 1823, by John Dunlap, J.P.	2	191
Sally, of Plainfield, m. Arnold **KING**, of Foster, R.I.,		

	Vol.	Page
SIMMONS, (cont.)		
Nov. 16, 1823, by Nathaniel Cole, Elder	2	192
SIMONS, [see also **SIMMONS**], Hezekiah, s. Horace, laborer, black, ae. 20, b. June 24, 1850	4	28
Horace, laborer, black, ae. 20, b. Griswold, res. Plainfield, m. Jane **PAIN[E]**, ae. 17, black, b. Griswold, res. Plainfield, [1850], by Joseph Hutchins	4	5
Joseph, laborer, Indian, b. Preston, res. Plainfield, d. Oct. 5, 1848, ae. 43	4	62
SISSON, Nathan P., trader, b. Thompson, res. Plainfield, d. May 28, 1848, ae. 43 y.	4	61
Silas, of Seekank, Mass., m. Elizabeth C. **BAKER**, of Plainfield, July 23, 1826, by Orin Fowler, V.D.M.	2	199
SKILLION, Lucy, m. Timothy **SPAULDING**, Dec. 25, 1766	2	74
Marcy, m. John **KEN[N]ADY**, Nov. 3, 1763	2	53
SKINNER, Mary, d. John & Mary, b. May 27, 1820	2	133
Samuel, s. John & Mary, b. Nov. 16, 1822	2	173
SLADE, Josiah, of Sterling, m. Lydia H. **DAWLEY**, of Coventry, R.I., Nov. 3, 1852, by Peleg Peckham, Elder	3	76
Otis H., m. Sophia **HARRIS**, b. of Plainfield, Nov. 26, 1827, by Orin Fowler, V.D.M.	2	204
Thomas S., of Woodstock, m. Hannah **KENYON**, of Sterling, Sept. 29, 1839, by Peleg Peckham, Elder	2	248
Thomas S., of Woodstock, m. Hannah **KENYON**, of Sterling, Sept. 29, 1839, by Peleg Peckham, Elder	3	1
SMALL, Lewis K., m. Lucinda **CASE**, Sept. 5, 1842, by John Read, Elder	3	16
SMART, Acsah, m. William Carr **HUTTON**, July 20, 1787	2	99
SMITH, Albert L., m. Mary J. **HOWARD**, b. of Scituate, Apr. 10, 1845, by James Smither, Elder	3	29
Barney, d. Sept. 7, [1847], ae. 3	4	61
Betsey, d. Luther & Ruth, b. Aug. 27, 1785	2	93
Betsey J., d. Peter J. & Celinda, b. Feb. 10, 1800	2	114
Celinda J., w. Peter J., d. Feb. 22, 1807	2	114
Daniel, m. Eliza **CONGDON**, b. of Plainfield, Sept. 10, 1837, by Rev. Samuel Rockwell	2	232
Edward, m. Mary **LAWSON**, b. of Plainfield, Oct. 7, 1827, by Orin Fowler, V.D.M.	2	203
Elizabeth, d. John & Susan[n]ah, b. July 30, 1706	1	4
Elvira A., m. Jeremiah **ARNOLD**, b. of Warwick, R.I., Sept. 17, 1848, by Rev. Geo[rge] W. Brewster	3	56
Fanny, m. Charles **HARRIS**, b. of Plainfield, Nov. 30, 1820, by Rev. Orin Fowler	2	132
George, of Salem, m. Huldah **ANDREW**, of Plainfield, July 21, 1823, by John Dunlap, J.P.	2	192
Harriet, d. May or June [1850 or 1851], ae. 55	4	66
Henrietta, d. William & Polly, b. Jan. 30, 1803	2	108

SMITH, (cont.)

	Vol.	Page
Horace A., m. Elizabeth H. **BENNETT**, b. of Sterling, May 21, 1854, by Peleg Peckham, Elder	3	83
Isaac Coit, s. Luther & Ruth, b. Mar. 1, 1781	2	93
Jeremiah B., of Canterbury, m. Martha **KENNEDY**, of Plainfield, Sept. 19, 1824, by Rev. James Porter, of Pomfret	2	195
John, m. Susannah **HALL**, d. Stephen, June 25, 169[ ]	1	1
John, s. John & Susan[n]ah, b. Dec. 18, 1708	1	10
John, m. Phebe **PEIRCE**, Nov. 24, 1736	1	66
John L., m. Olive **CORY**, Jan. 1, 1845, by V.R. Osborn, V.D.M.	3	26
John S., of Slatersville, R.I., m. Julia A. **HUMES**, of Plainfield, May 15, 1851, by Rev. John F. Sheffield	3	70
John S., of Canterbury, m. Frances C. **CORNELL**, of Plainfield, Mar. 27, 1854, by Rev. James Bates	3	86
Lemuell, s. John & Susan[n]ah, b. Feb. 25, 1710/11	1	10
Lucinda, of Plainfield, m. Alfred **ROUNDS**, of Foster, July 2, 1843, by Peleg Peckham, Elder	3	19
Luther, m. Ruth **HARWOOD**, Jan. 6, 1780	2	93
Magdalene, m. Robert **KENNEDY**, Feb. 9, 1797	2	116
Maria P., ae. 22, b. Sheffield, Mass., res. Canterbury, m. Alfred A. **BENNETT**, farmer, ae. 23, b. Plainfield, res. Canterbury, Apr. 12, 1848, by Rev. Mr. Bradford	4	1
Martha, d. Luther & Ruth, b. Nov. 30, 1787	2	93
Martha, m. William P. **KENYON**, June 27, 1847, by Peleg Peckham, Elder	3	45
Mary, m. Elkanah Cobb **EATON**, Apr. 19, 1812	2	123
Mary, of Canterbury, m. Nathan **KING**, of West Greenwich, R.I., May 9, 1830, by Francis B. Johnson, J.P.	2	211
Mary Ann, d. William & Polly, b. Nov. 26, 1804	2	110
Nancy J., d. Peter J. & Celinda, b. Sept. 27, 1805	2	114
Olive, d. Luther & Ruth, b. May 19, 1790	2	98
Olive, m. John **WITTER**, b. of Plainfield, Mar. 26, 1832, by Rev. Seth Bliss, of Jewett City	2	215
Olive J., d. Peter J. & Celinda, b. Mar. 27, 1803	2	114
Polly, d. Luther & Ruth, b. Aug. 29, 1783	2	93
Ruth, d. John & Susan[n]ah, b. Sept. 19, 1702	1	1
Ruth, d. John & Susan[n]ah, d. Dec. 28, 1715	1	15
Sally, of Plainfield, m. Simon **STONE**, of Griswold, June 5, 1825, by Rev. Orin Fowler	2	198
Susan A., of Scituate, m. William A. **STAFFORD**, of Plainfield, Jan. 5, 1846, by Peleg Peckham, Elder	3	35
Susan A., of Sterling, m. Hiram **HAWKINS**, of Plainfield, Jan. 1, 1852, by Rev. Henry Robinson	3	73

	Vol.	Page
SMITH, (cont.)		
Susan[n]ah, d. John & Susan[n]ah, b. Oct. 15, 1700	1	1
Susan[n]a, of Volluntown, m. Jonas **SHEPARD**, of Plainfield, May 29, 1722	1	26
Thomas, m. Jemimah **BUMP**, d. Philip, of Plainfield, May 9, 1706	1	4
William, of Plainfield, m. Esther **HOLWAY**, of West Greenwich, R.I., Apr. 4, 1841, by Rev. Hezekiah Thatcher	3	9
SNELL, Alice Ann, m. Nathaniel **ARNOLD**, July 1, 1847, by Rev. Fred[eri]c Charlton	3	49
Harriet, m. Ira **ARNOLD**, b. of Plainfield, Jan. 13, 1845, by James Smither, Elder	3	29
Mary, of Sterling, m. Gardiner **CHILSON**, of Providence, Oct. 8, 1826, by Rev. Orin Fowler	2	199
SPAULDING, SPALDING, Abel, s. Jonathan & Judeth, b. July 10, 1728	1	63
Abel, m. Mary **ANDERSON**, Nov. 23, 1749	2	48
Abel, s. Abel & Mary, b. Sept. 30, 1756	2	48
Abiah, m. Squire **CADY**, May 29, 1799	2	106
Abigaill, d. Samuel & Susan[n]ah, b. May 7, 1711	1	9
Abega[i]ll, d. Benjamin & Abega[i]l, b. Feb. 20, 1722/3	1	27
Abigaiel, w. Benjamin, d. Jan. 6, 1726	1	40
Abigaiel, d. Thomas & Marcy, b. Sept. 20, 1727	1	61
Abigail, d. Ephraim & Abigail, b. Mar. 16, 1736	2	27
Abigail, d. Eleazer, Jr. & Lois, b. Mar. 6, 1750; d. July 5, 1752	2	30
Abigail, m. Samuel **WARREN**, Feb. 8, 1753	2	22
Abigail, m. Ebenezer **GALLUP**, Mar. 27, 1755	2	44
Abigail, m. Samuel **HALL**, May 19, 1756	2	38
Abigail, d. Andrew & Delight, b. Mar. 19, 1758	2	63
Abigail, d. Oliver & Mary, b. May 4, 1765	2	94
Abigail, d. Samuel & Joanna, b. Oct. 27, 1773	2	91
Allice, d. Benjamin & Abigail, b. Jan. 25, 1724/5	1	32
Allis, m. Isaac **MORGAN**, Mar. 26, 1759	2	43
Allen Munro, s. Joseph & Mary, b. Jan. 17, 1830	2	170
Allen Munro, s. Joseph & Mary, b. Jan. 17, 1830	3	22
Alpheas, s. Phillip & Ann, b. Feb. 3, 1740	2	21
Amelia, of Plainfield, m. Ambrose **FRINK**, of Sterling, Mar. 3, 1822, by John Dunlap, J.P.	2	187
Ammesa, s. John & Elizabeth, b. Dec. 11, 1755	2	30
Amos, s. Nathaniel & Johan[n]ah, b. Mar. 12, 1715/16	1	16
Amos, m. Hannah **CARY**, Nov. 14, 1739	2	11
Amos, s. Amos & Hannah, b. Jan. 25, 1743/4	2	11
Amy, d. Isaac & Elisabeth, b. Dec. 13, 1717	1	18
Amey, m. Alexander **STEWERT**, Apr. 18, 1734	1	66
Andrew, [twin with Eunis], s. Thomas & Mercy, b. July		

	Vol.	Page
SPAULDING, SPALDING, (cont.)		
28, 1720	1	26
Andrew, s. Phillip & Ann, b. Apr. 28, 1722	1	27
Andrew, s. Curtis & Belle, b. July 11, 1760	2	49
Andrew, d. Apr. 14, 1806, ae. 86 y. (?)	2	114
Anna, d. Ele[a]zer & Abigail, b. May 7, 1717	1	33
Annah, m. Nath[anie]l **MAINE**, of Stonington, Jan. 10, 1737/8	1	70
Anna, d. Simon & Anne, d. Oct. 18, 1754	2	31
Anna, d. Jacob & Mathew, b. May 15, 1755	2	29
Anner, d. John & Elizabeth, b. Aug. 27, 1761	2	66
Anne, d. Simon & Anne, b. May 12, 1753	2	23
Anne, w. Simon, d. Nov. 10, 1754	2	31
Anne, d. Jacob & Mathew, b. May 15, 1755	2	12
Anne, d. Jonathan & Phebe, b. Apr. 23, 1767	2	64
Ardelia, ae. 19, of Plainfield, m. John H. **TANNER**, manufacturer, ae. 19, b. W. Greenwich, res. Griswold, May 6, 1850, by Rev. Henry Robinson	4	5
Asah, s. Benjamin & Deb[o]rah, b. Mar. 26, 1729	1	47
Azariah, s. Phillip & Ann, b. Jan. 19, 1724	1	39
Az[a]riah, s. Phillip & Ann, b. Jan. 19, 1724	1	69
Azariah, m. Molly **JEARAULD**, Sept. 7, 1744	2	16
Belle, w. Curtis, d. Feb. 23, 1769	2	67
Benjamin, Jr., m. Sarah **HALL**, d. Stephen, Oct. 21, 170[ ]	1	7
Benjamin, d. Sept. 17, 1712	1	11
Benjamin, m. Abega[i]ll **[W]RIGHT**, d. of Ebenezer, of Cheltsford, Mar. 7, 1719/20	1	22
Benjamin, s. Benjamin & Abega[i]ll, b. Feb. 22, 1720/21	1	24
Benjamin, m. Deborah **WHEELER**, Oct. 30, 1727	1	41
Benjamin, m. Rachel **CRARY**, Jan. 29, 1756	2	33
Benjamin, Jr., was executor of the last will of John Crery, Esq.	2	52
Caroline, d. Charles & Lydia, b. Feb. 17, 1811	2	172
Caroline, d. Aug. 5, [18]49, ae. 2 m.	4	62
Caroline, of Plainfield, m. Peter **FARNUM**, of Philadelphia, Pa., Jan. 26, 1852, by Rev. Joseph P. Brown	3	73
Cate, d. Curtis & Bette, b. Sept. 5, 1766	2	65
Champin, s. Phillip & Parnel, b. Sept. 23, 1753	2	41
Charles, s. Phillip & Ann, b. Dec. 12, 1735	1	70
Charles, s. Azariah & Molle, b. Mar. 12, 1764	2	59
Charles, m. Abigail **GATES**, Dec. 25, 1764	2	59
Charles, m. Eunice **WILSON**, b. of Plainfield, Dec. 6, 1829, by Rev. Orin Fowler	2	210
Charles, farmer, d. Aug. 20, 1850, ae. 81	4	66
Charles Henry, s. Morey B., farmer, & Elizabeth, b. Dec. 15, 1850	4	32

PLAINFIELD VITAL RECORDS 243

	Vol.	Page
SPAULDING, SPALDING, (cont.)		
Charles Hubbard, s. Joseph & Sarah, b. Oct. 1, 1837	2	241
Charles Hubbard, s. Joseph C. & Sarah, b. Oct. 1, 1837	3	13
Curtis, s. Phillip & Ann, b. Apr. 10, 1726	1	69
Curtis, s. Phillip & Ann, b. Apr. 11, 1726	1	39
Curtis, m. Hannah **SHEPARD**, Dec. 19, 1750	2	18
Curtis, m. Bette **SHEPHERD**, Dec. 26, 1753	2	25
Cyril, m. Martha **SABIN**, Feb. 14, 1809	2	173
Cyril, s. Cyril & Martha, b. Nov. 4, 1813	2	173
Cyrus, s. Andrew & Delight, b. Sept. 27, 1764	2	63
Daniel, s. Phillip & Ann, b. Dec. 12, 1731	1	70
Daniel, s. Azariah & Molley, b. Dec. 13, 1759	2	43
Daniel, s. Cyrel & Martha, b. Nov. 10, 1819	2	173
Daniel, m. Cleonna **PINK**, b. of Plainfield, Apr. 19, 1821, by Rev. Orin Fowler	2	133
Daniel, m. Dinah **MEDBERY**, b. of Plainfield, Apr. 7, 1822, by Rev. Nathaniel Cole	2	187
Darius, s. Eleazer, Jr. & Lois, b. July 2, 1753; d. Sept. 11, 1754	2	31
Darius, s. Phillip & Deborah, b. July 24, 1760	2	47
David, s. Ebenezer & Abigaiel, b. Dec. 23, 1728	1	47
David, s. Benjamin & Deb[o]rah, b. Mar. 27, 1736	1	66
David, s. Benjamin, Jr. & Rachel, b. May 23, 1759; d. Aug. 15, 1759	2	63
David, [twin with Jonathan], s. Timothy & Lucy, b. July 25, 1772	2	74
Debora[h], [twin with Rachal], d. Edward & Dorothy, b. Jan. 17, 1706/7	1	5
Deborah, d. Joseph & Lydia, b. Dec. 30, 1746	2	17
Deborah, d. Eleazer, Jr. & Lois, b. Oct. 30, 1758	2	55
Deborah, m. Ebenezer **CLAPP**, Sept. 15, 1773	2	226
Deborah, w. Phillip, d. Mar. 20, 1825	2	174
Delight, w. Andrew, d. Nov. 15, 1805, ae. 72 y. (?)	2	111
Deliverance, s. Nathaniel & Joanna, b. Nov. 12, 1733	1	60
Dennison, s. Simon & Anne, b. July 19, 1743; d. Oct. 10, 1749	2	9
Dennison, s. Curtis & Han[n]ah, b. July 8, 1752	2	18
Diah, s. Jonathan & Judeth, b. Nov. 18, 1732	1	63
Dinah, d. Jonathan & Judah, b. June 12, 1723	1	29
Dolle, d. Curtis & Belle, b. July 14, 1758; d. May 13, 1759	2	49
Dorcues, d. Eleazer & Abigaill, b. Feb. 8, 1712/13	1	11
Darkis, d. Ele[a]zer & Abigail, b. Feb. 8, 1713	1	32
Dorkis, m. Samuel **KINGSBURY**, May 12, 1730	2	17
Dorcas, d. John & Elizabeth, b. Dec. 25, 1744	2	30
Dorcas, m. Lemuel **PEIRCE**, Feb. 10, 1756	2	35
Dutee, s. Charles & Abigail, b. Nov. 29, 1765	2	59

	Vol.	Page
SPAULDING, SPALDING, (cont.)		
Ebenezer, s. Benjamin & Abigaiel, b. Dec. 31, 1726	1	39
Ebenezer, s. Benjamin & Abigaiel, d. Mar. 26, 1727	1	40
Edath, d. Jonathan & Eunis, b. Oct. 24, 1726	1	44
Edward, m. Elizabeth **HALL**, d. Stephen, Oct. 21, 1708	1	6
Edward, s. Isaac & Elisabeth, b. Aug. 18, 1722	1	27
Edward, m. Ruth **KINGSBURY**, July 9, 1744	2	15
Edward, d. Aug. 23, 1750	2	15
Ele[a]zer, m. Abigail **KINGSBURY**, Nov. 14, 1712	1	32
Eleazar, m. Abigail **KINGSBURY**, d. James, Nov. 17, 1712	1	11
Eleazer, s. Eleazer & Abigeel, b. July 3, 1721	1	33
Elisha, s. Anna, b. Apr. 6, 1809	2	173
Elisha Knight, s. Samuel K. & Lucy, b. June 6, 1821	2	173
Elisabeth, d. Sam[ue]ll & Susan[n]ah, b. July 16, 1714	1	15
Elisabeth, d. Isaac & Elisabeth, b. Jan. 13, 1715/16	1	16
Elisabeth, d. Tho[ma]s & Mercy, b. Apr. 20, 1719	1	21
Elisabeth, d. Edward & Elisabeth, b. June 23, 1727	1	51
Elizabeth, d. Andrew & Delight, b. May 2, 1752	2	31
Elizabeth, d. John & Elizabeth, b. Aug. 21, 1759	2	66
Elizabeth, m. Elisha **PAINE**, May 20, 1762, by Rev. Alex[ande]r Miller, in the Second Society	2	51
Elizabeth, d. Jonathan & Phebe, b. May 7, 1771	2	75
Ellen, d. Benja[mi]n, Jr. & Rachel, b. Aug. 28, 1760; d. June 19, 1762, by being drowned	2	63
Emma Sophia, d. Joseph C. & Sarah, b. Aug. 4, 1841	3	13
Ephraim, s. Ephraim & Abigail, b. May 24, 1747	2	27
Ephraim, s. Oliver & Mary, b. Sept. 21, 1777	2	94
Erastus, s. Oliver & Mary, b. May 28, 1775	2	94
Erastus S., m. Julia **SPAULDING**, b. of Plainfield, Mar. 19, 1848, by Rev. J. Mather	3	54
Easter, d. Edward, Jr. & Elizabeth, b. Jan. 25, 1711/12	1	9
Esther, d. Eleazer, Jr. & Lois, b. May 30, 1744	2	30
Esther, d. Timothy & Lucy, b. Sept. 16, 1774	2	81
Eunes, d. Ele[a]zer & Abigail, b. Dec. 22, 1713	1	32
[E]uniss, d. Edward & Dorithy, b. Aug. 16, 1715	1	15
Eunis, [twin with Andrew], d. Thomas & Mercy, b. July 28, 1720	1	26
[E]unis, d. Eleazer, d. Mar. 26, 1738	1	70
[E]unice, d. Simon & Anne, b. Feb. 23, 1740; d. Mar. 5, 1741	2	9
Eunis, d. Phillip & Anne, b. Mar. 10, 1743	2	21
Eunice, d. Andrew & Delight, b. Aug. 26, 1760	2	63
Eunice, d. Timothy & Lucy, b. May 30, 1768	2	74
Eunice C., d. Aug. 5, 1849, ae. 2 m.	4	64
Eunice W., of Plainfield, m. A. Leroy **PRINTICE**, of Lisbon, June 9, 1844, by Rev. D. Dorchester	3	24

	Vol.	Page
SPAULDING, SPALDING, (cont.)		
Experience, d. Nathaniel & Joannah, b. Jan. 16, 1726/7	1	40
Experience, m. Amos **STAFFORD**, Sept. 9, 1747	2	11
Ezekiel, s. Ephraim & Abigail, b. Sept. 30, 1731	2	27
Ezekiel, m. Jenne **MAT[T]HEWS**, Mar. 26, 1754	2	24
Ezarah, s. Edward & Ruth, b. Apr. 25, 1745	2	15
Ezra, s. Abel & Mary, b. Dec. 11, 1751	2	48
Ezra, s. Andrew & Delight, b. Nov. 5, 1754	2	31
Ezra, m. Hannah **EATON**, Mar. 10, 1781	2	87
Ezra had Ceazer, negro, s. Beulah, b. Jan. 14, 1789	2	96
Frances A., of Plainfield, m. John H. **TURNER**, of West Greenwich, R.I., May 6, 1850, by Rev. Henry Robinson	3	64
Francis, s. Amos & Hannah, b. May 18, 1753	2	29
Frank Willis, s. Joseph C. & Sarah, b. Nov. 26, 1839	3	13
Frederick, s. Oliver & Mary, b. July 23, 1772	2	94
Furies, s. Ephraim & Abigaiel, b. Mar. 25, 1726	1	43
George, s. Cyrel & Martha, b. Oct. 27, 1815	2	173
George Henry, s. Joseph & Mary, b. Dec. 4, 1838	2	170
George Henry, s. Joseph & Mary, b. Dec. 4, 1838	3	22
Gordis, s. Charles & Lydia, b. Mar. 11, 1804	2	117
Han[n]ah, d. Thomas & Mercy, b. July 15, 1722	1	28
Hannah, w. Curtis, d. July 8, 1752	2	18
Hannah, d. Curtis & Bette, b. Sept. 3, 1754	2	29
Hannah, w. Willard, d. Mar. 2, 1755, ae. 29 y. 9 m.	2	29
Hannah, d. Oliver & Mary, b. Mar. 22, 1763; d. Dec. 29, [1763]	2	83
Hannah, d. Oliver & Mary, b. Mar. 22, 1763; d. Dec. 29, [1763]	2	94
Hannah, d. Jonathan & Phebe, b. May 1, 1773	2	77
Hannah, m. Jonathan **HANN**, July 7, 1774	2	78
Hannah, d. Oliver & Rebecca, b. July 23, 1786	2	94
Harvey, s. Cyrel & Martha, b. Sept. 7, 1821	2	173
Henry Otis, s. Joseph & Sarah, b. Oct. 19, 1835	2	241
Henry Otis, s. Joseph C. & Sarah, b. Oct. 19, 1835	3	13
Hester, m. Sam[ue]ll **PARKHURST**, Jan. 20, 1731	1	60
Hester, d. Azariah & Molle, b. Apr. 20, 1762	2	43
Hester, d. Azariah & Molle, b. Apr. 20, 1762	2	59
Hezeciah, s. Ele[a]zer & Abigail, b. June 27, 1719; d. July 10, 1719	1	33
Hezeciah, s. Thomas & Marcy, b. Feb. 20, 1724	1	40
Hezekiah, m. Mary **WILLIAMS**, Aug. 24, 1790	2	98
Hezekiah, d. Feb. 9, 1808, ae. 84	2	116
Horace, s. Ezra **SPAULDING** & Hannah, b. July 25, 1783	2	89
Isaac, m. Elizabeth **HAINES**, of Haverell, Feb. 2, 1712/13	1	13
Isaac, s. Isaac & Elisabeth, b. Apr. 22, 1726	1	38

	Vol.	Page
SPAULDING, SPALDING, (cont.)		
Jabez, s. Jesse & Mary, b. Nov. 6, 1761	2	54
Jacob, s. Phillip & Ann, b. Nov. 14, 1729	1	69
Jacob, s. Isaac & Elisabeth, b. Dec. 6, 1733	1	60
Jacob, m. Mathew **JEARAULD**, May 1, 1753	2	26
Jacob, m. Mathew **GERAULD**, May 2, 1753	2	12
Jacob, m. Thankfull **BURGES[S]**, Nov. 27, 1760	2	45
James, s. Amos & Hannah, b. Oct. 9, 1746	2	11
Jedediah, s. Samuell & Susan[n]ah, b. Apr. 1, 1709	1	7
Jedediah, s. Samuel & Joanna, b. Nov. 13, 1777	2	91
Jedediah, s. Lemuel & Hannah, b. May 28, 1804	2	112
Jeremiah, s. Isaac & Elizabeth, b. Aug. 20, 1730	1	51
Jesse, s. Jonathan & Judeth, b. Sept. 12, 1730	1	63
Jesse, s. Nathaniel & Joanna, b. Aug. 5, 1731	1	59
Jesse, m. Mary **KIMBALL**, Feb. 28, 1757	2	48
Jesse, s. Amos & Hannah, b. Sept. 10, 1757	2	46
Joannah, d. Nath[anie]ll & Joan[n]ah, b. Dec. 13, 1722	1	27
Joanna, d. Azariah & Molley, b. June 21, 1755	2	35
Joannah, m. Reuben **JERAULD**, Jan. 1, 1757	2	39
Johannah, d. Phillip & Ann, b. Sept. 22, 1733	1	70
Johannah, m. James **HOW[E]**, Feb. 3, 1742	2	17
John, s. Samuell & Sarah, b. Apr. 2, 1701	1	4
John, s. Ephraim & Abigaiel, b. Aug. 8, 1724	1	43
John, s. Ephraim & Abigail, b. Aug. 8, 1724	2	27
John, s. Edward & Elizabeth, b. Nov. 27, 1732	1	68
John, m. Elizabeth **SANGER**, Jan. 22, 1744	2	30
John, s. John & Elizabeth, b. Dec. 13, 1751	2	30
John, s. Simon & Ruth, b. Nov. 14, 1765	2	73
John, s. Ephraim & Abigail, d. May 29, 1768, by the kick of a horse, ae. 43 y. 9 m.	2	66
John, s. Oliver & Rebecca, b. July 4, 1784	2	94
John Knight, s. Jos[eph] C., merchant, & Susan E., b. Mar. 30, 1851	4	32
John W., m. Mary Elizabeth **PALMER**, b. of Plainfield, Apr. 12, 1846, by Rev. Andrew Dunning	3	37
John W., m. Amanda M. **KING**, b. of Plainfield, Feb. 2, 1851, by Rev. W. Emerson	3	68
John Williams, s. Joseph & Mary, b. Mar. 6, 1824	2	170
John Williams, s. Joseph & Mary, b. Mar. 6, 1824	2	173
John Williams, s. Joseph & Mary, b. Mar. 6, 1824	3	22
Jonathan, m. Judah Billings **MAIN**, d. Han[n]a[h], Apr. 22, 1714	1	20
Jonathan, s. Elizabeth **DYAR**, b. May 1, 1738	2	10
Jonathan, s. Phillip & Anne, b. July 30, 1738	2	21
Jonathan, s. Eleazer, Jr. & Lois, b. Mar. 4, 1747	2	30
Jonathan, m. Phebe **BACKUS**, Mar. 20, 1765	2	59
Jonathan, [twin with David], s. Timothy & Lucy, b. July 25, 1772	2	74

PLAINFIELD VITAL RECORDS

	Vol.	Page
SPAULDING, SPALDING, (cont.)		
Jonathan, s. Phillip & Deberough, b. Oct. 23, 1774	2	100
Joseph, s. Nathaniel & Johan[n]ah, b. Feb. 28, 1717/18	1	19
Joseph, s. Edward & Dorothy, b. Sept. 3, 1718	1	19
Joseph, d. Apr. 3, 1740, ae. 96; had he lived until Aug. next, ae. 97	1	95
Joseph, m. Lydia **WHE[E]LER**, Mar. 4, 1742	2	17
Joseph, s. Joseph & Lydia, b. June 7, 1745	2	17
Joseph, s. Nathaniel & Marah, b. Feb. 26, 1746	2	10
Joseph, s. Amos & Hannah, b. June 29, 1748	2	11
Joseph, s. Abel & Mary, b. Mar. 11, 1753	2	48
Joseph, s. Hezekiah & Polly, b. June 22, 1797	2	116
Joseph, m. Bridget **FRINK**, b. of Plainfield, Nov. 16, 1809, by Rev. Joel Benedict	2	118
Joseph, s. Cyrel & Martha, b. Oct. 26, 1817	2	173
Joseph, of Plainfield, m. Mary **MUNRO**, of Seekonk, Mass., May 18, 1823	2	170
Joseph, of Plainfield, m. Mary **MUNRO**, of Seekonk, Mass, May 18, 1823	3	22
Joseph C., m. Sarah **WESTCOTT**, b. of Plainfield, Oct. 6, 1834, by Rev. Samuel Rockwell	2	219
Joseph C., m. Susan E. **WESCOTT**, b. of Plainfield, Sept. 3, 1849, by Rev. Joseph P. Brown	3	58
Joseph C., merchant, ae. 45, of Plainfield, m. 2d w. Susanna **WESTCOTT**, ae. 25, b. Sterling, res. Plainfield, Sept. 3, 1849, by Joseph P. Brown	4	6
Joseph Cary, s. Samuel K. & Nabby, b. Sept. 3, 1804	2	172
Joseph Francis, s. Joseph & Mary, b. Oct. 9, 1834	2	170
Joseph Francis, s. Joseph & Mary, b. Oct. 9, 1834	3	22
Joseph S., m. Susan **CADY**, b. of Plainfield, Apr. 23, 1817, by Rev. Daniel Dow, Thompson	2	130
Josephine A., d. Benjamin, merchant, ae. 25, & Lucinda, ae. 27, b. Dec. 24, 1849	4	28
Josiah, m. Sarah **WARREN**, d. Jacob & Sarah, Dec. 4, 1710	1	9
Josiah, s. Josiah & Sarah, b. Oct. 27, 1715	1	15
Josiah, d. Sept. 21, 1727	1	41
Josiah, s. Ephraim & Abigail, b. Dec. 7, 1729	2	27
Josiah, of Plainfield, m. Hannah **GROVER**, of Killingly, May 18, 1738	1	95
Josiah, s. Josiah & Hannah, b. June 29, 1740	1	98
Josiah, s. Joseph & Lydia, b. Dec. 19, 1750	2	18
Josiah, m. Prescilla **PAINE**, Dec. 24, 1755	2	36
Julia, m. Erastus S. **SPAULDING**, b. of Plainfield, Mar. 19, 1848, by Rev. J. Mather	3	54
Kezia, d. Josia[h] & Sarah, b. Apr. 15, 1721	1	25
Keziah, m. Eleazer **CADY**, Oct. 28, 1739	2	36

SPAULDING, SPALDING, (cont.)

	Vol.	Page
Kezia, d. Samuel K. & Nabby, b. July 23, 1806; d. Sept. 23, 1809	2	172
Lemuel, s. Amos & Hannah, b. Sept. 27, 1740	2	11
Lemuel, s. Samuel & Joanna, b. Sept. 18, 1771	2	91
Leonard, s. Eleazer, Jr. & Lois, b. Aug. 8, 1761	2	55
Lois, d. Jonathan & Juda, b. Mar. 16, 1720/21	1	25
Lois, d. Timothy & Lucy, b. July 17, 1770	2	74
Lois, d. Samuel & Joanna, b. Jan. 20, 1784	2	91
Louisa, twin with Lovisa, d. Charles & Lydia, b. May 11, 1813	2	172
Louisa, m. William **KENYON**, b. of Plainfield, [ ], by Rev. Joseph P. Brown	3	77
Lovel, s. Jesse & Mary, b. Oct. 29, 1757	2	48
Lovisa, twin with Louisa, d. Charles & Lydia, b. May 11, 1813	2	172
Luce, d. Phillip & Ann, b. Nov. 4, 1727	1	69
Lucy, d. Abel & Mary, b. May 27, 1761	2	48
Lucy, d. Capt. John & Lucy, b. Oct. 17, 1762	2	77
Lucy, d. Ezra & Hannah, b. Mar. 6, 1782	2	87
Lucy, m. Aaron **STARKWEATHER**, May 9, 1805	2	116
Lucy Kezia, d. Samuel K. & Nabby, b. Apr. 12, 1811	2	172
Lucy W., m. Charles W. **HOWLAND**, b. of Plainfield, Mar. 27, 1837, by Rev. Samuel Rockwell	2	229
Lydia, d. Joseph, m. Timothy **PEARCE**, May 27, 1696; d. Mar. 23, 1705/6	1	3
Lydiah, d. Thomas & Marcy, b. Dec. 9, 1729	1	61
Lydia, d. Joseph & Lydia, b. Aug. 16, 1743	2	17
Lydia, d. Amos & Hannah, b. June 2, 1761	2	46
Lydia, b. Killingly, res. Plainfield, d. Nov. 6, 1849, ae. 73	4	64
Lyman, m. Apphia **CLARK**, Apr. 24, 1823, by Rev. Orin Fowler	2	191
Magdelon, d. Azariah & Molly, b. June 18, 1747	2	16
Marah, d. Nathaniel & Marah, b. Feb. 3, 1744	2	10
Marah, d. R[e]uben & Marah, b. June 19, 1748	2	7
Marcy, w. Joseph, d. Aug. 7, 1728, in the 76th y. of her age	1	44
Marcy, d. Charles & Lydia, b. Sept. 17, 1807	2	117
Martha, d. Josiah & Sarah, b. Oct. 25, 1723	1	28
Ma[r]tha, m. Samuel **HOW[E]**, Jr., Oct. 30, 1740	1	100
Mary, w. Edward, d. Dec. 8, 1704	1	3
Mary, d. Josiah & Sarah, b. Oct. 12, 1711	1	9
Mary, d. Thomas & Mercy, b. July 7, 1716	1	17
Mary, m. Sam[ue]ll **SHEPARD**, Jan. 20, 1731	1	59
Mary, d. Benjamin & Deborah, b. Jan. 17, 1731/2	1	61
Mary, d. Ephraim & Abigail, b. May 16, 1744	2	27
Mary, m. Rev. David **ROWLAND**, Feb. 20, 1754	2	29

PLAINFIELD VITAL RECORDS 249

	Vol.	Page
SPAULDING, SPALDING, (cont.)		
Mary, m. John **LARRABEE**, Dec. 16, 1762	2	55
Mary, d. Samuel & Joanna, b. Aug. 24, 1775	2	91
Mary, w. Oliver, d. Apr. 24, 1781	2	95
Mary, wid. Thomas, d. Oct. 19, 1784	2	89
Ma[t]thew, d. Azariah & Molly, b. Mar. 22, 1749		
(Martha?)	2	16
Mathew, w. Jacob, d. Sept. 23, 1755	2	34
Mehetable, d. Isaac & Elizabeth, b. Feb. 7,		
1713/14	1	13
Mephebal, m. David **SHEPARD**, May 8, 1732 (Mehetable)	1	57
Mehetabel, m. Ephraim **WHE[E]LER**, Dec. 31, 1776	2	87
Mercy, d. Hezekiah & Mary, b. Nov. 16, 1791	2	99
Molly, d. Azariah & Molly, b. July 21, 1745	2	16
Molle, m. Aaron **WHE[E]LER**, June 13, 1764	2	71
Molle, d. Curtis & Belle, b. Dec. 15, 1764	2	49
Molle, d. Curtis & Bette, b. Dec. 15, 1764	2	65
Molle, d. Azariah & Molle, b. Mar. 5, 1767	2	59
Nancy, d. Cyrel & Martha, b. June 1, 1810	2	173
Nathan, s. Simon & Anne, b. Sept. 15, 1748; d.		
[ ]	2	9
Nathan, s. Charles & Lydia, b. June 5, 1809	2	117
Nathaniel, s. Nathaniel & Johan[n]ah, b. July 7, 1720	1	22
Nathaniel, Jr., m. Marah **STEVENS**, Feb. 15, 1741	2	10
Noah, s. Simon & Anne, b. Jan. 10, 1751	2	21
Olive, d. Benjamin, Jr. & Sarah, b. July 17, 1709	1	7
Olief, m. John **DOUGLAS**, Jan. 13, 1724/5	1	32
Olive, m. John **HALL**, June 23, 1744	1	2
Olive, d. John & Elizabeth, b. Apr. 3, 1750	2	30
Olive Prior, d. Samuel K. & Lucy, b. May 1, 1818	2	172
Oliver, s. Benjamin & Deborah, b. Jan. 25, 1730/31; d.		
Feb. 24, 1731	1	60
Oliver, s. Ephraim & Abigail, b. Sept. 30, 1739	2	27
Oliver, m. Mary **HUNTER**, June 17, 1762, in the 23rd y.		
of his age	2	83
Oliver, m. Mary **WINTER**, June 17, 1762, in the 23rd y.		
of his age	2	94
Oliver, m. 2d w. Rebecca **BOTTOM**, May 9, 1784	2	94
Otis, s. Samuel K. & Nabby, b. Sept. 17, 1808; d.		
Dec. 23, 1812	2	172
Palatiah, s. Ephraim & Abigail, b. Mar. 19, 1734	2	27
Palatiah, s. Ephraim & Abigail, d. Oct. 3, 1750	2	27
Parnel, w. Phillip, d. May 25, 1756	2	41
Parnel, d. Phillip & Deborah, b. Jan. 2, 1759	2	41
Parnel, d. Phillip, d. Oct. 26, 1761, ae. 2 y. 10 m.	2	47
Peneuel, s. Ele[a]zer & Abigail, b. June 20, 1720;		
d. July 5, 1720	1	33
Phebe, d. Jonathan & Phebe, b. Feb. 5, 1769	2	75

	Vol.	Page
SPAULDING, SPALDING, (cont.)		
Phebe Goff, d. Charles & Lydia, b. Nov. 1, 1814	2	172
Phillip, s. Edward & Mary, b. Mar. 6, 170[ ]	1	7
Phillip, m. Ann **CLEAVELAND**, d. Isaac & Elisabeth, Aug. 10, 1721	1	27
Phillip, s. Jonathan & Judeth, b. Feb. 26, 1726	1	39
Phillip, m. Parnel **CHAMPIN**, May 1, 1750	2	41
Phillip, Dea., d. May 2, 1752	2	21
Phillip, s. Joseph & Lidiah, b. May 11, 1753	2	28
Phillip, s. Phillip & Parnel, b. Nov. 22, 1755	2	41
Phillip, m. Deborah **WOODWARD**, Mar. 22, 1758	2	41
Phineas, s. Isaac & Elisabeth, b. Jan. 23, 1720/21	1	21
Phinehas, s. Ephraim & Abigail, b. Mar. 25, 1726	2	27
Phinehas, s. Ephraim & Abigail, d. Aug. 18, 1751	2	27
Phinehas, s. Curtis & Belle, b. Mar. 10, 1756; d. May 29, 1758	2	49
Polly, d. Oliver & Mary, b. Oct. 16, 1780; d. Apr. 2, 1781	2	94
Prissilla, d. Josia[h] & Sarah, b. Jan. 17, 1718/19	1	20
Prescilla, d. Josiah & Prescilla, b. Oct. 24, 1756	2	36
Prudence, m. David **REYNOLDS**, of Coventry, R.I., both residing in Plainfield, Oct. 19, 1828, by Peleg Peckham, Elder	2	207
Rachal, [twin with Debora], d. Edward & Dorothy, b. Jan. 17, 1706/7	1	5
Rachel, d. Nathaniel & Johanna, b. Sept. 14, 1724	1	31
Rachal, d. Isaac & Elizabeth, b. July 15, 1728	1	44
Rachal, m. Simon **SHEPHARD**, Dec. 25, 1751	2	28
Rachel, d. Timothy & Lucy, b. Jan. 9, 1777	2	81
Rachel, of Plainfield, m. Joseph **HAWKINS**, of Sterling, June 29, 1828, by John Dunlap, J.P.	3	3
Rebec[c]a, d. Edward, Jr. & Elisabeth, b. Oct. 20, 1721	1	25
Rebecka, d. Simon & Anne, b. Mar. 10, 1739	2	9
Rebeckah, m. Reuben **SHEPHARD**, Feb. 27, 1760	2	47
Rebecca, m. Reuben **SHEPHARD**, Feb. 27, 1760	2	75
R[e]uben, s. Ephraim & Abigaiel, b. Feb. 24, 1727/8	1	44
R[e]uben, s. Ephraim & Abigail, b. Feb. 26, 1728	2	27
R[e]uben, m. Mary **PEIRCE**, Oct. 1, 1747	2	7
R[e]uben, s. Joseph & Lydia, b. Dec. 7, 1748	2	17
Reuben, s. Josiah & Priscilla, b. Dec. 20, 1758	2	38
Reuben, d. Dec. 4, 1821, ae. 73	2	173
Rosilla, m. George **NEY**, b. of Plainfield, Feb. 1, 1832, by Nathaniel Cole, Elder	2	215
Royal, s. Benj[ami]n, Jr. & Rachel, b. Aug. 23, 1766	2	63
Rozell, s. John & Elizabeth, b. Nov. 1, 1756	2	37
Rozel, s. John & Elizabeth, b. Nov. 1, 1757	2	66
Rufus, s. Azariah & Molly, b. May 16, 1751	2	16

	Vol.	Page
SPAULDING, SPALDING, (cont.)		
Ruluff, s. Nathaniel & Mary, b. Nov. 13, 1750	2	12
Ruth, d. Edward, Jr. & Elisabeth, b. Apr. 30, 1719	1	25
Ruth, d. Simon & Anne, b. Apr. 21, 1745	2	9
Ruth, d. Nathaniel & Marah, b. July 5, 1748	2	10
Ruth, d. Simon & Ruth, b. July 2, 1771	2	73
Samuel, d. June 9, 1749	2	7
Samuel, s. Amos & Hannah, b. Nov. 20, 1754	2	29
Samuel, m. Joanna **KEE**, June 11, 1771	2	91
Samuel, s. Samuel & Joanna, b. May 1, 1781	2	91
Samuel K., m. Lucy **PRIOR**, May 1, 1816	2	172
Sarah, d. Benjamin & Sarah, b. Oct. 8, 1711	1	10
Sarah, d. Josiah & Sarah, b. Oct. 3, 1713	1	13
Sarah, d. Josiah & Sarah, b. Oct. 4, 1713	1	25
Sarah, wid. of Benjamin, Jr., m. William **BLOGGET**, Aug. 18, 1714	1	14
Sarah, d. Thomas & Mercy, b. Oct. 7, 1717	1	19
Sarah, d. Isaac & Elisabeth, b. Feb. 15, 1722/3	1	29
Sary, d. Benjamin, Jr., m. Sam[ue]ll **COIT**, Mar. 30, 1730	1	63
Sarah, d. Benjamin & Deborah, b. Dec. 5, 1733	1	61
Sarah, d. Nathaniel & Johannah, b. Apr. 30, 1736	1	65
Sarah, d. Josiah & Hannah, b. Feb. 8, 1738/9	1	95
Sarah, d. Simon & Anne, b. Dec. 4, 1746; d. Oct. 11, 174[ ]	2	9
Sarah, d. Edward & Ruth, b. Apr. 7, 1748	2	15
Sarah, m. David **STEVENS**, July 7, 1753	2	32
Sarah, m. Stephen **KINGSBURY**, Dec. 10, 1755	2	37
Sarah, d. Simon & Ruth, b. Jan. 31, 1763	2	73
Sarah, of Plainfield, m. Alvan **GALLUP**, of West Greenwich, R.I., Feb. 4, 1839, by Rev. Samuel Rockwell	2	239
Sarah, Mrs., b. Sterling, res. Plainfield, d. June 23, [18]48	4	61
Sarah, d. Cyrel, farmer, ae. 65, & Ruth, ae. 44, b. Sept. [ ], 1848	4	26
Sila, d. Jacob & Thankfull, b. Jan. 17, 1761	2	45
Silas, s. Phillip & Parnel, b. June 24, 1751	2	41
Simeon, s. Josiah & Sarah, b. Jan. 24, 1717/18; d. Feb. 4, 1717/18	1	18
Simon, s. Edward & Elizabeth, b. Nov. 7, 1714	1	14
Simon, m. Anne **BILLINGS**, June 1, 1737	2	9
Simon, Jr., s. Simon & Anne, b. Jan. 16, 1742	2	9
Simon, s. Edward & Elizabeth, d. Oct. 14, 1754	2	31
Simon, m. Ruth **SHEPHARD**, Apr. 15, 1761	2	73
Simon, s. Samuel K. & Nabby, by Sept. 9, 1813	2	172
Stephen, s. Edward, Jr. & Elizabeth, b. Aug. 2, 1709	1	7

	Vol.	Page
SPAULDING, SPALDING, (cont.)		
Surviah, see under Zerviah		
Susannah, d. Samuel & Susannah, b. Oct. 19, 1723	1	28
Susan[n]ah, d. Azariah & Molley, b. Sept. 20, 1753	2	35
Tho[ma]s, m. Marcy **WELTCH**, d. James. Dec. 9, 1714	1	16
Timothy, s. William & Lidia, b. Mar. 31, 1719	1	23
Timo[thy], s. Eleazer & Abigaiel, b. Jan. 14, 1725	1	33
Timothy, s. Ebenezer*, d. Dec. 15, 1737 (*Probably "Eleazer")	1	70
Timothy, s. Isaac & Elizabeth, b. Dec. 19, 1738	1	70
Timothy, s. Eleazer, Jr. & Lois, b. Nov. 15, 1741	2	30
Timothy, m. Lucy **SKILLION**, Dec. 25, 1766	2	74
Uriah, s. Jonathan & Judah, b. Nov. 24, 1719; d. Dec. 8, 1719	1	21
Willard, s. Edward & Elisabeth, b. Mar. 1, 1716/17	1	17
Willard, m. Hannah **BRADFORD**, Feb. 20, 1745	2	13
Willard, s. Eleazer, Jr. & Lois, b. July 30, 1755	2	55
William, d. Dec. 29, 1754, in the 60th y. of his age	2	28
William, s. Eleazer & Lois, b. July 30, 1755	2	32
William, s. Oliver & Mary, b. Nov. 18, 1767	2	94
William Peirce, s. Ezra & Hannah, b. Jan. 17, 1787	2	96
Wright, s. Benjamin & Rachal, b. Feb. 5, 1757	2	33
Wyman, s. Nathaniel & Johanna, b. Aug. 19, 1739; d. Mar. 7, 1739/40	1	95
Zadock, s. Willard & Hannah, b. May 8, 1746	2	13
Zerviah, d. Josiah & Sarah, b. Dec. 17, 1726	1	39
Zeviah, m. John **PAINE***, Dec. 24, 1750 (*correction **PIERCE** (?) handwritten in margin of original manuscript)	2	24
Surviah, d. Oliver & Mary, b. Mar. 1, 1770	2	94
Zilpah, d. Azariah & Molley, b. Nov. 23, 1757	2	43
Zilpah, d. Benj[ami]n, Jr. & Rachel, b. Nov. 9, 1763	2	63
Ziprah, d. Josiah & Hannah, b. Mar. 6, 1742	1	99
Zipporary, d. Josiah & Sarah, b. July 5, 1725	1	35
-----, child of Benjamin, b. Oct. 24, 1739	1	101
-----, child of Lyman, carpenter, ae. 49, & Alphia, ae. 45, b. June 13, 1848	4	21
-----, child of Simon & Anne, b. Nov. 5, 1754; d. same day	2	31
SPENCER, William, m. Jemima F. **LOVEGROVE**, b. of Plainfield, June 27, 1831, by Benjamin R. Allen, Minister	2	213
SPOONER, Jordan, m. Susan **MORSE**, May 22, 1842, by Lawton Cady, Elder	3	14
Philip C., of Lawrenceburgh, Ind., m. Lydia **COIT**, of Plainfield, Sept. 11, 1839, by Rev. Samuel Rockwell	2	247

	Vol.	Page
SPRAGUE, Edelia G., of Plainfield, m. John **BOSS**, of West Greenwich, R.I., Jan. 30, 1825, by Orin Fowler, V.D.M.	2	197
STAFFORD, Abel, s. Amos & Experience, b. Apr. 6, 1748	2	11
Amos, m. Experience **SPAULDING**, Sept. 9, 1747	2	11
William A., of Plainfield, m. Susan A. **SMITH**, of Scituate, Jan. 5, 1846, by Peleg Peckham, Elder	3	35
STANTON, Clark, m. Rachel **PICKET**, b. of Plainfield, Sept. 25, 1836, by Chester Tilden	2	227
Frank, s. Clarke, farmer, ae. 42, & Rachel, ae. 38, b. June 1, 1850	4	28
Freelove Ann, m. David **PRENTICE**, Nov. 18, 1824, by Rev. John Hyde, Preston	2	196
Olive, d. Joseph & Abigail, b. Nov. 11, 1748	2	6
STARKWEATHER, Aaron, s. Jabez & Martha, b. Nov. 2, 1777	2	82
Aaron, m. Lucy **SPAULDING**, May 9, 1805	2	116
Aaron, Jr., s. Aaron & Lucy, b. July 25, 1806	2	116
Aaron, m. Adaline **HARRIS**, b. of Plainfield, Mar. 10, 1840, by Rev. Tubal Wakefield	3	4
Calvin, s. Aaron & Lucy, b. Oct. 1, 1818	2	174
Daniel, s. Joseph & Lucy, b. Nov. 17, 1819	2	230
Daniel, m. Louisa **FRENCH**, b. of Plainfield, Feb. 19, 1846, by Rev. A. Dunning	3	35
Elizabeth, d. Jacob & Jean, b. Oct. 27, 1756	2	32
Elmira, m. James S. **HORTEN**, b. of Plainfield, Jan. 6, 1828, by Orin Fowler, V.D.M.	2	204
Ezra, m. Mercy **GALLUP**, June 8, 1797	2	102
Frances C., d. Daniel, farmer, ae. 40, & Louisa, ae. 27, b. Mar. 29, 1849	4	26
George E., s. Daniel, shoemaker, ae. 28, & Louisa, ae. 25, b. Oct. 25, [1848?]	4	22
Hannah, w. of a carpenter, d. July 28, 1849, ae. 37	4	62
Jared, s. Joseph & Lucy, b. Aug. 19, 1822	2	230
Jared, m. Mary **PHILLIPS**, b. of Plainfield, Jan. 15, 1854, by Rev. William Turkington	3	81
Jeremiah, farmer, d. Aug. 17, 1847, ae. 71	4	61
Joel, s. Joel & Joan, b. Mar. 21, 1754	2	32
Lucy, d. Jabez & Martha, d. June 8, 1806	2	116
Lydia, d. Aaron & Lucy, b. Mar. 6, 1812	2	126
Lydia S., of Plainfield, m. Royal S. **COLBURN**, of Brooklyn, Jan. 24, 1850, by Rev. Henry Robinson	3	64
Lydia S., ae. 38, b. Plainfield, res. Plainfield, m. Royal S. **COLBURN**, carpenter, ae. 40, b. Windham, Ct., res. Plainfield, June 24, 1850, by Henry Robinson	4	6
Lydia Spaulding, d. Aaron & Lucy, b. Mar. 6, 1812	2	126
Martha, d. Jabez & Martha, b. Jan. 1, 1773	2	82
Martha, m. Justus **BABCOCK**, Apr. 13, 1806	2	117

	Vol.	Page
STARKWEATHER, (cont.)		
Martha, w. Jabez, d. Oct. 3, 1809	2	117
Martha, w. Jabez, d. Oct. 4, 1809	2	117
Marvin, s. Aaron & Lucy, b. Dec. 28, 1808, in Mansfield, Conn.	2	126
Marvin, m. Almanda **CORBIN**, b. of Plainfield, Nov. 30, 1848, by Amos Witter, J.P.	3	56
Marvin, laborer, ae. 40, of Plainfield, m. Amanda **COLVIN**, ae. 46, b. Chaplain, Ct., res. Plainfield, Nov. 30, 1848, by Amos Witter, Esq.	4	3
Mary, d. Jabez & Martha, d. Mar. 3, 1806	2	116
Mary Ann, of Plainfield, m. Lovell W. **BALDWIN**, of Dalton, Mass., Nov. 25, 1839, by Rev. Samuel Rockwell	2	249
Mary Ann, of Plainfield, m. Lovell W. **BALDWIN**, of Dalton, Mass., Nov. 25, 1839, by Rev. Samuel Rockwell	3	2
Molly, d. Jabez & Martha, b. May 6, 1775	2	82
Samuel Spaulding, s. Aaron & Lucy, b. Nov. 19, 1814	2	127
Sarah, d. Jabez & Martha, b. Jan. 14, 1784; d. Mar. 3, 1785	2	96-7
Susan A., of Plainfield, m. Manser G. **THOMAS**, of Exeter, N.Y., Nov. 22, 1820, by Jonathan Gallup, J.P.	2	131
-----, st. b. s., Jeremiah, carpenter, ae. 40, & Hannah E., ae. 37, b. July 22, 1849	4	26
STAYSA, John, s. Stephen & Lucy, b. June 19, 1795	2	108
Joseph Avery, s. Stephen & Lucy, b. Apr. 20, 1793	2	108
STEARNS, STEARNES, STERNS, STURNS, Anna, d. Ebenezer & Mary, b. Nov. 8, 1754	2	30
Boaz*, [see **STEVENS**] (*correction entire entry handwritten in original manuscript)		
Cynthia, d. Ebenezer & Mary, b. Feb. 4, 1749/50	2	11
Hannah, m. Isaac **WHEELER**, Jr., June 5, 1729	1	50
Isaac, s. Ebenezer & Mary, b. Sept. 18, 1742; d. Sept. 21, 17[ ]	1	1X
Isaac, s. Ebenezer & Mary, b. Jan. 19, 1757	2	35
Mary, d. Ebenezer & Mary, b. Dec. 1, 1745	1	2X
Mathew, d. Ebenezer & Mary, b. June 25, 1759	2	35
Nathaniel, s. Nathaniel & Anna, b. Sept. 21, 1732	1	57
Nath[anie]ll, m. Mary **WARREN**, Aug. 6, 1761	2	48
Persilla, d. Ebenezer & Mary, b. Apr. 30, 1752	2	19
Samuel, s. Ebenezer & Mary, b. Dec. 1, 1745; d. Dec. 25, 1745	1	2X
Samuel, Dea., d. Aug. 25, 1759, in the 93rd y. of his age	2	48
Samuel, s. Nathaniel, Jr. & Mary, b. Aug. 11, 1768	2	65
Sibel, d. Ebenezer & Sarah, b. Dec. 13, 1740	1	96

PLAINFIELD VITAL RECORDS 255

	Vol.	Page
STEERE, Zadock J., of Plainfield, m. Robiah B. **HAWKINS**, of Sterling, Aug. 20, 1837, by Peleg Peckham, Elder	2	232
STEPHENS, [see under **STEVENS**]		
STERNS, [see under **STEARNS**]		
STERRY, Jane, of Norwich, m. Peleg **HUNT**, of Worcester, Mass, Mar. 25, 1823, by Rev. Orin Fowler	2	191
STEVENS, STEEVENS, STEEPHENS, STEVANS, Abel, s. Cyprian & Rachel, b. Mar. 23, 1752	2	24
Abigail, d. Willard & Deborah, b. Aug. 26, 1769	2	72
Abigail, d. Simon & Mercy, b. Mar. 24, 1754	2	30
Abigail, d. Simon & Mercy, b. Mar. 24, 1754	2	56
Ame, s. [sic] William & Allis, b. Apr. 20, 1758	2	34
Andrew, s. Tho[ma]s & Mary, b. Nov. 6, 1709	1	19
Anna, d. Thomas, Jr. & Amey, b. Mar. 25, 1719	1	21
Anna, d. Simon & Mercy, b. Mar. 17, 1756	2	56
Anne, d. Thomas, Jr. & Lydia, b. July 17, 1755	2	32
Asa, s. David & Sarah, b. Apr. 6, 1754	2	32
Benjamin, s. Tho[ma]s & Mary, b. Apr. 17, 1713	1	19
Boaz, [**STEARNS***], m. Lidiah **SHEPARD**, Nov. 18, [1725*] (*correction **STEARNS** handwritten in margin of original manuscript; *correction 1725 handwritten within brackets of original manuscript)	1	35
Siprian, s. Siprian & Abigail, b. Apr. 15, 1724	1	35
Siprian, Jr., m. Abigaiel **WARREN**, Nov. 26, 1727	1	51
Cyprian, m. Rachel **LYON**, Aug. 9, 1748	2	24
Daniel, s. Nehemiah & Hipzabah, b. Aug. 7, 1766	2	61
David, s. Cyprian, Jr. & Abigaiel, b. Aug. 23, 1731	1	64
David, m. Sarah **SPAULDING**, July 7, 1753	2	32
David, s. David & Sarah, b. Nov. 24, 1763	2	64
Deborah, d. David & Sarah, b. Jan. 25, 1759; d. Oct. 1, 1759	2	64
Ebenezer, m. Sarah **GOULD**, Feb. 28, 1740	1	96
Elias, s. Thomas & Amey, b. June 3, 1728	1	45
Elias, m. Sarah **SHEPHARD**, Feb. 27, 1754	2	24
Elias, s. Elias & Sarah, b. Oct. 15, 1755	2	29
Elisabeth, m. Nathaniel **PEIRCE**, Feb. 20, 1723	1	38
Elizabeth, m. Sam[ue]ll **HALL**, Aug. 27, 1729	1	48
Esther, d. Nehemiah & Hephsibah, b. Jan. 10, 1776	2	100
Hannah, w. Syperan, d. July 4, 1748	2	6
Hannah, d. Nehemiah & Rebecca, b. Oct. 19, 1750	2	6
Hannah, d. Syran & Rachal, b. Feb. 12, 1757	2	51
Hannah, d. William & Allis, b. Feb. 20, 1764	2	35
Henry, m. Elizabeth **FFELLOWS**, d. Ephraim, Mar. 2, 1708/9	1	7
Henery, s. Henery & Elizabeth, b. Dec. 18, 1709	1	9
Isaac, s. Cyprian, Jr. & Abigaiel, b. Feb. 16, 1734/5	1	64
Isaac, s. Ebenezer & Mary, b. Sept. 18, 1742	1	99

	Vol.	Page
STEVENS, STEEVENS, STEEPHENS, STEVANS, (cont.)		
Isaac, m. Sarah **CLARK**, Sept. 19, 1758	2	40
Jacob, s. Syperan & Abigail, b. Sept. 1, 1736	2	6
Jacob, m. Elizabeth **LEONARD**, May 26, 1757	2	37
Jeduchan, s. Thomas, 3rd, & Amey, b. Nov. 16, 1736	1	67
Jeduthan, s. Thomas & Lydia, b. Dec. 13, 1743	2	15
Jeduthan, m. Prudence **HAVENS**, Mar. 8, 1766	2	104
Jeduthan, d. July 27, 1799	2	104
Jesse, s. Tho[ma]s, 2d, & Abegall, b. Aug. 31, 1721	1	26
Jesse, s. Thomas & Abigaiel, d. Oct. 12, 1726	1	39
Jes[s]e, s. Thomas, 4th, & Elizabeth, b. Aug. 16, 1729	1	50
John, s. John & Elisabeth, b. Jan. 8, 1721/2	1	26
John, s. Ne[he]miah & Rebecca, b. Oct. 31, 1748	2	6
Jonathan, s. Thomas & Lydiah, b. Dec. 13, 1743	1	2X
Joseph, s. Sypran & Rachal, b. Oct, 23, 1754	2	51
Lowis, d. Thomas, Jr. & Amy, b. Aug. 21, 1717	1	21
Lois, m. Ezekiel **PARCE**, Feb. 11, 1736	1	101
Lois, m. Ezekiel **PEIRCE**, Feb. 11, 1736	2	5
Lois, d. Simon & Mercy, b. July 26, 1762	2	56
Lucy, d. David & Sarah, b. Feb. 22, 1756	2	32
Lucy, d. William & Allis, b. Oct. 6, 1766	2	35
Lydiah, d. Thomas & Lydiah, b. June 16, 1746	1	2X
Lydia, d. Thomas & Lydia, b. June 16, 1746	2	15
Lydia, m. Moses **SHEPHARD**, Oct. 15, 1765	2	62
Lydia, d. Jeduthan & Prudence, b. Feb. 5, 1781	2	104
Lydia, of Plainfield, m. William **PEIRCE**, of Troy, N.Y., Oct. 5, 1800	2	106
Marah, m. Nathaniel **SPAULDING**, Jr., Feb. 15, 1741	2	10
Mary, w. Thomas, Jr., d. May 30, 1719	1	21
Mary, d. John & Elisabeth, b. Sept. [ ], 1723	1	30
Mary, d. Thomas & Lydia, b. June 10, 1748	2	15
Mary, d. Simon & Mercy, b. Oct. 8, 1751, o.s.	2	30
Mehetable*, m. William **BLODGETT**, Mar. 31, 1737 (*correction "possibly **STERRY**" handwritten in margin of original manuscript. See **BLODGETT** entry.)	1	68
Molly, d. Simon & Mercy, b. Oct. 8, 1752	2	56
Ne[he]miah, s. Thomas, Jr. & Ame, b. Aug. [31], 1725	1	38
Nehemiah, m. Rebec[c]a **DOW**, Dec. 24, 1747	2	6
Nehemiah, m. Hiphzabah **KILLUM**, Jan. 24, 1766	2	61
Nehemiah, d. Feb. 13, 1776	2	100
Newel, s. David & Sarah, b. July 24, 1760	2	64
Perry, s. Isaac & Sarah, b. Sept. 20, 1768	2	72
Polle, d. William & Alice, b. May 1, 1769	2	76
Persiller, d. Siprian, Jr. & Abigaiel, b. Sept. 10, 1728	1	51

STEVENS, STEEVENS, STEEPHENS, STEVANS, (cont.)

	Vol.	Page
Priscella, d. Simon & Mercy, b. Mar. 9, 1758	2	56
Rachel, m. Ephraim **SANFORD**, b. of Plainfield, Apr. 1, 1838, by William Dyer, J.P.	2	234
Rebeckah, w. Nehemiah, d. Nov. 13, 1754, in the 26th y. of her age	2	28
Rebecka, d. Nehemiah & Hipzabah, b. Mar. 10, 1770	2	61
Roswel[l], s. Thomas, 3rd, & Amey, b. Dec. 3, 1733	1	61
Royal, s. Simon & Mercy, b. Mar. 31, 1760; d. Apr. 1, 1761	2	56
Rozell, s. William & Allis, b. Jan. 14, 1756	2	34
Russel[l], s. Nehemiah & Hipzabah, b. June 17, 1768	2	61
Ruth, d. Thomas & Ame, b. Feb. 4, 1721	1	30
Ruth, d. John & Elisabeth, b. May 20, 1726	1	37
Ruth, m. Capt. Beman **LEE**, July 8, 1746	1	2X
Ruth, m. Benjamin **LEE**, July 8, 1746	2	4
Samuel, s. Tho[ma]s & Mary, b. Mar. 6, 1714/15	1	19
Sam[ue]ll, s. Boaz & Lydiah, b. Sept. 2, 1726	1	40
Sarah, d. David & Sarah, b. July 31, 1767	2	64
Semeon, s. Henry & Elizabeth, b. Apr. 22, 1714	1	14
Simon, s. Siprian, Jr. & Abigaiel, b. Feb. 7, 1729/30	1	51
Simon, m. Mercy **BENNET**, June 20, 1751	2	56
Simon, s. Simon & Mercy, b. Feb. 27, 1765	2	59
Syla, d. William & Allis, b. Jan. 3, 1761	2	34
Sylvan, m. Abegell **JO[H]NSON**, b. of Plainfield, May 1, 1723	1	28
Thomas, Jr., m. Mary **HALL**, d. Stephen, May 26, 1702	1	3
Thomas, s. Thomas, Jr. & Mary, b. Jan. 12, 1703/4	1	7
Thomas, s. Thomas, Jr. & Mary, b. Dec. 30, 1705	1	7
Thomas, Jr., m. Amy **FFELLOWS**, Nov. 8, 1716	1	17
Thomas, 2d, m. Abegall **WINEWARD**, Mar. 14, 1719/20	1	22
Thomas, s. Thomas, Jr. & Ame, b. Apr. 16, 1723	1	30
Thomas, 4th, m. Elizabeth **WILLIAMS**, June 5, 1728	1	50
Thomas, Jr., m. Lydiah **PEIRCE**, Oct. [ ], 1742	1	2X
Thomas, m. Lydia **PEIRCE**, Oct. [ ], 1742	2	15
Thomas, s. Thomas & Lydia, b. Jan. 14, 1751	2	15
Thomas, Jr., d. Nov. 12, 1755	2	32
Timothy, s. Thomas, Jr. & Lydia, b. June 14, 1754	2	15
Uriah, s. Thomas, Jr. & Mary, b. Jan. 21, 1708	1	7
Whelthy, d. Willard & Deborah, b. Jan. 30, 1760	2	72
William, m. Allis **WEAVER**, Feb. 7, 1755	2	34
William, Jr., s. William & Alice, b. Dec. 6, 1771	2	76
Zebulon, s. Tho[ma]s & Mary, b. June 25, 1717	1	19

STEWARD, [see also STEWART and STUART]

	Vol.	Page
Elizabeth, of Plainfield, m. David **RITCHY**, of Saratoga, N.Y., July 18, 1852, by Rev. Joseph P. Brown	3	75
Henry F., of Norwich, m. Mary H. **FRY**, of Plainfield, Mar. 4, 1852, by Rev. Joseph P. Brown	3	74

	Vol.	Page
[STEWART], STEWERT, [see also **STEWARD** and **STUART**],		
Alexander, m. Amey **SPAULDING**, Apr. 18, 1734	1	66
Sarah, d. Alexander & Amey, b. Feb. 28, 1734/5	1	66
STEWELL, STUELL, [see also **STOWELL**], Aurelia, of Bolton, m. Hopkins **FISK**, of Plainfield, Sept. 3, 1827, by Enoch Burt, Manchester	2	203
Caroline, m. Arnold **DIXON**, b. of Plainfield, Nov. 27, 1836, by Chester Tilden	2	228
STODDARD, Hannah, of Canterbury, m. Grafton **BENNET**, of Plainfield, June 12, 1828, by Rev. James K. Wheelock, of Canterbury	2	206
STONE, Ann Eliza, b. Coventry, R.I., res. Plainfield, d. May 14, 1848, ae. 4	4	61
Godfrey, m. Mary **MOWRY**, b. of Killingly, July 17, 1823, by Orin Fowler, V.D.M.	2	191
Harris H., of Cranston, R.I., m. Abby Ann **PARKER**, of Coventry, R.I., Oct. 6, 1846, by Rev. J. Mather	3	39
Jason, of Sterling, m. Rhoda **FRY**, of Plainfield, Sept. 18, 1837, by Chester Tilden	2	232
Jeremiah, of West Killingly, m. Sarah **BURDICK**, of Plainfield, Jan. 16, 1848, by Rev. James Mather	3	50
Jeremiah, mechanic, of Killingly, m. Sarah J. **BURDICK**, b. Killingly, Feb. [ ], 1848, by Rev. James Mathew	4	2
John W., of West Greenwich, m. Betsey M. **REYNOLDS**, of Sterling, Nov. 13, 1843, by Peleg Peckham, Elder	3	21
Nathan, of Sterling, m. Elipha **POTTER**, of Plainfield, Nov. 24, 1839, by Rev. Hezekiah Thatcher	2	252
Nathan, of Sterling, m. Elipha **POTTER**, of Plainfield, Nov. 24, 1839, by Rev. Hezekiah Tha[t]cher	3	2
Simon, of Griswold, m. Sally **SMITH**, of Plainfield, June 5, 1825, by Rev. Orin Fowler	2	198
STORRS, STORES, Maria A., m. Albert G. **LESTER**, b. of Plainfield, Sept. 1, 1846, by A. Dunning	3	38
William, m. Elizabeth **DEAN**, b. of Plainfield, Feb. 26, 1823, by Orin Fowler, V.D.M.	2	190
STORY, Amarick, m. Lamira **DEAN**, b. of Plainfield, Sept. 17, 1832, by Rev. Samuel Rockwell	2	215
STOWELL, [see also **STEWELL**], Betsey, of Plainfield, m. Roswell W. **BAILEY**, of Bolton, Mar. 19, 1826, by Orin Fowler, V.D.M.	2	198
Harriet, m. Asa C. **GUILE**, b. of Plainfield, Aug. 24, 1835, by Peleg Peckham, Elder	2	222
Mary B., of Plainfield, m. George **MONTGOMERY**, of Sterling, Sept. 20, 1830, by Benj[ami]n R. Allen, Elder	2	211

	Vol.	Page
STOWELL, (cont.)		
Mary B., of Plainfield, M. George **MONTGOMERY**, of Sterling, Sept. 20, 1830, by Benj[ami]n R. Allen, Elder	2	212
STRAIGHT, Phebe D., m. Ira C. **MATTISON**, Jan. 3, 1841, by Sam[ue]l D. Hough. J.P.	3	9
STRANAHAN, Anthony, s. James & Martha, b. July 16, 1776	2	84
Freelove, d. James & Martha, b. Feb. 26, 1775	2	84
James, Jr., s. James & Martha, b. May 12, 1772	2	84
Jenne, d. James & Martha, b. Dec. 25, 1766	2	84
John, s. James & Martha, b. Apr. 25, 1769	2	84
Joshua, of Killingly, m. Mary **MASON**, Nov. 18, 1821, by Rev. Nathaniel Cole	2	134
Samuel, s. James & Martha, b. June 4, 1778	2	84
William, s. James & Martha, b. Nov. 27, 1770	2	84
STRINGER, Margaret, m. Rodman **JAMES**, b. of Plainfield, Nov. 25, 1802, by Rev. Joel Benedict	2	190
STUART, [see also **STEWARD** and **STEWART**], Joseph, s. Mary **BOYD**, b. Feb. 10, 1760	2	62
STUTSON, Isaac P., of Lysbon, m. Lucy R. **PALMER**, of Plainfield, Aug. 4, 1844, by Rev. Daniel Lyon, Packerville	3	25
SUMMERS, Dudley A., of Hartford, m. Mary M. **LATHROP**, of Plainfield, July 7, 1834, by Rev. Samuel Rockwell	2	219
SUMNER, Sally Maria, m. Henry S. **LOWELL**, b. of Plainfield, Nov. 24, 1846, by Rev. Jared C. Knapp, Central Village	3	41
SWAN, Mary, d. John & Jean, b. June 9, 1725	1	35
Nathan, s. John & Jean, b. Apr. 4, 1745	2	6
SWANSBROUGH, William, m. Rebecca **BOTTUM**, June 26, 1794	2	100
SWEET, Almira, of Scituate, R.I., m. Robert **WHIPPLE**, of Cranston, R.I., Oct. 14, 1849, by Rev. Joseph P. Brown	3	61
Alvan Abel, s. William & Betsey, b. Mar. 9, 1832	2	241
Amos C., m. Mary S. **YOUNG**, b. of Sterling, Apr. 13, 1845, by Peleg Peckham, Elder	3	31
Charlotte, m. Edmond **MATTESON**, b. of R.I., Feb. 15, 1830, by Peleg Peckham, Elder	2	210
Emeline, ae. 23, m. Thomas **RHODES**, farmer, ae. 30, b. Sterling, res. Vermont, Mar. 27, [18]48, by Rev. Frederick Charlton	4	2
Hepsbeth B., of West Greenwich, R.I., m. William H. **JACOY**, of Warwick, R.I., May 8, 1846, by Rev. James Mather	3	37
Jane, m. George **KEACH**, b. of Brooklyn, Feb. 10, 1850, by Rev. W. Emerson	3	63
Jay, of Canterbury, m. Thankful **TUCKER**, of Plainfield, Mar. 7, 1832, by Nathaniel Cole	2	215

	Vol.	Page
SWEET, (cont.)		
Mary R., m. Horace **READ**, b. of Warwick, R.I., Sept. 28, 1847, by Rev. J. Mather	3	46
Rhody, of Plainfield, m. Nathaniel **PULLMAN**, of West Greenwich, R.I., Jan. 31, 1822, by Rev. Nathaniel Cole	2	187
Stephen B., of Sterling, m. Andra Ann **GREEN**, of Plainfield, Nov. 30, 1843, by Peleg Peckham, Elder	3	21
William, Jr., s. William & Betsey, b. June 6, 1829	2	241
William A., of Worcester, Mass., m. Harriet **WEAVER**, of Plainfield, Oct. 11, 1835, by Rev. Samuel Rockwell	2	222
William C., of Smithfield, R.I., m. Freelove **CAREY**, of Providence, R.I., Nov. 28, 1846, by Rev. J. Mather	3	40
-----, st. b. twins, s. & d., Cha[rle]s, public lecturer, ae. 41, & Lucy T., ae. 37, of Middlebury, Mass., b. Aug. 26, [18]48	4	27
SYDLEMAN, Elisha R., of Canterbury, m. Sally **FISHER**, of Plainfield, May 9, 1841, by Rev. John Read	3	9
TALBOT, Anna, of Plainfield, m. Henry L. **ALDRICH**, of Worcester, Mass., Apr. 22, 1850, by Rev. J. O. Knapp	3	64
Annie W., ae. 25, b. N. Bridge, Mass., res. Plainfield, m. Henry L. **ALDRICH**, merchant, ae. 24, b. Plainfield, res. Worcester, Mass., Apr. 22, 1850, by Rev. J.O. Knapp	4	6
Sarah, b. Smithfield, R.I., res. Plainfield, d. Mar. 31, 1849, ae. 69	4	63
TANNER, Edwin M., tailor, ae. 21, b. R.I., res. Plainfield, m. Harriet B. **FULLER**, ae. 19, b. Thompson, Ct., res. Plainfield, July 1, 1849, by Frederic Coe	4	3
John H., manufacturer, ae. 19, b. W. Greenwich, res. Griswold, m. Ardelia **SPAULDING**, ae. 19, of Plainfield, May 6, 1850, by Rev. Henry Robinson	4	5
Pardon, taverner, b. R.I., res. Plainfield, d. Oct. 10, 1848, ae. 44	4	62
Russel[l], of Voluntown, m. Patty **PHILLIPS**, of Plainfield, Nov. 10, 1851, by Rev. Henry Robinson	3	72
Worthing J., s. Edwin, hotel keeper, b. Apr. 18, [1850]	4	30
TARBOX, Hiram, 2d, of Lisbon, m. Mary **CLARK**, of Canterbury, Dec. 1, 1839, by Rev. Tubal Wakefield	2	249
Hiram, 2d, of Lisbon, m. Mary **CLARK**, of Canterbury, Dec. 1, 1839, by Rev. Tubal Wakefield	3	2
TAYLOR, TAYLER, TAILOR, Christopher H., of Mass., m. Eliza **HENRY**, of Plainfield, Nov. 1, 1841, by Peleg Peckham, Elder	3	12
Cyfuantus (?) B., of Sterling, m. William B. **HOPKINS**, of R.I., now residing in Sterling, Apr. 28, 1844,		

	Vol.	Page
TAYLOR, TAYLER, TAILOR, (cont.)		
by Peleg Peckham, Elder	3	23
John E., m. Thankful **WILBUR**, b. of Coventry, R.I., Nov. 7, 1847, by Rev. Frederic Charlton	3	49
Joseph, of Scituate, R.I., m. Emely **GREEN**, of Plainfield, Jan. 1, 1822, by Rev. Orin Fowler	2	134
Roxana, m. Emory H. **TYLER**, b. of Plainfield, Nov. 26, 1835, by Rev. Ziba Loveland, Central Village	2	223
Sally M., m. Perry A. **POPPLE**, b. of Sterling, Nov. 15, 1847, by Peleg Peckham, Elder	3	47
William R., of Scituate, R.I., m. Amey A. **NICHOLS**, of West Greenwich, R.I., Nov. 15, 1846, by Rev. J. Mather	3	40
TEMPEL, Levy, s. William & Sarah, b. Dec. 24, 1729	1	54
TENNANT, Joseph, m. Paulina **ROANA**, b. of Plainfield, Dec. 7, 1835, by Rev. Samuel Rockwell	2	223
THA[T]CHER, R[h]oda A., of Plainfield, m. Eben[eze]r P. **DAVIS**, of Newbury, Mass., Sept. 17, 1844, by J.R. Osborn, V.D.M.	3	25
THAYER, Alexander, of Worcester, Mass., m. Lucinda **WEAVER**, of Plainfield, Jan. 8, 1837, by Chester Tilden	2	228
Dinah, m. Dick **FORTUNE**, Nov. 19, 1795	2	102
THOMAS, Alice, m. Willard **PARKHURST**, Feb. 9, 1773	2	77
John, m. Clista **BAKER**, b. of Plainfield, Nov. 20, 1831, by Peleg Peckham, Elder	2	214
Manser G., of Exeter, N.Y., m. Susan A. **STARKWEATHER**, of Plainfield, Nov. 22, 1820, by Jonathan Gallup, J.P.	2	131
THOMPSON, THOMSON, Hugh, s. Jonathan & Johannah, b. Sept. 16, 1754	2	29
Jonathan, s. Jonathan & Johannah, b. Nov. 16, 1757	2	37
Patience, d. of Tho[ma]s, of Providence, m. David **WARREN**, Mar. 24, 1718/19	1	22
Sarah E., of New Haven, m. William H. **CUTLER**, of Plainfield, June 16, 1851, by Rev. Henry Robinson	3	70
Sarah E., school teacher, ae. 22, b. Conn., m. William H. **CUTLER**, merchant, ae. 21, b. Conn., res. Plainfield, June 16, 1851, by Rev. Robinson	4	7
THURSTON, Ann E., m. Oliver W. **POLLARD**, b. of East Greenwich, R.I., Jan. 10, 1854, by Rev. Joseph P. Brown	3	82
Emily, m. Edward M. **PRIOR**, b. of Plainfield, Oct. 13, 1847, by Rev. James Mather	3	46
TIBBETTS, Benjamin, m. Betsey **HALL**, b. of Plainfield, Apr. 1, 1827, by Rev. Roswell Whitmore	2	201
TIDD, Pashal P., m. Martha R. **BROWN**, July 14, 1844, by William Dyer, J.P.	3	24

	Vol.	Page
TIFFANY, TIFANY, Henry F., d. June 5, 1851, ae. 3 y.	4	66
-----, child of Thomas A., farmer, & Deney, b. June 20, 1848	4	21
TIFT, Samuel R., of Foster, R.I., m. Topsye **DORING**, of Killingly, both now residing in Plainfield, June 24, 1827, by Rev. Nathaniel Cole	2	202
TILLINGHAST, Azubah D., of West Greenwich, R.I., m. Marcas F. **BENNETT**, of Sterling, Oct. 12, 1851, by Peleg Peckham, Elder	3	72
Betsey, of Voluntown, m. Dr. Henry **ALDRICH**, of South Kingstown, R.I., June 23, 1830, by Rev. Orin Fowler	2	211
Charles, d. Aug. 27, 1847, ae. 3 m.	4	61
Christopher A., m. Amey **FENNER**, b. of Sterling, Nov. 6, 1836, by Peleg Peckham, Elder	2	228
Joseph A., m. Caroline **PECKHAM**, b. of Plainfield, Sept. 17, 1837, by Peleg Peckham, Elder	2	232
Mary, m. Darius A. **FISH**, b. of Sterling, Sept. 4, 1843, by Peleg Peckham, Elder	3	20
Mary A., m. Joel **BURDICK**, Feb. 19, 1847, by Rev. Fred[eri]c Charlton	3	48
Thomas S., of Plainfield, m. Laura **KINNE**, of Voluntown, Feb. 26, 1843, by Peleg Peckham, Elder	3	18
TILLOTSON, George J., Rev., of Brooklyn, m. Elizabeth H. **LESTER**, of Plainfield, Nov. 15, 1848, by Rev. Jared O. Knapp, Central Village	3	54
Philena, m. Orin **DADD***, b. of Griswold, June 13, 1841, by Peleg Peckham, Elder (*Perhaps **LADD**?)	3	10
W[illia]m, Rev., pastor Cong. Church, ae. 45, res. Brooklyn, Ct., m. 3d w. Elizabeth **LESTER**, ae. 30, b. Plainfield, res. Brooklyn, Ct., Nov. 12, 1848, by Rev. J.C. Knapp	4	3
TITUS, Cyrus, m. Sarah H. **MILLER**, b. of Plainfield, Dec. 30, 1832, by Peleg Peckham, Elder	2	216
Harriet, d. Willard, farmer, ae. 32, & Nancy, ae. 26, of Killingly, b. May 6, 1850	4	28
TRACY, Hiram A., of Sutton, Mass., m. Mary Ann **SABIN**, of Plainfield, June 24, 1835, by Rev. Samuel Rockwell	2	221
Lucretia, m. Elias **PARKE**, Feb. 29, 1776	2	86
Lydia, d. Jabez & Hannah, b. July 26, 1785	2	90
Marian, m. Josiah **DEAN**, Feb. 12, 1769	2	66
Meriam, m. Josiah **DEAN**, Feb. 12, 1769	2	84
Olive, d. Stephen & Eunice, b. Jan. 21, 1769	2	74
Samuel, s. Stephen & Eunice, b. Nov. 14, 1770	2	74
Samuel R., m. Mary P. **MIDDLETON**, b. of Plainfield, Apr. 19, 1824, by Orin Fowler, V.D.M.	2	194
Sarah, m. Ebenezer **HARRIS**, Jr., June 5, 1732	1	60

	Vol.	Page

TRACY, (cont.)
    Stephen, m. Eunice **CLARK**, Oct. 13, 1768, by Isaac
        Coit, Esq. — 2, 74
TRANTUM, Sally, m. William **HOPKINS**, May 6, 1804 — 2, 125
TREAT, James S., of Preston, m. Frances A. **WITTER**, of
    Plainfield, Sept. 7, 1829, by Rev. Orin Fowler — 2, 210
    James S., of Voluntown, m. Lydia M. **WITTER**, of
    Plainfield, Nov. 18, 1839, by Rev. Nathan E.
    Sholes, of Preston — 2, 249
    James S., of Voluntown, m. Lydia M. **WITTER**, of
    Plainfield, Nov. 18, 1839, by Rev. Nathan E.
    Shaler, of Preston — 3, 2
TRIPP, Lucy A., m. Gilbert C. **ROLINS**, b. of Plainfield,
    Nov. 18, 1838, by Rev. Samuel Rockwell — 2, 237
    Perry G., s. Perry G., farmer, ae. 25, & Lidea A.,
    ae. 20, b. Feb. 25, 1847 — 4, 26
TRUESDELL, Rachel, m. Albert **BROWN**, b. of Killingly, Nov.
    10, 1844, by James Smither, Elder — 3, 28
TUCKER, Alvin, of South Kingstown, R.I., m. Lucetta W.
    HOWORTH, of Exeter, R.I., Sept. 17, 1848, by Rev.
    Geo[rge] W. Brewster — 3, 56
    Charles E., s. William C., farmer, ae. 28, & Happy
    C., ae. 25, b. June 14, 1849 — 4, 26
    Lucius, of Pomfret, m. Sarah Ann **PHILLIPS**, of Plain-
    field, Mar. 4, 1845, by Peleg Peckham, Elder — 3, 27
    Thankful, of Plainfield, m. Jay **SWEET**, of Canterbury,
    Mar. 7, 1832, by Nathaniel Cole — 2, 215
TUCKERMAN, Benjamin, of Sterling, m. Betsey **LEONARD**, of
    Plainfield, Jan. 18, 1824, by Orin Fowler, V.D.M. — 2, 193
    Mary E., m. Edward H. **GREEN**, b. of Sterling, Oct. 26,
    1845, by Peleg Peckham, Elder — 3, 32
    Penn, of New York, m. Hannah D. **PERKINS**, of Sterling,
    Sept. 14, 1840, by Peleg Peckham, Elder — 3, 7
TUMA, David, laborer, ae. 25, b. Ireland, res. Plainfield,
    m. Eliza **SHATDOW**(?), ae. 31, June 20, 1849 — 4, 3
TUNO, Bridget, m. John **HILLIS**, b. of Plainfield, Mar. 31,
    1839, by Rev. Samuel Rockwell — 2, 240
TURNER, James R., m. Mary A. **ARNOLD**, b. of Warwick, R.I.,
    Nov. 25, 1847, by Rev. Frederic Charlton — 3, 50
    John H., of West Greenwich, R.I., m. Frances A.
    SPAULDING, of Plainfield, May 6, 1850, by Rev.
    Henry Robinson — 3, 64
    Katharine, had d. Hannah **HERRINGTON**, b. Oct. 27, 1762 — 2, 64
    Oliver C., of Providence, R.I., m. Lucy H. **MEDBURY**, of
    Plainfield, May 22, 1843, by Rev. A.B. Wheeler — 3, 19
    William, m. Katharine **BOYD**, Feb. 7, 1759 — 2, 42
    William, s. William & Katharine, b. Sept. 6, 1759 — 2, 42
TYLER, Ann M., of Plainfield, m. Joseph A. **DEAN**, of Taunton,

	Vol.	Page
TYLER, (cont.)		
Mass., July 2, 1838, by Rev. Samuel Rockwell	2	235
Boaz, s. Nathaniel & Lydiah, b. Jan. 30, 1758	2	47
Delilah H., of Killingly, m. Jonah **YOUNG**, of Sterling, Apr. 6, 1845, by Peleg Peckham, Elder	3	27
Edward, b. Canterbury, Ct., res. Plainfield, d. July 18, 1851	4	66
Emory H., m. Roxana **TAYLOR**, b. of Plainfield, Nov. 26, 1835, by Rev. Ziba Loveland, Central Village	2	223
Mary E., of Plainfield, m. Andrew **EDMOND**, of Griswold, Mar. 20, 1845, by A. Dunning	3	27
Mehitable C., m. Edwin **AMES**, b. of Plainfield, Feb. 28, 1843, by Rev. A. Dunning	3	18
Nathaniel, m. Lydiah **WOODWARD**, Oct. 12, 1757	2	47
Thomas, of Manchester, m. Mary Ann **POTTER**, of Plainfield, Sept. 30, 1827, by Orin Fowler, V.D.M.	2	203
UNDERWOOD, Anne, d. Israel & Ruth, b. Feb. 5, 1747	2	42
Bette, d. William & Sarah, b. Mar. 14, 1771	2	72
Elizabeth, d. Israel & Ruth, b. Sept. 23, 1752	2	42
Isaac, s. Israel & Ruth, b. Aug. 29, 1744	2	42
Israel, s. Israel & Ruth, b. Apr. 4, 1746	2	42
Jesse, s. William & Sarah, b. Dec. 20, 1763; d. May 14, 1764	2	59
Josiah, s. Israel & Ruth, b. Feb. 9, 1757	2	42
Lott, s. William & Sarah, b. Mar. 1, 1765	2	59
Lott, s. William & Sarah, b. Mar. 1, 1765	2	97
Lucy, d. William & Sarah, b. June 23, 1773	2	98
Polly, d. William & Sarah, b. Mar. 14, 1771	2	98
Sarah, m. Eliphalet **BINGHAM**, Nov. 25, 1761	2	52
Sarah, d. William & Sarah, b. Feb. 11, 1767	2	62
Septemeas, s. William & Sarah, b. Apr. 27, 1769	2	72
Septimus, s. William & Sarah, b. Apr. 27, 1769	2	97
Timothy, s. Israel & Ruth, b. Sept. 15, 1755	2	42
William, m. Sarah **PHILLIPS**, Apr. 3, 1763	2	59
UPTON, George, of Chaplin, m. Maria B. **DIXON**, of Sterling, Jan. 30, 1843, by Rev. A.B. Wheeler	3	18
Lucy, of Plainfield, m. Lewis **EDWARDS**, of Warwick, R.I., Dec. 2, 1850, by Rev. Joseph P. Brown	3	68
Lucy, cotton weaver, ae. 23, b. Chaplin, res. Plainfield, m. Lucius* **EDWARDS**, farmer, ae. 25, b. Norwich, res. Plainfield, Dec. 2, 1850, by Rev. Joseph P. Brown (*correction Lucius is crossed out and Levias is handwritten in margin of original manuscript)	4	7
Sarah, d. Oct. [ ], 1849, ae. 3	4	63
UTLY, Abigaill, d. Samuell, of Stoningtown, m. John **SCRIPTURE**, formerly of Grotton, now of Plainfield, May 15, 1712	1	10

PLAINFIELD VITAL RECORDS 265

	Vol.	Page
VALENTINE, Edward Henry, of Sterling, m. Olive L. **PLACE**, of Foster, Sept. 2, 1843, by Peleg Peckham, Elder	3	20
VAUGHAN, VAUGHN, Almira, m. Allen **HARRIS**, b. of Plainfield, Sept. 21, 1827, by Orin Fowler, Clericus	2	202
Barbara J., m. Theron D. **WHITFORD**, b. of Sterling, Apr. 10, 1843, by Peleg Peckham, Elder	3	19
Bowen, of East Greenwich, R.I., m. Atlucy **ELLIS**, of West Greenwich, R.I., Aug. 23, 1841, by Peleg Peckham, Elder	3	10
Charles, b. Sterling, res. Plainfield, d. Mar. 16, 1849, ae. 78	4	62
Clark D., of Killingly, m. Juliett **HILL**, of Sterling, May 18, 1846, by Peleg Peckham, Elder	3	37
Colonel, of Bennington, Vt., m. Lydia **FRENCH**, of Plainfield, Sept. 16, 1827, by Elder George W. Appleton, Sterling	2	203
Edward, of Brooklyn, m. Alice M. **DOOLEY**, of Plainfield, Nov. 18, 1849, by Rev. J.O. Knapp	3	61
Eunice, m. Randall B. **WILCOX**, b. of Sterling, July 9, 1843, by Peleg Peckham, Elder	3	20
Hannah, b. Sterling, res. Plainfield, d. Feb. 21, 1849, ae. 78	4	62
Joseph, m. Thrsa **LADD**, b. of Sterling, Oct. 10, 1836, by Peleg Peckham, Elder	2	227
Russel[l], of Sterling, m. Sarah A. **PLACE**, of Foster, R.I., Apr. 22, 1849, by Peleg Peckham, Elder	3	58
Zeanah, m. Joseph **CHANDLER**, b. of Plainfield, Sept. 14, 1824, by Rev. Nathaniel Cole	2	196
VENNER, Sabina B., m. Benjamin J. **LAWTON**, b. of Notich, R.I., Apr. 25, 1847, by Rev. J. Mather	3	43
VIOL, Keziah, m. Thomas D. **CHILDS**, b. of Plainfield, June 8, 1828, by Rev. Orin Fowler	2	205
WALCH, [see also **WELCH**], Martha had d. Elisabeth **ROBSON**, b. Aug. 26, 1730; father, Joseph **ROBSON**	1	54
WALCOTT, [see also **WOLCOTT**], Sophia, b. Scituate, R.I., res. Plainfield, d. Nov. 15, 1848, ae. 78	4	62
WALDO, Eybert, of Norwich, m. Abby **MIDDLETON**, of Plainfield, Feb. 19, 1828, by Rev. Orin Fowler	2	205
WALKER, Albert C., s. Comfort, mason, ae. 43, & Betsey, ae. 44, b. July 4, 1850	4	29
Archibald A., of Newton, Mass. m. Esther S. **DENISON**, of Plainfield, Mar. 29, 1846, by Rev. Andrew Dunning	3	37
Benjamin, of Andover, Mass., m. Susan Perkins **WILBOUR**, of Plainfield, Aug. 7, 1825, by Orin Fowler, V.D.M.	2	198
John, s. Peter & Hanner, b. Feb. 4, 1752	2	17
Joseph A., m. Abby **CHAMPLAIN**, b. of Plainfield, June 21, 1852, by William Turkington	3	75

	Vol.	Page
WALKER, (cont.)		
Julius, s. Archibald, farmer, ae. 26, & Esther, ae. 27, b. Nov. 12, 1847	4	22
Mary, of Killingly, m. William **PECK**, of Coventry, R.I., Sept. 9, 1822, by Rev. Nathaniel Cole	2	189
WALLIS, Joshua, m. Hannah **WINTER**, Nov. 3, 1739	1	98
Joshua, s. Joshua & Hannah, b. Apr. 4, 1742	1	99
Sarah, d. Joshua & Hannah, b. Dec. 23, 1740	1	98
WALLS, Caroline, F., of Plainfield, m. Geo[rge] W. **HARRIS**, of German Flatts, N.Y., [ ], by Rev. John F. Sheffield	3	71
James, b. R.I., res. Plainfield, d. [1850], ae. 12	4	65
WARREN, Abigail, d. Jacob & Sarah, b. Sept. 9, 1708	1	6
Abega[i]ll, d. Jacob, Jr. & Abegall, b. June 16, 1721	1	24
Abega[i]ll, d. Jacob & Abegall, d. July 3, 1721	1	25
Abega[i]ll, w. Jacob, Jr., d. July 5, 1722	1	26
Abigaiel, m. Siprian **STEEVENS**, Jr., Nov. 26, 1727	1	51
Abigaiel, d. [Jacob or John?], b. Sept. 11, 1747 (L.B.B.)	1	1X
Abigail, d. Samuel & Abigail, b. Nov. 26, 1753	2	23
Abigail, m. James **HOW**, Jr., May 15, 1774	2	78
Abigail, w. Dea. Samuel, d. Dec. 8, 1795, ae. 73	2	128
Abigail, d. David & Peggy, b. June 6, 1796	2	102
Allis, d. Jacob, Jr. & Elizabeth, b. Dec. 21, 1749	2	11
Allis, d. Jacob, Jr., d. Nov. 10, 1754, ae. 4 y. 10 m. 20 d.	2	26
Betsey Butler, d. David & Peggy, b. Sept. 27, 1793	2	100
Dan, s. Jacob & Elizabeth, b. Aug. 16, 1755	2	31
David, s. Jacob & Sarah, b. Apr. 4, 1696	1	6
David, m. Patience **THOMSON**, d. of Tho[ma]s, of Providence, Mar. 24, 1718/19	1	22
David, s. Joseph & Martha, b. Mar. 24, 1732	1	93
David, s. Samuel & Abigail, b. June 3, 1761	2	97
David, m. Peggy **FOWLER**, Oct. 18, 1790	2	98
Ede, d. John & Elizabeth, b. Mar. 10, 1737	1	68
Eleazer, s. Ephraim & Abigail, b. Nov. 19, 1700	1	5
Elisha Olney, s. David & Peggy, b. Mar. 29, 1804	2	128
Elizabeth, d. Jacob & Sarah, b. June 7, 1693	1	6
Elizabeth, d. Jacob, of Plainfield, m. David **WHITNEY**, s. Joshua, of Growtown, Jan. 20, 1712/13	1	13
Elizabeth, d. Joseph & Ma[r]tha, b. Aug. 19, 1730	1	60
Elizabeth, m. Thomas **WELCH**, June 30, 1753	2	29
Elizabeth, d. Jacob & Elizabeth, b. June 15, 1757	2	36
Easter, d. David & Patience, b. Dec. 9, 1721	1	25
Ezra, s. Joseph & Eunis, b. Apr. 24, 1755	2	53
Hannah, d. Stephen & Hannah, b. Apr. 28, 1759	2	44
Jacob, s. Jacob & Sarah, b. July 13, 1691	1	6

	Vol.	Page
WARREN, (cont.)		
Jacob, Jr., m. Abigail **HAINES**, d. Samuell, of		
Haverell, Jan. 11, 1714/15	1	15
Jacob, s. Jacob, Jr. & Abega[i]ll, b. Apr. 16, 1719	1	21
Jacob, m. Abegill **CAREY**, of Windham, Mar. 12, 1723	1	28
Jacob, Dea., d. Sept. 3, 1727	1	41
Jacob, Jr., of Plainfield, m. Elizabeth **COOPER**, of		
Scituate, Dec. 27, 1739	1	98
Jacob, s. Steven & Hannah, b. Nov. 21, 1748	2	6
Jacob, s. Jacob & Elizabeth, b. Oct. 2, 1752	2	20
John, s. Jacob & Sarah, b. Jan. 31, 1702/3	1	1
John, m. Elisabeth **HUET**, Apr. 29, 1734	1	64
John, d. Aug. 31, 1745	2	12
Joseph, s. Jacob & Sarah, b. Aug. 4, 1701	1	4
Joseph, m. Martha **BERMAN***, Jan. 2, 1722/23 (*correction **BERMAN** crossed out and **BATEMAN** handwritten in		
margin of original manuscript)	1	29
Joseph, s. Joseph & Martha, b. Oct. 12, 1723	1	29
Joseph, s. Jacob & Abigaiel, b. Jan. 24, 1727/8	1	44
Joseph, s. Joseph & Ma[r]tha, b. May 24, 1733	1	60
Joseph, m. Eunis **HIDE**, May 29, 1754	2	53
Joseph, Dea., d. Feb. 16, 1757	2	35
Joseph, m. Anne **EATON**, June 6, 1759	2	43
Joseph, d. Oct. 2, 1762, at Havannah	2	54
Joseph, Dea., d. Feb. 21, 1764, in the 63rd y. of his		
age	2	55
Jotham, s. Joseph & Eunis, b. Sept. 4, 1759	2	53
Lada, d. Stephen & Hannah, b. June 24, 1755	2	30
Lemuel, s. Joseph & Eunis, b. June 22, 1756	2	53
Lurinda, d. Joseph & Eunis, b. Feb. 18, 1758	2	53
Lidah, d. Jacob, Jr. & Abigel, b. Apr. 12, 1724	1	29
Mancer, s. Jacob & Elizabeth, b. Aug. 16, 1741	1	98
Manser, s. Jacob, Jr., d. Nov. 22, 1762, in his		
passage from the Havannah	2	50
Mara[h], d. Jacob, Jr. & Abega[i]ll, b. July 5,		
1722	1	26
Margaret,d. Jacob, Jr. & Elizabeth, b. Sept. 22,		
1761	2	47
Martha, d. David & Patience, b. Mar. 13, 1719/20	1	22
Martha, d. Joseph & Martha, b. Aug. 22, 1735	1	64
Martha, w. Dea. Joseph, d. Dec. 3, 1756	2	35
Martha, d. Stephen & Hannah, b. Sept. 14, 1762	2	53
Mary, d. Ephraim & Abigaill, b. Feb. 25, 1703/4	1	4
Mary, d. Jacob, b. Jan. 11, 1705/6	1	4
Mary, m. Jonas **SHEPARD**, June 1, 1727	1	52
Mary, d. Oct. 18, 1736	1	65
Mary, m. Nath[anie]ll **STEARNES**, Aug. 6, 1761	2	48
Moses, s. Joseph & Ma[r]tha, b. June 10, 174[ ]	1	98

	Vol.	Page
WARREN, (cont.)		
Nehemiah Olney, s. David & Peggy, b. Sept. 20, 1798	2	104
Obed, s. Jacob & Elizabeth, b. Mar. 18, 1760	2	41
Perces, d. John & Elisabeth, b. Jan. 9, 1734/5	1	64
Prisilla, d. Jacob & Sarah, b. Oct. 8, 1711	1	9
Priscilla, m. Nathan **FELLOWS**, Jan. 29, 1750	2	26
Rachall, d. Jacob, Jr. & Abega[i]l, b. Aug. 23, 1717	1	17
Ruth, d. Joseph & Ma[r]tha, b. July [31], 1727	1	41
Ruth, d. Jos[eph] & Ma[r]tha, b. July 31, 1727	1	60
Ruth, m. Ezekiel **WILLIAMS**, June 27, 1748, by Thomas Stevens, Jr.	2	1
Ruth, d. Stephen & Hannah, b. Dec. 16, 1765	2	60
Samu[e]ll, s. Jacob & Abegael, b. Jan. 24, 1725/6	1	36
Samuel, m. Abigail **SPAULDING**, Feb. 8, 1753	2	22
Samuel, s. David & Peggy, b. Feb. 14, 1792	2	99
Samuel, Dea., d. Nov. 27, 1815, in the 91st y. of his age	2	128
Sarah, d. Jacob & Sarah, b. Sept. 18, 1687	1	6
Sarah, d. Jacob & Sarah, m. Josiah **SPAULDING**, Dec. 4, 1710	1	9
Sarah, d. Jacob, Jr. & Abega[i]ll, b. Apr. 17, 1716	1	16
Sarah, d. John & Elizabeth, b. Jan. 4, 1739/40	1	95
Solomon, s. Jacob & Abigaiel, b. Aug. 27, 1731	1	54
Solomon, s. Jacob & Abigaiel, d. Dec. 21, 1733	1	61
Steven, s. Joseph & Malha, b. Sept. 13, 1725	1	35
Steven, m. Han[n]ah **WILLIAMS**, Dec. 2, 1748, by Thomas Stevens	2	1
Theophilas, s. Stephen & Hannah, b. Oct. 18, 1751	2	14
Theophilus, s. Stephen & Hannah, b. Oct. 18, 1751	2	30
Thomas Jefferson, s. David & Peggy, b. June 12, 1805	2	128
William Clark, s. David & Peggy, b. Sept. 15, 1800	2	128
WASHBURN, Abby, m. William **WILLIAMS**, b. of Newport, R.I., May 16, 1844, by Rev. Daniel Lyon	3	23
John, s. Robert & Adah, b. Aug. 26, 1769	2	68
Lucy, w. Robert, d. Apr. 7, 1766	2	59
Noah, s. Robert & Adah, b. Oct. 15, 1773	2	77
Robert, m. Lucy **FARNUM**, Feb. 9, 1764	2	59
Robert, m. Adah **BENNET[T]**, Feb. 16, 1769	2	66
Stephen, s. Robert & Lucy, b. Feb. 28, 1766	2	59
Zeriah, d. Robert & Mary, b. Oct. 23, 1754	2	32
WASHINGTON, George, of Providence, m. Mary S. **RANDALL**, of Foster, R.I., Nov. 27, 1845, by Peleg Peckham, Elder	3	34
WATSON, Benjamin P., m. Hannah **COLE**, b. of Plainfield, Sept. 4, 1843, by Rev. Daniel Dorchester	3	22
Wealthy Ann, b. Norwich, res. Norwich, d. Mar. 28, 1848, ae. 18	4	61

	Vol.	Page
WATTS, Mary, of Plainfield, m. Wanton **SCOTT**, of Worcester, Mass., Aug. 29, 1836, by Chester Tilden	2	227
WEAVER, WEEVER, Albina, m. Ezekiel **REYNOLDS**, b. of Warwick, R.I., Dec. 16, 1846, by Rev. J. Mather	3	42
Allis, m. William **STEVENS**, Feb. 7, 1755	2	34
Alpheas, s. Remington & Esther, b. Sept. 17, 1827	3	13
Charles, m. Mary **WEAVER**, b. of Plainfield, June 10, 1849, by Amos Witter, J.P.	3	58
Charles, laborer, ae. 24, b. Plainfield, m. Mary Louisa **BROWN**, ae. 16, b. Lisbon, res. Plainfield, June 10, 1849, by Amos Witter, Esq.	4	3
Eliza A., of Plainfield, m. Timothy **RISLEY**, of Manchester, May 2, 1853, by Rev. William Turkington	3	78
Ella Patience, d. Reuben, 2d, merchant, ae. 27, & Betsey, ae. 26, b. Aug. 25, 1849	4	28
Elvira, m. George N. **NILES**, b. of Warwick, R.I., Feb. 2, 1848, by Rev. J. Mather	3	51
Emily D., d. Remington & Esther, b. Feb. 18, 1835	3	13
George, s. Remington & Esther, b. June 18, 1824	3	13
Geo[rge], m. Betsey **BURDIN**, b. of Plainfield, Oct. 31, 1847, by Rev. Fred[eri]c Charlton	3	49
George, laborer, ae. 21, b. Dudley, Mass., res. Providence, m. Betsey **BURDICK**, ae. 19, b. Brooklyn, res. Plainfield, Oct. 30, [18]48, by Rev. Frederic Charlton	4	1
Harriet, d. Remington & Esther, b. Mar. 4, 1817	3	12
Harriet, of Plainfield, m. William A. **SWEET**, of Worcester, Mass., Oct. 11, 1835, by Rev. Samuel Rockwell	2	222
Lucinda, d. Remington & Esther, b. Dec. 31, 1814	3	12
Lucinda, of Plainfield, m. Alexander **THAYER**, of Worcester, Mass., Jan. 8, 1837, by Chester Tilden	2	228
Mary, b. Killingly, res. Plainfield, d. Feb. 10, 1849, ae. 94	4	62
Mary, m. Charles **WEAVER**, b. of Plainfield, June 10, 1849, by Amos Witter, J.P.	3	58
Remington, m. Esther **DITCHFIELD**, Feb. 16, 1812, by John Parish, Esq. Brooklyn	3	12
Sally C., d. Remington & Esther, b. Mar. 5, 182[ ]	3	12
Spencer, of Coventry, R.I., m. Catharine **COREY**, of Plainfield, Sept. 26, 1824, by Orin Fowler, V.D.M.	2	195
Thomas, m. Olive **COLE**, b. of Plainfield, Sept. 8, 1828, by Peleg Peckham, Elder	2	207
-----, d. R[e]uben, merchant, ae. 29, b. Aug. 1, 1849	4	27
WEBB, Amos Wells, s. John & Polly, b. Sept. 17, 1817	2	180
Esther, w. Capt. Joshua, d. Feb. 17, 1818	2	180
George, s. John & Polly, b. June 5, 1805	2	180
Hannah, d. John & Polly, b. Nov. 7, 1808, in Woodstock,		

	Vol.	Page
WEBB, (cont.)		
Conn.	2	180
Hannah, m. Abram **SHEPERD**, b. of Plainfield, June 16, 1828, by Rev. Orin Fowler	2	206
Harriet S., of Plainfield, m. Caleb B. **ROGERS**, of Montville, May 10, 1830, by Benjamin R. Allen, Elder	2	211
Jeremiah S., m. Frances **COIT**, b. of Plainfield, Apr. 30, 1840, by Rev. Samuel Rockwell	3	4
Polly, w. John, d. July 15, 1824	2	180
Sally Ann, d. John & Polly, b. Dec. 17, 1820	2	180
Walter Palmer, s. John & Polly, b. Apr. 28, 1815	2	180
WEBSTER, Charles R., of Harwinton, Conn., m. Hannah P. **MILLER**, of Plainfield, Feb. 3, 1841, by Rev. Thomas Barber	3	9
WEEKS, William, m. Ellen **WIHAN**, b. of Providence, R.I., Sept. 15, 1839, by [ ], Packerville	2	247
WELCH, WELTCH, [see also **WALSH**], Amy, m. Jacob **HOARD**, Aug. 18, 1750	2	32
Ann, m. Daniel **HARRIS**, May 25, 1749	2	10
Daniel, s. Daniel & Elizabeth, b. Sept. 8, 1749	2	20
Eunice, d. John & Sarah, b. Sept. 4, 1760	2	79
Hannah, d. John & Sarah, b. Dec. 11, 1730	2	22
John, m. Abigail **DIB[B]AL**, Sept. 11, 1722	1	32
John, m. Sarah **ABBE**, Apr. 11, 1729	2	22
John, s. John & Sarah, b. June 12, 1732	2	22
John, s. Thomas & Elizabeth, b. Jan. 20, 1755; d. May 12, 1755, ae. 3 m. 22 d.	2	29
Marcy, d. James, m. Tho[ma]s **SPAULDING**, Dec. 9, 1714	1	16
Martha, d. James & Mary, b. Oct. 25, 1704	1	1
Mary, d. John & Abigail, b. July 2, 1723	2	22
Mary, d. John & Abigail, b. July 16, 1723	1	32
Rufus, s. John & Sarah, b. Apr. 2, 1766	2	79
Thomas, m. Elizabeth **WARREN**, June 20, 1753	2	29
WELLMAN, Mary O., d. Elijah & Mary, b. Mar. 10, 1828	2	180
Susan Elizabeth, d. Elijah & Mary, b. Mar. 26, 1826	2	180
WELLS, Albert, m. Delilah **ROUSE**, b. of Plainfield, Jan. 28, 1852, by Rev. Joseph P. Brown	3	74
Amey, d. John, Jr. & Amy, b. Dec. 15, 1732	1	58
Eliza A., m. Hezekiah **FRENCH**, Oct. 3, 1853, by Rev. W[illia]m Turkington	3	80
Ellen A., d. Amos, painter, ae. 26, & Eley, ae. 28, b. Apr. 26, 1848	4	22
George T., m. Elizabeth B. **HOLLEY**, b. of Plainfield, Dec. 4, 1854, by Rev. Joseph P. Brown	3	88
Hannah, d. Sam[ue]ll & Hannah, b. Mar. 19, 1739	1	92
John, Jr., of Plainfield, m. Amie **WILLCOKS**, of Stonington, Jan. 19, 1731/2	1	55

	Vol.	Page

WELLS, (cont.)

Lucinda S., of East Greenwich, R.I., m. Robert
  CASWELL, of Warwick, R.I., Sept. 7, 1846, by
  Rev. James Mather — 3 — 40
Samuel, m. Hannah **NEEDY**, Apr. 9, 1730 — 1 — 65
Sam[ue]ll, s. Samu[e]ll & Hannah, b. Aug. 9, 1735 — 1 — 66

WENTWORTH, [see under **WINTWORTH**]

WEST, Dean, m. Mary Ann KENNEDY, b. of Plainfield, Aug.
  29, 1837, by Chester Tilden — 2 — 232
James, carpenter, b. Scituate, R.I., res. Plainfield,
  d. Mar. 26, 1849, ae. 64 — 4 — 62
Mary, farmer, d. Apr. 24, 1850, ae. 14 — 4 — 64
Susan, of Plainfield, m. Alfred **FOSTER**, of Leicester,
  Mass., May 23, 1841, by Rev. John Read — 3 — 10
Susan, d. Dean, carpenter, ae. 40, & Mary, ae. 38, b.
  Nov. 30, 1850 — 4 — 31
William H., m. Jerusha **CONGDON**, b. of Plainfield,
  Dec. 25, 1842, at Mr. Thomas Harris' by Rev.
  Lawton Cady — 3 — 89
-----, d. David*, carpenter, ae. 38, & Mary, ae. 37,
  Feb. 17, 1849 (*Dean?) — 4 — 25

WESTCOTT, WESCOTT, Almy F., m. Charles D. **MORSE**, b. of
  Plainfield, Jan. 29, 1854, by Rev. William
  Turkington — 3 — 81
Harriet A., m. Allen J. **BURLESON**, b. of Plainfield,
  May 23, 1836, by Chester Tilden — 2 — 226
Henry, m. Eliza **MORY**, b. of Sterling, July 2, 1838,
  by Peleg Peckham, Elder — 2 — 235
John, m. Joan C. **GREENMAN**, b. of Plainfield, Oct. 21,
  1850, by Rev. Joseph P. Brown — 3 — 67
John, cotton mill, ae. 30, b. Sterling, res. Plain-
  field, m. Joanna **GRINMAN**, cotton mill, ae. 21, of
  Plainfield, Nov. [ ], 1850, by Joseph P. Brown — 4 — 7
Lucy, woolen finisher, ae. 20, of Plainfield, m.
  Augustus **HAMMETT**, clerk in store, ae. 21, of Plain-
  field, Apr. 7, 1851, by Rev. Joseph P. Brown — 4 — 7
Lucy N., m. Augustus J. **HAMMETT**, b. of Plainfield, Apr.
  13, 1851, by Rev. Joseph P. Brown — 3 — 69
Mary, m. Stephen **HALL**, Apr. 20, 1847, by Rev.
  Fred[eri]c Charlton — 3 — 48
Phebe Ann, m. Levi **RANDALL**, b. of Plainfield, Nov. 25,
  1830, by Benj[ami]n R. Allen, Elder — 2 — 212
Sarah, m. Joseph C. **SPAULDING**, b. of Plainfield, Oct.
  6, 1834, by Rev. Samuel Rockwell — 2 — 219
Sophia Maria Fanning, m. Jason **PRAY**, b. of Plainfield,
  July 27, 1828, by Rev. Orin Fowler — 2 — 206
Susan E., m. Joseph C. **SPAULDING**, b. of Plainfield,
  Sept. 3, 1849, by Rev. Joseph P. Brown — 3 — 58

	Vol.	Page
WESTCOTT, WESCOTT, (cont.)		
Susanna, ae. 25, b. Sterling, res. Plainfield, m.		
Joseph C. **SPAULDING**, merchant, ae. 45, of Plainfield, Sept. 3, 1849, by Joseph P. Brown	4	6
Thomas, m. Mary M. **CHAMPLAIN**, b. of Plainfield, Nov. 6, 1853, by Rev. W[illia]m Turkington	3	80
WHALEY, Susan A., m. Robert **ANDREW**, b. of Coventry, R.I., Nov. 29, 1847, by Rev. J. Mather	3	47
WHEAT, Solomon, s. Salmon & Mercy, b. Aug. 2, 1751	2	21
WHEELER, WHELER, WHEELLER, A[a]ron, s. Ephraim & Mary, b. July 4, 1742	2	5
A[a]ron, s. Isaac & Hannah, b. Nov. 2, 1748	2	6
A[a]ron, d. June 25, 1753	2	22
Aaron, m. Molle **SPAULDING**, June 13, 1764	2	71
Abega[i]ll, d. Isaac & Sarah, b. Jan. 29, 1711/12	1	13
Abigaiel, m. Thomas **HOW[E]**, May 28, 1729	1	62
Benjamin, s. Ephraim & Elizabeth, b. Jan. 29, 1703/4	1	4
Benjamin, m. Prudence **HUET**, Jan. 29, 1729/30	1	62
Benjamin, s. Benjamin & Prudence, b. Apr. 12, 1743	2	3
Benj[ami]n, s. Ephraim, Jr. & Experience, b. July 10, 1769	2	70
Benjamin, d. Apr. 11, 1770, in the 67th y. of his age	2	70
Daniel, s. Ephraim, Jr. & Experience, b. Aug. 26, 1766	2	70
Daniel, m. Ruth **MILLER**, b. of Plainfield, Aug. 19, 1801, by Rev. Joel Benedict	2	190
Daniel, s. Col. Daniel & Ruth, b. May 9, 1805	2	180
David, s. Jonas & Tabatha, b. Jan. 20, 1757	2	44
Deborah, m. Benjamin **SPAULDING**, Oct. 30, 1727	1	41
Dresilla, d. Timothy & Mary, b. Apr. 16, 1760	2	42
Drusilla, d. Timothy & Mary, b. Apr. 16, 1760	2	44
Edward, s. Ephraim & Elisabeth, b. May 13, 1715	1	15
Elizabeth (Bette), d. Isaac & Sarah, b. Sept. 28, 1708	1	6
Elisabeth, w. Joshua, d. Feb. 12, 1715/16, in the 80th y. of her age	1	15
Elisabeth, w. Ephraim, d. Sept. 4, 1724, in the 44th y. of her age	1	30
Elizabeth, d. Benjamin & Prudence, b. Feb. 6, 1731	1	62
Elizabeth, d. Benjamin & Prudence, b. Feb. 6, 1730/31	2	3
Elizabeth, m. Ebenezer **COLE**, Apr. 23, 1751	2	14
Elizabeth, d. Isaac & Lois, b. Jan. 12, 1758	2	40
Elizabeth, d. Ephraim, Jr. & Experience, b. Aug. 17, 1762	2	57
Ephraim, d. Apr. 19, 1725	1	34
Ephraim, s. Benjamin & Prudence, b. May 15, 1738	1	70
Ephraim, s. Benjamin & Prudence, b. May 15, 1738	2	3
Ephraim, Jr., m. Experience **HARRIS**, Apr. 16, 1761	2	57
Ephraim, m. Mehetabel **SPAULDING**, Dec. 31, 1776	2	87
Ephraim, d. Sept. 9, 1821, ae. 83	2	180

	Vol.	Page
WHEELER, WHELER, WHEELLER, (cont.)		
Est[h]er, d. Timothy & Mary, b. Oct. 28, 1762	2	51
Esther, d. Capt. Timothy & Mary, d. Nov. 3, 1778	2	83
Eunice, d. Benj[amin] & Prudence, b. Nov. 1, 1754	2	28
Experience, d. Isaac, of Stoningtown, m. Joseph **COITE**, Sept. 18, 1705	1	5
Experience, d. Ephraim & Experience, b. Oct. 31, 1773	2	79
Experience, w. Ephraim, Jr., d. Mar. 10, 1776	2	79
George B., of Mantua, O., m. Nancy G. **KENYON**, of Plainfield, Sept. 19, 1854, by Rev. James Bates	3	86
Hannah, d. Isaac, Jr. & Hannah, b. Apr. 8, 1739	1	94
Hezekiah, s. Jonas & Sarah, b. Mar. 6, 1768	2	67
Hulda[h], d. Joseph & Elizabeth, b. Dec. 6, 1747	1	1X
Isaac, s. Isaac & Sarah, b. Nov. 18, 1704	1	4
Isaac, Jr., m. Hannah **STERNS**, June 5, 1729	1	50
Isaac, s. Isaac, Jr. & Hannah, b. Feb. 22, 1735/6	1	65
Isaac, d. May 6, 1752	2	17
Isaac, Jr., m. Lois **ALLEN**, June 3, 1755	2	40
James, s. Aaron & Molle, b. Mar. 27, 1767	2	71
Job, s. Timothy & Mary, b. June 17, 1754	2	24
John, s. Isaac & Hannah, b. Nov. 23, 1731	1	55
John Hancock, s. Ephraim & Mehetable, b. Apr. 29, 1779	2	87
Jonas, s. Benjamin & Prudence, b. May 29, 1735	1	70
Jonas, s. Benjamin & Prudence, b. May 29, 1735	2	3
Jonas, m. Tabatha **BROWN**, Mar. 12, 1756	2	44
Jonas, m. Sarah **COLE**, Oct. 12, 1757	2	44
Jonas, m. Tabatha **BROWN**, [ ].	2	43
Jeshuay, d. Feb. 4, 1725 (Joshua?)	1	34
Joshua, s. Josiah & Elizabeth, b. Jan. 2, 1745/6	1	2X
Josiah, s. Isaac & Sarah, b. Apr. 18, 1719	1	20
Josiah, s. Josiah, Jr. & Hannah, b. June 2, [ ]	2	12
Lucy, d. Benjamin & Prudence, b. Sept. 2, 1752	2	20
Lucy, d. Jonas & Sarah, b. Aug. 19, 1772	2	76
Lidya, d. Isaac & Sarah, b. Jan. 23, 1720/21	1	24
Lydia, d. Benjamin & Prudence, b. Nov. 18, 1740	2	3
Lydia, m. Joseph **SPAULDING**, Mar. 4, 1742	2	17
Lydia, d. Timothy & Mary, b. Apr. 3, 1757	2	24
Magdalen, d. Aaron & Molle, b. Oct. 30, 1770	2	76
Maryetta, of Canterbury, m. Hiram **BENNET**, of Plainfield, Aug. 4, 1833, by Jonathan Goff, J.P.	2	218
Marsie, d. Isaac & Sarah, b. Nov. 21, 1706	1	4
Mary, d. Ephraim & Elisabeth, b. Dec. 23, 1720	1	23
Mary, m. Timo[thy] **PEIRCE**, Jr., June 12, 1723	1	37
Mary, d. Isaac, Jr. & Hannah, b. Mar. 5, 1729/30	1	50
Mary, d. Benjamin & Prudence, b. Sept. 22, 1747	2	3

WHEELER, WHELER, WHEELLER, (cont.)

	Vol.	Page
Mary, m. John **HOW[E]**, Dec. 25, 1755	2	44
Mary, m. Henry **PHILLIPS**, b. of Plainfield, Jan. 15, 1835, by Rev. Samuel Rockwell	2	220
Moses, s. Ephraim & Mary, b. Jan. 26, 1745/6	2	5
Nathaniel, s. Isaac, Jr. & Hannah, b. Oct. 7, 1741	1	99
Olive, d. Ephraim & Elizabeth, b. Jan. 13, 1708/9	1	6
Olive, m. Jeremiah **LAWRANCE**, Feb. 2, 1729	1	37
Olive, d. Ephraim & Mary, b. Jan. 18, 1739/40; d. Feb. 15, 1747/8	2	5
Olive(?), d. Thomas & Lucey, b. July 7, 1744	2	10
Olive, d. Benjamin & Prudence, b. Sept. 11, 1750	2	20
Olive, d. Aaron & Molle, b. Mar. 25, 1765	2	71
Olive, m. Stephen **FARNUM**, Mar. 10, 1768	2	66
Olive, m. Edward **CLARK**, b. of Plainfield, Feb. 24, 1839, by Rev. Samuel Rockwell	2	239
Phebe, d. Ephraim & Experience, b. May 5, 1771	2	79
Polly, d. Aaron & Polly, b. Feb. 19, 1788	2	100
Polly, of Plainfield, m. Joseph **BUTCHER**, of England, now residing in Plainfield, Mar. 21, 1833, by Peleg Peckham, Elder	2	217
Prudence, d. Isaac & Sarah, b. Feb. 9, 1709/10	1	13
Prudence, d. Benjamin & Prudence, b. May 20, 1745	2	3
Prudence, m. Robert **CARR**, Dec. 21, 1765	2	61
Rufus, s. Aaron & Molle, b. July 8, 1773	2	86
Ruth, d. Isaac & Sarah, b. Jan. 17, 1713/14	1	13
Sam[ue]ll, s. Isaac, Jr. & Hannah, b. Oct. 19, 1733	1	61
Samuel, m. Olive **HALL**, Dec. 26, 1765	2	63
Sarah, d. Ephraim & Elizabeth, b. Oct. 21, 1712	1	10
Sarah, d. Ephraim & Elisabeth, d. Aug. 24, 1724, in the 12th y. of her age	1	30
Sarah, d. Benjamin & Prudence, b. Apr. 4, 1733	1	62
Sarah, d. Benjamin & Prudence, b. Apr. 4, 1733	2	3
Sarah, m. Jonas **HOW[E]**, Jan. 24, 1750/51	2	12
Sarah, d. Dec. 25, 1760, in the 81st y. of her age	2	44
Sarah, d. Jonas & Sarah, b. Oct. 24, 1765	2	60
Sarah A., of Plainfield, m. William B. **MOORE**, of Charleston, S.C., Jan. 6, 1828, by Orin Fowler, V.D.M.	2	204
Shepard, s. Timothy & Mary, b. Mar. 15, 1752	2	17
Shepard, s. Timothy & Mary, d. Feb. 6, 1753	2	24
Spaulding, s. Ephraim & Mehetable, b. Oct. 15, 1777	2	87
Stephen, s. Samuel & Olive, b. Mar. 16, 1767	2	63
Susannah, d. Isaac & Sarah, b. Feb. 21, 1723/4	1	30
Susan[n]ah, m. Nathan **SHEPARD**, Feb. 15, 1743	2	4
Tabatha, w. Jonas, d. Jan. 25, 1757	2	44
Tabatha, d. Jonas & Sarah, b. Jan. 13, 1761	2	45
Thomas, s. Ephraim & Elizabeth, b. May 13, 1706	1	4

	Vol.	Page
WHEELER, WHELER, WHEELLER, (cont.)		
Thomas, s. Thomas & Luce, b. Jan. 13, 1737; d. Jan. 23, 1737	1	71
Thomas, s. Thomas & Luce, b. Mar. 29, 1738	1	71
Thomas, s. Ephraim, Jr. & Experience, b. July 17, 1764	2	57
Thomas, m. Luce **HOW[E]**, [ ]	1	71
Timothy, s. Isaac & Sarah, b. Mar. 15, 1717	1	17
Timothy, m. Mary **SHEPARD**, June 18, 1751	2	14
Timothy, s. Timothy & Mary, b. July 31, 1769	2	68
Zilpha, d. Aaron & Molle, b. Nov. 17, 1780	2	86
WHILDEN, Isaac N., m. Jane G. **JACOBS**, b. of Lisbon, Sept. 3, 1854, by Rev. Alfred Gates	3	86
WHIPPLE, Bethyah, d. Zebulon & Mehetabell, b. Mar. 16, 1747	2	51
Betsey, d. Anne, b. Jan. 14, 1780	2	92
Happy, m. Joseph **WHIPPLE**, Jr., b. of Plainfield, June 1, 1825, by Rev. Orin Fowler	2	198
John, s. Joseph & Katharine, b. Mar. 10, 1785	2	92
Jonathan, m. Anna **PETERS**, Apr. 15, 1781	2	86
Joseph, Jr., m. Happy **WHIPPLE**, b. of Plainfield, June 1, 1825, by Rev. Orin Fowler	2	198
Katharine, d. Joseph & Katharine, b. Oct. 6, 1782	2	92
Mary, d. Joseph & Katharine, b. Nov. 8, 1778	2	92
Mary Jane, of Cumberland, R.I., m. William **BRAINARD**, of Killingly, June 25, 1854, by Rev. E. Loomis	3	83
Robert, of Cranston, R.I., m. Almira **SWEET**, of Scituate, R.I., Oct. 14, 1849, by Rev. Joseph P. Brown	3	61
Samuel, s. Zebelon & Mehetabell, b. Mar. 28, 1762	2	51
Susannah, d. Zebulon & Mehetabell, b. Jan. 10, 1761	2	51
William, of Groton, m. Prudence **LAMB**, of Plainfield, Sept. 5, 1822, by Jonathan Gallup, J.P.	2	188
Zebulon, m. Mehetabell **GALLUP**, Mar. 1, 1759	2	40
Zebulon, m. Phebe A. **GLADDING**, b. of Plainfield, May 11, 1846, by A. Dunning	3	37
Zebulon, of Providence, R.I., m. Sarah **BURGESS**, of Plainfield, June 1, 1852, by Rev. Joseph P. Brown	3	75
WHIT, [see also **WHITE**], Prudence, m. John **CRARY**, Oct. 12, 1715	1	16
WHITE, [see also **WHIT**], Ebenezer, s. Robert & Jane, b. Nov. 12, 1718	1	20
James, of Cranston, R.I., m. Deborah E. **LEWIS**, of Scituate, R.I., Mar. 19, 1848, by Rev. James Mather	3	54
Robert, s. Robert & Jane, b. Apr. 16, 1715	1	20
WHITEHORN, Stephen, of South Kingstown, R.I., m. Silence **COZZENS**, of Plainfield, Oct. 22, 1837, by Rev. Samuel Rockwell	2	233
WHITFORD, Delilah, m. Ira **BARSTO[W]**, b. of Sterling, Apr.		

	Vol.	Page
WHITFORD, (cont.)		
28, 1833, by Peleg Peckham, Elder	2	217
Setilice D., of West Greenwich, R.I., m. Henry J. **HOLDEN**, of Warwick, R.I., Aug. 2, 1846, by A. Dunning	3	38
Theron D., m. Barbara J. **VAUGHAN**, b. of Sterling, Apr. 10, 1843, by Peleg Peckham, Elder	3	19
WHITING, Mary E., m. Gideon **CADY**, May 11, 1851, by John J. Penrose, J.P.	3	69
WHITMAN, Harris, m. Laura **YO[U]NG**, b. of Sterling, July 25, 1842, by Peleg Peckham, Elder	3	16
John, Jr., of Griswold, m. Weltha **ALLEN**, of Sterling, May 21, 1821, by Jonathan Gallup, J.P.	2	133
WHITMORE, Mary, d. Samuel, m. Jonas **SHEPARD**, Nov. 5, 1747	1	IX
Mary, m. Jonas **SHEPHARD**, Nov. 5, 1747	2	27
William H.R., m. Harriet M. **BISSELL**, b. of Warwick, R.I., Feb. 2, 1848, by Rev. J. Mather	3	51
WHITNEY, A[a]ron, s. Ezekiel & Sarah, b. Sept. 6, 1739	1	100
Caleb, s. William & Margeret, b. Sept. 10, 1721	1	27
David, s. Joshua, of Growtown, m. Elizabeth **WARREN**, d. of Jacob, of Plainfield, Jan. 20, 1712/13	1	13
David, s. David & Elisabeth, b. Sept. 16, 1716	1	16
Elisabeth, d. William & Marg[a]ret, b. Aug. 12, 1719	1	27
Elisabeth, d. David & Elisabeth, b. Feb. 26, 1720/21	1	24
Enoch, m. Thankfull **PARKE**, Dec. 21, 1732	1	67
Est[h]or, d. David & Elizabeth, b. May 1, 1714	1	13
Ezekiel, m. Elizabeth **KNIGHT**, Mar. 7, 1757	2	35
Ezekiel, s. Ezekiel & Elizabeth, b. May 15, 1758	2	35
Hester, d. Ezekiel & Sarah, b. Mar. 6, 1734	1	99
Jacob, s. David & Elisabeth, b. July 13, 1723	1	28
Jacob, s. Capt. Whitney, d. Sept. 20, 1738	1	71
John, s. William & Marg[a]ret, b. Jan. 30, 1717/18	1	27
Jo[na]than*, s. David & Elisabeth, b. Oct. 11, 1718 (*correction Jo[na]than is crossed out and Joshua is handwritten in margin of original manuscript)	1	20
Joshua, Jr., m. Ama **BLODGETT**, about the 8th of Apr., 1743	2	5
Joshewa, d. Feb. 10, 1761, ae. 42 y. 3 m. 29 d.	2	47
Josiah, s. David & Elizabeth, b. Aug. 11, 1731	1	61
Lydiah, d. Ezekiel & Sarah, b. May 2, 1737	1	99
Mary, d. David & Elizabeth, b. Mar. 13, 1727/8	1	44
Mary, d. David & Elizabeth, d. June 28, 1729	1	61
Moses, s. Ezekiel & Sarah, b. Sept. 10, 1742	1	100
Rosanna, d. Enoch & Thankfull, b. Aug. 29, 1740	1	96
Sam[ue]ll, s. Enoch & Thankful, b. May 24, 1734	1	67
Sarah, d. Joshua, of Grotton, m. Nathaniel **JEWELL**, Jr., July 11, 1704	1	9

	Vol.	Page
WHITNEY, (cont.)		
Sarah, d. Joshua, of Grotton, m. Nathaniel **JEWEL**, July 11, 1704	1	10
Suesanna, d. Enoch & Thankfull, b. Mar. 13, 1739	1	94
Tarbel, s. David & Elisabeth, b. Nov. 1, 1725	1	38
WICKES, WICKS, Calvin F., of Providence, R.I., m. Clarissa D. **ANGELL**, of Scituate, R.I., Nov. 14, 1844, by A. Dunning	3	25
Mary, m. Layton E. **SEAMANS**, b. of Coventry, R.I., Apr. 21, 1851, by Rev. Joseph P. Brown	3	69
Mary, b. R.I., res. Plainfield, m. Layton E. **SEAMANS**, physician, b. R.I., res. Plainfield, Apr. 21, 1851, by Rev. Joseph P. Brown	4	7
WIGHT, Sarah, m. Jesse **SHEPHARD**, Sept. 24, 1766	2	64
WIHAN, Ellen, m. William **WEEKS**, b. of Providence, R.I., Sept. 15, 1839, by [ ], Packerville	2	247
WILBUR, WILBOUR, Albert, m. Gethan G. **FREEMAN**, b. of Sterling, Oct. 3, 1847, by Peleg Peckham, Elder	3	53
Alpheas Hatch, s. John & Mehetabel, b. Dec. 20, 1796	2	119
Buel Stevens, s. Oliver & Elizabeth, b. June 23, 1788	2	99
Elizabeth, d. Oliver & Elizabeth, b. Nov. 13, 1794	2	101
George, woolen finisher, ae. 24, of Plainfield, m. Mary E. **SHEPARD**, ae. 21, b. Brooklyn, Dec. 24, [18]47, by William Shepard, Esq.	4	2
George, manufacturer, ae. 26, of Plainfield, m. Esther **SHEPARD**, ae. 26, b. Brooklyn, Dec. 26, 1847, by W[illia]m Shepard, Esq.	4	1
George, blacksmith, d. Sept. 9, 1848, ae. 67	4	63
Huldah, d. Oliver & Elizabeth, b. Sept. 28, 1790	2	99
Jared Fuller, s. John & Mehetabel, b. Nov. 18, 1805	2	119
Jared N., m. Abby A. **ROBINSON**, b. of Sterling, May 26, 1850, by Peleg Peckham, Elder	3	64
John, s. Jonathan & Hannah, b. Feb. 3, 1768	2	69
John, d. Nov. 11, 1810, from a blow on his head received while shoeing a horse	2	119
Johnson, s. William & Elizabeth, b. Mar. 25, 1766	2	60
Jonathan, s. Jonathan & Hannah, b. July 14, 1766, in Westerly, R.I.	2	69
Lydia A., of Scituate, R.I., m. David [ ], of Newtown, Conn., May 8, 1836, by Rev. Tubael Wakefield	2	226
Margaret, d. William & Elizabeth, b. Sept. 20, 1763	2	49
Maria, d. John & Mehetabel, b. Mar. 16, 1803	2	119
Maria, d. John & Mehetable, d. Nov. 20, 1811	2	120
Mary Ann, m. George **PARKIS**, b. of Plainfield, Apr. 3, 1837, by Rev. Samuel Rockwell	2	230
Mary E., d. George, wool manufacturer, ae. 26, & Esther, ae. 26, b. Mar. 2, 1848	4	22

	Vol.	Page
WILBUR, WILBOUR, (cont.)		
Mehitable, d. John & Mehitable, b. Apr. 3, 1811	2	119
Mehetable, of Plainfield, m. George W. **HEBARD**, of Willimantic, May 8, 1833, by Rev. Samuel Rockwell	2	217
Olive, d. William & Elizabeth, b. Apr. 2, 1761	2	48
Olive, d. Oliver & Elizabeth, b. Sept. 26, 1796	2	108
Oliver, m. Elizabeth **BENJAMIN**, Oct. 23, 1777	2	85
Samuel Rathbone, s. Oliver & Elizabeth, b. Dec. 20, 1782	2	88
Sarah Anna, d. Oliver & Elizabeth, b. Aug. 10, 1786	2	99
Susan Perkins, d. John & Mehitable, b. Nov. 22, 1798	2	119
Susan Perkins, of Plainfield, m. Benjamin **WALKER**, of Andover, Mass., Aug. 7, 1825, by Orin Fowler, V.D.M.	2	198
Thankful, m. John E. **TAILOR**, b. of Coventry, R.I., Nov. 7, 1847, by Rev. Frederic Charlton	3	49
William, s. Jonathan & Hannah, b. Feb. 9, 1770	2	69
William Benjamin, s. Oliver & Elizabeth, b. May 26, 1778	2	85
Woodbury Starkweather, s. Oliver & Elizabeth, b. Jan. 19, 1781	2	88
WILCOX, WILLCOKS, Abby, of Voluntown, m. Jonathan **JOHNSON**, of Plainfield, Nov. 8, 1840, by Amos Witter	3	8
Amie, of Stonington, m. John **WELLS**, Jr., of Plainfield, Jan. 19, 1731/2	1	55
Edward B., s. James M., tailor, ae. 29, & Susan E., ae. 30, b. Sept. 22, 1850	4	31
Hannah Ann, of Norwich, m. John M. **FULLER**, of Hanover, Jan. 31, 1854, by Rev. William Turkington	3	82
Henry, mechanic, ae. 26, b. Georgia, res. New Haven, m. Sarah M. **LESTER**, ae. 25, of Plainfield, Sept. 10, 1850, by Rev. Jared O. Knapp	4	5
Henry A., of New Haven, m. Sarah Maria **LESTER**, Apr. 10, 1850, by Rev. Jared O. Knapp	3	64
Randall B., m. Eunice **VAUGHAN**, b. of Sterling, July 9, 1843, by Peleg Peckham, Elder	3	20
William, manufacturer, ae. 26, b. Lisbon, res. Norwich, m. Esther S. **BRISHNELL**, ae. 25, b. Stafford, res. Plainfield, Feb. [ ], 1848, by Rev. Benton	4	1
WILKMAN, Brownwell, of Watertown, N.Y., m. Sarah B. **PHILLIPS**, of Plainfield, May 4, 1829, by Peleg Peckham, Elder	2	209
WILLIAMS, Abega[i]l, d. Richard & Abega[i]ll, b. Feb. 25, 1715/16	1	15
Abega[i]ll, d. Richard & Abega[i]ll, d. June 15, 1717	1	18
Abraham, [twin with Isaac], s. Nathan & Waightstill, b. May 14, 1765	2	58

	Vol.	Page
WILLIAMS, (cont.)		
Amy, d. Robert & Han[n]ah, b. Nov. 15, 1707	1	10
Anna, d. Thomas & Sarah, b. June 30, 1696; d. Aug. 4, 1696	1	12
Anna, d. Thomas & Sarah, b. Dec. 12, 1697; d. Feb. 22, 1698	1	12
Anne, d. Joseph & Suesanna, b. Aug. 14, 1728; d. Sept. 13, 1728	1	45
Ashur, s. Ebenezer & Abigail, b. Sept. 9, 1760	2	48
Attwood, m. Elizabeth **GALLUP**, Aug. 3, 1749	2	50
Attwood, s. Attwood & Elizabeth, b. Oct. 13, 1759	2	50
Barshebah, d. Richard & Abegall, b. Dec. 2, 1717	1	18
Bartholomew, s. Richard & Elizabeth, b. Mar. 9, 1707/8	1	6
Bartholome[w], d. Apr. 24, 1728	1	44
Bri[d]git, d. Thomas, Jr. & Han[n]ah, b. Mar. 25, 1719	1	21
Catharine, m. Eleazer **BARRET**, Dec. 25, 1730	1	54
Charles G., of Brooklyn, m. Lucy E. **GALLUP**, of Sterling, Feb. 25, 1846, by Peleg Peckham, Elder	3	36
David, s. Nathan & Grace, b. June 27, 1752	2	23
Delight, d. Thomas & Hannah, b. Jan. 15, 1735/6	1	66
Delight, m. Jonathan **WOODWARD**, Dec. 5, 1759	2	45
Ebenezeer, s. Thomas & Sarah, b. May 28, 1693	1	12
Ebenezer, m. Judah **BROWN**, May 14, 1723	1	29
Ebenezer, s. Joseph & Suesanna, b. Sept. 8, 1730	1	51
Ebenezer, m. Abigail **KIMBALL**, May 17, 1756	2	38
Ele[a]zer, s. Joseph & Suesanna, b. Sept. 8, 1730; d. same day	1	51
Eli, s. Ebenezer & Abigail, b. Mar. 28, 1766	2	83
Elihu, m. Desire **FISH**, Nov. 17, 1747	2	22
Elihu, s. Elihu & Desire, b. May 13, 1755	2	22
Elisha, s. Joseph & Susannah, b. May 23, 1725	1	34
Elizabeth, d. Thomas & Sarah, b. Aug. 25, 1707	1	12
Elizabeth, d. Robert & Han[n]ah, b. July 4, 1709	1	10
Elizabeth, d. Joseph & Susan[n]ah, b. Oct. 16, 1711	1	9
Elizabeth, m. Thomas **STEEVENS**, 4th, June 5, 1728	1	50
Elisabeth, d. Ebenezer & Judeth, b. Feb. 6, 1733	1	59
Elizabeth, d. Samuel & Dorcas, b. Mar. 3, 1742	2	18
Ezekiel, s. Thomas & Hannah, b. Dec. 10, 1724	1	31
Ezekiel, m. Ruth **WARREN**, June 27, 1748, by Thomas Stevens, Jr.	2	1
Fanny, m. Silvester H. **BRIG[G]S**, b. of Plainfield, Apr. 1, 1832, by Peleg Peckham, Elder	2	215
Grace, d. Nathan & Grace, b. Jan. 17, 1747/8	2	6
Hannah, d. Thomas & Hannah, b. Oct. 18, 1731	1	56
Han[n]ah, m. Steven **WARREN**, Dec. 2, 1748, by Thomas Stevens	2	1
Hannah, w. Thomas, d. Sept. 15, 1757, in the 62nd y. of her age	2	36

	Vol.	Page
WILLIAMS, (cont.)		
Hannah, m. John **HALL**, Feb. 25, 1762	2	77
Hepsabah, d. Richard & Elizabeth, b. Apr. 23, 1710	1	8
Isaac, s. Attwood & Elizabeth, b. Nov. 7, 1756	2	50
Isaac, [twin with Abraham], s. Nathan & Waightstill, b. May 14, 1765	2	58
Isaiah, s. Thomas & Sarah, b. Nov. 5, 1701	1	12
Isaiah, m. Deb[o]ra[h] **BILLINGS**, Aug. 8, 1725	1	56
Isaiah, s. Isaiah & Deb[o]rah, b. Jan. 11, 1737/8	1	71
Jacob, s. Ebenezer & Judeth, b. July 1, 1737	1	70
John, s. Ebenezer & Judeth, b. Feb. 20, 1724/5; d. Sept. 6, 1724	1	33
John, s. Isaiah & Deb[o]ra[h], b. Dec. 25, 1726	1	41
John, s. Isaiah & Deb[o]rah, b. Dec. 25, 1727	1	57
John, s. Ebenezer & Judeth, b. Sept. 13, 1728	1	47
John, m. Mary **DEAN**, Nov. 4, 1762	2	70
John, s. John & Mary, b. Oct. 24, 1765	2	70
Joseph, s. Thomas & Sarah, b. Oct. 28, 1679	1	12
Joseph, m. Susannah **LAWRANS**, d. Peleg, of Grotton, Oct. 13, 1710	1	9
Joseph, s. Joseph & Susan[n]ah, b. Apr. 18, 1713; d. May 24, 1713	1	12
Joseph, s. Joseph & Susan[n]ah, b. June 17, 1714	1	13
Joseph, s. Ebenezer & Judeth, b. Jan. 3, 1730	1	59
Joseph, s. Joseph & Susan[n]ah, d. May 10, 1730	1	50
Joseph, s. Nathan, b. Apr. 4, 1745	1	2X
Joseph, s. Nathan & Grace, b. Apr. 3, 1745	2	6
Joseph, m. Experience **LAWRANCE**, Mar. 6, 1758	2	45
Joseph, m. Experience **LAWRENCE**, Apr. 5, 1758	2	39
Joseph, Jr., s. Joseph & Abyga[i]l, b. Aug. 9, 1769	2	68
Joseph, m. Louisa **CONGDON**, b. of Plainfield, Aug. 13, 1850, by Rev. Warren Emerson	3	65
Judah, d. Joseph & Experience, b. Aug. 31, 1760	2	45
Judah, twin with Mary, d. John & Mary, b. Jan. 6, 1768	2	70
Julia A., ae. 26, b. Foster, R.I., res. Plainfield, m. Albert H. **WOOD**, depot master, ae. 40, b. Foster, R.I., res. Plainfield, Dec. 30, 1849, by Rev. Jared O. Knapp	4	5
Julia Ann, m. Albert H. **WOOD**, b. of Plainfield, Dec. 30, 1849, by Rev. J. O. Knapp	3	62
Laury A., of Plainfield, m. Alfred S. **HUDSON**, of Providence, R.I., May 1, 1853, by Rev. Joseph P. Brown	3	78
Lemuel, s. Isaiah & Deb[o]rah, b. Dec. 19, 1729	1	57
Lois, d. Ebenezer & Abigail, b. Feb. 25, 1758	2	38
Lucy, d. John & Mary, b. June 26, 1763	2	70
Luther, s. Ebenezer & Abigail, b. Aug. 26, 1771	2	83
Lydiah, d. Thomas & Hannah, b. Jan. 6, 1733/4	1	61

PLAINFIELD VITAL RECORDS 281

	Vol.	Page
WILLIAMS, (cont.)		
Mary, d. Isaiah & Deb[o]rah, b. Apr. 4, 1730	1	57
Mary, d. Samuel & Dorcas, b. Mar. 26, 1744	2	18
Mary, twin with Judah, d. John & Mary, b. Jan. 6, 1768	2	70
Mary, w. John ,d. Jan. 6, 1768, in the 40th y. of her age	2	70
Mary, m. Hezekiah **SPAULDING**, Aug. 24, 1790	2	98
Meriam, d. Samuel & Darkis, b. Feb. 28, 1740	1	97
Miriam, d. Samuel & Dorcas, b. Feb. 28, 1740	2	18
Nathan, s. Thomas & Sarah, b. May 13, 1699	1	12
Nathan, s. Tho[ma]s & Sarah, d. June 2, 1720, ae. 21 y. 21 d.	1	22
Nathan, s. Joseph & Susan[n]ah, b. Mar. 1, 1722/3	1	28
Nathan, m. Waightstill **DAVENPORT**, Aug. 26, 1755	2	35
Noah, s. Joseph & Experience, b. June 20, 1762	2	45
Obediah, s. Samuel & Dorcas, b. Mar. 2, 1749	2	19
Olive, d. Elihu & Desire, b. Sept. 9, 1752	2	22
Phebe, d. Isaiah & Deb[o]rah, b. June 3, 1735	1	71
Philemon, s. Thomas & Hannah, b. Feb. 26, 1738	2	29
Priscilla, d. Attwood & Elizabeth, b. June 27, 1751, in Stoningtown	2	50
Robert, s. Robert & Hannah, b. Mar. 1, 1706/7	1	9
Rozel, s. Sam[ue]ll & Dorkis, b. Aug. 20, 1757	2	19
Rufus, s. Elihu & Desire, b. Mar. 7, 1750	2	22
Samuel, s. Joseph & Susan[n]ah, b. Nov. 14, 1717	1	18
Samuel, of Plainfield, m. Darkhorse **CLEAVELAND**, Apr. 11, 1739	1	97
Samuel, m. Dorkas **CLEAVELAND**, Apr. 11, 1739	2	18
Samuel, s. Samuel & Dorcas, b. July 24, 1746	2	18
Samuel, s. Attwood & Elizabeth, b. Mar. 19, 1754, in Stoningtown	2	50
Sam[ue]ll, d. Oct. 14, 1759	2	19
Sarah, d. Thomas & Sarah, b. Dec. 6, 1704	1	12
Sarah, d. Richard & Abega[i]ll, b. Oct. 31, 1719	1	21
Sarah, m. Daniel **LAWRANCE**, Mar. 4, 1724/5	1	32
Sarah, d. Ebenezer & Judeth, b. Oct. 30, 1740	1	97
Sarah, w. Capt. Thomas, d. Aug. 8, 1751	2	20
Sarah, m. William **PARKS**, Jr., Dec. 28, 1758	2	39
Sarah, m. William **PARKE**, Jr., Dec. 28, 1758	2	53
Shubal, s. Isaiah & Deb[o]rah, b. Apr. 29, 1733	1	58
Simeon, s. Thomas & Han[n]ah, b. Apr. 18, 1715	1	15
Simeon, s. Ezekiel & Ruth, b. May 19, 1750	2	12
Suesannah, d. Joseph & Suesannah, b. Nov. 28, 1732	1	56
Susannah, d. Samuel & Dorcas, b. Nov. 10, 1751	2	19
Susannah, m. Ebenezer **PARISH**, Feb. 13, 1752	2	23
Theofeles, s. Tho[ma]s & Han[n]ah, b. Jan. 20, 1716/17	1	17

	Vol.	Page
WILLIAMS, (cont.)		
Thomas, s. Thomas & Sarah, b. July 19, 1677	1	12
Thomas, s. Thomas, m. Han[n]ah **DOUGLAS**, d. William, Feb. 9, 1713/14	1	13
Thomas, Capt., d. Feb. 3, 1722/3, in the 58th y. of his age	1	27
Thomas, s. Ebenezer & Judeth, b. Sept. 5, 1726	1	46
Thomas, s. William & Lydia, b. Apr. 27, 1765	2	90
Warren, of Brooklyn, m. Olive **FRENCH**, of Plainfield, Nov. 25, 1847, by Rev. Henry Robinson	3	47
Warren, farmer, ae. 23, of Brooklyn, m. Olive **FRENCH**, ae. 20, b. Plainfield, Nov. 25, [18]47, by Rev. Henry Robinson	4	1
We[a]lthy, d. Attwood & Elizabeth, b. Oct. 16, 1761	2	50
We[a]lthy, of Woodstock, m. George B. **GASKILL**, of Sterling, Feb. 22, 1854, by Peleg Peckham, Elder	3	82
William, s. Thomas & Hannah, b. Sept. 10, 1728	1	45
William, m. Lydia **CADY**, b. of Plainfield, Apr. 8, 1764, by Alex[ande]r Miller, V.D.M.	2	54
William, of Newport, R.I., m. Abby **WASHBURN**, of Newport, R.I., May 16, 1844, by Rev. Daniel Lyon	3	23
Zadock, s. Ezekiel & Ruth, b. Apr. 26, 1752	2	19
WILSON, WILLSON, Abraham, s. John & Mary, b. Apr. 24, 1750	2	60
Charles, m. Susan **CRAWFORD**, of Coventry, R.I., Apr. 16, 1847, by Rev. Fred[eri]c Charlton	3	48
Charles P., s. Caleb P., laborer, ae. 35, & Harriet A., ae. 30, by June 21, 1848	4	21
Charles P., d. July 7, 1848, ae. 16 d.	4	61
Clarissa, m. Robert **KINNIE**, b. of Plainfield, Mar. 14, 1824, by Orin Fowler, V.D.M.	2	193
Electa, d. Aug. 9, 1849, ae. 1	4	62
Ella L., d. Aug. 9, 1849, ae. 9 m.	4	64
Ellen W., d. Phillip, manufacturer, ae. 27, & Susan, ae. 25, b. Nov. 22, 1848	4	25
Eunice, m. Charles **SPAULDING**, b. of Plainfield, Dec. 6, 1829, by Rev. Orin Fowler	2	210
Isaac, s. John & Mary, b. Feb. 17, 1752	2	61
Jacob, s. John & Mary, b. Jan. 14, 1754	2	61
James, s. John & Mary, b. July 23, 1757	2	61
James, of Griswold, m. Esther **HALL**, of Plainfield, Feb. 21, 1830, by Orin Fowler, V.D.M.	2	210
Jane, m. John **KENNEDY**, Apr. 6, 1797	2	221
Jared, m. Abigail B. **WRIGHT**, b. of Coventry, R.I., Apr. 19, 1847, by Rev. J. Mather	3	43
John, s. John & Mary, b. Mar. 18, 1746	2	60
John F., m. Mary F. **PARKER**, b. of Plainfield, Sept. 2, 1845, by Peleg Peckham, Elder	3	32
Joshua, s. John & Mary, b. Aug. 19, 1761	2	61

	Vol.	Page
WILSON, WILLSON, (cont.)		
Judah, m. Jonathan **PARKHURST**, May 12, 1761	2	69
Louisa, m. Obed **MATTISON**, Nov. 8, 1840, by Samuel L. Hough, J.P.	3	8
Louisa, m. George **MATHEWSON**, b. of Sterling, July 30, 1854, by Peleg Peckham, Elder	3	85
Lidea, ae. 19, m. Jacob **BENNETT**, laborer, ae. 28, b. Foster, R.I., res. Plainfield, July 20, 1849	4	3
Mary, d. John & Mary, b. June 30, 1742	2	60
Mary, d. John & Mary, d. Apr. 18, 1763, in the 23rd y. of her age	2	61
Meriam, d. John & Mary, b. Apr. 22, 1738	2	60
Meriam, m. Abijah **CADY**, May 24, 1763	2	54
Olive, m. Ira **HYDE**, b. of Plainfield, Oct. 24, 1841, by John Read, Elder	3	11
Orilla, m. Jeremiah **SHEPERD**, b. of Plainfield, Dec. 31, 1826, by Elder George W. Appleton, of Sterling	2	200
Rachel, m. Ephraim **PRENTICE**, b. of Plainfield, June 30, 1845, by Peleg Peckham, Elder	3	31
Robert, s. John & Mary, b. Apr. 15, 1740	2	60
Rufus, of Sterling, m. Phebe **YOUNG**, of Killingly, June 6, 1849, by Peleg Peckham, Elder	3	59
Rufus, farmer, ae. 42, of Plainfield, m. Phebe **YOUNG**, ae. 38, b. Killingly, res. Plainfield, June 6, 1849, by Peleg Peckham	4	4
Sally, of Plainfield, m. Thimot[h]y J. **BACKUS**, of Ashford, July 15, 1838, by William Dyer, J.P.	2	235
Samuel, farmer, d. May 29, 1849, ae. 64	4	63
Seth A., of Killingly, m. Mary A. **CURTIS**, of Plainfield, Dec. 5, 1849, by Rev. Joseph P. Brown	3	62
Thomas, s. John & Mary, b. May 31, 1744	2	60
Thomas, m. Jerusha **GAIL**, June 27, 1749	2	8
Thomas, m. Susan W. **HERRINGTON**, b. of Plainfield, Sept. 9, 1838, by Peleg Peckham, Elder	2	237
Walter, of Providence, R.I., m. Elizabeth **BROWN**, of Plainfield, Sept. 5, 1848, by Rev. Frederic Charlton	3	55
Walter, butcher, ae. 26, b. Plainfield, res. Providence, R.I., m. Elizabeth **BROWN**, ae. 21, b. Plainfield, res. Providence, R.I., Sept. 17, 1848, by Rev. Frederic Charlton	4	3
William, s. John & Mary, b. Mar. 13, 1748	2	60
William H., of Dartmouth, Mass., m. Mary E. **MASON**, of Plainfield, Sept. 25, [ ], by Rev. A. B. Wheeler	3	17
Zilphia, of Plainfield, m. George H. **CLARK**, of Ashford, Apr. 16, 1845, by Peleg Peckham, Elder	3	31
-----, s. Philip, cotton spinner, ae. 27, & Caroline,		

	Vol.	Page
WILSON, WILLSON, (cont.)		
ae. 27, b. July 10, 1850	4	29
WINDSOR, WINSOR, Horace W., m. Sabra **GALLUP**, b. of Sterling, Apr. 7, 1845, by Peleg Peckham, Elder	3	27
Naomi Ann, of Sterling, m. Warren **DAWLEY**, of Griswold, Mar. 6, 1837, by Peleg Peckham, Elder	2	230
WINEWARD, Abega[i]ll, m. Thomas **STEEVENS**, 2d, Mar. 14, 1719/20	1	22
WINTER, Hannah, m. Joshua **WALLIS**, Nov. 3, 1739	1	98
Mary, m. Oliver **SPAULDING**, June 17, 1762, in the 23rd y. of his age	2	94
WINTWORTH, Mary, m. Stephen **HARRIS**, Mar. 17, 1761	2	45
WISE, Catharine, d. Charles & Catharine, b. Oct. 28, 1810	2	124
Charles Collins, s. Charles & Catharine, b. Jan. 20, 1817	2	130
Mary Ann, d. Charles & Catharine, b. Dec. 25, 1808	2	124
Nancy, housekeeper, b. Conn., res. Plainfield, d. July 30, [18]49, ae. 27	4	62
William, m. Nancy **MATTESON**, Dec. 13, 1840, by Solomon Payne, J.P.	3	8
William Henry, s. Charles & Catharine, b. Apr. 25, 1806	2	124
WITTER, WHITTER, Amos, m. Mary J. **AMES**, Apr. 13, 1828, by Rev. Orin Fowler	2	205
Frances A., of Plainfield, m. James S. **TREAT**, of Preston, Sept. 7, 1829, by Rev. Orin Fowler	2	210
John, m. Olive **SMITH**, b. of Plainfield, Mar. 26, 1832, by Rev. Seth Bliss, of Jewett City	2	215
Lydia M., of Plainfield, m. James S. **TREAT**, of Voluntown, Nov. 18, 1839, by Rev. Nathan E. Sholes, of Preston	2	249
Lydia M., of Plainfield, m. James S. **TREAT**, of Voluntown, Nov. 18, 1839, by Rev. Nathan E. Shaler, of Preston	3	2
Martha L., of Plainfield, m. Charles H. **BREWER**, of Norwich, Sept. 30, 1847, by Rev. Henry Robinson	3	45
Martha L., ae. 18, b. Plainfield, m. Charles **BROWN**, bank clerk, ae 25, of Norwich, Sept. 30, 1847, by Rev. Henry Robinson	4	1
Mary Ann, of Plainfield, m. Francis S. **PALMER**, of Lownesbow, Ala., Feb. 4, 1846, by Rev. A. Dunning	3	35
WOLCOTT, [see also **WALCOTT**], Caroline, of Plainfield, m. James M. **KIMBALL**, of Rockland, N.Y., Feb. 17, 1847, by Rev. Jared C. Knapp, Central Village	3	42
WOOD, WHOOD, Alared, m. Jonathan **DAVIS**, b. of Plainfield, June 19, 1837, by Chester Tilden	2	231
Albert H., m. Julia Ann **WILLIAMS**, b. of Plainfield, Dec. 30, 1849, by Rev. J. O. Knapp	3	62
Albert H., depot master, ae. 40, b. Foster, R.I., res.		

PLAINFIELD VITAL RECORDS 285

	Vol.	Page
WOOD, WHOOD, (cont.)		
Plainfield, m. Julia A. **WILLIAMS**, ae. 26, his 2d w., b. Foster, R.I., res. Plainfield, Dec. 30, 1849, by Rev. Jared O. Knapp	4	5
Elexander, s. Russel[l] & Kata, b. Jan. 1, 1802 (Alexander)	2	111
Deborah, d. Russel[l] & Kata, b. July 5, 1796	2	111
Deborah, m. Daniel **HILL**, b. of Plainfield, Dec. 11, 1814, by Rev. Nath[anie]l Cole	2	132
E., of Plainfield, m. Albert **ROTH**, of Norwich, Apr. 19, 1852, by Rev. Joseph P. Brown	3	74
Earl P., of Coventry, R.I., m. Lucindal **HALL**, of Plainfield, Jan. 7, 1827, by Nathaniel Cole, Elder	2	200
Emeline E., of Brookfield, Mass., m. George R. **HENRY**, of Plainfield, Sept. 8, 1851, by Rev. Henry Robinson	3	70
Harry, s. Russel[l] & Kata, b. Nov. 2, 1794	2	111
Jason, of Sterling, m. Almira **GREEN**, of Plainfield, Dec. 22, 1839, by Peleg Peckham, Elder	2	250
Jason, of Sterling, m. Almira **GREEN**, of Plainfield, Dec. 22, 1839, by Peleg Peckham, Elder	3	2
Julian, m. Cyrus **MITCHELL**, b. of Killingly, Sept. 21, 1845, by James Smither, Elder	3	34
Louisa A., d. June 30, 1847, ae. 34	4	63
Maria B., of Plainfield, m. Thomas M. **FRAZIER**, of Norwich, Apr. 2, 1843, by Rev. A. B. Wheeler	3	18
Mary, d. Russel[l] & Kata, b. Dec. 15, 1798	2	111
Mary Ann, d. Russel[l] & Kata, b. Aug. 6, 1805	2	111
Mary Ann, m. Welcom[e] **BABCOCK**, Apr. 6, 1842, by Rev. John Read	3	14
Mason, rag bleacher, ae. 21, b. Foster, R.I., res. Plainfield, m. Maria **BACON**, ae. 22, b. Canterbury, Ct., res. Plainfield, Sept. 12, 1849, by Rev. Leonard	4	5
Polly, of Plainfield, m. Alvah **GROVER**, of Killingly, Dec. 23, 1827, by Rev. Roswell Whitmore	2	204
-----, s. Darius, merchant, ae. 32, & Clarinda, ae. 32, b. May 17, 1850	4	29
WOODWARD, Abigaiel, d. Jonathan & Marg[a]ret, b. Oct. 17, 1736	1	66
Abigail, d. Jonathan & Sarah, b. Oct. 17, 1736	2	80
Abigail, d. Jonathan & Delight, b. Jan. 17, 1766	2	55
Anne, d. Jonathan & Delight, b. Feb. 25, 1764	2	55
Asa, s. Daniel & Hannah, b. Nov. 18, 1736; d. Feb. 11, 1751	2	13
Asa, s. Daniel & Hannah, b. Mar. 1, 1751	2	12
Daniel, s. Daniel & Hannah, b. Mar. 8, 1742/3	2	12
Daniel, d. Jan. 22, 1772	2	78

	Vol.	Page
WOODWARD, (cont.)		
Deb[o]rah, d. Jonathan & Marg[a]ret, b. Aug. 20, 1738	1	71
Deborah, d. Jonathan & Margaret, b. Aug. 20, 1738	2	81
Deborah, m. Phillip **SPAULDING**, Mar. 22, 1758	2	41
Elija[h], s. Daniel & Hannah, b. Jan. 23, 1740/41	2	13
Elizabeth, d. Jonathan & Sarah, b. Aug. 13, 1731	1	54
Elizabeth, d. Jonathan & Sarah, b. Aug. 13, 1731	2	80
Elizabeth, d. Daniel & Hannah, b. Mar. 16, 1748/9	2	12
Elizabeth, m. Eliphalet **KIMBALL**, May 10, 1759	2	47
Hannah, d. Daniel & Hannah, b. Feb. 5, 1744/5	2	12
John, s. Daniel & Hannah, b. Aug. 7, 1757	2	78
Jonathan, s. Jonathan & Sarah, b. June 4, 1726	1	37
Jonathan, Jr., s. Jonathan & Sarah, b. June 4, 1726	2	80
Jonathan, m. Anna **HARRIS**, of Oxford, Jan. 15, 1752	2	20
Jonathan, s. Jonathan, Jr. & Anne, b. Oct. 28, 1752	2	20
Jonathan, m. Delight **WILLIAMS**, Dec. 5, 1759	2	45
Jonathan, s. Jonathan, Jr. & Delight, b. Mar. 25, 1762	2	45
Josiah, s. Jonathan & Delight, b. Mar. 9, 1768	2	55
Julia Ann, of Plainfield, m. Daniel **GALLUP**, of Sterling, Oct. 14, 1835, by Geo[rge] Perkins, Minister, of Griswold	2	223
Lemuel, farmer, d. May 25, [1851?], ae. 74	4	66
Luce, d. Daniel & Hannah, b. Sept. 19, 1738; d. May 5, 1746	2	13
Luce, d. Daniel & Hannah, b. Feb. 1, 1746/7	2	12
Lydiah, d. Jonathan & Marg[a]rat, b. Oct. 19, 1734	1	63
Lydiah, m. Nathaniel **TYLER**, Oct. 12, 1757	2	47
Lydia C., m. Luther **CLEVELAND**, b. of Plainfield, Oct. 15, 1834, by Rev. Samuel Rockwell	2	219
Mehetibel, d. Jonathan & Mehetibel, b. May 18, 1749	2	8
Mehatabal, d. Jonath[an] & Margaret, b. May 18, 1749	2	81
Mehetabel, w. Jonathan, d. Aug. 31, 1783	2	90
Mercy, d. Jonathan & Mehetable, b. Dec. 1, 1752	2	20
Olive, d. Daniel & Hannah, b. Oct. 18, 1758	2	78
Rachel, d. Daniel & Hannah, b. Mar. 27, 1753	2	78
Sarah, d. Jonathan & Sarah, b. Nov. 18, 1729	1	49
Sarah, w. Jonathan, d. May 2, 1733	1	58
Suesannah, d. Jonathan & Marg[a]ret, b. Apr. 17, 1740	1	95
Susanna, d. Jonathan & Margaret, b. Apr. 17, 1740	2	81
Susan[n]ah, m. Jonathan **KINGSBURY**, Nov. 14, 1764	2	57
Thankfull, d. Daniel & Hannah, b. May 6, 1755	2	78
William, s. Jonathan, Jr. & Delight, b. Aug. 29, 1760	2	45
WRIGHT, RIGHT, RIGHTE, Abega[i]ll, d. Ebenezer, of Cheltsford, m. Benjamin **SPAULDING**, Mar. 7, 1719/20	1	22
Abigail B., m. Jared **WILSON**, b. of Coventry, R.I., Apr. 19, 1847, by Rev. J. Mather	3	43
Hannah, d. Dec. 26, 1728	1	47

	Vol.	Page
WRIGHT, RIGHT, RIGHTE, (cont.)		
Jonathan, d. May 11, 1725, in the 26th y. of his age	1	41
Margaret, see under Margaret **WRIGHT** **MARDENBOROUGH**	2	144
Susannah, d. Jonathan & Hannah, b. Feb. 1, 1725	1	41
Suesanna, d. Jonathan & Hannah, d. May 8, 1729, in the 5th y. of her age (Arnold Copy has the name "**RIGBE**". Corrected by L.B.B.)	1	50
WYLIE, Joseph, m. Eliza **BROWN**, b. of Plainfield, May 18, 1845, by James Smither, Elder	3	29
YEAW, James B., of R.I., residing in Sterling, m. Eliza **ANGELL**, of Scituate, Dec. 2, 1838, by Peleg Peckham, Elder	2	238
YENCKES, Dwight A., of Coventry, R.I., m. Nancy M. **JOHNSON**, of Sterling, Mar. 1, 1846, by Peleg Peckham, Elder	3	36
YORK, Speedy, m. William **FISHER**, b. of Plainfield, Mar. 17, 1839, by Rev. Samuel Rockwell	2	240
YOUNG, YONG, Caroline, d. William F., dresser tender, ae. 37, & Amey, ae. 39, b. May 30, 1851	4	31
Edward, s. Zelotes, blacksmith, b. Feb. 2, 1848	4	22
Ellen Frances, d. Lewis & Elizabeth, b. Feb. 5, 1848	3	59
Frances P., m. Jason J. **POTTER**, Oct. 1, 1837, by Peleg Peckham, Elder	2	233
Horace P., m. Eliza G. **CONGDON**, b. of Griswold, Oct. 19, 1851, by [ ]. Witness: John Paine	3	71
Jonah, of Sterling, m. Delilah H. **TYLER**, of Killingly, Apr. 6, 1845, by Peleg Peckham, Elder	3	27
Laura, m. Harris **WHITMAN**, b. of Sterling, July 25, 1842, by Peleg Peckham, Elder	3	16
Lewis, of Killingly, m. Elizabeth D. **HUTCHINSON**, of Plainfield, Aug. 7, 1842, by Andrew Dunning	3	16
Lewis Kimball, s. Lewis & Elizabeth, b. Oct. 24, 1842	3	59
Louisa, m. Jeremiah **HILL**, b. of Sterling, Nov. 10, 1844, by Peleg Peckham, Elder	3	25
Mary Elizabeth, d. Lewis & Elizabeth, b. Sept. 6, 1844	3	59
Mary S., m. Amos C. **SWEET**, b. of Sterling, Apr. 13, 1845, by Peleg Peckham, Elder	3	31
Nelson, b. Sterling, res. Plainfield, d. July 29, 1847, ae. 7	4	63
Phebe, of Killingly, m. Rufus **WILSON**, of Sterling, June 6, 1849, by Peleg Peckham, Elder	3	59
Phebe, ae. 38, b. Killingly, res. Plainfield, m. 2d h. Rufus **WILSON**, farmer, ae. 42, of Plainfield, June 6, 1849, by Peleg Peckham	4	4
Stephen G., m. Mary **HILL**, b. of Sterling, Dec. 8, 1835, by Peleg Peckham, Elder	2	224
William P., Jr., of Sterling, m. Laury A. **HILL**, of		

	Vol.	Page
YOUNG, YONG, (cont.)		
Griswold, Nov. 25, 1851, by Rev. Joseph P. Brown	3	72
-----, child of Lewis, blacksmith, & Elizabeth, b. Feb. 5, 1848	4	21
NO SURNAME		
David, of Newtown, Conn., m. Lydia A. **WILBOUR**, of Scituate, R.I., May 8, 1836, by Rev. Tubael Wakefield	2	226
Dolly, m. Edward [**MEDBERY**], Dec. 26, 1811	3	88
Ed, negro s. Seacer & Hagar, negros, b. Apr. 24, 1754	2	66
Elizabeth, m. John **PEIRCE**, Dec. 9, 1779	2	87
Elizabeth, m. James **DOUGLASS**, Oct. 7, 1782	3	3
Hannah, m. Asa **SHEPERD**, Nov. 25, 1778	2	87
Hannah, m. Peirce **PARKIS**, Feb. 12, 1784	2	123
Jemima, m. John **HARRISON**, Oct. 10, 1813, by Thomas Backus, J.P.	2	124
Jen[n]y, m. William **EVENS**, July 9, 1747, by Rev. Thomas Stevens	2	9
Lydia, of Foster, R.I., m. Sanford **BASS**, of Olneyville, R.I., May 8, 1836, by Rev. Tubael Wakefield	2	226
Martha, m. Benjamin **GALLUP**, Dec. 6, 1781	2	90
Mary, m. Ephraim **FELLOWS**, Dec. 3, 1711	1	11
Mary, m. Archibald [**MEDBERY**], Oct. 14, 1839	3	88
Polly, b. Attleborough, res. Killingly, d. May 6, 1850, ae. 81	4	64
Rebecca, m. Henry **DOW**, Dec. 6, 1787	2	95

www.ingramcontent.com/pod-product-compliance
Lightning Source LLC
Chambersburg PA
CBHW062002220426

43662CB00010B/1205